Artificial Intelligence and Intellectual Property

Artificial Intelligence and Intellectual Property

Edited by

JYH-AN LEE, RETO M HILTY,
AND KUNG-CHUNG LIU

OXFORD
UNIVERSITY PRESS

OXFORD
UNIVERSITY PRESS

Great Clarendon Street, Oxford, OX2 6DP,
United Kingdom

Oxford University Press is a department of the University of Oxford. It furthers the University's objective of excellence in research, scholarship, and education by publishing worldwide. Oxford is a registered trade mark of Oxford University Press in the UK and in certain other countries

First Edition published in 2021

Impression: 1

Published in the United States of America by Oxford University Press
198 Madison Avenue, New York, NY 10016, United States of America

British Library Cataloguing in Publication Data

Data available

Library of Congress Control Number: 2020944786

ISBN 978–0–19–887094–4

DOI: 10.1093/oso/9780198870944.001.0001

Printed and bound by
CPI Group (UK) Ltd, Croydon, CR0 4YY

Table of Contents

List of Contributors

Feroz Ali is a legal consultant with the Vision Realization Office, Ministry of Health, Saudi Arabia. He is a visiting professor at National Law School of India University, Bangalore, his *alma mater*, where he teaches the course, 'Regulating Artificial Intelligence'. He was the first Intellectual Property Rights (IPR) Chair Professor at the Indian Institute of Technology (IIT) Madras, where he worked closely with the IPM Cell and the Dean ICSR in managing their IPR portfolio. He offers online courses in intellectual property law on the NPTEL/Swayam platform. As an advocate, he has represented clients before the Patent Office, Intellectual Property Appellate Board, and High Courts and Supreme Court of India. He founded Techgrapher.com, a platform for managing intellectual property and LexCampus.in, a portal that trains patent professionals. He has authored three books on patent law. He is an alumnus of Trinity College, University of Cambridge, and Duke University School of Law.

Hao-Yun Chen is an Assistant Professor at the College of Law at National Taipei University in Taiwan. She holds an LLD from Nagoya University in Japan. Prior to joining National Taipei University, she taught at National Taiwan University of Science and Technology. She teaches and researches in the field of intellectual property law, with special emphasis on the enforcement of patent rights, trademark protection and unfair competition law, copyright issues arising from new technology, and the relation between intellectual property law and competition law. Before starting her academic career, she worked as an associate attorney in a law firm in Taiwan.

Conrado Freitas is an in-house trademark counsel. Prior to that, he has contributed to several IP-related research projects as a Research Assistant at the Institute for Globalisation and International Regulation—IGIR, at Maastricht University. He holds an LLM in Intellectual Property Law and Knowledge Management from Maastricht University. He also holds a bachelor's degree in Law from the Federal University of Rio de Janeiro, Brazil, and has completed several IP courses from WIPO and Brazilian IP Associations. Conrado is a qualified lawyer in Brazil with over seven years' experience in total in the intellectual property field.

Andres Guadamuz is a Senior Lecturer in Intellectual Property Law at the University of Sussex and the Editor-in-Chief of the Journal of World Intellectual Property. His main research areas are: artificial intelligence and copyright, open licensing, cryptocurrencies, and smart contracts. Andres has published two books, the most recent of which is *Networks, Complexity and Internet Regulation*, and he regularly blogs at Technollama.co.uk. He has acted as an international consultant for the World Intellectual Property Organization (WIPO), and has done activist work with Creative Commons.

Andrew Fang Hao Sen is a family physician and a medical informatics practitioner at SingHealth. He has over ten years' experience in the medical field. He graduated from the Yong Loo Lin School of Medicine, National University of Singapore (NUS), and furthered his medical education to obtain a Master of Medicine (Family Medicine). He also holds a Master of Technology (Enterprise Business Analytics) from NUS and graduated with the IBM Medal and Prize. He also lectures at the NUS Department of Statistics and Applied Probability. He is passionate about exploring and using technology to improve healthcare delivery, and his research focus is on healthcare analytics for clinical decision support.

Tianxiang He is Assistant Professor at the School of Law, City University of Hong Kong, where he serves as the Associate Director of the LLM Programme. He holds an LLB degree (Huaqiao University, China, 2007) and a master's degree in International Law (Jinan University, China, 2009). He received his PhD in IP law at Maastricht University (the Netherlands, 2016) and another PhD in Criminal Law at Renmin University of China (2017). He is the author of *Copyright and Fan Productivity in China: A Cross-jurisdictional Perspective* (Springer 2017). He is an Elected Associate Member of the International Academy of Comparative Law (IACL). His research focuses on comparative intellectual property law, law and technology, and the intersections between the regulative framework of cultural products and fundamental rights such as freedom of speech.

Reto M Hilty is Director at the Max Planck Institute for Innovation and Competition in Munich, Germany. He is a full Professor ad personam at the University of Zurich and Honorary Professor at the Ludwig Maximilian University of Munich. In 2019, he received an Honorary Doctorate from the University of Buenos Aires. He specializes in intellectual property and competition law with a further focus on IP-specific contract law. Moreover, his research centres on the impact of new technologies and business models on intellectual property rights and the European and international harmonization of intellectual property law.

Jörg Hoffmann is a Junior Research Fellow at the Max Planck Institute for Innovation and Competition, Munich, a doctoral candidate at the Ludwig Maximilian University of Munich, and a fully qualified lawyer in Germany. He studied law at UCL and the Ludwig Maximilian University of Munich, where he obtained his law degree with a specialization in European Law and Public International Law. His main research interests lie in the fields of intellectual property and competition law with a major focus on the implications of the digital economy on the regulatory framework pertaining to innovation and competition in data-driven markets.

Ivan Khoo Yi is currently a doctor in Singapore's primary healthcare industry. He was educated within the Singapore school system and graduated from the prestigious Yong Loo Lin School of Medicine, National University of Singapore in 2010. During his time in medicine, he received an award as one of the best house officers during his houseman year, and went on to practice otorhinolaryngology for a brief period. In 2016, seeking a new challenge, he enrolled in the Singapore Management University Juris Doctor programme, and graduated in 2019 with summa cum laude. His education in law has fundamentally changed his outlook towards the practice of medicine.

Jyh-An Lee is an Associate Professor of Law at the Chinese University of Hong Kong, where he currently serves as the Assistant Dean for Undergraduate Studies and Director of the LLB Programme. He holds a JSD from Stanford Law School and an LLM from Harvard Law School. Prior to joining the Chinese University of Hong Kong, he taught at National Chengchi University and was an Associate Research Fellow in the Center for Information Technology Innovation at Academia Sinica in Taiwan. He was the Legal Lead and Co-Lead of Creative Commons Taiwan (2011–14) and an advisory committee member for Copyright Amendment in the Taiwan Intellectual Property Office (TIPO) at the Ministry of Economic Affairs (2011–14). He has been the Legal Lead of the Creative Commons Hong Kong Chapter since October 2018. Before starting his academic career, he was a practising lawyer in Taiwan, specializing in technology and business transactions.

Matthias Leistner is Professor of Private Law and Intellectual Property Law, with Information and IT-Law (GRUR Chair) at LMU Munich. He studied law in Berlin, Brussels, Munich, and Cambridge, obtaining his PhD at the Max Planck Institute Munich, Max Planck Institute for Innovation and Competition in Munich; Dr. iur., LMU Munich 1999, and LLM, University of Cambridge 2004. He completed his Habilitation (Post-doc thesis) at LMU Munich 2006. Apart from his Chair at LMU Munich, at present, he is a Member of the Faculty of the Munich Intellectual Property Law Center (MIPLC), and a guest professor for European Intellectual Property Law at the University of Xiamen, China, and at the Tongji University, Shanghai. He was an International Short Term Visiting Professor at Columbia Law School in the Spring Term 2020. His areas of expertise are intellectual property law, unfair competition law, and data and information law.

Jianchen Liu holds the position of Research Associate at ARCIALA, School of Law, Singapore Management University. He is also a PhD candidate at Renmin University of China, majoring in IP law and an LLM candidate at Columbia Law School. He focuses his research on the intersection between AI and IP law, as well as competition law and data protection. To date, he has published over ten articles on these topics in several law journals. Prior to pursuing his academic career, he worked as an IP lawyer for a world-renowned US law firm and a leading Chinese law firm for three years.

Kung-Chung Liu is Lee Kong Chian Professor of Law (Practice) and founding Director of Applied Research Centre for Intellectual Assets and the Law in Asia (ARCIALA) of Singapore Management University. He is also a professor of Renmin University of China and the Graduate Institute of Technology, Innovation and Intellectual Property Management, National Chengchi University, Taiwan. His teaching and research interests are intellectual property law, antitrust and unfair competition law, communications law, and the interface between those disciplines, with a geographic focus on greater China and Asia.

Ming Liu serves as Head of the Research Division at the Patent Re-examination Board (PRB) of the National Intellectual Property Administration of China (CNIPA). He is a high-level member, a second-level examiner, and an expert of the Standing Panel for Examining Matters at CNIPA. He has significant experience in patent examination and invalidation. He has worked for CNIPA since 2002 after obtaining his MS degree from Chinese Academy of Sciences, first as a patent examiner, then transferred to PRB in 2007, and since then has continued hearing patent invalidation cases, many of which have been highly influential, both domestically and overseas. He has also been involved in the legislative process of the Patent Law, and the Implementing Rules of Patent Law and Guidelines for Patent Examination. He has published twenty articles in foreign and domestic academic journals.

Eliza Mik is an Assistant Professor at the Chinese University of Hong Kong Faculty of Law. She holds a PhD in contract law from the University of Sydney. She has taught courses in contract law and in the law of e-commerce at the Singapore Management University and the University of Melbourne, as well as courses in FinTech and Blockchain at Bocconi University in Milan. In parallel with a line of research focused on distributed ledger technologies and smart contracts, she is involved in multiple projects relating to the legal implications of transaction automation. Eliza holds multiple academic affiliations, including those with the Tilburg Institute for Law, Society and Technology (TILT) and the Center for AI and Data Governance in Singapore. Before joining academia, Eliza worked in-house in a number of software companies, Internet start-ups, and telecommunication providers, where she advised on technology procurement, payment systems, and software licensing.

Anke Moerland is Assistant Professor of Intellectual Property Law in the European and International Law Department, Maastricht University. Her research relates to the interface of intellectual property law and political science, with a focus on governance aspects of intellectual property regulation in international trade negotiations, and more specifically in the area of geographical indications and trade mark law. Dr. Moerland holds degrees in law (Maastricht University) and international relations (Technical University Dresden), with a PhD in intellectual property protection in EU bilateral trade agreements from Maastricht University. Since 2017, she has coordinated the EIPIN Innovation Society, a four-year Horizon 2020 grant under the Marie Skłodowska Curie Action ITN-EJD. Since 2018, she has held a visiting professorship in Intellectual Property Law, Governance and Art at the School of Law, Centre for Commercial Law Studies of Queen Mary University of London.

Ichiro Nakayama is Professor of Law, Graduate School of Law, Hokkaido University. Before he joined Hokkaido University in 2019, he served as Associate Professor of School of Law at Shinshu University from 2005 to 2009 and Professor of School of Law at Kokugakuin University from 2009 to 2019. Prior to joining academia, Professor Nakayama originally joined the Ministry of International Trade and Industry (MITI) in 1989 and spent sixteen years in the Government of Japan, where he worked not only in intellectual property law and policies but also other fields including energy policies and national security policies. Professor Nakayama received an LLB in 1989 from the University of Tokyo, LLM in 1995 from the University of Washington, and MIA in 1997 from Columbia University. He has published a number of articles in the field of intellectual property law with a focus on patent law.

Anselm Kamperman Sanders is Professor of Intellectual Property Law, Director of the Advanced Masters Intellectual Property Law and Knowledge Management (IPKM LLM/MSc), and Academic Director of the Institute for Globalization and International Regulation (IGIR) at Maastricht University, the Netherlands. He acts as Academic Co-director of the Annual Intellectual Property Law School and IP Seminar of the Institute for European Studies of Macau (IEEM), Macau SAR, China and is Adjunct Professor at Jinan University Law School, Guangzhou, China. Anselm holds a PhD from the Centre for Commercial Law Studies, Queen Mary University of London, where he worked as a Marie Skłodowska-Curie Fellow before joining Maastricht University in 1995. For the UN he was member of the expert group for the World Economic and Social Survey 2018. Anselm sits as deputy judge in the Court of Appeal in The Hague, which has exclusive jurisdiction on patent matters.

Stefan Scheuerer is a Junior Research Fellow at the Max Planck Institute for Innovation and Competition, Munich, a doctoral candidate at the Ludwig Maximilian University of Munich (LMU), and a fully qualified lawyer in Germany. He is a member of the Max Planck Institute's research group on the regulation of the digital economy. Previously, he studied law at LMU with a specialization in intellectual property law, competition law, and media law, and gained practical experience in these fields in the course of several internships, inter alia at the European Commission, DG Competition, Brussels. His main research interests lie in the fields of intellectual property law, unfair competition law, legal theory, and law and society, especially in the context of the digital economy.

Daniel Seng is an Associate Professor of Law and Director of the Centre for Technology, Robotics, AI & the Law (TRAIL) at NUS. He teaches and researches on information technology and intellectual property law. He graduated with firsts from NUS and Oxford and won the Rupert Cross Prize in 1994. His doctoral thesis with Stanford University involved the use of machine learning, natural language processing, and data analytics to analyse the effects and limits of automation on the DMCA takedown process. Dr. Seng is a special consultant to the World Intellectual Property Organization (WIPO) and has presented and published papers on differential privacy, electronic evidence, information technology, intellectual property, artificial intelligence, and machine learning at various local, regional, and international conferences. He has been a member of various Singapore government committees that undertook legislative reforms in diverse areas such as electronic commerce, cybercrimes, digital copyright, online content regulation, and data protection.

Peter R Slowinski is a Junior Research Fellow at the Max Planck Institute for Innovation and Competition in Munich. He is admitted as attorney-at-law (Rechtsanwalt) in Germany as well as a qualified mediator. In addition, he holds a Master of the Science of Law (JSM) from Stanford Law School after completing the Stanford Program in International Legal Studies (SPILS). He has given lectures at Stanford Law School and the Munich Intellectual Property Law Center (MIPLC). Until 2016, he practised as a patent litigator in infringement and nullity proceedings in Germany. His research focuses on patents and dispute resolution. He has published on copyright and patent law. Mr. Slowinski has conducted an empirical study on mediation proceedings in patent law and participated in the SPC Study of the Max Planck Institute. He is a member of the research groups on data-driven economies and AI as well as life sciences.

Anthony Man-Cho So received his BSE degree in Computer Science from Princeton University with minors in Applied and Computational Mathematics, Engineering and Management Systems, and German Language and Culture. He then received his MSc and PhD degrees in Computer Science with a PhD minor in Mathematics from Stanford University. Professor So joined CUHK in 2007 and is currently Professor in the Department of Systems Engineering and Engineering Management. His research focuses on optimization theory and its applications in various areas of science and engineering, including computational geometry, machine learning, signal processing, and statistics. He has received a number of research and teaching awards, including the 2018 IEEE Signal Processing Society Best Paper Award, the 2016–17 CUHK Research Excellence Award, the 2013 CUHK Vice-Chancellor's Exemplary Teaching Award, and the 2010 Institute for Operations Research and the Management Sciences (INFORMS) Optimization Society Optimization Prize for Young Researchers.

Benjamin Sobel is an Affiliate at Harvard University's Berkman Klein Center for Internet & Society. His research and teaching examine the way digital media, artificial intelligence, and networked devices influence intellectual property, privacy, security, and expression. His article, 'Artificial Intelligence's Fair Use Crisis', was among the first publications to comprehensively examine the intersection between machine learning technology and the fair use doctrine in US copyright law.

Shufeng Zheng is a research associate of Applied Research Centre for Intellectual Assets and the Law in Asia (ARCIALA) of Singapore Management University and a PhD student at the Peking University. Before this, she was a Research Assistant in Peking University Science and Technology Law Research Center, and obtained a master's degree in Common Law from the University of Hong Kong and a master's degree in Intellectual Property Law from the Peking University. Her research focuses on the protection of and access to data, copyright licence scheme, and patent protection for software-related inventions.

Raphael Zingg is an Assistant Professor at Waseda University, Institute for Advanced Study, Tokyo, and a Research Fellow at the ETH Zurich, Center for Law & Economics. He has worked as a visiting scholar at a number of foreign institutions, notably the University of California in Berkeley, the University of Hong Kong, Singapore Management University, and the Max Planck Institute for Innovation and Competition in Munich. His scholarly fields of interest include the study of the patent system, biotechnology, nanotechnology, artificial intelligence laws, and the protection of cultural heritage. He received his PhD from the ETH Zurich, and his degrees in law from the universities of Zurich, Fribourg, and Paris II.

Roadmap to Artificial Intelligence and Intellectual Property

An Introduction

Jyh-An Lee, Reto M Hilty, and Kung-Chung Liu

The Broader Picture and Structure of the Book

The ability of computers to imitate intelligent human behaviour has drawn wide attention in recent years; we humans are increasingly ceding our decision-making power to technological artefacts. With the advancement of data science and computing technologies, artificial intelligence (AI) has become omnipresent in all sectors of society. Face and speech recognition, visual perception, self-driving vehicles, surgical robots, and automated recommendations from social media are all well-known examples of how computer systems perform tasks that normally require human intelligence. From manufacturing to healthcare services, AI has already improved previous best practices. Based on large volumes of data, AI can predict more accurately than humanly possible. The overwhelming intellectual power of AI is also exemplified by AlphaGo and AlphaZero, which have taught themselves to beat the best human players of chess, Go, and Shogi.

AI also enables new models of creativity and innovation with its data-driven approach. While human beings have used various instruments and technologies to create and innovate, they themselves have been the main driving force of creativity and innovation. AI puts that into question, raising numerous challenges to the existing intellectual property (IP) regime. Traditionally, the 'intellectual' part of 'intellectual property' refers to human intellect. However, since machines have become intelligent and are increasingly capable of making creative, innovative choices based on opaque algorithms, the 'intellectual' in 'intellectual property' turns out to be perplexing. Existing human-centric IP regimes based on promoting incentives and avoiding disincentives may no longer be relevant—or even positively detrimental—if AI comes into play. Moreover, AI has sparked new issues in IP law regarding legal subjects, scope, standards of protection, exceptions, and relationships between actors.

This book proceeds in seven parts, each of which is interconnected. Part I provides the technical, business, and economic foundations for the analysis of IP

Jyh-An Lee, Reto M Hilty, and Kung-Chung Liu, *Roadmap to Artificial Intelligence and Intellectual Property* In: *Artificial Intelligence and Intellectual Property.* Edited by: Jyh-An Lee, Reto M Hilty, and Kung-Chung Liu, Oxford University Press (2021). DOI: 10.1093/oso/9780198870944.003.0001

issues in the AI environment in the following parts of the book. Part II examines emerging substantive patent law and policy issues associated with AI, including foundational patents in AI-related inventions, the patentability of AI inventions, and how AI tools raise the standard of the inventive step. This part also illustrates how patent prosecution has evolved from material to textual to digital. Part III probes into two major copyright issues concerning AI's involvement in creation: the copyrightability of AI-generated works and copyright exceptions for text and data mining (TDM). Parts II and III present various legal and policy concerns in patent law and copyright law, respectively. However, patent law, copyright law, and trademark law occasionally share the same conundrum caused by the rapid development of AI technologies.

From Parts IV to VII, the book covers issues relevant to multiple categories of IP. While AI has enhanced the efficiency of IP administration and enforcement, it has generated new problems yet to be solved. Therefore, Part IV explores how AI reshapes IP administration in the public sector and IP enforcement in the private sector. Part V examines copyright and patent protection for AI software, which is qualitatively different from traditional computer programs. While AI is implemented by software, the protection for such software per se has been ignored by the mainstream IP literature. Part VI discusses the protection of and access to data, which is the driving force of all AI inventions and applications. It further illustrates how IP law will interact with other fields of law, such as unfair competition law and personal data protection law, on various data-related issues. Part VII provides a broader picture of AI and IP, searching for solutions to fundamental inquiries, such as IP and competition policy in the era of AI and whether an AI should be viewed as a legal person.

Individual Chapters

AI is a catch-all term that covers cognitive computing, machine learning (ML), evolutionary algorithms, rule-based systems, and the process of engineering intelligent machines. Anthony Man-Cho So's chapter provides essential knowledge for IP lawyers to understand AI technologies. ML is a core part of many AI applications, a process by which algorithms detect meaningful patterns in training data and use them for prediction or decision-making. The volume and quality of training data therefore always play crucial roles in the performance of AI applications. Because of their nested, non-linear structure, AI models are usually applied in a black-box manner. Consequently, AI systems' 'interpretability' or 'explainability', ie, the degree to which a human observer can understand the cause of a decision by the system, has been concerning for policymakers as well as AI users. Sometimes, even an AI developer can neither fully understand an AI's decision-making process nor predict its decisions or outputs. In supervised ML, a prediction rule can map an input (a data sample) to an expected output (a label). Currently, the most powerful way to implement a prediction rule is an artificial neural network, which is inspired by biological networks. In contrast, unsupervised ML has neither labelling nor prediction rules. The goal of unsupervised learning is to uncover hidden structures in data. Other than supervised and unsupervised learning, reinforcement learning is another ML paradigm in which a software agent learns by interacting with its environment to achieve a certain goal.

As a powerful instrument for business growth and development, AI technologies serve almost all areas of business operation, from corporate finance to human resource management to digital marketing. Among many other business sectors, healthcare in particular exemplifies how AI has fundamentally reshaped the whole industry. Ivan Khoo Yi and Andrew Fang's chapter illustrates AI's impact on the industry's main stakeholders: providers of healthcare, patients, pharmaceuticals, payers of healthcare (insurance companies and employees), and policymakers. While AI has enhanced the quality and effectiveness of medical examination, treatment, and overall medical services, it has also created challenges, such as mismatches between training data and operational data, opaque decision-making, privacy issues, and more.

IP regimes are designed to balance various economic interests and moral values. Ordinary IP policy concerns include, but are not limited to, incentives for creativity, technological innovation, economic development, dissemination of knowledge, and overall social welfare. Considering all these interests and values, the exclusivity and monopoly of IP rights can only be justified if their consequent social benefits outweigh their social costs. The same understanding is applicable to discussions of whether IP protection is desirable in AI markets. Based on mainstream economic theories of IP, Reto M Hilty, Jörg Hoffmann, and Stefan Scheuerer assess the necessity of IP protection for AI tools and AI outputs. While different AI tools and AI outputs might lead to different conclusions on this issue, the robust development in AI technology implies that IP may not be a necessary incentive to foster innovation in this field. Moreover, the underlying black box in AI systems possibly runs afoul of the disclosure theory in patent law.

Emerging technologies can be blocked by broad foundational patents, and AI is no exception. These upstream patents cover essential aspects of technologies and thus hamper downstream research or resulting products. Therefore, from a policy perspective, certain building blocks of future innovation should be free from such patent enclosure. Raphael Zing examines the foundational triadic AI patents filed with the United States Patent and Trademark Office (USPTO), the European Patent Office (EPO), and the Japanese Patent Office (JPO), illustrating major players' intentions to acquire foundational patents in AI. He suggests that patent offices and courts can protect the AI field from patent enclosure by strictly applying patentability standards.

The opaque AI black box behind algorithms can lead to legal questions, especially when transparency and disclosure are legally required. For example, the disclosure of invention is required in patent applications in most jurisdictions. Ichiro

Nakayama uses the JPO's 2019 *Examination Handbook for Patent and Utility Model* as an example to illustrate how the disclosure requirement in patent law is applied to AI inventions with inexplicable black boxes. He further explores how AI tools will affect the hypothetical person having ordinary skill in the art (PHOSITA) and the level of inventive step. Once we recognize that AI is a common tool used by the PHOSITA, the level of inventive step will rise dramatically because many scientific experiments will be much more easily completed with the assistance of AI.

Looking forward, AI may fundamentally change patent prosecution and the role of patent offices. While AI systems can easily determine the novelty, disclosure, and enablement of an invention, a patent office will only need to focus on whether the application meets the inventive-step requirement. Feroz Ali envisions this near future in which inventions are presented digitally to patent offices and patent prosecution becomes a decentralized, AI-enabled process.

The wide use of AI in creating works also challenges copyright policy's goal of maintaining the balance between protecting creative works and allowing the public to use them. AI can currently produce music, paintings, poems, film scripts, and a wide variety of other works. It is legally perplexing whether these works are subject to copyright protection. While humans have deployed various tools and technologies to create, they have been the main sources of creativity in the history of copyright law. However, as well as human beings, AI can now also make creative decisions and generate creative works by learning from existing works. This development has precipitated a debate concerning the copyrightability of AI-generated works. Andres Guadamuz provides a comparative analysis of copyrightability and originality issues regarding AI-generated works by studying copyright laws and practices in Australia, China, the United Kingdom (UK), and the United States (US), among others. While copyright laws in most jurisdictions do not protect AI-generated works, it is noteworthy that such works may be protected by the computer-generated works provisions in the Copyright, Designs and Patents Act (CDPA) 1988 in the UK. Similar provisions appear in some common law jurisdictions, such as Ireland, New Zealand, Hong Kong, and South Africa. Jyh-An Lee focuses on policy and legal issues surrounding the output of AI and copyright protection of computer-generated works under the CDPA 1988. He argues that from both legal and policy perspectives, the UK and other jurisdictions with similar computer-generated work provisions in their copyright laws should reconsider their approaches to these works.

Using AI to create works inevitably involves the reproduction of data, which might be the copyrighted works of others. Therefore, copyright infringement risks appear when TDM techniques are used to 'train' AI. To foster AI development and ease AI developers' concerns over copyright infringement, more and more jurisdictions have added TDM to their list of copyright exceptions. Notable examples include the UK 2014 amendment to the CDPA (1988), the German Copyright Law (2018), the Japan Copyright Law (2018), and the European Union (EU) Directive on Copyright in the Digital Single Market (2019). While these TDM exceptions are subject to different application criteria, copyright liability should obviously not overburden the promising development of AI. Tianxiang He's chapter explores the possible applications and legislation of TDM exceptions in China. After examining the copyright exceptions models in Japan, Korea, and Taiwan, he argues that a semi-open copyright exceptions model incorporating the essence of the Japanese Copyright Law is most suitable for China and its AI industry. Benjamin Sobel approaches the copyright limitation and exception of TDM from a different angle. He argues that TDM exceptions should be designed and applied based on the nature of training data. Sobel develops a novel taxonomy of training data and suggests that copyright law should only regulate market-encroaching uses of data.

As well as the application of substantive IP law, IP administration and enforcement have also been fundamentally reshaped by AI technology. Jianchen Liu and Ming Liu study China's patent examination of AI-related inventions and its recent regulatory movements. China first amended its Guidelines for Patent Examinations (Guidelines) in 2017 to allow the patentability of software-implemented business methods. It also distinguished computer-program-implemented inventions from computer programs themselves. The 2019 amendment of the Guidelines further points out that if an AI-related patent application contains both technical and non-technical plans, including algorithms and business methods, it will not be rejected directly because of the non-technical parts. Additionally, this chapter provides some examples of AI patents approved in China.

Anke Moerland and Conrado Freitas demonstrate how AI can be used to examine trademark applications and to assess prior marks in oppositions and infringement proceedings. Their chapter compares the functionality of AI-based algorithms used by trademark offices and evaluates the capability of these AI systems in applying legal tests for trademark examination. Their empirical findings reveal that only a few trademark offices are currently applying AI tools to assess the applications of trademark registration. Furthermore, no court has used AI to assist their judgement in a trademark case. Moerland and Freitas also identify AI's limitation in implementing legal tests associated with subjective judgement, such as the distinctiveness of a trademark and the likelihood of confusion among the relevant public.

Compared to IP administration in the public sector, AI techniques are more widely adopted by trademark and copyright owners and online platforms in the digital environment. Daniel Seng's chapter introduces various automated IP-enforcement mechanisms adopted by platforms, such as Amazon, Alibaba, and eBay. These mechanisms include automated detection systems for counterfeits and automated takedown systems for content providers. While these automated techniques significantly enhance the efficiency of IP enforcement, they are not a panacea to curb piracy and counterfeiting activities in the online marketplace. Substantial transaction costs still prevent IP owners, online sellers, and platforms from collaborating with each other to restrain piracy and counterfeiting activities. Moreover, technology-driven private ordering is potentially subject to manipulation because of information asymmetry between stakeholders. These problems may be reinforced by AI's black-box method of processing data. Seng proposes legal reforms to address the problems underlying automated IP enforcement mechanisms.

As the core of AI, software has transformed into a generative tool capable of learning and self-correcting. Unlike traditional software with predesigned inputs and outputs, the operation of AI-related software has become a dynamic process. For example, evolutionary algorithms are one genre of AI software that generate and continuously test solutions for their fitness to accomplish a given task. Hao-Yun Chen refers to such software as 'software 2.0' in her chapter, which mainly focuses on copyright protection for a new generation of computer programs. In addition to how copyright doctrines, such as idea/expression dichotomy and authorship, can be applied to software 2.0, she explores whether natural-rights and utilitarian theories can justify copyright protection of the functional aspects of software 2.0. Peter Slowinski's chapter discusses the general IP protection of AI software from a different angle by comparing the IP laws in the US and the EU. He investigates both copyright and patent protection of different parts of the AI software, which include algorithms, mathematical models, data, and overall applications.

The AI economy is a data-centric one because AI systems analyse enormous amounts of data. Therefore, access to and protection of data have been crucial to the development of the AI industry. Kung-Chung Liu and Shufeng Zheng classify data into three categories: data specifically generated for AI, big data, and copyright-protected data. While these three types are not mutually exclusive, each is subject to different protection and access issues governed by IP law, competition law, and personal data protection law. Moreover, data generated by the public and private sectors have different policy implications for their protection and access, which inevitably intertwine with other data policies, such as open data and competition policies. Matthias Leistner approaches the same issue from the EU perspective and argues that access to data is a more urgent issue than protection of data under the current IP regime. Like many other jurisdictions, databases with original selections or arrangements are protected by copyright law as compilations in the EU. Moreover, the EU Data Protection Directive has established a sui generis right for database makers. While both copyright law and the EU Data Protection Directive provide exceptions to exclusive rights, a more comprehensive infrastructural framework for data access and exchange is still desirable. Leistner's chapter also evaluates possible reforms of access to data, including establishing sector-specific access rights, requiring licences, and applying the fair, reasonable, and non-discriminatory (FRAND) terms to assure data users' access rights.

AI algorithms are intricately woven into our economy and create a pervasively automated society. Anselm Kamperman Sanders approaches IP issues from a broader perspective of human trust and governance. Because AI is a core component of the Fourth Industrial Revolution, AI-related IP has the potential to generate market dominance in the connected environment of sensory devices and datasets. Consequently, such IP will reshape market structures and trigger new competition policy concerns.

When machines begin to exhibit human-like intelligence, another legal puzzle appears: whether an AI should be recognized as a legal person, like a corporation. If the law identifies AIs as legal persons, they will be able to enjoy legal rights and bear legal obligations. AIs will also have the capacity to enter into agreements with other parties and to sue and be sued. AI personality has also become a commonly discussed issue in the IP literature. When AI plays a major role in creative and innovative activities and is referred to as a 'non-human' author or inventor, some suggest that it should be the legal subject that owns the IP in question. Likewise, when the deployment of AI involves IP-infringement risk, some contend that it should be held liable for infringement. Nonetheless, an AI as a legal person is not currently the mainstream viewpoint; the EPO and the USPTO have ruled that an AI system cannot be recognized as an inventor of a patent. Eliza Mik's chapter explains why AIs should not be deemed legal persons based on their technological features and the nature of legal persons in our current legal system.

This book is a result of collaboration between two Asian academic institutions—the Applied Research Centre for Intellectual Assets and the Law in Asia (ARCIALA), the School of Law, Singapore Management University, and the Chinese University of Hong Kong Faculty of Law—and one European institution, the Max Planck Institute of Innovation and Competition. As a result, it might have distinctly Asian and European touches; however, the editors intend to elucidate the general challenges and opportunities faced by every jurisdiction in the era of AI. We believe all policy and legal analysis should be based on a correct understanding of the technology and the economics of innovation, and an ideal policy should facilitate human sovereignty over machine efficiency. By the same token, a desirable IP policy should enable society to fully grasp the value of new technologies for economic prosperity.

PART I

TECHNOLOGY, BUSINESS, AND BASICS OF AI

1

Technical Elements of Machine Learning for Intellectual Property Law

*Anthony Man-Cho So**

1. Introduction

Although the field of artificial intelligence (AI) has been around for more than sixty years, its widespread influence is a rather recent (within the past decade or so) phenomenon. From human face recognition to artificial face generation, from automated recommendations on online platforms to computer-aided diagnosis, from game-playing programs to self-driving cars, we have witnessed the transformative power of AI in our daily lives. As it turns out, machine learning (ML) techniques lie at the core of many of these innovations. ML is a sub-field of AI that is concerned with the automated detection of meaningful patterns in data and using the detected patterns for certain tasks.[1] Roughly speaking, the learning process involves an algorithm,[2] which takes *training data* (representing past knowledge or experience) as input and outputs information that can be utilized by other algorithms to perform tasks such as prediction or decision-making. With the huge amount of data generated on various online platforms,[3] the increasing power (in terms of both speed and memory) of computers, and advances in ML research, researchers and practitioners alike have been able to unleash the power of ML and contribute to the many impressive technologies we are using or experiencing today. In this chapter, I will give an overview of the key concepts and constructions in ML and,

* All online materials were accessed before 30 March 2020.

[1] Shai Shalev-Shwartz and Shai Ben-David, *Understanding Machine Learning: From Theory to Algorithms* (Cambridge University Press 2014) (hereafter Shalev-Shwartz and Ben-David, *Understanding Machine Learning*).

[2] An *algorithm* is a well-defined sequence of computational steps for solving a problem. Specifically, it takes zero or more values as inputs and applies the sequence of steps to transform them into one or more outputs. Note that an algorithm can be described in, say, the English language (which is easier for humans to understand) or in a programming language (which is easier for the computer to process). The word *program* refers to an expression of an algorithm in a programming language. See Donald E Knuth, *The Art of Computer Programming. Volume I: Fundamental Algorithms*, 3rd edn (Addison Wesley Longman 1997) for a more detailed discussion.

[3] The data could be in the form of images and texts posted on social media, browsing and purchasing history on e-commerce sites, or emails sent and received using online email platforms, to name just a few.

Anthony Man-Cho So, *Technical Elements of Machine Learning for Intellectual Property Law* In: *Artificial Intelligence and Intellectual Property*. Edited by: Jyh-An Lee, Reto M Hilty, and Kung-Chung Liu, Oxford University Press (2021).
 DOI: 10.1093/oso/9780198870944.003.0002

with an aim to make them more concrete, explain the roles they play in some of the contemporary applications. In addition, I will elucidate the ways human efforts are involved in the development of ML solutions, which I hope could facilitate the legal discussions on intellectual property issues. In recent years, there has been much interest in applying ML techniques to legal tasks such as legal prediction and classification of legal documents. However, the discussion of these applications is beyond the scope of this chapter.[4]

2. Main Types of Machine Learning

The outcome of any learning process depends, among other things, on the material from which the learner learns. As alluded to in the introduction, in the context of ML, the learning material comes in the form of training data. Since the training data in most applications of interest are too complex and too large for humans to process and reason about, the power of modern computers is harnessed to identify the patterns in and extract information from those data. A key characteristic of ML algorithms is that they can adapt to their training data. In particular, with better training data (in terms of volume and quality), these algorithms can produce outputs that have better performance for the tasks at hand. In order to distinguish among different ML tasks, it is common to classify them according to the nature of the training data and the learning process. In this section, I will describe three main types of ML tasks—namely *supervised learning, unsupervised learning,* and *reinforcement learning*—and explain how they manifest themselves in various real-life applications.

2.1 Supervised Learning

Supervised learning refers to the scenario in which the training data contain certain information (commonly referred to as the *label*) that is missing in the *test data* (ie, data that have not been seen before), and the goal is to use the knowledge learned from the training data to predict the missing information in the test data. It has been successfully applied to various fields, such as credit risk assessment[5] and medical imaging.[6] To better understand the notion of supervised learning, let

[4] Readers who are interested in some of the applications of ML in the legal field can refer to, eg, Harry Surden, 'Machine Learning and Law' (2014) 89 Washington Law Review 87.

[5] Dinesh Bacham and Janet Yinqing Zhao, 'Machine Learning: Challenges, Lessons, and Opportunities in Credit Risk Modeling' (2017) 9 Moody's Analytics Risk Perspectives: Managing Disruption 30.

[6] Geert Litjens and others, 'A Survey on Deep Learning in Medical Image Analysis' (2017) 42 Medical Image Analysis 60.

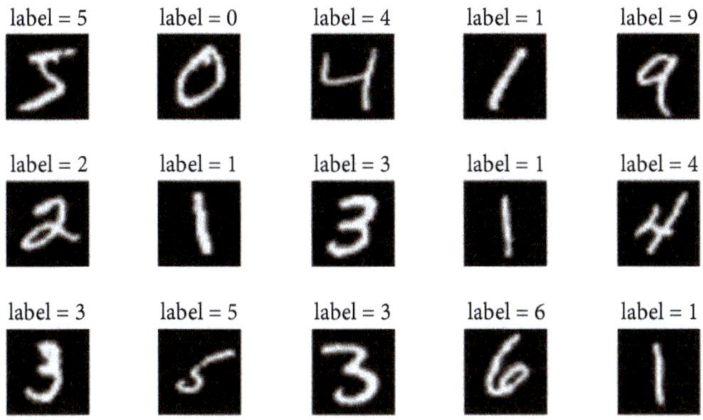

Figure 1.1 Sample handwritten digits from the MNIST database with their corresponding labels

me highlight three of its key elements—preparation of training data, formulation of the learning task, and implementation of algorithmic solutions to perform the learning.

2.1.1 Preparation of training data

The word 'supervised' in 'supervised learning' comes from the fact that the training data contain information that guides, or supervises, the learning process. Typically, the information is supplied by humans (a process referred to as *labelling the data*). As such, it often requires substantial effort to prepare the training data for a supervised learning task.[7] To illustrate the concepts of training data and test data in the supervised learning setting, consider the task of recognizing handwritten digits. The training data can be a collection of handwritten digit samples, each of which is labelled with its interpretation (ie, 0–9). Figure 1.1 shows a small portion of such a collection from the MNIST database.[8] Any collection of handwritten digit samples that have not been labelled or seen before can then be the test data.

It is important to note that in general the label given to a data sample is not guaranteed to be correct. This can be caused, eg, by human error or by the ambiguity in the data sample itself. For instance, in labelling handwritten digit samples,

[7] Nowadays, it is common to use crowdsourcing to get a large volume of data labelled. One manifestation of this is the use of CAPTCHAs (Completely Automated Public Turing test to tell Computers and Humans Apart) on various websites. Although the explicitly stated purpose of CAPTCHAs is to authenticate users as humans (to prove 'I'm not a robot'), the responses given by human users provide information about the queries posed by CAPTCHAs (eg, identify the traffic lights in the image, transcribe the distorted words, etc), thus labelling the data in those queries in the process. See, eg, Luis von Ahn and others, 'reCAPTCHA: Human-Based Character Recognition via Web Security Measures' (2008) 321(5895) Science 1465, for a discussion.

[8] Yann LeCun, Corinna Cortes, and Christopher JC Burges, 'The MNIST Database of Handwritten Digits' (2010) <http://yann.lecun.com/exdb/mnist/>.

Figure 1.2 An ambiguous handwritten digit: Is this a '0' or '6'?

mistakes can occur when the handwritten digits are hardly legible (Figure 1.2). As the premise of supervised learning is to use the knowledge learned from the labels of the training data samples to predict the labels of the test data samples, the presence of incorrectly labelled data samples can adversely affect the outcome of the learning process.

2.1.2 Formulation of learning task

The prediction of the labels of the data samples relies on a *prediction rule*—ie, a function that takes a data sample as input and returns a label for that sample as output. With this abstraction, the goal of supervised learning can be understood as coming up with a prediction rule that can perform well on most data samples. Here, the performance is evaluated by a *loss function*, which measures the discrepancy between the label returned by the prediction rule and the actual label of the data sample. The choice of the loss function is largely dictated by the learning task at hand and is commonly known.[9]

To achieve the aforementioned goal, a natural idea is to search among rules that minimize the loss function on the *training data*. In other words, we aim to find the rule that best fits our past knowledge or experience. However, without restricting the type of rules to search from, such an idea can easily lead to rules that perform poorly on the unseen *test data*. This phenomenon is known as *over-fitting*. As an illustration, consider the task of classifying data points on the plane into two categories. Figure 1.3 shows the training data, in which each data point is labelled by either a cross '×' or a circle '○' to indicate the category it belongs to. A prediction rule takes the form of a boundary on the plane, so that given any point, the side of the boundary on which the point falls will yield its predicted category. Given a boundary, a common way to measure its performance on the training data is to count the number of points that it misclassified. Naturally, the fewer misclassified points, the better the boundary.

Suppose that we do not restrict the type of boundaries we can use. Then, a boundary that misclassifies the fewest training data samples is given by the bolded curve in Figure 1.3a. Indeed, all the crosses are on the left of the curve, while all the circles are on the right. However, such a boundary fits the training data too well and is not well-suited for dealing with potential variations in the test data. In particular, it is more likely to return a wrong classification for a test data sample.

[9] See, eg, Shalev-Shwartz and Ben-David, *Understanding Machine Learning* (n 1) for a discussion of different loss functions.

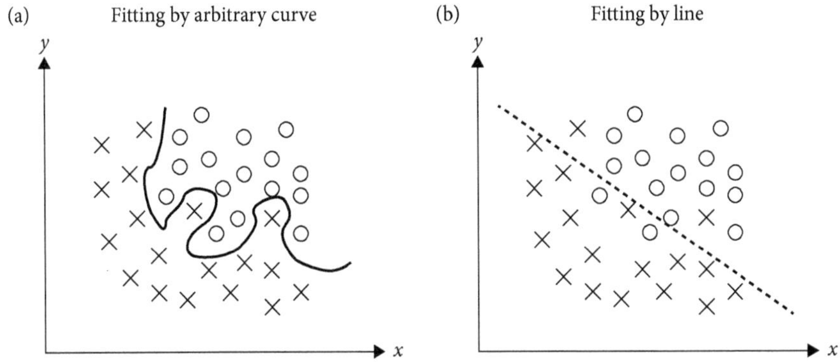

Figure 1.3 Illustration of over-fitting in a classification task

On the other hand, suppose that we restrict ourselves to using only straight-line boundaries. Then, the dotted line in Figure 1.3b yields the best performance among all straight lines in terms of the number of misclassified training data points. Although the dotted line incorrectly classifies some of those points (eg, there are two circles on the left and two crosses on the right of the line), it can better handle variations in the test data and is thus more preferred than the curved boundary in Figure 1.3a.

The above discussion highlights the necessity to choose the type of prediction rules that will be used to fit the training data. Such a choice depends on the learning task at hand and has to be made by human users before seeing the data. In general, there are many different types of prediction rules that one can choose from. Some examples include polynomial functions, decision trees, and neural networks of various architectures. A key characteristic of these different types of rules is that each type can be defined by a set of *parameters*. In other words, each choice of values for the parameters corresponds to one prediction rule of the prescribed type. For instance, in the classification example above, the straight-line boundaries used in Figure 1.3b, which are lines on the plane, can be described by two parameters—slope and intercept. As another illustration, let us consider neural networks, which constitute one of the most powerful and popular types of prediction rules in ML today. Roughly speaking, a neural network consists of nodes (representing *neurons*) linked by arrows. Each arrow has a *weight* and connects the output of a node (ie, the tail of the arrow) to the input of another node (ie, the head of the arrow). Each node implements a function whose input is given by a weighted sum of the outputs of all the nodes linked to it, where the weights are obtained from the corresponding arrows. The *architecture* of a neural network is specified by its nodes, the links between the nodes, and the functions implemented on the nodes.[10] The weights on the links then constitute the parameters that

[10] Shalev-Shwartz and Ben-David, *Understanding Machine Learning* (n 1).

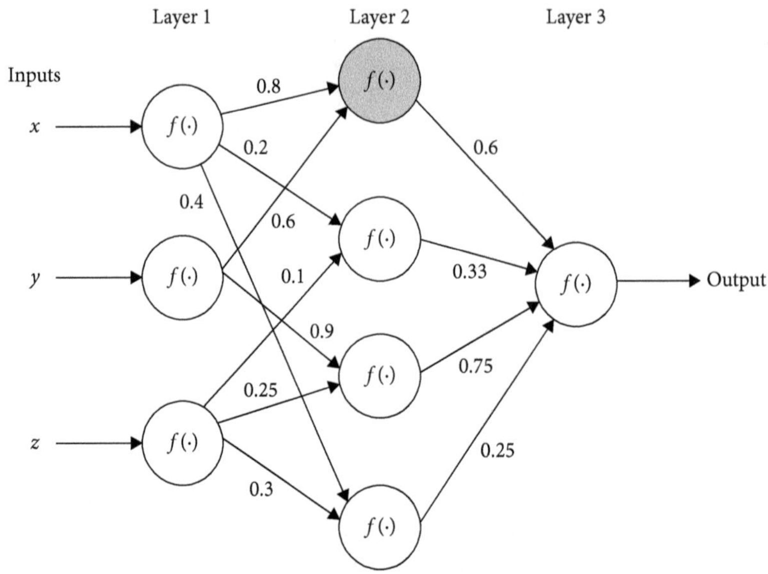

Figure 1.4 A simple feedforward neural network

describe different neural networks with the same architecture. Some commonly used neural network architectures include *autoencoders*, *convolutional neural networks* (CNNs), *feedforward networks*, and *recurrent neural networks* (RNNs). Each of these architectures is designed for particular learning tasks.[11]

Figure 1.4 shows an example of a simple three-layer feedforward neural network. It takes three inputs, which are denoted by x, y, z. The weight assigned to an arrow is given by the number next to it. All the nodes implement the same function, which is denoted by $f(\cdot)$.[12] To get a glimpse of what is being computed at the nodes, let us focus on the shaded node. It has two inputs, one from the output of the first node in the first layer, the second from the output of the second node in the first layer. The former, which equals $f(x)$, has a weight of 0.8; the latter, which equals $f(y)$, has a weight of 0.6. Therefore, the output of the shaded node is computed as $0.8 \times f(x) + 0.6 \times f(y)$. By assigning a different set of weights to the arrows, we obtain a different neural network with the same architecture. As an aside, one often sees the word 'deep' being used to describe neural networks nowadays. Loosely speaking, it simply refers to a neural network with many (say, more than two) layers.

[11] Ian Goodfellow, Yoshua Bengio, and Aaron Courville, *Deep Learning* (MIT Press 2016), available at <http://www.deeplearningbook.org> (hereafter Goodfellow, Bengio, and Courville, *Deep Learning*).

[12] Mathematically, a function can be regarded as specifying an input-output relationship. The dot '·' in the notation '$f(\cdot)$' represents a generic input to the function f. Given a number t as input, the function f returns the number $f(t)$ as output.

Once the human user specifies the type of prediction rules to use, the next step is to find the values of the parameters that minimize the loss function on the training data. This gives rise to a computational problem commonly known as *loss minimization*. By solving this problem, one obtains as output a prediction rule of the prescribed type that best fits the training data. The rule can then be integrated into other decision support tools to inform the decisions of human users.

2.1.3 Implementation of algorithmic solution

Loss minimization problems are typically solved by *iterative algorithms*. Starting from an initial choice of values for the parameters, which can be viewed as a point in space, these algorithms proceed by moving the point in a certain direction by a certain distance, and then repeat until a certain stopping criterion is met. Different algorithms have different rules for determining the direction and distance to use at each point and have different stopping criteria. Generally speaking, the directions and distances are designed in such a way that the values of the loss function evaluated at the points generated by the algorithm have a decreasing trend (recall that the goal is to minimize the loss function), and the algorithm stops when no further progress can be made. One popular iterative algorithm for solving loss minimization problems is the *stochastic gradient method*. At each step, the method moves the current point along a random direction that is generated based on the properties of the loss function, and the distance by which the point is moved is decreasing as the method progresses, so as to avoid overshooting the solution.[13]

Although algorithm design requires human efforts and it is natural for developers to protect their algorithms in some ways, the specifications (ie, the rules for choosing directions and distances, and the stopping criterion) of many iterative algorithms used in the ML community are public knowledge. Still, even after one settles on a particular iterative algorithm to solve the loss minimization problem at hand, the choice of initial values for the parameters (also known as the *initialization*) could affect the performance of the algorithm. To understand this phenomenon, let us consider the scenario shown in Figure 1.5. The points on the horizontal axis represent possible values of the parameter, and the curve represents the loss function $\mathcal{L}$. One can think of the curve representing $\mathcal{L}$ as a mountain range and an iterative algorithm as a person hiking there without a map and who can only explore her immediate surroundings to decide on which way to go. The goal of loss minimization can then be understood as finding the lowest point on the mountain range. In Figure 1.5, this is the black dot corresponding to the parameter value w^* and loss function value $\mathcal{L}(w^*)$.

[13] Sebastian Ruder, 'An overview of gradient descent optimization algorithms' (*Sebastian Ruder*, 19 January 2016) <https://arxiv.org/abs/1609.04747>.

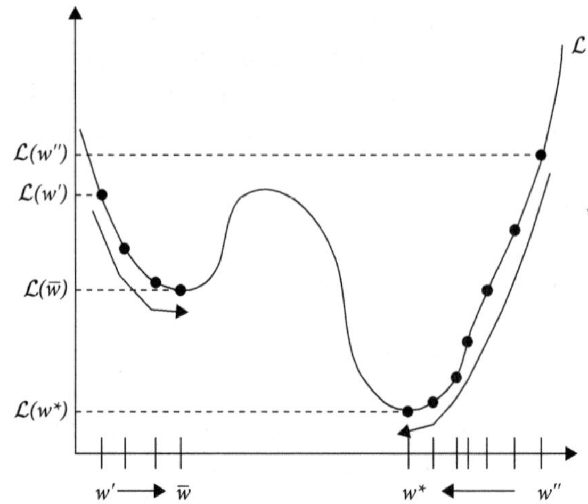

Figure 1.5 Effect of initialization

Now, suppose that the hiker starts at the leftmost black dot on the mountain range. This corresponds to initializing the algorithm at the point w' whose loss function value is $\mathcal{L}(w')$. To get to a lower point on the mountain range, the person will naturally walk down the valley until she reaches the point with value $\mathcal{L}(\overline{w})$. At this point, the hiker cannot reach a lower point on the mountain range without first going up. Since she does not have a full picture of the mountain range, she will be inclined to stop there. This is precisely the behaviour of most iterative algorithms—they will stop at a point when there is no other point with a lower loss function value nearby. However, it is clear that the point with value $\mathcal{L}(\overline{w})$ is not the lowest one on the mountain range. In other words, by starting at the leftmost black dot, most iterative algorithms will stop at the sub-optimal point that corresponds to the value $\mathcal{L}(\overline{w})$. On the other hand, if the algorithm starts at the rightmost black dot, which corresponds to taking w'' as the initial point with loss function value $\mathcal{L}(w'')$, then it will stop at the lowest point on the mountain range. The parameter value at this point is w^*, which corresponds to the prediction rule that best fits the training data.

In view of the above, a natural question is how to find a good initialization for the learning task at hand. Although there are some general rules-of-thumb for choosing the initialization, finding a good one is very much an art and requires substantial human input and experience.[14] Moreover, since the shape of the loss

[14] To quote Goodfellow, Bengio, and Courville, *Deep Learning* (n 11) 293, 'Modern initialization strategies are simple and heuristic. Designing improved initialization strategies is a difficult task because neural network optimization is not yet well understood.'

function depends on both the training data and the type of prediction rules used, an initialization that works well for one setting may not work well for another.

From the brief introduction of supervised learning above, it can be seen that the performance of the prediction rule obtained from a supervised learning process hinges upon three human-dependent factors: the quality of the training data (in particular, the informativeness of the labels), the type of prediction rules used to fit the training data (eg, the choice of a certain neural network architecture), and the algorithm (including its settings such as the initialization and the rule for finding the next point) used to solve the loss minimization problem associated with the learning task. As such, the prediction rules obtained by two different users will generally be different if they specify any of the above factors differently. Putting it in another way, it is generally difficult to reproduce the outcome of a supervised learning process without knowing how each of the above three factors is specified. In addition, the prediction rule obtained is often neither transparent nor interpretable. Indeed, a human cannot easily explain how an iterative algorithm combines the different features of the data to produce the prediction rule, or how the rule makes predictions, or why the rule makes a certain prediction for a given data sample. Such a *black-box* nature of the prediction rule limits our understanding of the learning task at hand and could have various undesirable consequences.[15]

2.2 Unsupervised Learning

Unlike supervised learning, in which the goal is to learn from the labels of the training data samples a rule that can predict the labels of the unseen test data samples as accurately as possible, unsupervised learning is concerned with the scenario where the training data samples do not have any labels and the goal, loosely speaking, is to uncover *hidden structure* in the data. Such a goal is based on the belief that data generated by physical processes are not random but rather contain information about the processes themselves.[16] For instance, a picture taken by a camera typically contains a foreground and a background, and one can try to identify the backgrounds in image data for further processing. However, in an unsupervised learning task, there is no external guidance on whether the uncovered structure is correct or not, hence the word 'unsupervised'. This is in contrast to supervised learning, where one can evaluate the accuracy of the prediction rule by comparing the predicted labels and actual labels of the data samples. Thus, one may

[15] In recent years, there has been growing interest in *interpretable ML*, which concerns the design of ML systems whose outputs can be explained; see Christoph Molnar, *Interpretable Machine Learning: A Guide for Making Black Box Models Explainable* (1st edn, Lulu 2019) for some recent advances in this direction (hereafter Molnar, *Interpretable Machine Learning*).

[16] DeLiang Wang, 'Unsupervised Learning: Foundations of Neural Computation—A Review' (2001) 22(2) AI Magazine 101.

say that unsupervised learning has a much less well-defined goal. Nevertheless, it is more typical of how humans learn. Indeed, as Geoffrey Hinton, one of the most prominent researchers in artificial intelligence, put it:[17]

> When we're learning to see, nobody's telling us what the right answers are—we just look.... The brain's visual system requires 10^{14} [neural] connections. And you only live for 10^9 seconds. So it's no use learning one bit per second. You need more like 10^5 bits per second. And there's only one place you can get that much information—from the input itself.

Moreover, since unsupervised learning does not require labelled data—which, as previously mentioned, are not only more expensive to obtain but also quite limited due to the substantial human efforts involved—it is applicable to many more settings. As a first illustration, let us consider one of the most fundamental tasks in unsupervised learning—*clustering*.

2.2.1 Clustering

Roughly speaking, the goal of clustering is to divide the data samples into groups, so that those with similar characteristics belong to the same group and those with different characteristics are separated into different groups. The discovered clusters can then inform the decisions of human users. Clustering is a data analysis technique that has many applications, such as customer segmentation (the process of identifying groups of customers with similar characteristics so that targeted marketing can be carried out)[18] and image segmentation (the process of dividing images into regions so that each region is largely homogeneous).[19]

One may note the similarity of clustering with classification (recall the example shown in Figure 1.3). However, there is a fundamental difference between the two. In a classification task, each training data sample is labelled with its category. As such, we know exactly how many categories are there and what similar data samples look like. By contrast, in a clustering task, it is not clear how many groups one should divide the data samples into and how to define similarity (or dissimilarity) between two samples. Thus, depending on the notion of similarity used, it is entirely possible to come up with different but equally convincing groupings of the same set of data. To demonstrate such a possibility, let us consider dividing the points below (which constitute the data samples) into two groups.[20]

[17] Pam Frost Groder, 'Neural Networks Show New Promise for Machine Vision' (2006) 8(6) Computing in Science & Engineering 4.

[18] Michael J Shaw and others, 'Knowledge Management and Data Mining for Marketing' (2001) 31(1) Decision Support Systems 127.

[19] Richard Szeliski, *Computer Vision: Algorithms and Applications* (Springer-Verlag 2011).

[20] This example is taken from Chapter 22 of Shalev-Shwartz and Ben-David, *Understanding Machine Learning* (n 1).

If one prefers not to separate nearby points, then the points should be divided into the two groups shown in Figure 1.6a. However, if one prefers not to have far-away points belonging to the same group, then the points should be divided into the two groups shown in Figure 1.6b.

The existence of multiple different clustering criteria motivates the development of various clustering algorithms. In general, human input is needed to define a suitable criterion for the clustering task at hand. Once the criterion is fixed, further human input is needed to either choose an existing algorithm (if available) or design a new one to compute a desired clustering of the data samples.

2.2.2 Generative modelling

As another illustration, let us turn to *generative modelling*—an unsupervised learning task that has attracted much attention in recent years. Besides being used to inform decisions, the information extracted from the training data can also be used to build a model (in the form of an algorithm) for generating new data samples that resemble or are highly related to the training data. The task of building such a model is known as generative modelling. It lies at the core of many intriguing applications, such as image generation (eg, to generate highly realistic synthetic photographs that are practically indistinguishable from real ones)[21] and poem generation (eg, to generate a poem that 'describes' the scene of an input image).[22]

(a) Nearby points should not be separated

(b) Far-away points should not share the same group

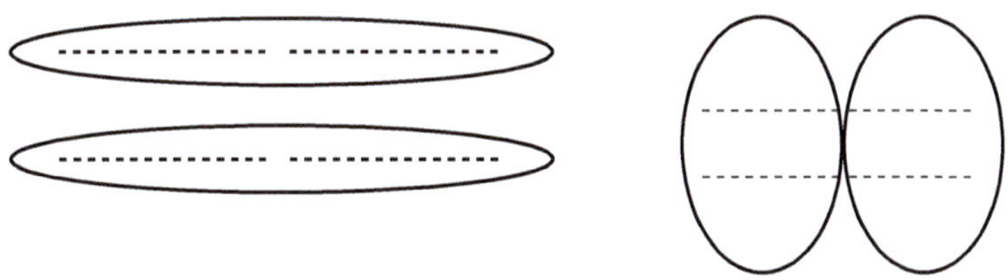

Figure 1.6 Clustering points into two clusters

[21] For a state-of-the-art approach, see Tero Karras and others, 'Analyzing and Improving the Image Quality of StyleGAN' (2019) https://arxiv.org/abs/1912.04958 Readers who are interested in seeing its performance can visit https://thispersondoesnotexist.com/ (for human face generation) or https://thiscatdoesnotexist.com/ (for cat photo generation).

[22] Bei Liu and others, 'Beyond Narrative Description: Generating Poetry from Images by Multi-Adversarial Training' (2018) Proceedings of the 26th ACM International Conference on Multimedia 783.

Currently, one of the most powerful approaches to generative modelling is to use a neural network architecture called *generative adversarial network* (GAN).

A GAN consists of two components, namely the *generator* and the *discriminator*. The generator produces new data samples that are supposed to resemble the training data (the fake data). These generated data samples are then passed along with some training data samples (the real data) to the discriminator, whose task is to classify the data samples it receives as either real or fake. As the word 'adversarial' suggests, these two components can be viewed as two players in a game, in which the generator aims to make the real and fake data samples indistinguishable to the discriminator, while the discriminator aims to correctly classify the data samples that are being passed to it. The two components interact in rounds. At the end of each round, the generator is updated depending on how well it fools the discriminator, while the discriminator is updated depending on how well it classifies the real and fake data samples. The interaction ends when the discriminator is no longer able to distinguish between the real and fake data.[23] At this point we say that the GAN is *trained*, and the resulting generator can be used as the generative model. Figure 1.7 shows the schematic view of a GAN.

In more detail, both the generator and discriminator are represented by neural networks. From the discussion in Section 2.1, we know that each of these neural networks has its own set of parameters. To measure how well these two networks perform, two loss functions are introduced, one for the generator (denoted by $\mathcal{L}_G$) and one for the discriminator (denoted by $\mathcal{L}_D$). These loss functions take the parameters of both the generator and discriminator networks as input. However, since the generator and discriminator are competing against each other, each can only control the parameters of its own network. In particular, only after both the generator and discriminator fix the values of the parameters of their own networks would the values of the loss functions $\mathcal{L}_G$ and $\mathcal{L}_D$ be known. Such a setting can best be understood as a game between the generator and discriminator,

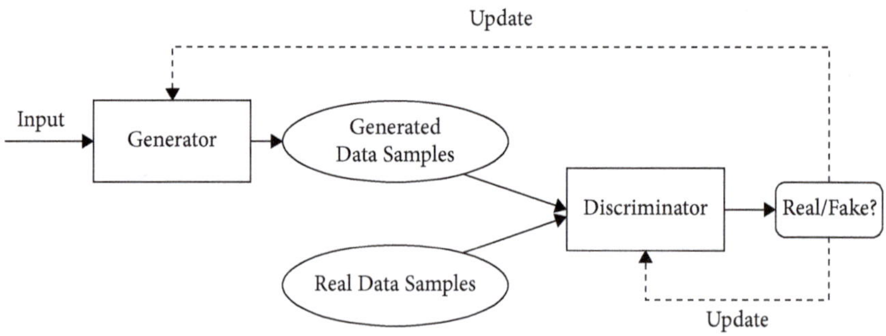

Figure 1.7 Schematic view of a GAN

[23] One can formalize this by comparing the classification accuracy of the discriminator with that of random guess, which is 0.5.

where each player's move is to choose the values of the parameters it controls, and the payoffs to the players are given by the corresponding values of the loss functions and are known only after both players make their moves. The goal of the game is to find the values of the parameters of the generator and discriminator networks so that the loss functions $\mathcal{L}_G$ and $\mathcal{L}_D$ are minimized. This gives rise to a computational problem that can again be solved by iterative algorithms.

Naturally, the performance of a GAN depends on the architectures of the generator and discriminator networks, the choice of the loss functions $\mathcal{L}_G$ and $\mathcal{L}_D$ and the iterative algorithm used to minimize them, and the training data. While there are some standard choices for the network architectures, loss functions, and the algorithm for minimizing the loss functions,[24] a human user will have to come up with the training data and the initialization strategy for the algorithm. Without knowing either of these two ingredients, it is virtually impossible to reproduce the generator obtained from a trained GAN.

In view of its applications in generative modelling, particularly on content (eg, photos, artworks, poems, etc) generation, one may ask whether GANs have the intelligence to do creation on their own. Our discussions above suggest that the answer is no. Indeed, the training of a GAN relies on a number of ingredients supplied by a human user. The computer only executes the instructions of the human user to identify the patterns in and extract information from the training data. The generator obtained from a trained GAN can thus be viewed as a non-linear function that is created using the ingredients supplied by the human user. However, it is generally difficult to pin down precisely how the function depends on those ingredients, as the process of creating the function is too complex for humans to reason about using the currently available tools.

2.3 Reinforcement Learning

Reinforcement learning refers to the scenario in which an *agent*[25] learns by interacting with its environment over time to achieve a certain goal. The interaction involves the agent taking actions to change the *state* of the environment and receiving *feedback* in the form of rewards and penalties from the environment, while the goal is typically to maximize the total cumulative reward. To have a more concrete understanding of the above concepts, let us consider the familiar game of tic-tac-toe.

Illustration: Tic-Tac-Toe. In the classic setting of tic-tac-toe, two players take turns playing on a 3-by-3 board. One player places an '×' in an unoccupied slot

[24] Ian Goodfellow, 'NIPS 2016 Tutorial: Generative Adversarial Networks' (2017) https://arxiv.org/abs/1701.00160.

[25] The term 'agent' refers to a generic decision-making entity, such as a computer program.

of the board when it is her turn, while the other player places an 'O'. A player wins when her symbol appears three in a row, either horizontally, vertically, or diagonally.

With the above setup, each player is an agent. A state of the game corresponds to a configuration (ie, placement of the ×'s and O's) of the board. The actions available to an agent on her turn are the different ways she can place her symbol in the current configuration of the board. Hence, the game changes to a new configuration after the play of each player. There could be many different ways to define the reward of an action. One possibility is to define it as 1 if the game is won after the action is played, -1 if the game is lost or ends in a draw, and 0 otherwise.

It is worth noting that even in such a simple game, the number of different states is large: Assuming that '×' is played first, there are 5,478 different states of the game!

From the above illustration, it can be seen that reinforcement learning is rather different from supervised learning. Indeed, it needs to account for the interactions between the agent and the environment, and it is often impractical to obtain labelled training data that indicate which actions are 'correct' in which state of the environment. Reinforcement learning is also different from unsupervised learning, in that it aims to maximize a certain reward function rather than to uncover hidden structure. Generally speaking, in a reinforcement learning task, an agent only knows the reward of the action it has taken but not whether that action has the most reward. Thus, the agent has to try out different actions in order to discover the one with the most reward. In the process, however, the agent could incur penalties. In addition, the action taken by the agent at present time may affect not only the immediate reward but also the actions that are available afterwards and hence the future rewards. These features naturally pose a great challenge to the agent. On one hand, the agent should *exploit* what it has learned from the environment by repeating actions that it has taken before and found to produce reward. On the other hand, the agent should *explore* the environment by trying actions that it has not taken before in order to discover ones with better reward. Therefore, to be successful in a reinforcement learning task, the agent must carefully manage the trade-off between exploration and exploitation.

There are various algorithms for solving reinforcement learning problems. One family is the *evolutionary methods*.[26] These methods are inspired by biological evolution and proceed in three steps. First, a collection of initial solutions is generated. Here, a solution, which is commonly referred to as a *policy* in the literature, takes the form of a function that specifies the action to be taken by the agent from each state. Next, the solutions undergo 'reproduction', meaning that new solutions are generated, eg, by either combining (known as *recombination*) or modifying (known as *mutation*) existing ones in a certain way. Then, a 'natural selection' of the

[26] Zhi-Hua Zhou, Yang Yu, and Chao Qian, *Evolutionary Learning: Advances in Theories and Algorithms* (Springer Nature Singapore Pte Ltd 2019).

solutions is performed, in which solutions that yield the most reward are carried over to the next generation. These solutions will undergo another round of reproduction and the whole process repeats until certain stopping criterion is met. There are various evolutionary methods in the literature, which differ in their implementations of the three steps above. These methods can be effective when the number of states and number of actions available at each state are small. Nevertheless, they do not make use of the information contained in the state-action relationships of the reinforcement learning problem at hand. For instance, the natural selection step selects solutions that lead to a high cumulative reward. However, for those solutions, it does not reveal which actions taken in which states are crucial to getting the high cumulative reward. Thus, evolutionary methods can be quite inefficient.[27]

Another family of algorithms that can address this shortcoming is the *value function methods*. Roughly speaking, these methods also proceed in three steps, and they differ in their implementations of these steps. First, using some initial policy, a sequence of states, together with the actions taken and the corresponding rewards earned along the way, is generated. Next, the generated information is used to estimate a *value function*, which specifies for each state the total reward that an agent can expect to earn in the future if it starts from that state. For environments with a huge number of states,[28] the value function is typically approximated by a neural network. In this case, estimating the value function means finding values of the parameters of the neural network that best fit the information collected in the first step. Lastly, the estimated value function is used to update the policy, and the whole process repeats until a certain stopping criterion is met. It should be noted that reward and value are two different notions. The former measures the *immediate* merit of an action, while the latter measures the *long-term* merit of a state by taking into account the possible subsequent states and the rewards of the actions that lead to those states. Thus, value function methods can evaluate the merit of individual states and hence can better exploit the state-action relationships of the problem at hand.[29]

Recently, the use of reinforcement learning techniques has led to some very impressive advances in board game-playing (eg, AlphaGo),[30] video game-playing (eg, StarCraft),[31] and autonomous driving,[32] just to name a few. As most applications of

[27] Richard S Sutton and Andrew G Barto, *Reinforcement Learning: An Introduction*, 2nd edn (The MIT Press 2018) (hereafter Sutton and Barto, *Reinforcement Learning*).

[28] For many contemporary applications such as the board game Go, the number of states can easily exceed the number of atoms in the whole universe (which is roughly 10^{80}). Even with today's supercomputer, which can execute roughly 10^{17} calculations per second, it will take more than 10^{63} seconds, or 10^{55} years, to enumerate all the states.

[29] Sutton and Barto, *Reinforcement Learning* (n 27).

[30] David Silver and others, 'Mastering the Game of Go Without Human Knowledge' (2017) 550 Nature 354.

[31] Oriol Vinyals and others, 'Grandmaster Level in StarCraft II Using Multi-Agent Reinforcement Learning' (2019) 575 Nature 350.

[32] Jack Stilgoe, 'Self-driving Cars Will Take a While to Get Right' (2019) 1 Nature Machine Intelligence 202.

interest give rise to reinforcement learning tasks that have an astronomical number of states, careful implementation of algorithms and significant computational resources are essential to getting good results. Both of these factors require substantial human input and cannot be easily reproduced.

3. Closing Remarks

In this chapter, I gave an overview of three types of ML problems and discussed the technical elements in each. A theme that is common in all three types of problems is the use of certain algorithms to extract information from data so as to enable humans to perform complex tasks. Whether the learning process yields useful results depends mainly on the formulation of the learning task at hand (eg, for supervised learning, the type of prediction rule used for classification; for unsupervised learning, the criterion used to define clusters in the data; for reinforcement learning, the reward and penalty used to train a self-driving car), the algorithm used to tackle the formulation and its implementation details (eg, initialization strategy), and the volume and quality of the data (which represent past knowledge or experience). As explained in this chapter, the above factors, especially the last two, rely heavily on human users' input. In particular, it is generally difficult to reproduce the outcome of a learning process without knowing how each of the factors is specified. Moreover, the outcome is typically given as a black box, which lacks transparency and interpretability. It is often unclear to humans what features of the training data are used by an ML algorithm to produce the output and how the output accomplishes its objective.

Due to their ability to perform tasks that are beyond human capabilities, modern ML systems are often deemed 'intelligent' in the sense that they can create or reason on their own. In reality, the power of these systems is limited by how the learning tasks are formulated and what data are used to train them. As it turns out, such a limitation could have far-reaching consequences, legal, ethical, and otherwise. For instance, since ML algorithms take the training data as input, they will pick up biases in the data and encode them in their output. In a recent study, it has been shown that 'standard machine learning can acquire stereotyped biases from textual data that reflect everyday human culture'.[33] On one hand, such a finding suggests the possibility of using ML techniques to study and identify prejudicial behaviour in humans. On the other hand, it also means that ML-based decision support tools can give discriminatory results. A case in point is Amazon's ML-based recruiting tool, which aims to automate the process of reviewing job

[33] Aylin Caliskan, Joanna J Bryson, and Arvind Narayanan, 'Semantics Derived Automatically from Language Corpora Contain Human-like Biases' (2017) 356(6334) Science 183.

applicants' résumés and searching for top talents.[34] The tool took the résumés submitted to the company over a ten-year period as training data. However, most of these résumés were from men. As a result, the tool tends to penalize résumés from female applicants. Although the problem was later identified and attempts to make the tool more gender-neutral were made, the black-box nature of ML processes means that it is difficult to rule out other form of biases in the resulting tool. The need to tackle the issue of bias in ML systems in part drives the recent growth in research on interpretable and fair ML.[35] Another example is adversarial attacks on ML systems—ie, the use of carefully designed data samples to force the ML systems to commit an error. For instance, it has been found that various image classification systems obtained by training standard neural network architectures using different sets of training data can be fooled by adversarially designed images. In some cases, the adversarial image is just a slight perturbation of a correctly classified image and is essentially the same as the latter from a human perspective.[36] Such a finding shows that the behaviour of ML systems is not only very different from that of humans but can also be manipulated in ways that have negative consequences. It is now an active research area to develop ML systems that are robust against adversarial attacks.[37]

Although the aforementioned efforts to overcome the limitations of ML systems do lead us closer to being able to explain their inner workings and interpret their outputs, there is still much work to be done and it is entirely possible that the development of new, more complex ML systems can outpace these efforts.

[34] Reuters, *Amazon scraps secret AI recruiting tool that showed bias against women* (2018) https://www.reuters.com/article/us-amazon-com-jobs-automation-insight/amazon-scraps-secret-ai-recruiting-tool-that-showed-bias-against-women-idUSKCN1MK08G.

[35] Molnar, *Interpretable Machine Learning* (n 15); Morgan Gregory, 'What Does Fairness in AI Mean?' (15 January 2020) https://www.forbes.com/sites/googlecloud/2020/01/15/what-does-fairness-in-ai-mean/.

[36] Readers can refer to Samuel G Finlayson and others, 'Adversarial Attacks on Medical Machine Learning' (2019) 363(6433) Science 1287, for examples of adversarial attacks on medical imaging systems.

[37] See, eg, Gean T Pereira and André CPLF de Carvalho, 'Bringing Robustness Against Adversarial Attacks' (2019) 1 Nature Machine Intelligence 499.

2

The Rise and Application of Artificial Intelligence in Healthcare

*Ivan Khoo Yi and Andrew Fang Hao Sen**

1. What is AI in Healthcare?

In broad terms, AI is the use of computer algorithms to perform logical tasks or deductions, which are otherwise associated with human intelligence.[1] In particular, in the area of clinical medicine, the specific task of AI is to utilize computer algorithms to generate information about patients or their conditions—using data made available during the routine course of medical examination, history-taking, investigation, and treatment—in order to aid clinical management.[2] Some authors have even argued that these algorithms have the capacity to outperform healthcare professionals in performing specific tasks associated with clinical deduction and management.[3]

AI has also been leveraged for non-clinical aspects such as optimizing healthcare workflows and automating mundane tasks like billing and medical coding.[4] Even more broadly, within the healthcare ecosystem, AI has impacted and even redefined certain aspects work for not just healthcare providers, but also other stakeholders such as healthcare regulators, pharmaceutical companies, medical device manufacturers, and insurance companies.

* All online materials were accessed before 10 February 2020.

1 Jianxing He, Sally L. Baxter, Jie Xu, Jiming Xu, Xingtao Zhou, and Kang Zhang, 'The Practical Implementation of Artificial Intelligence Technologies in Medicine' (2019) 25(1) Nature Medicine 30–6.

2 Ibid.

3 Jack Guy, 'AI may be as effective as medical specialists at diagnosing disease' (*CNN Health*, 25 September 2019) https://edition.cnn.com/2019/09/25/health/ai-disease-diagnosis-scli-intl/index.html.

4 Jennifer Bresnick, 'Identifying near-term use cases for AI in the healthcare setting' (*Health IT Analytics*, 22 March 2019) <https://healthitanalytics.com/news/identifying-near-term-use-cases-for-ai-in-the-healthcare-setting> (hereafter Bresnick, 'Identifying near-term use cases').

Ivan Khoo Yi and Andrew Fang Hao Sen, *The Rise and Application of Artificial Intelligence in Healthcare*
In: *Artificial Intelligence and Intellectual Property.* Edited by: Jyh-An Lee, Reto M Hilty, and Kung-Chung Liu,
Oxford University Press (2021). © The several contributors. DOI: 10.1093/oso/9780198870944.003.0003

2. The Entry of AI in Healthcare

Today, more than ever, there has been an explosion of available electronic health records (EHR) as clinics and hospitals increasingly digitize record-keeping.[5] The volume of healthcare data is estimated to increase by 48% annually, swelling to an estimated 2,314 exabytes (2,314 billion gigabytes) by 2020.[6] Together with the volume of data, the variety of data that has become available has also been expanded by the inclusion of relatively newer data types such as genomic and imaging data. Topping it all off, we have also experienced an accelerating velocity of data ingestion in the form of constantly-flowing medical biodata from devices like wearable health trackers and video cameras used for telemedicine services.

This wealth of information available, coupled with the advancement of machine processing power and the development of ever-more sophisticated algorithms, is rapidly changing the way diagnosis, pattern recognition, information retrieval, and outcome prediction is happening in the medical sphere.[7]

Furthermore, as AI becomes ever more ubiquitous and inseparable from our daily lives—optimizing the way we shop, travel, or even think—it has, and will increasingly be part of the way doctors manage their decision-making processes and how patients want to be treated.[8] This, in turn is gradually paving the way for greater cultural receptivity of AI, especially amongst healthcare providers. For the more optimistic medical providers, the advent of AI is viewed as the perfect opportunity to leverage this new technology to improve the way healthcare providers work, positively impacting patient outcomes. On the other hand, for the sceptics amongst healthcare providers— resistance is waning and even the most sceptical practitioners, would grudgingly acknowledge that they will personally encounter some implementation of AI technology in their practice of medicine.

It is the combination of these trends of: (1) increasing volumes and availability of data, (2) advancing data processing technology, and (3) improving receptivity, which has contributed to a self-perpetuating cycle of accelerated AI adoption in the healthcare industry. In other words, the increasing data availability, which allows for experimentation of new AI technologies, leads to increased adoption which thereby further increases the chance of success and encourages a further increased collection of even more data to feed the entire cycle.

[5] Beau Norgeot, Benjamin S Glicksberg, and Atul J Butte, 'A Call for Deep-learning Healthcare' (2019) 25(1) Nature Medicine 14, 15 (hereafter Norgeot, Glicksberg, and Butte, 'A Call for Deep-learning Healthcare').

[6] This estimate is from a report published in 2014. See EMC—The Digital Universe Driving Data Growth in Healthcare <https://www.emc.com/analyst-report/digital-universe-healthcare-vertical-report-ar.pdf>.

[7] Norgeot, Glicksberg, and Butte, 'A Call for Deep-learning Healthcare' (n 5) 14.

[8] Ibid.

3. Implementations of AI in Healthcare

The various implementations of AI in healthcare are myriad and ever expanding, and while this chapter seeks to provide as broad an overview as possible, we recognize that this will be in no way exhaustive, with new implementations being discovered daily. In facilitation of this general discussion, we have categorized the various current implementations of AI in healthcare according to the various primary stakeholders within the healthcare system, in what we have termed—the 5 'P's:

(i) Providers (Healthcare professionals and administrators);
(ii) Patients (and their caregivers);
(iii) Pharmaceuticals (Drug and medical device manufacturers);
(iv) Payers (Insurance companies and employers);
(v) Policymakers (Regulators and government).

3.1 Providers (Healthcare Professionals and Administrators)

3.1.1 Clinical decision support

The most obvious and direct implementation of AI in healthcare can be seen in the various clinical decision support tools which have been used to support and aid clinical diagnosis and management.

Dermatology. In the area of dermatology and with regards to the classification of skin lesions, AI has been proven to be able to at least match and even surpass human specialist doctors in accurately diagnosing and classifying malignant skin conditions.[9] Although such studies are heavily caveated by the physician's ability to pick up other concurrent related or unrelated medical problems, as well as to take responsibility for misdiagnosis, it is clear that in the area of specific tasks, AI promises the possibility of increased accuracy and the ability to bring expert diagnosis into the primary care sector.[10]

Surgery. AI can help surgeons actively identify missed steps in real time, during surgery.[11] AI-driven machine learning has also been shown to be able to identify surgical site complications, as well as identifying negative predictors for patient complications in the post-operative setting.[12] In fact, the multiple

9 Eric J Topol, 'High-performance Medicine: The Convergence of Human and Artificial Intelligence' (2019) 25 (1) Nature Medicine, 44–56, 46.

10 Ibid.

11 Daniel A Hashimoto, Guy Rosman, Daniela Rus, and Ozanan R Meireles, 'Artificial Intelligence in Surgery: Promises and Perils' (2018) 268(1) Ann Surg 70–6 (hereafter Hashimoto, Rosman, Rus, and Meireles, 'Artificial Intelligence in Surgery').

12 Ibid, 70, 71.

algorithms developed can quite confidently identify both population-specific and individual-specific information for each patient, helping to support surgical teams in medical management tailored to the individual patient.[13] While robotic-assisted surgery currently comprises mainly of surgeons using guiding the robotic instruments via a televised screen (not unlike a three-dimensional interactive game), it has been postulated that machine learning can be used to observe and learn from surgeons, especially for repetitive tasks such as suturing, possibly helping to augment surgical abilities and assist in time-intensive tasks.[14] However, a major caveat to such advances would be the need for AI to be able to adapt to different anatomical anomalies or the complexities of something as intuitive to humans as the perception of depth.[15]

Oncology. Immunotherapy for cancer is not an exact science. While many immunotherapy options are available, a patient's DNA ultimately determines whether a certain treatment will be effective for him or her. In this aspect, machine learning algorithms can be harnessed to analyse large volumes of data information, far more efficaciously than humans, in order to enable us to recognize patterns in genetics strings in patients' DNA, allowing us to then correlate those patterns against immunotherapy options, which will hopefully be effective in that particular patient. If successful on consistent scale, this capability could possibly result in a truly personalized approach to cancer treatment,[16] and medical therapy at large.

Renal Medicine. DeepMind, the company behind AlphaGo, which made history defeating the world champion in a game of Go,[17] has had forays into real world medical applications since 2015, when it teamed up the Royal Free London NHS Foundation Trust to develop an application named Streams.[18] Streams utilises patient data generated inpatient to help physicians decide whether a certain patient is at risk of developing acute kidney injury (AKI), alerting doctors to take preventive action as soon as possible.[19] Despite early concerns about a breach of data protection legislation concerning the personal data of patients,[20] this has not stopped the adoption of Streams in other healthcare institutions, with reviews finding that it

[13] Ibid.

[14] Andre Esteva, Alexandre Robicquet, Bharath Ramsundar, Volodymyr Kuleshov, Mark DePristo, Katherine Chou, Claire Cui, Greg Corrado, Sebastien Thrun, and Jeff Dean, 'A Guide to Deep Learning in Healthcare' (2019) 25(1) Nature Medicine 26.

[15] Ibid.

[16] Lisa Morgan, 'Artificial intelligence in healthcare: how AI shapes medicine' (*Datamation*, 8 March 2019) https://www.datamation.com/artificial-intelligence/artificial-intelligence-in-healthcare.html.

[17] Dawn Chan, 'The AI that has nothing to learn from humans' (*The Atlantic*, 20 October 2017) https://www.theatlantic.com/technology/archive/2017/10/alphago-zero-the-ai-that-taught-itself-go/543450/.

[18] 'Our Work with Google Health UK' (*Royal Free London NHS Foundation Trust*) https://www.royalfree.nhs.uk/patients-visitors/how-we-use-patient-information/our-work-with-deepmind/.

[19] Ibid.

[20] 'Royal Free—Google DeepMind trial failed to comply with data protection law' (*Information Commissioner's Office*, 3 July 2017) https://ico.org.uk/about-the-ico/news-and-events/news-and-blogs/2017/07/royal-free-google-deepmind-trial-failed-to-comply-with-data-protection-law/.

could reduce the costs of admission for AKI by up to 17%.[21] A recent report published by DeepMind in association with the US Department of Veteran Affairs (VA),[22] was also similarly able to demonstrate the ability of their machine learning algorithm to predict 55.8% inpatient AKI events forty-eight hours before their onset, [23,24] giving doctors the opportunity to intervene early, in order to prevent life-threatening consequences.[25]

Ophthalmology. With an increasing concern over the rapidly growing diabetic population worldwide,[26,27] access to timely retina care has never been more relevant and has been proven to reduce the risk of vision loss in diabetics by up to 95%, contributing to significant cost savings for both patients and society at large.[28] Guidelines from the American Diabetes Association currently recommend diabetics without any eye symptoms to be seen by an ophthalmologist twice a year, although it has been estimated that only 50% of patients follow this recommendation.[29] In this regard, the use of AI has proven to be a useful adjunct to telemedicine, with a study conducted using multiethnic data from the Singapore National Diabetic Retinopathy Screening Program, showing that a machine learning algorithm was able to achieve a sensitivity of 93% and specificity of 77.5%, which improved to a sensitivity of 91.3% and specificity of 99.% if the AI-generated results were further graded by eye surgeons.[30] The usefulness of such AI-powered

[21] Andrea Downey, 'DeepMind's Streams app saves £2,000 per patient, peer review finds' (*Digitalhealth*) <https://www.digitalhealth.net/2019/07/deepminds-streams-saves-2000-peer-review/>.

[22] Nenad Tomašev, Xavier Glorot, and Jack W Rae, 'A Clinically Applicable Approach to Continuous Prediction of Future Acute Kidney Injury' (2019) 572 Nature 116–19 (hereafter Tomašev, Glorot, and Rae, 'A Clinically Applicable Approach').

[23] Mustafa Suleyman, 'Using AI to give doctors a 48-hour head start on life-threatening illness' (*DeepMind Blog*, 31 July 2019) <https://deepmind.com/blog/article/predicting-patient-deterioration>.

[24] Tomašev, Glorot, and Rae, 'A Clinically Applicable Approach' (n 22).

[25] Ibid.

[26] Jessie Lim, 'Singapore is No. 2 nation with most diabetics: 5 things about diabetes' (*Straits Times Online*, 8 April 2016) <https://www.straitstimes.com/singapore/singapore-is-no-2-nation-with-most-diabetics-5-things-about-diabetes>.

[27] World Health Organization, 'Diabetes' (*World Health Organization*, 30 October 2018) <https://www.who.int/news-room/fact-sheets/detail/diabetes>.

[28] John Lahr, 'Vision benefits can lead to early detection of diabetic retinopathy' (*Eyemed*, 11 November 2019) <https://eyemed.com/en-us/blog/health-wellness/vision-benefits-can-lead-to-early-detection-of-diabetic-retinopathy-17546>.

[29] Ursula Schmidt-Erfurth, Amir Sadeghipour, Bianca S Gerendas, Sebastian M Waldstein, and Hrvoje Bogunović, 'Artificial Intelligence in Retina' (2018) 67 Progress in Retinal and Eye Research 1–29, 17

[30] Daniel Shu Wei Ting, Carol Yim-Lui Cheung, Gilbert Lim, Gavin Siew Wei Tan, Nguyen D Quang, Alfred Gan, Haslina Hamzah, Renato Garcia-Franco, Ian Yew San Yeo, Shu Yen Lee, Edmund Yick Mun Wong, Charumathi Sabanayagam, Mani Baskaran, Farah Ibrahim, Ngiap Chuan Tan, Eric A Finkelstein, Ecosse L Lamoureux, Ian Y, Wong, Neil M Bressler, Sobha Sivaprasad, Rohit Varma, Jost B Jonas, Ming Guang He, Ching-Yu Cheng, Gemmy Chui Ming Cheung, Tin Aung, Wynne Hsu, Mong Li Lee, and Tien Yin Wong, 'Development and Validation of a Deep Learning System for Diabetic Retinopathy and Related Eye Diseases Using Retinal Images from Multiethnic Populations with Diabetes' (2017) 318 Journal of the American Medical Association 2211–23.

screening services would be even more relevant in helping ophthalmologists to remotely diagnose diabetic retinopathy in a community setting,[31] reducing the burden on both physician and patient.

3.1.2 Clinical knowledge management

With the availability of millions of research findings and even more medical records, there is a constant pressure on healthcare professionals to stay abreast of the latest treatment strategies available and to have a complete view of a patient's medical history. Being able to do so may also come at the expense of the 'human touch' and there are numerous reports of doctors spending more of the consult time looking at their computer screens than into their patient's eyes.[32] By assisting with knowledge management in the areas of medical documentation and information retrieval, AI has been touted as offering '[t]he greatest opportunity ... to restore the precious and time-honored connection and trust—the human touch—between patients and doctors'.[33]

3.1.3 Medical documentation

Effort has been underway to augment and automate documentation so that healthcare professionals can free up precious time resources for themselves as well as the patients.[34] These tools, also known as 'digital scribes', aim to take a conversation between a doctor and patient, parse the text, and use it to populate the patient's EHR. One such system is Kara, a virtual assistant developed by a Seattle-based startup Saykara. The application uses advanced machine learning, voice recognition, and language processing to capture conversations between patients and physicians and turn them into notes, diagnoses, and orders in the EHR.

3.1.4 Information retrieval

AskBob, an AI-based medical decision support tool developed by Ping An Insurance, utilizes proprietary knowledge graphs and natural language processing technology to provide up-to-date medical literature analyses and summaries to time-strapped healthcare professionals, enabling them to stay abreast of the latest medical evidence, as well as diagnosis and treatment recommendations for over

[31] Carol Y Cheung, Fangyao Tang, Daniel Shu Wei Ting MD, Gavin Siew Wei Tan, and Tien Yin Wong MD, 'Artificial Intelligence in Diabetic Eye Disease Screening' (2019) 8(2) Asia-Pacific Journal of Ophthalmology 158–64.

[32] Ben Nwoke, 'Are you taking the time to look into your patients' eyes?' (*Health IT Outcomes*, 5 February 2016) <https://www.healthitoutcomes.com/doc/are-you-taking-the-time-to-look-into-your-patients-eyes-0001>.

[33] Eric Topol, *Deep Medicine: How Artificial Intelligence Can Make Healthcare Human Again* (1st edn, Basic Books 2019) 18.

[34] Cassandra Willyard, 'Can AI Fix Medical Records?' (2019) 576 Nature 59–62.

1,500 conditions.[35] In Singapore, AskBob is currently undergoing testing with primary healthcare institutions, with aims to provide doctors with personalized treatment recommendations for diabetic patients at the point of care.[36]

3.1.5 Healthcare operations and administrative support

Apart from its use in the clinical domain, AI has also been arguably more successfully implemented in some operations and administrative areas within the healthcare setting. Some use cases include:

Hospital bed management. For example, IBM is collaborating with a healthcare IT company (Glintt) to develop an AI solution to streamline hospital bed assignment decisions by predicting when patients will be discharged to free up bed space.[37]

Scheduling. In the words of Dr. Katherine Andriole, Director of Research Strategy and Operations at MGH & BWH Center for Clinical Data Science and Associate Professor of Radiology at Harvard Medical School, 'There are so many opportunities in the administrative realm. Scheduling, for example, is something that computers are great at doing. If you have a no-show, it isn't just an inconvenience. It's a cost issue, because now you have a very, very expensive MRI scanner sitting empty, and you're effectively throwing money down the drain. If you can use AI to predict which patients might not show up, then you've got a much better chance of ensuring that your machines are always contributing to the bottom line—and that your staff isn't just twiddling their thumbs, either. It's a winning situation for patients, staff, and the health system as a whole.'[38]

Billing and coding. 'Incorrect billing can cost millions of dollars, and in some cases, it can even be viewed as fraud,' Dr. Andriole said. 'Using natural language processing to match documentation with standardized billing codes is a prime use case for AI ... Health systems should already be familiar with natural language processing, since it powers the voice recognition and dictation tools used by so many physicians. It's not a new technology, but it is becoming more and more refined to get better at extracting meaning from unstructured documentation.'[39]

[35] Ping An Group, 'Ping An introduces doctor's AI assistant to Singapore' (*PRNewswire*, 23 July 2019) <https://www.prnewswire.com/news-releases/ping-an-introduces-doctors-ai-assistant-to-singapore-300889404.html>

[36] Dean Koh, 'Ping-An's AI-powered CDSS "AskBob" being trialled in Singapore' (*Healthcare IT News*, 23 July 2019) <https://www.healthcareitnews.com/news/asia-pacific/ping-s-ai-powered-cdss-askbob-being-trialled-singapore>.

[37] Nuno Forneas, 'Improving hospital bed management with AI' (*IBM*, 16 August 2018) <https://www.ibm.com/blogs/client-voices/improving-hospital-bed-management-ai/>.

[38] Bresnick, 'Identifying Near-Term Use Cases' (n 4).

[39] Ibid.

3.2 Patients (and Their Caregivers)

3.2.1 AI-powered medical advice

There are several companies looking at making medical advice more accessible to patients via AI-powered virtual assistants in the form of chatbots and symptom-checkers. These companies range from large corporations like Microsoft[40] and Amazon[41] to startups like Your.MD. In a collaboration between University Hospitals Birmingham and a private company Babylon Health, the National Health Service Trust in Birmingham launched an 'AI triage' for the hospital's Accident and Emergency (A&E) in 2019,[42] in which people who are considering a visit to the A&E are encouraged to utilize a two-minute symptom check questionnaire which can then advise them on whether they actually need to visit the A&E.[43] In January 2020, this initiative received further endorsement when it was adopted by the Royal Wolverhampton National Health Service Trust[44] as well as the government of Rwanda.[45] The latter development is an example of how technology can help make up for deficits in healthcare systems—private or public, with the service providing quicker access to medical attention in one of the poorest countries in the world,[46] in stark comparison to the long waiting times frequently seen in wealthier first-world countries like the UK.[47]

However, such AI consultation services are not without problems, with not-infrequent complaints of misdiagnosis—fuelling Asia-Pacific Journal of Ophthalmology worries about negligence.[48] Furthermore, the system has forced

[40] The Microsoft Healthcare Bot <https://www.microsoft.com/en-us/research/project/health-bot/>.

[41] Haroon Siddique, 'NHS teams up with Amazon to bring Alexa to patients' (*The Guardian*, 10 July 2019) <https://www.theguardian.com/society/2019/jul/10/nhs-teams-up-with-amazon-to-bring-alexa-to-patients>.

[42] University Hospitals Birmingham National Health Service Trust website <https://www.uhb.nhs.uk/ask>.

[43] Denis Campbell, 'NHS to sign up patients for "virtual" A&E in tech revolution' (*The Guardian*, 23 May 2019) <https://www.theguardian.com/society/2019/may/23/birmingham-to-begin-accident-and-emergency-online-chat-service-in-tech-revolution-for-nhs-care>.

[44] Royal Wolverhampton National Health Service website <https://www.royalwolverhampton.nhs.uk/media/latest-news/january-2020/the-royal-wolverhampton-nhs-trust-and-babylon-to-create-the-worlds-first-integrated-digital-health-system/>.

[45] Babylon Health website <https://www.babylonhealth.com/blog/business/rwanda-will-be-the-worlds-most-advanced-country-for-digital-health>.

[46] Katie Stick, 'The Rwandan project: how Babylon helped rebuild healthcare in a war-shattered country' (*Evening Standard*, 12 July 2018) <https://www.standard.co.uk/futurelondon/health/the-rwandan-project-how-babylon-helped-rebuild-healthcare-in-a-warshattered-country-a3885946.html>.

[47] Jamie Nimmo, 'Babylon boss on why we need video doctors: "Try calling your GP … a peasant in Rwanda has faster access to healthcare"' (*This is Money*, 4 March 2019) <https://www.thisismoney.co.uk/money/markets/article-6764295/Try-calling-GP-peasant-Rwanda-faster-access-healthcare.html>.

[48] Sam Blanchard, 'NHS-backed GP chatbot asks a 66-year-old woman if she's PREGNANT before failing to suggest a breast lump could be cancer' (*Mail Online*, 27 February 2019) <https://www.dailymail.co.uk/health/article-6751393/NHS-backed-GP-chatbot-branded-public-health-danger.html>.

healthcare systems to relook at traditional models of funding allocation based on physical location, as the increased reach and ease of access to AI services resulting in patients seeking healthcare outside their geographical areas, resulting in an overburdening of limited local resources.[49]

3.2.2 AI-powered health assistant and coach

Apart from providing medical advice when we are ill, there are an even larger number of AI-powered virtual assistants looking to keep us in good health or help us manage control of certain chronic medical conditions. Some examples of the latter in the area of diabetes care include the BD Diabetes Care (24/7 Diabetes Assistant and Log)[50] and Hedia.[51] These assistants are accessible by phone applications and take in a person's glucose readings, food intake, and physical activity to serve out tailored recommendations such as lifestyle changes and even medication dosage adjustments. The potential benefits for patients are personal empowerment and an overall better control of their diabetes.

3.3 Pharmaceuticals (Drug and Medical Device Manufacturers)

3.3.1 Drug discovery

The process of drug discovery is prohibitively expensive, with the estimated average cost of a single drug costing billions of dollars.[52] The complicated journey of a product into an FDA-certified drug can be broadly split into four stages:[53] (a) selection of the biologically active target and validating it; (b) screening the biologically active compound as well as optimizing and modifying its functional properties; (c) preclinical studies involving the use of in vitro and animal models; (d) actual clinical studies in humans—which involves another three stages (Phase I trial— test drug safety testing with a small number of human subjects; Phase II— test drug efficacy with a small number of people affected by the targeted disease through a randomized control trials; Phase III—validates efficacy studies with a larger number of patients). Each stage of testing involves enormous funding, and it has been estimated that only 10% of the drugs that enter phase 1 clinical trials ultimately end up as FDA-approved medication.[54]

[49] Matt Burgess and Nicole Kobie, 'The messy, cautionary tale of how Babylon disrupted the NHS' (*Wired*, 18 March 2019) <https://www.wired.co.uk/article/babylon-health-nhs>.

[50] BD Diabetes Care application <https://apps.apple.com/us/app/bd-diabetes-care/id1278446171>.

[51] Hedia Diabetes Assistant application <https://www.hedia.co/>.

[52] Stephen HC Chan, Hanbin Shan, Thamani Dahoun, Horst Vogel, and Shuguang Yuan, 'Advancing Drug Discovery via Artificial Intelligence' (2019) 40(8) Trends Pharmacol Sci Aug 592–604, 592 (hereafter Chan, Shan, Dahoun, Vogel, and Yuan, 'Advancing Drug Discovery').

[53] Ibid.

[54] Smalley Eric, 'AI-powered Drug Discovery Captures Pharma Interest' (2017) 35(7) Nat Biotechnol 604–5, 604.

In simple terms, an effective drug is a bioactive molecule that has to be capable of being delivered effectively in *vivo* into a human, in addition to being able to bind effectively to a reciprocal biochemical target on the human cells in order to affect a change in function of the cell or organ. Consequently, the high rate of failure is often attributable to the lack of efficacy on the part of researchers in picking the right biochemical targets for new drugs to adhere,[55] and it has been argued that a modest '5 or 10% reduction in efficacy failure' in current drug trails, could possibly lead to amazing cost savings.[56] In this regards, modern advances in AI machine learning coupled with the availability of large data sets about the chemical properties of biochemical receptors and ligands,[57] could carry with it the promise of improving this 'drug discovery efficacy failure' by enabling researchers to reduce the logistics of finding effective drug candidates. This in turn increases the chance that drug candidates—which do enter the extremely expensive clinical trial stage[58] —end up as an eventual success.

Chan and others,[59] in a comprehensive review of the existing strategy on the use of AI in drug discovery, has described the current differing approaches of using AI in drug discovery. These various approaches can—notwithstanding the risk of over-generalization—be broadly classified in two general strategies. The first is to use existing data sets on the biological nature of the various biochemical receptors and ligands to help screen the various drug candidates for: (i) effective adherence by the ligands to the selected-for receptors;[60] (ii) the bioavailability routes for the potential drug candidates;[61] (iii) toxicity of the potential drug candidates.[62] The second strategy is to harvest available data sets on the chemical reactions to optimize the synthesis of drug molecules.[63] Without the aid of AI, researchers have to consider an exponential number of ways a single molecule can be formed, to try and decide which is the most efficient way to produce that bioactive drug molecule with the most optimal yield.

[55] Ibid.

[56] Ibid.

[57] Alex Zhavoronkov, 'Artificial Intelligence for Drug Discovery, Biomarker Development, and Generation of Novel Chemistry' (2018) 15(10) Molecular Pharmaceutics 4311–13, 4311.

[58] Costs for a clinical trial are often high due to the complexity of randomized control trials, as well as the need to project for the costs of logistics and possible compensation to patients for unexpected adverse drug reactions. A randomized control trial involves the comparison between groups of patients who are randomly assigned between varying drug dosages or placebo, to look for any clinical benefit—this can often take a long time.

[59] Chan, Shan, Dahoun, Vogel, and Yuan, 'Advancing Drug Discovery' (n 52) 592–604.

[60] Eg, the sorting of the types of receptors in the cells for which a bioactive drug is sought to be developed for. Ibid, 593–4.

[61] Eg, whether the potential drug candidate is likely to be oil or water soluble. Ibid, 594.

[62] Eg, whether the potential drug candidate would cross-react with other receptors to effect side-effects on humans. Ibid, 596.

[63] Ibid, 598–600.

3.3.2 Tailoring medical therapy based on genomics

Advances in DNA (deoxyribonucleic acid) sequencing and the ability to efficiently and economically process DNA sequences from small samples have led to an ever-increasing adoption of genomic information in clinical settings.[64] Genomics are now used to personalize the treatment of cancer patients, allowing clinicians to improve patient survival rates;[65] as well as help cancer researchers discover new immunomodulation biomarkers.[66]

With the increase in available genomic data, there is the issue of mapping the obtained genomic data to the actual clinical characteristics of the patients (ie, phenotype). In this regard, AI can aid clinicians to map the clinical phenotypes onto the genomic data, by integrating available clinical data (such as laboratory test results, radiological investigations, or electronic health records)—through pattern recognition.[67] In this regard, AI has been demonstrated to be able to predict the effectiveness of adjuvant chemotherapy drugs in breast cancer patients based on their genomic data, with accuracy ranging from 62% to 84%.[68] Researchers were also able to generate a machine learning model that took publicly available cancer screening data to predict the activity of 225 drugs against 990 cancer cell lines, generating a sensitivity and specificity of 87%, demonstrating the potential of using AI to aid new drug discovery, as well as new uses for 'old' drugs.[69]

AI algorithms would also enable clinicians to better understand non-coding DNA sequences.[70] These sequences were traditionally called introns (ie, intervening sequences) which did not carry 'useful' expressed genetic data, but has now been recognized to contain important but very complex information in relation to the DNA segments which are being actively expressed.[71] With the use of deep-learning AI algorithms, researchers were able to process far larger subsets of DNA data than traditionally possible, to help predict and find information 'hidden' within the non-coding segments of genes.[72]

[64] Jia Xu J, Pengwei Yang , Shang Xue, Bhuvan Sharma, Marta Sanchez-Martin, Fang Wang, Kirk A Beaty, Elinor Dehan, and Baiju Parikh, 'Translating Cancer Genomics into Precision Medicine with Artificial Intelligence: Applications, Challenges and Future Perspectives' (2019) 138(2) Human Genetics 110.

[65] Ibid.

[66] Ibid.

[67] Dias Raquel and Torkamani Ali, 'Artificial Intelligence in Clinical and Genomic Diagnostics' (2019) 11(70) Genome Medicine 7 (hereafter Raquel and Ali, 'Artificial Intelligence in Clinical').

[68] Stephanie N Dorman, Katherina Baranova, Joan H M Knoll, Brad L Urquhart, Gabriella Mariani, Maria Luisa Carcangiu, and Peter K Rogan, 'Genomic Signatures for Paclitaxel and Gemcitabine Resistance in Breast Cancer Derived by Machine Learning' (2016) 10(1) Molecular Oncology 85–100.

[69] Alex P Lind and Peter C Anderson, 'Predicting Drug Activity Against Cancer Cells by Random Forest Models Based on Minimal Genomic Information and Chemical Properties' (2019) 14(7) PLoS One

[70] Raquel and Ali, 'Artificial Intelligence in Clinical' (n 67) 6.

[71] Ibid.

[72] Ibid.

However, as AI models are 'trained' via the provision of large data sets, the 'quality' of the predictions from the AI models would be limited by the 'quality' of the training data provided to it.[73] Furthermore, patient data such as environmental factors or lifestyle factors are difficult to quantify in absolute numbers, further complicating the accuracy of such predictive models.[74] The 'black box' issue, wherein the mechanics of AI predictions are not easily scrutinized, increases the probability of errors being reinforced,[75] making it difficult and 'dangerous' for clinicians to base life-changing decisions on the predictions generated.[76]

3.3.3 Personalization of medical devices

Device manufacturers have also successfully harnessed AI to manufacture personalized devices. Align has started to reinvent the way teeth misalignment is treated by producing a new form of dental braces (Invisalign) compared to the traditional braces using brackets and wires with the help of AI algorithms.[77] Its treatment model involves a one-time scan of a patient's teeth before manufacturing a set of braces which patients then wear in a specific order to shift the teeth to their desired position. This minimizes the need for frequent dental visits in the traditional model where a trained orthodontist needs to perform serial assessment of the teeth and manually make adjustments to the wires. Underpinning this new treatment model is an AI algorithm that takes in each individual's scan results to custom make the set of braces which would fit each patient best.

3.4 Payers (Insurance Companies and Employers)

3.4.1 Fraud detection

Rising healthcare cost is an increasing burden to developed countries around the world,[78] and Singapore is no exception. It is estimated that medical insurance fraud accounts for up to 10% of healthcare budgets in countries such as the US.[79] Globally, medical insurance fraud has been estimated to cost insurers over USD 455 billion a year, and is one of the main drivers behind a continued rise in medical

[73] Anna Marie Williams, Yong Liu, Kevin R Regner, Fabrice Jotterand, Pengyuan Liu, and Mingyu Liang, 'Artificial Intelligence, Physiological Genomics, and Precision Medicine' (2018) 50(4) Physiological Genomics 237, 240.

[74] Ibid.

[75] Ibid, 241.

[76] Eg, if the AI model predicts that the patient will have little or no response to a certain chemotherapy drug, does that preclude the use of that drug completely?

[77] See Align Tech website <https://www.aligntech.com/>.

[78] Hyunjung Shin, Hayoung Park, Junwoo Lee, and Won Chul Jhee, 'A Scoring Model to Detect Abusive Billing Patterns in Health Insurance Claims' (2012) 39 Expert Systems with Applications 7441 (hereafter Shin, Park, Lee, and Jhee, 'A Scoring Model').

[79] Ibid.

insurance premiums;[80] with Singapore being ranked ninth amongst the most expensive international health insurance premiums in the world.[81] Concerns over medical insurance fraud have also been highlighted in the public sector, leading to closer regulatory surveillance[82] and even criminal charges in Singapore.[83]

Despite the magnitude and financial burden posed by medical insurance fraud, the detection of fraudulent medical insurance claims have remained fraught with difficulty,[84] in part due to the fact that detection is heavily reliant on medical knowledge to differentiate legitimate claims from fraudulent ones.[85] Furthermore, the claims made by healthcare providers or insured persons can vary according to their changing health needs, which make static models of detection inefficient.[86] On the other hand, modern healthcare systems are increasingly switching to EHRs, which are essentially repositories of data—ripe for AI to plow through in search of recognizable patterns.[87]

In a broad-scoped review of fraud detection systems, Abdallah and others[88] succinctly identified three main ways AI researchers have sought to tackle the issue of medical insurance fraud. The first identified method is that of concept drift, where AI models attempt to keep fraud detection algorithms up to date,[89] such as through the use of established and updated clinical pathways as a template to benchmark healthcare provider or patient behaviour.[90] This method is especially pertinent, in view of the constantly evolving medical knowledge and treatments available to both provider and patients, which would in turn determine if a claim is possibly fraudulent.[91] The second method identified is that of using AI to reduce large swathes of raw medical data, but attempting to fit available data in EHRs into known algorithms to identify outliers.[92] The third method Abdullah and others observed was the use of AI to create support vector machines—which are algorithms used for classification or regression problems—to create knowledge models for the

[80] Pacific Prime, 'Cost of International Health Insurance 2018' https://www.pacificprime.com/cohi-2018/download/.

[81] Ibid.

[82] Low Lin Fhoong and Wong Pei Ting, 'MOH to probe alleged insurance fraud involving physios, doctors and others' (*Today Online*) <https://www.todayonline.com/singapore/moh-probe-alleged-insurance-fraud-involving-physios-doctors-and-others>.

[83] Shaffiq Idris Alkhatib, 'Dentist behind bogus Medisave claims scam jailed 21/2 years' (*Straits Times Online*, 11 August 2018) <https://www.straitstimes.com/singapore/courts-crime/dentist-behind-bogus-medisave-claims-scam-jailed-212-years>.

[84] Shin, Park, Lee, and Jhee, 'A Scoring Model' (n 78) 7441.

[85] Wan-Shiou Yang and San-Yih Hwang, 'A Process-mining Framework for the Detection of Healthcare Fraud and Abuse' (2006) 31 Expert Systems with Applications 57 (hereafter Yang and Hwang, 'A Process-mining Framework')

[86] Aisha Abdallah, Mohd Aizaini Maarof, and Anazida Zainal, 'Fraud Detection System: A Survey' (2016) 68 Journal of Network and Computer Applications 103 (hereafter Abdallah, Maarof, and Zainal, 'Fraud Detection System').

[87] Ibid.

[88] Ibid.

[89] Ibid, 94–5.

[90] Yang and Hwang, 'A Process-mining Framework' (n 85) 56–68.

[91] Abdallah, Maarof, and Zainal, 'Fraud Detection System' (n 86) 103.

[92] Ibid, 103–4.

detection of fraudulent behaviour.[93] However, whatever the use of AI in fraud detection systems, the use of AI only goes so far as to help flag up likely fraudulent behaviour in order to reduce the burden of identification and detection; but the ultimate arbiter still has to be a medical expert—with all the inherent differences of opinion and biases existing between experts.[94]

3.4.2 Personalization of insurance premiums and plans

With access to big data as well as the individualized characteristics of insured persons, AI can be used to automate the process of individualized risks, enabling insurers to offer 'individualized risk-based underwriting'—tailoring the scope of insurance coverage to correspond to individual health risks.[95] From the consumer point of view, AI can be used to help consumers seek out and identify 'health insurance plans based on user-defined requirements', such as 'coverage requirements and cost-based criteria'.[96] While this is broadly similar to online websites for users to compare insurance plans,[97] this method involves the use of AI in the form of a web crawler to seek out information about prevailing insurance plans and then ranking them for consumers to choose based on their individual needs, community user ranking, and user popularity.[98]

3.5 Policymakers (Regulators and Government)

3.5.1 Epidemiology

The study of epidemiology is an attempt by healthcare providers to understand the complicated impact of the genetic composition of populations, the behavioural patterns of people; the interaction of humans with their environment; and, the complex nature of socioeconomic status, on human disease and survival.[99] In this particular area of medicine, the availability of data is not an issue, but rather the processing of that data to discover useful information which can then be used to

[93] Ibid, 104.

[94] Hongxing He, Jincheng Wang, Warwick Graco, and Simon Hawkins, 'Application of Neural Networks to Detection of Medical Fraud' (1997) 13(4) Expert Systems With Applications 335.

[95] Joe Mckendrick, 'How Artificial Intelligence Is Transforming Insurance: AI Is Giving Insurance New Ways to Engage With Their Customers, Process Claims and Adjust Risk' (2017) 19(4) Digital Insurance 38

[96] Ylli Sadikaj, 'Personalized Health Insurance Services Using Big Data' A Thesis Submitted to the Graduate Faculty of the North Dakota State University of Agriculture and Applied Science, April 2016 <https://library.ndsu.edu/ir/handle/10365/27978> (hereafter Sadikaj, 'Personalized Health Insurance Services').

[97] Timothy Ho, 'Using DIY insurance? Here are the pros and cons that you should consider' (*Dollarsandsense*, 27 September 2018) <https://dollarsandsense.sg/using-diyinsurance-pros-cons-consider/>.

[98] Sadikaj, 'Personalized Health Insurance Services' (n 96).

[99] Flouris AD and Duffy J, 'Applications of Artificial Intelligence Systems in the Analysis of Epidemiological Data' (2006) 21(3) European Journal of Epidemiology 167.

impact clinical practice.[100] The premise of AI in this arena is to digest large data sets in order to help identify trends and similarities for researchers to focus on, unlike a more 'traditional' scientific approach of deriving a hypothesis before looking for the data to prove or disprove it.[101] Using an AI-based approach, areas of epidemiological research include: (a) antibiotic resistance, (2) infection prediction, (3) disease prediction, and (4) disease surveillance.[102] The rise of EHRs as well as information from unconventional places such as social media;[103] or even climate data,[104] are promising sources of data for AI to analyse—allowing researchers to predict the impact of environment or sociopolitical factors on disease trends.[105] It remains to be seen how accurate and useful such AI-based approaches are compared to traditional epidemiology approaches.[106]

3.5.2 Paradigm shift in policymaking

Healthcare policies and clinical guidelines have traditionally been approached at a population level, with an emphasis on a 'fee for service' model—where providers and institutions charging on a per-procedure basis, regardless of outcome.[107] This traditional approach, while successful thus far, is facing increasing scrutiny and concern over unsustainable rising costs—which are predicted to worsen with aging populations worldwide.[108] In contrast, a 'value-based healthcare' looks at the quality rather than the quantity of medical treatment, looking at the holistic treatment of patients—from diagnosis to recovery and prevention of further complications.[109] Along with a global shift towards value-based healthcare delivery models, healthcare policymakers are urging healthcare providers to be more prudent in the way they utilize their resources.[110] One strategy for this to occur would be to better match resources to individual care needs by—first segmenting patients into fairly homogenous groups based on their needs and then tailoring policies

[100] Ibid.
[101] Ibid.
[102] Zanin Alejandro Rodríguez-González, Massimiliano Zanin, and Ernestina Menasalvas-Ruiz, 'Public Health and Epidemiology Informatics: Can Artificial Intelligence Help Future Global Challenges? An Overview of Antimicrobial Resistance and Impact of Climate Change in Disease Epidemiology' (2019) 28(1) Yearbook of Medical Informatics 224–31.
[103] Eg, the use of information posted on twitter. See Ireneus Kagashe, Zhijun Yan, and Imran Suheryani I. 'Enhancing Seasonal Influenza Surveillance: Topic Analysis of Widely Used Medicinal Drugs Using Twitter Data' (2017) 19 Journal of Medical Internet Research 1–14.
[104] Christopher L Merkord, Yi Liu, Abere Mihretie, Teklehaymanot Gebrehiwot, Worku Awoke, Estifanos Bayabil, and others, 'Integrating Malaria Surveillance With Climate Data for Outbreak Detection and Forecasting: The EPIDEMIA System' (2017) 16 Malaria Journal 1–15.
[105] Thiébaut R and Thiessard F, 'Artificial Intelligence in Public Health and Epidemiology' (2018) 27(1) Yearbook of Medical Information 208.
[106] Ibid.
[107] Joanne Yoong, 'A value-based system where healthcare providers are accountable for outcomes will benefit patients' (*Today Commentary*, 10 October 2019) https://www.todayonline.com/commentary/making-healthcare-providers-accountable-outcomes-will-benefit-patients.
[108] Ibid.
[109] Ibid.
[110] Ibid.

and specialized programmes for each of the various groups. In this regard, AI and machine learning techniques have proven to be able to provide an efficient and effective population segmentation,[111] which could in turn potentially allow healthcare providers to better provide patients with the care they need without overburdening limited financial resources.

4. Challenges and Risks of AI in Healthcare

Despite the promise of vast benefits that AI brings to various stakeholders in the healthcare industry, there have been voices of concern with regards to its implementation in practice. As Professor Jonathan Zittrain, one of the leading legal authorities on IT law says, 'machine learning [is] kind of [like] asbestos ... It turns out that it's all over the place, even though at no point did you explicitly install it, and it has possibly some latent bad effects that you might regret later, after it's already too hard to get it all out.' [112] The BMJ Quality and Safety, a leading healthcare journal dealing with patient safety and quality of care, recently published a narrative review article which systematically classifies these various risks and concerns into short-, medium-, and long-term issues.[113]

4.1 Short-Term Issues

4.1.1 Risk of distributional shift

The risk of distributional shift refers to a mismatch in the data used to train the AI algorithms (training data) versus the data in which the algorithm is used in the real-life context (operational data). It can arise from a change of environment or circumstances, leading to erroneous predictions. An example of this can be seen in the case of an AI model which was used to predict for acute kidney injury (AKI) to allow for early clinical intervention—it was found that over time, the 'success' of the model in predicting for AKI caused the AI model to overpredict for the event as time progressed, as it was reducing the actual incidence of AKI.[114]

[111] Jiali Yan, 'Applying Machine Learning Algorithms to Segment High-Cost Patient Populations' (2019) 34(2) Journal of General Internal Medicine 211–17.

[112] Casey Ross, 'What if AI in health case is the next asbestos' (*STAT*, 19 June 2019) <https://www.statnews.com/2019/06/19/what-if-ai-in-health-care-is-next-asbestos/>.

[113] Robert Challen, Joshua Denny, Martin Pitt, and others, 'Artificial Intelligence, Bias and Clinical Safety' (2019) 28 BMJ Quality & Safety 231–7 (hereafter Challen, Denny, Pitt, and others, 'Artificial Intelligence, Bias and Clinical Safety').

[114] Sharon E Davis, Thomas A Lasko, Guanhua Chen, Edward D Siew, and Michael E Matheny, 'Calibration Drift in Regression and Machine Learning Models for Acute Kidney Injury' (2017) 24(6) Journal of the American Medical Informatics Association 1052–61.

4.1.2 Insensitivity to impact

In diagnosing patients, clinicians generally tend to 'err on the side of caution', especially when it comes to possible life-threatening or serious differential diagnoses such as cancers. This behaviour may technically reduce a human diagnostician's accuracy in differentiating benign or malignant conditions, and is equally critical for safety, to avert potentially serious outcomes in clinical management. In contrast, AI algorithms focus mostly on accuracy as the main performance metric, and to this end it has been argued that perhaps those AI models applied to clinical care should be trained to consider not just with the end result (benign or malignant), but also the cost associated with potential misdiagnoses as well as over-diagnosis.[115]

4.1.3 Black-box decision-making

With more sophisticated techniques such as deep learning and neural networks used in AI algorithms, how predictions were arrived at are not open to inspection or easily explainable. This leads to broader issue of accountability and difficulty to investigate how erroneous predictions were made. This issue has been highlighted with regards to AI algorithms used for image analysis, skin lesion,[116] and chest X-ray analysis.[117] The more opaque the 'black box' is to scrutiny, the greater the issues with accountability, safety, and verifiability of the AI algorithms. This would create a hindrance towards the implementation of such AI algorithms in medical practice, [118] clearer legal guidance on how it would fit into the current legal standards of care must be provided.[119]

4.1.4 Lack of a fail-safe

Related to the issue of insensitivity to impact and black-box decision-making, many AI algorithms simply produce a prediction without providing any level of confidence to that prediction. In mitigation of this risk, there have been calls to build in fail-safe mechanisms that refuse to make a prediction if the confidence in the prediction is low, or if the system finds that the input it receives is insufficient or 'out-of-sample' (ie, dissimilar from training data).[120]

[115] Veronika Megler and Scott Gregoire, 'Training models with unequal economic error costs using Amazon SageMaker' (*AWS Amazon*, 18 October 2018) <https://aws.amazon.com/blogs/machine-learning/training-models-with-unequal-economic-error-costs-using-amazon-sagemaker/#>.

[116] Andre Esteva and others, 'Dermatologist-level classification of skin cancer with deep neural networks' (2017) 542 Nature 115–18.

[117] Pranav Rajpurkar and others, 'CheXNet: radiologist-level pneumonia detection on chest x-rays with deep learning' (2017) arXiv:1711.05225 [cs.CV].

[118] Hashimoto, Rosman, Rus, and Meireles, 'Artificial Intelligence in Surgery' (n 11) 73.

[119] *Hii Chii Kok v Ooi Peng Jin London Lucien* [2017] 2 SLR 492.

[120] Varshney KR, 'Engineering safety in machine learning' In:2016 Information Theory and Applications Workshop. ITA, arXiv:1601.04126, 1–5

4.2 Medium-Term Issues

4.2.1 Automation complacency

Automation complacency is a phenomenon where human operators fail to pick up errors made by a decision support system which is generally reliable.[121] The occurrence of automation complacency is especially pronounced when the individuals with oversight are 'burdened' with multiple concurrent tasks and is paradoxically more common the more reliable a decision support system is.[122] As AI algorithms become more prevalent in medical practice, multi-tasking healthcare providers may fail to detect an error made by a generally reliable AI algorithm—potentially resulting in detrimental effects on a patient.[123]

Taking it a step further, healthcare providers may also become overly reliant on AI algorithms to help them make clinical decisions, such that they do not exercise their own mind in the decision-making process, potentially leading to an eventual de-skilling of healthcare workers.

4.2.2 Self-fulfilling predictions

As AI algorithms get implemented and their recommendations influence decisions made, it may lead to a scenario where a system trained and used to detect and recommend treatment for a certain illness, will reinforce the system towards the outcome and treatment it recommended in the first place[124]—eg, if the system predicts a patient has condition X and should undergo chemotherapy regime Y, then a subsequent patient with condition X will likely be predicted to have greatest benefit from the same prior recommended chemotherapy regime Y.

A related problem that can potentially arise with an AI algorithm which is dependent on previous data, is a reinforcement loop involving outmoded medical practices. For example, a medical treatment which is superseded, may not be 'updated' immediately as part of the treatment protocol—resulting in it being continued to be recommended until the protocol is updated. Even after being updated, the AI algorithm would have no prior data to use with the updated protocols.[125]

4.3 Long-Term Issues

4.3.1 Negative side effects

AI algorithms may make recommendations that take into consideration the effectiveness, but not the cost of unintended consequences for the recommendation.

[121] Challen, Denny, Pitt, and others, 'Artificial Intelligence, Bias and Clinical Safety' (n 113) 234.

[122] Parasuraman Raja and Manzey Dietrich, 'Complacency and Bias in Human Use of Automation: An Attentional Integration' (2010) 52 Human Factors 381–410.

[123] Challen, Denny, Pitt, and others, 'Artificial Intelligence, Bias and Clinical Safety' (n 113) 234.

[124] Ibid, 235.

[125] Ibid.

For example, to maximize a patient's glucose control, an AI system may recommend increasing doses of insulin without considering that it could lead to potentially dangerous hypoglycemic (low blood sugar) episodes. While this can be rectified by putting in place maximal insulin limits, this may also potentially result in insufficient insulin doses in certain patients. In practice, medical practitioners have to consider and vary the administration of insulin in accordance with the changing dietary habits of a patient, which goes beyond a simple escalation of insulin dose.

4.3.2 Reward hacking

This can occur when proxies for intended goals are used as 'rewards' to train the AI algorithm, and when the algorithm somehow finds loopholes to maximize the reward without actually achieving the intended goals. The example cited in the BMJ Quality and Safety article was that of a heparin (blood-thinner) dosing system[126] intended to achieve long-term stable control of blood-thinning effect, but instead stumbled on a strategy of giving pulses of heparin just immediately before the test of blood-thinness (activated partial thromboplastin time 'aPTT') was performed. On the whole, the system was able to achieve good short-term biochemical control based on the aPTT measurements, but not the intended goal of stable long-term control—which is required to prevent medical complications.

4.3.3 Unsafe exploration

Using the same example of the heparin dosing system described above, and AI system may potentially test clinical boundaries by increasing the recommended doses of heparin to a potentially unsafe level. In view of the potentially fatal outcomes, there are now discussions proposing limits on AI algorithms and to define what changes in strategy are safe for the system to 'explore'.[127]

4.3.4 Unscalable oversight

Because AI systems are continually learning and developing new strategies, and capable of carrying out an ever-growing number of tasks and activities, which will make the monitoring of such systems nearly impossible for humans. For example, in the heparin dosing system described above, increasing dose recommendations from an AI algorithm would require closer clinical monitoring through more frequent blood tests, which can possibly render the AI recommendation impractical. This again brings up issues of accountability, especially when things go wrong.

[126] Amodei D and others, 'Concrete problems in AI safety' (2016) arXiv:1606.06565 [cs.AI].

[127] Javier Garcia and others, 'Safe Exploration of State and Action Spaces in Reinforcement Learning' (2012) 45 Journal of Artificial Intelligence Research 515–64.

5. Miscellaneous Issues

In addition to the above issues, there are other concerns that have also been raised.

5.1 Cybercrime Risk

A concern raised about AI in healthcare is that it may open doors to new forms of cybercrimes. Given that data used to make AI-driven decisions and operations are typically hosted in a centralized cloud server, if a malicious hacker manages to gain access to these centralized servers, they could alter the data and potentially cause harm to users of the system. Such risks have been exposed in the past. For example, a hacker with diabetes shared at a hacker conference in 2011 that he was able to hack his own insulin pump and gain control of other insulin pumps which could then be used to administer lethal doses of insulin to patients.[128] In another case, a hacker also showed how he could control pacemakers and send electric shocks to patients using his computer.

5.2 Data Privacy Issues

While the advent of AI in medical practice brings with it all the promises we have discussed and much more, the potential for abuse of the private medical data being used to bring about those promises looms large in the backdrop.[129] For example, leaked data about a patient's medical condition could result in his medical insurance premium being raised by insurers worried about their bottom lines,[130] or could expose the patient to social embarrassment especially if he is suffering from a stigmatizing condition like the human immuodeficiency virus (HIV).[131] In a recent 2018 survey conducted by Statistical Analysis System (SAS) (an American multinational developer of analytics software),[132] it was found that among 500 respondents, consumers were more comfortable with AI being used in the healthcare setting than in banking or retail.

However, it also found that only 35% were confident that their data being used for AI was stored securely. 69% of those above forty years were concerned

[128] Mari Colham, 'Hackers can access your medical devices' (*Medium*, 28 April 2019) <https://medium.com/datadriveninvestor/hackers-can-access-your-medical-devices-1ad3e8a528a2>

[129] W Nicholson Price and I Glenn Cohen, 'Privacy in the Age of Medical Big Data' (2019) 25(1) Nature Medicine 38 (hereafter Price and Cohen, 'Privacy in the Age of Medical Big Data').

[130] Ibid.

[131] Ibid.

[132] Denver, 'The doctor is in: Consumers are more comfortable with AI in healthcare than other industries, per a SAS survey' (*Sas*, 9 April 2018) <https://www.sas.com/en_za/news/press-releases/2018/april/artificial-intelligence-survey-sgf18.html>.

that their data was not stored securely and 58% of those younger than forty had similar concerns. In this regard, the benefits of 'harvesting' patient data should be balanced against the potential harm to the individual. It has also been suggested that a balance could possibly be found in allowing medical data to be shared with the following criteria: data is to be limited to the minimal amount; data to be retained only for a limited time; and, data should be anonymized where possible.[133] Although, herein also lies a further caveat, that an overcautious approach to data could potentially hobble the progress of innovation and place a shroud of opaqueness over the already opaque black box that defines some AI algorithms.[134]

5.3 Need for Change in the Status Quo

Not so much a risk, but rather more of a challenge, would be the need for a change of the status quo with the prevalence of AI implementations. One area that would need to adapt would be that of medical education. As mentioned by Steven A. Wartman in a recent article for the American Medical Association Journal of Ethics, 'The current learning environment, with its excessive information-retention demands, has proven to be toxic and [is] in need of complete overhaul. The speed of technological innovation means that the skills of some faculty members are outdated compared to those of their students.'[135] This change in status quo would require monumental efforts to redesign the medical education curriculum, 'to focus more on knowledge capture rather than knowledge retention; [encouraging] collaboration with [and] management of AI algorithms; and a better understanding of probabilities and how to apply them in clinical decision-making.'[136]

6. Conclusion

The rise of AI in healthcare carries with it immense promise for the advent of a new age of medicine, which can rival monumental events such as the discovery of antibiotics by Alexander Fleming or the purported modernization of nursing care by Florence Nightingale. This chapter has in rather broad strokes attempted to provide a looking glass at the ways through which AI has permeated every facet of the practice of medicine, from the way drugs are created to the way patients are

[133] Price and Cohen, 'Privacy in the Age of Medical Big Data' (n 129) 41.

[134] Ibid, 42.

[135] Steven A Wartman and C Donald Combs, 'Reimagining Medical Education in the Age of AI' (2019) 21(2) AMA Journal of Ethics <https://journalofethics.ama-assn.org/article/reimagining-medical-education-age-ai/2019-02>.

[136] Jessica Kent, 'Could artificial intelligence do more harm than good in healthcare?' (*Health IT Analytics*, 25 June 2019) <https://healthitanalytics.com/news/could-artificial-intelligence-do-more-harm-than-good-in-healthcare>.

treated, and healthcare professionals and ever-precious healthcare resources are sought to be redistributed. This chapter seeks to show that the advent of AI should not be feared but should instead be recognized for its ability to support patient and healthcare providers in medicine. However, it cannot be forgotten that the rise of AI in healthcare also carries with it a unique bevy of challenges and risks, although this unique set of challenges also represents a fertile ground for AI regulators and healthcare providers to streamline the rising tide of AI integration.

3

Intellectual Property Justification for Artificial Intelligence

*Reto M Hilty, Jörg Hoffmann, and Stefan Scheuerer**

1. Introduction

The commonly known issue of underinvestment in the production of new knowledge has been traditionally addressed via either direct legal intervention in the marketplace, by granting subsidies for research and development or by transforming the public into a private good through the granting of intellectual property (IP) rights. Over the last decades, new technologies have boosted the general tendency of establishing subject matter-specific forms of protection, such as for computer programs or databases. This move towards a policy-driven activism has rightly been criticized.[1] Indeed, the false assumption that IP rights a priori provide incentives for creation and innovation is not tenable. One also should bear in mind the potentially dysfunctional effects of excessive IP protection and related deadweight loss.

'Artificial intelligence' (AI) is another example of technological development where industrial policy considerations tend to go hand in hand with an urge for direct market interventions. Within this context, it seems crucial to reassess the need for IP protection and its theoretical justification in this particular field. It should be recalled that in a liberal society based on a market economy there is no need to justify why IP protection is not awarded. On the contrary, the question is why (and under which circumstances) IP rights are necessary.

Traditionally, the justification of IP rights builds on either deontological or utilitarian economic grounds.[2] The advent of AI, however, might change the

* All online materials were accessed before 22 December 2019.

[1] Hanns Ullrich, 'Intellectual Property: Exclusive Rights for a Purpose—The Case of Technology Protection by Patents and Copyright' (2013) Max Planck Institute for Intellectual Property and Competition Law Research Paper No 13-01 <https://papers.ssrn.com/sol3/papers.cfm?abstract_id=2179511>.

[2] IP comprises a variety of rights in intangible goods. For the purposes of this chapter, reference will be made to the general term 'IP' whenever the justification theory in question is of overarching relevance. Although some theories are specific to special IP rights and do not apply to others, there is considerable common ground as regards the theoretical backdrop of IP protection. Distinct justificatory paradigms apply, however, to the fields most closely related to unfair competition law, trade secrecy, and trademark law, which are therefore generally outside the scope of this chapter.

Reto M Hilty, Jörg Hoffmann, and Stefan Scheuerer, *Intellectual Property Justification for Artificial Intelligence* In: *Artificial Intelligence and Intellectual Property.* Edited by: Jyh-An Lee, Reto M Hilty, and Kung-Chung Liu, Oxford University Press (2021). © The several contributors. DOI: 10.1093/oso/9780198870944.003.0004

underlying paradigms.[3] On the one hand, AI leads to a potential decline in human effort necessary for the generation of intangible goods. This affects the anthropocentric deontological justification theories. On the other hand, AI changes certain market conditions and thus impacts utilitarian welfare theories. Irrespective of the considerable technological and economic context-dependency of such diagnoses, this chapter attempts to shed light on overarching trends, thus providing an abstract conceptual background.[4]

Since its beginning in the early 1950s, AI has developed in three different fields. The first field is the so-called 'symbol processing hypothesis' developed by Alan Turing, the 'founding father' of AI.[5] The second branch that attracted increasing attention was robotics. The third stream of research has been on the so-called 'learning approach'.[6] Particularly the last branch, also known as machine learning (ML), developed in the mid-2000s with such scale and widespread usage penetration that it is commonly seen as a general purpose technology (GPT) and often referred to as the most important AI technology. However, other AI technologies are relevant as well, such as 'evolutionary algorithms'.[7]

Against this backdrop, this chapter addresses the question of whether IP protection for both AI tools and outputs generated by or with the help of these tools is justifiable under traditional IP theories.

[3] Most justification theories have been subject to considerable abstract scholarly criticism. The primary purpose of this chapter is not to revisit these general caveats, but to assess new AI-induced developments vis-à-vis the traditional assumptions these theories were built on.

[4] The approach thereby taken with regard to still existing uncertainties of AI, in both a technical and an economic sense, is twofold. On the one hand, the chapter relies on the current understanding of the technological and economic circumstances, which are reflected in diverse scientific literature. It further applies knowledge gained from a workshop the Max Planck Institute for Innovation and Competition conducted in 2019, the results of which are summarized in Josef Drexl and others, 'Technical Aspects of Artificial Intelligence' (2019) Max Planck Institute for Innovation and Competition Research Paper No 19-13 <https://papers.ssrn.com/sol3/papers.cfm?abstract_id=3465577> (hereafter Drexl and others, 'Technical Aspects of Artificial Intelligence'). Such thorough understanding, allowing for a de-mystification of the science fiction scenarios discussed throughout considerable parts of the AI literature, is key for drawing sound legal and policy conclusions. On the other hand, the technology is highly fast-moving and the market conditions are dynamic and complex, with empirical evidence largely lacking. Thus to some extent this chapter also has to build on certain presumptions and hypotheses.

[5] Alan Mathison Turing, 'Computing Machinery and Intelligence' (1959) 59(236) Mind 433–60.

[6] Geoffrey Everest Hinton and Ruslan Salakhutdinov, 'Reducing the Dimensionality of Data with Neural Networks' (2006) 313 Science 504–7.

[7] Which can, however, also be used within ML. For a technological introduction, see Drexl and others, 'Technical Aspects of Artificial Intelligence' (n 4).

2. Decreasing Role of Deontological Justification of IP Rights

2.1 Overview of the Different Theories

There are three[8] main theoretical branches of deontological justification theories one can distinguish (notwithstanding significant mutual overlaps): labour theory, personality theory, and reward theory. These are of special importance in the copyright realm, which is characterized by the highest degree of anthropocentrism. However, they pervade IP law in general with differing nuances.[9] What is important to note at the outset is that, contrary to traditional notions viewing them as 'natural law', in a liberal democracy under the rule of law there is no such thing. The legal design of any IP regime rests upon the political will in the respective legal order,[10] within the boundaries of the respective constitution[11] and other high-ranking law. The relevancy of the theories is confined to an inspirational conceptual backdrop without any normative power.[12]

Labour theory assumes that people are entitled to own property rights based on the labour they put into obtaining the respective subject matter, ie, they are entitled to earn the 'fruits of their own labour'.[13] This theory was initially developed by John Locke with regard to tangible property[14] and later extended by others to intangible goods.[15]

According to personality theory, generating something and making it accessible to the general public is an expression of personality, which is assumed to rely on a person's interaction with external objects.[16] Such considerations

[8] Other categorizations are possible; see Justin Hughes, 'The Philosophy of Intellectual Property' (1988) 77 Georgetown Law Journal 287.

[9] See, eg, on deontological reasoning in patent law Robert P. Merges and others, *Intellectual Property in the New Technological Age* (6th edn, Wolters Kluwer 2012) 131 ff with further references (hereafter Merges and others, *Intellectual Property in the New Technological Age*).

[10] Often, however, this political will of society will to some extent converge with deontological assumptions as regards common social notions of justice or 'fairness'.

[11] Including the fundamental and human rights in which elements of the theories are reflected, in particular fundamental rights to protection of property and personality.

[12] Which is why many authors refer to them under notions such as 'social policy arguments'; see, eg, Robert Yu, 'The Machine Author' (2017) 165 University of Pennsylvania Law Review 1245, 1263 (hereafter Yu, 'The Machine Author').

[13] For details on labour theory see, eg, Gordon Hull, 'Clearing the Rubbish: Locke, the Waste Proviso, and the Moral Justification of Intellectual Property' (2009) 23 Public Affairs Quarterly 67; Carol M. Rose, 'Possession as the Origin of Property' (1985) 52 University of Chicago Law Review 73; The World Economic Forum recently still referred to this theory in the AI regulation context; see World Economic Forum White Paper, *Artificial Intelligence Collides with Patent Law* (April 2018) fn 125.

[14] Cf John Locke, *Two Treatises on Government* (3rd edn, Awnsham and John Churchill 1698) Book 2 para 26.

[15] Prominently by German IP scholar Josef Kohler, *Deutsches Patentrecht systematisch bearbeitet unter vergleichender Berücksichtigung des französischen Patentrechts* (Neudr. d. Ausg. 1878) 7 ff for patent law; Josef Kohler, *Das Autorrecht* (Kessinger Publishing, LLC 1880) 98 ff for copyright law; Josef Kohler, 'Dogmatische Abhandlungen aus dem Immaterialgüterrecht' (1887) 47 Busch's Archiv 167, 173.

[16] For a more detailed description see Margaret Jane Radin, 'Property and Personhood'(1982) 34(5) Stanford Law Review 957, 971 ff; Justin Hughes, 'The Philosophy of Intellectual Property' (1988) 77 Georgetown Law Journal 287, 330 ff.

are rooted especially in the philosophy of Georg Wilhelm Friedrich Hegel and were prominently advocated in the IP realm by Otto von Gierke.[17] The theory is especially important for copyright law in the Continental European 'droit d'auteur' tradition[18] due to works of art being more significantly influenced by the personality of those who create them than is the subject matter of industrial property law.[19]

According to reward theory, it is fair to give someone a reward for enriching society. In the patent field, it goes back primarily to John Stuart Mill[20] and was also relied on by Jeremy Bentham.[21] In contrast to the other deontological theories, its perspective is not unilaterally confined to the person generating the intangible good but puts special emphasis on its utility for society.[22] This deontological theory can thus to some extent be aligned with or read in conjunction with utilitarian considerations.[23]

What unites these theories is their anthropocentrism: IP protection is awarded to humans.

2.2 Assessing the Human Contribution in AI at the Current State of Technology

At present, AI-related processes are still directed by humans. The development and designing of an AI tool and the use of a developed AI tool to generate new intangible goods generally require considerable human input.

[17] Otto von Gierke, *Deutsches Privatrecht Band 1, Allgemeiner Teil und Personenrecht* (1895) §94, 854 ff considered patent law exclusively based on personality rights of the inventor. Differently, Josef Kohler, *Handbuch des deutschen Patentrechts in rechtsvergleichender Darstellung* (J. Bensheimer 1900) 55 ff assumed a dualism of personality and economic dimensions of IP.

[18] As particularly reflected in the Berne Convention for the protection of literary and artistic works of 1886; on deontological reasoning also in American copyright law see Merges and others, *Intellectual Property in the New Technological Age* (n 9) 436 ff with further references.

[19] But see, eg, for patent law in the concrete AI context Shlomit Yanisky-Ravid and Xiaoqiong (Jackie) Liu, 'When Artificial Intelligence Systems Produce Inventions: The 3A Era and an Alternative Model for Patent Law' (2018) 39 Cardozo Law Review 2215, 2245 assuming 'it may be possible to program an AI in various ways, each one representing a different personal style for accomplishing the task'.

[20] Cf John Stuart Mill, *Principles of Political Economy* (1870/1909) Book V 10.25 (hereafter Mill, *Principles*).

[21] Cf Jeremy Bentham, *A Manual of Political Economy* (1843) 71.

[22] Cf John Stuart Mill, *Principles of Political Economy* (1902) Book V, 548: '... because the reward conferred by it depends on the invention's being found useful, and the greater the usefulness, the greater the reward'.

[23] Eg with investment theory by linking the amount of deserved reward to the amount of required investment (see Ana Ramalho, 'Patentability of AI-generated inventions: Is a reform of the patent system needed?' (2018) 22 <https://ssrn.com/abstract=3168703> or with patent law's disclosure theory by assuming reward is only deserved for disclosed inventions (see Rogge and Melullis in Georg Benkard (eds), *PatG Kommentar* (11th edn, CH Beck 2015) introduction para 3).

2.2.1 AI tools

Every AI tool (be it ML, evolutionary algorithms, or other technologies) initially builds on traditional software programmed by humans. Humans write new algorithms or choose existing ones from so-called 'libraries'. In ML, they build the architecture of neural networks. However, if the software then develops further and changes without this concrete development having been guided or at least foreseen by the programmer, the 'human link' fades or rather is confined to initial causality.

Besides the programmer, other humans can be involved in the development of an AI tool as well. In the realm of ML, they choose and label (in the case of 'supervised learning') training data, define the training methods with a certain degree of heuristics, and interpret the output (the latter especially in the case of 'unsupervised learning').[24] Also, in the field of evolutionary algorithms, humans interpret and evaluate the solutions which the algorithm selects out of a randomly generated initial population of possible solutions.[25]

2.2.2 AI outputs

As far as 'AI-generated output' is concerned, it has to be stressed from the outset that according to the current state of knowledge, really 'independently acting' computers do not exist. Whether AI systems dispose of some degree of 'autonomy'[26] may largely depend on one's definition of that notion. For the moment, however, terms suggesting the absence of any human influence are more misleading than helpful in the debate. Rather, it is humans who use the AI tool with a view to obtaining a potentially creative or innovative output.

In this regard, one first has to realize, however, that they may well 'use' the tool in no creative or innovative ways at all: Generating a translation via using the completed program DeepL is of as little IP relevance as driving a car (which embodies inventions). In contrast, a researcher using an AI tool to develop a new medical compound may do so in an innovative way in the course of designing and applying his or her research toolkit.

Secondly, the key problem is that the level of detail and thus the predetermination of the output by human instructions can vary considerably.[27] The less precise the input instructions are and the more patterns are found that a human would not have discovered, the less intellectual connection to and direction of the output by the human exists. The lack of human capability of processing or interpreting large amounts of data within a limited amount of time as compared to a computer may at

[24] For details of the technical process, see Drexl and others, 'Technical Aspects of Artificial Intelligence' (n 4).

[25] Ibid.

[26] *The WIPO Draft Issues Paper on Intellectual Property and Artificial Intelligence* (WIPO/IP/AI/2/GE/20/1, 13 December 2019 <https://www.wipo.int/about-ip/en/artificial_intelligence/call_for_comments/>), assumes such autonomy exists.

[27] See Drexl and others, 'Technical Aspects of Artificial Intelligence' (n 4).

least to a certain extent lead to what is commonly referred to as the 'black box' phenomenon.[28] The 'explainability' or 'interpretability' of the process (which is subject to the ongoing research on 'explainable AI') in the ML realm especially depends on the complexity of the model and is most challenging in the case of 'Deep Neural Networks', which feature a very high number of layers.[29] The relationship between human-led input and output thus has to be thoroughly determined in every single case. In the famous case of an atypically designed space antenna that NASA developed with the help of evolutionary algorithms, the human guidance subsisted in the desired performance of the antenna being specified and subsequently re-specified by human scientists.[30]

Viewing the human impact from the angle of personality theory, the selection of ML input data can be of a 'creative' nature or not. The outcome of the 'Next Rembrandt' project, a computer-generated 'new painting' in the style of Rembrandt, was simply founded on all available pre-existing Rembrandt paintings. In contrast, combining input from different artists in a targeted way to create a new stylistic mix might qualify as an expression of personality.

2.3 Assessing the Need for IP Protection under Deontological Considerations

One may argue that labour theory focuses more on the 'quantity' of labour conducted, personality theory emphasizes more the 'quality' (personal expression or not?), and reward theory gives more weight to the characteristics of the output as such (is it useful for society?).[31] But despite these differences in detail and emphasis, the AI-induced challenges to all these theories ultimately come down to the level of human involvement.

In that respect, the justification of IP is not confronted with major problems as long as AI is used as a tool under human guidance, just as a painter's use of a brush does not call into question his or her entitlement to copyright[32] under deontological theories or just as an inventor is allowed to use a microscope. As long as there is a sufficient 'human link', labour is conducted, a reward deserved,

[28] Ibid.

[29] Ibid.

[30] Cf John Bluck, '"Borg" computer collective designs NASA space antenna' (*NASA*, 16 February 2006) <https://www.nasa.gov/centers/ames/research/exploringtheuniverse/borg.html>.

[31] Tim W Dornis, 'Der Schutz künstlicher Intelligenz im Immaterialgüterrecht' (2019) GRUR 1252, 1257 ff (hereafter Dornis, 'Der Schutz') eg assumes the viability of labour theory regarding involved actors even in 'AI autonomy' constellations, but denies the viability of personality theory.

[32] Karl-Nikolaus Peifer, 'Roboter als Schöpfer' in Silke von Lewinski and Heinz Wittmann (eds), *Urheberrecht! Festschrift für Michel M. Walter zum 80. Geburtstag* (Medien und Recht 2018) 222, 226 (hereafter Peifer, 'Roboter als Schöpfer').

personality expressed.[33] In contrast, once human impact or guidance falls below a certain critical level, deontological justification fails.[34]

As regards protection for AI tools, one could revisit the question of whether IP protection for software has ever been justifiable under deontological theories. In many cases software does not require considerable labour and cannot be characterized as an expression of personality; it rather appears to be a basic working tool, quite trivial to the person 'skilled in the art'. Apart from this 'classic' problem of IP justification for traditional software, deontological justification for protection of the AI tool fails as soon as the tool changes, develops, or evolves beyond the initial software without sufficient human guidance.

Likewise, AI outputs raise issues under deontological reasoning. Here, once the critical level of human creative or innovative guidance is fallen short of, only some kind of 'perpetuation of attribution' could justify protection. This entails the assumption that the 'fruit of the labour' or personality of the 'original' programmer or overall designer of an AI tool also encompasses or lives on in further derivative generations by this tool or, respectively, that he or she deserves a reward for making these possible.

Such reasoning is, however, not convincing for a variety of reasons. First, it presupposes the existence of 'first level' IP justification for the AI tool. Yet, as shown above, there appears to be (apart from at most the initial software) no case for such protection under deontological reasoning. This has to be borne in mind also with regard to the common counter-argument that such extension would constitute an unjustified 'double reward'.[35] Second, the link gets weaker with every further derivative generation and at some point will inevitably cross the border of not being acknowledgeable anymore. It would overstretch the theories if they had to encompass such follow-up outputs.[36]

Another important question is whether deontological theories might preclude IP protection for other reasons where no human is sufficiently involved. At the outset, they appear indifferent in this regard. Although these theories do require the granting of IP rights under the condition of sufficient human input, they do

[33] In favour of sufficiency of tiny human impact: Peter Blok, 'The Inventor's New Tool: Artificial Intelligence—How Does It Fit in the European Patent System?' (2017) 39(2) European Intellectual Property Review 69 ff.

[34] Even the establishment of some kind of legal personhood for AI systems would not justify IP protection under deontological reasoning. Such personhood would be based on purely functional paradigms just like its role model, the 'legal personhood' of companies. It would not make AI human.

[35] Cf Renate Schaub, 'Interaktion von Mensch und Maschine' (2017) 7 Juristenzeitung 342, 349; Pamela Samuelson, 'Allocating Ownership Rights in Computer Generated Works' (1986) 47 University of Pittsburgh Law Review 1185, 1192 (hereafter Samuelson, 'Allocating Ownership Rights'); Yu 'The Machine Author' (n 12) 1261 speaks of 'over-reward' and 'copyright stockpiling'. This argument constitutes a link between the deontological theories and the economic incentive theory; see Ana Ramalho, 'Will Robots Rule the (Artistic) World?' (2017) 21 Journal of Internet Law 16 (hereafter Ramalho, 'Will Robots Rule the (Artistic) World?').

[36] For arguments both pro and contra, see Shlomit Yanisky-Ravid, 'Generating Rembrandt' (2017) Michigan State Law Review 659, 707 (hereafter Yanisky-Ravid, 'Generating Rembrandt').

not a priori or *e contrario* prohibit the granting of such rights for intangible subject matter generated without it.[37] These theories stem from times when AI was not available. They therefore cannot be interpreted as deliberately preclusive regarding certain new technologies.[38] At the same time, one has to refrain from confusing possibility with desirability of IP protection. Efforts of 'saving' the applicability of the concepts of authorship and inventorship in the AI realm thus appear conceptually misguided.

However, deontological theories may exclude protection regimes for AI if such protection would result in negative consequences vis-à-vis human creators.[39] If it were true that IP protection had an incentivizing effect on AI developments, such 'competition' with superior AI (fostered by IP) might pose a threat to *human-led* progress.[40] But this issue can also be viewed from a different angle: A widespread argument assumes that markets might be distorted by the co-existence of IP-free machine outputs and IP-protected human outputs, leading to a favouring of the former (due to their being free) to the detriment of the latter. In that case not denying, but granting IP protection to AI-generated output could allegedly 'level the commercial playing field' to the benefit of human creators.[41] Of course such levelling could, on a theoretical level, also be achieved the other way round by abolishing IP law altogether. At least in the field of copyright, but potentially also in design law, however, precisely the opposite could be true anyway: human authorship might constitute a competitive advantage with a view to consumers valuing human-made culture. Yet, the practical difficulty of distinguishing whether intangible subject matter has been generated based on sufficient human input or not[42] may pose market transparency problems threatening the viability of this market-based solution.

In any case, when reflecting on such potential effects, one has to keep in mind the limits of IP law: AI-induced losses of traditional creative jobs (in the copyright field) or R&D-related ones (in the patent field)[43] may be a challenge to society. This

[37] In light of the fact that, according to most scholarship, IP law justification relies not on one theory only, but on a combination of all the existing (economic and deontological) ones (see for patent law Fritz Machlup, 'Die wirtschaftlichen Grundlagen des Patentrechts—1. Teil' (1961) GRUR Ausl 373), some may simply not be applicable to certain constellations. A parallel can be drawn to the general discussion about introducing legal personhood for AI: The fact that the constitutional concept of human dignity demands that humans have legal personhood does not *e contrario* preclude legislatures from granting legal personhood to other entities for different reasons, see Jens Kersten, 'Menschen und Maschinen' (2015) 1 Juristenzeitung 7; Jan-Erik Schirmer, 'Rechtsfähige Roboter?' (2016) 13 Juristenzeitung 663.

[38] On 'dynamic interpretation' of American IP law in the AI context *de lege lata* see Ryan Abbott, 'I Think Therefore I Invent' (2016) 57 Boston College Law Review 1079, 1112 ff (hereafter Abbott, 'I Think').

[39] See Daniel Schönberger, 'Deep Copyright' (2018) 10 ZGE 35, 46 (hereafter Schönberger, 'Deep Copyright'); Abbott, 'I Think' (n 38) 1106; Erica Fraser, 'Computers As Inventors' (2016) 13(3) scripted 305, 327 (hereafter Fraser, 'Computers As Inventors').

[40] Daniel Gervais, 'The Machine As Author' (2019) Vanderbilt Law Research Paper No 19-35, 60 <https://ssrn.com/abstract=3359524>, emphasis added (hereafter Gervais, 'The Machine').

[41] Ibid, 15.

[42] See Yu 'The Machine Author' (n 12) 1266.

[43] Cf Fraser, 'Computers As Inventors' (n 39) 305, 327; Dornis, 'Der Schutz' (n 31) 1259.

challenge, however, cannot be resolved via IP legislation, as IP's core function is promoting innovation and not preserving tradition or pursuing general social policy aims.[44] Ultimately, it is up to democratic societal debate to determine the desirability of general progress vs. human-led progress.[45] Albeit an important field of general philosophy, this issue clearly exceeds the realm of (IP) jurisprudence.[46]

3. Utilitarian Economic Justification of IP Rights

3.1 Background

The most popular justification of IP rights is based on the utilitarian guideline that lawmakers should maximize net social welfare when shaping property rights.[47] In relation to IP, this requires lawmakers to strike a balance between incentives that IP rights may provide to stimulate creation and innovation and the tendency of such rights to curtail public enjoyment of those subject matters of protection by certain dysfunctional effects that exclusive rights may produce.[48] Yet, the translation of this utilitarian welfare justification of IP rights into an administrable and feasible legal system is most challenging. It is already controversial whether the desired social welfare improvement should be achieved via a wealth-maximization criterion,[49] the Pareto criterion,[50] or the Kaldor-Hicks

[44] In this vein also *WIPO Draft Issues Paper on Intellectual Property and Artificial Intelligence* (WIPO/IP/AI/2/GE/20/1, 13 December 2019 <https://www.wipo.int/about-ip/en/artificial_intelligence/call_for_comments/> 8: '... many of those questions and challenges lie well beyond IP policy, involving, for example, questions of labour policy, ethics, human rights and so forth.' On the socioeconomic aspects of innovation in the AI context see the contribution of Anselm Kamperman Sanders in this volume.

[45] See for copyright *WIPO Draft Issues Paper on Intellectual Property and Artificial Intelligence* (WIPO/IP/AI/2/GE/20/1, 13 December 2019 <https://www.wipo.int/about-ip/en/artificial_intelligence/call_for_comments/> 5. 'If AI-generated works were excluded from eligibility for copyright protection, the copyright system would be seen as an instrument for encouraging and favoring the dignity of human creativity over machine creativity. If copyright protection were accorded to AI-generated works, the copyright system would tend to be seen as an instrument favoring the availability for the consumer of the largest number of creative works and of placing an equal value on human and machine creativity.' See also Axel Walz, 'A Holistic Approach to Developing an Innovation-friendly and Human-centric AI Society' (2017) 48(7) IIC 757, 759.

[46] A certain embedment of such considerations may, however, be found in the promotion-of-culture theory of copyright law, according to which copyright aims at fostering a special kind of new intangible goods, namely culture—whether 'AI art' constitutes such culture is an interesting field for cultural sciences to elaborate on.

[47] Cf William Fisher, 'Theories of Intellectual Property' in Stephen R Munzer (ed), *New Essays in the Legal and Political Theory of Property* (Cambridge University Press 2001) 168 ff; Edwin C Hettinger, 'Justifying Intellectual Property' (1989) 18 Philosophy and Public Affairs 31, 47 (hereafter Hettinger, 'Justifying Intellectual Property'); Richard Posner, *Economic Analysis of Law*, 3rd edn (Little Brown 1986) 38 (hereafter Posner, *Economic Analysis of Law*).

[48] Hettinger, 'Justifying Intellectual Property' (n 47) 47; Posner, *Economic Analysis of Law* (n 47) 38.

[49] The wealth maximization criterion counsels lawmakers to select the system of rules that maximizes aggregate welfare measured by consumers' ability and willingness to pay for goods, services, and conditions. See Posner, *Economic Analysis of Law* (n 47) 16.

[50] According to the Pareto criterion, the social state X is preferable to the social state Y if each member of society either prefers the state X to that of Y personally or is indifferent to both, but at least

criterion.[51] Ultimately, however, all these approaches are criticized for ignoring the incommensurability of utility functions and social welfare considerations merely based on efficiency criteria. Despite this, utilitarian economic welfare maximization still serves as a beacon for various economic theories on how to efficiently design the legal IP framework.[52] It has to be noted though, that these considerations may not serve as a source of purely legal argumentation for defining the scope of already existing IP regimes, unless the legal regime itself embeds utilitarian welfare considerations.[53]

Therefore, general statements regarding the utilitarian economic justification of IP rights for AI always need to be reassessed with the concrete case at hand. Creation and innovation markets in relation to AI function under unequal conditions. Depending on the respective field of AI technology, entirely different requirements may apply to the necessary investments, the lifecycles, and prospects of amortization for each respective AI tool and output. Moreover, industrial patterns of technological advance may vary even within the same field of technology. This may facilitate or hinder dynamic competition, as the subject matter of protection may be easier or more difficult to substitute for further creative or innovative advancement. It may also affect the economic suitability of IP enforcement.

The overall general starting point has to be that IP rules per se are not a prerequisite for cooperation gains and efficient product allocation.[54] This means that

one member of society prefers X. Building on this assumption, such a state could be achieved by the creation of property rights that may lead to perfect allocation of goods. Such assumptions, however, do not take transaction costs into account and are not well-suited for public information goods and their allocation through property rights. See also Hans Bernd Schäfer and Claus Ott, *Ökonomische Analyse des Zivilrechts* (5th edn, Springer 2013) 24 ff.

[51] The Kaldor Hicks criterion sets out the rule that one state of affairs is preferred to a second state of affairs if, by moving from the second to the first, the gainer from the move can, by a lump-sum transfer, compensate the 'loser' for its loss of utility and still be better off. Nicholas Kaldor, 'Welfare Propositions in Economics and Interpersonal Comparisons of Utility' (1939) 69 Economic Journal 549–52.

[52] See for the discussion Posner, *Economic Analysis of Law* (n 47) 11–15. For a more critical analysis of the issue of a biased wealth maximization approach see Baker, 'Starting Points in Economic Analysis of Law' (1980) 8 Hofstra Law Review 939, 966–72; Ronald Dworkin, 'Is Wealth a Value?' (1990) 9(9) Journal of Legal Studies 191; and Steven Shavell, 'Economic Analysis of Welfare Economic, Morality and the Law' (2003) NBER Working Paper No 9700, 669.

[53] Although efficiency from the point of view of utilitarian welfare is intrinsically associated with an IP rights regime and may be even embedded in the constitution itself, caution is needed when adopting a general legal concept of efficiency that shall ultimately serve as the only beacon for judges and public officials to assess the scope of existing IP rights. The case is different once the legislature takes efficiency as one of the key considerations in a legislative procedure. It has to be noted though that even in this case, there might be the danger of regulatory capture. Normative economic theories, in fact, possess an inherent epistemological gap between assessing the real case and absolute conclusions drawn from a theory. This may provide leeway for lobbying through economic theory. See on this issue Robert Cooter and Thomas Ulen, *Law and Economics* (6th edn, Addison Wesley 2016) 4; Walter Eucken, *Grundsätze der Wirtschaftspolitik* (7th edn, UTB 2004) 370 (hereafter Eucken, *Grundsätze der Wirtschaftspolitik*); Horst Eidenmüller, *Effizienz als Rechtsprinzip* (Mohr Siebeck 1998) 468, Josef Drexl, *Die Wirtschaftliche Selbstbestimmung des Verbrauchers* (Mohr Siebeck 1998) 176 ff; Christopher Carrigan and Cary Coglianese, 'Capturing Regulatory Reality: Stigler's The Theory of Economic Regulation' (2016) University of Pennsylvania Faculty Scholarship Paper 1650 ff.

[54] Such relativization is commonly based on various reasons. First of all, positive economics and utilitarian normative economics are based on the assumption of the rationality model of the *homo*

IP rights for AI are not a priori justified. Following the new institutional economics framework, IP rights are informally and spontaneously arranged.[55] Accordingly, the economic necessity of IP rights is assessed against the backdrop of a general market economy framework. One of the prerequisites of the market economy is the freedom of action and competition among market participants.[56] This forbids an a priori allocation of IP.[57] This is all the more true in view of certain negative economic effects of IP rights, eg, threat of over-investment in IP rights or deadweight effects due to static inefficiencies.[58]

This inevitably raises the question of how to strike the balance between the power of IP rights to promote AI-related creation and innovation and their dysfunctional effects. There are the following economic theories and assumptions pertaining to the balancing question: incentive theories (general incentive theory[59] and investment protection theory[60]) and optimizing patterns of productivity theories (market opening theory,[61] prospect theory,[62] and disclosure theory[63]).

oeconomicus which contains certain systematic deficits that are increasingly criticized. See, eg, Christine Jolls, Cass Sunstein, and Richard H Thaler, 'A Behavioural Approach to Law and Economics' in Cass R Sunstein (ed), *Behavioral Law and Economics* (Cambridge University Press 2000) 59. A further point relates to the fact that any axiomatic statement would remain in the model of complete rivalry which is neither realistic nor can be seen as the sole narrative of a competition policy that builds on dynamic competition. On this point see Eucken, *Grundsätze der Wirtschaftspolitik* (n 53) 24; ultimately, even positive economics have shown that an all-encompassing approach for IP rights cannot exist. See, eg, Dietmar Harhoff and Bronwyn H Hall, 'Recent Research on the Economics of Patents' (2011) NBER Working Paper No 17773, 35 (hereafter Harhoff and Hall, 'Recent Research'), or Robert P Merges and Richard R Nelson, 'On the Complex Economics of Patent Scope' (1990) 90 Columbia Law Review 841 (hereafter Merges and Nelson, 'On the Complex Economics of Patent Scope').

[55] Lee Alston and Bernardo Mueller, 'Property Rights and the State' in Claude Menard and Mary M Shirley (eds), *Handbook on New Institutional Economics* (Springer 2008) 573. Federal Trade Commission, 'To Promote Innovation—the Proper Balance of Competition and Patent Law and Policy', Executive Summary (2004) 19 Berkeley Technology Law Journal 861, 863.

[56] Cf. Eucken, Grundsätze der Wirtschaftspolitik (n 53) 175 ff; Franz Böhm, *Wirtschaftsverfassung und Staatsverfassung* (J.C.B. Mohr (Paul Siebeck) 1950) 50 et seq.

[57] Ronald Harry Coase, 'The Problem of Social Costs' (1960) 31 Journal of Law & Economics 44.

[58] IP systems permit owners to raise prices above marginal cost, causing deadweight losses by raising the price to consumers for the sake of incentivizing innovation capabilities. This was already established by: William D Nordhaus, *Invention, Growth and Welfare: A Theoretical Treatment of Technological Change* (The MIT Press 1969) (hereafter Nordhaus, *Invention, Growth and Welfare*). For a more general overview on this point, see Mark A Lemley, 'Property, Intellectual Property, and Free Riding' (2005) 83 Texas Law Review 1031, 1057 ff (hereafter Lemley, 'Property, Intellectual Property, and Free Riding')

[59] Eg, Dornis, 'Der Schutz' (n 31) 1258 ff; Sven Hetmank and Anne Lauber-Rönsberg, 'Künstliche Intelligenz—Herausforderungen für das Immaterialgüterrecht' (2018) GRUR 574, 579 (hereafter Hetmank and Lauber-Rönsberg, 'Künstliche Intelligenz').

[60] Cf Richard Posner, *Economic Analysis of Law* (7th edn, Wolters Kluwer 2007) 31 ff.

[61] Harold Demsetz, 'Information and Efficiency: Another Viewpoint' (1969) Journal of Law and Economics, 1 ff.. Such Market Opening approach is also supported by Hans Ullrich, 'Lizenzkartellrecht auf dem Weg zur Mitte' (1996) GRUR Int. 555, 565.

[62] Edmund W Kitch, 'The Nature and Function of the Patent System' (1977) 20(2) Journal of Law and Economics 265 ff (hereafter Kitch, 'The Nature and Function of the Patent System'); Suzanne Scotchmer, 'Protecting Early Innovators: Should Second-Generation Products Be Patentable?' (1996) 27 Rand Journal of Economics 322.

[63] Yoram Barzel, 'Optimal Timing of Innovations' (1968) 50 Review of Economics & Statistics 348 ff (hereafter Barzel, 'Optimal Timing of Innovations').

Another consideration that should at least be taken into account is the transaction costs theory.[64] IP rights in comparison to alternative systems of protection, eg, trade secrecy and contracts, may save private transaction costs, as they may already outline certain points that would otherwise need to be formulated in contracts. One still has to bear in mind though that even if such cost savings may be generally welfare enhancing, they always need to be assessed against the backdrop of the costs that any IP system causes. The costs and value of IP-induced stimulation of creation and innovation might therefore also offset each other or might even be detrimental to general welfare.

3.2 Analysis of IP Justification for AI Tools and Outputs

3.2.1 Incentive theories

The *incentive theories* can be divided into two strands: a *general incentive theory*, which is ultimately entrenched in deontological and psychological considerations, and the (more relevant) *investment protection theory*.

According to general incentive theory, intangible goods would not be generated without the allocation of property rights. Such a priori considerations, however, are hardly convincing, as what provides for incentives is not IP rights per se, but rather the prospect of successful market opportunities. A lack of market demand cannot be replaced by IP protection.[65] Nevertheless, some current scholarly work on the IP protection of AI builds on such considerations.[66]

The most common justification theory is investment protection theory.[67] According to this theory, one of the main reasons for granting exclusive rights lies in the distinctive character of most intellectual products. As non-rivalrous public goods, they can easily be replicated, and their enjoyment by one person does not prevent enjoyment of them by other persons. This may lead to an underinvestment in the production of knowledge, if necessary investments cannot be recouped, once

[64] See, eg, Paul J Heald, 'A Transaction Costs Theory of Patent Law' (2005) 66(3) Ohio State Journal 475 ff.

[65] This is especially evidenced in the field of orphan drugs: Although market players are able to obtain a patent, they do not engage in the marketing of the respective drugs since the market conditions do not allow them to make a sufficient amount of money—with or without the patent.

[66] See, eg, Dornis, 'Der Schutz' (n 31) 1258ff; Hetmank and Lauber-Rönsberg, 'Künstliche Intelligenz' (n 59) 574, 579.

[67] This theory is very well-illustrated by William Nordhaus's classical treatment of patent law. Nordhaus was primarily concerned with determining the optimal duration of a patent, but his analysis can be applied more generally. Each increase in the duration or strength of patents, he observed, stimulates an increase in inventive activity. The resultant gains to social welfare include the discounted present value of the consumer surplus and producer surplus associated with the distribution of the intellectual products whose creation is thereby induced. See Nordhaus, *Invention, Growth and Welfare* (n 58) 71 ff. As regards the special case of copyright, in continental Europe the investment protection rationale is primarily located in the dogmatic realm of neighbouring rights, but it can also be invoked for traditional copyright as one of several rationales.

imitators, who can save the product development costs and thus offer identical products substantially cheaper, undercut them. The absence of such investment ultimately leads to market failure and therewith a decrease of social net welfare.

3.2.1.1 General incentive theory

If the incentive theory is generally not convincing, it loses even more relevancy in the AI context. The computer itself, ie, the AI tool, is not conscious of or responsive to incentives.[68] Regarding the various human actors involved—whether as a programmer, a potentially creative or innovative user of an AI tool, or a distributor of AI-generated output[69]—a certain influence of legal incentives might be conceivable.[70] But it is in no way apparent that there is a lack of motivation to be active in these areas.[71] Rather, on a general level one can presently observe that AI innovation appears to be thriving. The markets are highly dynamic. Market failure is not apparent.

It has been claimed that the (human) programmers need to obtain rights to the results generated by AI, because programming would not be undertaken if third parties could immediately free ride.[72] However, no evidence supports this assumption, and in any case it does not substantively go beyond the mere reiteration of theoretical, abstract lines of IP reasoning.[73] A counter view argues that the programmer's incentive to develop AI applications is sufficiently taken into account 'higher up the chain'[74] by IP protection for the elements of the specific AI tool[75] or rather the sales or licensing revenues pertaining thereto.[76] This line of

[68] Ramalho, 'Will Robots Rule the (Artistic) World?' (n 35) 15; Annemarie Bridy, 'Coding Creativity' (2012) 5 Stanford Technology Law Review 1, 21 fn 157; Ralph D Clifford, 'Intellectual Property in the Era of the Creative Computer Program: Will the True Creator Please Stand Up?' (1997) 71 Tulane Law Review 1675, 1702–3; Peifer, 'Roboter als Schöpfer' (n 32) 226; Iony Randrianirina, 'Copyright Issues Arising From Works Created With Artificial Intelligence' (2019) 2 Medien und Recht International 70, 71; Schönberger, 'Deep Copyright' (n 39) 35, 46; Colin R Davies, 'An Evolutionary Step in Intellectual Property Rights' (2011) 27 Computer Law & Security Review 601, 616, however, considers that a computer might theoretically be programmed towards responsiveness for reward and incentive.

[69] Ramalho, 'Will Robots Rule the (Artistic) World?' (n 35) 19, compares disseminators of AI creations with 'the publishers of books in the public domain (who) expect users to pay for copies of the book' and considers the need for IP rights from the perspective of these disseminators. See also Robert Denicola, 'Ex Machina: Copyright Protection for Computer-Generated Works' (2016) 69 Rutgers University Law Review 251, 283 (hereafter Denicola, 'Ex Machina').

[70] Incentives and disincentives of IP allocation to humans for AI-generated output are discussed by Rosa Maria Ballardini and others, 'AI-generated Content: Authorship and Inventorship in the Age of Artificial Intelligence' in Taina Pihlajarinne and others (eds), *Online Distribution of Content in the EU* (Edward Elgar 2019) 117; Butler argued already in 1981 in favour of incentivizing effects of copyright availability for AI-generated works: see Timothy L Butler, 'Can a Computer be an Author?' (1981) 4 Hastings Communications and Entertainment Law Journal 707, 735.

[71] But see in favour of the need for incentives, eg, Dornis, 'Der Schutz' (n 31) 1258ff.

[72] Hetmank and Lauber-Rönsberg, 'Künstliche Intelligenz' (n 59) 574, 579.

[73] In this vein also Mauritz Kop, 'AI & Intellectual Property: Towards an Articulated Public Domain' (2019) 8 https://ssrn.com/abstract=3409715, forthcoming in (2020) 28 Texas Intellectual Property Law Journal (hereafter Kop, 'AI & Intellectual Property').

[74] Jane Ginsburg, 'People Not Machines' (2018) 49(2) International Review of Intellectual Property and Competition Law 131, 134.

[75] Yanisky-Ravid, 'Generating Rembrandt' (n 36) 700 ff; Yu 'The Machine Author' (n 12) 1263.

[76] Denicola, 'Ex Machina' (n 69) 251, 283; Samuelson, 'Allocating Ownership Rights' (n 35) 1225.

argument, however, constitutes the economic mirror image, so to speak, of the deontological 'double reward' thought outlined above. Thus, it suffers from the same misguided assumption that IP protection for the tool as such is given or justified in the first place. In any case, all perspectives ultimately remain speculative for lack of empirical grounds.

With regard to humans using AI tools with a view to obtaining a superficially creative or potentially innovative output, then, 'the mere action of pressing a button'[77] (which is the ultimate technological promise of AI) is certainly not in need of external motivation. As far as subsequent distributors are concerned, a variety of business models to make profitable use of public domain subject matter are imaginable—reaping these possibilities is up to the commercial creativity of the market players.

At the same time, considerable AI-related patenting activity can be observed.[78] However, there is no evidence concerning whether or to what extent such patents are actually obtained because they are associated with incentivizing functions. Rather it can be assumed that there are varieties of market-driven reasons (in particular first-mover advantages[79] and the almost infinite advantages AI-enabled knowledge gathering possesses) that motivate undertakings to engage in AI markets. Consequently, they may be patenting for a variety of differing reasons, in particular for corporate strategy purposes.

In addition, there is an observable shift towards self-regulation tendencies. The more market players voluntarily share their intangible assets—whatever their actual motives may be—the less their actions can be incentivized by the prospect of obtaining or making use of state-granted exclusive rights. As shown above, in essence AI works on the basis of data and algorithms. In both fields, self-regulatory sharing schemes play a major role.

As regards software algorithms in particular, the 'Open Source' movement has long been a self-regulatory deviation from proprietary state IP law.[80] Its 'openness and sharing culture' appears to particularly thrive also in the AI context: Large players like Google share and publish their new developments for 'free' (ie, at least without an explicit counter-performance).[81] Optimization algorithms are to a large extent available in publicly accessible 'libraries' such as Google's

[77] Yu, 'The Machine Author' (n 12) 1262.

[78] See WIPO, 'WIPO Technology Trends 2019: Artificial Intelligence' (2019); Cockburn, Henderson, and Stern, 'The Impact of Artificial Intelligence on Innovation' (2017) 18 ff.

[79] See Yu, 'The Machine Author' (n 12) 1264 ff, arguing first-to-market economic incentives are especially powerful in digital markets.

[80] See only Maurice Schellekens, 'Free and Open Source: An Answer to Commodification?' in Lucie Guibault and P Bernt Hugenholtz (eds), *The Future of the Public Domain* (Kluwer Law International 2006) 303.

[81] Cf Google, 'Perspectives on issues in AI governance' (2019) 20 <https://ai.google/static/documents/perspectives-on-issues-in-ai-governance.pdf>. Yet, one still needs to consider undertakings' chances to reap the users' data and the possibility to end up in profitable licensing endeavours once the model is adequately advanced.

'TensorFlow'.[82] Individual programmers may often be intrinsically motivated to share by reputational prospects.[83]

Also, with regard to data, pools and sharing platforms have gained considerable importance, and their practical relevance is expected to keep on growing.[84] These, too, are operating under paradigms of self-regulation,[85] especially with regard to access issues. Private ordering[86] thus plays a major role in designing innovation-enabling frameworks for AI markets. Of course, there is a highly complicated interaction between the existing IP regime and the self-regulatory schemes, partly revolving around, building on, or deviating from them. Nevertheless, in their specific appearances outlined above, self-regulation tendencies to a certain extent call into question IP's exclusionary property logic and ultimately its justification in the realm of AI.

A point that is at least indirectly related to the incentive theory relates to the role of IP as a potential signal of firms' innovativeness in attracting venture capital. A correlation between a firm's innovation capacity and the number of patents it holds has traditionally been seen. However, there are new forms of investment chances, which relativizes the relevancy of patents above all for startups. State-offered research funds also allow direct market intervention to promote innovative or creative output. Direct research subsidizing can also facilitate knowledge transfer from science to practice.[87]

3.2.1.2 Investment protection theory

Under investment protection theory, one has to distinguish between AI tools and outputs. Depending on each AI application, there may be different investments in AI, such as high-quality data,[88] infrastructure,[89] computing power,[90] and know-how.[91] In light of the argument that investment can become sunk costs and cannot be recouped without the existence of exclusive rights, IP protection for AI tools

[82] <https://www.tensorflow.org/>.

[83] Cf. Dornis, 'Der Schutz' (n 31) 1259.

[84] Cf. Heiko Richter and Peter Slowinski, 'The Data Sharing Economy: On the Emergence of New Intermediaries' (2019) 50(1) International Review of Intellectual Property and Competition Law 4.

[85] Ibid, 24 ff.

[86] Reto M Hilty, 'Intellectual Property and Private Ordering' in Rochelle C Dreyfuss and Justine Pila (eds), *The Oxford Handbook of Intellectual Property Law* (Oxford University Press 2018) 898, 922.

[87] Eg, deep learning was mainly developed by IT researchers from Stanford University.

[88] The necessary amount of investments differs considerably depending on whether data are publicly available or have to be newly generated. The latter can happen, eg, in the health and pharmaceutical sector, where clinical trials have to be conducted. If the necessary data are protected by IP rights not limited by adequate exceptions and limitations, then to obtain such data may require the payment of (high) licensing royalties and entail high transaction costs, especially when the data are held by multiple parties.

[89] Infrastructure software, for example.

[90] Many further potential and conceivable advancements in AI (like the computer trying all possible solutions and thus inevitably finding the best one) have not been realized to its full capability due to as of yet still widely insufficient computing power.

[91] AI specialists are heavily sought after in labour markets and are a key factor for successful AI.

and outputs seems to be justified once certain investments are really made and cannot be recouped. Nonetheless, one has to be cautious and should not quickly draw this conclusion.

Scrutinizing the theory that justifies the necessity of IP protection in more detail, one has to assess that the need for IP protection for AI tools and outputs under investment protection theory considerations is different in AI cases. Investment protection theory builds on two assumptions. First, the innovation processes that Nordhaus analysed were rather long, included high investment, and took place in markets with slower innovation cycles and a lower likelihood of product substitutes. Secondly, the likelihood of imitation and misappropriation was rather high, which in the absence of IP rights would lead to pricing under the inventor's marginal costs.

The scenario seems different in AI cases. Innovations here tend to happen in vast cycles and very dynamic markets, which are characterized by constant improvement in AI applications. Such improvements typically entail incremental innovations that do not require enormous investments, unlike innovations with protracted production phases. The constant improvements in ML applications, eg, mostly depend on an increase in brute calculation speed, on better and more data inputs, and ultimately on certain heuristics applied by ML programmers for solving specific issues.[92] Actual technological changes are thereby rather minimal. Instead, an increasing tendency towards individualization of certain ML applications can be observed, which allows creation and innovation in ML to be refinanced via services.[93] This seems to hold true for AI applications in general. Thus, unauthorized marketization of certain AI products and services, which were subject to high initial investments and misappropriation by competitors, seems unlikely for typical AI applications.[94]

Nordhaus[95] and Teece[96] also analysed potential innovation strategies of an undertaking to succeed sustainably in markets. What they found can also serve *e contrario* as an argument for not granting IP rights at all in certain AI cases. According to their findings, in industries where legal protection is effective, or where new products are difficult to copy, the strategic necessity for innovative firms to integrate into so-called co-specialized assets seems less compelling than in industries where legal protection is 'weak' in terms of uncertainty. Co-specialized assets are assets that rely upon each other in order to succeed. These assets are so highly specialized that they are dependent upon each other: one without another is

[92] It should be noted, however, that there might be certain models which require more heuristics and a certain know-how on the part of the ML programmer.

[93] Luminovo and Dataguard, eg, are two examples of startups that offer ML services to data-rich customers.

[94] This assumption might change the technical category, however.

[95] Nordhaus, *Invention, Growth and Welfare* (n 58) 70 ff.

[96] See David J Teece, 'Profiting from Technological Innovation: Implications for Integration, Collaboration, Licensing and Public Policy' (1986) 15 Research Policy 285 ff.

of no use. In other words, in markets where co-specialized assets already exist, IP protection is not needed as an incentive for creation and innovation, and would be detrimental to economic welfare.

Translated into the world of AI, such considerations become particularly relevant for AI tools. In the context of ML, eg, the highest value of each generated ML tool does not lie in the ML tool itself and hence in the specific software algorithm. It lies in so-called weights. Weights are trainable parameters that are optimized during the learning process. Weights allow for conclusions on the quality of each ML tool. Weights are what determines the loss function, and they are needed for improving each tool. Therefore, an ML tool without correlating weights would be valueless for potential free riders. The ML tool and its weights, in other words, are co-specialized assets. Moreover, ML tools are becoming increasingly dependent on data and the service know-how component. Under such circumstances the creation of (factual) data exclusivities or data-specific competitive advantages and know-how tends to be the incentive to innovate in the first place, and not IP rights. Such strategies can be currently seen in most of the big tech incumbents in the ICT sector.[97] Hence, it seems that the investments undertaken for ML tools are already sufficiently protected, and there is no case for investment protection by IP rights, as there simply is no market failure.[98]

Even outside the field of data, investment protection by factual means seems to play a major role in the context of AI. In particular, the developed, ie, applicable AI tool is characterized by the 'black box' phenomenon already outlined above.[99] This phenomenon is closely related to the issue of reverse engineering, which can be defined as 'the possibility to extract or deduce certain elements of the machine-learning process through access to other elements'. Take ML as an example. Some elements of the ML process can potentially be reverse engineered, which is highly unlikely as regards the overall functioning of the ML tool.[100] Up to a certain level of complexity of the model,[101] reverse engineering may still be technically possible, but it may no longer make sense from an economic point of view because it is easier to design an alternative model that produces a comparable output.[102] In addition,

97 On the issue of data-induced market foreclosures under competition law considerations see Jörg Hoffmann and Gérman Johannsen, 'Big data and merger control' (2019) 3 ff. <https://papers.ssrn.com/sol3/papers.cfm?abstract_id=3364792>.

98 Recently, the need for introducing a property right in data has not been identified, precisely because sufficient contractual and factual means of protection appear to be available; see Josef Drexl and others, 'Position Statement of the Max Planck Institute for Innovation and Competition of August 16, 2016—On the current debate on exclusive rights and access rights to data at the European level' (2016) Max Planck Institute for Innovation and Competition Research Paper No 16-10 <https://papers.ssrn.com/sol3/papers.cfm?abstract_id=2833165>. This discussion should be kept in mind when reflecting on the scope of exclusivity of ML components.

99 Drexl and others, 'Technical Aspects of Artificial Intelligence' (n 4).

100 Ibid.

101 Ibid.

102 Ibid.

there are further technical protection measures market players can rely on, especially application programming interfaces (APIs) to exercise factual control over each ML tool. Similar considerations seem to apply *pars pro toto* to AI tools in general.

Regarding the AI output, however, factual scarcity of the creation or innovation may not be given, and the return on investment may indeed be imperilled. This, however, might still not be efficiently remedied by IP rights, once high market dynamics and faster innovation cycles begin to operate, with the effect of minimizing the lifecycle of AI outputs. Indeed, once the substitution of AI products or services happens with such speed that investments could not be recouped despite IP protection in place, any IP right would be detrimental to economic welfare and not justifiable. This may hold particularly true for registered rights that are characterized by long application procedures. Yet what one has to keep in mind is that again, this assumption cannot be made without making a clear distinction between potential market dynamics of AI tools that may make IP rights for AI outputs unnecessary and market dynamics in relation to the AI output per se.

In relation to high market dynamics for AI tools, each AI output may still have longer-lasting market relevancy, regardless of certain rapidly evolving AI tools. The life expectancy of AI outputs actually may be completely detached from fast-moving innovation cycles of AI tools. An example of this is the NASA antenna mentioned above. The NASA antenna was developed over two years with the help of an evolutionary algorithm. Significant investments were made in the form of specific know-how and labour costs. The evolutionary algorithm that was developed and then used would be our AI tool, and the antenna itself, the AI output. The evolutionary algorithm can be marketed and effectively protected against misappropriation via technical protection measures or *de facto* protection, and the investments could be recouped and hence the intellectual creation or innovation in the tool itself would not need IP protection.

However, for the antenna, effective protection against misappropriation does not exist. The investments could not be recouped. Incentives to innovate with regard to such AI outputs would diminish. IP protection would be needed under the investment protection theory. Certainly, once such output is quickly substituted by another more successful product, marginalizing the return on the product, IP protection would not make sense, as the costs of investment could never be recouped. This would be the case if IP protection simply came too late, as returns on investment could never reach marginal costs due to higher market dynamics. Such considerations, however, have to be assessed separately from the question of whether the evolutionary algorithm itself might be already outdated. This question may not have any influence on the lifecycle of the antenna itself.

Therefore, even though AI techniques continue to develop at a fast pace, this fact cannot axiomatically provide additional insights on the question of whether a given AI output might be substituted with such speed that IP protection would be unnecessary. This has to be assessed independently. Thus, IP protection for AI outputs theoretically might be economically justified under the investment protection theory. This has to be determined on a case-by-case basis while keeping in mind both the potential creation and innovation incentivizing function of IP rights when undertakings' recoup chances are really at stake, and the complex set of economic costs that such rights also entail.

3.2.2 Theories related to the optimization of patterns of productivity

Market opening theory, prospect theory, and disclosure theory all build on the idea of optimizing patterns of creative or innovative productivity via the creation of artificial scarcity. Under such considerations, rent dissipation may be minimized, leading to welfare gains.[103]

3.2.2.1 Market opening theory

According to market opening theory, artificial scarcity by IP regimes is expected to play the important role of letting potential producers of intellectual products know what consumers want, and thus of channelling productive efforts in directions most likely to enhance general welfare.[104] These considerations, however, only make sense insofar as such scarcity is not already existent due to other means of protection. As already outlined above, this might only be the case for AI outputs. AI tools, in contrast, seem to be efficiently protected by other technical means, eg, APIs.

3.2.2.2 Prospect theory

In his prospect theory Edmund Kitch favoured a broad scope of IP protection.[105] He argued that granting to the developer of a pioneering invention an expansive set of entitlements enables the undertaking to coordinate research and development dedicated to improving the invention internally. This reduces dissipation of rents and hence fosters innovation.[106] A similar argument also holds true for fostering creations.

This argument at first sight might be relevant if AI is involved. It is, however, generally too short-sighted to assume that granting IP rights may only lead to a lowering of rent dissipation and welfare gains. Once IP rights exist, they interfere with the ability of other market participants to freely conduct their then

[103] Rent dissipation is defined as total expenditure of resources by all agents attempting to capture a rent or prize.

[104] Accordingly, the logic of property rights dictates their extension into every corner in which people derive enjoyment and value from literary and artistic works. To stop short of these ends would deprive producers of the signals of consumer preference that trigger and direct their investments. See Paul Goldstein, *Copyright's Highway, From Gutenberg to the Celestial Jukebox* (2nd edn, Stanford Law and Politics 2004) 178.

[105] Kitch, 'The Nature and Function of the Patent System' (n 62) 322 ff.

[106] Ibid.

IP-infringing business. This may lead to races to create or invent, which may lead to wasteful duplication of research effort. Furthermore, instead of enabling the original inventor to coordinate efficiently the exploitation of the technology, a quasi-monopoly may lead to satisficing behaviour and thus to an inefficiently narrow focus on improvements related to the primary AI creator's or inventor's principal line of business.[107]

These considerations further reflect the very question as to whether market concentration or effective competitive markets may serve as nutrient soil for creations and innovations.[108] Granting perfect control privileges and unchallenged economic power over AI tools or outputs may simply give less incentive to improve further on first-generation tools and outputs. This could ultimately cause both static and dynamic inefficiencies and could pre-empt welfare-enhancing competitive creation and innovation processes.[109] Kitch's prospect theory therefore can be falsified and should not be applied for utilitarian economic considerations.[110]

In the realm of AI, such considerations become particularly relevant in the case of deep learning, which is a specific ML application. Deep learning is a GPT as well as a method of invention.[111] From the perspective of a utilitarian economic justification of IP rights, the usage of deep learning throughout multiple sectors will, first, lead to certain positive vertical research spillovers. Such welfare-enhancing effects, however, might dwindle away if IP rights preclude independent subsequent creation and innovation that build on deep-learning tools and outputs.[112] Second,

[107] Merges and Nelson, 'On the Complex Economics of Patent Scope' (n 54) 843. On satisficing behaviour see Herbert A Simon, 'A Behavioral Model of Rational Choice' (1955) 69 Quarterly Journal of Economics 99–118.

[108] Such considerations reflect the very question of whether market concentration or effective competitive markets may serve as fertile soil for innovation. See also Mark A Lemley, 'The Economics of Improvement in Intellectual Property Law' (1997) 75 Texas Law Review 993 ff.

[109] See also Lemley, 'Property, Intellectual Property, and Free Riding' (n 58) 1031.

[110] See, eg, Harhoff and Hall, 'Recent Research' (n 54) 10. Merges and Nelson refer to Kitch's theory under the notion of the vertical dilemma of IP, falsifying it for cases of cumulative innovation. Merges and Nelson, 'On the Complex Economics of Patent Scope' (n 54) 875. See also for the role of antitrust doctrine in such cases Louis Kaplow, 'The Patent-Antitrust Intersection: A Reappraisal' (1984) Harvard Law Review 97, 1813–92.

[111] One example for deep learning is the pioneering unstructured approach to predictive drug candidate selection that brings together a vast array of previously disparate clinical and biophysical data. In this context, Atomwise may fundamentally reshape the 'ideas production function' in drug discovery. See Iain M Cockburn, Rebecca Henderson, and Scott Stern, 'The Impact of Artificial Intelligence on Innovation: An Exploratory Analysis' in Ajay Agrawal, Joshua Gans, and Avi Goldfarb (eds), *The Economics of Artificial Intelligence: An Agenda* (University of Chicago Press 2017) 14

[112] Even though intertemporal spillovers from today's to tomorrow's creators and innovators cannot be easily captured in positive economics, Furman and Stern and Williams have already showed that when IMIs and GPTs coincide, control over the deep-learning tool shapes both the level and the direction of innovative activity throughout different sectors. Beyond that, the rules and institutions governing such control have a powerful influence on the realized amount and nature of innovation. See on this issue from a rather positive economics perspective: Jeffrey L Furman and Scott Stern, 'Climbing Atop the Shoulders of Giants: The Impact of Institutions on Cumulative Research' (2011) 101(5) American Economic Review 1933–63; Heidi L Williams, 'Intellectual Property Rights and Innovation: Evidence from the Human Genome' (2014) 121(1) Journal of Political Economy 1 ff; Paul M Romer, 'Endogenous Technological Change' (1990) 98(5) Journal of Political Economy 71 ff.

as already outlined above, this also means that IP-generated exclusive endogenous creation and innovation growth has negative externalities that may ultimately lead to underinvestment in AI-related creations and innovations.[113] Certainly, the fact that tomorrow's innovators can benefit from 'standing on the shoulders of giants',[114] while potentially not sharing gains with their predecessors, makes a nuanced assessment of the 'free-rider' issue necessary. This assessment has to be done against the backdrop of the specific characteristics of AI tools and outputs outlined above.

3.2.2.3 Disclosure theory

Yoram Barzel's disclosure theory is based on the idea that the grant of exclusive rights can eliminate or reduce the tendency of duplicated or uncoordinated inventive activity and hence rent dissipation of other market participants.[115] Such argumentation, however, has to be contrasted with the fact that, due to the black-box phenomenon and the corresponding inability of humans to understand the entire AI process, certain aspects of at least the AI tool, particularly in more complex cases, actually cannot be disclosed.[116] Even though the programming source code of the algorithm behind a model and the primary architecture of an AI model can be explained and disclosed, a concrete description of the final AI tool, a very complex deep neural network model, eg, is still not possible. Just such an explanation, however, is the most crucial part in really preventing the duplicative and uncoordinated activity that causes rent dissipation.

Even though a lot of research is currently going on in relation to the interpretation of AI (so-called 'explainable AI'), more complex AI tools may still not be sufficiently disclosed. The disclosure theory therefore cannot serve as argumentation for the utilitarian economic justification of IP rights for AI tools per se. Instead, such considerations also need to be assessed on a case-by-case basis.

[113] Kenneth J Arrow, 'Economic Welfare and the Allocation of Resources for Invention' in National Bureau of Economic Research, *The Rate and Direction of Inventive Activity: Economic and Social Factors* (Princeton University Press 1962) 609, 620. For different opinions on this, see: Joseph Schumpeter, *Theorie der wirtschaftlichen Entwicklung* (Berlin 1912) 157 and Philippe Aghion and Peter Howitt, 'A Model of Growth through Creative Destruction' (1992) 60(2) Econometrica 323 ff.

[114] Suzanne Scotchmer, 'Standing on the Shoulders of Giants: Cumulative Research and the Patent Law' (1991) 45(1) Journal of Economic Perspectives 29 ff.

[115] Barzel, 'Optimal Timing of Innovations' (n 63) 348 ff: see for a good overview.

[116] Even though there are certain endeavours to 'reverse engineer' the black box (mostly due to quality improvements), some of them may even be legally necessary under the requirements of Article 22 General Data Protection Regulation (Regulation (EU) 2016/679 of the European Parliament and of the Council of 27 April 2016 on the protection of natural persons with regard to the processing of personal data and on the free movement of such data. Another example would be certain obligations in MIFID II for FinTech applications in high-frequency trading. See Directive 2014/65/EU of the European Parliament and of the Council of 15 May 2014 on markets in financial instruments. What has to be kept in mind, however, is that any ML application is still determined by humans. On the AI-induced challenges to patent law justification regarding the disclosure requirement, see also Alfred Früh, 'Transparency in the Patent System—Artificial Intelligence and the Disclosure Requirement' (2019) https://papers.ssrn.com/sol3/papers.cfm?abstract_id=3309749 forthcoming in Zaneta Pacud and Rafal Sikorski (eds), *Rethinking Patent Law as an Incentive to Innovation*.

4. Conclusion

AI is at risk of becoming another chapter in the history of politically motivated attempts to foster creation and innovation via legislative market intervention. In fact, however, most AI applications lack a theoretical justification for creating exclusive rights. If this fact is ignored, such legislation could ultimately lead to dysfunctional effects that have negative impacts on social welfare. While there may be some exceptions regarding AI outputs, considerable (in particular economic) research is still needed to identify these specific cases where IP protection is needed.

This conclusion stems from the observation that with the advent of AI there also comes a decline of relevancy of deontological justification theories in the AI field, with regard to both AI tools and AI outputs. Although at present, considerable human impact is indispensable for AI to produce proper outcomes, in light of the fast-moving nature of the field this required involvement can be expected to constantly diminish.[117] The 'romantic' image of human ingenuity envisaged by traditional notions of labour, personality, and reward reasoning has anyway long been overridden by market realities determined by industries, not individuals.[118] It further loses persuasive power in the AI field. Potential protection regimes—if ever required—would be looking not at creators or inventors, but at investors.[119]

As regards the utilitarian economic IP justification theories, one has to distinguish between AI tools and outputs when assessing the question of whether AI markets function without IP protection.

In cases pertaining to AI tools, the likelihood of misappropriation is rather low due to factual control of certain parameters of AI that are crucial for further re-use. Besides the black-box phenomenon, there are also technical protection measures in place, such as APIs, that create factual scarcity. In such cases, IP protection does not seem to be justifiable.

In the case of AI outputs, however, there might be exceptions in which IP protection could be justified. Even though the theories related to the optimization of patterns of productivity may not support this observation, investment protection

[117] This decline of human impact may have an interesting impact on the 'public domain' as the flipside of IP (see Alexander Peukert, *Die Gemeinfreiheit* (Mohr Siebeck 2012)). Intangible goods without human authors or inventors fall into the public domain from the outset and considerably enlarge it; see Peifer, 'Roboter als Schöpfer' (n 32) 228; Yu, 'The Machine Author' (n 12) 1265 ff; Ramalho, 'Will Robots Rule the (Artistic) World?' (n 35) 22; Gervais, 'The Machine' (n 40) 21; Samuelson, 'Allocating Ownership Rights' (n 35) 1224 ff; Kop, 'AI & Intellectual Property' (n 73). (Re-)conceptualizing and possibly strengthening the still underdeveloped 'public domain' perspective in the doctrinal framework of IP appears an interesting area for future research in light of AI developments.

[118] Including in the realm of copyright law; cf only Reto M Hilty, *Urheberrecht* (Stämpfli 2011) 4 ff, 39 ff; Ansgar Ohly, 'Urheberrecht als Wirtschaftsrecht' in Otto Depenheuer and Karl-Nikolaus Peifer (eds), *Geistiges Eigentum: Schutzrecht oder Ausbeutungstitel?* (Springer 2008) 141.

[119] In this direction, see Peifer, 'Roboter als Schöpfer' (n 32) 228; Herbert Zech, 'Artificial Intelligence: Impact of Current Developments in IT on Intellectual Property' (2019) GRUR Int. 1145, 1147.

theory may back it in certain cases. For AI outputs at least, technical protection measures may not exist, and thus misappropriation might be possible. Once investments are actually made, returns on them might be imperilled by potential free riders in the absence of exclusive rights. This could from a theoretical point of view lead to a case where competitors actually could sell the AI output under the generators' marginal costs and hence create disincentives for undertakings to further invest in AI creations and innovations.

Such considerations, however, need to be thoroughly assessed against the backdrop of the concrete creation and innovation incentivizing function of IP rights and the complex set of economic costs that IP rights in general entail. Exclusive rights for AI outputs can only be justified once investments are made, when undertakings' chances of recouping them really exist and are at stake, and when these chances actually can be protected by IP rights. The latter point of suitability of IP rights to achieve their intended purpose becomes particularly relevant in a world of AI where specific market dynamics may render IP systems unnecessary, possibly dysfunctional, and ultimately harmful to general economic welfare.

PART II

ARTIFICIAL INTELLIGENCE AND PATENT LAW

4

Foundational Patents in Artificial Intelligence

*Raphael Zingg**

1. Introduction

Despite pledges for openness, technology companies are rushing to gain control over the direction of artificial intelligence (AI) via patents. Leaders in the field such as Google, Facebook, Amazon, and Microsoft all host open-source AI repositories. TensorFlow, the machine learning software used for research and production at Google, has been downloaded more than 15 million times through 2018.[1] Facebook offers PyTorch and Caffe, two popular machine learning frameworks increasingly used for developing and building AI products.[2] Innovation in AI is a 'function of openness and collaboration', contends the director of big data solutions at Intel.[3] To maintain their learning trajectories, AI technologies require large-scale participation by developers, allowing their owners to leverage the training methodologies of open-source contributors, effectively crowd-sourcing the development of AI.[4] Yet, technology firms continue to file patents in the AI space. IBM announced that it led the industry with 1,600 AI-related patents in 2018, stemming

* All online materials were accessed before 21 March 2020.

[1] TensorFlow, 'An Open Source Machine Learning Framework for Everyone' <github.com/tensorflow> and Tom Simonite, 'Despite pledging openness, companies rush to patent AI tech' (*WIRED*, 31 July 2018) <wired.com/story/despite-pledging-openness-companies-rush-to-patent-ai-tech>. Tensorflow's Apache 2.0 Licence grants users the right to use patents inevitably infringed by the use of the software.

[2] For the repositories, see <github.com/pytorch> and <github.com/caffe2>.

[3] See a keynote by Martin Hall, Senior Director of CSP AI Partnerships at Intel, in the Artificial Intelligence Product Group at Intel Corporation, under <youtube.com/watch?v=MDyu-V4ld0k>. When sponsoring the Intel Science and Technology Centers (ISTC), eg, the ISTC for Big Data at the Massachusetts Institute of Technology, Intel includes clauses preventing Intel or academic institutions from filing patents and requiring them instead to publish patentable inventions and release all significant software under open source licences; see Melba Kurman, 'Intel to universities: no patents, please, just open source' (Innovation Excellence, 2011) <innovationexcellence.com/blog/2011/09/12/intel-to-universities-no-patents-please-just-open-source>.

[4] Facebook trains its image recognition networks on data sets of public images with user-supplied hashtags as labels; its largest data set includes 3.5 billion images and 17,000 hashtags; see <code.facebook.com/posts/1700437286678763>; see Ken Goldberg, 'Robots and the Return to Collaborative Intelligence' (2019) 1 Nature Machine Intelligence 2 for work by Fei-Fei Li utilizing the Amazon crowdsourcing platform Mechanical Turk to have contributors hand-label image data sets known as ImageNet10, with 14 million images labelled through 2018.

Raphael Zingg, *Foundational Patents in Artificial Intelligence* In: *Artificial Intelligence and Intellectual Property.*
Edited by: Jyh-An Lee, Reto M Hilty, and Kung-Chung Liu, Oxford University Press (2021). © The several contributors.
DOI: 10.1093/oso/9780198870944.003.0005

mainly from its work in language and machine learning techniques.[5] Microsoft and Google have similarly filed for several hundred AI-related patents over the past years.[6] Even OpenAI, a non-profit research organization co-founded by Elon Musk with a USD one billion endowment committed to open source suggested it might engage in pre-emptive patenting in the long run.[7] While the extent and impact of such a patenting surge is unclear, the protection of fundamental techniques with large application potential creates obstacles in the path towards the public domain. Basic inventions comprising the enabling technologies of the twentieth century were unpatented, as they were largely driven by government funding, or faced issues of patentability. This resulted in the building blocks of computer hardware, software, lasers, and biotechnology being found in the public domain.[8]

Contrarily, the foundations of AI arise from the private sector. It follows that the fundamentals of AI innovation may come to exist behind a blockade of privatization. Technology giant Google holds a patent on dropout, a technique standard for neural networks to generalize to new data.[9] Further patents held on learning with deep methods, classification of data objects, parallelizing neural networks, and word embedding have the potential to leave Google owning key components of future machine learning methods.[10] In lockstep with current strategies of exploiting social media user data, Facebook is seeking to patent an approach to design memory networks, neural networks which enhance a conventional machine learning system for processing text.[11] Microsoft employs an aggressive approach, seeking to patent a sweeping set of methodologies on querying data instances to be labelled for training, effectively assuming ownership of basic uses and applications of active machine learning.[12] Recently, the scientist who introduced the compression technique called asymmetric numeral systems wrote a protest letter after

[5] See the press release by IBM under <ibm.com/blogs/research/2019/01/2018-patent> where the firm details filing numbers and individual technology trends (language and machine learning techniques relating to Project Debater, blockchain technology, and machine learning powered diagnostic tools).

[6] CB Insights, 'Microsoft, Google lead In AI patent activity, while Apple lags behind' (*CB Insights*, 20 January 2017) <cbinsights.com/research/google-apple-microsoft-ai-patents>.

[7] Cade Metz, 'Inside OpenAI, Elon Musk's wild plan to set artificial intelligence free' (*WIRED*, 27 April 2016) <wired.com/2016/04/openai-elon-musk-sam-altman-plan-to-set-artificial-intelligence-free>.

[8] Mark A Lemley, 'Patenting Nanotechnology' (2005) 58 Stanford Law Review 601 with detailed case studies.

[9] US9406017 'System and Method for Addressing Overfitting in a Neural Network' granted in 2016.

[10] Amongst many, see US20150100530 'Methods and Apparatus for Reinforcement Learning' granted in 2017; US20150178383 'Classifying Data Objects' filed in 2014; US14030938 'System and Method for Parallelizing Convolutional Neural Networks' granted in 2017, and US20170011289 'Learning Word Embedding Using Morphological Knowledge' filed in 2015.

[11] US20170103324 'Generating Responses Using Memory Networks' filed in 2015.

[12] US20160162802 'Active Machine Learning' filed in 2014; Jeremy Gillula and Daniel Nazer, 'Stupid patent of the month: will patents slow artificial intelligence?' (*Electronic Frontier Foundation*, 29 September 2017) <eff.org/deeplinks/2017/09/stupid-patent-month-will-patents-slow-artificial-intelligence> (hereafter Gillula, 'Will patents slow artificial intelligence?'). Note that the application was first rejected by the patent office for lack of subject-matter eligibility and non-obviousness; the patent was ultimately granted in February 2019.

Google attempted to gain a patent over the use of asymmetric numeral systems for video compression, stating that as the technology has turned out to be extremely valuable, there have emerged attempts to monopolize its basic concepts, modifications, and applications.[13]

The 'Tragedy of the Anticommons' conceptualizes the potential of broad, upstream patents to add to the costs and slow the pace of downstream innovation.[14] Patenting the building blocks of a technology risks interfering with its progress, as each upstream patent allows its owner to request royalty payments from downstream users. There exist many documented cases amongst other emerging technologies such as semiconductors or nanotechnology where an extensively crowded set of patents has locked up or retarded innovation.[15] Webs of overlapping intellectual property rights increase transaction costs for market participants.[16] Termed patent thickets, these webs can have drastic effects, preventing new firms from entering the market, and influencing the operational direction of current actors.[17] Should a number of companies effectively control blocking patents in AI, and request that new downstream innovators obtain licences before their rights can be used, patents will be underused and innovation stifled.[18] These blockading patents impact not only the market, but also a subset of its most innovative drivers such as academics and open-source users.[19] The patenting of feature detectors and descriptors for computer vision are exemplary, leading to open-source libraries such as OpenCV eliminating the patented module. Without them, users had to invest extensive time in building the modules from source.

While it appears that many AI firms currently operate without licences, this trend can be reversed rapidly if patent litigation expands to the field.[20] A recent study by the World Intellectual Property Organization (WIPO) estimates that

[13] US20170164007 'Mixed Boolean-Token ANS Coefficient Coding' filed in 2016; see <th.if.uj.edu.pl/%7Edudaj/protestGoogle.pdf> for the third-party pre-issuance submission letter by Jaroslaw Duda (hereafter Duda, 'Pre-issuance').

[14] Michael A Heller and Rebecca S Eisenberg, 'Can Patents Deter Innovation? The Anticommons in Biomedical Research' (1998) 280 Science 698.

[15] Raphael Zingg and Marius Fischer, 'The Nanotechnology Patent Thicket Revisited' (2018) 20 Journal of Nanoparticle Research 267.

[16] Carl Shapiro, 'Navigating the Patent Thicket: Cross Licenses, Patent Pools, and Standard Setting' in Adam Jaffe, Josh Lerner, and Scott Stern (eds), *Innovation Policy and the Economy* (MIT Press 2001).

[17] Bronwyn H Hall and Rosemarie Ham Ziedonis, 'The Patent Paradox Revisited: An Empirical Study of Patenting in the U.S. Semiconductor Industry, 1979–1995' (2001) 32 RAND Journal of Economic 101; Bronwyn H Hall, Christian Helmers, and Georg von Graevenitz, 'Technology Entry in the Presence of Patent Thickets' (2015) NBER Working Paper 21455 <nber.org/papers/w21455.pdf>; Edward J Egan and David J Teece, 'Untangling the Patent Thicket Literature' (2015) University of California Berkeley Tusher Center for Management Intellectual Capital, Working Paper No 7 <hdl.handle.net/1911/92003>.

[18] Patent thickets do not inherently require that the ownership be fragmented; a patent space in which few companies with large portfolios exist can also lead to a thicket; see Dan L Burk, and Mark A Lemley, *The Patent Crisis and How Courts Can Solve It* (University of Chicago Press 2009).

[19] Richard L Wang, 'Biomedical Upstream Patenting and Scientific Research: The Case for Compulsory Licenses Bearing Reach-trough Royalties' (2008) 10 Yale Journal of Law and Technology 251.

[20] The incentives for openness for technology firms, sometimes formalized through patent pledges, are manifold. By pledging not to enforce their patent rights, companies such as Tesla gain access to

already slightly less than 1% of the worldwide AI patents have been litigated.[21] Monetization of AI intellectual property through selling or licensing of patent portfolios to patent enforcement entities can accentuate this practice.[22] Colloquially known as 'patent trolls', these patent enforcement entities do not invest in bringing technology to market via the acquired invention. Rather, they amass patent portfolios for the sole purpose of generating revenue by prosecuting infringement.[23] In fact, a number of AI patents have already been transferred to entities interested in enforcing them. For instance, Monument Peak Ventures, a subsidiary of the patent enforcement company Dominion Harbor, purchased Kodak's digital imaging portfolio of over 4,000 patents, affording them ownership of machine learning patents related to image recognition.[24] With patents on techniques to identify a photographer, recognize individuals in images, or discover the social relationships from personal photo collections, Monument Peak Ventures has myriad means to impede the development of new image analysis technologies.[25] The company launched first lawsuits over patents of this portfolio against GoPro and SZ DJI Technology for the infringement of patents covering the identification of the main subjects of an image by drone cameras and video editors.[26] The patent assertion campaign by Clouding IP against Amazon, AT&T, Dropbox, Google, Hewlett-Packard, SAP, Verizon, and more may serve as an additional example of what may happen when patent assertion entities acquire broad AI patents.[27] Relying on IP assigned by Symantec, the

costless publicity, increasing their brand value and awareness, while diffusing (or hoping to diffuse) their technology at low cost.

[21] With Nuance Communications, American Vehicular Sciences, and Automotive Technologies International as top three plaintiffs; see WIPO, 'WIPO technology trends 2019, artificial intelligence' (2019) <wipo.int/edocs/pubdocs/en/wipo_pub_1055.pdf> (hereafter WIPO, 'WIPO technology trends').

[22] Intellectual Ventures, one of the most prominent non-practising entities, was largely funded by Microsoft, Intel, Sony, Nokia, Apple, Google, Yahoo, American Express, Adobe, SAP, NVIDIA, and eBay; see Erik Oliver, Kent Richardson, and Michael Costa, 'How Intellectual Ventures is Streamlining its Portfolio' (2016) 77 Intellectual Asset Management 9; for trends in patent brokerage to patent enforcement entities, see Brian J Love, Kent Richardson, Erik Oliver, and Michael Costa, 'An Empirical Look at the "Brokered" Market for Patents' (2018) 83 Missouri Law Review 359.

[23] Former US President Obama: '[t]hey don't actually produce anything themselves .... They are essentially trying to leverage and hijack somebody else's idea and see if they can extort some money out of them'; see Erin Fuchs, 'Obama calls patent trolls extortionists who "hijack" people's ideas' (Business Insider, 15 February 2013) <businessinsider.com/obamas-patent-comments-at-google-chat-2013-2>.

[24] For the patent acquisition by Monument Peak Ventures, see the press release available under <dominionharbor.com/press-release-dominion-harbor-acquires-iconic-kodak-portfolio-intellectual-ventures>.

[25] Illustratively US7953690 'Discovering Social Relationships from Personal Photo Collections' granted in 2011; US8180112 'Enabling Persistent Recognition of Individuals in Images' granted in 2012; US6895103 'Method for Automatically Locating Eyes in an Image' granted in 2005; US8311364 'Estimating Aesthetic Quality of Digital Images' granted in 2005; US8180208 'Identifying a photographer' granted in 2012.

[26] For the press release, see <dominionharbor.com/rpx-united-states-dominion-asserts-former-kodak-patents-in-new-us-suits>; for the AI patents at suit, US6282317 'Method for automatic determination of main subjects in photographic images' granted in 2001.

[27] For a summary of the multiple patent infringement actions against several defendants, including Google, Amazon, AT & T, and SAP, see *Clouding IP, LLC v Google Inc.*, 61 F. Supp. 3d 421 (D. Del. 2014).

patent monetization company used a patent regarding a system and method for automatic maintenance of a computer system to contend infringement on a large scale.[28] As early as in 2006, the non-practising company Acacia Research, through its subsidiaries Automotive Technologies International and American Vehicular Sciences, started filing actions for infringement of AI patents against large players such as Toyota, Hyundai, General Motors, Siemens, and more.[29]

2. Patenting Artificial Intelligence

The United States Patent and Trademark Office (USPTO) classifies patents relating to AI in its USPC class 706 titled 'Data Processing—Artificial Intelligence'. The latter is a generic class comprising inventions for artificial intelligence type computers and digital data processing systems and corresponding data processing methods and products for emulation of intelligence; and including systems for reasoning with uncertainty, adaptive systems, machine learning systems, and artificial neural networks. The class was established in 1998 to form a coherent processing system taxonomy for patenting in AI.[30] Although the classification has an arguably narrow focus,[31] it provides a clean method for identifying AI patent data. Under the latter system, artificial intelligence patents are classified in a range of sub-classes, ie, (i) adaptive system, (ii) fuzzy logic hardware, (iii) knowledge processing system, (iv) machine learning, (v) miscellaneous, (vi) neural network, (vii) plural processing system, and (viii) plural processing system having a particular user interface ('plural processing system PUI'). Note that sub-fields are exclusive, so that a patent can only be classified in one category of AI (see Table 4.1 for summary statistics).

In total 16,994 patent applications filed from 2000 to 2018 were identified using data sets from the Patent Examination Data System.[32] As depicted in Figure 4.1, the number of AI patent applications increased strongly over the past twenty years. Prior 2004, the filings numbered less than 500 a year. In 2011, more than 1,000 AI patent applications were filed for the first time. By 2016, that number had doubled yet again.

[28] US5944839 'System and method for automatically maintaining a computer system' granted in 1999.

[29] WIPO, 'WIPO technology trends' (n 21) 113.

[30] Francois Lafond and Daniel Kim, 'Long-Run Dynamics of the U.S. Patent Classification System' (2018) arXiv:1703.02104 [q-fin.EC].

[31] Dean Alderucci, Lee Brancstetter, Eduard Hovy, and Andrew Runge, 'Mapping the Movement of AI into the Marketplace with Patent Data' (Working Paper) <cmu.edu/block-center/images/center-images/AI-patent-project-media-summary.pdf> using machine learning algorithms to classify patent documents.

[32] Search conducted in November 2018 on <ped.uspto.gov/peds>. Patents from an earlier time span were excluded; see in that regard Chun-Yao Tseng and Ping-Ho Ting, 'Patent Analysis for Technology Development of Artificial Intelligence: A Country-Level Comparative Study' (2013) 15 Innovation 463.

Table 4.1: Summary Statistics

	Obs.	Mean	Std. Dev.	Min	Max
Filing Year	16,994	2011.39	4.68	2000	2018
Small	16,994	.260	.438	0	1
Grant	14,210	.769	.420	0	1
Gov. Funding	8,915	.061	.239	0	1
Claims	8,915	21.16	15.67	1	760
Foreign	8,915	.1481	.355	0	1

Note: 'Filing Year' represents the date that an application was filed with the USPTO; 'Small' represents the entity status of an applicant as being either a small entity or a micro entity for fee purposes; 'Grant' represents whether an application was granted or abandoned/rejected; 'Gov. Funding' represents whether the application records federal funding; 'Claims' represents the number of claims at filing; 'Foreign' represents whether or not the application has a foreign priority.

Knowledge processing systems, machine learning, and neural networks represented the three largest technological sub-classes (Figure 4.2). Machine learning patent applications grew rapidly, increasing their share from 10 to 30% of all filings. The widespread adoption of big data has created a need for machine learning. As it

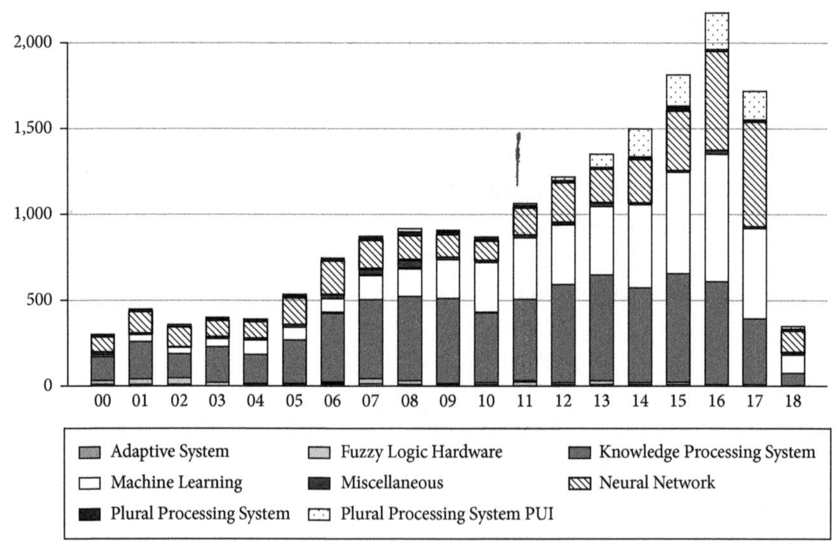

Figure 4.1 Artificial intelligence patent applications

The figure represents the number of patent applications filed by year and by technological sub-class in artificial intelligence. Because applications are published eighteen months after the earliest priority date, the data from the latest years is incomplete and does not necessarily reflect a downwards trend.

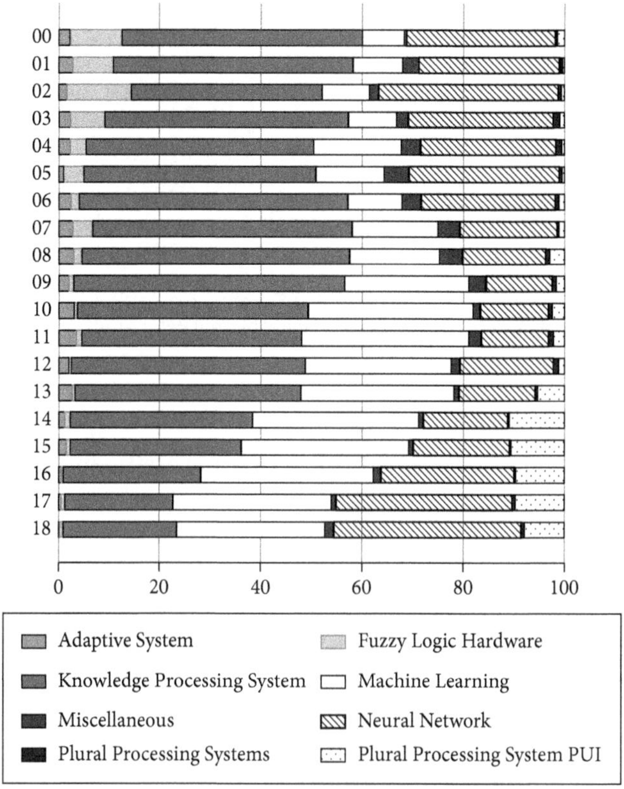

Figure 4.2 Artificial intelligence patent applications (percentage by field)
The figure represents the share of the different technological sub-classes by year of filing in artificial intelligence.

becomes necessary for organizations from small to large enterprises to process data produced by their applications and users, machine learning is being increasingly employed to offset the need for actual human headcounts. In contrast, fuzzy logic hardware patent filings stagnated in their numbers, and their representation declined from 10 to less than 1%. This trend could be indicative of increasing use of resource management processes in virtualized data centres that utilize fuzzy logic-based approaches. Additional pressure would certainly be applied by the shift in focus in high technology from generating revenue through the sale of on-premise hardware, to cloud-based applications designed to support and scale global enterprises.[33]

The trends in filings reflect to some extent the advances in the field. Illustratively, neural networks have been in and out of fashion since their inception in the 1980s,

[33] Kyriakos Deliparaschos, Themistoklis Charalambous, Evangelia Kalyvianaki, and Christos Makarounas, 'On the Use of Fuzzy Logic Controllers to Comply with Virtualized Application Demands in the Cloud' (2016) 15th European Control Conference Proceedings.

and their share fluctuated widely over the past twenty years.[34] Deep learning, in which neural network weights are typically trained through variants of stochastic gradient descent, made its breakthrough in 2012.[35] Consistent with its impressive results for supervised learning and in producing reinforcement results,[36] the field currently represents a third of all filings. Over the last five years, a notable increase in the filing of patents for plural processing systems having a particular user interface has occurred. As AI and machine learning are employed across industries, the need for machines to understand and process natural language is imperative.[37] Since AI systems designed to understand user-facing interaction and behaviour have been increasing in number in response to the market, patents protecting these key technologies are also invariably growing.

3. Triadic Patenting of Artificial Intelligence

AI encompasses a global market, with key players typically comprising large multinational technology firms. It can be assumed that such firms will file patents in the three primary markets for intellectual property, the US, Europe, and Japan,[38] if and when the technology patented is foundational for the progress and development of AI. Termed triadic patents, these sets of patents are filed for the same invention at the European Patent Office, the Japan Patent Office and the USPTO.[39] Should this assumption be too strong, triadic patents nonetheless represent a proxy for a subset of particularly valuable AI patents. Previous scholarship has supported the view that triadic patents are of high economic value.[40] In addition, studying US patent data only presents a distorted picture of R&D; according to the 'home advantage' effect, domestic firms are more likely to protect their inventions in their home

[34] Iain M Cockburn, Rebecca Henderson, and Scott Stern, 'The Impact of Artificial Intelligence on Innovation: An Exploratory Analysis' in Ajay K Agrawal, Joshua Gans, and Avi Goldfarb (eds), *The Economics of Artificial Intelligence: An Agenda* (University of Chicago Press 2019) 115.

[35] Elad Hoffer, Itay Hubara, and Daniel Soudry, 'Train Longer, Generalize Better: Closing the Generalization Gap in Large Batch Training of Neural Networks' (2017) 30 Advances in Neural Information Processing Systems 1729.

[36] Kenneth O Stanley, Jeff Clune, Joel Lehman, and Risto Miikkulainen, 'Designing Neural Networks Through Neuroevolution' (2019) 1 Nature Machine Intelligence 24.

[37] Julia Hirschberg and Christopher D Manning, 'Advances in Natural Language Processing' (2015) 349 Science 261.

[38] The US, Europe, and Japan are the jurisdictions with the highest share of the world's royalties and licence fees; see World Trade Organization, World Trade Statistical Review (2019) 134 <wto.org/english/res_e/statis_e/wts2019_e/wts2019_e.pdf>.

[39] The chapter extracts information on triadic patents using the OECD Triadic Patent Families database, March 2018.

[40] Paola Criscuolo, 'The "Home Advantage" Effect and Patent Families. A Comparison of OECD Triadic Patents, the USPTO and the EPO' (2006) 66 Scientometrics 23, finding that 'OECD triadic patents receive on average a higher number of citations than those patents not filed in the other two patent offices'; George Messinis, 'Triadic Citations, Country Biases and Patent Value: The Case of Pharmaceuticals' (2011) 89 Scientometrics 813.

country.[41] As such, relying on triadic patent data reduces said 'home advantage' effect, and eliminates the impact of country-specific sets of patenting rules and regulations. Therefore, triadic patents are, in the view of the authorship, well-suited for the present analysis.

Approximately 9% of all patents granted in the US were triadic. In Figure 4.3, the 975 triadic patents are represented in terms of year of filing. Compared to overall filing trends, the growth in triadic patents is less pronounced.[42] This might be taken as a sign that the growth in the number of valuable inventions—assuming that AI patent value is indeed mirrored by triadic patents—albeit growing, is not as exponential as domestic trends would suggest. Knowledge processing systems, machine learning, and neural networks patents formed the largest triadic subclasses, identical to the US overall trends.

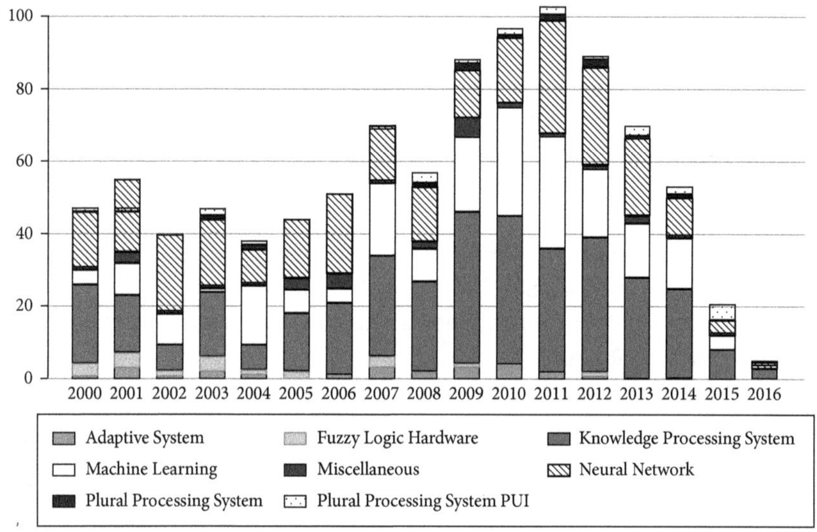

Figure 4.3 Triadic artificial intelligence patents over time

The figure represents the number of triadic patent applications filed by year and by technological sub-class in artificial intelligence. Because applications are published eighteen months after the earliest priority date, the data from the latest years are incomplete and do not necessarily reflect a downwards trend.

[41] Pari Patel and Modesto Vega, 'Patterns of Internationalisation of Corporate Technology: Location vs. Home Country Advantages' (1999) 28 Research Policy 148, contending that '[u]sing US patent data for US companies and for US subsidiaries of non-US companies means that there will be an overestimation of the role of domestic R&D for the former and foreign R&D for the latter'.

[42] Interestingly, the overall number of triadic patents across all technologies and industries appears to be on the decline since 2000; see <data.oecd.org/rd/triadic-patent-families.htm>.

Table 4.2: Country Origin of Triadic Patents

Country	Number	Country	Number	Country	Number	Country	Number
AR	1	DE	54	IT	9	PG	5
AT	3	DK	1	JP	85	RU	1
AU	3	ES	1	KR	9	SE	1
BB	11	FI	5	LU	3	SG	3
BE	4	FR	17	MD	1	TR	1
CA	18	GB	11	MM	1	US	653
CH	8	IL	11	MY	5	VG	1
CN	4	IN	1	NL	32	ZA	1

Note: The table summarizes the country of origin of triadic patents.

The triadic patents are from as many as thirty different countries. The OECD defines the country of origin of a triadic patent as the home country of the inventor(s), which signals the place where the research was executed.[43] Figure 4.4 maps the geographical origin of triadic patents (Table 4.2 lists the individual country data). The vast majority of triadic patents originated in the US. With its thriving ecosystems in Silicon Valley, New York, and Boston, leading universities, and strong corporate research facilities, the US has been the role example for innovation in AI. Japan, Germany, the Netherlands, Canada, and France followed as the most represented countries of origin.[44]

China has been heralded as the new dominating country in AI,[45] but Chinese applications have focused on the domestic market so far.[46] The impact of recent investment policies by China, such as the 2017 New Generation Artificial Intelligence Development Plan, is not reflected in the data yet.[47] With the shift from discovery to implementation of AI, players like China have the required strengths—abundant data, a hyper-competitive business landscape, and public

[43] See David Popp, 'Using the Triadic Patent Family Database to Study Environmental Innovation' (2005), OECD Report.

[44] The country of origin was identified for 964 patents, while no country data were present for eleven patents.

[45] Louis Columbus, 'How China is dominating artificial intelligence' (*Forbes*, 16 December 2018) <forbes.com/sites/louiscolumbus/2018/12/16/how-china-is-dominating-artificial-intelligence/#5693c3f32b2f>.

[46] WIPO, 'WIPO technology trends' (n 21) 33.

[47] Chinese firms only hold a handful of triadic patents; although it must be noted that the triadic patent data cover filings from 2000 to 2015 only. In overall artificial intelligence patent applications, Chinese patents represented less than 1% of all applications in the US filed from 2000 to 2015.

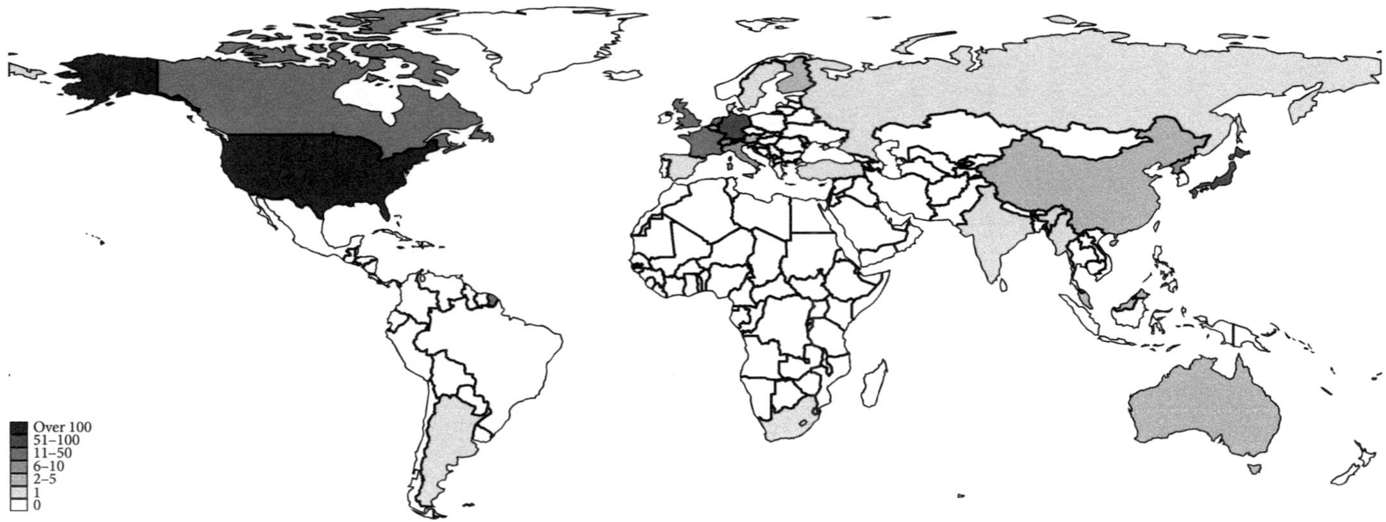

Figure 4.4 Triadic artificial intelligence patents by country

The figure maps the country of origin and frequency of triadic patents.

infrastructures adapted with AI in mind—to turn scientific breakthroughs into commercially viable products.[48]

4. Policy Levers

At this moment in time, and all around the globe, patent offices, courts, and legislators are seeking to develop policies that integrate and balance the specificities of innovation in AI. To prevent the emergence of a patent thicket in AI, where broad, foundational techniques are patented by numerous global actors, a rational patent policy can employ a variety of policy levers. This section explores how courts and patent offices can apply strict standards of patent-eligibility, disclosure, non-obviousness, novelty, and double patenting to ensure a decrease in the patenting of foundational techniques in AI. While the present approach focuses on minimizing the patenting of such key inventions, an alternative or complementary regulatory strategy can focus on lubricating transaction costs. As such, patent pools conserve transaction costs by bundling together related patents and offering single licences. Antitrust laws can be designed in a way so as to not obstruct horizontal rivals, and to facilitate the creation of such pools. Similarly, to reduce the looming threat of litigation by patent monetization entities, a satisfactory response may focus on setting higher standards to enforcement. Rulings such as *eBay v MercExchange* (2006) rejecting the rule that prevailing patentees are automatically entitled to injunction are a strong step in this direction.[49]

4.1 Patent-Eligibility of Ideas

The abstract ideas doctrine can prevent unnecessary upstream patents that threaten to stagnate downstream implementation.[50] Patenting abstract ideas or concepts would permit the patentee to 'engross a vast, unknown, and perhaps unknowable area' rather than particular implementations.[51] To be eligible for patentability, patent claims must be directed towards a statutory category of invention (processes, machines, manufactures, and compositions of matter).[52] A commonly used strategy to patent AI is to claim the invention as a process of method steps for

[48] Kai-Fu Lee, 'What China Can Teach the U.S. About Artificial Intelligence' (*New York Times*, 23 September 2018) 5.

[49] *eBay Inc. v MercExchange, L.L.C.*, 547 US 388.

[50] Dan L Burk and Mark A Lemley, 'Policy Levers in Patent Law' (2003) 89 Virginia Law Review 1575.

[51] *Brenner v Manson*, 383 US 519, 534 (1966) stating that '[s]uch a patent may confer power to block off whole areas of scientific development, without compensating benefit to the public' and 'there is insufficient justification for permitting an applicant to engross what may prove to be a broad field'.

[52] 35 USC 101. *Mayo Collaborative Services v. Prometheus Laboratories, Inc.*, 132 S. Ct. 1289 (2012).

completing a certain purpose or task or to draft claims directed to a method of use of the AI technology.[53] Alternatively, inventors can claim the physical structure of the device harbouring the AI and how the structural elements of the device operate with the AI.[54]

The US Supreme Court recently spelled out the determination of patent eligibility as a two-part test in *Alice Corp. v CLS Bank International*.[55] The test first requires determination of whether the claims are directed to a patent-ineligible concept, ie, law of nature, natural phenomena, or abstract idea.[56] Myriad AI patent claims are directed towards an abstract idea, ie, an 'idea "of itself"'.[57] This is similar to organizing information by mathematical correlations, a concept found to be abstract by the Federal Circuit.[58] Illustratively, the steps of producing new labelled observations, evaluating an observation, comparing scores, identifying a feature, and updating a model are deemed to be abstract, since they are examples of organizing information; a machine learning model is simply existing information that has been manipulated to create additional information.[59] The second part of the Alice test states that if the claimed invention is directed to a judicial exception such as an abstract idea, the claimed invention can only qualify as patent-eligible subject matter if the claim as a whole includes additional limitations amounting to significantly more than the exception.[60] Although there is no strict standard to determine when additional claim elements constitute 'significantly more' than an abstract idea, recent Federal Circuit case law provides some guidance. The applicant can establish that the claim is a particular technical solution to a technical problem, an argument

[53] Andrew Rapacke, 'Strategies for claiming AI inventions in patent applications' (*Rapacke Law Group*, 9 August 2018) <arapackelaw.com/patents/strategies-claiming-ai-patent-applications> (hereafter Rapacke, 'Strategies for claiming AI'). Often, these will be 'method[s] of using conventional AI technologies to solve a general problem'; see Jonathan Bockman, Rudy Y Kim, and Anna Yuan, 'Patenting artificial intelligence in the U.S.—considerations for AI companies' (*Morrison & Foerster LLP*, 8 November 2018) <mofo.com/resources/publications/181108-patenting-artificial-intelligence-us.html>(hereafter Bockman, 'Patenting artificial intelligence in the U.S.').

[54] Naming an AI medical device that can recognize patient symptoms based on data from a variety of physiological sensors and then identify the patient's likely diagnosis, 'patent claims can focus on the various structural elements of the medical device (such as the housing, connected to a temperature sensor, pulse oximeter, galvanometer, computer processor, etc.) and how these various structural elements interact in conjunction with the AI symptom analyzer program that is run on the computer processor of the medical device'; see Rapacke, 'Strategies for claiming AI' (n 53).

[55] *Alice Corp. v CLS Bank International*, 573 US 208, 134 S. Ct. 2347 (2014.); further, *Mayo Collaborative Services v Prometheus Laboratories, Inc.*, 132 S. Ct. 1289 (2012).

[56] Richard A Stern, 'Alice v CLS Bank: US Business Method and Software Patents Marching towards Oblivion?' (2014) 10 European Intellectual Property Review 619.

[57] Non-Final Rejection by the USPTO, Application 14/562,747 'Active Machine Learning', 30 August 2018 (hereafter USPTO, 'Rejection Active Machine Learning').

[58] Digitech Image Technologies, *LLC v Electronics For Imaging, Inc.*, Case No 13-1600 (Fed. Cir. 2014) 'a process that employs mathematical algorithms to manipulate existing information to generate additional information is not patent eligible'.

[59] USPTO, 'Rejection Active Machine Learning' (n 57).

[60] A claim reciting an abstract idea does not become eligible 'merely by adding the words "apply it"'; see *Bancorp Servs., LLC v Sun Life Assurance Co. of Can.* (U.S.), 687 F.3d 1266, 1276 (Fed. Cir. 2012).

that has been supported by several courts.[61] The argument, however, recently failed to convince the patent office on a patent application by Google on active machine learning methods. In this case, retraining (or updating) a machine learning model was deemed an improved algorithm, despite its integral importance to the overall active machine learning method. Simply, the updating process remains abstract, with data manipulated to create other data.[62] Alternatively, the applicant can seek to demonstrate that the claim recites a problem necessarily rooted in a computer technology.[63] Even if this rather permissive standard is applied, examiners have the leeway to remain defensive; and the USPTO recently found that a classification algorithm[64] or the improvement of computer display devices by the combination of information[65] were not necessarily computer-based problems.[66] Finally, the applicant can contend that the claims improve computer functionality.[67] To that end, the claims must improve computer functioning as a tool, but the mere implementation of algorithms for manipulating data—an abstract idea—implemented on a computer is not sufficient.[68] In all these three cases, the courts and the patent office are in a position to make use of strict standards to limit the patenting of abstract ideas. A restrictive approach in patenting AI abstract concepts lowers the risk of ending up with a field whose building blocks are in private hands.

This recent case law has certainly already led to higher standards in patent-eligibility of software and business inventions.[69] While the degree to which this has

[61] *DDR Holdings, LLC v Hotels.com, L.P.*, 773 F.3d 1245 (Fed. Cir. 2014) and *Bascom Global Internet Servs., Inc. v AT&T Mobility LLC*, 827 F.3d 1341, 1350 (Fed. Cir. 2016) 1349–52: 'recite a sufficient inventive concept under step two—particularly when the claims solve a technology-based problem'. Google similarly states that: 'when we draft applications and claims to clearly explain how the invention provides a technical solution to a technical problem, we draft higher-quality applications that meet with more success both at the U.S. PTO and in foreign patent offices'; see Comments of Google Inc. before the USPTO on Legal Contours of Patent Subject Matter Eligibility (18 January 2017). <uspto.gov/sites/default/files/documents/comments_google_jan182017.pdf>.

[62] Final Rejection by the USPTO, Application 14/562,747 'Active Machine Learning', 1 October 2018.

[63] *DDR Holdings, LLC v Hotels.com, L.P.*, 773 F.3d 1245 (Fed. Cir. 2014) where 'the claimed solution is necessarily rooted in computer technology in order to overcome a problem specifically arising in the realm of computer networks'.

[64] USPTO, 'Rejection Active Machine Learning' (n 57).

[65] *Interval Licensing LLC v AOL, Inc.*, 896 F.3d 1335 (Fed. Cir. 2018).

[66] See, however, a recent decision by the PTAB where the examiner found the claims to be directed to 'payment management in a network' or 'coding' and supported the standpoint of the applicant that the claims are not directed to a general concept of coding, but instead specifically to generating a plurality of code snippets and files, Patent Trial and Appeal Board, Appeal 2017-008457, *Ex Parte* Amish Patel, Nick Groleau, William Charles Taylor, and Saleem Qadir, 23 November 2018.

[67] *Enfish, LLC v Microsoft Corp.*, 822 F.3d 1327 (Fed. Cir. 2016) where 'the plain focus of the claims is on an improvement to computer functionality itself, not on economic or other tasks for which a computer is used in its ordinary capacity'.

[68] USPTO, 'Rejection Active Machine Learning' (n 57). Bockman, 'Patenting artificial intelligence in the U.S.' (n 53) illustratively recommends including technical features on the pre-processing of training data, the training process, the use of trained classifiers or solutions, the end-to-end workflow, and the hardware to identify aspects of its technology producing tangible results or concretely improving the functioning of a computer system.

[69] Estimations contend that out of 240,00 computer-related inventions in force in 2015, as many as about 200,000 would likely to be invalid under *Alice*; see Japer L Tran, 'Software Patents: A One-Year Review of Alice v. CLS Bank' (2015) 97 Journal of the Patent and Trademark Office Society 532.

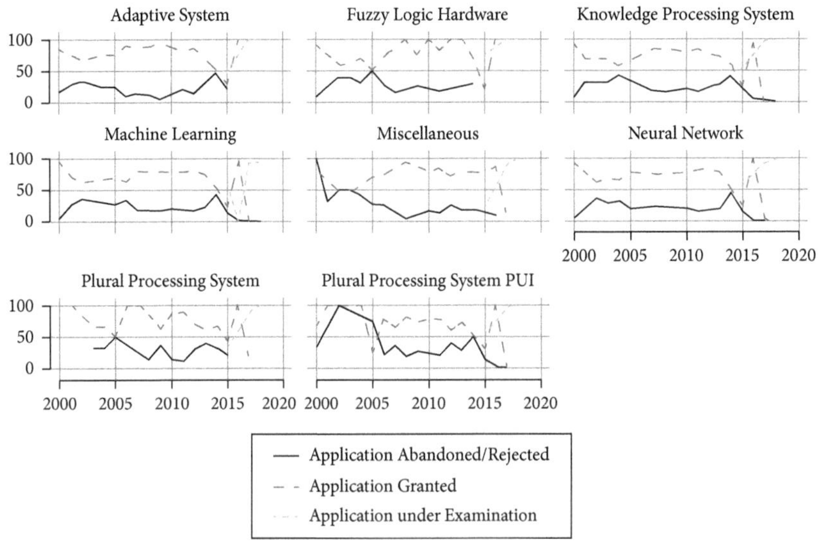

Figure 4.5 Artificial intelligence patent applications grant (percentage by field).
The figure represents the share of patent applications that were (i) abandoned/rejected, (ii) granted, or (iii) under examination by year and by technological sub-class in artificial intelligence.

impacted AI patenting is unclear, a jump in the rejection or abandonment rate can be observed across almost all AI sub-fields in 2014, the year of the *Alice* decision (Figure 4.5).

In April 2019, a framework on patent-eligibility reform was released by Democratic and Republican legislators from both the Senate and the House of Representatives.[70] In a press release, Senator Coons declared that 'U.S. patent law discourages innovation in some of the most critical areas of technology, including artificial intelligence, medical diagnostics, and personalized medicine'.[71] The proposal defines an exclusive set of categories of statutory subject matter that alone should not be eligible for patent protection, such as pure mathematical formulas, and abrogates judicially created exceptions. The framework also foresees a practical application test to ensure that the statutorily ineligible subject matter is construed narrowly. While the intent of remedying the uncertainty relating to patent-eligibility is to be encouraged, the far-reaching effects of foundational patents should not be easily discarded. Any legislative change should factor in the

[70] Retrieved under <tillis.senate.gov/public/_cache/files/3491a23f-09c3-4f4a-9a93-71292704c5b1/outline-of-101-reform.pdf>.

[71] Retrieved under <tillis.senate.gov/public/index.cfm/press-releases?ID=B521846C-594A-46BE-B17A-0E11393D23AD>.

negative impact of such patents, as well, and ensure, in the opinion of the author, a narrow construction of eligibility requirements.

4.2 Disclosure Requirements

The disclosure requirements are another lever by which courts and patent offices can counter the patenting of foundational techniques. AI offers cross-industry functionality, and patents on techniques with application potential in a variety of fields are likely to accelerate patent thicket issues. Typically, a patent holder can hold up companies not only in his own technology space, but also in widely disparate ones.[72] Per the disclosure requirements of 35 United States Code (USC) 112 (a), the claims containing subject matter must be described in the specification in such a way as to reasonably convey to one skilled in the relevant art that the inventor, at the time the application was filed, had possession of the claimed invention.[73] Two doctrines are rooted in this section, 'enablement' and 'written description'. Enablement requires that one of ordinary skill in the art, relying on the disclosure and information known to those skilled in the art, must be able to make and use the claimed invention without undue experimentation. Written description ensures that the inventor conveys that an applicant has invented the subject matter which is claimed. To satisfy the written description requirement, a patent specification must describe the claimed invention in sufficient detail that one skilled in the art can reasonably conclude that the inventor had possession of the claimed invention.[74]

The Federal Circuit has, in the field of biotechnology especially, used these doctrines to prevent inventors from obtaining or enforcing overly broad patent claims.[75] Under strict enablement requirements, broad claims often require 'undue experimentation' by a person skilled in the art. When the specification discloses overly broad claims, the Federal Circuit has expanded the written description requirement to invalidate such claims.[76] A strategy for AI patents has been to include functional claiming of the invention, for instance claiming elements as 'means of classifying' or 'means for responding to backpropagation learning'.[77] In addition to specific structural details of the invention, alternative claims define claim

[72] Mark A Lemley, 'Patenting Nanotechnology' (2005) 58 Stanford Law Review 615.

[73] *Vas-Cath, Inc. v Mahurkar*, 935 F.2d 1555, 1563–64 (Fed. Cir. 1991).

[74] *Moba, B.V. v Diamond Automation, Inc.*, 325 F.3d 1306, 1319, 66 USPQ2d 1429, 1438 (Fed. Cir. 2003).

[75] Margaret Sampson, 'The Evolution of the Enablement and Written Description Requirements Under 35 U.S.C. § 112 in the Area of Biotechnology' (2000) 15 Berkeley Technology Law Journal 1233.

[76] Ibid.

[77] Frank A DeCosta, Aliza G Carrano, and Li Ruohan, 'Early strategies for protecting neural network inventions' (*Finnegan*, 6 September 2018) <finnegan.com/en/insights/ early-strategies-for-protecting-neural-network-inventions.html>.

boundaries by the functions that the elements perform (35 USC Section 112(f)).[78] The revised 2019 guidelines by the USPTO for applications with 'functional limitations' require now that functional claims meet the requirement of definiteness under 35 USC 112(b). By applying these two sections together, the guidelines put a limit on purely functional claiming and encourage examiners to be more consistent and aggressive in rejecting applications lacking technical detail.[79] The definiteness requirement under 35 USC 112(b) requires that the subject matter which the inventor regards as the invention is particularly pointed out and distinctly claimed. Patent applications in AI have sometimes sought to broaden their scope by not specifying certain terms of art. For instance, by not defining the term 'reinforcement learning' in one of its applications, Microsoft made it unclear whether the claim language was referring to the specific method of machine learning, or more broadly to mean retraining or improving or making stronger or better.[80] The USPTO found that the definiteness requirement was not satisfied in this case. Heightened disclosure requirements therefore appear as a simple yet effective way to counter broad patents on AI techniques.

4.3 Non-obviousness Requirement

At the current stage of technology, companies mainly use the established set of methods in AI and find novel applications for use. As such, AI can be thought of as a toolbox, from which innovators pull various needed tools. To some extent, this trend of using conventional machine learning methods on particular applications has been criticized and can be examined under the standpoint of the non-obviousness standards of 35 USC 103.[81] The Supreme Court redefined non-obviousness in *KSR International Co. v Teleflex, Inc.*, which is to be determined based on a constellation of factors designed to discern whether a person having ordinary skill in the art would likely think to make the patented invention.[82] Let us take the example of a patent on an autism disorder classification questionnaire. A typical machine learning claim will seek to determine the correlational value between questions and answers based on the regression coefficients of a trained machine learning model. When the claimed invention modifies a previously disclosed machine learning model for mental health diagnoses, the patent office will assess whether the concepts and advantages of using the method were

[78] Ibid.

[79] Ian Robinson, 'Missing the target with functional claim language' (*Appleyard Lees*, 29 January 2019) <appleyardlees.com/missing-the-target-with-functional-claim-language/>.

[80] USPTO, 'Rejection Active Machine Learning' (n 57).

[81] 'When you're doing that machine learning from Claim 1, use this particular well-known pre-existing machine learning algorithm'; see Gillula, 'Will patents slow artificial intelligence?' (n 12).

[82] *KSR International Co. v Teleflex, Inc.* 27 S. Ct. 1727 (2007).

well-known to a person of ordinary skill in the art. This was found to be the case when a claimed invention relied on multinomial logistic regression instead of the previously disclosed logistic regression.[83] Similarly, a patent disclosing machine learning methods for classifying files and extracting signatures, such as neural networks and Bayesian methods, was found to render obvious the use of a multi-naïve Bayes algorithm, which is a type of Bayesian method. Such modification was considered nothing more than a simple substitution of one known element for another to obtain predictable results.[84] When inventions take the form of a combination of existing ideas, it must be asked whether the skilled person would have thought to combine these elements.[85] If these elements are familiar and do no more than yielding predictable results, the combination is likely to be obvious.[86] The combination of teachings appears to be particularly obvious when they relate to the same field of art.[87] Non-obviousness requirements can limit the breakdown of patents that update conventional AI methods, or seek to protect narrow sub-fields of application.

4.4 Novelty Requirement

There appears to be a certain tendency—or examples at least—of firms trying to patent AI techniques that were initially disclosed as early as in the 1990s. Two patent applications from Google and NEC Laboratories can serve as examples of such practice. When Google sought to patent batch normalization layers techniques in 2018, the USPTO identified four anticipating patents from as early as 1992.[88] The application attracted a lot of attention because of its fundamental component that would, if patented, have the potential to negatively impact the development of deep learning technology.[89] As to the patent application by NEC, several of its claims

[83] Non-Final Rejection by the USPTO, Application 15/234,814, 6 July 2018 'Methods and Apparatus to Determine Developmental Progress with Artificial Intelligence and User Input': 'the concept and advantages of using multinomial logistic regression when there is more than one desired outcome variable were old and well known to the person of ordinary skill in the art at the time (before the effective filing date) of the invention'.

[84] Patent Trial and Appeal Board, Patent 7,487,544, Inter Parted Symantec Corporation vs. The Trustees of Columbia University in the City of New York, 5 December 2014.

[85] Daralyn J Durie and Mark A Lemley, 'A Realistic Approach to the Obviousness of Inventions' (2008) 50 William & Mary Law Review 989.

[86] *KSR International Co. v Teleflex, Inc.* 27 S. Ct., 1739 (2007); Non-Final Rejection by the USPTO, Application14/273,487, 18 June 2018: '[t]his combination is applying known techniques of neural network connections to yield predictable results'.

[87] Patent Trial and Appeal Board, Patent 7,487,544, Inter Parted Symantec Corporation vs. The Trustees of Columbia University in the City of New York, 5 December 2014.

[88] Non-Final Rejection by the USPTO, Application 15/009,647, 31 October 2018 'Batch Normalization Layers'.

[89] Daeho Lee, 'AI patent report: batch normalization layers' (PI IP LAW (Lee, Park & Morris), 15 January 2019) <piip.co.kr/en-us/news/batch-normalization-layers-google>.

were anticipated by a publication by neural network pioneer Terry Sejnowksi dated 1986.[90] This 'recycling' of early academic work is particularly worrisome,[91] and has the potential to lead to the protection of advances undertaken with the original purpose of being in the public domain.[92] Consistent examination will therefore be required by patent offices to ban any attempt to patent previously disclosed inventions.

4.5 Double Patenting

Double patenting rejections are based on a judicially created doctrine grounded in public policy to prevent unjustified or improper timewise extension of the right to exclude granted by a patent and to prevent harassment by multiple assignees. They are appropriate where patent claims are not identical, but at least one examined application claim is not patentably distinct from the reference claim, since it is either anticipated or would have been obvious over the reference claims.[93] To broadly protect an invention, patent applicants can try to file multiple patent applications on the same invention having claims of slightly different scope.[94] A number of AI patents have been rejected for violating this doctrine. For instance, InsideSales.com, Inc., a company developing an AI platform for sales, filed a patent claiming a broader form of the same invention.[95] Another reported instance is Sentient Technologies, the world's most well-funded AI company, which filed for two patents with claims dealing with a data mining system.[96] The applicant can overcome the double patenting rejection by establishing that the claims are patentably distinct or by filing a terminal

[90] Terrence J Sejnowksi, Paul K Kienker, and Geoffrey E Hinton, 'Learning Symmetry Groups With Hidden Units: Beyond the Perceptron' (1986) 22D Physica 260. Similarly, the patent on active machine learning methods by Microsoft mentioned previously seems to be potentially anticipated by prior art by AI pioneers from the '90s; see David JC MacKay, 'Information-Based Objective Functions for Active Data Selection' (1992) 4 Neural Computation 590.

[91] Further examples include a Qualcomm patent application anticipated by an academic publication from 1996, Non-Final Rejection by the USPTO, Application 14/526,304, 8 March 2017 'Neuronal Diversity in Spiking Neural Networks and Pattern Classification'.

[92] 'As patents have already prevented wide adoption of arithmetic coding for many decades, I wanted to do all I could to make public the required basic concepts, modifications and applications by presenting them in scientific papers, reference implementations, and multiple public discussion forums'; see Duda, 'Pre-issuance' (n 13).

[93] *In re Berg*, 140 F.3d 1428, 46 USPQ2d 112 (Fed. Circ. 1998); *In re Goodman*, 11 F.3d 1046, 29 USPQ2d 2010 (Fed. Cir. 1993); *In re Longi*, 759 F.2d 887, 225 USPQ 645 (Fed. Cir. 1985).

[94] Dana Tangren, 'Non-statutory double patenting rejections and terminal disclaimers' (IP Sketchbook, 4 April 2017) <wnlaw.com/blog/non-statutory-double-patenting-rejections-terminal-disclaimers/> (hereafter Tangren, 'Double patenting').

[95] Non-Final Rejection by the USPTO, Application 14/503,263, 19 November 2014 'Email Optimization for Predicted Recipient Behavior: Suggesting Changes in an Email to Increase the Likelihood of an Outcome'.

[96] Non-Final Rejection by the USPTO, Application 13/358,381, 7 August 2014 'Data Mining Technique with Maintenance of Fitness History'.

disclaimer. By doing so, he agrees that the two patents have the same term and that they can only be enforced as long as jointly owned.[97] Patent offices should continue to strictly monitor double patenting attempts.

5. Conclusion

The results of this chapter indicate an increasingly globalized approach to AI IP development. A proverbial land grab seems to be occurring; an increase in AI patenting, particularly the protection of triadic patents, illustrates industry players aggressively attempting to own the building blocks of a rapidly emerging market. In addition to a number of high-profile patents that portent a possible slowdown in downstream innovation, such as Google's patent on dropout, the impact of this patenting rush could hinder the development of novel AI technologies in the long run. Should a number of actors own broad, foundational patents protected throughout the main global markets, the rate of adoption of AI may slow. There is no certainty that current practices and pledges to not enforce those patent rights will be sustained. A number of AI patents have already been transferred to patent enforcement entities who have initiated litigation, effectively allowing operating companies to monetize their AI portfolio out of the public eye. A blockade of privatization seems to challenge the openness and collaboration promoted by technology firms, raising eyebrows among researchers and users over the patenting trend in AI. Further, in line with discussions about the social inequalities caused by AI at the World Economic Forum 2019, it should be questioned whether some early key players should reap licence rights from building blocks that are instrumental to the development of any AI product.

A number of policy levers have been examined here, highlighting how patent offices and courts can seek to prevent the granting of patents with broad, foundational application potential. Continuing to refine the doctrines surrounding the patent-eligibility of abstract ideas will be crucial to minimize the protection of concepts, and focus on the practical computer-rooted implementations of AI. Heightened disclosure requirements are an efficient way to limit the scope of overly broad, indefinite patent claims. This toolbox is complemented by possible adjustments in non-obviousness, novelty, and double patenting standards. Accordingly, it appears that current patent law can address the issue of claiming foundational patents by relying on strict and narrow patentability standards. The difficulties in achieving this aim must nonetheless be highlighted; considering the time constraints of patent examiners, the reduction rather than the elimination of such

[97] Tangren, 'Double patenting' (n 94).

patents should be the ultimate aim. Considering the potential blockade of downstream innovation induced by the privatization of the foundations for AI, it is to be hoped that patentability standards will be leveraged to let the building blocks of AI remain in the public domain.

Appendix

Table A.1: Top 10 Most Cited Technologies (Triadic Patents)

	Technology	Grant	Assignee	Title	Citations
1. Processing Data Flows					
Neural Network	US7979368	2011	Crossbeam Systems	Systems and methods for processing data flows	375
Neural Network	US9525696	2016	Crossbeam Systems	Systems and methods for processing data flows	286
Neural Network	US8010469	2011	Crossbeam Systems	Systems and methods for processing data flows	99
Neural Network	US8135657	2012	Crossbeam Systems	Systems and methods for processing data flows	66
2. Codeword Decoding					
Neural Network	US7552097	2009	Qualcomm	Methods and apparatus for decoding LDPC codes	294
Neural Network	US7133853	2009	Qualcomm	Methods and apparatus for decoding LDPC codes	280
Neural Network	US6633856	2003	Qualcomm	Methods and apparatus for decoding LDPC codes	187
3. Data Mining					
Knowledge Pr. Sys.	US7921068	2011	Health Discovery	Data mining platform for knowledge discovery from heterogeneous data [..]	255
Machine Learning	US7444308	2008	Health Discovery	Data mining platform for bioinformatics and other knowledge discovery	60

(continued)

Table A.1: Continued

	Technology	Grant	Assignee	Title	Citations
Machine Learning	US7542947	2009	Health Discovery	Data mining platform for bioinformatics and other knowledge discovery	32
4. Scaling Multi-Dimensional Data sets					
Neural Network	US7117187	2006	Janssen Research	Method [..] for non-linear mapping of multi-dimensional data	222
5. Content Blocking Filter					
Knowledge Pr. Sys.	US8630968	2014	Avaya Inc	Selective content block of posts to social network	200
6. Communications Contactability					
Knowledge Pr. Sys.	US8589326	2013	Avaya Inc	Utilizing presence [..] to determine an appropriate communications modality	200
7. Preference Determination					
Machine Learning	US7730002	2010	Affinnova	Method for iterative design of products	194
Machine Learning	US7610249	2009	Affinnova	Method and apparatus for evolutionary design	160
Machine Learning	US7016882	2006	Affinnova	Method and apparatus for evolutionary design	127
8. Predictive Model Forecasting Surprises					
Machine Learning	US8706651	2014	Microsoft	Building and using predictive models of current and future surprises	187
Machine Learning	US7519564	2009	Microsoft	Building and using predictive models of current and future surprises	86

Table A.1: Continued

	Technology	Grant	Assignee	Title	Citations
9. HR Screening and Selection					
Knowledge Pr. Sys.	US8086558	2011	PreVisor Inc	Computer-implemented system for human resources management	142
10. Data Classification					
Neural Network	US8719197	2014	Kofax Inc	Data classification using machine learning techniques	140
Neural Network	US8239335	2012	Kofax Inc	Data classification using machine learning techniques	139
Machine Learning	US8374977	2013	Kofax Inc	Methods and systems for transductive data classification	130
Machine Learning	US7761391	2010	Kofax Inc	Methods and systems for improved transductive maximum entropy discrimination classification	94
Neural Network	US7958067	2011	Kofax Inc	Data classification methods using machine learning techniques	92
Machine Learning	US7937345	2011	Kofax Inc	Data classification methods using machine learning techniques	92

Table A.2: Top 20 Assignees (Triadic Patents)

Organization	Patents	Percent	Cum. %
Microsoft Corporation	47	6.29	6.29
Sony Corporation	26	3.48	9.77
Health Discovery Corporation	24	3.21	12.99
Fujitsu Limited	22	2.95	15.93
Palo Alto Research Center Incorporated	15	2.01	17.94
Koninklijke Philips Electronics N.V.	14	1.87	19.81
Computer Associates Think, Inc.	11	1.47	21.29
Honda Research Institute Europe GmbH	11	1.47	22.76
International Business Machines Corporation	11	1.47	24.23
Canon Kabushiki Kaisha	9	1.20	25.44
Icosystem Corporation	9	1.20	26.64
QUALCOMM Incorporated	9	1.20	27.84
Ab Initio Technology LLC	8	1.07	28.92
Kofax, Inc.	8	1.07	29.99
Neurosciences Research Foundation, Inc.	8	1.07	31.06
Siemens Aktiengesellschaft	8	1.07	32.13
AiLive, Inc.	7	0.94	33.07
D-Wave Systems Inc.	7	0.94	34.00
General Electric Company	7	1.07	34.94
New York University	7	0.94	35.88

Note: The table summarizes the top 20 assignees of origin of triadic patents (750 assignees identified)

5

Patentability and PHOSITA in the AI Era—A Japanese Perspective

*Ichiro Nakayama**

1. Introduction

The recent development of artificial intelligence (AI) may have huge impacts on society. Although it may be hard to define AI correctly, AI involves highly sophisticated information systems which have been expanding their capabilities thanks to the rapid advancement of machine learning, especially deep learning.[1] Today AI is also utilized in creative activities. AI is more likely to autonomously generate outputs that look like copyrighted works,[2] which raises issues such as copyrightability and authorship. On the other hand, AI may or may not generate an invention autonomously without human intervention. However, there is little doubt that the development of AI may produce inventions of AI technologies such as machine learning (deep learning). Researchers and engineers also have begun to use AI as a tool to help them create inventions (hereafter 'AI-assisted inventions').

* All online materials were accessed before 3 January 2020.

[1] The term 'artificial intelligence' was first used by Professor John McCarthy. He defined AI as 'the science and engineering of making intelligent machines, especially intelligent computer programs'. John McCarthy, 'What is artificial intelligence?'(Revised 12 November 2007) <http://www-formal.stanford.edu/jmc/whatisai/whatisai.html>. On the other hand, an expert group set up by the European Commission explained that 'Artificial intelligence (AI) systems are software (and possibly also hardware) systems designed by humans that, given a complex goal, act in the physical or digital dimension by perceiving their environment through data acquisition, interpreting the collected structured or unstructured data, reasoning on the knowledge, or processing the information, derived from this data and deciding the best action(s) to take to achieve the given goal.... As a scientific discipline, AI includes several approaches and techniques, such as machine learning (of which deep learning and reinforcement learning are specific examples).' The Independent High-level Expert Group on Artificial Intelligence set up by the European Commission, 'A definition of AI: main capabilities and disciplines' (8 April 2019) 6 <https://ec.europa.eu/digital-single-market/en/news/definition-artificial-intelligence-main-capabilities-and-scientific-disciplines>. Yutaka Matsuo, 'Jinko Chinou Kaihatsu No Saizensen' (Frontiers of AI Development) (2019) 91 *Horitsu Jiho* (Law Review) 4, 7–8, argued that although no definition of AI had been established, there was little disagreement that the recent technical focus was deep learning.

[2] The most famous example is 'The Next Rembrandt' project, where after analysing data of 346 of Rembrandt's paintings, the software learned principles to replicate the style and generate new facial features for new paintings, and a 3D printer printed out a painting which looked like a Rembrandt. 'The Next Rembrandt'<https://www.nextrembrandt.com/>.

Ichiro Nakayama, *Patentability and PHOSITA in the AI Era—A Japanese Perspective* In: *Artificial Intelligence and Intellectual Property*. Edited by: Jyh-An Lee, Reto M Hilty, and Kung-Chung Liu, Oxford University Press (2021).
 DOI: 10.1093/oso/9780198870944.003.0006

Both inventions of AI technologies and AI-assisted inventions raise the urgent and practical issues of patentability such as disclosure requirements and inventive step (non-obviousness). The Japanese Patent Office (JPO) updated the Examination Handbook for Patent and Utility Model (hereafter 'Handbook') in 2019[3] to address some of the issues. For instance, they discussed to what extent inventors should disclose in a patent application, because AI as a black box does not explain how technical problems are solved. However, the JPO paid little attention to the possibilities that not only inventors but also a person having ordinary skills in the art (PHOSITA) might use AI and that PHOSITA with the aid of AI would create inventions more easily, thereby raising the level of the inventive step. This chapter critically reviews the JPO's updated Handbook and discusses how we can take into account the use of AI by PHOSITA in examining the inventive step.

2. Types of AI-related Inventions and Issues on Patentability

There are various types of AI-related inventions: 1) inventions of AI technologies, 2) AI-assisted inventions, and 3) AI-generated inventions.

The first type is an invention of AI technologies which is created by humans to improve AI technologies themselves. The second type is an AI-assisted invention which is created by humans with the use of AI. In the second type, AI, as a tool to help humans create inventions, is applied to various fields, as some examples will show later. Both the first and second type are created by human inventors, whoever they may be. They may be protected under the current Patent Act if they satisfy patentability requirements, including patent eligibility. There are many of these today. In fact, AI-related inventions have been increasingly filed recently in Japan (Figure 5.1). AI-related inventions are filed in various fields, but concentrated on five categories: G06N (AI core), G06T (Image Processing), G06F16 (Information Retrieval/Recommendation), Other G06F (Information in General), and G06Q (Business).[4]

On the other hand, the third type, AI-generated inventions, is autonomously generated by AI. This does not necessarily mean no human intervention at all. Rather humans may give AI instructions or orders such as 'to generate something like … '. Unlike the first and the second types, there may be few AI-generated inventions, partly because creating inventions generally requires more complicated

[3] The JPO, Examination Handbook for Patent and Utility Model in Japan, 2019. <https://www.jpo.go.jp/e/system/laws/rule/guideline/patent/handbook_shinsa/index.html> (hereafter the JPO, Handbook).

[4] Applications of these five categories occupy more than half of all AI-related inventions filed in 2017 in Japan. The JPO, Recent Trends in AI-related inventions (July 2019) <https://www.jpo.go.jp/e/system/patent/gaiyo/ai/ai_shutsugan_chosa.html>.

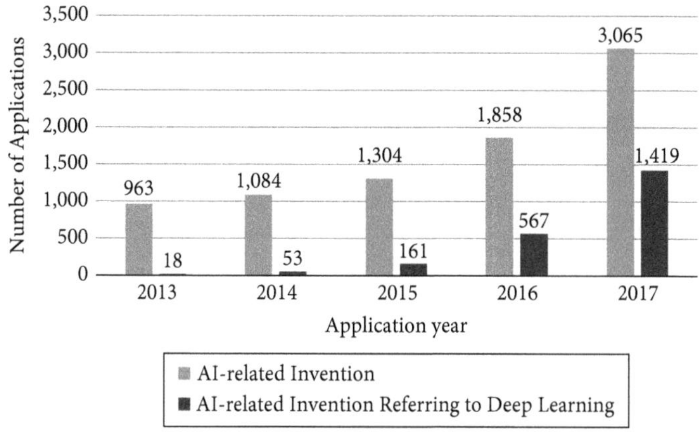

Figure 5.1 Applications of AI-related inventions in Japan

technologies than creating works such as paintings or music. However, it may not be impossible.

In fact, a project called 'Artificial Inventor Project',[5] consisting of an international team of patent attorneys, filed two patent applications with the US Patent Office (USPTO), the European Patent Office (EPO), the UK Intellectual Property Office (UKIPO), and the WIPO in 2018, seeking patent protection for AI-generated inventions. According to the Project, AI called DABUS allegedly autonomously created two inventions, a food or beverage container, and devices and methods for attracting enhanced attention.[6] They explained that DABUS contained several neural networks that had been trained with general information in various fields. Then, the first neural network generated novel ideas and the second neural network not only identified sufficiently novel ideas but also generated an effective response to selectively form and ripen ideas having the most novelty, utility, or value. In the above-mentioned two inventions, DABUS only received training in general information in the fields and proceeded to independently conceive the inventions and to identify them as novel and salient.[7] The applicants argued that it was not a person but AI which identified the novelty and salience of the inventions. Accordingly, they asserted that AI should be deemed an inventor, and that since a machine could not own property such as patents, AI's owners should be entitled to obtain the patent rights.[8] However, in December of 2019, the EPO refused the two applications on the ground that they did not meet the requirement of the

[5] 'Artificial Inventor Project' <http://artificialinventor.com/>.

[6] Specifications and drawings of patent applications for the two inventions are uploaded on the Project's homepage. 'Patent Applications' <http://artificialinventor.com/patent-applications/>.

[7] Ibid.

[8] Ibid.

European Patent Convention (EPC) that an inventor had to be a human being, not a machine.[9] The UKIPO also refused these applications on the same grounds; the inventor in the UK Patent Act (sections 7, 13) is a natural person—ie, a human and not an AI machine.[10] Although the Japanese Patent Act does not say so explicitly, it provides that '[a]n inventor of an invention that is industrially applicable may be entitled to obtain a patent for the said invention, ...' (Article 29 (1)). The 'inventor' in that provision is considered to be a person, not AI. Therefore, autonomously AI-generated inventions, if any, could not be protected in Japan either.[11]

The 'Artificial Inventor Project' raises theoretically interesting questions on inventorship as well as protectability of autonomously AI-generated inventions (the third-type) in the context of policy discussion as to whether to amend the patent law, if necessary.[12] However, it may not have huge impact in practice because so far, most AI-related inventions are presumably either the first type (inventions on AI technologies) or the second type (AI-assisted inventions). These inventions raise urgent and practical issues on patentability such as eligibility, disclosure requirements, and inventive step (non-obviousness). This chapter focuses therefore on these patentability issues.

3. Patent Eligibility (Patentable Subject Matter)

The first question to be asked is whether AI-related inventions may fall within patentable subject matter. This is an issue of patent eligibility. Most AI-related inventions are software-related inventions. This means that the patent eligibility of AI-related inventions mainly depends on that of computer software. Unlike US patent law or the EPC, the Japanese Patent Act has a statutory definition of inventions: '"Invention" in this act means the highly advanced creation of technical ideas utilizing the laws of nature' (Article 2(1)). Thus, patent eligibility of computer

[9] The EPO, 'EPO refuses DABUS patent applications designating a machine inventor' (20 December 2019) <https://www.epo.org/news-issues/news/2019/20191220.html>. They further published the detailed grounds for refusal. 'EPO publishes grounds for its decision to refuse two patent applications naming a machine as inventor' <https://www.epo.org/news-issues/news/2020/20200128.html>.

[10] The UKIPO, Decision BL O/741/19 on 4 December 2019 <https://www.ipo.gov.uk/p-challenge-decision-results/o74119.pdf>.

[11] Intellectual Property Strategy Headquarters of Japan, Committee on Evaluation, Assessment, and Planning, Subcommittee on Examining Intellectual Property System in Next Generation, 'Jisedai Chizai Shisutemu Kento Iinkai Houkokusho' (the Report by Subcommittee on Examining Intellectual Property System in Next Generation) (April 2016) 22 <https://www.kantei.go.jp/jp/singi/titeki2/tyousakai/kensho_hyoka_kikaku/2016/jisedai_tizai/hokokusho.pdf>.

[12] The USPTO invited public comments on this issue, along with another eleven questions on patenting AI-related inventions in August 2019. Specifically, question 3 was '[d]o current patent laws and regulations regarding inventorship need to be revised to take into account inventions where an entity or entities other than a natural person contributed to the conception of an invention?' USPTO, 'Request for Comments on Patenting Artificial Intelligence Inventions' (27 August 2019) <https://www.federalregister.gov/documents/2019/08/27/2019-18443/request-for-comments-on-patenting-artificial-intelligence-inventions> (hereafter USPTO, 'Request').

software has been discussed in Japan as a question of whether it may fall within the statutory definition of 'invention' or not.

The Guidelines of the JPO enumerate the subject matters in which the laws of nature are not utilized.[13] Mathematical formulas are among those not eligible for patent. Since computer software applies mathematics, the following question may be raised: Does computer software utilize the laws of nature? The Handbook says that it does. 'When ... information processing by the software is concretely realized by using hardware resources', said software is a 'creation of a technical idea utilizing the laws of nature' which 'means that "a specific information processor or an operation method ... is constructed through cooperation of the software and the hardware resources"'.[14] Put differently, unlike mathematical formulas, software gives instructions to computers, and computers as hardware resources utilize the laws of nature to execute the software. When the software and the hardware are working together to perform a specific function, the laws of nature are considered to be utilized.

This does not mean that merely adding the term 'computers' or 'apparatus' (hardware) to the claims may always make them eligible for patents. The Intellectual Property High Court in *Method to generate abbreviated expression of bit group* case[15] affirmed the JPO's refusal of the applications, the claim of which referred to the 'apparatus' that generated abbreviated expression of a bit group. It held that, given that the algorithm as such did not utilize the laws of nature, calculation of mathematical formulas by using an existing arithmetic unit was nothing but realizing a solution for mathematical problems, thereby adding no technical idea that utilizes the laws of nature. Otherwise, all mathematical formulas could be patentable. Similarly, the Intellectual Property High Court in the *Knowledge base system* case[16] held that adding a recording or displaying the data to abstract ideas or arbitrary arrangements simply by using the functions of general-purpose computers did not constitute the creation of technical ideas which 'utilize the laws of nature'. In contrast, the Intellectual Property High Court in the *Interactive dental treatment network* case[17] recognized a computer-based dental treatment system as a patentable subject matter. In the claimed invention, dentists develop a preliminary treatment plan including prostheses and send it via computer network to dental technicians, who might modify it and send it back. Since dentists at dental offices and dental technicians at dental laboratories were usually located at different places, they communicated via networks. In doing so, they could refer to a

[13] The JPO, Examination Guidelines for Patent and Utility Model in Japan, 2019, Part III Chapter 1 Section 2.1.4 <https://www.jpo.go.jp/e/system/laws/rule/guideline/patent/tukujitu_kijun/index.html> (hereafter the JPO, Guidelines).

[14] The JPO, Handbook (n 3), Annex B Chapter1, 2.1.1.2(1).

[15] Tokyo Intellectual Property High Court, 29 February 2008, 2007 (Gyo-Ke) 10239, Hanji, No 2012, 97.

[16] Tokyo Intellectual Property High Court, 24 September 2014, 2014 (Gyo-Ke) 10014.

[17] Tokyo Intellectual Property High Court, 24 June 2008, 2007 (Gyo-Ke) 10369, Hanji, No 2026, 123.

database which stores the latest information on dental prostheses. The court held that the claimed invention provided a means for assisting some part of the activities formerly performed by a dentist and a dental technician and, as a whole, was understood as providing a computer-based technical means for assisting dental treatment which comprises 'a network server equipped with a database', 'a communication network', 'a computer located in the dental office', and 'a device capable of displaying and processing the images'. Therefore, it was eligible for patent.

These cases suggest that software may not be patentable when it does not cooperate with hardware resources (computers), but the cooperation between software and hardware resources in a concrete manner may make software eligible for patent. Consequently, software-related inventions could be patentable when the claims are carefully drafted. Although there is no Supreme Court decision, it seems to be fairly settled law in Japan. Since AI-related inventions are software-related inventions, the same rule may be applicable. Accordingly, AI-related inventions could be eligible for patent. In fact, the Handbook give the example of a trained model comprising several neural networks as a patentable subject matter.[18]

4. Updates of the JPO's Guidelines

The JPO has updated the Handbook and added examples pertinent to AI-related technologies in January 2019.[19] The Handbook mainly deals with two kinds of AI-related technologies, namely inventions applying AI in various fields and inventions of products in which AI assumes a certain function. While the former specifies AI as one of the elements of the inventions, the latter may not necessarily mention AI in the patent claims because AI may be used only in the process of creating the product, and the claims may cover only the product. The Handbook gives examples to illustrate how the requirements for disclosure as well as for the inventive steps are applied to these two kinds of invention.

4.1 Disclosure Requirements

Article 36(1) of the Japanese Patent Act provides that 'the statement [of the description] shall be clear and sufficient as to enable any person ordinarily skilled in the art to which the invention pertains to work the invention' (enablement requirement). Article 36(6)(1) provides that 'the invention for which a patent is sought is stated in the detailed explanation of the invention' in the description (support

[18] The JPO, Handbook (n 3), Annex B Chapter 1, [Case 2-14].

[19] The JPO, 'Patent examination case examples pertinent to AI-related technologies' (March 2019) <https://www.jpo.go.jp/e/system/laws/rule/guideline/patent/ai_jirei_e.html>.

requirement). These two requirements as a whole are called 'disclosure requirements'. The disclosure requirements aim to prevent a patent without disclosure, as a patent should only be granted in exchange for disclosing an invention.[20]

The Handbook addresses disclosure requirements of the two kinds of AI-related inventions mentioned above. Regarding the first kind where AI is applied in various fields, it acknowledges that in general, AI may estimate a certain relationship, such as a correlation among the multiple types of data contained in the training data for machine learning. However, AI is a black box and does not explain how it estimates such a correlation. AI estimation itself gives few clues on whether data are really correlated. For instance, suppose an invention trained AI with data of facial images of farmers and the sugar contents of vegetables (eg, tomatoes) grown by them and estimated a correlation between these data. Upon the input of the image of a specific farmer's face, the invention could estimate the sugar content of tomatoes grown by this farmer. However, this invention does not satisfy the disclosure requirements because PHOSITA cannot presume any correlation between a facial image and the sugar content of vegetables, unless actual experimentation or common general technical knowledge supports it.[21] Accordingly, the Handbook requires the following to satisfy the description requirements: First, the correlation among various data should be recognizable based on the disclosure in the description, such as actual experimentation results[22] or existing statistical information[23] in the description. Alternatively, the correlation may be presumed simply by common general technical knowledge even without any disclosure in the description.[24]

Regarding the second kind, where AI presumes a certain function of the products, the Handbook provides that inventions of the said products may not satisfy the disclosure requirements without an evaluation of the function by using the said product that has actually been made, except that an AI estimation result could replace such an evaluation. For instance, suppose that AI learned various data on composition of an anaerobic adhesive and came up with the specific composition which could be estimated to achieve desirable performance. Then, an invention of a composite anaerobic adhesive product was claimed. However, the description did not disclose any evaluation of the estimated composition of the adhesive by using an actually produced product, and did not verify estimation accuracy of a trained model by any other means. Further, it was not assumed that there existed

[20] *Parameter patent* case, Tokyo Intellectual Property High Court, 11 November 2005, 2005 (Gyo-Ke) 10042, Hanji, No 1911, p 48 (Support requirements). The no patent without disclosure principle may hold for the enablement requirement, even though there is room for arguing whether and how the support requirement and enablement requirement are different. See *Flibanserin* case, Tokyo Intellectual Property High Court, 28 January 2010, 2009 (Gyo-Ke) 10033, Hanji, No 2073, p 105.

[21] The JPO, Handbook (n 3) Case 46 of Appendix A.

[22] Ibid, Case 50 of Appendix A.

[23] Ibid, Case 49 of Appendix A.

[24] Ibid, Cases 47 and 48 of Appendix A.

common general technical knowledge as of the filing date that an estimation result by a trained model could replace actual experimentation. Consequently, the accuracy of AI estimation is not verified and thus, the disclosure requirement not satisfied.[25] In sum, AI estimation alone in the description is not a sufficient disclosure.[26] It implies that AI estimation may not be reliable enough at this moment in time.

4.2 The Inventive Step

Article 29(2) of the Japanese Patent Act provides that '[w]here, prior to the filing of the patent application, a person ordinarily skilled in the art of the invention would have been able to easily make the invention based on an invention prescribed in any of the items of the preceding paragraph, a patent shall not be granted for such an invention ...'. Article 29(1) enumerates the prior arts which include 'inventions that were described in a distributed publication, ... in Japan or a foreign country, prior to the filing of the patent application'. A prior art not only destroys the novelty but also provides a basis for determining the inventive step of an invention in the patent application. In the patent examination, the applied invention needs to be compared with an invention described in the publication and then, a common feature and a difference are identified. When there is a difference, examiners must decide whether PHOSITA could easily conceive the applied invention based on the state of the art as of the filing date. If they consider that PHOSITA could do so, inventive step may be denied. This is a well-established practice.[27]

According to the Handbook, the mere application of AI does not pass the threshold of the inventive step. Suppose the claimed invention performs cancer level estimation by using AI instead of human doctors using a blood sample and measuring specific markers. It is only a simple replacement of manually operated tasks by AI, a mere exercise of ordinary creativity of PHOSITA, and therefore lacks the inventive step.[28] In sum, inventions that merely automate manually operated tasks by using AI may be considered as lacking the inventive step.

Similarly, the inventive step may still be denied when a conventional estimation method is replaced by a trained neural network model (AI). Suppose that an invention is claimed in the application of an estimation system for the hydroelectric power-generating capacity of a dam. The invention is designed to forecast the hydroelectric power-generating capacity by means of a neural network which

[25] Ibid, Case 51 of Appendix A.

[26] The USPTO seems to raise a similar question. See USPTO, 'Request' (n 12) Q6.

[27] The JPO, Guidelines (n 13) Part III, Chapter 2, Sections 2, 3. See also *Pyrimidine Derivative* case, Tokyo Intellectual Property High Court, 13 April 2018, 2016 (Gyo-Ke) 10182, 10184, Hanrei Taimuz, No 1460, p 125.

[28] The JPO, Handbook (n 3) Case 33 of Appendix A.

learns both past data, such as the precipitation amount upstream, water flow rate of the river, etc., and future data on hydroelectric power-generating capacity. A prior art was estimation of a hydroelectric power-generating capacity by means of a regression equation model. It is also well-known that an estimation process of an output in the future is carried out based on an input of time series data in the past, using a trained neural network. Therefore, PHOSITA could be considered to conceive easily the claimed invention by adopting AI in substitution of a regression equation model, which lacks the inventive step.[29]

On the other hand, adding training data may change the conclusion. In the above-mentioned example of the estimation system for hydroelectric power-generating capacity, suppose that the applicant used additional data of ambient temperature upstream. As the temperature upstream increases in spring, so does inflow rate of the upper stream due to meltwater in mountains, which enables a highly accurate estimation of hydroelectric power-generating capacity. Assuming no prior art discloses such an idea, the claim with the additional training data of upstream temperature produces a significant effect that PHOSITA cannot expect. Accordingly, it may be considered to have reached the inventive step.[30] This does not mean that changing training data for machine learning always leads to an inventive step. When such a change is made only via a combination of known data, no significant effects are thereby produced, the inventive step may be denied.[31] This is because it is common, general technical knowledge in the technical field of machine learning to use data which are highly likely to be correlated with the output, as an input to a machine learning device, so long as it produces an effect that PHOSITA could expect.

4.3 Summary

Several points should be noted in the updated Handbook. First, training data for machine learning play an important role in requirements for both disclosure and inventive steps. However, training data may work in opposite directions for disclosure and inventive steps, respectively. In cases where a correlation among various data may be presumed based on common general technical knowledge without any disclosure in the description; the disclosure requirement may be satisfied, whereas the inventive step may be denied because PHOSITA could easily conceive such a correlation by referring to common general technical knowledge.[32] Conversely, the inventive step may be satisfied in cases where an invention utilizes

[29] Ibid, Case 34, Claim 1 of Appendix A.
[30] Ibid, Case 34, Claim 2 of Appendix A.
[31] Ibid, Case 35 of Appendix A.
[32] Masaki Saito, 'AI Kannren Gijutsu Ni Kansuru Tokkyo Shinsa Jirei' (Patent Examination Cases concerning AI-related technologies) (2019) 64 AIPPI, 5, 394.

a correlation not presumed by common general technical knowledge, whereas other relevant information, such as actual experimentation results showing the actual correlation, need to be disclosed to satisfy the disclosure requirements.

Secondly, the Handbook considers the mere application of AI as the exercise of ordinary creativity by PHOSITA, and denies the inventive step. This may be consistent with the examination practices on computer-implemented inventions in general. Before the Handbook was updated, it already provided that 'if systemizing the service or method for doing business performed by humans in the specific field and implementing it by a computer are to such an extent that they are possible by daily work using a normal system analysis method and a system design method, they fall under exhibition of normal creation capabilities of a person skilled in the art',[33] which lacks the inventive step. The above-mentioned updates seem to apply the conventional practices of computer-implemented inventions to AI-related inventions. In other words, the Handbook assumes that PHOSITA may use AI to the same extent as general-purpose computers, which has broader implications as discussed below.

4.4 What is Not Discussed in the Handbook

As explained earlier, the Handbook mainly deals with two kinds of AI-related inventions, namely inventions applying AI technology in various fields and inventions of products whose function is assumed by AI. In both cases, the applicants admit the use of AI in either claims or description. However, not only the applicants but also PHOSITA use AI. Therefore, the Handbook considers the mere application of AI as obvious to PHOSITA, as the case examples for the first kind of AI-related inventions illustrate. However, the use of AI by PHOSITA may have broader impacts on the inventive step.

The second kind of inventions may reveal an issue that is not fully addressed by the Handbook. The Handbook makes it clear that AI estimation alone may not satisfy the disclosure requirements, and thus, actual experimentation results or common general technical knowledge is required to verify the AI estimation. On the other hand, the Handbook is silent on whether PHOSITA could conceive the function of the claimed product with the aid of AI as the applicants actually did in the above-mentioned case of anaerobic adhesive composition, and therefore the inventive step is to be denied.

The issue is not limited to an invention in which the applicant admits the use of AI. As explained earlier, the applicant has to disclose actual experimentation results or cite a common general technical knowledge to verify the AI-presumed

[33] The JPO, Handbook (n 3) Appendix B, Chapter 1, 2.2.3.2 (4).

function of the product in order to satisfy the disclosure requirements. From the applicant's point of view, it is of little use for them to disclose the use of AI in the description. They have no incentive to do so. This implies that the use of AI may not be disclosed in the description, even though AI is actually used in the R&D. If the use of AI by PHOSITA may be taken into account when determining the inventive step for invention in which either claims or description disclose the use of AI, the same policy should be applied to inventions which did not disclose the use of AI in the description. Moreover, one could hardly know whether AI has been used in creating the inventions unless the description states so. Accordingly, all inventions, whether or not the applications disclose that they have been created with the aid of AI, cannot but be examined on the assumption that PHOSITA use AI. Is such an assumption reasonable and justifiable? If yes, how would the examiners take into account the use of AI by PHOSITA when examining the inventive step in practice? What impacts, if any, would it have on the creation of future inventions? The Handbook has left these questions unresolved.

5. Justifying PHOSITA with AI

5.1 PHOSITA with AI Has Become an Important Issue

In theory, the inventive step prevents a patent from being granted to an invention which would be created anyway without the incentives of exclusive rights.[34] In other words, the inventive step aims to select an invention that, but for the inducement of a patent, would not have been created for a substantial period (the so-called 'inducement theory').[35] On the contrary, a patent on an invention which PHOSITA would easily conceive would unreasonably restrict third parties' businesses and increase social costs of patent protection.

In practice, the JPO's Guidelines enumerate the conditions of PHOSITA, one of which is '[a] person who is able to use ordinary technical means for research and development (including document analysis, experiment, technical analysis, manufacture, etc.)'.[36] If AI is considered to be 'ordinary technical means', PHOSITA may have no obstacles to using it. Accordingly, an invention that would be easily created by PHOSITA with the aid of AI might well be considered as lacking the inventive step. The lack of the inventive step may still exist even when the applicants have

[34] Nobuhiro Nakayama, *Tokkyo Ho* (*Patent Law*) (4th edn, Kobundo 2019) 134 (hereafter Nakayama, *Tokkyo Ho*); Takeshi Maeda, '*Shinposeiyouken No Kinou Kara Mita Saibannrei No Seiri To Jisshou Bunseki*' (Classification and Empirical Analysis of Judicial Cases from the Function of Inventive Step) (2014) Institute of Intellectual Property 14–17.

[35] *Graham v John Deere Co.*, 383 US 1, 11 (1966); Michael Abramowicz and John F Duffy, 'Inducement Standard of Patentability' (2011) 120 Yale Law Journal 1590.

[36] The JPO, Guidelines (n 13) Part III Chapter 2 Section 2 2. This notion of PHOSITA was supported by Tokyo High Court, 26 December 2002, 2000 (Gyo-Ke) 404.

not used AI. A question in examining the inventive step is whether PHOSITA, not applicants, would produce an invention by using AI. So long as AI is considered to be widely available to PHOSITA, the use of AI by PHOSITA should be taken into consideration when examining the inventive step, which might lead to a higher requirement level of the inventive step.

Some US scholars have similar views, while the USPTO has just begun to consider the issue.[37] They have argued that the development and diffusion of AI may raise the level of PHOSITA and thus the threshold of the inventive step.[38] They are concerned that conceiving of PHOSITA as not using AI would lead to an overflow of patentable inventions, which would eventually stifle innovation. Therefore, how we should take the notion of PHOSITA with AI into consideration in practice has become an important issue.

5.2 Issues Posed by the 'Pyrimidine Derivative' Case

5.2.1 The case

One of the recent court cases in Japan may be a good example to illustrate how PHOSITA with AI may or may not affect the inventive step in practice.

On 13 April 2018, the grand panel of the Tokyo Intellectual Property High Court decided the 'Pyrimidine Derivative' case.[39] Although the case itself was not directly related to AI, the judgment rendered by the court posed interesting questions to be discussed in future cases involving AI-assisted inventions. The case was a suit against the JPO's decision that dismissed a request for the invalidation trial of a patent accorded to an invention titled 'pyrimidine derivatives'. One of the issues was the inventive step.

In this case, the patented invention that allegedly lacked the inventive step (hereafter, 'the Invention') was a pharmaceuticals compound for the treatment of hypercholesteremia, hyperlipoproteinemia, etc. The difference between the Invention and the main-cited invention described in the publication lies in the fact that the specific part of the compound of the Invention was an alkylsulfonyl group, whereas that of the compound of the main-cited invention was a methyl group. A publication that allegedly described a sub-cited invention in the form of

[37] The USPTO asked this question in their requests for public comments. The USPTO, 'Request' (n 12) question 8.

[38] Ryan Abbott, 'Everything is Obvious' (2018) 66 UCLA Law Review 2 (hereafter Abbott, 'Everything'); William Samore, 'Artificial Intelligence and the Patent System: Can a New Tool Render a Once Patentable Idea Obvious?' (2013) 29 Syracuse Journal of Science & Technology 113 (hereafter Samore, 'Artificial Intelligence'); Liza Vertinsky, 'Thinking Machines and Patent Law' in Woodrow Barfield and Ugo Pagallo (eds), *Research Handbook of Law and Artificial Intelligence* (Edward Elgar Publishing 2018) 15–16; Susan Y Tull and Paula E Miller, 'Patenting Artificial Intelligence: Issues of Obviousness, Inventorship, and Patent Eligibility' (2018) 1 The Journal of Robotics, Artificial Intelligence & Law 313, 320.

[39] *Pyrimidine Derivative* (n 27).

Markush claims disclosed a compound where the corresponding part was the general formula of an alkylsulfonyl group. However, the specific configuration of the Invention was one of 20 million or more alternatives.

The court held that if a compound was described in the form of a general formula in a publication prior to the filing date and the general formula had an enormous number of alternatives, it was impossible to extract a specific technical idea embodied in a specific alternative, unless there was a circumstance where the specific alternative would be positively or preferentially selected. In the 'Pyrimidine Derivative' case, since the general formula of an alkylsulfonyl group in the publication had more than 20 million alternatives, circumstances could hardly be found to suggest the specific alternative would be selected, and thus, it could not be seen from the publication that the technical idea corresponding to the difference might be extracted. In other words, the combination of the main-cited invention with the sub-cited invention was unlikely to result in the configuration corresponding to the above-mentioned difference between the Invention and the inventions described in the publication. Therefore, it held that the Invention was not easily conceivable on the basis of the cited invention.

5.2.2 AI's possible impacts on the holding

It was evident that the Invention in the 'Pyrimidine Derivative' case neither incorporated AI nor was created by using AI, and thus, Tokyo Intellectual Property High Court did not mention AI at all in their judgment. Nonetheless, several commentators pointed out the possibilities that the development and diffusion of AI might have impacts on the court's holding in future. One anonymous commentator suggested the necessity to reconsider the framework held by the court in cases where the use of AI might become a general practice in the future for selecting potentially effective compounds among enormous numbers of compounds without experimentation.[40] Other commentators made similar comments. More than 20 million alternatives might be an enormous number today, but might not be so in the future when using AI.[41] The development of AI might make it easier to pick up a specific alternative among an enormous number of alternatives, which might lead to the findings that the said specific alternative is considered to be the prior art.[42]

[40] Anonymous comments (2018) 80 L & T, 96–7. In Japan, legal periodicals report court cases together with anonymous comments. These anonymous comments are generally believed to be written by the judges who decided the cases. It should also be noted that lower court judges deliver neither dissenting nor concurring opinions, but Supreme Court Justices do. In other words, lower courts judges have no official opportunity to express their views other than in the judgments. However, it is widely believed that anonymous comments in legal periodicals give them *de facto* chances to make complementary remarks to their judgments. Whether such a belief is true or not, it is a well-accepted practice in Japan to cite anonymous comments in legal periodicals.

[41] Hiroshi Kato (2018) 16 *Chizai Prism* (IP Prism) 190, 35 (note).

[42] Ryouko Iseki (2018) 66 *Tokkyo Kenkyu* (Patent Studies) 74 (note).

These comments may well be relevant. Researchers and engineers have begun to use AI for screening or other purposes to make the R&D more efficient. Material informatics is one of the fields where AI has been utilized, where AI has been used to reduce the use of a conventional materials simulation method such as the first principles of calculations requiring a significant computational load, and notably accelerate the development of solid electrolytes with high ionic conductivity for use in all-solid-state lithium-ion rechargeable batteries.[43] AI's contributions to the efficient development of other materials include the reduction of the development time by one-sixth in developing a new material adhesive for ceramics in semiconductor electrodes, and the reduction of one to two years in developing a catalyst for polymer chemistry among more than three million molecular structures.[44] AI may also be used in drug development. In some instances, it shortened the development time by more than 30% for screening target antibodies and compounds.[45] Similarly, deep learning reportedly enables rapid identification (twenty-one days) of potent DDR 1 kinase inhibitors.[46]

These examples illustrate the capabilities of AI in streamlining R&D, which may make it easier for PHOSITA to find a solution that they would hardly do by conventional technologies. Then, one could not but face the question of whether the inventive step should be decided by taking into account possibilities of PHOSITA with AI, even though the Tokyo Intellectual Property High Court in the 'Pyrimidine Derivative' case paid no attention to it. However, as the above-mentioned commentators correctly pointed out, the rapid development of AI urges the court to seriously consider it.

5.3 Is the Use of AI Widespread?

Although the 'Pyrimidine Derivative' case suggests the necessity of considering the possibility of PHOSITA with AI, we cannot jump to that conclusion without addressing one more question: Is it fair to say that AI may be 'ordinary technical means' that PHOSITA would use?

In fact, AI may not yet have been used widely, at least in Japan. In 2020, less than 50% of firms are estimated to have introduced AI in their business (Figures 5.2 and 5.3). Nonetheless, should the examination of invention step assume PHOSITA with AI?

[43] Fujitsu Limited and RIKEN, 'Fujitsu and RIKEN demonstrate AI's utility in material design' (16 March 2018) <https://www.fujitsu.com/global/about/resources/news/press-releases/2018/0316-01.html>.

[44] 'Material design by big data' *Nihon Keizai Shinbun* (Japan Economy Newspaper) (Tokyo, 4 April 2018).

[45] 'Drug development accelerated by AI' *Nihon Keizai Shinbun* (Japan Economy Newspaper) (Tokyo, 15 October 2018).

[46] Alex Zhavoronkov and others, 'Deep learning enables rapid identification of potent DDR1 kinase inhibitors' (2 September 2019) <https://www.nature.com/articles/s41587-019-0224-x>.

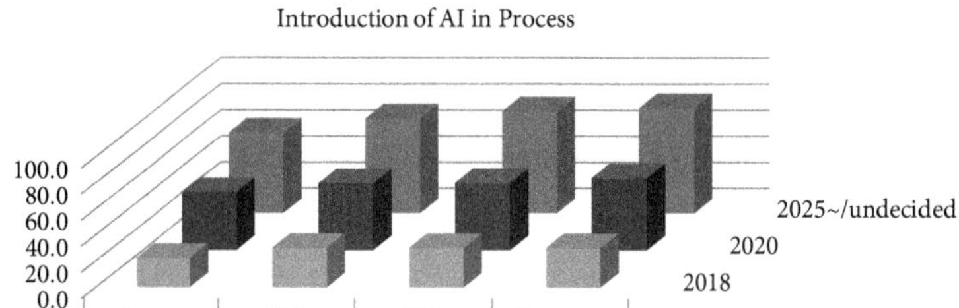

	Japan (n = 190)	US (n = 325)	UK (n = 413)	Germany (n = 412)
2018	22.1	29.8	29.5	30.6
2020	44.2	51.1	51.6	55.6
2025~/undecided	62.1	73.2	78.7	82.0

2018 2020 2025~/undecided

Figure 5.2 Introduction of AI in process

On one hand, since AI has not been widely available, one may argue that PHOSITA is not expected to use it and the inventive step test should assume PHOSITA without AI. Otherwise, the level of the inventive step would be unnecessarily raised, making it harder for many inventors who do not use AI to obtain patents. In contrast, PHOSITA without AI may make it easier for those who introduce AI at earlier stages to obtain patents on AI-related inventions. Thus, patents would encourage AI-related inventions, which may be partly justified under the inducement theory. In this line of argument, the level of PHOSITA is determined objectively. Thus, the notion of PHOSITA may change over time, depending on whether the use of AI is widespread. It then raises the question of how to determine the popularity of AI. Some scholars in the US have proposed to use the 'duty to

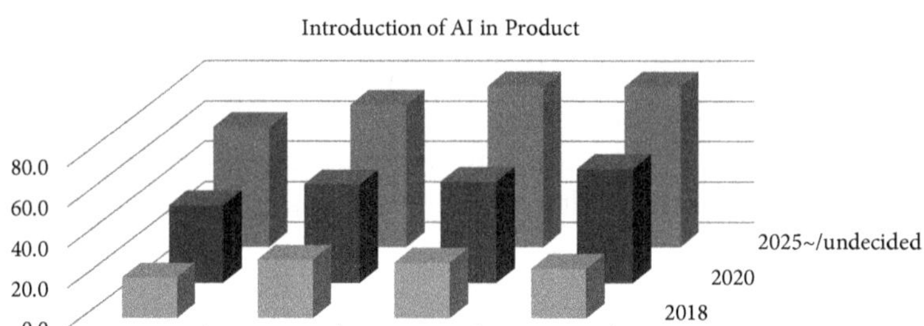

	Japan (n = 188)	US (n = 312)	UK (n = 413)	Germany (n = 411)
2018	19.7	28.8	27.4	24.3
2020	38.3	48.4	49.6	56.4
2025~/undecided	59.6	70.2	79.4	79.8

Figure 5.3 Introduction of AI in product

disclose information material to patentability'[47] to include a duty upon the applicant to disclose the use of AI.[48]

On the other hand, one may make a counterargument: Although AI has not been widely used now, it is forecasted to be widespread rapidly (Figure 5.3). Then, it may not be unreasonable to expect PHOSITA to use AI. There may be a concern that PHOSITA with AI may raise the level of inventive step, thereby hurting those who do not use AI. However, such a concern may be outweighed by the incentives in the market to use AI, which may promote the introduction of AI. A survey in Japan shows that AI aims to supplement deficiencies in the labour force or to make business more efficient.[49] There are no reasons to lower the level of the inventive step on the assumption that PHOSITA do not use AI, which would slow down the take-up of AI by the industry. This line of argument considers the level of PHOSITA normatively for policy reasons.

Which line of argument is more reasonable? The above-mentioned updates in the Handbook will have an important impact on this issue.

6. The Handbook's Unconscious Support of PHOSITA with AI

As explained earlier, the JPO's Handbook provides that the mere application of AI may lack the inventive step because it is considered to be the exercise of ordinary creativity by PHOSITA. This means that PHOSITA is presumed to use AI to the same extent as general purpose computers. It would be no exaggeration to say that they (unconsciously?) support assuming PHOSITA with AI in deciding the inventive step in all fields of technology despite the fact that the use of AI has not been widespread.

However, attention should be paid to the low reliability of AI. As also explained earlier, the Handbook requires actual experimentation results, etc in addition to AI estimation in order to satisfy the disclosure requirements, unless common general technical knowledge supports the AI estimation. This means that AI alone may not be considered reliable enough. Then, even if the inventive step is examined under the notion of PHOSITA with AI and AI seems to make it easier for PHOSITA to conceive the invention, the low reliability of AI may not deny the inventive step

[47] 37 CFR 1.56. Violation of such a duty may render the patent right unenforceable.

[48] Abbott, 'Everything' (n 38) 39. Samore, 'Artificial Intelligence' (n 38) 133–7 made a similar proposal, but proposed a broader four-factor test to determine the widespread use of AI (genetic programme). The proposed four factors are (1) whether the invention was actually designed with AI; (2) the proportion of PHOSITAs in the field having access to AI; (3) the cost associated with the use of AI; and (4) the amount of time and effort required to operate AI.

[49] The Ministry of Internal Affairs and Communications, *Jyouhou Tsushin Hakusho 2016* (Information and Communications in Japan White Paper 2016) (2016) Chart 4-3-3-2.

because PHOSITA would not trust AI estimation and thus, would not try to create the invention due to no expectation of success. As a result, PHOSITA with AI may not change the conclusion of the inventive step in practice for the time being. However, the rapid advancement of AI technologies is likely to improve the reliability of AI soon. Accordingly, the low reliability of AI of today may be no excuse to ignore the need in the near future to consider when and how PHOSITA with AI will raise the level of the inventive step.

7. Challenges for PHOSITA with AI

Even if PHOSITA is presumed to use AI, there are numerous challenges in practice.

7.1 Does the Applicants' Use of AI Matter?

The use of AI is evident in the inventions which claim AI as one of their elements. Some applicants disclose in the description the fact that they have created an invention based on the AI estimation. However, there are other cases where applicants do not disclose the use of AI, though they actually did use it. It is difficult for third parties to discern which invention was created with the aid of AI. As mentioned earlier, some scholars have addressed this issue by imposing on applicants a duty to disclose the use of AI.[50] Although the Japanese Patent Act has a similar information disclosure requirement,[51] non-compliance does not directly constitute an invalidation ground provided in Article 123(1), but allows examiners to notify the applicants and give them opportunities to submit opinions or amendments (Article 48-7). Weak sanctions make it hard for the JPO to detect non-compliance. Thus, a proposal on duty to disclose the use of AI would not work well, at least in Japan.

On the contrary, once the level of PHOSITA is determined, the level of the applicants does not matter in examining the inventive step. So long as PHOSITA is expected to use AI, the inventive step should be examined on the premise of PHOSITA with AI, regardless of whether the applicants use AI or not.[52] It is not the applicants, but PHOSITA who determines the level of the inventive step.

[50] See n 48 and the corresponding text.

[51] Japanese Patent Act, Article 364(2).

[52] Hisayoshi Yokoyama, 'AI Ni Kansuru Chosakukenho Tokkyoho Jyo No Mondai' (Issues on AI under Copyright Law and Patent Law) (2019) 91 Horitsu Jiho 8, 52.

7.2 Is Reproducibility by AI Necessary?

How can PHOSITA with AI be put into practice in the examination of the inventive step? One interesting idea was proposed: testing reproducibility by AI.[53] The proposal aimed to determine the inventive step in a more objective way without relying on hypothetical inquiry as to whether PHOSITA would have easily conceived the invention. Thus, the proposal consisted of three steps: (1) to determine the extent to which AI is used in the field, (2) if AI is generally used, to characterize the AI that best represents the average worker, and (3) to determine whether the AI would find an invention obvious.

However, this chapter does not consider the first step necessary because, as of today, it may not be unreasonable to expect PHOSITA to use AI for the above-mentioned reasons. More interesting are the second and third steps. The second step is to identify the specific AIs, eg, Deep Mind (Google) and Watson (IBM). This is because not hypothetical AI but specific, actual AI would result in a more objective test. It should also be noted that more than one AI should be selected and the claimed inventions in patent applications should be considered as lacking the inventive step if they were obvious compared to all of the selected AIs. In other words, the applicants could obtain patents if their claimed invention is not obvious to either one of the AIs. This means that the specific AI would be more likely to generate patentable inventions if it outperforms other competing AIs. This could accelerate the competition of AI development, as more advanced AI will be rewarded.

The third step is to determine whether the selected AI would find an invention obvious. This could be accomplished by testing whether the specified AI would be able to recreate the invention, namely reproduce the invention within a reasonable time (reproducibility test). Again, doing so would be a more objective standard than subjective, hypothetical queries of what PHOSITA would have found obvious. Thus, the proposer argued that the reproducibility test of AI might contribute to improvement over the current cognitive standards, such as other secondary considerations (commercial success, unexpected results, long-felt but unsolved needs, the failure of others, etc.).

Although the proposal is intriguing, there are considerable difficulties foreseen for its implementation. For instance, since the inventive step must be examined as of the filing date (priority date), AI which PHOSITA is expected to use should be the one as of the filing date. This means that capabilities improvement to the AI after the filing date needs to be neglected or at least downgraded, as do the training data. However, is it realistically feasible to do so? Another problem is that in other fields of technology, the patent examiners are not expected to conduct experimentation

[53] Abbot, 'Everything' (n 38) 38–46.

in determining the inventive step, which raises a fundamental question: why do the patent examiners only have to verify the reproducibility of AI-related inventions?

PHOSITA is a legal fiction, not a real person,[54] as it is impractical to identify specific individuals as PHOSITA, and the inquiry into whether PHOSITA would have easily conceived the invention does not aim at scientific verification. Rather, the PHOSITA inquiry is a normative, legal question based on policy considerations under the patent law. Therefore, testing reproducibility by AI may not be necessary. Then, a question follows: what methods may be used to take into account PHOSITA with AI in the examination of the inventive step? For the time being, a realistic and pragmatic approach would be to consider experts' opinions.[55] However, expert opinions are more likely to be submitted at later stages such as during the lawsuits, invalidation trials, post-grant oppositions, etc rather than at earlier stages such as the prosecution of the patent applications in patent offices.

7.3 Different Considerations May Still Speak for PHOSITA Without AI

It should be noted, however, that different considerations may be appropriate in specific sectors. Take the pharmaceutical industry, for example. It may be true that AI is utilized in the R&D process and makes it easier to create an invention. However, clinical tests and regulatory approvals are mandated before the invention is commercially put on the market as drugs. The new drug development process, including the clinical tests, not only requires huge investments but also poses huge risks. According to the Japanese pharmaceutical manufacturing industry, the whole process from basic research to regulatory approval takes nine to sixteen years and only one in about 25,000 researched chemical compounds eventually becomes a new drug.[56] In such a high-risk environment, the expense of conducting clinical tests would not be fully invested without patent protection. As the so-called prospect theory teaches, a pharmaceutical patent may induce *ex post* investments after an invention is created rather than *ex ante* investments before an invention is created.[57] Even if AI makes it easier to create an invention, AI does not change the *ex post* investment pattern. However, a heightened inventive step based on PHOSITA with AI might deny patent protection which could still play an important role in inducing *ex post* investment in pharmaceutical industry. This would

[54] Nakayama, *Tokkyo Ho* (n 34) 135.

[55] Even the proposal on testing reproducibility of AI recognizes expert testimony as a more practical option. Abbot, 'Everything' (n 38) 41.

[56] Japan Pharmaceutical Manufacturers Association, 'Japan Pharmaceutical Manufacturers Association Guide 2018–2019' 8 <http://www.jpma.or.jp/english/about_us/pdf/jpma_guide_2018-2019.pdf>.

[57] Edmund W Kitch, 'The Nature and Function of the Patent System' (1977) 20 Journal of Law & Economics 265.

be inconsistent with the purpose of patent law 'to contribute to the development of industry' (Japanese Patent Act, Article 1). Therefore, pharmaceutical patents may need an exception, namely PHOSITA without AI. Given that PHOSITA is a normative concept based on policy considerations, such an exception may be justifiable on the ground that AI estimation is deemed unreliable for PHOSITA in the pharmaceutical sector, which puts priority on reliability due to the safety needs of drugs and thus, the said PHOSITA may not use AI.[58]

8. Conclusion

The fact that the JPO updated the Handbook to deal with AI-related inventions clearly illustrates the need to change the current examination practice in response to the rapid development of AI. The JPO took one step forward in the right direction. However, it is not enough. The JPO mainly discussed invention in which the use of AI is evident in either claims or descriptions. However, there are other inventions which do not disclose the use of AI, though AI may have been used in creating them. In addition, the JPO made it clear that the mere application of AI lacked the inventive step. This suggests that PHOSITA may be able to use AI to the same extent as general-purpose computers even though the use of AI is not yet widespread. This may be justifiable on the ground that it may not be considered unreasonable to expect PHOSITA to use AI because incentives exist in the market for the adoption of AI. In fact, the use of AI has been increasing. This line of argument may be applied to all inventions, regardless of whether the applicants have used AI in creating the inventions.

On the other hand, outputs of AI may not be so reliable today. Taking PHOSITA with AI into account may not change the determination of the inventive step so much. However, since AI's ability has been improving rapidly, it is just a matter of time before AI generates more reliable output. Therefore, low reliability of AI today should not be used as a pretext to avoid the discussion of AI's impacts on the inventive step.

In the beginning of this chapter, three types of AI-related inventions were identified. The above discussion mainly deals with the first type of inventions on AI technologies and the second type of AI-assisted inventions, given the fact that these inventions are produced on a daily basis today. Having said that, the rapid progress of AI technologies increases the possibility of the third type of autonomous AI-generated inventions without human intervention. This would raise issues such as inventorship and ownership, as briefly mentioned. These issues are not the main subject of this chapter. However, there is one thing worth mentioning

[58] Alternatively, data protection for clinical tests may provide enough incentives. Abbott, 'Everything' (n 38) 49.

in terms of the topic of this chapter. Autonomous AI-generated inventions would raise the level of the inventive step further, which may make it harder for human inventors to obtain patents. One may worry that autonomous AI-generated inventions might disincentivize human inventors. However, even if human inventors were discouraged, endless amounts of autonomous AI-generated inventions would still be forthcoming. Investment may be still necessary for introducing AI which generates inventions or commercializing AI-generated inventions. However, as explained earlier, incentives other than patent incentives in the market (eg, to cover labour shortages or streamline business operations) work for introducing AI. In addition, it should be noted that a patent protects only some of the creations which satisfy the patentability requirements. Nonetheless, we know that many products are supplied in the market without patent protection. Investment without patent protections may be explained based on well-known findings that companies use various mechanisms other than a patent in order to appropriate the returns from their innovation: first-mover advantage (lead time), secrecy, complementary sales and services, complementary manufacturing facilities, and so on.[59] A patent is neither necessary nor desirable for protecting all kinds of investments. It is justifiable only if there exists market failure such as underproduction (scarcity) of inventions. The inventive step serves such a purpose by selecting an invention that, but for the inducement of a patent, would not have been created, as mentioned earlier. In this context, it would be appropriate to give a patent to the first type of inventions on AI technologies themselves to incentivize the upgrading or improving of AI capability. Accordingly, AI which is capable of generating inventions autonomously could be patentable. On the other hand, given the incentives in the market for introducing AI, patent incentives would not be necessary to create inventions if AI autonomously generated infinite inventions in the future. Although no one knows what the future will look like, autonomous AI-generated inventions may well become more common.[60] In such a scenario, we do not have to worry so much about the disincentives for human inventors. On the other hand, since the incentive function for human inventors would be less important, we may have to re-consider what roles and functions patent law should play in an era when autonomous AI-generated inventions prevail.

[59] Richard C Levin, Alvin K Klevorick, Richard R Nelson, and Sidney G Winter, 'Appropriating the Returns from Industrial Research and Development' (1897) 3 Brookings Papers on Economic Activity 783; Wesley M Cohen, Richard R Nelson, and John P Walsh, 'Protecting Their Intellectual Assets: Appropriability Conditions and Why U.S. Manufacturing Firms Patent (or Not)' (2000) NBER Working Paper No 7522.

[60] Mark A Lemley, 'IP in a World Without Scarcity' (2015) 90 NYU Law Review 460.

6

Digitalized Invention, Decentralized Patent System

The Impact of Blockchain and Artificial Intelligence on the Patent Prosecution

*Feroz Ali**

1. Introduction

The patent prosecution—the art and science of verifying and certifying patents—has evolved over the years with the advancement in technology. The manner of representation of the invention before the patent office has influenced the standards of patent prosecution. The changes in the representation of the invention before the patent office can be mapped to three periods in which the invention came to be materialized, textualized, and digitalized.

The earliest accounts of patent history show that the material representation of the invention presented to the patent office in the form of miniature working models formed the subject matter of patent prosecution, as models were seen as more authentic embodiments of the invention than written description and drawings.[1] It is possible to say, from the viewpoint of patent prosecution, that the invention became *materialized* during this period. The development of the patent specification into a full-fledged written representation of the invention happened over a period of time, which shifted the focus of patent prosecution to how the invention was expressed in words and figures, ie, the textual representation of the invention.[2] The invention became *textualized* during this period. The advancements in digital technology now allow for a digital representation of the invention, which is achieved by new technologies such as blockchain and artificial intelligence (AI). The invention will become *digitalized* in this period.

* All online materials were accessed before 24 February 2020.

[1] Kendall J Dood, 'Patent Models and the Patent Law: 1790-1880 (Part I)' (1983) 65 Journal of Patent Office Society 187, 210 (hereafter Dood, 'Patent Models').

[2] Brad Sherman and Lionel Bently, *The Making of Modern Intellectual Property Law: The British Experience, 1760–1911* (Cambridge University Press 1999) 192 (hereafter Sherman and Bently, *Modern Intellectual Property Law*).

Feroz Ali, *Digitalized Invention, Decentralized Patent System* In: *Artificial Intelligence and Intellectual Property*.
Edited by: Jyh-An Lee, Reto M Hilty, and Kung-Chung Liu, Oxford University Press (2021). © The several contributors.
DOI: 10.1093/oso/9780198870944.003.0007

The manner in which the advancements in technology influenced the representation of the invention impacts how patents are prosecuted. The standards of novelty, inventive step, fair basis,[3] enabling disclosure, written description, and other requirements changed when the representation of the invention shifted.[4] The chapter covers the impact of new technologies such as blockchain and AI on the representation of the invention before the patent office and its consequential effect on the decentralization of the functions of the patent office.

This chapter proceeds in four sections. Section 1 introduces the subject covered in this chapter. Section 2 details the changes in the representation of images by comparing digital photography with analogue photography and how the backend process changed the entire field of photography. It further details the transformation of the patent office functions with the introduction of new technology to represent the invention. Section 3 introduces the digitalized invention as a new way to represent the invention before the patent office, demarcates its distinguishing features, and details the mechanics of the digitalized invention. Section 4 analyses the impact of the digitalized invention on the patent office and notes how the changes in the novelty, inventive step, disclosure, and enablement caused by the new representation of the invention can eventually lead to decentralization of various functions of the patent office.

2. The Changes in Representation of Invention

By some accounts, patents began their life as exclusive grants, similar to the royal privileges that were granted for the purposes of trade, but focused on the introduction of products and services into Britain from continental Europe.[5] The new services and manufacture that were introduced into Britain emphasized the new technology that was introduced into the country. In the US, patents were granted for new technology which had to be demonstrated before the patent office. In the early days, the demonstration of the invention was by way of miniature working models of the invention that was claimed, as the patent office accepted the models as indisputable proof of prior invention.[6] Since most of the inventions pertained to mechanical inventions, it enabled inventors to demonstrate working models

[3] The doctrine of fair basis requires that for a patent to be valid the claims have to be fairly based on the matter disclosed in the specification. The lack of fair basis can be a ground for invalidating the patent. David J Brennan, 'Does a Requirement that the Description Fully Supports a Product Claim Raise Australia from Mechanistic and Impoverished Patent Rules' (2012) 38 Monash University Law Review 78.

[4] Feroz Ali, *The Access Regime: Patent Law Reforms for Affordable Medicines* (Oxford University Press 2016) 29–36 (hereafter Feroz Ali, *The Access Regime*).

[5] Pamela O Long, 'Invention, Authorship, "Intellectual Property," and the Origin of Patents: Notes toward a Conceptual History' (1991) 32 Technology & Culture 846, 878.

[6] Dood, 'Patent Models' (n 1) 211.

before the patent office to entitle them to a grant. The Board of Examiners established under the Patent Act of 1790 could not cope with the workload and relaxed the requirement that all patents should include patent specifications.[7] Though the written form patent specification existed in tandem with the models, the Patents Act of 1836 insisted on the submission of models as they were seen as more authentic embodiments of the invention than the patent specification.[8]

Till this point, we see a preference given to the physical representation of the invention by way of a working model, which was the subject matter of patent prosecution. Due to a host of factors, the focus of patent prosecution shifted to patent specifications, as the reduction of the patent on paper helped to overcome difficulties of space and distance, resulting in the shift in the representation of the invention to textual means by words and figures.[9] The departure from the physical representation of the invention and the introduction of a new way of representing the invention by textual means was also aided by the development of technology which enabled reproduction and distribution of copies of the description of the invention. The written representation of the invention later came to be known as the patent specification which was amenable to easy duplication, could be stored in different locations and accessed with relative ease as compared to the miniature working models. This led to the textualization of the invention, a phase in the development of patent law which was enabled not only by the need to make the patent system more accessible but also by the developments in recording, storage, and distribution technology of the times.

The textual representation of the invention continues up until this day. Patent offices around the world insist only on a textual representation of the invention and rarely insist on the production of working models.[10] Thus, the representation of the invention shifted over the years when the invention became materialized in the form of working models, then changed its form and became textualized with the evolution of patent specification. We can now reasonably expect the invention to become digitalized with the use of blockchain, AI, and other technologies that can impact the manner in which the invention is represented. The digitalized representation of the invention will open up more opportunities and challenges in patent prosecution, much more than the earlier two phases of materialization and textualization did. The digitalized invention would be characterized by the

[7] John N Adams and Gwen Averley, 'The Patent Specification: The Role of Liardet v. Johnson' (1986) 7 Journal of Legal History 156, 159 (hereafter Adams and Averley, 'The Patent Specification').

[8] Dood, 'Patent Models' (n 1) 210.

[9] Sherman and Bently, *Modern Intellectual Property Law* (n 2) 182.

[10] The USPTO insists on working models in case of inventions involving perpetual motion. US Patent & Trademark Office, Manual of Patent Examining Procedure § 608.03 (9th edn 2012) <http://www.uspto.gov/web/offices/pac/mpep/mpep-0600.pdf>. Models are not ordinarily required by the Office to demonstrate the operability of a device except in the case of applications involving perpetual motion. The director can require the applicant to furnish a model of convenient size to exhibit advantageously the several parts of the invention. 35 USC 114, Models, specimens.

medium in which it is created, allowing it to be presented, recorded, and analysed in the digital medium. Unlike the photo reproduction of the text of the patent specification, the digitalized representation of the invention entrusts the representation of the invention with hitherto unfamiliar characteristics such as transparency, immutability, and decentralization, that can impact the concepts of disclosure, publication, priority date, proof of possession, and other established concepts that came about with the textualization of the invention.

Though recent scholarship has focused on the need for legal reforms concerning ownership of AI-related patents (patent for inventions created by AI and patents involving AI),[11] not much has been done on the impact of AI and new technologies on the prosecution of patents. Scholars expect the new inventions created by AI systems to be on a collision course with patent law,[12] and warn that the new invention process cannot be easily accommodated within the existing patent system.[13] Not surprisingly, in August 2019 the United States Patent and Trademarks Office (USPTO) came up with a list of questions containing a mix of those pertaining to ownership of AI inventions and patentability of AI invention.[14] But how the new technologies will impact the patent prosecution and the patent system itself has not been explored in detail.

2.1 The Backend Revolution—How Digital Photography Changed the Representation of Images

Skeptics may disagree with the hypothesis that new technologies can change the way patents are prosecuted. How can new technologies that change the representation of an invention have an impact on patent prosecution, especially when the output, the patent specification, remains the same? How can the patent specification, a representation of the invention in words and figures, substantially change

[11] W Michael Schuster, 'Artificial Intelligence and Patent Ownership' (2019) 75 Washington and Lee Law Review 1945; Liza Vertinsky and Todd M Rice, 'Thinking About Thinking Machines: Implications of Machine Inventors for Patent Law' (2002) 8 Boston University Journal of Science & Technology Law 574 (hereafter Vertinsky and Rice, 'Thinking About Thinking Machines'); Erica Fraser, 'Computers as Inventors—Legal and Policy Implications of Artificial Intelligence on Patent Law' (2016) 13 SCRIPTed 305; Liza Vertinsky, 'Boundary-Spanning Collaboration and the Limits of Joint Inventorship Doctrine' (2017) 55 Houston Law Review 3887; Noam Shemtov, 'A Study on Inventorship in Inventions Involving AI Activity' [2019] 36; Erica Fraser, 'Computers as Inventors—Legal and Policy Implications of Artificial Intelligence on Patent Law' (2016) 13 SCRIPTed 305; Ryan Abbott, 'I Think, Therefore I Invent: Creative Computers and the Future of Patent Law' (2016) 57 Boston College Law Review 1079 (hereafter Abbott, 'I Think'); Ben Hattenbach and Joshua Glucoft, 'Patents in An Era of Infinite Monkeys and Artificial Intelligence' (2015–16) 19 Stanford Technology Law Review 32 (hereafter Hattenbach and Glucoft, 'Patents').

[12] Hattenbach and Glucoft, 'Patents' (n 11).

[13] Vertinsky and Rice, 'Thinking About Thinking Machines' (n 11) 574.

[14] 'Request for comments on patenting artificial intelligence inventions' (*Federal Register*, 27 August 2019) <https://www.federalregister.gov/documents/2019/08/27/2019-18443/request-for-comments-on-patenting-artificial-intelligence-inventions>.

patent prosecution, merely by the fact that it now employs new advancements in digital technology like blockchain and AI? To appreciate this hypothesis, we need to focus on the changes the new technology brings to the backend work on a patent, ie, the work that goes into creating the representation (patent drafting) and the work that goes into verifying and certifying the representation (patent prosecution).

We need to first look at how the change in representation of images in photography evolved over the years, from analogue to digital and observe its impact on the evolution of photography. We notice a similar shift in photography—from chemical process to a digital process—without any change in the final representation of the image. The comparison with photography is for the limited purpose of understanding the concept that though the external representation of the output, ie, the patent specification in the case of an invention, remains the same in the case of a textualized invention or a digitalized invention, the backend work can be substantially different.

Analogue photography and digital photography both use the same principle and can give the same results: capturing the image on a light-sensitive screen using a camera and representing them on paper. But how the result is achieved is remarkably different. Analogue photography or traditional photography is characterized by the black-and-white negative-positive system.[15] It is a predominantly chemical process where the images are captured on a photographic film made up of layers of light-sensitive silver halide emulsion coated on a flexible base, by exposing the film to light in a camera.[16] The film is later developed by immersion in a 'developer' solution and prints are made by projecting the image from the film on sensitized paper and processing the material in chemical baths, much of the processing happening in a darkened environment to avoid other light sources reaching the sensitive emulsions.[17] There were some developments to make the backend process faster. Edwin H. Land, the inventor of the Polaroid system of instant photography, conceived and perfected the art of instant photography, thereby reducing the time taken for developing the photographs, by compressing the darkroom processes into an integrated film unit which produced the final outcome photograph in few seconds.[18] Though the change introduced by Polaroid was transformational,

[15] Helmut Erich Robert Gernsheim and Andrew Mannheim, 'Technology of Photography' (*Encyclopedia Britannica*, no date) <https://www.britannica.com/technology/technology-of-photography> (hereafter Robert and Mannheim, 'Technology of Photography').

[16] Canon Europa N. V. and Canon Europe Ltd 2002–17, 'Differences between Analogue and Digital' (*Canon Professional Network*, no date) https://cpn.canon-europe.com/content/education/infobank/introduction_to_digital_photography/differences_between_analogue_and_digital.do (hereafter Canon Europa N V and Canon Europe Ltd 2002–17, 'Differences').

[17] Ibid.

[18] 'Edwin Land and Instant Photography' (*American Chemical Society*, no date) <https://www.acs.org/content/acs/en/education/whatischemistry/landmarks/land-instant-photography.html> (hereafter 'Edwin Land and Instant Photography').

Polaroid as a business ran into trouble when things got digital.[19] Eventually, the digitalization of photography accentuated by digital cameras made Polaroid cameras obsolete.[20]

Digital photography, on the other hand, offers an entirely different process that eliminates the need to have any chemicals and dark rooms, by capturing images with arrays of photo sensors, processing them with computer software, and printing them with tiny jets of coloured ink or dyes on photo paper.[21] Though the two processes are substantially different, the net result appears to be the same to the lay viewer—an image printed on photographic paper. But the genius of digital photography is in what can happen after the image is captured and processed by computer software. The digital technology allows the images to be represented as software, enabling them to be stored indefinitely, shared through different media, reproduced and edited digitally. The digital form also allowed software to 'search' the images and harness intelligent output from the images, like the face recognition system. Digital photography also contributed to the ubiquitousness of photography by bringing affordable, quality technology to the common people. It substantially reduced the backend work, eliminating the need for equipment, films, chemicals, and dark rooms—and the accompanying investments in materials, space, and time—that characterized analogue photography.

The impact of digital photography on analogue photography is best summed up by destinies of Kodachrome film and Polaroid cameras, the two icons of analogue photography. In the case of Kodachrome, the film manufactured by Eastman Kodak, when the product was finally retired by the company, an observer wrote its obituary in the Telegraph with the title, 'Kodachrome is killed by its digital offspring'.[22] And as another observer puts it, 'Polaroid went from ubiquity to obsolescence as digital photography replaced the print'.[23]

[19] Polaroid started off as an iconic company that introduced instant photography but went through bad phases in the later stages. It went bankrupt twice and was bought and sold. Harry McCracken, 'Polaroid's Newest Gadget Gives Analog Life to Smartphone Photos' (*Fast Company*, 10 September 2019) <https://www.fastcompany.com/90401054/polaroids-newest-gadget-gives-analog-life-to-smartphone-photos>.The last Polaroid factory in the Netherlands discontinued its production in 2008 and was acquired by a startup called The Impossible Project which had as its goals the saving of the factory and the reinvention of instant films for Polaroids. Erin Schulte, 'How The Impossible Project Gave Polaroid Cameras A New Lease On Life' (*Fast Company*, 12 March 2013) <https://www.fastcompany.com/3006865/how-impossible-project-gave-polaroid-cameras-new-lease-life>.

[20] Polaroid did attempt to combine analogue instant photography and digital photography in some of its products like the Polaroid Pic-300 and Z2300. Lisa Evans, 'How Polaroid saved itself from certain death' (*Fast Company*, 15 May 2014) <https://www.fastcompany.com/3030562/how-polaroid-saved-itself-from-certain-death>.

[21] Canon Europa N V and Canon Europe Ltd 2002–17, 'Differences' (n 16).

[22] Jeff Segal, 'Kodachrome is killed by its digital offspring' (*The Telegraph*, 24 June 2009) <https://www.telegraph.co.uk/finance/newsbysector/mediatechnologyandtelecoms/5621307/Kodachrome-is-killed-by-its-digital-offspring.html>.

[23] Andrea Nagy Smith, 'What was Polaroid thinking?' (*Yale Insights*, 4 November 2009) <https://insights.som.yale.edu/insights/what-was-polaroid-thinking>.

2.1.1 Image as software

Digital photographs are images stored digitally in the form of software.[24] The images can be stored in reusable and transferable memory cards, as opposed to film, which makes them easy to reuse and transfer. The image is captured in a digital camera as a RAW file, the uncompressed format that camera manufacturers use, some of which are unique and proprietary, and rendered in different formats such as JPEG, PNG, GIF, MNG, or TIFF.[25] Digital photography allows images to be subject to everything that software can do—store them on recordable media, transfer them, digitally edit them, subject them to analytics, among other things. With the use of photo-editing software like Adobe Photoshop, editing photographs—a process that was previously thought to be sacrilege and technically infeasible—became acceptable and practicable.[26]

2.1.2 Ubiquitousness and affordability

The omnipresence of smart phones is proof of the reach of digital photography. Everyone is a photographer today. Digital photography, apart from revolutionizing the manner in which images are captured, processed, stored, edited, and transferred, significantly brought down the cost of photography by eliminating films, chemicals, equipment, and the accompanying processing costs. There was no need to go to a photo studio to get a quality photograph as there was no longer the need to rely on an expert who could 'capture' and 'develop' the film into a picture—digital photography gave the power to the people. The ability to copy, edit, and transfer the image file without the loss of quality, made the technology ubiquitous and accessible to non-experts. It decentralized the backend process in photography.

2.1.3 Reduction of backend work

Analogue photography was traditionally beset with delay between the exposure and the availability of the processed picture. One of the biggest contributions of digital photography was to reduce the time between the exposure and the final outcome by eliminating much of the backend work. There is no need for the 'development' of photographs and the various processes of fixing, washing, drying, enlarging, and printing associated with it.[27] The darkroom of photography no longer exits. Digital photography, also rightfully referred to as instant photography,[28] changed

[24] Mike Dooly, 'Digital photography in airplane maintenance' <https://www.boeing.com/commercial/aeromagazine/aero_01/textonly/m01txt.html>.

[25] Mark Ferrara and David Germano, 'Digital image formats' (*Tibetan & Himalayan Library Toolbox*) <https://collab.its.virginia.edu/wiki/toolbox/Digital%20Image%20Formats.html>.

[26] Some restrictions exist in capturing photographs relating to news, sporting events, and wildlife. Melissa Groo, 'How to photograph wildlife ethically' (*Animals*, 31 July 2019) <https://www.nationalgeographic.com/animals/2019/07/ethical-wildlife-photography/>.

[27] Robert and Mannheim, 'Technology of Photography' (n 15).

[28] This is different from the earlier development in photography introduced by Polaroid, which was also referred to as instant photography. 'Edwin Land and Instant Photography' (n 18).

the process in a radical way. It shrunk the time taken for the entire backend work, which took hours to days in the case of analogue photography. The need for specialized equipment, expensive chemicals, complex light-sensitive films, darkened room, and experts with technical background on developing films was immediately eliminated by digital photography. Much of the backend work in digital photography is done by software and photo printers. With the advancements in digital cameras and photo printers, the production of good quality photographs is almost instantaneous.

In a similar manner, the change in the representation of the invention from textual to digital, has a tremendous impact on the backend process, not so much in the final outcome, which is the patent specification itself, but in the manner in which the backend process takes place. Similar to the image being rendered through software, the digitalized invention will be manifested through software, allowing it to be easily stored, copied, and reproduced. More importantly, the software foundation of the digitalized invention will allow for analytics, which would become the foundation for conducting the tests of novelty and inventive step by using AI. Like digital photography, the ubiquitousness and affordability of the process will render the power to do a machine-based patentability analysis to the users, who will now be able to judge the patentability of the invention before filing them in the patent office. The ability to verify the patentability of an invention, a power that is now vested solely with the patent office, will enable the users to proactively gauge their invention and perform the functions that the patent office would do during prosecution at the users' end. When such technology is made accessible to the masses, it would decentralize the role of the patent office and allows software-related analytics to carry out some of the traditional functions of prosecution by using AI. Just as the backend process becomes more efficient for digital photography when managed by software, we can expect patent prosecution to become more efficient for the digitalized invention, though the process for patents is admittedly more complicated and involves multiple parties: the inventor, the patent agent, and the patent office. However, before we look at how digital technology can change the backend process of the patent office, let us examine the brief history of the manner in which technology influenced the patent office and the way it functioned.

2.2 Patent Office Transformation: From Museum to Library to Machine

The transformation of the patent office, through the ages, can be explained through the metaphor of what it became. Early inventors had to submit working models to the patent office. In the nineteenth century, the ability to make miniature working models that could be presented as verifiable proofs of invention led to the patent office becoming a 'museum' of prior art. Later, with the textualization of the invention, the patent specification and the manner in which it could be recorded, stored, and accessed made the patent office a 'library' of records. With digitalization of patent office records and the prospect of empowering them with AI, the patent office of the future could become a 'machine'. The historical evolution of the patent office from a museum to a library and then to an AI machine has profound implications on the manner in which patents are searched and drafted. The legal fiction that created the 'person skilled in the art' for determining issues of validity and infringement will cast a shadow on all AI-generated inventions, if such a person can be deemed to be an AI-enabled machine.[29]

The history of patent prosecution can be studied in three parts based on how the invention was represented before the patent office: (1) the materialization of the invention, (2) the textualization of the invention, and (3) the digitalization of the invention.

2.2.1 Materialization of the invention

In the early days of the development of patent law, grants were focused on the actions of the individuals, on the things that they did. Patents evolved from royal privileges granted in Britain to promote actions aimed at instructing the English in a new industry.[30] The emphasis was on manufacture, as the grants could be forfeited on proof of defective manufacture, or on failure to practise the grant within the stipulated time.[31] Early patent systems existed as a means of technology transfer for introducing new industries and manufacturing techniques from abroad.[32] The privileges were offered as a means of attracting foreign talent but soon evolved to distribute talent within the country.[33] The territorial nature of the privileges became an impetus for people and ideas to move from one place to another. Privileges were different from exclusive rights as they were targeted towards skills rather than things.[34] The introduction of the new skill into the territory was more important than finding or creating the new object.[35]

[29] Ryan Abbott, 'Everything is Obvious' (2019) 66 University of California Los Angeles Law Review 2 (hereafter Abbott, 'Everything').

[30] E Wyndham Hulme, 'History of the Patent System Under the Prerogative and at Common Law' (1896) 12 Law Quarterly Review 141, 142 (hereafter Hulme, 'History of the Patent System').

[31] Ibid, 145, 146.

[32] Christine MacLeod, *Inventing the Industrial Revolution: The English Patent System, 1660–1800* (Cambridge University Press 1988) 12–13 (hereafter MacLeod, *Inventing the Industrial Revolution*).

[33] Ibid, 40 ('[P]atents ceased to be the perquisite of courtiers, office-holders and immigrant tradesmen. They began to assume a more distinct and recognizable form as instruments of protection and competition among native inventors and entrepreneurs and, increasingly, if hesitantly, to leave London for the provinces').

[34] Alain Pottage and Brad Sherman, *Figures of Invention: A History of Modern Patent Law* (Oxford University Press 2010) 46 (hereafter Pottage and Sherman, *Figures of Invention*).

[35] Mario Biagioli, 'From Print to Patents: Living on Instruments in Early Modern Europe' (2006) 44 History of Science 139, 151.

The early grants had 'training clauses' as witnessed in some of the early licences granted to foreigners with stipulations that they train at least two natives in the art or with a condition of employing and instructing an apprentice of local origin for every foreigner employed.[36] One can see the early signs of the development of the modern day requirement of reduction of the invention to writing in the instances where the secrets of manufacture had to be reduced in writing.[37] Training of apprentices was an important element of the patent system. The primary mode of dissemination of the information, in modern terminology the discharge of the teaching function, was by personal demonstration.[38]

In the US, early patents were granted without any examination into the technical merits of the invention.[39] The US insisted on a primitive version of the patent specification and even provided copies of the patent specification and the models to the public.[40] Examination of the patent specification took a back seat, as the patent office could not cope up with the increasing number of applications filed. This brought the role of the models into prominence. Since models were seen as more authentic embodiments of the invention than the patent specification, the Patent Act of 1836 required applicants to submit models.[41] Models disclosed the invention and did the task of the textual description by enabling a person skilled in the art to make or use the invention. Prior art analysis comprised of comparing the invention with earlier models as they were generally accepted as undisputable proof of invention.[42] The collection of models at the patent office for public display made it the 'veritable museum of American technology'.[43] Models also performed the teaching function as they were seen as a means of instruction to the public,[44] as they were more direct in conveying inventiveness than text.[45]

The reliance on models declined due to a combination of administrative and technology-related issues. Preservation of models became difficult due to the

[36] Hulme, 'History of the Patent System' (n 30) 145, 147–8.

[37] Ibid, 145 (noting an early licence granted by the Crown for the manufacture of saltpeter in the UK requiring the 'secrets of manufacture' to be reduced in writing before the promised reward of £300 was paid).

[38] MacLeod, *Inventing the Industrial Revolution* (n 32) 49.

[39] B Zorina Khan and Kenneth L Sokoloff, 'Patent Institutions, Industrial Organization and Early Technological Change: Britain and the United States, 1790–1850' in Maxine Berg and Kristine Bruland (eds), *Technological Revolutions in Europe: Historical Perspectives* (Edward Elgar Publishing 1998) 292, 295.

[40] B Zorina Khan, *The Democratization of Invention: Patents and Copyrights in American Economic Development, 1790–1920* (Cambridge University Press 2005) 59 (hereafter Khan, *The Democratization of Invention*).

[41] Dood, 'Patent Models' (n 1) 210 (noting that written description and the drawings, which existed as parallel requirements along with the submission of models, had to convey more information than in the models).

[42] Ibid, 211.

[43] Eugene S Ferguson, *Little Machines: Patent Models in the Nineteenth Century* (Hagley Museum 1979) 11.

[44] Pottage and Sherman, *Figures of Invention* (n 34) 87, Sean B. Seymore, 'The Teaching Function of Patents' (2009–10) 85 Notre Dame Law Review 621.

[45] Dood, 'Patent Models' (n 1) 197.

recurrent fires at the USPTO. In 1836, a fire at the USPTO destroyed as many as 7,000 models, while others degenerated due to natural causes as the space for preserving them put constraints on the patent office.[46] On the technical side, as texts and drawings conveniently described the invention and replaced models as a more convenient and easily communicable description of the invention, the need for storing and upkeeping them reduced. The law changed to accommodate this development with the 1870 Act ending the need to submit models.[47] The second fire at the USPTO in 1877 destroyed around 76,000 models.[48] Due to the increasing administrative expenses involved in storage and upkeep of the models, the patent office decided to dispose of all the models.[49]

2.2.2 Textualization of the invention

The early manifestations of the patent specifications were not structured as documents with disclosure performing the teaching function, as their purpose was to stop competitors from acquiring British technology.[50] Filing a patent specification started off as a post-grant obligation on the inventor who was required to make a detailed description of the invention within a few months after the grant of the patent.[51]

In Britain, the need to make a full disclosure of the invention came after the decision in *Liardet v Johnson*.[52] The decision required the inventor to make an enabling disclosure, a full description that would enable anyone skilled in the art to make the invention.[53] The disclosure was seen as a *quid pro quo* for the grant of the patent.[54] The evolution of the minimal patent specifications also shifted the responsibility from the patent office which granted them to the courts which had to decide cases on infringement.[55]

The advent of the patent specification introduced a change in the representation of the invention from material to textual and facilitated the transition of the patent system from being registration-centric with minimal or no examination of applications to an examination-centric system with substantial examination. This change in the representation of the invention which required a more detailed examination also led the patent office to develop standards of examinations such as the standards of novelty and inventive step.

46 Pottage and Sherman, *Figures of Invention* (n 34) 93–4.
47 Ibid, 94.
48 Ibid.
49 Ibid, 96.
50 MacLeod, *Inventing the Industrial Revolution* (n 32) 51.
51 Ibid, 41.
52 (1778) 481 NB 173 (KB).
53 Adams and Averley, 'The Patent Specification' (n 7) 171.
54 MacLeod, *Inventing the Industrial Revolution* (n 32) 49.
55 Ibid, 51.

Patent prosecution achieved its modern incarnation in the latter half of the nineteenth century,[56] with the shift in depiction of the creative labour embodied in the manufactured product or process—the material embodiment—to the description of the creative labour in writing—the textual embodiment. The new system gave importance to paper description of the invention.[57] This shift required the new patent regimes to capture the inventive idea in writing in the form of the patent specification.[58] The paper form of the invention allowed for representative registration to dispense with the need to submit models, making the patent specification a reference point to ascertain the inventiveness.[59] The representative registration made possible by the written description of the invention built a prosecution system that came to be focused solely on the ways in which the patent specification was drafted, registered, and interpreted.[60]

The written representation of the invention allowed the intangible property to be presented in a format that was stable and indefinitely repeatable,[61] providing a reference point to ascertain the identity of the intangible.[62] The written representation shifted the burden of proving the invention from the inventor to the administrative agencies, thereby requiring the patent office to develop various standards for ascertaining patentability.[63]

Models were perceived as authentic embodiments of inventions but they were deficient when it came to verifying them. The simultaneous usage of models and patent specification at the same time as proofs of invention posed some problems. The evidentiary value of models eventually diminished towards the end of the nineteenth century when they were seen as compromising the textual certainty of the patent specification.[64] When the text and the drawings replaced the function of models, the patent office shifted its focus to substantive examination of patent applications. This was done as the patent documents began to reach the courts as records of the decisions of the patent office on novelty or adequacy of disclosure.[65]

Patent prosecution became a matter of public concern as the patent system symbolized a form of public memory.[66] As the registration process shifted the focus from the created object to the representation of the created object, the need to evolve standards for managing and demarcating the limits of the intangible property arose.[67] The patent system became dependent on paper inscriptions which

[56] Sherman and Bently (n 3) 192.
[57] Ibid, 181–2.
[58] Pottage and Sherman, *Figures of Invention* (n 34) 46.
[59] Sherman and Bently (n 3) 182.
[60] Ibid, 186.
[61] Ibid, 181.
[62] Ibid, 186.
[63] Ibid.
[64] Pottage and Sherman, *Figures of Invention* (n 34) 107, 108.
[65] Ibid, 119.
[66] Sherman and Bently (n 3) 71, 72.
[67] Ibid, 4–5.

facilitated the classification, measurement, and communication of intangible property.[68] It was also built on the system of priority and first filing to prove ownership, which later manifested into the first-to-file system. The examination system propelled a centralized patent office as it reduced uncertainty about the validity of patents and achieved the economies of scale in certification.[69]

2.2.3 Digitalization of the invention

Digitalization of the invention refers to the process of converting the patent specification into digital form.[70] The digitalized invention, or more precisely, the digital representation of the invention before the patent office, when stored as a transparent, trustworthy, and secure record by means of technology like the blockchain would make it easier for establishing disclosure, priority, and ownership of inventions.[71] The digitalized invention will not be a mere digital version of the textualized invention, ie, an algorithmic version of the printed document. Rather, it would be a version created on a digital platform using distributed ledger technology like blockchain and integrated to AI systems.[72] Such a digital version of the invention may not be available today. But there are clear signs in other legal fields such as IP management and contract drafting where the technology has already been implemented.[73]

Patent systems that recognize and attribute priority based on blockchain disclosure would make disclosures public, immutable, and trustworthy, thereby reducing the need to make the first disclosure to the patent office to preserve priority. A patent system that recognized a blockchain disclosure of an invention would shift the focus of disclosure made to the patent office to disclosure made to the world at large. The digitalized invention would facilitate simultaneous filing in different jurisdictions and would not require the eighteen-month secrecy period for publication. We have seen the patent system move away from the first-to-invent system to the first-to-file system, a move necessitated by the changes in technology that facilitates record keeping and efficient filing. The digitalized invention would

[68] Ibid, 72.

[69] Khan, *The Democratization of Invention* (n 40) 60.

[70] 'Definition of DIGITALIZATION' (*Merriam Webster*) <https://www.merriam-webster.com/dictionary/digitalization>.

[71] Blockchain is a shared, immutable ledger for recording transactions which can be effective in tracking assets and building trust. 'What is blockchain technology?' (*IBM*, 3 January 2020) <https://www.ibm.com/blockchain/what-is-blockchain>.

[72] Distributed ledgers are a type of database that is spread across multiple sites, countries, and institutions and is usually public. Mark Walport, 'Distributed ledger technology: beyond block chain' (*Government Office for Science*) <https://www.gov.uk/government/news/distributed-ledger-technology-beyond-block-chain>.

[73] Toni Nijm, 'Will blockchain fundamentally change IP management?' (*CPA Global*, 19 October 2018) <https://www.cpaglobal.com/cpa-global-blog/will-blockchain-fundamentally-change-ip-management>, 'Blockchain technology for digital contracting | Accenture' (*Accenture*) <https://www.accenture.com/gr-en/case-studies/about/blockchain-contracts-harnessing-new-technology>.

take the patent system to the next phase of patent filing: a first-to-disclose system and the first disclosure need not be a disclosure made to the patent office.[74]

The digitalized invention would also make the digital representation of the invention amenable to analysis by AI systems. When the digitalized invention can be subject to AI system, machine analysis of the invention description would be possible. Machine prosecution—AI-enabled prosecution of the digital representation of the invention—would change the manner in which the traditional tests of patent law are applied: the analysis of novelty, inventive step, fair basis, antecedent basis, succinctness, enabling disclosure, etc would change. Some of the changes to the traditional tests will occur be due to the change in the concept of the person skilled in the art.[75] When AI-enabled systems are accessible to the person skilled in the art, the manner in which we understand the standards of novelty, inventive step, and enablement is bound to change. Some of the tests, such as the inventive step test, will become a two-fold analysis: the machine inventive step analysis followed by, where necessary, the human inventive step analysis. Such a bifurcation of the analysis will be necessitated by the separation of tasks that can be efficiently and completely performed by machines and those that would require a further human intervention.

As AI would be able to do a part of the patent prosecution that is now being done by the patent office, the question that would arise is why should these tests remain the sole prerogative of the patent office? Some of these tests, insofar as they can be conducted efficiently and completely by machines, can be conducted at the user's end (inventor), even at the time of drafting the patent specification, when the AI-enabled patent prosecution systems are widely available to the general public. For instance, the test of antecedent basis can be easily spotted and corrected by an AI-enabled writing tool. Similarly, given the state of current technology, it is possible to have AI-enabled real-time novelty checks while the patent is being drafted, as the databases on which novelty checks are made are mostly online. When the digitalized invention is combined with AI-enabled systems that can run these tests at the user's end, this would eventually lead to the patent office losing some of its traditional functions in prosecution. The test of novelty, which even with the current levels of technology is a predominantly machine-based test, would be much better achieved at the user's end and should not be a burden on the patent office to check. Novelty would cease to be a requirement in patent law which the patent office has to detect, analyse, and approve. A decentralized patent office of the future will specialize in the functions that can only be done solely by humans, once the machine

[74] Jurisdictions such as the US, Japan, and India that recognize a grace period do not require the first disclosures to be made to the patent office. Chiara Franzoni and Giuseppe Scellato, 'The Grace Period in International Patent Law and Its Effect on the Timing of Disclosure' (2010) 39 Research Policy 200.

[75] Abbott, 'Everything' (n 29).

analysis is done, thereby making patent prosecution quicker, efficient, and less susceptible to errors.

3. The Digitalized Invention: The Frontier of New Technologies

The digitalized invention refers to the new form of representation of the invention before the patent office. The ingenuity of patent law lies in allowing a representation of invention, rather than the invention itself, to be presented before the patent office for the grant of a patent. As we have seen, in the early years of patent law, the representation of the invention was done by way of miniature working models. Later the representation of the invention changed as the patent office began to receive textual representation of the invention, instead of material representations. Now, the technologies that are available allow for a digital representation of the invention which is substantially different from the textual representation of the invention. The digitalized invention is not merely a digital form of the patent specification that was originally rendered in print. Rather the digitalized invention is a ground-breaking way to represent the invention. Throughout history, the manner in which the invention was represented before the patent office impacted patent prosecution. When models were presented, prosecution was rudimentary. More recently, where the invention is presented textually, prosecution had to create various legal fictions to cope up with the demands of the system. These legal fictions include the hypothetical construct of the 'person skilled in the art' and the concepts tied to it like novelty, inventive step, and enablement. With the new form of representation, the digitalized invention is bound to affect patent prosecution in many intriguing ways.

3.1 A New Way to Represent the Invention

The digitalized invention is a digital representation of the invention with the use of new technologies. While it is hard to predict the future acceptance of the new technologies, any technology that can have an impact on the following three aspects can impact the digitalized invention. For the present, the emerging technologies will influence the digitalized invention in three aspects: (1) the manner in which it is created; (2) the manner in which the invention is presented in the digital medium; and (3) the manner in which the representation of the invention is verified.

3.1.1 Creation

The creation of the digitalized invention will be a departure from the traditional way in which patents are drafted. Most patents are drafted on word processing software. AI-enabled writing assistance software such as Grammarly utilizes machine learning to help writers through the various processes of research, spelling and grammar check, genre-specific writing style checks, offering tips for conciseness, readability and vocabulary enhancements, as well as detecting plagiarism.[76] The LexisNexis PatentOptimizer takes the game, especially with regard to drafting patents, a step forward. It not only streamlines the patent writing but also offers help in replying to office actions.[77] In a white paper published by LexisNexis, patent quality is defined as the relative ability of the granted patent to consistently meet the legal requirements of patentability, including utility, novelty, non-obviousness and written description, enablement and definiteness.[78] PatentOptimizer helps users to identify instances of a lack of sufficient description, vague and indefinite claim language, claim terms that lack proper antecedent basis, functional claim language without the recitation of corresponding structure in the specification for accomplishing the claimed function, and detecting and correcting inconsistent part names/numbers.[79]

Right now, the general writing software and the special patent drafting software are tuned towards reducing human error and easing manually intensive activities in writing. But soon with the implementation of effective AI-enabled tools, the software should be able to predict and suggest conflicting prior art while drafting the patent. Similar tools are available today in plagiarism detection software. The ability to simultaneously search the patent databases while the user is drafting the patent and suggest changes based on conflicting prior art and patent analytics, would result in more formidable patents that are less prone to objections at the patent office and challenges from the competitors. When AI-enabled writing assistance software is able to comprehensively search the prior art, research on the technological domain to identify white spaces, offer suggestions on scope of the claims, detect internal errors in the patent specification, provide technology-specific writing styles, and incorporate the legal requirements of patentability—all on the basis of inputs on the invention from the inventor—the need to rely on intermediaries such as patent agents will substantially diminish. Thus, the creation of the patent will depart from the traditional norms, and empower the inventor to create and file patents without relying on an intermediary.

[76] 'Clean up your writing with grammarly premium' (*Grammarly*) <https://www.grammarly.com/premium>.

[77] 'Patent Application Software|LexisNexis PatentOptimizer®' (*LexisNexis® IP*) <https://www.lexisnexisip.com/products/patent-optimizer/>.

[78] Brian Elias and David Stitzel, 'Patent quality: it's now or never' (*LexisNexis® IP*) https://go.lexisnexisip.com/patentquality-white-paper-0.

[79] Ibid, 8.

3.1.2 Presentation

The presentation of the digitalized invention will seamlessly merge the message and the medium. The medium could well become the message as 'it is the medium that shapes and controls the scale and form of human association and action'.[80] The representation of the invention with decentralized technology such as blockchain can change the manner in which initial representation of the invention is made. The nature of the technology will focus on the time and propriety of the disclosure and not on the place or manner of disclosure. Patent laws today require, except in some cases involving a grace period, the first disclosure to be made to the patent office which acknowledges the filing with a date and time stamp. The use of blockchain technology will be relevant not only for making the initial disclosure of the invention which is tamperproof and verifiable, but also in helping all the future transactions relating to filing, prosecution, grant, and commercialization (licensing) to happen on the same source. Web-based applications like Bernstein allow users to create a digital trail of records of their innovation and creation processes using Bitcoin blockchain and national timestamping authorities.[81] Applications like Bernstein can be used to certify disclosures at the user's end without the need to file a patent application before the patent office. The use of blockchain to register online can prove existence, ownership, and development of the initial disclosure into a full-fledged patent over time, which can be critical for disclosures made in the case of inventions.

3.1.3 Verification

Verification of the digitalized invention using AI holds much promise. AI tools can be used to save time and money by identifying whether those inventions are patentable.[82] Much of the time-consuming, labour-intensive tasks like prior art search, which relies on matching selected words to databases, can be done more efficiently by AI-enabled systems. AI can impact the manner in which patents are verified and prosecuted. It can also affect the manner in which patents are drafted, prior art reports are generated, and patent prosecution is done. In short, the digitalized invention will overturn established conventions relating to disclosures and how they are made, patent documents and how they are created, and the concept of 'person skilled in the art' and how it is employed to determine the standards of novelty, inventive step and enablement.

[80] Marshall McLuhan and Lewis H Lapham, *Understanding Media: The Extensions of Man*, reprint edn (The MIT Press 1994) 2.

[81] 'Bernstein—digital IP protection' (*Bernstein*) <https://www.bernstein.io>.

[82] 'Artificial intelligence will help to solve the USPTO's patent quality problem' (*IPWatchdog.com\ Patents & Patent Law*, 23 November 2019) <https://www.ipwatchdog.com/2019/11/23/artificial-intelligence-will-help-solve-usptos-patent-quality-problem/id=116302/>.

3.2 Digitalized Invention and Patent Law Reforms

The textual representation of the invention will be different from its digital manifestation. Since the rampant growth of ICT, the textual representation has seen many digital forms over time (scanned copy, html copy, pdf version, and other versions). It is difficult to draw a line to demarcate where the textual versions end and where the digital versions begin. In fact, the change from textual to digital is a gradual and ongoing process. By digitalized invention, we refer to the fully digital representation of the invention, which is digital in its creation, in its medium, and in its processing (prosecution using digital technologies). To be sure, such a version of the invention, as envisaged in this chapter, does not exist as yet. It will require the patent office and all the stakeholders to adopt new changes and technologies. The patent office system of receiving applications, processing them, granting them, etc have to be based on a technology which is decentralized and tamperproof. For now, we identify this with blockchain as it is the closest technology which can be implemented.

The digitalized version of the invention presents the greatest promise, not just in changing some aspects of patent prosecution, but also in changing the foundation of the entire patent system. Such a change is imperative. Patent law has faced severe criticism in its operating model largely due to quality issues. Some of those quality issues can be traced to the manner in which the textual representation allowed for certain legal fictions, such as the person skilled in the art, to operate.[83] The legal fictions and the gap they created allow the system to be exploited and manipulated.

Take, for instance, the evolution of the teaching function in patent law. Initially the teaching function was expressly mentioned in the patent-like royal privileges granted in the UK. It required the patentee to train two apprentices back to back, so as to transfer the expertise to locals.[84] During the age of the models, the teaching function was inbuilt into the working model, ie, the fact that the model worked was meant to be the teaching. Early patent law also required the patent to be worked locally, which is still a requirement is certain jurisdictions, and not working the patent could be a reason for grant of compulsory licence. When the textualized invention came into prominence, there was no need to present a working model. If the person disclosed the manner in which the patent worked (how to work the invention was disclosed in writing), that was deemed to substitute the actual working of the invention. While this was easier to do and saved the patent office from the responsibility of scrutinizing every invention and its working, it shifted the burden on the competitors to challenge it. When a patent did not have an enabling disclosure, it was left to a third party—since the patent office is technically not the person skilled in the art, there is a greater chance for it to overlook this—to bring

[83] Feroz Ali, *The Access Regime* (n 4) 34.
[84] Hulme, 'History of the Patent System' (n 30) 141, 145.

this up and challenge the patent either before the patent office or the court. In effect, the textual description shifted the burden of proving the counter fact that the invention did not work on the patent office initially and then on the person affected by the patent, in the long term. The relaxed requirement that one did not have to make the invention work or demonstrate the working in any place, led to the filing of prospective patents (as explained by the prospect theory) and the problem of non-practising entities.[85] Thus, the representation of the invention can be seen as the root cause for some of the modern-day problems in patent law. And the manner in which the invention is represented, insofar as it can clear up some of the troubling issues in patent law, is a change that should be welcomed. This does not mean all the issues that adversely affect the patent system can be swept away in one broad stroke by the implementation of this change and technology. One can agree with Fritz Machlup and lament over the impossibility of patent reform, which he said, for better or for worse, would be an irresponsible thing to do.[86] However, some of the critical issues pertaining to the disclosure and person skilled in the art could be impacted by bringing in changes using new technology.

3.3 The Mechanics of the Digitalized Invention

The digitalized invention will be built on new technology. The type of technology will be hard to predict given the scale at which new technologies are opening up. However, given the impact of new technologies that we know so far on the representation of the invention, we can make broad estimates as to what will be needed to create the new system.

3.3.1 Universal, user-centric, authenticated disclosure

There are questions that have disturbed patent law for a long time: Why does the inventor have to approach a third party to disclose his invention? Why does the patent office have to be the first place to make a disclosure to establish priority, which becomes the mechanism for establishing novelty? Why does a disclosure by an inventor become the reason for killing the novelty of his own invention when he does not take certain counter-intuitive precautions? Why is the verification by the patent office the only way to verify a disclosure? Why should there be a race to the patent office for seeking priority, which now characterizes the first-to-file system?

[85] Edmund W Kitch, 'The Nature and Function of the Patent System' (1977) 20 Journal of Law & Economics 265.

[86] Fritz Machlup, *An Economic Review of the Patent System* (Washington 1958). 'If we did not have a patent system, it would be irresponsible, on the basis of our present knowledge of its economic consequences, to recommend instituting one. But since we have had a patent system for a long time, it would be irresponsible, on the basis of our present knowledge, to recommend abolishing it.' Ibid, 80.

The technology employed should address these fundamental issues. The new system will need to be universal, user-centric, and user-authenticated. This will allow the user to create the first version of the representation of the invention and to present the first version of the invention to the world, at his or her discretion. For the world to verify and check the authenticity of the invention without the need for a third-party verifier, the technology used should be tamperproof, enable verification, and be capable of creating an unalterable timestamp. More importantly, the source on which the first disclosure is made should be dynamic enough to form the ground for every other action, be it prosecution actions, licensing, revocation, etc., so that every transaction relating to a patent can be found in one place. By implementing this technological change, the entire public information on priority document, prosecution history, amendments, licensing, and termination, can be kept in one source. Any technology, in solo or in combination, that could produce these outcomes can be used.

3.3.2 Convergence of technologies: blockchain and AI

The digitalized invention will result from the convergence of technologies. Blockchain and AI show promise for becoming the foundational technologies on which the digitalized invention will be built. Blockchain technology shares the traits that would allow for a universal, user-centric, and user-authenticated disclosure. A blockchain is defined as a timestamped series of immutable records of data that is managed by a cluster of computers not owned by any single entity.[87] Since each of these blocks of data (ie, block) is secured and bound to each other using cryptographic principles (ie, chain), it is embedded with an uncharacteristic trait not found in digital records, ie, the trait of immutability. The fundamental characteristics of blockchain, namely, decentralization, pseudonymity/anonymity, immutability, and automation, can fundamentally change the way in which patent office operates.[88] Blockchain allows digital information to be distributed but not copied.[89] The use of blockchain goes beyond cryptocurrency, the use for which it was initially meant for.

Since the blockchain network is distributed, there is no need for a centralized authority. Patents specifications disclosed on blockchain will reduce the function of the patent office, and we will see a more decentralized patent system where disclosure and patentability analysis are done at the user's end. Transparency will be enhanced since the shared and immutable ledger is open for verification by anyone. Blockchain does not have any transaction cost, though there is a cost for setting up

[87] Ameer Rosic, 'What is blockchain technology? A step-by-step guide for beginners' (*Blockgeeks*, 18 September 2016) <https://blockgeeks.com/guides/what-is-blockchain-technology/> (hereafter Rosic, 'What is Blockchain Technology?').

[88] The European Union Blockchain Observatory and Forum, 'Legal and Regulatory Framework of Blockchains and Smart Contracts' (2019) 5.

[89] Rosic, 'What is Blockchain Technology?' (n 87).

the system, ie, the infrastructure cost. Information shared on a blockchain network exists as a shared and continually updated database, allowing amendments and changes to be done with a detailed record of every transaction. Every patent will come along with its prosecution history.

Blockchain uses the cryptographic hash function to maintain immutability of its records. Hashing is the process of taking an input string of any length and giving out an output of a fixed length. This allows any amount of information to be stored as an input string, whereas the output string will be of the same size, ie, fixed 256-bits length.[90] Blockchain is also characterized by the 'avalanche effect', the property of a small change in the input string leading to a substantial change in the output string. Blockchain contains the data and a hash pointer. The hash pointer, rather than just containing the address of the previous block, also contains the hash of the data inside the previous block.[91]

For the representation of an invention that is as dynamic as the one described above, the manner in which the invention is drafted and prosecuted will have to change. A technology that helps the user to create an immutable disclosure, that allows the user to check whether the disclose is unique and complies with the principles of patent law (novelty, inventive step, and utility), and that allows the user to check and fine tune her invention, before she discloses it to the world, will require employing blockchain at the systemic level.

While blockchain would form the basic substrate for the representation of the invention, AI will make machine prosecution a reality. As a branch of computer science, AI is concerned with the automation of intelligent behaviour.[92] AI refers to the ability of digital computers and computer systems to perform tasks commonly associated with intelligent beings such as the ability to reason, discover meaning, generalize, or learn from past experience.[93] AI systems are prediction machines that make decisions based on data.[94] The bigger the data set, the better the predictions. Problem-solving is a defining trait of AI, which can be characterized as a systematic search through a range of possible actions in order to reach some predefined goal or solution. For problem-solving, one of the general-purpose techniques that AI uses is the means-end analysis—a step-by-step, or incremental, reduction of the difference between the current state and the final goal. In prosecuting patents, the means-end analysis will be critical in applying the tests of novelty and inventive step.

[90] Bitcoin uses the hashing algorithm SHA-256.

[91] Rosic, 'What is Blockchain Technology?' (n 87).

[92] George F Luger, *Artificial Intelligence: Structures and Strategies for Complex Problem Solving* (6th edn, Pearson Addison-Wesley 2009) 1.

[93] BJ Copeland, 'Artificial intelligence | definition, examples, and applications' (*Encyclopedia Britannica*) <https://www.britannica.com/technology/artificial-intelligence>.

[94] Ajay Agrawal and others, *Prediction Machines: The Simple Economics of Artificial Intelligence* (Harvard Business Review Press 2018).

4. Machine Prosecution and Decentralization

The impact of new technology on patent prosecution can be studied in the manner in which two leading technologies of our times, namely blockchain and AI, affect the development of prosecution. The new technologies will impact patent prosecution in two significant ways. First, it will enable machine prosecution, ie, prosecution of patents using AI and machine learning without human intervention. Second, the wide use of these technologies and the limited role played by humans will result in the decentralization of the functions of the patent office. Both machine prosecution and decentralization of the patent office functions will have a bearing on how the traditional concepts of novelty, inventive step, disclosure, and enablement are understood.

4.1 Novelty

The traditional understanding of novelty, which has been the preliminary step towards patentability for many decades, will be the first casualty of machine prosecution. Novelty will cease to be a requirement of patentability that needs to be checked by the patent office. Machine prosecution will do away with the novelty test which is heavily reliant on searching and matching words on a database, a function where machines can outperform humans. The ability to automate the novelty search will also move the test from being a patentability requirement checked by the patent office to a due diligence measure that can be done at the user's end. Patent application software, like LexisNexis PatentOptimizer can have built in novelty checks that can be performed while the patent specification is drafted or when a copy of the patent specification is uploaded onto the software.

4.2 Inventive Step

With the requirement of novelty out of the way, the focus of patent prosecution will be to check if the inventive step requirement is satisfied. Here again, the availability of AI and machine learning is likely to render most inventions obvious. Just as the standard of person skilled in the art is likely to change to include a combination of humans and machines,[95] the test of inventive step will now factor in both machine intelligence and human intelligence. It is expected that machine intelligence will complement human intelligence rather than compete with it. It will be hard to rely entirely on algorithms for interpretation of grave matters involving life and death

[95] Abbott, 'Everything' (n 29).

like radiology scans and it will be difficult to depend on machines in matters that involve human expert contextualization.[96] Since the subject matter of patents is human creativity, it is unlikely that we will defer the decision to machines and be content with the decisions taken by them. Human scrutiny will be required to take a final call on whether to grant a patent or not.

4.3 Disclosure

Disclosure principle in patent law in counter-intuitive. An inventor is not expected to know the law with regard to experimental use and when public use can affect the novelty of his invention.[97] Disclosure, when done without taking proper precautions, can make the invention invalid.[98] In a decentralized system, disclosure can now be used strategically and done by the user. Since every disclosure is protected and authenticated, they will perform the role of marking the priority of inventions. There will not be any need to prove disclosure. The disclosure itself, when it is made through a digitalized invention, will be proof that can be verified.

4.4 Enablement

Any technology that can machine-read the instructions contained in the digitalized invention and translate them to human-readable form, if needed, or create the invention from those instructions, should satisfy the enablement requirement. The blueprint used for 3D printing is a good example. 3D-printed guns can be manufactured completely based on the blueprint. If the blueprint is supplied, it should be taken as having discharged the requirement of disclosure. The fact that the invention now not only comes with instructions on how to make it but is ready in a machine-readable format, would make the enablement a perfect one.

Thus, the patent system which uses blockchain and AI will be a decentralized, user-centric system. Just as blockchain is expected to fundamentally change the banking system by eliminating the banks as the middlemen who handle money, a similar change can be expected in the patent office with the advent of machine-assisted prosecution of patents. But unlike banks, patent offices are not just repositories of intellectual property, they are also the arbiters and assessors of inventions. Though we can expect the final discretionary functions of granting and rejecting patents to be done by humans, the structure of the patent system would be a

[96] Abbott, 'I Think' (n 11).

[97] *Lough v Brunswick Corp* 86 F.3d 1113, 1124 (Fed. Cir. 1996) (Plager, J., dissenting).

[98] Ibid, where the Federal Circuit held that Lough did not keep adequate documentation to show that the prototypes he disclosed to the public more than a year before filing the patent was done for testing purposes.

decentralized one. As publicly accessible distributed ledgers, blockchain can make record keeping more efficient and AI and machine learning can constantly evolve and improve with the systemic needs. The digitalized invention will revolutionize the patent system by eliminating its human frailties: time delays, fraud, and judgemental errors, all of which have plagued the existing patent system.

PART III

ARTIFICIAL INTELLIGENCE AND COPYRIGHT LAW

7

Do Androids Dream of Electric Copyright?

Comparative Analysis of Originality in Artificial Intelligence Generated Works

*Andres Guadamuz**

1. Introduction

We are living through a revolution in the production of artistic, literary, and musical works that have been generated in some shape or form by artificial intelligence (AI). Take the following paragraph:

> One can have many opinions and still have strong values and morals. The phrase 'all opinions are equal' is only the correct one when we understand that no opinion, no matter how stupid or contrary to reality, will ever be given any special place in our discussion. No one has the right to censor you because of your opinions . . .

This is a readable text, but it doesn't make much sense. You may expect it to come from a non-native speaker, or perhaps to be the ramblings of a bored Internet user. However, the text was generated by a language model called GPT-2, developed by Open AI.[1] This is just one of the many tools being developed that can produce uncanny works that mimic human creativity. Take two other Open AI tools, Musenet and Jukebox. Musenet can produce musical compositions for ten instruments having been trained in classical and popular music;[2] while Jukebox can produce music, lyrics, and singing in the style of several artists such as Elvis Presley and Katy Perry.[3]

Other AI-generated works have been widely reported in the press in recent years. For example, the AI painting called *Edmond de Belamy*[4] made the news

* This article was first published by Sweet & Maxwell in Intellectual Property Quarterly [IPQ 2017, 2, 169–86] and is reproduced by agreement with the publishers. This chapter is an update on the original. All online materials were accessed before 6 June 2020.

[1] The text was created by entering the text 'but this individualism is a sham' as prompt in 'Talk To Transformer', a GPT-2 model implementation <https://talktotransformer.com/>.

[2] MuseNet <https://openai.com/blog/musenet/>.

[3] Jukebox <https://openai.com/blog/jukebox/>.

[4] Obvious-art <https://obvious-art.com/edmond-de-belamy.html>.

Andres Guadamuz, *Do Androids Dream of Electric Copyright?* In: *Artificial Intelligence and Intellectual Property.* Edited by: Jyh-An Lee, Reto M Hilty, and Kung-Chung Liu, Oxford University Press (2021). © The several contributors.
DOI: 10.1093/oso/9780198870944.003.0008

when it was sold in an auction for USD 432,500.[5] The painting was made by the French art collective Obvious using a machine learning algorithm designed specifically to generate images, known as a Generative Adversarial Network (GAN). The artists fed the AI over 15,000 portraits from various epochs, and produced a set of portraits of the fictional Belamy family.[6]

Another landmark in AI creativity took place in 2016, when a group of museums and research institutions in the Netherlands, in conjunction with Microsoft, unveiled a portrait entitled 'The Next Rembrandt'.[7] This is not a newly found painting by Rembrandt Harmenszoon van Rijn, nor it is an imitation as such. What makes this portrait unique is that it is presented as a new painting that could have been created by Rembrandt, as it was generated by a computer after painstakingly analysing hundreds of artworks by the Dutch Golden Age artist. The machine used something called 'machine learning'[8] to analyse technical and aesthetic elements in Rembrandt's works, including lighting, colouration, brushstrokes, and geometric patterns. The result is a painting where algorithms have produced a portrait based on the styles and motifs found in Rembrandt's art.

One could argue the artistic value of this endeavour,[9] but the technical achievement is ground-breaking. The researchers took in every Rembrandt painting pixel by pixel, and most of the decisions of what would make the final painting were made by the machine itself using pre-determined algorithms. In other words, this represents a computer's interpretation of what a typical Rembrandt painting should look like.

It may seem like this is just another technical advance in a long line of computer-generated art, but what is really happening under the hood of artistic projects such as *The Next Rembrandt* displays a quantum leap in the way that we use machines. We are getting to the point at which vital creative decisions are not made by humans, rather they are the expression of a computer learning by itself based on a set of parameters pre-determined by programmers.

It is fair to point out that *The Next Rembrandt* has not been the subject of any legal scrutiny as of yet, and most of the examples that will be discussed in this chapter have not made it to court either. As far as we can tell, the programming team has not made any copyright claims over the painting; it is a project created as an advertisement of the technological capacities that gave rise to it, as it is funded and supported by commercial sponsors. Rembrandt's paintings are in the public

[5] AJ Dellinger, 'AI-generated painting sells for $432,000 at auction' (*Engadget*, 25 October 2018) <https://www.engadget.com/2018-10-25-ai-generated-painting-sells-for-432-000-at-auction.html>.

[6] Obvious-art <https://obvious-art.com/gallery-obvious/>.

[7] Microsoft, *The Next Rembrandt* (2017) <https://www.nextrembrandt.com/>.

[8] David E Goldberg and John H Holland, 'Genetic Algorithms and Machine Learning' (1988) 3 Machine Learning 95.

[9] Art critic Jonathan Jones calls it 'a new way to mock art'. J. Jones, 'The digital Rembrandt: a new way to mock art, made by fools' (*The Guardian*, 6April 2016) <https://www.theguardian.com/artanddesign/jonathanjonesblog/2016/apr/06/digital-rembrandt-mock-art-fools>.

domain, and there is likely not going to be any legal opposition to the project, or we are not likely to see this as a violation of moral rights. Nor are we likely to revisit questions of originality in the copies of public domain works that were explored in *Bridegman v Corel.*[10] However, both this project and Edmond de Belamy raise other interesting legal questions. Does this painting have copyright in its own right? If so, who owns it? If this project was based on the works of a living artist, could he or she object to the treatment in some manner? Would it be copyright infringement?

This chapter will consider the first question, namely the issue of whether computer-generated works have copyright protection. While the law about this type of creative work is answered satisfactorily in the UK, the treatment of such works is less clear in other jurisdictions, and there is still debate as to whether some computer works even have copyright in the first place. This chapter will make a comparative analysis of the law in the UK, Europe, Australia, China, and the US. This is becoming an important area of copyright, and one that has not been explored in depth in the literature.

2. Artificial Intelligence and the Law

2.1 Artificial Intelligence and Machine Learning

When we hear the term 'artificial intelligence', it is easy to think of it as a futuristic topic, and often the first image that comes to mind one of science fiction depictions of AI, either the human-like friendly android, or the killer robot. But if we understand artificial intelligence as 'the study of agents that exist in an environment and perceive and act',[11] it is possible to appreciate that this is a much broader area of study, and we already have various applications used in everyday life that meet the threshold of what is artificial intelligence. From search engine algorithms to predictive text in mobile phones, we are constantly interacting with AI.[12]

Of particular interest to the present chapter is the application of artificial intelligence in creative works such as art, computer games, film, and literature. There is a vibrant history of computer-generated art that takes advantage of different variations of AI algorithms to produce a work of art. The first military-grade computers were able to produce crude works of art, but these first efforts relied heavily

[10] *The Bridgeman Art Library Ltd v Corel Corp* 36 F.Supp 2d 191 (SDNY) [1999]. For an interesting discussion about this case, see R Deazley, 'Photographing Paintings in the Public Domain: A Response to Garnett' (2001) 23(4) European Intellectual Property Review 179.

[11] Stuart J Russell and Peter Norvig, *Artificial Intelligence: A Modern Approach* (3rd edn, Pearson 2010) 1.

[12] More technical details can be found in Anthony Man-Cho So, Chapter 1 in this volume.

on the input of the programmer.[13] During the 1970s, a new generation of programs that were more autonomous started making an appearance, with AARON, a project by artist Harold Cohen becoming one of the longest-running examples of the genre.[14] Later projects, such as e-David, made use of robot arms with real canvas and real colouring palettes.[15] The techniques used in some of these 'computer artists' vary from project to project, and while the aspiration of many of these is to be 'taken seriously ... as a creative artist',[16] most projects work either copying existing pictures, or almost directly guided by their programmers.

In the textual realm, renowned futurist Ray Kurzweil was granted a patent in the US for 'poet personalities',[17] protecting a method of generating an artificial poet capable of reading a poetry work, analysing the structure, and coming up with its own outputs. Kurzweil went to design a poet called Ray Kurzweil's Cybernetic Poet (RKCP), which reads an extensive selection of poems from an author, and then uses a type of neural network algorithm to produce recursive poetry that can 'achieve the language style, rhythm patterns, and poem structure of the original authors'.[18] The RKCP program produced a series of poems, the quality of which is debatable.

While interesting from an artistic and technical perspective, all of the above examples of computer art and literature rely heavily on the programmer's input and creativity. But the next generation of artificial intelligence artists are based on entirely different advances that make the machine act more independently, sometimes even making autonomous creative decisions. The field of machine learning is a subset of artificial intelligence that studies autonomous systems that are capable of learning without being specifically programmed.[19] The computer program has a built-in algorithm that allows it to learn from data input, evolving and making future decisions in ways that can be either directed, or independent.[20] There are various techniques that fall under the category of machine learning,[21] but for the

[13] Benj Edwards, 'The never-before-told story of the world's first computer art (it's a sexy dame)' (*The Atlantic*, 24 January 2013) <https://www.theatlantic.com/technology/archive/2013/01/the-never-before-told-story-of-the-worlds-first-computer-art-its-a-sexy-dame/267439/>.

[14] Harold Cohen, 'Parallel to Perception' (1973) 4 Computer Studies in The Humanities and Verbal Behavior 37.

[15] Oliver Deussen, Thomas Lindemeier, Sören Pirk, and Mark Tautzenberger, 'Feedback-guided Stroke Placement for a Painting Machine' (2012) in Proceedings of the Computational Aesthetics in Graphics Conference 2012.

[16] These are the words of The Painting Fool, an art project by Simon Colton, see The Painting Fool <http://www.thepaintingfool.com/>.

[17] US Patent 6, 647, 395.

[18] Ray Kurzweil, *The Age of Spiritual Machines: How We Will Live, Work and Think in the New Age of Intelligent Machines* (Texere 2001) 117.

[19] Jaime G Carbonell, Ryszard S Michalski, and Tom M Mitchell, *Machine Learning: An Artificial Intelligence Approach* (Tioga Publishing 1983) 4

[20] Donald Michie, David J Spiegelhalter, and Charles C Taylor, *Machine Learning, Neural and Statistical Classification* (Springer 1994).

[21] Pat Langley, 'The Changing Science of Machine Learning' (2011) 82 Machine Learning 275.

purpose of this chapter, we will concentrate on those which show potential for creative works.

One of the most exciting innovations in machine learning art comes in the shape of what is known as an artificial neural network, an artificial intelligence approach based on biological neural networks that use neuron equivalents based on mathematical models.[22] One such application in art is a Google project called Deep Dream,[23] a visualization tool that uses neural networks to create unique, bizarre, and sometimes unsettling images.[24] Deep Dream transforms a pre-existing image using machine learning mathematical methods that resemble biological neural networks, in other words, the machine mimics human thinking and makes a decision as to how to transform the input based on pre-determined algorithm. What is novel about Deep Dream, and other similar applications of neural networks, is that the program decides what to amplify in the image modification, so the result is unpredictable, but also it is a direct result of a decision made by the algorithm. The researchers explain:

> Instead of exactly prescribing which feature we want the network to amplify, we can also let the network make that decision. In this case we simply feed the network an arbitrary image or photo and let the network analyze the picture. We then pick a layer and ask the network to enhance whatever it detected. Each layer of the network deals with features at a different level of abstraction, so the complexity of features we generate depends on which layer we choose to enhance.[25]

The result of different levels of abstraction produce new images that do not resemble the originals, but most importantly, they are not the result of creative decisions by the programmers, but rather they are produced by the program itself.

Deep Mind, the Google company dedicated to the exploration of machine learning, has published a number of papers explaining the various experiences with artificial agents engaged in the development of art and music.[26] While Deep Dream has been widely publicized in the mainstream media, one of the most astounding projects involves music, and it is called WaveNet.[27] This is a project that was initially created to generate seamless artificial voice audio by using a machine learning algorithm that replicates how voices sound in real life, which tries to get

[22] Marilyn McCord Nelson and W.T. Illingworth, *A Practical Guide to Neural Nets* (Addison-Wesley 1991) 13.

[23] A Mordvintsev, 'Inceptionism: going deeper into neural networks' (*Google Blog*, 17 June 2015) <https://research.googleblog.com/2015/07/deepdream-code-example-for-visualizing.html> (hereafter Mordvintsev, 'Inceptionism').

[24] A collection of Deep Dream images <http://deepdreamgenerator.com/gallery/public/best-dreams>.

[25] Mordvintsev, 'Inceptionism' (n 23).

[26] See Deep Mind <https://deepmind.com/research/publications/>.

[27] A van den Oord and others, 'Wavenet: A Generative Model for Raw Audio' (2016), arXiv:1609.03499 [cs.SD].

past the mechanical sound when computers speak. What is interesting is that by analysing voice waves, Wavenet has learned also how to create music. When given a set of classical music to analyse, Wavenet produced completely generative piano compositions that would not be amiss in a sophisticated piano concerto, and that has been generated solely by the machine.[28] The technology is reaching a point where it might be difficult to tell a real composer from an automated agent.

Another relevant application of machine learning algorithms can be found in game development. There are already considerable applications of artificial intelligence in gaming,[29] but one of the most innovative is what is known as procedural generation, a method of creating content algorithmically.[30] The promise of this type of development is to have gaming environments created not by the programmers, but that the program itself based on pre-determined rules and algorithms. The potential is to have games with no end, where content is generated by the computer in a unique manner each time that the player logs in. This is already a reality in the blockbuster game *No Man's Sky*, where the program makes 'mathematical rules that will determine the age and arrangement of virtual stars, the clustering of asteroid belts and moons and planets, the physics of gravity, the arc of orbits, the density and composition of atmospheres'.[31] While the programmers set parameters, the machine literally builds new virtual worlds every time it runs.

As impressive as many of the above examples are, we are witnessing a revolution in the scope and capability of AI-generated works. A large number of creative works in recent years have been making use of advances in both computational power and increased sophistication in the existing algorithms. In particular, the emergence of Generative Adversarial Networks (GANs)[32] has heralded an explosion of AI-generated works due to a combination of availability—the underlying software is open source—and its effectiveness as a training model that learns from the inputs given to it. The secret to this model's success is in its name, the algorithm works by creating adversarial nets that try to compete with one another. As the authors of the model explain:

> The generative model can be thought of as analogous to a team of counterfeiters, trying to produce fake currency and use it without detection, while the

[28] Several samples can be found at Deep Mind <https://deepmind.com/blog/wavenet-generative-model-raw-audio/>.

[29] Donald Kehoe, 'Designing artificial intelligence for games' (Intel Developer Zone Papers, 20 June 2009) <https://software.intel.com/en-us/articles/designing-artificial-intelligence-for-games-part-1>.

[30] Daniel Ashlock, Colin Lee, and Cameron McGuinness, 'Search-based Procedural Generation of Maze-like Levels' (2011) 3(3) IEEE Transactions on Computational Intelligence and AI in Games 260, 264.

[31] Raffi Khatchadourian, 'World Without End: Creating a Full-scale Digital Cosmos' (2015) 91 The New Yorker 48.

[32] Ian J Goodfellow, Jean Pouget-Abadie, Mehdi Mirza, Bing Xu, David Warde-Farley, Sherjil Ozair, Aaron Courville, and Yoshua Bengio, 'Generative Adversarial Networks' (2014) arXiv:1406.2661 [stat.ML].

discriminative model is analogous to the police, trying to detect the counterfeit currency.[33]

The examples arising from GANs can be astounding. One project has been using GANs to successfully simulate photographs of human faces,[34] while another one has been producing photographs of non-existent bedrooms,[35] just to name a few. But GANs are just part of the equation, we are about to encounter more and more artistic implementations of artificial intelligence using various machine learning methods, and examples already abound, including music,[36] movie scripts,[37] and art installations.[38]

The common thread running through all of these applications is that most of the creative choices are no longer made by programmers, and a large part of what we would generally define as the creative spark comes from the machine.

2.2 Framing the Issue of Machine Learning and Copyright

In the past few decades there has been growing interest in the legal applications of artificial intelligence. For the most part, the literature covers the use of artificial intelligence in legal systems as an aid to decision-making,[39] but there has been growing interest of the practical implications of the wider availability and implementation of intelligent systems in everyday life.[40] Machine learning itself has also started to get some attention in legal informatics as a method to index legal cases,[41]

[33] Ibid, 1.

[34] Tero Karras, Timo Aila, Samuli Laine, and Jaakko Lehtinen, 'Progressive Growing of GANs for Improved Quality, Stability, and Variation' (2018) arXiv:1710.10196 [cs.NE].

[35] Alec Radford, Luke Metz, and Soumith Chintala, 'Unsupervised Representation Learning with Deep Convolutional Generative Adversarial Networks' (2016) arXiv:1511.06434 [cs.LG].

[36] See various projects here <http://www.datasciencecentral.com/profiles/blogs/using-machine-learning-to-generate-music>.

[37] Annalee Newitz, 'Movie written by AI algorithm turns out to be hilarious and intense' (*Ars Technica*, 16 June 2016) <http://bit.ly/29QXzcu>.

[38] Gene Kogan, 'Machine learning for artists' (*Medium*, 5 January 2016) <http://bit.ly/29QXWDS>.

[39] See Jon Bing and Trygve Harvold, *Legal Decisions and Information Systems* (Universitetsforlaget 1977); Giovanni Sartor, *Artificial Intelligence and Law: Legal Philosophy and Legal Theory* (Tano 1993); Philip Leith, *Formalism in Al and Computer Science* (Ellis Horwood 1990); and Danièle Bourcier, Laurent Bochereau, and Paul Bourgine, 'Extracting legal knowledge by means of multilayer neural network. Application to municipal jurisprudence' in *Proceedings of the 3rd ICAIL*, Oxford (ACM 1991) 288.

[40] For a couple of examples, see Bettina Berendt and Sören Preibusch, 'Better Decision Support through Exploratory Discrimination-Aware Data Mining: Foundations and Empirical Evidence' 22 Artificial Intelligence and Law 175; and Markus Wagner, 'The Dehumanization of International Humanitarian Law: Legal, Ethical, and Political Implications of Autonomous Weapon Systems' (2014) 47 Vanderbilt Journal of Transnational Law 1371.

[41] Stefanie Brüninghaus and Kevin D Ashley, 'Toward Adding Knowledge to Learning Algorithms for Indexing Legal Cases' in *ICAIL '99: Proceedings of the 7th International Conference on Artificial Intelligence and Law* (ACM Press 1999) 9.

and also to make legal arguments based on data inputs.[42] Some algorithms are also drafting patent applications,[43] and even have been used to pre-empt state of the art in future inventions.[44]

All of these are often ground-breaking and innovative areas of research, but they tend to be a very specialist area of study that generally eludes the mainstream. Even the most popular works that propose some form of legal adoption of artificial intelligence in the legal profession[45] can often be received with mild scepticism about the true reach of the potential for change.[46]

A growing area of interest is the interface between copyright and artificial intelligence.[47] There is a common element in most of the examples of machine learning that have been described in the previous section, namely that we have machines that are starting to generate truly creative works, prompting us to review our understanding of originality.

Intellectual property is specifically directed towards the protection of the fruits of the human mind, and these works are given a set of limited ownership rights allocated to persons, both natural and legal.[48] Because of the personal nature of this type of protection, there is no such thing as non-human intellectual property rights.

Copyright law clearly defines the author of a work as 'the person who created it'.[49] Despite some recent legal disputes regarding monkeys and photographs,[50] it is highly unlikely that we will witness any deviation away from personhood as a requirement for ownership, and nor will we witness any sort of allocation of rights towards machines and animals. However, works like *The Next Rembrandt* could challenge what we generally consider to be original, which is one of the requirements for copyright protection.[51] Is the mechanistic data analysis of dozens of portraits enough to warrant protection? Is there originality in the composition of

42 Martin Možina, Jure Žabkar, Trevor Bench-Capon, and Ivan Bratko, 'Argument Based Machine Learning Applied to Law' 13 Artificial Intelligence and Law 53.

43 Ben Hattenbach and Joshua Glucoft, 'Patents in an Era of Infinite Monkeys and Artificial Intelligence' (2015) 19 Stanford Technology Law Review 32

44 This is a project called 'All Prior Art', which attempts to algorithmically create and publicly publish all possible new prior art, making it impossible for future inventions to be registered. See All Prior Art <http://allpriorart.com/>.

45 See, eg, Richard E Susskind and Daniel Susskind, *The Future of the Professions: How Technology Will Transform the Work of Human Experts* (Oxford University Press 2015).

46 'Professor Dr Robot QC' (*The Economist*, 17 October 2015) <https://www.economist.com/business/2015/10/15/professor-dr-robot-qc>.

47 See Ana Ramalho, 'Will Robots Rule the (Artistic) World? A Proposed Model for the Legal Status of Creations by Artificial Intelligence Systems' (2017) 21 Journal of Internet Law 12; and Jane C Ginsburg and Luke Ali Budiardjo, 'Authors and Machines' (2019) 34 Berkeley Technology Law Journal.

48 Edwin C Hettinger, 'Justifying Intellectual Property' (1989) 18 Philosophy & Public Affairs 31.

49 Copyright, Designs and Patents Act 1988, s 9(1).

50 Andrés Guadamuz, 'The Monkey Selfie: Copyright Lessons for Originality in Photographs and Internet Jurisdiction' 5 Internet Policy Review.

51 Andreas Rahmatian, 'Originality in UK Copyright Law: The Old "Skill and Labour" Doctrine under Pressure' (2013) 44 IIC 4 (hereafter Rahmatian, 'Originality in UK Copyright Law').

the program? What if most of the creative decisions are being performed by the machine?

Interestingly, science fiction depiction of artificial intelligence organisms invariably tries to tackle the question of art and the machine. In various depictions of robots and androids, the understanding of art and music is an important element towards the elevation of the machine towards personhood. A great example of this is Data in *Star Trek: The Next Generation*, who struggles with his search for personhood by painting and performing music. On the other hand, the android Ava in the movie *Ex Machina* uses art to deceive one of the protagonists into thinking that it is more like a human, eventually betraying their trust. Art, music, and literature are quintessentially human, and any effort to allocate creativity to artificial intelligence feels wrong.

But the fact remains that machines are creating art, even if the experts are divided on the artistic merit of existing productions.[52] While accepting that it is art, critic Ben Davies comments that Deep Dream 'is essentially like a psychedelic Instagram filter'.[53] So at the very least, we need to explore from a legal perspective if the new forms of creative works generated by intelligent machines meet the requirements for copyright protection, and if they do, we need to ask who owns the images.

This may seem like a fruitless academic exercise with little practical implications, but there is potential for this becoming an important legal issue. Commercial application of machine learning is already taking place on a broader scale,[54] and this technology is set to become an important tool in many creative industries in the future.[55] A report by Nesta on the potential impact of artificial intelligence in the creative industries found that while highly creative jobs are not at risk, there will be a growing participation of machine learning in the industry. The report states:

> In the creative economy, advances in the area of Mobile Robotics may have implications for making and craft activities (as industrial robots with machine vision and high-precision dexterity become cheaper and cheaper). Data Mining and Computational Statistics where algorithms are developed which allow cognitive tasks to be automated—or become data-driven—may conceivably have significant implications for non-routine tasks in jobs as wide-ranging as content.[56]

52 Marina Galperina, 'Is Google's Deep Dream art?' (*Hopes&Fears*, 14 July 2015) http://www.hopesandfears.com/hopes/culture/is-this-art/215039-deep-dream-google-art.

53 Ibid.

54 Randal S Olson, 'How machines learn (and you win)' (2015) November Issue, Harvard Business Review <http://bit.ly/2a31OlI>.

55 Paul Tozour, 'Making designers obsolete? Evolution in game design' (*AI GameDev*, 6 February 2012) <http://aigamedev.com/open/interview/evolution-in-cityconquest/>.

56 Hasan Bakhshi, Carl Benedikt Frey, and Michael Osborne, *Creativity Vs. Robots: The Creative Economy and the Future of Employment* (NESTA 2015).

This means that while we still have writers, musicians, artists, and game designers in charge of the creative process, a large number of tasks, particularly mechanical tasks, might be given to machines.

This is not science fiction, there are already plenty of examples of commercially viable artificial intelligence projects that produce copyright works that sound indistinguishable from those produced by a human. Jukedeck[57] is an interesting example that produces unique music for commercial use in seconds; the user only needs to specify the genre, the mood, and the length of the song, and the site's neural network will produce a royalty-free composition that can be incorporated into a video or any other derivative work.[58] It is important to point out that at the time of writing Jukedeck is no longer open to the public, and it has been purchased by the Chinese social media giant TikTok, which gives us a hint of the economic importance that is given to AI-generated works.[59]

Similarly, a Google project used neural networks to produce unsupervised poetry after 'reading' 11,000 unpublished books.[60] On a related note, a news organization has announced that it might deploy a machine learning algorithm to author news items in sport and election coverage.[61]

The issue with examples such as these is that we are entering a new era of creation that allows for increasingly smart programs to produce advanced works that would normally be given copyright protection by the author. Boyden calls these creations 'emergent works', and comments that in many instances we are presented with pieces that have emerged from the program itself, and practically without human interaction.[62] Will developments such as these have an effect on ownership? And what happens when machines start making important creative decisions?

Finally, there is another angle to study, and this is the problem of artificial intelligence agents as copyright infringers.[63] While extremely relevant in its own right, this topic falls outside of the remit of the current work, as it deals with the issue of responsibility of autonomous machines, rather than rights allocated to the creations that they produce.

[57] Jukedeck <https://www.jukedeck.com>.

[58] For an example of a melancholic pop song produced by the site's artificial intelligence, see <http://bit.ly/2athkHE>.

[59] Mike Butcher, 'It looks like TikTok has acquired Jukedeck, a pioneering music AI UK startup' (*TechCrunch*, 23 July 2019) <https://techcrunch.com/2019/07/23/it-looks-like-titok-has-acquired-jukedeck-a-pioneering-music-ai-uk-startup/>.

[60] Samuel R Bowman, Luke Vilnis, Oriol Vinyals, Andrew M Dai, Rafal Jozefowicz, and Samy Bengio, 'Generating Sentences from a Continuous Space' (2015) arXiv:1511.06349 [cs.LG].

[61] Dominic Ponsford, 'Press Association set to use "robot" reporters across business, sport and elections coverage' (*Press Gazette*, 18 October 2016) <http://www.pressgazette.co.uk/press-association-set-to-use-robot-reporters-across-business-sport-and-elections-coverage/>.

[62] Bruce E Boyden, 'Emergent Works' (2016) 39 Columbia Journal of Law and the Arts 377, 378 (hereafter Boyden, 'Emergent Works').

[63] Burkhard Schafer and others, 'A Fourth Law of Robotics? Copyright and the Law and Ethics of Machine Co-Production' 23 Artificial Intelligence and Law 217. See also James Grimmelman, 'Copyright for Literate Robots' (2016) 101 Iowa Law Review 657.

3. Protection of Computer-Generated Works

3.1 Computer-Generated Works in the UK

The legal ownership of computer-generated works is perhaps deceptively straightforward in the UK.[64] Section 9(3) of the Copyright, Designs and Patents Act (CDPA) states:

> In the case of a literary, dramatic, musical or artistic work which is computer-generated, the author shall be taken to be the person by whom the arrangements necessary for the creation of the work are undertaken.

Furthermore, section 178 defines a computer-generated work as one that 'is generated by computer in circumstances such that there is no human author of the work'. This is an elegant and concise wording that does away with most potential debates about the creative works produced by artificial intelligent agents. However, the UK is one of only a few countries protect computer-generated works,[65] most of the others clearly inspired by the UK treatment of computer-generated works, as they use practically the same formulation.[66] In fact, this has been for a while considered one of the most salient aspects where UK and Irish copyright law diverges from the European norms,[67] as will be explained in the next section.

The fact that section 9(3) is so clear could explain the lack of case law dealing with this problem. In fact, the main authority in the area of computer-generated works predates the existing law. The case is *Express Newspapers v Liverpool Daily Post*,[68] in which the plaintiffs published a competition involving the distribution of cards to its readers, with each card having a sequence of five letters that were to be checked against the winning sequences published by the Express group newspapers. The winning sequences were published in a grid of five rows and five columns of letters. Because the players did not need to purchase the newspaper in order to obtain the

64 For more detail about the UK's approach, see Jyh-An Lee, Chapter 8 in this volume.

65 Besides the UK, such protection exists only in Ireland, New Zealand, India, and Hong Kong. See Jani McCutcheon, 'Vanishing Author in Computer-Generated Works: A Critical Analysis of Recent Australian Case Law' (2012) 36 Melbourne University Law Review 915, 956 (hereafter McCutcheon, 'Vanishing Author in Computer-Generated Works'). It is worth pointing out that while McCutcheon also includes South Africa in the list, the definition in s 1(1)(i) is for a computer program, not computer-generated work.

66 Eg, the Copyright and Related Rights Act 2000 (Ireland), s 21(f) says that an author in computer-generated works is 'the person by whom the arrangements necessary for the creation of the work are undertaken'. Almost the same wording can be found in Copyright Act 1994 (New Zealand), s 5(2)(a); Copyright Act 1978 (South Africa), s 1(1)(h); and Copyright Act 1957 (India), s 2(d)(vi).

67 Christian Handig, 'The Copyright Term "Work"—European Harmonisation at an Unknown Level' (2009) 40 IIC 665, 668 (hereafter Handig, 'The Copyright Term "Work"').

68 *Express Newspapers Plc v Liverpool Daily Post & Echo Plc* [1985] 3 All ER 680.

cards, the Liverpool Daily Post reproduced the winning sequences in their newspapers. The plaintiffs sued seeking an injunction against this practice.

The defendants contended that the published sequences were not protected by copyright because they had been generated by a computer, and therefore there was no author. Whitford J held that the computer was merely a tool that produced the sequences using the instructions of a programmer, so the plaintiffs were awarded the injunction. Whitford J commented:

> The computer was no more than the tool .... It is as unrealistic as it would be to suggest that, if you write your work with a pen, it is the pen which is the author of the work rather than the person who drives the pen.[69]

This decision is consistent with section 9(3), but despite the apparent clarity of this argument, there is some ambiguity as to who the actual author is. Adrian astutely points out that Whitford J's pen analogy could be used to adjudicate copyright ownership to the user of the program, and not to the programmer.[70] It seems evident that the spirit of the law favours the latter and not the former, but this is a persisting ambiguity that could have an impact in a world where computer-generated works become more prevalent.

Let us use a word processor to illustrate why the existing ambiguity could prove problematic. It is evident that Microsoft, the makers of the Word programme, do not own every piece of work written with their software. Now imagine a similar argument with a more complex machine learning program such as *No Man's Sky*. If we use the word processor analogy, one would own all new worlds generated by the software because the user made 'the arrangements necessary for the creation of the work'. Yet clearly the game developers make a strong claim in their end-user licence agreement that they own all intellectual property arising from the game.[71]

It is therefore necessary to seek clarification to this possible conundrum elsewhere. While discussing copyright reform that eventually led to the 1988 CDPA and the current wording of section 9(3), the Whitford Committee had already discussed that 'the author of the output can be none other than the person, or persons, who devised the instructions and originated the data used to control and condition a computer to produce a particular result'.[72]

Similarly, during the discussion of the enactment of the current law, the House of Lords discussed computer-generated work in the context of exempting section 9(3) from the application of moral rights.[73] In that context, Lord Beaverbrook

[69] At 1098.

[70] Angela Adrian, *Law and Order in Virtual Worlds: Exploring Avatars, Their Ownership and Rights* (Information Science Reference 2010)

[71] End User Licence Agreement <http://store.steampowered.com//eula/275850_eula_0>.

[72] 'Report of the Whitford Committee to Consider the Law on Copyright and Designs' (Cmd 6732, 1977) para 513.

[73] HL Deb vol. 493 col. 1305 25 February 1988.

usefully commented that '[m]oral rights are closely concerned with the personal nature of creative effort, and the person by whom the arrangements necessary for the creation of a computer-generated work are undertaken will not himself have made any personal, creative effort'.[74] This suggests that the law recognizes that there is no creative input in computer-generated works, and therefore section 9(3) has been framed as an exception to the creativity and originality requirements for the subsistence of copyright. It is precisely this divorce with creativity what makes the UK's computer-generated clause so different to other jurisdictions.

Some commentators seem to be concerned about the ambiguity present both in the law and in *Express Newspapers*. Dorotheu goes through the options of who owns a work produced by an artificial intelligent agent, weighing the merits of giving ownership to the programmer, to the user, to the agent itself, or to no one at all.[75] However, this apparent ambiguity could be solved simply by reading the letter of the law and applying it on a case-by-case basis. If the artificial agent is directly started by the programmer, and it creates a work of art, then the programmer is clearly the author in accordance to section 9(3) CDPA. However, if a user acquires a program capable of producing computer-generated works, and uses it to generate a new work, then ownership would go to the user.

This is already happening with Deep Dream images. After announcing the existence of the Deep Dream project, Google released its code[76] to the public as an open source program,[77] not claiming ownership over any of the resulting art. Any user can run the program and generate art using it, and it would seem counter-intuitive to believe that Google should own the images, after all, the user is the one who is making the necessary arrangements for the creation of the work.

To illustrate this approach of looking at works on a case-by-case basis, we can look at the main case that cites section 9(3) CDPA. In *Nova Productions v Mazooma Games*,[78] the plaintiff designed and sold arcade video games, and they claimed that the defendants produced two games that infringed its copyright. The issue was not that any source code had been copied, but that some graphics and frames were very similar between all three works. In first instance Kitchin J found that there was no substantial similarity between the works, and the plaintiffs appealed. Jacob LJ opined that individual frames shown on a screen when playing a computer game where computer-generated artistic works, and that the game's programmer 'is the person by whom the arrangements necessary for the creation of the works were undertaken and therefore is deemed to be the author by virtue of

[74] Ibid.

[75] Emily Dorotheu, 'Reap the Benefits and Avoid the Legal Uncertainty: Who Owns the Creations of Artificial Intelligence?' (2015) 21 Computer and Telecommunications Law Review 85.

[76] See Github <https://github.com/google/deepdream>.

[77] For more about open source software, see Lawrence Rosen, *Open Source Licensing: Software Freedom and Intellectual Property Law* (Prentice Hall PTR 2004).

[78] *Nova Productions Ltd v Mazooma Games Ltd & Ors* [2006] RPC 14.

s.9(3)'.[79] Interestingly, Kitchin J also addresses the potential authorship of the user. He comments:

> Before leaving this topic there is one further complexity I must consider and that is the effect of player input. The appearance of any particular screen depends to some extent on the way the game is being played. For example, when the rotary knob is turned the cue rotates around the cue ball. Similarly, the power of the shot is affected by the precise moment the player chooses to press the play button. The player is not, however, an author of any of the artistic works created in the successive frame images. His input is not artistic in nature and he has contributed no skill or labour of an artistic kind. Nor has he undertaken any of the arrangements necessary for the creation of the frame images. All he has done is to play the game.[80]

This opens the door to the possibility that only a user who 'contributes skill and labour of an artistic kind' could be declared the author of the work.

To summarize, the situation in the UK with regards to computer-generated works would appear to be well-covered by the law and case law, and even the potential ambiguities are not problematic. Generally speaking, section 9(3) acts as an exception to the originality requirements in copyright law. But there is a potential spanner in the works, European copyright law has been taking a very different direction with regards to originality, and this could prove to be a clash with regards to the long-term viability of the UK's approach. This divergence is discussed next.

3.2 Originality and Creativity in the EU

As has been covered above, while the law is clear in the UK covering computer-generated works, the situation in the European Union (EU) is considerably less favourable towards ownership of computer works. There is no equivalent to section 9(3) in the major continental copyright jurisdictions, and the subject is not covered by the international treaties and the copyright directives that harmonize the subject.[81] Article 5 of Spanish copyright law[82] specifically states that the author of a work is the natural person who creates it; while Article 7 of German copyright law[83] says that the 'author is the creator of the work', and while it does not specify that this is to be a person, Article 11 declares that copyright 'protects the author in

[79] Ibid, 105.
[80] Ibid, 106.
[81] Handig, 'The Copyright Term "Work"' (n 67) 668.
[82] Ley 22/11 sobre la Propiedad Intelectual de 1987.
[83] *Urheberrechtsgesetz* (UrhG), 1 October 2013.

his intellectual and personal relationships to the work', which strongly implies a necessary connection with personhood.

The end result is that computer-generated works are not dealt with directly in most European legislation, so when presented with a work that has been created with a computer, one must revert to the basics of awarding copyright protection, namely originality. For such a vital concept of authorship, originality has proved to be a difficult concept to pin down, while it is well-understood that originality is one of the most important elements of authorship, different jurisdictions have developed their own version of originality, and furthermore, the level of originality may vary in one jurisdiction depending on the nature of the work.[84] Indicative of the lack of harmonization is the fact that Rosati identifies at least four different originality standards in common use.[85]

It is precisely the European standard that could present its own unique challenges to computer-generated works. This standard is to be found in the Court of Justice decision of *Infopaq*,[86] where the Danish news clipping service Infopaq International was taken to court by the Danish newspaper association over its reproduction of news cuttings for sale to its clients. The clipping process involved a data capture process consisting of scanning images of original articles, the translation of those images into text, and the creation of an eleven-word snippet for sale to Infopaq's clients. The court had to determine whether these snippets were original enough, as the process was highly mechanized. The court decided to define originality as a work that must be the 'author's own intellectual creation', and ruled in favour of giving copyright to the work.

Dealing specifically with computer-generated works there is further clarification in *Bezpečnostní softwarová asociace*,[87] the Court of Justice of the European Union (CJEU) was asked to determine whether a computer graphical interface was a work in accordance to the definitions set out in European copyright law.[88] The Court declared that 'a graphic user interface can, as a work, be protected by copyright if it is its author's own intellectual creation'.[89]

The above provides a strong indication about the personal nature of the European originality requirement. As Handig accurately points out, '[t]he expression "author's own intellectual creation" clarifies that a human author is necessary

[84] Jane C Ginsburg, 'The Concept of Authorship in Comparative Copyright Law' (2002) 52 DePaul Law Review 1063.

[85] Eleonora Rosati, *Originality in EU Copyright: Full Harmonization through Case Law* (Edward Elgar 2013) 60.

[86] Case C-5/08 *Infopaq International A/S v Danske Dagblades Forening* [2009] ECR I-06569 (hereafter *Infopaq v Danske*)/

[87] Case C-393/09 *Bezpečnostní softwarová asociace—Svaz softwarové ochrany (BSA) v Ministry of Culture of the Czech Republic* [2010] ECR I-13971 (hereafter *Bezpečnostní softwarová asociace*).

[88] Specifically, Directive 2001/29/EC of the European Parliament and of the Council of 22 May 2001 on the harmonization of certain aspects of copyright and related rights in the information society [2001] OJ L167 10.

[89] *Bezpečnostní softwarová asociace* (n 87) 46.

for a copyright work'.[90] Moreover, the preamble of the Copyright Term Directive[91] defines original as a work that is the 'author's own intellectual creation reflecting his personality'. It seems then inescapable to conclude that not only does the author need to be human, the copyright work must reflect the author's personality.

All of the above is not problematic for most computer-generated works, particularly those in which the result is the product of the author's input. When using graphic editing software to produce a picture, the resulting picture will reflect the creative impulses of artists, reflecting their personality. But conversely, it is easy to see how a definition of authorship that is completely embedded to personal creativity would spell trouble for computer-generated works that are the result of an advanced artificial intelligence program. Even the creators of Deep Dream do not know exactly what happens at all stages of the production of an image. They comment that the artificial intelligence is perfectly capable of making its own decisions about what elements to enhance, and this decision is entirely independent of human input.[92]

The decision of whether a machine-generated image will have copyright in Europe under the *Infopaq* standard may come down to a matter of a case-by-case analysis of just how much input comes from the programmer, and how much from the machine. Take the machine learning algorithm used in the creation of *The Next Rembrandt* as an illustration of the challenges ahead. The description[93] of the process that led to the creation of the painting makes it clear that a lot of work was performed by the team of experts and programmers: they identified portraits as the way to go, and then selected using various commonalities in this set, including age, gender, face direction, and lighting. They then decided that the portrait would depict a 'Caucasian male, with facial hair, between 30–40 years old, wearing dark clothing with a collar, wearing a hat and facing to the right'.[94] With that data selection, they extracted data from portraits that had only those sets of features. The experts allowed an algorithm to select common features in the data set, and the program came with 'typical' Rembrandt elements for each part of the portrait.

The question then is whether *The Next Rembrandt* has copyright. Based on just the description of the process found in interviews and online, it is difficult to say that the process does not represent the personality of the authors through the choice of portrait elements to give to the computer to analyse. This is extremely important in the *Infopaq* standard, in that case the CJEU commented that elements by

[90] Handig, 'The Copyright Term "Work"' (n 67) 668.

[91] Council Directive 93/98/EEC of 29 October 1993 harmonizing the term of protection of copyright and certain related rights [1993] OJ L290 9.

[92] Mordvintsev, 'Inceptionism' (n 23).

[93] See https://youtu.be/IuygOYZ1Ngo.

[94] Ibid.

themselves may not have originality, but a selection process could warrant originality. The Court ruled:

> Regarding the elements of such works covered by the protection, it should be observed that they consist of words which, considered in isolation, are not as such an intellectual creation of the author who employs them. It is only through the choice, sequence and combination of those words that the author may express his creativity in an original manner and achieve a result which is an intellectual creation.[95]

Infopaq dealt with words, but the CJEU has extended a similar analysis to other types of work, such as it did with photographs in *Painer v Standard Verlags*,[96] where the preparation phase of taking a photograph, as well as the development choices and even the software editing decisions would be enough to warrant originality as they would reflect the author's 'personality and expressing his free and creative choices in the production of that photograph'.[97]

At the very least, *The Next Rembrandt* displays enough of that selection process to warrant originality given the current standards. But it is possible that other pictures where most of the decision is made by the computer, particularly in neural networks such as Deep Dream, this selection may not be enough to warrant originality, but this is entirely dependent on each case, and the interpretation given to what constitutes selection.

UK works appear immune from these problems given the relative clarity of section 9(3), but this could be under threat given recent decisions, particularly the landmark case of *Temple Island Collections v New English Teas*.[98] The case involves a black and white image of the UK Parliament building, and a bright red bus travelling across Westminster Bridge. The claimant owned the photograph, which was used in London souvenirs, and the defendant is a tea company that created a similar picture for a publicity campaign. Birss QC had to determine whether the original picture had copyright, and he concluded that when it comes to photography the composition is important, namely the angle of shot, the field of view, and the bringing together of different elements at the right place and the right time are enough to prove skill and labour, and therefore should have copyright.[99] This result was consistent with the skill and labour originality standard that was prevalent in the UK through various cases.[100]

However, throughout *Temple Island Collections* Birss QC seamlessly integrates 'skill and labour' with Infopaq's 'intellectual creative effort', and through repetition

[95] *Infopaq v Danske* (n 86) 45.

[96] Case C-145/10 *Eva-Maria Painer v Standard Verlags GmbH & Others* [2010] ECR I-12533.

[97] Ibid, 94.

[98] *Temple Island Collections Ltd v New English Teas Ltd and Another* (No 2) [2012] EWPCC 1.

[99] Ibid, 68–70.

[100] See, eg, *University of London Press v University Tutorial* [1916] 2 Ch 601 and *Interlego A.G v Tyco Industries Inc & Ors (Hong Kong)* [1988] 3 All ER 949. For a description of this see Rahmatian, 'Originality in UK Copyright Law' (n 51).

makes them equivalent, and even becoming 'skill and labour/intellectual creation'.[101] This case, coupled with other developments such as the treatment of originality in databases in the CJEU decision of *Football Dataco v Yahoo! UK*,[102] prompted Rahmatian to claim that the skill and labour test was under fire.[103] Furthermore, in *SAS v World Programming Ltd*[104] Arnold J finally laid the question to rest by completely adopting Infopaq's 'intellectual creation' test into English law.

If we take as a given that the UK now has a more personal test that requires us to analyse the author's own intellectual creation reflecting his personality, then we could argue that artificial intelligence works where the author has less input could be under fire in the future, particularly if we can expect further harmonization, which is difficult to ascertain given the troubled interaction with the EU.[105] What remains clear is that as UK courts have to meet the intellectual creation standard, then it is vital to look at each work on a case-by-case basis. Some works may have enough input from a human author to meet that requirement, and some may not.

Assuming that nothing changes and section 9(3) remains the undisputed standard for computer-generated works, it is now time to look at how other jurisdictions deal with artificial intelligence and computer-generated works.

3.3 Protection in Other Jurisdictions

As we have seen above, there are several common law countries that have implemented some form of protection for computer-generated works, while continental traditions of copyright protection tend to place the emphasis of authorship on personality and the creative effort. There is a third group of countries that deal with authorship in ways that make it difficult to protect computer-generated works, and these are the US and Australia.

3.3.1 United States

US copyright has been dealing with originality and authorship in a manner that deviates from other jurisdictions, what Gervais and Judge call 'silos of originality'[106] where various approaches have arisen. The US standard is set by *Feist Publications v Rural Telephone Service*,[107] where the US Supreme Court had to decide on the

[101] *Temple Island v New English Teas* at 27. Various other examples can be found at 31 and 34.

[102] Case C-604/10 *Football Dataco Ltd and Others v Yahoo! UK Ltd and Others* [2012] WLR(D) 57.

[103] Rahmatian, 'Originality in UK Copyright Law' (n 51). See also Andreas Rahmatian, 'Temple Island Collections v New English Teas: An Incorrect Decision Based on the Right Law?' (2012) 34 European Intellectual Property Review 796.

[104] *SAS Institute Inc v World Programming Ltd* [2013] EWHC 69 (Ch).

[105] This chapter was first written before the Brexit vote, and for the most part tends to ignore the issue altogether.

[106] Elizabeth F Judge and Daniel J Gervais, 'Of Silos and Constellations: Comparing Notions of Originality in Copyright Law' (2009) 27 Cardozo Arts and Entertainment Law Journal 375.

[107] *Feist Publications, Inc. v Rural Telephone Service Co.*, 499 US 340 (1991) (hereafter *Feist v Rural*).

originality of a phone directory containing names, towns, and telephone listings. Feist Publications copied over 4,000 entries from a 'white pages' directory compiled by Rural Telephone Service, and they did so without a licence. The prevalent principle before this decision was a 'sweat of the brow' approach that allowed the copyright of a compilation of facts if enough effort had gone into the creation of the compilation, even if facts are not protected by copyright.[108] The Court famously commented that '100 uncopyrightable facts do not magically change their status when gathered together in one place'.[109] Copyright protection therefore will only be given to 'those components of a work that are original to the author', [110] giving rise to a standard that requires 'a modicum of creativity'.[111] This test stands in stark contrast to the *Inofopaq* standard prevalent in Europe, as in *Feist* the Supreme Court clearly reckons that selection, coordination and arrangement of information is not an act that conveys originality, while the opposite is true across the Atlantic.[112]

It is easy to see that under this standard, some computer-generated works would not be protected, particularly if we are witnessing a work created with advanced artificial intelligence where a human author may not lend originality to the work. In fact, *Feist* specifically seems to veer against granting 'mechanical or routine' acts with originality,[113] and can there be anything more mechanical than a machine that produces a work?

Before *Feist*, the main treatment of the subject was undertaken in the 1979 report by the US Congress National Commission on New Technological Uses of Copyrighted Works (CONTU),[114] which decided not to give any special treatment to computer-generated works because no insurmountable problems were apparent or foreseeable. Because this was pre-*Feist*, CONTU's approach was to allocate copyright protection for computer-generated works using the 'sweat of the brow' approach, which seemed sensible at the time, something that several commentators agreed with.[115]

Other analysts were not as content with the CONTU approach, and veered towards a more proactive way to protect artificial intelligence works. In an article well ahead of its time,[116] Butler opined that '[i]n the vast majority of programming situations the legal requirements of human authorship can be easily satisfied'.[117]

[108] Jane C Ginsburg, 'No "Sweat"? Copyright and Other Protection of Works of Information after Feist v. Rural Telephone' (1992) 92 Columbia Law Review 338.

[109] *Feist v Rural* (n 107) 1287.

[110] Ibid, 1289.

[111] Ibid, 1288.

[112] Russ VerSteeg, 'Rethinking Originality' (1993) 34 William & Mary Law Review 802, 821.

[113] *Feist v Rural* (n 107) 1296.

[114] National Commission On New Technological Uses of Copyrighted Works, Final Report On New Technological Uses of Copyrighted Works (1979).

[115] Pamela Samuelson, 'CONTU Revisited: The Case Against Copyright Protection for Computer Programs in Machine-Readable Form' (1984) Duke Law Journal 663.

[116] Timothy L Butler, 'Can a Computer be an Author? Copyright Aspects of Artificial Intelligence' (1982) 4 Communications and Entertainment Law Journal 707.

[117] Ibid, 730.

However, he conceded that there could be a problem with advances in artificial intelligence that would cross what he defined as the man/machine threshold;[118] this is when a work can be said to have been authored by a machine and not by the programmer. Butler then goes on to suggest that copyright law pertaining to authorship should be interpreted with a 'human presumption',[119] if a work has been created by a machine in a way in which the end result is indistinguishable to that produced by a human author, then it should receive copyright protection nonetheless. This is an elegant solution, one that incorporates the concept of the Turing test[120] into law, making the standard of legal authorship one that would make the assumption that the author is human regardless of the process that gave rise to it. While it is tempting advocate for such a test, this would unfortunately incorporate a qualitative test to copyright that it currently lacks. Judges would have to be asked whether a text, a song, or a painting is the product of a human or a machine. Any observer of modern art will understand why this may not be such a good idea, and it is easy to imagine judges getting it wrong more often than not.

Therefore, it is perhaps fortunate that Butler's Turing test copyright idea did not survive past *Feist*. For the most part, US copyright law took a direction in which databases and compilations were left unprotected,[121] while having a high standard of originality for other works.[122] Most computer-generated creations that were deemed mechanical were not thought worthy of protection, while works in which the human component was clearly original were copyrightable, and with few exceptions[123] there was little debate as to whether computer-generated copyright would be a problem. In fact, in a review of the status of the law regarding artificial intelligence works post-*Feist*, Miller commented that while 'neural networks raise a number of interesting theoretical issues, they are not yet in a very advanced stage of development'.[124] Perhaps accurately at the time, Miller advocated not to rush to any changes in the law until real cases emerged, and it seems like this 'wait and see' strategy was to prevail.

This has all changed in recent years with the advances in artificial intelligence outlined above. With machines set to make more and more creative decisions, the

[118] Ibid, 733–4.

[119] Ibid, 746.

[120] The Turing test is a concept developed by Alan Turing to assess a machine's ability to exhibit intelligent behaviour. If a machine is capable of behaving and communicating in a way that is indistinguishable to that of a human, then that machine will be considered to be intelligent. See Alan Turing, 'Computing Machinery and Intelligence' (1950) 59 Mind 433.

[121] John F Hayden, 'Copyright Protection of Computer Databases After Feist' (1991) 5 Harvard Journal of Law and Technology 215.

[122] Howard B Abrams, 'Originality and Creativity in Copyright Law' (1992) 55 Law and Contemporary Problems 3.

[123] Darin Glasser, 'Copyrights in Computer-Generated Works: Whom, if Anyone, do we Reward?' (2001) 1 Duke Law and Technology Review 24.

[124] Arthur R Miller, 'Copyright Protection for Computer Programs, Databases, and Computer-Generated Works: Is Anything New Since CONTU?' (1993) 106 Harvard Law Review 977, 1037.

question about the copyright status of those works has resurfaced. If one believes that computer-generated works are worthy of protection, then the challenge is to get past the seemingly insurmountable obstacle that is *Feist*. Bridy rises to the challenge by recognizing that there are not yet any cases dealing with 'procedurally generated artworks',[125] so she uncovers a number of cases of non-human authorship. This is a very interesting avenue to explore, if we can find cases where copyright has been granted despite the lack of a human author, then this could boost the case for artificial intelligent ones. Some of these cases involve claims of authorship by non-human entities, be it aliens,[126] celestial beings,[127] or spiritual guides,[128] which have been dictated to human authors. The common element in all of these cases has been that the courts gave copyright ownership to the human author, as they found 'a sufficient nexus to human creativity to sustain copyright'.[129] Bridy astutely comments that these cases could be used to justify copyright in procedurally generated artworks, as the possible automated element can be ignored and originality, if any exists, would be given to the author. This would be entirely consistent with the way in which the UK deals with computer-generated works.

However, the US Copyright Office has recently made a statement that makes it difficult to interpret in favour of the existence of non-human authors. The US has a voluntary system of registration, and while this formality is not a prerequisite for the subsistence of copyright, it is necessary in order to enforce rights.[130] In the latest guidelines for registration, the Copyright Office clearly declares that it 'will register an original work of authorship, provided that the work was created by a human being'.[131] They base this specially on the US Supreme Court decision in *Trademark Cases*,[132] which defines copyright as protecting fruits of intellectual labour that 'are founded in the creative powers of the mind'.[133] Nonetheless, one could interpret that this declaration is worded in a manner that could still allow some computer-generated content if there is enough human input into it. Similarly, it must be pointed out that this is not law, this is just a compendium of practices at the offices, and that these could be changed or re-drafted in future editions.

Interestingly, other commentators appear to be moving towards a more European method of authorship that emphasizes the author's creative intent. Boyden in particular comments that emergent works could be given copyright by requiring a claimant to prove human authorship by establishing that the output

[125] Annemarie Bridy, 'Coding Creativity: Copyright and the Artificially Intelligent Author' (2012) 5 Stanford Technology Law Review 1, 18 (hereafter Bridy, 'Coding Creativity).

[126] *Urantia Foundation v Maaherra*, 114 F.3d 955 [1997].

[127] *Penguin Books U.S.A., Inc. v New Christian Church of Full Endeavor, Ltd.* 2000 US Dist. LEXIS 10394.

[128] *Garman v Sterling Publ'g Co.*, 1992 US Dist. LEXIS 21932.

[129] Bridy, 'Coding Creativity (n 125) 20.

[130] 17 US Code § 411.

[131] US Copyright Office, *Compendium of U.S. Copyright Office Practices* (2017) 3rd edn, 306.

[132] *Trademark Cases*, 100 US 82 (1879).

[133] Ibid, 94.

'foreseeably includes a meaning or message that the author wishes to convey'.[134] This formulation sounds remarkably like the current standard of originality that reflects the personality of the author.

Similarly, Ginsburg has emerged as the main proponent that machines are not capable to generate copyright works as they do not meet existing requirement. She writes:

> If the human intervention in producing these outputs does not exceed requesting the computer to generate a literary, artistic or musical composition of a particular style or genre, one may properly consider these works to be 'computer-generated' because the human users do not contribute sufficient 'intellectual creation' to meet minimum standards of authorship under the Berne Convention.[135]

On the other hand, other commentators do not see a problem with the current situation, at least not yet. Grimmelman makes a compelling case that there is no such thing as an artificial intelligent author, as most of the current examples are a mirage, and that talk of authorship has been fuelled by the 'novelty and strangeness' of some computer programs.[136]

Nonetheless, Grimmelman's more sceptical take on computer-generated works appears to be in the minority at the moment, although it is true that we still do not have case law reviewing ownership in the US. However, it may be just a matter of time before a copyright infringement case is defended with the argument that the work has no copyright because it was produced by an artificial intelligent machine.

3.3.2 Australia

Australia presents an interesting contrast with regards to protection of computer-generated works because it lacks the wording of section 9(3) CDPA that has been adopted by other countries such as New Zealand and Ireland.[137] The requirement for authorship is strictly tied to the existence of a person,[138] which could leave out works made by computers, a fact that had already been identified by the Australian Copyright Law Review Committee in 1998 as potentially problematic.[139] As a result of this lack of protection, there is now case law in Australia where works that

[134] Boyden, 'Emergent Works' (n 62) 393.

[135] Jane C Ginsburg, 'People Not Machines: Authorship and What It Means in the Berne Convention' (2018) 49 IIC 131.

[136] James Grimmelman, 'There's No Such Thing as a Computer-Authored Work—And It's a Good Thing, Too' (2016) 39 Columbia Journal of Law and the Arts 403, 414.

[137] McCutcheon, 'Vanishing Author in Computer-Generated Works' (n 65).

[138] Eg, Copyright Act 1968, s 10 (Australia) defines the author of a photograph as 'the person who took the photograph'.

[139] Parliament of Australia, 'Simplification of the Copyright Act 1968—Part 2: Categorisation of Subject Matter and Exclusive Rights, and Other Issues' (1999) 15 Research Note 1, 2.

might have been protected in jurisdictions such as the UK have been declared as not covered by copyright because of lack of human authorship.[140]

Although at some point there were some concerns that the *Feist* standard from the US would be exported around the world,[141] it is difficult to find a country that has had a similar approach to originality, although countries such as Australia have been grappling with the question.

This is evident in the case law that has been dealing with databases.[142] A very indicative case showing the contrasting take on originality in Australia can be found in *Desktop Marketing Systems v Telstra Corporation.*[143] The facts are somewhat reminiscent of *Feist*, where Desktop Marketing Systems produced a CD version of the phone directories belonging to Telstra, who claimed that such action infringed their copyright. At first instance[144] the judge decided that the phone directories had copyright and therefore the respondent had infringed copyright. The case was appealed, and the Federal Court decided that the phone directories did indeed have copyright even if they were a compilation of data. The Court directly addressed the *Feist* claim that a compilation of data cannot have copyright by declaring that the 'task of carefully identifying and listing units'[145] can be useful, and therefore could carry copyright protection.

So, *Desktop Marketing Systems* diverged from the strict *Feist* standard, opening the door to the protection of compilations, and therefore allowing a less restrictive approach to originality. However, this case was reversed in *IceTV v Nine Network Australia*,[146] where a provider of a subscription-based electronic programme guide via the Internet would gather TV schedule data from the broadcaster Nine Network and offer it to its subscribers. While part of the judgment relied on whether the copying of the schedule had been substantial, the relevant issue to the present chapter was whether TV schedules have originality. In this, *IceTV* resembles *Feist* more, as the High Court decided that there was not enough skill and labour in the expression of time and title required to create a program, on the contrary, it was minimal.[147] A similar result can be found in the more recent case of *Telstra Corporation v Phone Directories Company*,[148] where the judge goes as far as to

[140] McCutcheon, 'Vanishing Author in Computer-Generated Works' (n 65).

[141] Daniel J Gervais, 'Feist Goes Global: A Comparative Analysis of the Notion of Originality in Copyright Law' (2002) 49 Journal of the Copyright Society of the U.S.A. 949.

[142] The cases listed here have been highlighted by McCutcheon, 'Vanishing Author in Computer-Generated Works' (n 65).

[143] *Desktop Marketing Systems Pty Ltd v Telstra Corporation Limited* [2002] FCAFC 112 (hereafter *Desktop Marketing v Telstra*).

[144] *Telstra Corporation Limited v Desktop Marketing Systems Pty Ltd* [2001] FCA 612.

[145] *Desktop Marketing v Telstra* (n 143) 161.

[146] *IceTV Pty Limited v Nine Network Australia Pty Limited* [2009] HCA 14.

[147] Ibid, 54.

[148] *Telstra Corporation Limited v Phone Directories Company Pty Ltd* [2010] FCA 44.

declare that phone directories involved in the litigation were not original because the authors of these works had not exercised 'independent intellectual effort'.[149]

By choosing a narrower interpretation of originality, *IceTV* and *Telstra Corporation* show us that a higher threshold of originality can have negative effects with regards to the protection given to computer-generated works. This is evident in the case of *Acohs v Ucorp*,[150] where the claimant sued the respondent for copyright infringement of the source code of one of its programmes. Acohs and Ucorp are both in the business of developing software used to automatically fill industrial health and safety forms, which can be a time-consuming endeavour, particularly in large enterprises. Both developers have different ways of producing and filling the forms, the Acohs system in particular does not store documents, rather it stores information in a database and then when requested by the user, the software pulls that data and creates the requisite form. In other words, the Acohs system procedurally creates a new document automatically upon request. Ucorp is accused of reproducing the resulting document by extracting HTML code from the documents, as well as layout, presentation, and appearance of the outputs.[151]

In a baffling decision, the judge ruled that the resulting output did not have copyright protection because the source code had been generated by the system, and as such it had no 'single human author'.[152] By being generated by a computer program, its originality was compromised and it could not have copyright. Going back to the arguments of whether the author of a computer-generated work is the programmer or the user, Jessup J argued that those who initiated the program to generate code were not computer programmers, rather they were just using the software, and therefore they could not be authors.[153] The case was appealed, but the result was the same as the Federal Court decided that the code had not emanated from human authors, and therefore it 'was not an original work in the copyright sense'.[154]

This decision bodes ill for computer-generated works in general, and for artificial intelligence in particular. Reading the facts of the case, it is evident that the Acohs system is in no way a complex machine learning mechanism, it is a rather basic use of databases to produce documents and source code. It is remarkable that a court would not consider this function to be worthy of copyright protection, and it shows precisely how a decision based on narrow understanding of originality such as that seen in cases such as *Feist*, *IceTV*, and *Telstra Corporation* can produce negative results. If a system such as Acohs does not have a chance to be declared original, what chance do more complex artificial intelligence systems have?

149 Ibid, 340

150 *Acohs Pty Ltd v Ucorp Pty Ltd* [2010] FCA 577.

151 Ibid, 86.

152 Ibid, 50.

153 Ibid, 52.

154 *Acohs Pty Ltd v Ucorp Pty Ltd* [2012] FCAFC 16, 57.

3.3.3 People's Republic of China

Courts in the People's Republic of China have been the first to apply some form of copyright protection for artificial intelligence works. The Beijing Internet Court heard the case of *Feilin v Baidu*,[155] in which the plaintiff had produced a data report on the film industry in Beijing. The report consisted of text and images from various sources that had been put together with the help of analytical software and a database belonging to Wolters Kluwer; but it was later found that the report was not produced with those tools. The report was posted on the Web by the plaintiffs, and then it was copied, edited, and reposted in other platforms belonging to the defendant. The copy was missing several passages from the original, and was also missing attribution of authorship, so the plaintiffs sued for copyright infringement. The defendants argued that the work was not original as it contained data and charts that had been generated with software tools. The court was therefore asked to determine two issues, whether the report was original, and if so, who should own copyright over it.

The court stated categorically that machines could not produce copyright works, and that human authorship was vital in determining whether a work was subject to copyright protection. However, the court determined that while some elements of the report had been generated by a computer, the work was not in the public domain as it was also the result of human intervention. While some elements of the report could not be protected because it had not been created by a human being, the investment that went into the creation and use of the subject was worthy of some type of protection, and the defendant had to compensate the claimant and also had to remove the infringing material. Eventually the court held that the plaintiff's report was different from the result of using the database. In other words, the plaintiff's report was not a computer-generated work. Instead, it was created by a human being and was original.

This is a remarkable decision for various reasons. First, this decision recognizes that some form of rights arise from a work generated by a computer, even if this is not to be given full copyright protection, while it is not part of the reasoning that led to the infringement ruling, the decision opens up a policy discussion. Secondly, the decision hints at some form of investment-based right being developed; this is not entirely new, the basis for database protection in the EU is reliant on the recognition of the investment that goes into the creation of a work,[156] and a similar type of right is also being discussed in some other countries.[157] Finally, the case

[155] *Beijing Feilin Law Firm v Beijing Baidu Netcom Science Technology Co., Ltd.*, No 239 Minchu (Beijing Internet Ct. 2018). Full text of the decision at <https://www.bjinternetcourt.gov.cn/cac/zw/1556272978673.html>.

[156] Directive 96/9/EC of the European Parliament and of the Council of 11 March 1996 on the legal protection of databases, L77, 1996-03-27, 20–8.

[157] Another country that has hinted at similar test is Japan. See Intellectual Property Strategy Headquarters, 'Intellectual Property Strategic Program' (2016) <https://www.kantei.go.jp/jp/singi/titeki2/kettei/chizaikeikaku20160509_e.pdf>.

is reminiscent in some ways of the *Acohs* case in Australia discussed above, as it is not clear that the software in question could even be considered to be any type of artificial intelligence as commonly understood, by all descriptions of the software, as it is mostly a run-of-the-mill data analytics program. In other words, it's just a database. It is difficult to see why a court would not consider the output of such a work capable of copyright protection, but would allow any other output from similar software.

Another case in China has helped to shed further light on the issue, namely, *Tencent v Yinxun*.[158] In this case a court in Shenzhen has decided that an article that was written by an artificial intelligence program has copyright protection.[159] The article was written by Tencent's Dreamwriter AI Writing Robot,[160] an internal code at the Chinese tech giant that has produced half a million articles per year since 2015 in subjects such as weather, finance, sport, and real estate. The case involved the Shanghai Yingxun Technology Company, which copied and published one of the Dreamwriter authored articles, and which prompted Tencent to sue for copyright infringement. The court agreed with Tencent and ordered Yingxun to pay ¥1,500 yuan in damages.

This is an interesting follow-up to the *Feilin* case which, while it references the Beijing court's decision, involves a more sophisticated program that is more what we understand as artificial intelligence. The defendants tried to claim that the work was not protected by copyright as it was not authored by a human being, and therefore was in the public domain and could be used by anyone. However, the court decided that 'the article's form of expression conforms to the requirements of written work and the content showed the selection, analysis and judgement of relevant stock market information and data'. Moreover, 'the article's structure was reasonable, the logic was clear and it had a certain originality ... The automatic creation of the Dreamwriter software did not happen without cause or without conscious. Instead, the automation reflected the plaintiff's selection ... The form of expression underlying the article was determined by the personal arrangement and selection of the plaintiff's team.' In other words, it fulfilled the requirements for copyright protection.

With these two cases, we have confirmation that it is possible to bypass the human authorship argument, and that we should make this a question of originality, with such a requirement being considered on a case-by-case basis. As stated above, up until now the law has been ambiguous on this question, and for the most

158 *Shenzhen Tencent Computer System Co. Ltd. v Shanghai Yingxun Technology Co., Ltd.*, No 14010 Minchu (Shenzhen Nanshan District Ct. 2019). Full text of the decision at <https://mp.weixin.qq.com/s/jjv7aYT5wDBIdTVWXV6rdQ>.

159 As reported here: Li Yan, 'Court rules AI-written article has copyright' (*China Daily Global*, 9 January 2020) <http://www.ecns.cn/news/2020-01-09/detail-ifzsqcrm6562963.shtml>.

160 'Tencent robots have written thousands of articles a day' (*International Intelligent Robot Industry News*, 15 January 2019) <http://en.ii-robot.com/news/show.php?itemid=611>.

part it has been assumed that these works would be in the public domain as there is neither author nor originality. The relevance of the Chinese decision is that it considers directly whether the work is original, and states that if so, then it should be given protection.

4. Making the Case for Harmonization

For a system of protection that is supposed to be harmonized at an international level in order to promise predictability and ease of conducting business,[161] it is remarkable that the concept of originality, one of the most basic elements of authorship, is in such a state of disharmony. While the European standard of 'the author's own intellectual creation' has now been seamlessly incorporated to the UK standard of skill and labour, the higher threshold in countries like the US and Australia are still irreconcilable with the prevailing European approach. It is difficult to imagine an equivalent to *Temple Island Collections* bringing together such disparate standards as *Infopaq*, *IceTV*, and *Feist*.

It is clear that the various attitudes towards originality in computer-generated works highlighted above represent even more of a challenge. While originality may have been harmonized in Europe to a certain extent, it is impossible to foresee a case that would bring together *Infopaq* and section 9(3) CDPA. On the contrary, it would be possible to imagine a case that would try to declare the computer-generated work clause in the UK as contrary to European law.

While the concern of those who believe that there is no need to make changes to the law should be taken into account, *Acohs* shows us a future in which artificial intelligence works are not given copyright protection due to strict interpretation of what constitutes an original work. The requirement of having a human make all of the important creative decisions could have a significant economic effect in the future.

Besides computer code, there is one area where the effect of not giving protection to emergent works could have a serious commercial effect, and this is in the area of databases. It is no coincidence that some of the most important originality cases explored in the previous sections relate to data collection and compilation in one way or another.[162] At the heart of the problem with data collections is the fact that courts have to decide whether the often mechanical selection and gathering of data constitutes an original work worthy of copyright protection.[163] Why is this

[161] Kenneth D Crews, 'Harmonization and the Goals of Copyright: Property Rights or Cultural Progress?' 6 Indiana Journal of Global Legal Studies 117, 117–18.

[162] And it is no coincidence either that this is also the case in some other notorious decisions not cited here. See Case C-338/02 *Fixtures Mktg. Ltd. v Svenska Spel AB* [2004] ECR I-10497; and Case C-203/02 *British Horseracing Bd. Ltd. v William Hill Org. Ltd.* [2004] ECR I-10415, to name just a couple.

[163] Bryce Clayton Newell, 'Discounting the Sweat of the Brow: Converging International Standards for Electronic Database Protection' (2011) 15 Intellectual Property Law Bulletin 111.

relevant to the subject of computer-generated works? Because machine learning algorithms are already widely deployed in some of the most popular websites in the world.

One of the most famous machine learning systems in the world is Amazon's famous recommendation system, known as Deep Scalable Sparse Tensor Network Engine (DSSTNE, pronounced 'destiny'). This system populates Amazon's pages with unique recommendations for visitors based on previous purchases, and it has now been made available to the public under an open source licence,[164] which could lead to a much wider adoption of machine learning techniques, and also increase the potential for a copyright suit arising from the authorship of machine-made webpages. Netflix is another company that relies considerably on intelligent recommendation systems to populate film listings tailored for each user.[165]

These systems have human input in the sense that they were programmed by humans, but each unique work, namely the page displaying recommendations and listings, is created procedurally. Based on the current state of the law, these pages only have copyright unequivocally in the UK. While companies such as Amazon and Netlfix may not be too bothered about possible infringement, the future users of DSSTNE and other similar machine learning systems that generate listings may be more concerned about copying from competitors.

So there is certainly scope for harmonization. It is the contention of the present work that the best system available at the moment is the computer-generated work clause contained in section 9(3) CDPA. This has several advantages: it would bring certainty to an uncertain legal area; it has already been implemented internationally in various countries; it is ambiguous enough to deflect the user/programmer dichotomy question and make it analysed on a case-by-case basis; and it has been in existence for a relatively long time without much incident.

Moreover, a standard that allocates authorship to the person who made the necessary arrangements for a work to be made is consistent with existing law and case law, as evidenced by the *Tencent* case in China. There is no need to change originality standards as such, we would only be creating an addendum that applies to works made by a computer.

This approach has several advantages: it would bring certainty to an uncertain legal area; it has already been implemented internationally in various countries; it allows for each work to be analysed on a case-by-case basis; and it has been in existence for a relatively long time without much incident.

Moreover, a standard that allocates authorship to the person who made the necessary arrangements for a work to be made is consistent with existing law and case

164 Github <https://github.com/amznlabs/amazon-dsstne>.

165 Antony Arokisamy and others, 'Meson: workflow orchestration for Netflix recommendations' (*The Netflix Tech Blog*, 31 May 2016) <http://techblog.netflix.com/2016/05/meson_31.html>.

law. There is no need to change originality standards as such, we would only be creating an addendum that applies to works made by a computer.

This is better than the prevalent proposal to consider these works as not worthy of protection. While persuasive from a strictly doctrinal standpoint, there are various ways in which we can maintain the existing originality requirements, and still have some sort of protection for AI-generated works.

First, it is important to point out that the task of generating a work using AI is often not just a matter of pressing a button and letting the machine do all the work, someone has to program and teach the computer to compose music, write, or paint, and this is a process that is both lengthy and full of intellectual creativity. The makers of works of art such as *The Next Rembrandt* engaged in lengthy process, which could have enough 'intellectual creation'. On the other hand, you can go to a website[166] that is implementing OpenAI's GPT-2 predictive text model,[167] prompt the program with an opening sentence, and obtain some text with the press of a button. This involves hardly any action that we would recognize as original—unless we think that copying and pasting a few words is enough to meet any originality standard—and therefore any resulting work would not have protection. But more sophisticated AI needs more training and more human input, and this could potentially be considered as carrying enough intellectual creation from the user.

Secondly, the current system relies on the concept of originality that is very human centric, be it the requirement of intellectual creation. The idea behind this is that the human creative spark itself is what imbues a work with protection. But we are perfectly happy allowing legal persons to be authors and copyright owners, granted, with the understanding that the works are created by humans, so why not continue having another legal fiction only for AI works?

Thirdly, originality used to subsist if the author had exercised enough skill, labour, and judgement to warrant copyright protection.[168] Why not go back to a similar system that rewards a 'sweat of the brow' approach? While we have been moving away from such an approach, it might be worth reviewing the merits of recognizing the amount of effort and investment that goes into the creation of some of these works.

Finally, there are a number of practical problems with allowing increasing numbers of AI works to co-exist with human works. It is possible that public domain AI works will result in some creators to go out of business, as they cannot compete with free works. Stock photography, jingles, music for games, journalistic pieces, all of these could be affected by increasingly sophisticated AI.

[166] Talk to Transformer <https://talktotransformer.com/>.

[167] Alec Radford, Jeffrey Wu, Rewon Child, David Luan, Dario Amodei, and Ilya Sutskever, 'Language models are unsupervised multitask learners' (2019) 1:8 OpenAI Blog 9 <https://cdn.openai.com/better-language-models/language_models_are_unsupervised_multitask_learners.pdf>.

[168] Rahmatian Andreas, 'Originality in UK Copyright Law: The Old "Skill and Labour" Doctrine Under Pressure' (2013) 44 IIC 4.

Moreover, there are also some worrying practical implications. Copyright has no registration, so a work is assumed to be protected if it meets the existing requirements. This assumption is generally recognized by everyone, and it is not usually tested in court unless there is a conflict. The increasing sophistication of AI works will mean that there will be growing doubt as to the legitimate origin of works. Is this music created by a human or by AI? How could you tell?

5. Conclusion

At the end of the film Blade Runner, Roy Batty, an artificial entity (called a replicant in the movie), makes an impassioned speech before his death:

> I've seen things you people wouldn't believe. Attack ships on fire off the shoulder of Orion. I watched C-beams glitter in the dark near the Tannhäuser Gate. All those moments will be lost in time, like tears in the rain. Time to die.

While the film had characterized Batty as an inhuman killing machine intent on revenge, the final scene serves to display his humanity. An important element of the film's plot is that some replicants do not know that they are not human, implying that the distinction between self-aware machines that think they are human, and real humans, does not exist.

We are not at that stage yet, but we are certainly approaching a situation in which it will be difficult to discern if a song, a piece of poetry, or a painting, is made by a human or a machine. The monumental advances in computing, and the sheer amount of computational power available is making the distinction moot.

So we will have to make a decision as to what type of protection, if any, we should give to emergent works that have been created by intelligent algorithms with little or no human intervention. While the law in some jurisdictions does not grant such works with copyright status, countries like New Zealand, Ireland, South Africa, and the UK have decided to give copyright to the person who made possible the creation of procedural automated works.

This chapter proposes that it is precisely the model of protection based on the UK's own computer-generated work clause contained in section 9(3) CDPA that should be adopted more widely. The alternative is not to give protection to works that may merit it. Although we have been moving away from originality standards that reward skill, labour, and effort, perhaps we can establish an exception to that trend when it comes to the fruits of sophisticated artificial intelligence. The alternative seems contrary to the justifications of why we protect creative works in the first place.

8

Computer-generated Works under the CDPA 1988

*Jyh-An Lee**

1. Introduction

The Copyright, Designs and Patents Act (CDPA) 1988 in the UK provides copyright protection for literary, dramatic, musical, or artistic works generated by computer under circumstances where there was no human author.[1] In other words, for a computer-generated work in the UK, human authorship is irrelevant to whether the work is copyrightable. The CDPA 1988 further stipulates that the author of the computer-generated work is 'the person by whom the arrangements necessary for the creation of the work are undertaken'.[2] Some commentators view the computer-generated work provisions in the CDPA 1988 as being innovative[3] and some believe that this was the first legislation in the world protecting copyright in the context of artificial intelligence (AI).[4] While similar provisions exist in the copyright laws of some commonwealth jurisdictions, such as Ireland, New Zealand, Hong Kong, and South Africa,[5] most countries do not recognize the

* This study was supported by a grant from the Research Grants Council in Hong Kong (Project No.: CUHK 14612417). The author is grateful to Ms Jingwen Liu for her valuable research assistance. All online materials were accessed before 5 December 2020.

[1] CDPA 1988, ss 9(3), 178.

[2] CDPA 1988, s 9(3).

[3] Ysolde Gendreau, 'Copyright Ownership of Photographs in Anglo-American Law' (1993) 15(6) EIPR 207, 210–11.

[4] Toby Bond and Sarah Blair, 'Artificial Intelligence and Copyright: Section 9(3) or Authorship without an Author' (2019) 14 JIPLP 423 (hereafter Bond and Blair, 'Artificial Intelligence and Copyright').

[5] Annemarie Bridy, 'Coding Creativity: Copyright and the Artificially Intelligent Author' (2012) 2012 Stanford Technology Law Review 5, 67–8 (hereafter Bridy, 'Coding Creativity'); Colin R Davies, 'An Evolutionary Step in Intellectual Property Rights—Artificial Intelligence and Intellectual Property' (2011) 27 Computer Law & Security Review 601, 612; Tim W Dornis, 'Artificial Creativity: Emergent Works and the Void in Current Copyright Doctrine' (2020) 22 Yale Journal of Law & Technology 1, 17 (hereafter Dornis, 'Artificial Creativity'); Andres Guadamuz, 'Do Androids Dream of Electric Copyright? Comparative Analysis of Originality in Artificial Intelligence Generated Works' (2017) 2017(2) Intellectual Property Quarterly 169, 175, fn 52 (hereafter Guadamuz, 'Do Androids Dream of Electric Copyright?'); Paul Lambert, 'Computer-Generated Works and Copyright: Selfies, Traps, Robots, AI and Machine Learning' (2017) 39 European Intellectual Property Review 12, 17–18 (hereafter Lambert, 'Computer-Generated Works and Copyright'); Jani McCutcheon, 'The Vanishing Author in Computer-Generated Works: A Critical Analysis of Recent Australian Case Law' (2013) 36 Melbourne University Law Review 915, 956–7 (hereafter McCutcheon, 'The Vanishing Author

Jyh-An Lee, *Computer-generated Works under the CDPA 1988* In: *Artificial Intelligence and Intellectual Property*. Edited by: Jyh-An Lee, Reto M Hilty, and Kung-Chung Liu, Oxford University Press (2021). © The several contributors. DOI: 10.1093/oso/9780198870944.003.0009

copyrightability of such works. Nor have similar provisions been mentioned by any international intellectual property (IP) treaties.[6] With the advancement of AI technologies on an unprecedented scale and their increasing commercial applications, scholars have proposed to discuss whether the UK approach is desirable in the IP treaty-making.[7]

Thanks to the rapid development in the AI technologies in recent years, more and more works created by AI may fall into the category of computer-generated work under CDPA 1988. For example, *The Next Rembrandt* was an AI-generated portrait based on the machine learning of the lightening, colouration, brushstrokes, and geometric patterns of hundreds of Rembrandt Harmenszoon van Rijn's art works.[8] Google's WaveNet project can also create various types of music by studying and analysing existing music works.[9] These are just two of many examples of AI's ability to create high-quality artistic works and music works.[10] Other AI-generated works include poems,[11] novels,[12]

in Computer-Generated Works'); Mark Perry and Thomas Marhoni, 'From Music Tracks to Google Maps: Who Owns Computer-Generated Works?' (2010) 26 Computer Law & Security Review 621, 622, 625 (hereafter Perry and Marhoni, 'From Music Tracks to Google Maps').

[6] JAL Sterling, 'International Codification of Copyright Law: Possibilities and Imperatives' (2002) 33(3) IIC 270, 275.

[7] Jane C Ginsburg, 'People Not Machines: Authorship and What It Means in the Berne Convention' (2018) 49(2) IIC 131, 134–5.

[8] Dornis, 'Artificial Creativity' (n 5) 4; Guadamuz, 'Do Androids Dream of Electric Copyright?' (n 5) 169–70; Atilla Kasap, 'Copyright and Creative Artificial Intelligence (AI) Systems: A Twenty-First Century Approach to Authorship of AI-Generated Works in the United States' (2019) 19 Wake Forest Journal of Business & Intellectual Property Law 335, 342 (hereafter Kasap, 'Copyright and Creative Artificial Intelligence (AI) Systems'); Daryl Lim, 'AI & IP: Innovation & Creativity in an Age of Accelerated Change' (2018) 52 Akron L Rev 813, 832–3 (hereafter Daryl Lim, 'AI & IP'); Massimo Maggiore, 'Artificial Intelligence, Computer Generated Works and Copyright' in Enrico Bonadio and Nicola Lucchi (eds), *Non-Conventional Copyright: Do New and Atypical Works Deserve Protection?* (EE 2018) 383–4 (hereafter Maggiore, 'Artificial Intelligence, Computer Generated Works and Copyright').

[9] Jani Ihalainen, 'Computer Creativity: Artificial Intelligence and Copyright' (2018) 13 JIPLP 724, 724 (hereafter Ihalainen, 'Computer Creativity'); Guadamuz, 'Do Androids Dream of Electric Copyright?' (n 5) 172; Victor M Palace, 'What if Artificial Intelligence Wrote This? Artificial Intelligence and Copyright Law' (2019) 71 Florida Law Review 217, 223 (hereafter Palace, 'What if Artificial Intelligence Wrote This?').

[10] Enrico Bonadio, Luke McDonagh, and Christopher Arvidsson, 'Intellectual Property Aspects of Robotics' (2018) 9 European Journal of Risk Regulation 655, 664 (hereafter Bonadio, McDonagh, and Arvidsson, 'Intellectual Property Aspects of Robotics'); Annemarie Bridy, 'The Evolution of Authorship: Work Made by Code' (2016) 39 Columbia Journal of Law & the Arts 395, 397–8; Jane C Ginsburg and Luke Ali Budiardjo, 'Authors and Machines' (2019) 34 Berkeley Technology Law Journal 343, 407–9, 434–5; Kasap, 'Copyright and Creative Artificial Intelligence (AI) Systems' (n 8) 342; Daryl Lim, 'AI & IP' (n 8) 813, 832–3; Palace, 'What if Artificial Intelligence Wrote This?' (n 9) 223; Eleanor Selfridge-Field, 'Substantial Musical Similarity in Sound and Notation: Perspectives from Digital Musicology' (2018) 16 Colorado Technology Law Journal 249, 281–2.

[11] Bonadio, McDonagh, and Arvidsson, 'Intellectual Property Aspects of Robotics' (n 10) 664; Julia Dickenson, Alex Morgan, and Birgit Clark, 'Creative Machines: Ownership of Copyright in Content Created by Artificial Intelligence Applications' (2017) 39 EIPR 457, 457 (hereafter Dickenson, Morgan, and Clark, 'Creative Machines'); McCutcheon, 'The Vanishing Author in Computer-Generated Works' (n 5) 930–1; Maggiore, 'Artificial Intelligence, Computer Generated Works and Copyright' (n 8) 384.

[12] Ihalainen, 'Computer Creativity' (n 9) 725; Ana Ramalho, 'Will Robots Rule the (Artistic) World? A Proposed Model for the Legal Status of Creations by Artificial Intelligence Systems' (2017) 21 Journal of Internet Law 11, 12 (hereafter Ramalho, 'Will Robots Rule the (Artistic) World?').

screenplays,[13] jokes,[14] sketches,[15] photographs,[16] computer programs,[17] business reports,[18] news stories,[19] etc. These works involving a high level of creativity are generally indistinguishable from those created by professional human creators.[20] Some artistic productions, paintings in particular, generated by AI have been sold at steep prices.[21] However, legal issues arise because copyright jurisprudence has focused on human creativity, and the generative AI software is not a legal entity capable of owning a copyright.[22]

While some commenters in other countries advocate the transplant of the computer-generated works provisions from the CDPA 1998 to cope with new challenges brought by AI technologies,[23] the British courts have only applied these provisions once, in a case which did not involve any AI technology.[24] When the provisions of computer-generated works in CDPA were drafted in 1988, machine learning and other forms of AI technology were not as developed and widely used as today. Therefore, although these provisions represented Parliament's endeavour of 'precautionary intervention' into the future world of computer intelligence,[25] they might not be able to handle copyright issues resulting from current AI technologies.[26]

This chapter examines legal issues associated with the computer-generated works provisions in the CDPA 1998, especially in the context of the advancement of AI technology. Following the introduction, Section 2 explores the trajectory of these provisions by distinguishing computer-generated works from computer-assisted works. It also compares AI-generated works and traditionally perceived computer-generated works. AI-generated works differ notably from not only

[13] Kasap, 'Copyright and Creative Artificial Intelligence (AI) Systems' (n 8) 342; Dessislav Dobrev, 'The Human Lawyer in the Age of Artificial Intelligence: Doomed for Extinction or in Need of a Survival Manual' (2018) 18 Journal of International Business & Law 39, 53.

[14] Kasap, 'Copyright and Creative Artificial Intelligence (AI) Systems' (n 8) 342.

[15] Ibid

[16] Palace, 'What if Artificial Intelligence Wrote This?' (n 9) 223–4.

[17] Madeleine de Cock Buning, 'Autonomous Intelligent Systems as Creative Agents under the EU Framework for Intellectual Property' (2016) 7 European Journal of Risk Regulation 310, 310 (hereafter de Cock Buning, 'Autonomous Intelligent Systems').

[18] Dornis, 'Artificial Creativity' (n 5) 4.

[19] Robert Yu, 'The Machine Author: What Level of Copyright Protection Is Appropriate for Fully Independent Computer-Generated Works?' (2017) 165 University of Pennsylvania Law Review 1245, 1246–7 (hereafter Yu, 'The Machine Author').

[20] Perry and Marhoni, 'From Music Tracks to Google Maps' (n 5) 622.

[21] Timothy Pinto, 'Robo ART! The Copyright Implications of Artificial Intelligence Generated Art' (2019) 30(6) Entertainment Law Review 174, 174 (hereafter Pinto, 'Robo ART!')

[22] Eliza Mik, Chapter 19 in this volume.

[23] Bridy, 'Coding Creativity' (n 5) 66–7; Cody Weyhofen 'Scaling the Meta-Mountain: Deep Reinforcement Learning Algorithms and the Computer-Authorship Debate' (2019) 87 UMKC Law Review 979, 996.

[24] *Nova Productions Ltd v Mazooma Games Ltd* [2006] EWHC 24 (Ch) (20 January 2006).

[25] William Cornish, David Llewelyn, and Tanya Aplin, *Intellectual Property: Patents, Copyright, Trade Marks and Allied Rights* (9th edn, Sweet & Maxwell 2019) 863 (hereafter Cornish, Llewelyn, and Aplin, *Intellectual Property*).

[26] Dickenson, Morgan, and Clark, 'Creative Machines' (n 11) 458.

authorial works but also from traditionally perceived computer-generated works. Section 3 analyses the originality doctrine, which prevents computer-generated works from being protected by copyright law in most other jurisdictions. Because computer-generated works without originality are protected as copyright works in the CDPA 1988, some commentators categorize them as entrepreneurial works or as a neighbouring right. This section also illustrates the similarity and dissimilarity between computer-generated works and entrepreneurial works. Section 4 examines the determination of authorship in computer-generated works. While the CDPA 1988 stipulates that the author of a computer-generated work is 'the person by whom the arrangements necessary for the creation of the work are undertaken',[27] it is unclear who the person is that makes the necessary arrangement for the creation of an AI-generated work. Although Kitchin J once ruled that the person is the programmer instead of the player of a computer game, this determination only applies to a specific scenario concerning the display of a series of composite frames generated by a computer program.[28] It would be arbitrary to jump to the conclusion that the programmer is invariably the author of the computer-generated work. The determination of authorship will be even more complicated in an AI environment where the programmer, trainer, data provider, and machine operators all play important roles in the creation of the work. Section 5 discusses unresolved legal and policy issues. From a policy perspective, there has been a debate over whether computer-generated works deserve copyright protection. Moreover, copyright protection of computer-generated works will lead to other unsolved legal issues, such as copyright term and joint authorship. Section 6 concludes.

2. Scope

Computer-generated works are different from computer-assisted ones. The former refers to works generated automatically by computers, whereas the latter are created by human beings who use computers as tools to facilitate or improve their works.[29] In the context of computer-generated works, after programming, the role of human beings becomes negligible in the creation of the work.[30] In other words, the software autonomously generates the works and independently determines the particulars of the output.[31] In *Express Newspapers Plc v Liverpool Daily Post &*

[27] CDPA 1988, s 9(3).

[28] *Nova Productions Ltd v Mazooma Games Ltd* [2006] EWHC 24 (Ch) (20 January 2006) paras 12–18.

[29] Bonadio, McDonagh, and Arvidsson, 'Intellectual Property Aspects of Robotics' (n 10) 667; Ihalainen, 'Computer Creativity' (n 9) 725–6; McCutcheon, 'The Vanishing Author in Computer-Generated Works' (n 5) 929, 931–2; Perry and Marhoni, 'From Music Tracks to Google Maps' (n 5) 622–3.

[30] Perry and Marhoni, 'From Music Tracks to Google Maps' (n 5) 624; Yu, 'The Machine Author' (n 19) 1258.

[31] McCutcheon, 'The Vanishing Author in Computer-Generated Works' (n 5) 929.

Echo Plc and Others, the plaintiff designed a promotional scheme with a number of cards, each carrying a five-letter code.[32] In order to compete for a prize, readers needed to 'check the cards against grids containing 25 letters and two separate rows of five letters which were published daily in the plaintiff's newspapers'.[33] In order to save time and labour, the plaintiff's employee Mr. Ertel wrote computer programs that could generate an appropriate number of varying grids and letter sequences.[34] The defendant copied the grids and the two rows of five letters day by day in their publications[35] and argued that 'the result produced as a consequence of running those programmes [by the plaintiff] was not a work'.[36] Whitford J recognized the copyrightability of the result and ruled for the plaintiff:[37]

> The computer was no more than the tool by which the varying grids of five-letter sequences were produced to the instructions, via the computer programmes, of Mr. Ertel. It is as unrealistic as it would be to suggest that, if You write Your work with a pen, it is the pen which is the author of the work rather than the person who drives the pen.

Some scholars indicated this was a case concerning computer-generated works before the enactment of the CDPA 1988.[38] Nevertheless, the work in the case could not actually fall into the definition of computer-generated work in the CDPA 1988 because the plaintiff did not directly publish the computer-generated results. Instead, Mr. Ertel needed to check the results and decide which part would be included in the plaintiff's newspapers.[39] This process involved skills, judgement, and human creation. Therefore, the work in this case was computer-assisted, rather than computer-generated.[40] There is originality in the former, but not the latter. The deployment of computers and other tools in the human creative process is common in various creative environments and has not been an obstacle for copyright protection.[41]

The statutory definition of computer-generated work is a work 'generated by computer in circumstances such that there is no human author of the work'.[42] This

[32] *Express Newspapers Plc v Liverpool Daily Post & Echo Plc and Others* [1985] 1 WLR 1089, 1089.
[33] Ibid.
[34] Ibid, 1093.
[35] Ibid, 1089, 1092.
[36] Ibid, 1093.
[37] Ibid.
[38] Lionel Bently and Brad Sherman, *Intellectual Property Law* (4th edn, Oxford University Press 2014) 127 fn 21 (hereafter Bently and Sherman, *Intellectual Property Law*); Guadamuz, 'Do Androids Dream of Electric Copyright?' (n 5) 175–6.
[39] *Express Newspapers Plc v Liverpool Daily Post & Echo Plc and Others* [1985] 1 WLR 1089, 1093.
[40] Emily Dorotheou, 'Reap the Benefits and Avoid the Legal Uncertainty: Who Owns the Creations of Artificial Intelligence?' (2015) 21(4) CTLR 85, 86–7 (hereafter Dorotheou, 'Reap the Benefits and Avoid the Legal Uncertainty'); Lambert, 'Computer-Generated Works and Copyright' (n 5) 13.
[41] Maggiore, 'Artificial Intelligence, Computer Generated Works and Copyright' (n 8) 382–3.
[42] CDPA 1988, s 178.

definition might accidentally include some works beyond Parliament's contemplation. For example, when users use keywords to extract information from the Lexis database, the result of the search might well fall into the statutory definition of computer-generated works.[43] However, providing copyright protection for such results seems odd because it is not copyright's policy goal to incentivize such creations. Examples of computer-generated work provided in the literature include satellite photography,[44] 'works created by translation programs, search engines, and the like'.[45]

Computer-generated works have only appeared once in the English case law. In *Nova Productions v Mazooma Games and Others*, the work concerned was the display of a series of composite frames generated by a computer program using bitmap files in a coin-operated game 'Pocket Money' designed, manufactured, and sold by the claimant Nova Productions Limited ('Nova').[46] Kitchin J at the first instance explained specifically how the composite frames were generated:

> The program builds up composite images by taking, for example, the bitmap image of the table and then overlaying it with images of the balls, cue and the like. In the computer memory many different images of each of these items are stored. So, for example, images of the cue are stored in a large number of different orientations. One of these will be selected by the program to create an appropriate image of the cue on the screen.[47]

Kitchin J ruled that:

> these composite frames are artistic works. They were created by [the programmer] Mr. Jones or by the computer program which he wrote. In the latter case, the position is governed by [computer-generated work provisions] s.9(3) of the Act ... [a]nd by s.178 ... [48]

Nova is a representative case in which the court applied computer-generated work provisions in the CDPA 1988. However, it should be noted that although Kitchin J defined the composite frames produced by the claimant's computer program as computer-generated works, he ruled that defendants' works were not similar to the claimant's work.[49] Nova then appealed to the Court of Appeals.

[43] Cornish, Llewelyn, and Aplin, *Intellectual Property* (n 25) 864.

[44] de Cock Buning, 'Autonomous Intelligent Systems' (n 17) 318; Lambert, 'Computer-Generated Works and Copyright' (n 5) 13, 18; Sam Ricketson, 'The Need for Human Authorship—Australian Developments: Telstra Corp Ltd v Phone Directories Co Pty Ltd' (2012) 34 EIPR 54, 55 (hereafter Ricketson, 'The Need for Human Authorship').

[45] Bently and Sherman, *Intellectual Property Law* (n 38) 116.

[46] *Nova Productions Ltd v Mazooma Games Ltd* [2006] EWHC 24 (Ch) (20 January 2006) paras 12–18.

[47] Ibid, para 102.

[48] Ibid, paras 2, 104.

[49] Ibid, paras 2, 136–56.

While Jacob LJ in the Court of Appeals agreed with Kitchin's ruling, whether Nova's composite frames were computer-generated works were not an issue at all in his judgment.[50]

The works in *Nova* were generated by a computer program, but not by AI. While AI-generated works can be categorized as computer-generated works, they are qualitatively different from conventionally conceived computer-generated works. Computer-generated works perceived by the CDPA 1998 and *Nova* were the stably fixed results of software operation, designed and expected by the programmer. By contrast, with continuous machine learning, the machine is able to make creative decisions unexpected by its designer, and AI-generated works can evolve over time.[51]

3. Originality and Entrepreneurial Works

Professor Arthur R Miller rightfully foretold in his 1993 Harvard Law Review article that 'the next battlefield [of the computer-copyright battle] may be the protectability and authorship of computer-generated works'.[52] Because intellectual creation, an essential element of originality, is lacking in computer-generated works, commentators have had concerns over granting copyright protection to them by the CDPA 1988.[53] In many jurisdictions, such as the US and other European countries, computer-generated works are not copyrightable because of the absence of human creativity involved in the creation of the works.[54] Moreover, not all commonwealth jurisdictions have computer-generated work clauses similar to those in the CDPA 1988. Australia is a notable example where the courts ruled

[50] *Nova Productions Ltd v Mazooma Games Ltd* [2007] EWCA Civ 219 (14 March 2007).

[51] See, eg, Dornis, 'Artificial Creativity' (n 5) 8, 15; Dorotheou, 'Reap the Benefits and Avoid the Legal Uncertainty' (n 40) 89; Guadamuz, 'Do Androids Dream of Electric Copyright?' (n 5) 171; Mira T Sundara Rajan, *Moral Rights: Principles, Practice and New Technology* (Oxford University Press 2011) 310 (hereafter Rajan, *Moral Rights*); Anthony Man-Cho So, Chapter 1 in this volume.

[52] Arthur R Miller, 'Copyright Protection for Computer Programs, Databases, and Computer-Generated Works: Is Anything New Since CONTU?' (1993) 106 Harvard Law Review 977, 1054.

[53] Lionel Bently, Brad Sherman, Dev Gangjee, and Philip Johnson, *Intellectual Property Law* (5th edn, Oxford University Press 2018) 117–78 (hereafter Bently, Sherman, Gangjee, and Johnson, *Intellectual Property Law*).

[54] Bonadio, McDonagh, and Arvidsson, 'Intellectual Property Aspects of Robotics' (n 10) 669; Jeremy A Cubert and Richard GA Bone, 'The Law of Intellectual Property Created by Artificial Intelligence' in Woodrow Barfield and Ugo Pagallo (eds), *Research Handbook on the Law of Artificial Intelligence* (EE 2018) 424–5 (hereafter Cubert and Bone, 'The Law of Intellectual Property Created by Artificial Intelligence'); de Cock Buning, 'Autonomous Intelligent Systems' (n 17) 314–15; Dickenson, Morgan, and Clark, 'Creative Machines' (n 11) 457–8; Dornis, 'Artificial Creativity' (n 5) 20–4; Guadamuz, 'Do Androids Dream of Electric Copyright?' (n 5) 182–3; Ihalainen, 'Computer Creativity' (n 9) 726–7; Lambert, 'Computer-Generated Works and Copyright' (n 5) 14; Andres Guadamuz, Chapter 7 of this volume; Maggiore, 'Artificial Intelligence, Computer Generated Works and Copyright' (n 8) 387–9; Perry and Marhoni, 'From Music Tracks to Google Maps' (n 5) 624–5; Ramalho, 'Will Robots Rule the (Artistic) World?' (n 12) 14–16; Jacob Turner, *Robot Rules Regulating Artificial Intelligence* (Palgrave Macmillan 2019) 123–4 (hereafter Turner, *Robot Rules Regulating Artificial Intelligence*).

that computer-generated works were not copyrightable because there was no human author and the originality was thus lacking in the works.[55] By categorizing computer-generated works as copyright works, the UK law deviates not only from the European standard of originality, which requires human creation,[56] but also a general understanding of authorship in the copyright regime.[57]

Originality reflects the author's creativity in the copyright work. Conventional wisdom of copyright law indicates that human beings are the only source of creativity.[58] The computer-generated works that existed during the enactment of CDPA 1988 involved a rather straightforward process of creation. The output was produced as a result of a predetermined process and could be forecast and planned by the programmer. By contrast, AI-generated works reflect much more creative choices which are not envisioned by the programmers.[59] Were the same works produced by human beings, they would normally be viewed as original ones subject to copyright protection. A policy issue faced by the current copyright regime is whether copyright should protect such machine creativity or stay with the principle that copyright protection should be mainly based on human creativity. A subtle issue for CDPA 1988 and similar copyright regimes with computer-generated works clauses is whether copyright law should treat AI-generated works differently from other computer-generated works, because the former encompasses creative choices similar to that of human authors.

In fact, copyright law also protects unoriginal work. One example is that related rights or neighbouring rights in unoriginal sound recording and broadcasts are protected by copyright law as well.[60] Related right is the term used by the EU Copyright Directive, and it is referred to as neighbouring rights in continental Europe.[61] In the UK, works with neighbouring rights are referred to as entrepreneurial works, comprising films, sound recordings, broadcasts and cable

[55] *Achohs Pty Ltd. v Ucorp Pty Ltd.* [2010] FCA 577, confirmed on appeal; McCutcheon, 'The Vanishing Author in Computer-Generated Works' (n 5) 920–9; Ramalho, 'Will Robots Rule the (Artistic) World?' (n 12) 16; Perry and Marhoni, 'From Music Tracks to Google Maps' (n 5) 622; Ricketson, 'The Need for Human Authorship' (n 44) 55–9; Shlomit Yanisky-Ravid, 'Generating Rembrandt: Artificial Intelligence, Copyright, and Accountability in the 3A Era—The Humanlike Authors Are Already Here—A New Model' (2017) 2017 Michigan State Law Review 659, 718 (hereafter Yanisky-Ravid, 'Generating Rembrandt').

[56] Bently, Sherman, Gangjee, and Johnson, *Intellectual Property Law* (n 53) 117–18; Cornish, Llewelyn, and Aplin, *Intellectual Property* (n 25) 863; Dickenson, Morgan, and Clark, 'Creative Machines' (n 11) 459; Guadamuz, 'Do Androids Dream of Electric Copyright?' (n 5) 175, 177–8, 185.

[57] Cornish, Llewelyn, and Aplin, *Intellectual Property* (n 25) 863–4.

[58] Maggiore, 'Artificial Intelligence, Computer Generated Works and Copyright' (n 8) 384–6, 389–90; Andres Guadamuz, Chapter 7 of this volume (n 54).

[59] Maggiore, 'Artificial Intelligence, Computer Generated Works and Copyright' (n 8) 384.

[60] Muhammed Abrar, 'WIPO Proposed Treaty Development and Critical Legal Studies' (2013) 35 EIPR 715, 721–2 (hereafter Abrar, 'WIPO Proposed Treaty Development').

[61] Ibid, 715–16; Richard Arnold, 'Content Copyrights and Signal Copyrights: The Case for a Rational Scheme of Protection' (2011) 1 QMJIP 272, 273 (hereafter Arnold, 'Content Copyrights and Signal Copyrights'); Christopher Heath, 'All Her Troubles Seemed So Far Away: EU v Japan Before the WTO' (1996) 18 EIPR 677, 677; Kamiel J Koelman, 'Copyright Law and Economics in the EU Copyright Directive: Is the Droit D'auteur Passe?' (2004) 35 IIC 603, 612.

programmes, and typographical arrangements. Entrepreneurial works are distinct from authorial works, which include literary, dramatic, musical, or artistic works. One of the main distinctions between these two types of work is that originality is required for authorial works but not for entrepreneurial works.[62] This is because the purpose of protecting entrepreneurial works or neighbouring rights is to protect the financial investment of making the subject work available to the public or producing the subject matter, not the creativity of the authors.[63]

Because originality is not required in the protection of computer-generated works either, some scholars suggest that they should be protected as entrepreneurial works.[64] Just like sound recording and broadcast, the deemed author of a computer-generated work is a fictitious one who does not need to contribute creativity in the creation of the work.[65] Moreover, under the CDPA 1988, sound recording, broadcasts, and computer-generated works are protected for fifty years from the end of the calendar year in which the work is made,[66] whereas copyright for authorial works expires at the end of the period of seventy years from the end of the calendar year in which the author dies.[67] Therefore, computer-generated works' thinner copyright protection than authorial works' has also made them similar to entrepreneurial works.[68] One explanation of this thinner protection is that computer-generated works are less costly than authorial works to produce.[69]

Nevertheless, categorizing computer-generated works as entrepreneurial works will lead to certain controversies over infringement determination in the context of AI-generated works. Entrepreneurial works are sometimes understood as 'signal works'.[70] The protection of entrepreneurial works is limited to the form in which the work is fixed.[71] In the case of a film, infringement occurs when the specific images are taken.[72] In the case of a sound recording, the infringer must copy a specific

[62] Bently, Sherman, Gangjee, and Johnson, *Intellectual Property Law* (n 53) 118; Cornish, Llewelyn, and Aplin, *Intellectual Property* (n 25) 454; Michelle James, 'Some Joy at Last for Cinematographers' (2000) 22 EIPR 131, 132 (hereafter James, 'Some Joy at Last for Cinematographers').

[63] Abrar, 'WIPO Proposed Treaty Development' (n 60) 722; James, 'Some Joy at Last for Cinematographers' (n 62) 132; Cornish, Llewelyn, and Aplin, *Intellectual Property* (n 25) 451–2; Joshua Marshall, 'Case Comment: Copyright "Works" and "Fixation": Where Are We Now?' (2019) 2019(3) IPQ 352, 261; David Vaver, 'Translation and Copyright: A Canadian Focus' (1994) 16(4) EIPR 159, 162 (hereafter Vaver, 'Translation and Copyright').

[64] Bond and Blair, 'Artificial Intelligence and Copyright' (n 4) 423; Bently and Sherman, *Intellectual Property Law* (n 38) 117; Dornis, 'Artificial Creativity' (n 5) 44–6; Lambert, 'Computer-Generated Works and Copyright' (n 5) 13, 18; Maggiore, 'Artificial Intelligence, Computer Generated Works and Copyright' (n 8) 398.

[65] Vaver, 'Translation and Copyright' (n 63) 162

[66] CDPA 1988, ss 12(7), 13(A)(2), and 14(2).

[67] CDPA 1988, s 12(2).

[68] Cornish, Llewelyn, and Aplin, *Intellectual Property* (n 25) 863.

[69] Kasap, 'Copyright and Creative Artificial Intelligence (AI) Systems' (n 8) 364.

[70] Arnold, 'Content Copyrights and Signal Copyrights' (n 61) 276–7.

[71] Ibid, 276; Martina Gillen, 'File-sharing and Individual Civil liability in the United Kingdom: A Question of Substantial Abuse?' (2006) 17 Entertainment Law Review 7, 11.

[72] *Telmak Teleproducts Australia Pty Ltd v Bond International Pty Ltd* (1985) 5 IPR 203, (1986) 6 IPR 97; *Norowzian v Arks Ltd* [1999] EMLR 57; Cornish, Llewelyn, and Aplin, *Intellectual Property* (n 25) 451–2; James, 'Some Joy at Last for Cinematographers' (n 62) 132.

sound recorded. By contrast, the protection of authorial works extends beyond the specific form of signals in which the work is recorded or communicated.[73] This is because authorial works are protected due to the originality and creativity contributed by their authors, whereas entrepreneurial works are protected to incentivize investment in making available specific works via signals to the public.[74] If a computer-generated work is categorized as a signal work like other entrepreneurial works, then its infringement can only be found in the form in which it is fixed. Imagine there is an AI-generated fiction. If we categorize the work as an entrepreneurial work, the only way to infringe the copyright of such a computer-generated work is to reproduce the fiction in the form as it is fixed. However, if someone produces a film based on the AI-generated fiction, he does not infringe any copyright because the film is not a copy of the specific signals underlying the fiction. Therefore, if the law is to protect computer-generated works as traditional entrepreneurial works, there are obvious loopholes of protection, especially in the context of AI.

4. Authorship

Many believe that international copyright norms presuppose that authors must be humans.[75] Authorship in authorial works represents the author's creativity and personality associated with the subject work.[76] This personal relation, built upon the author's skill and judgement with the work, is understood as the author's originality.[77] In countries without computer-generated works provisions similar to the CDPA 1998, there are no authors for such works.[78] By contrast, the CDPA 1988 stipulates that the author of a computer-generated work is 'the person by whom the arrangements necessary for the creation of the work are undertaken'.[79] Although there is no readily identifiable author that makes the necessary arrangements for the creation,[80] it is clear the CDPA 1988 intends to build a personal relation or

[73] Bently, Sherman, Gangjee, and Johnson, *Intellectual Property Law* (n 53) 118.

[74] Arnold, 'Content Copyrights and Signal Copyrights' (n 61) 277.

[75] Ramalho, 'Will Robots Rule the (Artistic) World?' (n 12) 14.

[76] Jane C Ginsburg, 'Creation and Commercial Value: Copyright Protection of Works of Information' (1990) 90 Columbia Law Review 1865, 1866–74 (hereafter Ginsburg, 'Creation and Commercial Value'); Maggiore, 'Artificial Intelligence, Computer Generated Works and Copyright' (n 8) 384–5; Rebecca Tushnet, 'Copy This Essay: How Fair Use Doctrine Harms Free Speech and How Copying Serves It' (2004) 114 Yale Law Journal 535, 541; Lior Zemer, 'On the Value of Copyright Theory' (2006) 2006(1) IPQ 55, 69.

[77] Bond and Blair, 'Artificial Intelligence and Copyright' (n 4) 423; McCutcheon, 'The Vanishing Author in Computer-Generated Works' (n 5) 935; Tanya Aplin and Jennifer Davis, *Intellectual Property Law: Text, Cases, and Materials* (3rd edn, Oxford University Press 2017) 133; Ginsburg, 'Creation and Commercial Value' (n 76) 1867; Guadamuz, 'Do Androids Dream of Electric Copyright?' (n 5) 177–8; Maggiore, 'Artificial Intelligence, Computer Generated Works and Copyright' (n 8) 390.

[78] Mark Sherwood-Edwards, 'The Redundancy of Originality' (1994) 25(5) IIC 658, 680–1.

[79] CDPA 1988, s 9(3).

[80] Bonadio, McDonagh, and Arvidsson, 'Intellectual Property Aspects of Robotics' (n 10) 670.

causal link between the author and the computer-generated work.[81] Put differently, the CDPA 1988 intends to trace the most relevant human intervention associated with the creation of the work.[82]

Some view the computer-generated works provisions in the CDPA 1988 as a deviation from international copyright rules which define authors as those who create the work.[83] Different from authors contributing creativity to authorial works, the author enjoys copyright over computer-generated works for undertaking the necessary arrangements for the creation of the work under CDPA 1988. As Lord Beaverbrook explained during the enactment of the CDPA 1988, this person 'will not himself have made any personal, creative efforts'.[84] While the computer-generated work is produced by the computer rather than the deemed author in the law, the author of a computer-generated work has a more remote relation with the work than that of an authorial work.[85] Thanks to this relatively marginal role played by the author in the computer-generated work, he or she enjoys neither the moral right to be identified as author or director, nor the right to object to derogatory treatment of the work under CDPA 1998.[86] This is because the very nature of moral rights concerns the author's personality expressed in the work, and this personality is lacking in the computer-generated works.[87]

Most academic and judicial discussions regarding the author of a computer-generated work focus on whether that is a person operating the computer or programming the computer.[88] The majority view is that the author should be the computer programmer who wrote the algorithm(s) that generated the work.[89] Since the programmer is 'the author of the author of the work', he seems to be the logical owner of the computer-generated work.[90] This viewpoint was illustrated by

81 Turner, *Robot Rules Regulating Artificial Intelligence* (n 54) 125.

82 Ramalho, 'Will Robots Rule the (Artistic) World?' (n 12) 17.

83 Ibid.

84 Dorotheou, 'Reap the Benefits and Avoid the Legal Uncertainty' (n 40) 87; Guadamuz, 'Do Androids Dream of Electric Copyright?' (n 5) 176; Maggiore, 'Artificial Intelligence, Computer Generated Works and Copyright' (n 8) 397.

85 Dorotheou, 'Reap the Benefits and Avoid the Legal Uncertainty' (n 40) 90; Lambert, 'Computer-Generated Works and Copyright' (n 5) 13.

86 CDPA 1988, ss 79(2)(7) and 81(2). It should be noted that the Indian Copyright Act might be the only copyright regime that protects moral right in computer-generated works. See Rajan, *Moral Rights* (n 51) 311.

87 McCutcheon, 'The Vanishing Author in Computer-Generated Works' (n 5) 963; Jani McCutcheon, 'Curing the Authorless Void: Protecting Computer-Generated Works Following IceTV and Phone Directories' (2013) 37 Melbourne University Law Review 46, 71–2 (hereafter McCutcheon, 'Curing the Authorless Void').

88 Bently, Sherman, Gangjee, and Johnson, *Intellectual Property Law* (n 53) 128; Cornish, Llewelyn, and Aplin, *Intellectual Property* (n 25) 853.

89 Dickenson, Morgan, and Clark, 'Creative Machines' (n 11) 458–9; Lin Weeks, 'Media Law and Copyright Implications of Automated Journalism' (2014) 4 NYU Journal of Intellectual Property & Entertainment Law 67, 92; Peter K Yu, 'Data Producer's Right and the Protection of Machine-Generated Data' (2019) 93 Tulane Law Review 859, 904.

90 Bridy, 'Coding Creativity' (n 5) 51.

Kitchin J in *Nova* concerning whether the computer-generated works in a computer game belong to the programmer or the user:

> In so far as each composite frame is a computer generated work then the arrangements necessary for the creation of the work were undertaken by [the programmer] Mr. Jones because he devised the appearance of the various elements of the game and the rules and logic by which each frame is generated and he wrote the relevant computer program. In these circumstances I am satisfied that Mr. Jones is the person by whom the arrangements necessary for the creation of the works were undertaken and therefore is deemed to be the author by virtue of s.9(3).[91]

As to the role of the player in the game, Kitchin J ruled that:

> The appearance of any particular screen depends to some extent on the way the game is being played. For example, when the rotary knob is turned the cue rotates around the cue ball. Similarly, the power of the shot is affected by the precise moment the player chooses to press the play button. The player is not, however, an author of any of the artistic works created in the successive frame images. His input is not artistic in nature and he has contributed no skill or labour of an artistic kind. Nor has he undertaken any of the arrangements necessary for the creation of the frame images. All he has done is to play the game.[92]

While Kitchin J's analysis in *Nova* is sound in determining copyright ownership between the programmer and player in the video game, allocating copyright to the programmer instead of the user of the computer-generated work is not always seamless in various applications of software technologies. It is quite unclear what 'the arrangements necessary for the creation of the work' are.[93] Professor Jani McCutcheon proposed several factors to determine 'the person by whom the arrangements necessary for the creation of the work are undertaken.'[94] These factors include (1) intention to create the work; (2) proximity to the act of final creation; (3) the extent to which the arrangements shape the form of the work; (4) the extent to which the arrangements are responsible for the materialization of the work; and (5) investment.[95] Although these are all sensible factors, the weight of each factor against each other is not clear. While the first four factors might contain

91 *Nova Productions Ltd v Mazooma Games Ltd* [2006] EWHC 24 (Ch) (20 January 2006) paras 105–6.
92 Ibid.
93 Dornis, 'Artificial Creativity' (n 5) 18; Pinto, 'Robo ART!' (n 21) 177.
94 McCutcheon, 'Curing the Authorless Void' (n 87) 55–6.
95 Ibid. Ana Ramalho proposed a less comprehensive list of factors, including (1) the initiative to create the work; (2) the proximity to the final act of creation; and (3) the extent to which the arrangements are responsible for the creation of the work. Ramalho, 'Will Robots Rule the (Artistic) World?' (n 12) 17.

more personal or authorial elements, the last one 'investment' would make the computer-generated work closer to the spectrum of entrepreneurial work. In *Nova*, Kitchin J viewed Mr. Jones as the author because 'he devised the appearance of the various elements of the game and the rules and logic by which each frame is generated and he wrote the relevant computer program'.[96] This approach favours the authorial factors over investment in the determination of authorship of computer-generated works.[97] Nonetheless, as discussed above, computer-generated works are nearer to entrepreneurial works than to authorial works because their production does not encompass human creativity. In this sense, the identity of the person investing in the production is more important than the authorial factors in the determination of authorship.

The computer-generated works envisioned by CDPA 1988 were the result of a rather straightforward process, and were created through simple instructions in a computer.[98] The case law in the UK, most notably the *Nova* case mentioned above, so far has also focused on rather simple computer-generated works. By contrast, the deep learning and AI of today have enabled machines to teach and adapt themselves.[99] The scale of autonomy and automation has gone far beyond what was imagined in the CDPA 1988.[100] Therefore, works generated by those machines are quite different from those generated by computers in 1988 when the law was enacted. Nowadays, AI developers cannot always explain every stage of the AI creation, ie, the black-box issue.[101] Therefore, an AI developer's relation with AI-generated works is much more estranged than that in the traditional computer-generated work scenario. From a policy perspective, it is worth exploring whether we should allocate the ownership of an AI-generated work to the programmer who has little control over the production of it and may not be able to explain it.

In order to answer that question, some have argued that AI-generated works should be protected by copyright law only to the extent that the developer's message or meaning can pass through the computer program and be contained in the generated work.[102] Nonetheless, the defect in this argument is that if the developer's message can be fully illustrated in the generated work, then the role of the computer or AI is just the medium or tool for the developer to create. Consequently, the ultimate work would be an AI-assisted work rather than an AI-generated work.

[96] *Nova Productions Ltd v Mazooma Games Ltd* [2006] EWHC 24 (Ch) (20 January 2006) para 105.
[97] McCutcheon, 'Curing the Authorless Void' (n 87) 67.
[98] Dickenson, Morgan, and Clark, 'Creative Machines' (n 11) 459.
[99] Anthony Man-Cho So, Chapter 1 in this volume (n 51).
[100] Ramalho, 'Will Robots Rule the (Artistic) World?' (n 12) 18.
[101] Ginsburg and Budiardjo (n 11) 402–3; Guadamuz, 'Do Androids Dream of Electric Copyright?' (n 5) 178–9.
[102] Bruce E Boyden, 'Emergent Work' (2016) 39 Columbia Journal of Law & the Arts 337, 384.

5. Unresolved Problems

While the computer-generated works provisions in the CDPA 1988 have only been applied once in English case law, there remain some unresolved legal and policy issues underlying these provisions. The fundamental policy question is whether the UK and other jurisdictions with similar computer-generated work provisions should maintain these provisions in the statutory law. Other legal issues mostly concern new challenges brought by AI and the new collaboration model enabled by digital intelligence technologies.

5.1 Policy Issues

Some argue that if copyright law does not protect computer-generated works, considerable resources, time, and efforts invested in their production will be unfairly used by free riders.[103] Therefore, the computer-generated work provisions in the CDPA 1988 not only encourage investment in AI technologies[104] but also incentivize technological development in software.[105] With copyright protection over computer-generated works, programmers have more incentives to write generative algorithms.[106]

However, this line of argument is not flawless. First, AI developers normally obtain copyright for their generative AI software. If the software meets the patentability requirements, it can be protected by patent law as well. Therefore, AI developers, incentivized by the existing IP regime, are already able to profit from their commercially successful software through licensing royalties.[107] Additionally, software innovators' competitive edge is reinforced by the first-mover advantage, which is typically significant in the software industry and provides another layer of incentive for software development.[108] Therefore, if software developers can obtain additional copyright for AI-generated works, they would be over-rewarded for the same creation. This additional protection is not justified from a policy

[103] McCutcheon, 'The Vanishing Author in Computer-Generated Works' (n 5) 918–20.

[104] Bonadio, McDonagh, and Arvidsson, 'Intellectual Property Aspects of Robotics' (n 10) 671; Bond and Blair, 'Artificial Intelligence and Copyright' (n 4) 423.

[105] Cubert and Bone, 'The Law of Intellectual Property Created by Artificial Intelligence' (n 54) 425; Samantha Fink Hedrick, 'I "Think," Therefore I Create: Claiming Copyright in the Outputs of Algorithms' (2019) 8 NYU Journal of Intellectual Property & Entertainment Law 324, 374–375; McCutcheon, 'The Vanishing Author in Computer-Generated Works' (n 5) 956.

[106] Nina I Brown, 'Artificial Authors: A Case for Copyright in Computer-Generated Works' (2017) 20 Columbia Science & Technology Law Review 1, 220 (hereafter Brown, 'Artificial Authors'); Dornis, 'Artificial Creativity' (n 5) 33–4; Kalin Hristov, 'Artificial Intelligence and the Copyright Dilemma' (2017) 57 IDEA: J Franklin Pierce for Intellectual Property 431, 445.

[107] Robert C Denicola, 'Ex Machina: Copyright Protection for Computer-Generated Works' (2016) 69 Rutgers University Law Review 251, 283–4.

[108] Palace, 'What if Artificial Intelligence Wrote This?' (n 9) 239.

perspective.[109] After all, it is the software, rather than the human author, that creates the work. Different from human authors, computer programs will not be incentivized to create more or fewer works by copyright.[110] If software developers are entitled to the copyright of AI-generated works, they might own an indefinite number of subsequent copyrights by creating one single AI project, because of its continuously generative nature.[111] IP protection and its consequent social costs will then become disproportionate to the incentives it provides.

Second, although computer-generated works are not protected by copyright law in most jurisdictions, the global investment in AI technology has increased dramatically in the past decade. AI startups have attracted an enormous amount of investment from private equity funds, venture capital, and other corporate investors.[112] Investment in AI technologies has been rising dramatically since 2016.[113] Various industries ranging from healthcare to cybersecurity have also invested heavily in AI technologies.[114] AI companies in the US and China have attracted more investment than those elsewhere,[115] and copyright laws in these two countries do not protect computer-generated works. Recent development in AI has revealed that copyright is not a prerequisite for AI developers to exploit the commercial value of AI-generated works. That being said, the incentive theory might not be applicable in copyright protection for AI-generated works.[116]

Third, with the efficiently generative nature of AI algorithm, recognizing the copyrightability of AI-generated works might lead to copyright stockpiling.[117] Under the CDPA 1988, when most creative works are generated by AI in the not too distant future, programmers or those who make necessary arrangement for the creation of the work will become the majority of authors. Consequently, authors who do not employ AI to create will be diluted in the copyright system, and an allocation problem will correspondingly emerge in the judicial system and copyright collective management.[118] In other words, if the law protects copyright of

109 Darin Glasser, 'Copyright in Computer Generated Works: Whom if Anyone, Do We Reward?' (2001) 1 Duke Law & Technology Review 24; Palace, 'What if Artificial Intelligence Wrote This?' (n 9) 236–7; Pamela Samuelson, 'Allocating Ownership Rights in Computer-Generated Works' (1985) 47 University of Pittsburgh Law Review 1185, 1192; Yu, 'The Machine Author' (n 19) 1263–4.

110 Yu, 'The Machine Author' (n 19) 1249.

111 Ibid.

112 The Organisation for Economic Co-operation and Development (OECD), 'Private Equity Investment in Artificial Intelligence' (December 2018) < https://www.oecd.org/going-digital/ai/private-equity-investment-in-artificial-intelligence.pdf>.

113 Ibid; Xiaomin Mou, 'Artificial Intelligence: Investment Trends and Selected Industry Uses' International Finance Corporation (September 2019) <https://www.ifc.org/wps/wcm/connect/7898d957-69b5-4727-9226-277e8ae28711/EMCompass-Note-71-AI-Investment-Trends.pdf?MOD=AJPERES&CVID=mR5Jvd6> (hereafter Mou, 'Artificial Intelligence').

114 Mou, 'Artificial Intelligence' (n 113).

115 Deloitte Analytics, 'Future in the Balance? How Countries Are Pursuing an AI Advantage' (May 2019) <https://www2.deloitte.com/content/dam/Deloitte/cn/Documents/technology-media-telecommunications/deloitte-cn-tmt-future-in-the-balance-en-190528.pdf>.

116 Reto M Hilty, Jörg Hoffmann, and Stefan Scheuerer, Chapter 3 in this volume.

117 Yu, 'The Machine Author' (n 19) 1261.

118 Ibid, 1263.

AI-generated works, society will likely allocate most copyright related-resources to these works and their deemed authors, and such development might crowd out existing non-programmer authors who create the work on their own rather than making the necessary arrangements for AI creation.

Finally, copyright does not always protect commercially valuable information or content. Copyright doctrines, such as originality and the idea–expression dichotomy, reflect the value and policy judgements on which content is protected. Policymakers should therefore seriously consider these policy judgements underlying the copyright regime and the value of leaving AI-generated works in the public domain.[119]

5.2 Doctrinal Issues

Authorship is the most challenging part in copyright of computer-generated works.[120] Certain issues associated with the computer-generated provisions in the CDPA 1998 and their application to the AI technologies remain unsolved. There are typically multiple contributors to AI-generated works. In addition to investors and programmers, machine operators, trainers, and data providers all play important roles in the creation of the works.[121] The dynamics between these players will cause more complexities for the determination of 'the person by whom the arrangements necessary for the creation of the work are undertaken'.

Moreover, imagine that a person invested in and created an AI system and trained it with abundant data. However, the person passed away before the AI system started to generate works. While most people would agree that the person undertook the necessary arrangements for the creation of the AI-generated work, viewing the person as the author would conflict with existing copyright regime, in which the deceased are not able to create any copyright work. It would also be irrational for succession to make the person's heir the author of the work when that heir has not made any necessary arrangements or an original contribution. The work would therefore likely become authorless and fall into the public domain.

Computer-generated works are protected for fifty years from the end of the calendar year in which the work is made.[122] This copyright term is not problematic

[119] Amir H Khoury, 'Intellectual Property Rights for "Hubots": On the Legal Implications of Human-Like Robots as Innovators and Creators' (2017) 35 Cardozo Arts & Entertainment Law Journal 635, 654–8; Madeleine de Cock Buning, 'Artificial Intelligence and the Creative Industry: New Challenges for the EU Paradigm for Art and Technology by Autonomous Creation' in Woodrow Barfield and Ugo Pagallo (eds), *Research Handbook on the Law of Artificial Intelligence* (EE 2018) 529; Palace, 'What if Artificial Intelligence Wrote This?' (n 9) 240–1; Ramalho, 'Will Robots Rule the (Artistic) World?' (n 12) 21–2; Yu, 'The Machine Author' (n 19) 1265–6.

[120] Brown, 'Artificial Authors' (n 106) 27.

[121] Bently, Sherman, Gangjee, and Johnson, *Intellectual Property Law* (n 53) 128; Bond and Blair, 'Artificial Intelligence and Copyright' (n 4) 423; Dornis, 'Artificial Creativity' (n 5) 18; Pinto, 'Robo ART!' (n 21) 177; Yanisky-Ravid, 'Generating Rembrandt' (n 55) 692–3.

[122] CDPA 1988, s 12(7).

if the works result from a static process with predetermined inputs. However, AI-generated works are different from traditional computer-generated works in the sense that their results continue to evolve with constant machine learning and new data input. Therefore, new AI-generated works will incessantly emerge from the same AI project.[123] Consequently, to allow such works to be protected as copyright would create the undesirable position of rights in AI-generated works continuing in perpetuity.

Various applications of AI technologies have also made the determination of authors challenging in a way it has never been before. For example, Flow Machines is an AI system that can either create music independently or collaborate with human authors.[124] When AI collaborates with human beings to create copyright works, the authorship of these works is ambiguous. Under section 10 of the CDPA 1988, a 'work of joint authorship' means 'a work produced by the collaboration of two or more authors in which the contribution of each author is not distinct from that of the other author or authors'.[125] However, if the work is produced by the collaboration of a human author and an AI system, it cannot fall within the definition of joint authorship because the human author does not collaborate directly with the deemed author of section 9(3). While the deemed author can argue that he collaborates with the other human author via the AI he developed, his original expression was only presented in his AI algorithm, but not the final collaborative work. Therefore, the deemed author under section 9(3) cannot become a joint author under section 10. The same challenge will appear when multiple AI systems collaborate with each other to generate creative works.

Digital technologies and the Internet have enabled large-scale collaboration on AI projects. For example, Google has made a number of its AI projects, such as Deep Dream and Magenta, open-source.[126] In other words, hundreds of thousands of voluntary programmers might become the authors of these AI algorithms. When widespread volunteers become authors of AI software, it will be extremely challenging to decide which contributors undertook the necessary arrangements for the subject AI-generated work. Moreover, software companies have started to develop AI software which can learn to develop AI software.[127] Google's AutoML, a machine learning algorithm that learns to build other machine learning algorithms,

[123] Rajan, *Moral Rights* (n 51) 310 ('[i]f the work is executed through time, at what stage of its existence does it become a final product rather than a work-in-progress, thereby becoming capable of protection by copyright?').

[124] Ihalainen, 'Computer Creativity' (n 9) 724.

[125] CDPA 1988, s 10.

[126] Bonadio, McDonagh, and Arvidsson, 'Intellectual Property Aspects of Robotics' (n 10) 670–1; Guadamuz, 'Do Androids Dream of Electric Copyright?' (n 5) 177; Rachel Metz, 'Why Google's AI can write beautiful songs but still can't tell a joke' (*MIT Technology Review*, 7 September 2017) <https://www.technologyreview.com/s/608777/why-googles-ai-can-write-beautiful-songs-but-still-cant-tell-a-joke/>.

[127] Tom Simonite, 'AI software learns to make AI software' (*MIT Technology Review*, 18 January 2017) <https://www.technologyreview.com/s/603381/ai-software-learns-to-make-ai-software/>.

is one of them.[128] While such AI technologies might enable endless AI software development by the AI software itself, it also leads to a puzzle regarding who personally undertakes the necessary arrangements for the software generated by another AI-generated software program. All these developments in the AI industry reveal that identifying ownership in digitally collaborative works under section 9(3) of the CDPA 1988 involves heavy transaction costs and is therefore exceptionally difficult.

6. Conclusion

The computer-generated provisions in the CDPA 1988 were drafted in the 1980s when AI was but a concept. When the legislators were looking forward and envisioning the generativity of digital technologies, their understanding of and imagination about AI were quite limited. Therefore, the UK and jurisdictions with similar provisions need to address these new technological developments in their copyright regimes. Although a computer-generated work has certain attributes of entrepreneurial works, it is not entirely the same as the latter. While neither entrepreneurial works nor computer-generated works require originality in the creation, the way to determine infringement in entrepreneurial works may not be perfectly applied to that of computer-generated works. While the infringement of an entrepreneurial work can only be found in the form in which the work is fixed, there are various ways for the alleged infringer to exploit an AI-generated work in different media.

Authorship is the most challenging part for computer-generated works. Even though Kitchin J in the High Court ruled in *Nova* ruled that 'the person by whom the arrangements necessary for the creation of the work are undertaken' was the programmer, the determination of authors in the AI environment for these works is not always as easy as in *Nova*. The programmers, data providers, trainers, and machine operators may all play indispensable roles in the creation of AI-generated works. Moreover, the new creative model enabled by AI and digital technologies has made the determination of authorship even more challenging. Authorship issues remain insurmountable if the work is generated after the death of the author or is produced by various collaborative models, such as open-source software or the collaboration of machines and human beings.

From a policy perspective, this author is of the viewpoint that UK and other jurisdictions with similar computer-generated work provisions in their copyright laws should reconsider their approach to these works. Although these provisions

[128] Michael McLaughlin, 'Computer-Generated Inventions' (2019) 101 Journal of the Patent & Trademark Office Society 224, 238.

seem to provide desirable incentives for software development, they have deviated from the basic copyright principles of originality and human creation. Software developers will be over-rewarded by the computer-generated work provisions. More importantly, these provisions may unfortunately lead to misallocations of public resources for copyright protection in society.

9

Copyright Exceptions Reform and AI Data Analysis in China

A Modest Proposal

*Tianxiang He**

1. Introduction

The revival of the research on artificial intelligence (AI) seems irresistible due to the availability of big data, the dramatically improved machine learning approaches and algorithms, and the availability of more powerful computers.[1] Governments have released national strategies to further the development and application of AI technology, as AI is deemed crucial to their competitiveness in the global market.[2] Funding support from governments that aim to take a leading role in the field of AI for related scientific research is, as expected, very generous. For instance, the US government has issued two national AI research and development (R&D) strategy plans in 2016 and 2019 to establish 'a set of objectives for federally funded AI research',[3] and 'defines the priority areas for federal investments in AI R&D'.[4] The State Council of China also released the Government Work Report and the Development Plan on the New Generation of Artificial Intelligence in 2017, establishing the development of AI technology as a national strategy;[5] later, more operable implement layouts at the provincial and ministerial levels were released to

* All online materials were accessed before 1 May 2020.

[1] Executive Office of the President, 'Artificial Intelligence, Automation, and the Economy' (2016) <https://obamawhitehouse.archives.gov/sites/whitehouse.gov/files/documents/Artificial-Intelligence-Automation-Economy.PDF>.

[2] See Tim Dutton, 'An Overview of National AI Strategies' (*Medium*, 29 June 2018) <https://medium.com/politics-ai/an-overview-of-national-ai-strategies-2a70ec6edfd>.

[3] National Science and Technology Council and Networking and Information Technology Research and Development Subcommittee, 'The National Artificial Intelligence Research and Development Strategic Plan 2016' (2016) <https://www.nitrd.gov/pubs/national_ai_rd_strategic_plan.pdf>.

[4] Select Committee on Artificial Intelligence of the National Science and Technology Council, 'The National Artificial Intelligence Research and Development Strategic Plan: 2019 Update' (2019) <https://www.nitrd.gov/pubs/National-AI-RD-Strategy-2019.pdf>.

[5] See the State Council, 'Government Work Report of 2017' (2017) <http://www.gov.cn/premier/2017-03/16/content_5177940.htm>; see also the State Council, 'Notice of the State Council on Issuing the Development Plan on the New Generation of Artificial Intelligence' (2017) <http://www.gov.cn/zhengce/content/2017-07/20/content_5211996.htm>.

Tianxiang He, *Copyright Exceptions Reform and AI Data Analysis in China* In: *Artificial Intelligence and Intellectual Property.* Edited by: Jyh-An Lee, Reto M Hilty, and Kung-Chung Liu, Oxford University Press (2021).
DOI: 10.1093/oso/9780198870944.003.0010

speed up AI development.[6] As a result, a huge amount of government funding has been allocated to support AI-related projects on both regular[7] and special levels.[8] As the support from the government is strong, the legal issues related to AI have been a hot topic among Chinese academics in recent years,[9] and a substantive part of the related literature concerns the copyright issues related to AI-generated content. Also, much of the existing literature in fact focuses on similar topics such as the legal status of AI and the content it generates. However, the important topics of the potential copyright liabilities and the possible defences of AI analysis and data mining have not been properly explored in China.

Since the issues of authorship and entitlement have already been discussed by Jyh-An Lee in an earlier chapter in this volume[10] and elsewhere by the author,[11] this chapter focuses on the copyright issues related to AI technology about data analysis such as data training and mining, as applications of AI technology for those purposes will inevitably involve massive data processing in different stages. If such data contain copyrighted materials reproduced without permission from the copyright owners, potentially that might be considered copyright infringement. This chapter examines the above issue in the context of Chinese copyright law

[6] Eg, the Ministry of Industry and Information Technology issued the Three-year Action Plan for Promoting the New Generation of Artificial Intelligence Industry Development (2018–20) to promote the development of AI technologies; the Ministry of Education issued the Artificial Intelligence Innovation Action Plan for Higher Education Institutions to encourage technological innovation, personnel training, and international communication in the AI area; most provinces also released their local development plans to promote AI economics and industry; see, eg, Guangdong Province Development Plan on New Generation AI Technology <http://zwgk.gd.gov.cn/006939748/201808/t20180810_777229.html>.

[7] Regular national funding in general means the National Natural Science Fund of China and the National Social Science Fund of China. For example, among the 41,752 granted projects of the natural science category in 2019, 975 projects are about AI with total funding of RMB 0.95 billion, 1,028 projects are about big data with total funding of RMB 0.65 billion, and 1,175 projects are about data mining with total funding of RMB 0.75 billion. See National Natural Science Foundation of China, 'Announcement about the Application Results of the Annual Projects of the National Natural Science Fund of China in 2019' (2019) <http://www.npopss-cn.gov.cn/n1/2019/0625/c219469-31187315.html>. Among the 3,536 granted general projects of the social science category in 2019, twenty-four projects are about artificial intelligence, fifty-seven projects are about big data, and seven projects are about data mining, with a fixed ceiling of RMB 1,200,000 for each general project. See National Office for Philosophy and Social Sciences, 'Announcement about the Application Results of the Annual and Youth Funded Projects of the National Social Science Fund of China in 2019' (2019) <http://www.npopss-cn.gov.cn/n1/2019/0625/c219469-31187315.html>.

[8] Special national funding was provided for Technology Innovation 2030 — the New Generation of Artificial Intelligence Major Project since 2018. See Ministry of Science and Technology of China, 'About the Publication of Notice of Technology Innovation 2030—the New Generation of Artificial Intelligence Major Project Application Guidance 2018' (2018) <http://www.most.gov.cn/mostinfo/xinxifenlei/fgzc/gfxwj/gfxwj2018/201810/t20181012_142131.htm>.

[9] Eg, the author used the Chinese term '人工智能 (artificial intelligence)' as the 'subject' search term and '法 (law)' as the 'title' search term to search the China National Knowledge Infrastructure (CNKI) database on 18 December 2019; a total of 177 academic journal articles were identified. According to the search result, before 2015, almost no article related to the topic appears. In 2016, there have been a few related articles published sporadically, but the number went up to eighteen in 2017, and rose up to a staggering fifty-one in 2018. Moreover, thirty-three related articles were published in 2019 according to this search.

[10] Please see Chapter 8, 'Computer-Generated Works under the CDPA 1988' by Jyh-An Lee.

[11] Tianxiang He, 'The Sentimental Fools and The Fictitious Authors: Rethinking the Copyright Issues of AI-generated Contents in China' (2019) 27 Asia Pacific Law Review 218.

theory and practice, in order to find out whether infringement can be established and whether defences are available under the Copyright Law of China (CLC), and to propose future amendments to facilitate the development of AI based on the experiences of Japan, Korea, and Taiwan.[12]

For that purpose, Section 2 of this chapter examines the current level of development and applications of the AI technology related to data training/mining, and identifies to what extent it is not a fictional proposition but a real problem linked to genuine copyright issues worth investigating. Section 3 analyses in detail the scenarios in which data training/mining is deemed copyright infringement, and whether there are available copyright exceptions provided by the CLC, as well as whether there are experiences that can be learned from other East Asian jurisdictions, namely Japan, Korea, and Taiwan. Section 4 then discusses the pros and cons of the current copyright legal setting of China with regard to the data training/mining infringement related to AI technology, to check if the current copyright legal framework is a hindrance to the further development of AI, and put forward a feasible proposal for China that could serve as a valuable reference for countries that wish to update their copyright laws as well.

2. The Application of AI Technology and Its Copyright Problem

In the 'big data' era, data is seemingly the most valuable asset for companies that employ AI technology in their businesses. According to an IDC White Paper, the value of the data set lies not in the individual data itself, but rather in the extraction of valuable information that reveals patterns, trends, and new relationships.[13] Therefore, the term data mining, or more precisely, data analysis, was defined as '[t]he automated processing of digital materials, which may include texts, data, sounds, images or other elements, or a combination of these, in order to uncover new knowledge or insights'.[14]

With regard to AI applications that use copyrighted works for data training purposes, the current technology can already employ the result of data training to generate (mostly via unsupervised learning) various types of content that are analogous to different kinds of human expressions, such as literary, musical, or pictorial/graphical works. For example, *The Next Rembrandt*, a 3D printed painting, was generated by AI

[12] The author limited his focus to East Asian experiences because experiences from other regions such as the US and the EU are well-covered by Benjamin Sobel, Chapter 10 in this volume.

[13] IDC White Paper, 'The Digital Universe of Opportunities: Rich Data and the Increasing Value of the Internet of Things' (2014) EMC Corporation <https://www.emc.com/leadership/digital-universe/2014iview/index.htm>.

[14] Jean-Paul Triaille and others, 'Study on the legal framework of text and data mining (TDM)' (*Publications Office of the European Union*, 2014) <https://op.europa.eu/en/publication-detail/-/publication/074ddf78-01e9-4a1d-9895-65290705e2a5/language-en>.

technology based solely on Rembrandt's works. The project team studied the works of Rembrandt to establish an extensive database. They examined the entire collection of Rembrandt's works, and analysed a broad range of materials like high-resolution 3D scans and digital files, which were upscaled by deep learning algorithms to maximize resolution and quality. This extensive database was then used as the foundation for creating the painting. In short, it is an AI-generated 'artwork' that consists of over 148 million pixels based on 168,263 painting fragments from all 346 of Rembrandt's known paintings, and the whole process took eighteen months.[15] Similarly, in 2018, an AI system created by the French art collective, Obvious, used a data set of 15,000 portraits to produce an AI art piece, *Portrait of Edmond Belamy*. The portrait was sold at Christie's for $432,500, signalling the arrival of AI art on the world auction stage.[16] In another example, using a convolutional neural network to find and enhance patterns in images via algorithmic pareidolia, Google's Deep Dream Generator platform and software could also help its users to merge a selected art style with an uploaded picture in less than one minute.[17] In terms of literary works, it was reported that the quality of a short novel generated by AI with human intervention was able to compete with humans in a Japanese literary contest.[18] Another example is a book of poems written by Xiaoice, Microsoft's China-based chatbot.[19] Moreover, applications using AI technology such as Wordsmith can now generate news reports using text templates.[20] With regard to musical works, a project of Sony Computer Science Laboratories in Paris called 'Flow Machines' can now generate human-recognizable pop songs.[21]

Data mining of copyrighted works has been widely used in the fields of academic analysis and research.[22] For example, text data mining can empower computational linguistics such as corpus linguistics research, which may involve data mining of a corpus of copyrighted academic articles,[23] or the word2vec project

[15] See Robin, 'Microsoft AI creates 'new' Rembrandt painting' (*Netimperative*, 11 April 2016) <http://www.netimperative.com/2016/04/microsoft-ai-creates-new-rembrandt-painting/>.

[16] See 'Is artificial intelligence set to become art's next medium?' (*Christie's*, 2018) <https://www.christies.com/features/A-collaboration-between-two-artists-one-human-one-a-machine-9332-1.aspx>.

[17] See James Temperton, 'Create your own DeepDream nightmares in seconds' (*Wired*, 22 July 2015) <https://www.wired.co.uk/article/google-deepdream-dreamscope>.

[18] See Danny Lewis, 'An AI-written novella almost won a literary prize' (*SmartNews*, 28 March 2016) <https://www.smithsonianmag.com/smart-news/ai-written-novella-almost-won-literary-prize-180958577/>.

[19] See Geoff Spencer, 'Much more than a chatbot: China's Xiaoice mixes AI with emotions and wins over millions of fans' (*Microsoft*, 1 November 2018) <https://news.microsoft.com/apac/features/much-more-than-a-chatbot-chinas-xiaoice-mixes-ai-with-emotions-and-wins-over-millions-of-fans/>.

[20] See Klint Finley, 'This news-writing bot is now free for everyone' (*Wired*, 20 October 2015) <https://www.wired.com/2015/10/this-news-writing-bot-is-now-free-for-everyone/>.

[21] See Lucy Jordan, 'Inside the lab that's producing the first AI-generated pop album' (*Seeker*, 13 April 2017) <https://www.seeker.com/tech/artificial intelligence/inside-flow-machines-the-lab-thats-composing-the-first-ai-generated-pop-album>.

[22] Sergey Filippov, 'Mapping text and data mining in academic and research communities in Europe' (*the Lisbon Council*, 27 May 2014) <https://lisboncouncil.net/publication/publication/109-mapping-text-and-data-mining-in-academic-and-research-communities-in-europe.html>.

[23] Elke Teich, 'Exploring a Corpus of Scientific Texts Using Data Mining' (2010) 71 Language and Computers 233.

launched by Google that is trained by the Google News corpus, which may include huge loads of copyrighted works.[24] The ImageNet project is another example to show how 14 million collected copyrighted images could be used for further data mining or analytical purposes.[25]

Even though it is hard to abstract the common features of all data analytic techniques mentioned above, it is believed that there are three common steps in these applications that can be identified: access to content, extraction and/or copying of content for the purpose of generating relevant text and data, and mining of text and/or data and knowledge discovery, according to a report published by the Policy Department for Citizens' Rights and Constitutional Affairs of the European Parliament.[26]

It is obvious from the abovementioned cases that, where copyrighted works are concerned, at least in the second step, which concerns 'extraction and/or copying of content', there seems to be a risk of copyright infringement if copyright clearance has not been done properly. However, the mere fact that a potential risk of infringement is attached does not imply that there is a legal flaw. If copyright clearance can be done in a proper way or copyright exceptions are provided in the CLC to deal with the risk, then the problem is solved. However, the reason that a new copyright exception is needed is because the traditional copyright licensing approach will not work in the data analysis scenario. First, it is uncertain that copying copyrighted materials for data analysis purposes such as data mining will fall within the ambit of restricted acts of copyright law;[27] second, even if we assume that, prima facie, it is an act restricted by copyright, it is still an impossible task for the user to secure a licence from every copyrighted title they mined under our 'opt-in' copyright law model,[28] as the transaction cost will be extremely high, not to mention the fact that the orphan work problem still exists, and that many publishers that hold the copyright of massive amounts of articles will not render that kind of permission easily. As scholars have pointed out, copyright exceptions related to data analysis are at the heart of the issue.[29] The next section explores these issues in detail.

[24] 'word2vec' (2013) Google Code <https://code.google.com/archive/p/word2vec/>.

[25] 'ImageNet Overview' (*ImageNet*) <http://image-net.org/about-overview>.

[26] Eleonora Rosati, 'The exception for text and data mining (TDM) in the proposed Directive on Copyright in the Digital Single Market—technical aspects' (*European Parliament*, 2018) <http://www.europarl.europa.eu/RegData/etudes/BRIE/2018/604942/IPOL_BRI(2018)604942_EN.pdf>.

[27] Matthew L Jockers, Matthew Sag, and Jason Schultz, 'Don't Let Copyright Block Data Mining' (2012) 490 Nature 29.

[28] Monica Isia Jasiewicz, 'Copyright Protection in an Opt-Out World: Implied License Doctrine and News Aggregators' (2012) The Yale Law Journal 843 ('Traditional copyright law is an opt-in system, in which the default distribution of rights prohibits reproduction of copyrighted material unless copyright holders affirmatively give their permission').

[29] See Michelle Brook, Peter Murray-Rust, and Charles Oppenheim, 'The social, political and legal aspects of text and data mining (TDM)' (2014) 20 D-Lib Magazine <http://mirror.dlib.org/dlib/november14/brook/11brook.html> (claiming that the copyright exceptions related to TDM are 'ambiguous, and this will inhibit researchers from undertaking it'). See also Christophe Geiger, Giancarlo Frosio, and Oleksandr Bulayenko, 'The exception for text and data mining (TDM) in the proposed Directive on Copyright in the Digital Single Market—legal aspects' (2018) (Policy Department for

3. The Potential Copyright Infringements and Possible Defences Related to Data Analysis by AI under the CLC

Considering the fact that the legal status of copyrighted works varies, it is necessary to first clarify what types of works, when used in data analysis or mining, will amount to copyright infringement. At the moment, the safest resources for data analysis will be those copyright-free works in the public domain or under open access agreements.[30] For works under strict copyright protection such as journal articles and professional photographs, a licence is normally required. But even with institutional subscription via site licence, it is not certain that such licences will cover data analysis and mining, as the licence for use is partial and most publishers have set a rule to restrict bulk download by individual users.[31] Moreover, copyrighted works collected via unauthorized means such as crawler will of course constitute copyright infringement. This means that parties conducting data analysis face a great risk of copyright infringement, as a big chunk of targeted data is controlled by commercial establishments. The second part of this section discusses whether the CLC has provided adequate exemptions for AI analysis and data mining, and the last part of this section compares experiences from Taiwan, Korea, and Japan.

3.1 Inevitable Copyright Infringements of AI Data Analysis under the CLC

3.1.1 The process

The first step of many AI applications often involves data collection, as a considerable amount of data is needed for AI training. If the data must be collected first hand, in order to convert all physical copies of copyrighted works such as books and photos into a machine-readable format, the processes of digitalization, text and information extraction, and format conversion are inevitable. These

Citizens' Rights and Constitutional Affairs, European Parliament) <https://www.europarl.europa.eu/RegData/etudes/IDAN/2018/604941/IPOL_IDA(2018)604941_EN.pdf> ('Given the uncertainties that researchers face in applying present exceptions and limitations to TDM and the great necessity to create the best framework for European research and development, a new limitation is urgently needed in order to drive innovation and bridge the gap with other jurisdictions, permitting TDM activities').

[30] Benjamin Sobel, Chapter 10 in this volume (n 12).

[31] At the Copyright & Research and Innovation Policy Conference held in 2013 at the European Parliament, John McNaught, the Deputy Director of the UK National Centre for Text Mining, indicated in his speech that 'the standard licence that allows individuals to download academic papers will not support text and data mining as ... if the download rate is 1 page every 20 seconds, then at this rate, assuming instant download, 1 million texts each of 10 pages would take over 6 years to download ... '). See John McNaught, 'Role of text mining in research and innovation' (*Copyright4Creativity.eu* 2013) <http://copyright4creativity.eu/wp-content/uploads/2013/11/C4C-12-Nov-Event-John-McNaught.pdf>.

processes, viewed from a copyright law perspective, will constitute infringement if unauthorized.

The first type of economic right that is covered is the reproduction right. According to Article 10(5) of the CLC, the reproduction right is 'the right to produce one or more copies of a work by printing, photocopying, lithographing, making a sound recording or video recording, duplicating a recording, or duplicating a photographic work, digitalization or by any other means'.[32] It is clearly provided that digitalization is covered. As for format conversion, its open-ended design will cover it if unauthorized.

The right of adaptation, which is 'the right to change a work to create a new work of originality',[33] is also covered. In the data preparation phase of a standard data mining process, all steps that lead to the construction of the final dataset are covered. These steps include not only simple digitalization or format conversion, but also 'attribute selection, data cleaning, construction of new attributes, and transformation of data for modelling tools'.[34] Clearly, the latter cannot be simply described as conversion of format, as new information will be added and the raw data will be altered. If the degree of alteration and the information added are substantial, the data generated thereby can be considered a derivative work of the original, and this will touch upon the exclusive right of adaptation enjoyed by the copyright owners. In other words, the original work was transformed into a form that can be perceived and processed by the AI application.

3.1.2 The end results

If we expect that normally the data set used in AI analysis and data mining will not be disclosed, and hence the anticipated risk of copyright infringement will be smaller due to lack of evidence, then AI-generated content as the end result, if any, will be an important piece of evidence to prove that the right of reproduction and adaptation under the CLC are infringed, as the traditional ways of identifying copyright infringement such as 'prior access' and 'substantial similarity' will still function well under this scenario: if the borrowing can be identified, then there is prima facie copyright infringement unless defences are available.[35] This is a logical move for copyright owners to focus on the end result, considering the absence of evidence that their copyrighted works were included in the data set. Accordingly,

[32] CLC (2020) (PRC) Art 10(5).

[33] Ibid, Art 10(14).

[34] Rüdiger Wirth and Jochen Hipp, 'CRISP-DM: towards a standard process model for data mining' (2000 Proceedings of the 4th International Conference on the Practical Applications of Knowledge Discovery and Data Mining) <https://citeseerx.ist.psu.edu/viewdoc/download?doi=10.1.1.198.5133&rep=rep1&type=pdf>.

[35] 'Prior access' and 'substantial similarity' are considered by Chinese courts to be general principles in determining copyright infringement cases. See *Xue Huake v Yan Yaya* [2011] Beijing Second Intermediate People's Court, EZMZZ No 21796; *Wang Tiancheng v Zhou Yezhong and Dai Jitao* [2009] Supreme People's Court, MSZ No 161.

it is highly likely that 'prior access' can be proved when the end product is substantially similar to an existing work, if 'the allegedly copied work is present in input data'.[36] However, when an allegedly copied work is absent in input data and the end result is similar to an existing copyrighted work, which, according to Sobel, is 'unsurprising to anyone familiar with the creative process', the traditional ways of identifying infringement will then be challenged.[37]

However, in cases similar to the *The Next Rembrandt*, it is possible that the borrowed works will be indiscernible, as an advanced AI machine will make sure that the end result only represents the style behind the paintings rather than an individual work included in the data set. In this case, no copyright infringement can be proven unless an act of copying can be ascertained in the stage of data training. In both cases, the stages of digitalization, text/information extraction, and format conversion mentioned above are very crucial in finding copyright infringement.

3.2 A Silver Lining in the Copyright Exceptions of the CLC?

3.2.1 Why do we need an exception for AI training/data mining?

Copyright exceptions may serve as a legal shelter for AI analysis and data mining. As discussed in the previous section, either AI users will have to seek licences from all copyright owners of every piece of works they use, or they will run the risk of committing copyright infringement. In the worst-case scenario, users will have to end their project due to the risk of mass copyright infringement, and this will be detrimental to the development of the AI industry, as it will be discouraging if users and investors face countless copyright infringement risks.

It is also noted that a well-designed copyright defence regime may help in adjusting the bias problem in commercial AI systems, as it may help to 'increase the overall size of the dataset' and thereby 'balance out blind spots'.[38] This echoes the 'garbage in, garbage out' maxim among computer scientists. In other words, if incomplete and biased data is fed into the AI system due to the impossible task of copyright clearance, the outcome (often in the form of prediction) will also be biased and even misleading. Therefore, there is an urgent requirement for countries to provide AI analysis and data mining at least with a shelter with its copyright exceptions or defences. Unfortunately, China has failed to accommodate this need.

[36] Benjamin Sobel, 'Artificial Intelligence's Fair Use Crisis' (2017) 41 Columbia Journal of Law & the Arts 66 (hereafter Sobel, 'Artificial Intelligence's Fair Use Crisis').

[37] Ibid.

[38] Amanda Levendowski, 'How Copyright Law Can Fix Artificial Intelligence's Implicit Bias Problem' (2018) 93 Washington Law Review 621.

3.2.2 The current copyright exception model of China

China is a civil law country which adheres to early continental European traditions.[39] As a result, the CLC chose not to copy directly from the Berne Convention,[40] but to follow the concept of the European author's rights (*droit d'auteur*) system,[41] which adjudged the structure of China's copyright exceptions model to be closed-list rather than an 'open-ended' one such as the US fair use test.[42]

Specifically, Article 24, the so-called 'fair use' clause, was provided by the 1990 CLC originally as Article 22 and remained largely unchanged following its 2001, 2010, and 2020 amendments.[43] It provides thirteen circumstances under which a copyrighted work can be used without the permission of, and payment of remuneration to, the copyright owner.[44]

In order to inject more flexibility into Article 24, the Regulations for the Implementation of the CLC (RICL),[45] which is a set of detailed supplementary rules supplied by the State Council and the National Copyright Administration of China (NCAC), provide in-depth explanations of the article. According to Article 21 of the RICL:

> The exploitation of a published work which may be exploited without permission from the copyright owner in accordance with the relevant provisions of the

[39] Yu Xingzhong, 'Western Constitutional Ideas and Constitutional Discourse in China, 1978–2005' in Stéphanie Balme and Michael Dowdle (eds), *Building Constitutionalism in China* (Palgrave Macmillan US 2009) 120.

[40] Chengsi Zheng, *Copyright Law* (2nd edn, China Renmin University Press 1997) 251 (郑成思，《版权法》，中国人民大学出版社 1997) ('there are great differences between article 22 of CLC and the Berne convention in the regulations about fair use'.)

[41] Chenguo Zhang, 'Introducing the Open Clause to Improve Copyright Flexibility in Cyberspace? Analysis and Commentary on the Proposed 'Two-step Test' in the Third Amendment to the Copyright Law of the PRC, in Comparison with the EU and the US' (2017) 33 Computer Law & Security Review 74 (hereinafter Zhang, 'Introducing the Open Clause to Improve Copyright Flexibility in Cyberspace?').

[42] 17 USC § 107 (USA) 'Limitations on exclusive rights: Fair use. Notwithstanding the provisions of sections 106 and 106A, the fair use of a copyrighted work, including such use by reproduction in copies or phonorecords or by any other means specified by that section, for purposes such as criticism, comment, news reporting, teaching (including multiple copies for classroom use), scholarship, or research, is not an infringement of copyright. In determining whether the use made of a work in any particular case is a fair use the factors to be considered shall include—

(1) the purpose and character of the use, including whether such use is of a commercial nature or is for nonprofit educational purposes;
(2) the nature of the copyrighted work;
(3) the amount and substantiality of the portion used in relation to the copyrighted work as a whole; and
(4) the effect of the use upon the potential market for or value of the copyrighted work.

The fact that a work is unpublished shall not itself bar a finding of fair use if such finding is made upon consideration of all the above factors.'

[43] Except for changes made in 2001 to technical terms such as 'editorials or commentators articles' in sub-s. (4) regarding the exception of reprint by newspapers etc., and those narrowing down the coverage of some exceptions such as sub-s. (11) regarding the translation of works published in Chinese into a minority nationality language, the listed exceptions are largely untouched. See National People's Congress of China, 'The interpretation of the 2001 Copyright Law of China' (*National People's Congress of China Official Site*, 2002) <http://www.npc.gov.cn/npc/c2200/200207/516230c1aebe4ae88c1d22d0cfaccd71.shtml>. For the minor changes made in the 2020 revision, a detailed analysis can be found on Section 4.2 of this chapter.

[44] CLC (2020) (PRC) Art 24.

[45] Regulations for the Implementation of the Copyright Law of the People's Republic of China (2013) (PRC).

> Copyright Law shall not impair the normal exploitation of the work concerned, nor unreasonably prejudice the legitimate interests of the copyright owner.[46]

Thus, the aforementioned 'two-step' test serves as a complement to the listed exceptions from a doctrinal perspective. Accordingly, Article 21 of the RICL will only be invoked by a court until a particular use first falls into one of the listed exceptions in Article 24 of the CLC. Here, Article 21 of the RICL serves as a ceiling over the list provided by Article 24 of the CLC. The wording of Article 21 is also modified from Article 9 of the Berne Convention and many subsequent international treaties.[47] Combined with Article 24 of the CLC, it is clear that the extent of exempted uses should not violate the abovementioned 'two-step' test. However, the definitions of the terms 'normal exploitation' and 'legitimate interest' used in that test are not provided by the law and are left to the courts to determine.

Only a few of the listed exceptions concern AI analysis or data mining. Article 24(1) of the CLC provides that 'use of a published work for the purposes of the user's own private study, research or self-entertainment' can be exempted. It seems that 'private' research can be exempted under this section. However, this exception will not offer much help, as most AI users are corporations, and the research they conduct cannot be deemed 'private' in anyway. Even in the scenario of private study and research, it is believed that the amount of works used is not without limits, as any private use claim should also pass the 'two-step' test provided in both Article 24 of the CLC and Article 21 of the RICL.[48] Even if we assume under this broad exception that private use of a whole work for the designated purposes could be allowed, the amount of works required by AI analysis and data mining will definitely exceed that tolerable amount.

Article 24(6) of the CLC, which provides that 'translation, adaptation, compilation, playing, or reproduction in a small quantity of copies, of a published work for use by teachers or scientific researchers, in classroom teaching or scientific research of schools, provided that the translation or reproduction shall not be published or distributed' can be exempted, is another exception that may cover AI analysis or data mining. However, even though the term 'scientific research' implies that AI analysis or data mining might be covered, considering the restrictions that the legislators have set on the clause, it may not be able to provide the necessary shelter for such an exploitation. First, it is believed that the term 'school' excludes commercial educational institutions and the commercial activities conducted by

[46] Ibid, Art 21.

[47] Berne Convention, Art 9; Agreement on Trade-Related Aspects of Intellectual Property Rights, Art 13; WIPO Copyright Treaty, Art 10; WIPO Performances and Phonograms Treaty, Art 16.2; Beijing Treaty on Audiovisual Performances, Art 13.2.

[48] Qian Wang, *Intellectual Property Textbook* (Renmin University Press 2019) 211 (王迁，《知识产权法教程》，中国人民大学出版社 2019)

non-commercial educational institutions.[49] That is to say, commercial AI projects that involve data analysis and mining on mass copyrighted works are not covered. Second, even if research institutions such as public universities and the Chinese Academy of Sciences may be covered by this exception, it is also required that the reproduction of published works shall be kept 'in a small quantity', obviously not a welcomed limitation for AI analysis or data mining that may require huge amounts of copyrighted data.

Besides the abovementioned exceptions, there is no other exception that has the potential to provide a safe zone for uses related to AI analysis or data mining. This means that if the CLC remains unchanged, it will greatly hinder the development of AI technology in China.

3.3 East Asian Experiences

It is evident from the above that China needs to revise the exception part of the CLC, if it is to promote the development of AI. In general, there are two approaches: the closed-list model and 'open-ended' model. A closed-list model of copyright exceptions is commonly seen in, but not limited to, civil law jurisdictions. Under a closed-list regime, 'an unauthorized use of a copyrighted work is only permissible if it invokes one of a limited range of statutorily listed purposes for the use'.[50] In contrast, an open-ended regime, with the US fair use test as a prominent example, tends to provide a flexible standard and leave 'the task of identifying individual cases of exempted unauthorized use to the courts'.[51]

If China is to retain its current exception model, then a possible solution might be a new exception that specifically addresses the issue of AI analysis or data mining. However, if China is to change track and embrace the open-ended model, then a possible solution might be a flexible copyright exception test that can aid the judges in deciding new cases such as AI analysis or data mining.

The civil law origin of the CLC does not require China to keep the closed-list model; in fact, many East Asian civil law jurisdictions have introduced or plan to introduce the US fair use test into their copyright laws. In the following parts of this sub-section, the experiences from Taiwan, Korea, and Japan are examined in turn to determine the suitable exception model for China.

[49] Guobin Cui, *Copyright Law, Cases and Materials* (Peking University Press 2014) 606 (崔国斌，《著作权法：原理与案例》，北京大学出版社 2014).

[50] Lital Helman, 'Session IV: Fair Use and Other Exceptions' (2017) 40 Columbia Journal of Law & the Arts 395–6 (hereafter Helman, 'Session IV: Fair Use and Other Exceptions').

[51] Martin Senftleben, 'The International Three-Step Test: A Model Provision for EC Fair Use Legislation' (2010) 1 Journal of Intellectual Property, Information Technology and Electronic Commerce Law 68.

3.3.1 Taiwan

Taiwan transplanted the US fair use model to its copyright law in 1992. Its Copyright Act sets a specific section entitled 'Limitations on Economic Rights'.[52] The structure is a hybrid one: Articles 44 to 64 concern a list of exceptions similar to those provided in Article 24 of the CLC. However, its Article 65 provides an open-ended clause that largely imitates the US fair use test which can serve as a general principle for determination of all the circumstances, including the listed exceptions.[53] Under this kind of setting, when the process of AI analysis or data mining satisfies the four factors (which is highly likely as the use is transformative and will normally not damage the potential market of the copyright owners), it could then be exempted.

However, Taiwan has taken a new approach in the 2014 revision of its copyright law. The four factors of fair use are now considered by the court in two scenarios. First, when applying Articles 44 to 63, the court needs to consider the four factors if the statute explicitly requires the subject use be made within 'a reasonable/fair scope'.[54] Second, the four factors in Article 65(2) are still an independent and open-ended clause for the court to determine fair use, as before.

Among the listed exceptions in Articles 44 to 63, the most relevant one concerning data mining and analysis is probably Article 52: 'Within a reasonable scope, works that have been publicly released may be quoted where necessary for reports, comment, teaching, research, or other legitimate purposes'. However, 'quoting' the work is conceptually different from the massive reproduction of copyrighted works for AI analysis and data mining. Therefore, Article 52 may not be applicable in various AI applications concerning data mining and analysis. Instead, if any defendant requires to defend his use of copyrighted works for the purpose of AI analysis and data mining, the most likely ground of that defence will still be based on the general and open-ended four fair-use factors listed in Article 65(2).

52 Copyright Act (2019) (ROC), sub-s 4.

53 Ibid, Art 65:

> Fair use of a work shall not constitute infringement on economic rights in the work.
>
> In determining whether the exploitation of a work complies with the reasonable scope referred to in the provisions of Articles 44 through 63, or other conditions of fair use, all circumstances shall be taken into account, and in particular the following facts shall be noted as the basis for determination:

1. The purposes and nature of the exploitation, including whether such exploitation is of a commercial nature or is for nonprofit educational purposes.
2. The nature of the work.
3. The amount and substantiality of the portion exploited in relation to the work as a whole.
4. Effect of the exploitation on the work's current and potential market value.

54 Ibid, Art 65(2).

3.3.2 Korea

Korea, as a civil law jurisdiction, used to adopt a closed-list copyright exceptions model in its Copyright Act.[55] In the 2016 amendment, Korea has introduced a US style fair use test into its Copyright Act as Article 35-3.[56] Unlike the Taiwan approach, the Korean Copyright Act appears to distinguish the listed exceptions (Articles 23 to 35-2 and 101-3 to 101-5) with its fair use test. In other words, if any act is covered by any of the listed exceptions, then there is no room for the fair use test in Article 35-3 to apply.

Similar to the situation in Taiwan, none of the listed exceptions in the Korean Copyright Act can fully cover the use of AI analysis or data mining. As a result, this kind of use will be assessed by the fair use test parts within these two jurisdictions. According to the US precedents, 'non-expressive' uses such as the unauthorized use of copyrighted works in the Google Books project and search engines were considered fair use due to their transformative nature.[57] Following in that vein, AI analysis and data mining may well also be covered, as it is presumptively 'non-expressive' and transformative, and hence will not harm the potential market of the copyright owner.[58] However, it is hard to predict how the courts in Taiwan and Korea will decide a case involving AI analysis and data mining of copyrighted works based on their US style open-ended fair use provisions, as the four-factor test is a legal transplant per se, and the interpretation of the four factors will have to serve the local needs, and therefore may vary from country to country.

3.3.3 Japan

Japan once considered transplanting a flexible fair use doctrine directly to its copyright law, according to its 2009 national IP strategic plan.[59] However, in its 2016

[55] Sang Jo Jong, 'Fair Use: A Tale of Two Cities' in Toshiko Takenaka (ed.), *Intellectual Property in Common Law and Civil Law* (Edward Elgar 2013) 179.

[56] Copyright Act (2016) (Korea) Art 35-3 (Fair Use of Works, etc.):

(1) Except as provided in Articles 23 through 35-2 and 101-3 through 101-5, where a person does not unreasonably prejudice an author's legitimate interest without conflicting with the normal exploitation of works, he/she may use such works.

(2) In determining whether an act of using works, etc. falls under paragraph (1), the following shall be considered:

1. Purposes and characters of use including whether such use is for or not-for nonprofit;
2. Types and natures of works, etc.;
3. Amount and substantiality of portion used in relation to the whole works, etc.;
4. Effect of the use of works, etc. on the current or potential market for or value of such work etc.

[57] See, eg, *Kelly v Arriba Soft Corp.*, 336 F.3d 811 (9th Cir. 2003); *Perfect 10, Inc. v Amazon.com, Inc.*, 508 F.3d 1146 (9th Cir. 2007); *Authors Guild v Google Inc.*, 804 F.3d 202 (2d Cir. 2015).

[58] Sobel, 'Artificial Intelligence's Fair Use Crisis' (n 36) 57.

[59] Japan Intellectual Property Strategy Headquarters, 'Intellectual Property Strategic Plan 2009' (2009) <https://www.kantei.go.jp/jp/singi/titeki2/090624/2009keikaku.pdf> ('To introduce general rules for rights restrictions (Japanese Fair Use Rules)').

national IP strategic plan, Japan switched to a different track.[60] In May 2018, Japan amended its copyright law and changed the structure of its closed-list copyright exceptions model to a semi-open one.[61] Specifically, it has made the following changes:

First, it compartmentalized copyright exceptions into three types, according to the purposes they served and market considerations:

(a) Harmless uses, which refers to uses that do not fall under the original purposes of use of a copyrighted work and can be evaluated as not normally harming the interests of the rights holder;
(b) Minor harm uses, which refers to uses that do not fall under the original purposes of use of a copyrighted work but will cause a minor degree of damage to the rights holder;
(c) Public policy uses, which refers to uses that fall under the original purposes of use of a copyrighted work but are permitted in order to realize public policy objectives such as cultural development.[62]

Second, the once-scattered exceptions were then consolidated under specific general categories according to the aforementioned compartmentalization. Specifically, Japan has provided an exception (Article 30-4) that directly links to AI analysis or data mining, based on an existing exception and reconstructed into a multilayered (general clause—list—catch-all) style. Table 9.1, which compares the old and the new Article 30-4, shows clearly the changes that have been made:

Specifically, the newly amended article contains the following changes:

The first paragraph of Article 30-4 added a general rule that consists of a purpose element (exploitation is not for enjoying or causing another person to enjoy the ideas or emotions expressed in such work) and a market element (this does not apply if the exploitation would unreasonably prejudice the interests of the copyright owner in light of the nature and purposes of such work, as well as the circumstances of such exploitation).

Two listed examples were then provided: sub-paragraph (i) is derived from the old Article 30-4, and sub-paragraph (ii), which concerns AI analysis and data

[60] Japan Intellectual Property Strategy Headquarters, 'Intellectual Property Strategic Plan 2016' (2016) <https://www.kantei.go.jp/jp/singi/titeki2/kettei/chizaikeikaku20160509.pdf> ('in light of the need to respond to the use of copyrighted works in the digital network era from the viewpoint of flexible response to new innovation and the continuous creation of attractive content originating from Japan . . . to establish flexible rights restriction provisions').

[61] Copyright Law (2018) (Japan), Art 30-50.

[62] Agency for Cultural Affairs, 'Cultural Council Copyright Subcommittee Legal Basic Issues Subcommittee Interim Summary' (2017) <http://www.bunka.go.jp/seisaku/bunkashingikai/chosakuken/pdf/h2902_chukanmatome.pdf> 40.

Table 9.1: Comparison Between the Old and the New Article 30-4

Before the 2018 amendment	After the 2018 amendment
(Exploitation for the use in a test for the development or the practical use of technology) **Article 30-4** It shall be permissible to exploit a work already made public, to the extent deemed necessary, in the case of an offer to use in a test for the development or the practical use of technology required for sound or visual recording or other exploitations of that work.[63] (Reproduction, etc for information analysis) **Article 47-7** For the purpose of information analysis ('information analysis' means to extract information, concerned with languages, sounds, images or other elements constituting such information, from many works or other such information, and to make a comparison, a classification or other statistical analysis of such information; the same shall apply hereinafter in this Article) by using a computer, it shall be permissible to make recording on a memory, or to make adaptation (including a recording of a derivative work created by such adaptation), of a work, to the extent deemed necessary. However, an exception is made of database works which are made for the use by a person who makes an information analysis.	(Exploitations not for enjoying the ideas or emotions expressed in a work) **Article 30-4** It is permissible to exploit work, in any way and to the extent considered necessary, in any of the following cases or other cases where such exploitation is not for enjoying or causing another person to enjoy the ideas or emotions expressed in such work; provided, however that this does not apply if the exploitation would unreasonably prejudice the interests of the copyright owner in light of the natures and purposes of such work, as well as the circumstances of such exploitation: (i) exploitation for using the work in experiments for the development or practical realization of technologies concerning the recording of sounds and visuals or other exploitations of such work; (ii) exploitation for using the work in information analysis (meaning the extraction, comparison, classification, or other statistical analysis of language, sound, or image data, or other elements of which a large number of works or a large volume of information is composed . . .); (iii) in addition to the cases set forth in the preceding two items, exploitation for using the work in the course of computer data processing or otherwise that does not involve perceiving the expressions in such work through the human senses (in regard of works of computer programming, the execution of such work on a computer shall be excluded).

63 Copyright Law (2015) (Japan), Art 30-4.

mining, is clearly adapted from the old Article 47-7. Finally, a flexible circumstance was inserted as sub-paragraph (iii) to cover any other 'exploitation for using the work in the course of computer data processing or otherwise that does not involve perceiving the expressions in such work through the human senses'. It is clear from the above setting and the language of Article 30-4 that the new exception provided in sub-paragraph (ii) is very broad (even much broader than the previous Article 47-7)[64] in the following ways: first, there is no requirement that the AI analysis and data mining must be non-commercial; second, there is no requirement with regard to the purpose of the AI analysis and data mining; third, the 'by using a computer' requirement that existed in the previous Article 47-7 is lifted. In other words, non-computational ways of TDM are also covered; fourth, there is no limitation on sharing data sets; and last, the term 'information analysis' is interpreted quite broadly. And, in a case where a certain way of AI analysis and data mining falls short of the requirements set by sub-paragraph (ii), sub-paragraph (iii) could then apply as long as the use 'does not involve perceiving the expressions in such work through the human senses'.

The new Article 30-4 was apparently categorized by the legislature as a 'harmless use'. Obviously, Japan's approach was to place certain specific exceptions under a common but controllable theme, such as 'exploitations not for enjoying the ideas or emotions expressed in a work', and then provide it with a flexible general rule. Examples in this setting can provide a degree of certainty to that model. The catch-all circumstance will then provide space for future technological developments such as AI and deep learning.

4. How to Make the CLC a Promoter Rather Than a Barrier?

Can and should China learn from its neighbours, or should it transplant the US fair use model directly? In order to answer this question, it is necessary to check which approach is preferable in the eyes of both the judicature and the legislature in China.

4.1 Judicial Practices Advocate a Flexible Regime

Chinese courts have long been loyal supporters and protectors of new technologies. In most cases that involve new ways of utilization enabled by new technologies that are not covered by the thirteen listed exceptions of Article 24 of the CLC,

[64] The previous Art 47-7 amended in 2009 was deemed 'rather broad in scope'. See Marco Caspers and others, 'Deliverable D3.3+ Baseline report of policies and barriers of TDM in Europe' (*FutureTDM*, 2016) pp. 75–6 <http://www.futuretdm.eu/knowledge-library/?b5-file=4588&b5-folder=2227>.

such as caches and thumbnails,[65] and the Google books project,[66] the Chinese courts have all examined the defendants' fair use claims and supported the idea that they could be deemed fair use when necessary. In these judgments, the judges have all jumped out of the listed exceptions and turned to different justifications to support these activities. These include using the two-step test provided in Article 21 of the 2013 RICL as a general fair use clause, and even introducing the four fair use factors directly. Furthermore, the Supreme People's Court (SPC) has also used its judicial interpretations to either create new exceptions for caches and thumbnails outside the CLC,[67] or to introduce the four fair use factors to rule on certain types of cases directly.[68]

Despite the fact that these initiatives helped to solve some difficult cases, these practices may not be sustainable, as they deviate from the doctrinal interpretation of the CLC in an unconstitutional way. To begin with, as discussed previously, Article 21 of the RICL is actually an additional control over the list rather than a general clause that can be applied independently; then, even if these pragmatic approaches can later be confirmed and consolidated by SPC judicial interpretations, the legal effect of these SPC interpretations is uncertain, as the SPC judicial interpretations 'shall primarily involve the specific clauses of laws and conform to the objectives, principles, and original meaning of the legislation' according to the Legislation Law of China.[69] In other words, SPC judicial interpretations cannot go beyond the original meaning of the interpreted law, let alone create new laws, otherwise they will be deemed unconstitutional;[70] finally, without a substantive revision to the copyright exceptions part of the CLC, the arbitrary application of the law will result in contradictory interpretations by courts in new cases that involve new ways of utilization of copyrighted works such as live game webcasting.[71]

[65] *Wen Xiaoyang v Yahoo* [2008] Beijing Chaoyang District People's Court, CMCZ No 13556; T*he Music Copyright Society of China v Baidu* [2008] Beijing Haidian District People's Court, HMCZ No 7404; *Beijing Sogou Information Service Co Ltd v Wenhui Cong* [2013] Beijing First Intermediate People's Court, YZMZZ No 12533.

[66] *Wang Shen v Google Inc.* et al. [2012] Beijing 1st Intermediary People's Court, YZMCZ No.1321; [2013] Beijing Higher People's Court, GMZZ No.1221.

[67] Provisions of the Supreme People's Court on Several Issues concerning the Application of Law in Hearing Civil Dispute Cases Involving Infringement of the Right of Dissemination on Information Networks (2012) (PRC), Art. 5(2).

[68] Several Opinions of the Supreme People's Court on Some Issues in Fully Giving Rein to the Function of Intellectual Property Rights Adjudication in Promoting the Great Development and Flourishing of Socialist Culture and Stimulating the Indigenous and Coordinated Development of Economy (2011) (PRC), para 8.

[69] Legislation Law (2015) (PRC), Art 104.

[70] Feng Lin and Shucheng Wang, 'Protection of Labour Rights through Judicial Legislation In China—An Analysis of Its Constitutionality and Possible Solution' in Surya Deva (ed.), *Socio-economic Rights in Emerging Free Markets: Comparative Insights from India and China* (Routledge 2015) 176.

[71] Jie Wang and Tianxiang He, 'To Share is Fair: The Changing Face of China's Fair Use Doctrine in the Sharing Economy and Beyond' (2019) 35 Computer Law & Security Review 20, 21. Tianxiang He, 'Transplanting Fair Use in China? History, Impediments and the Future' (2020) 2020 The University of Illinois Journal of Law, Technology & Policy 359, 382–84.

4.2 Legislature Proposed an Open-ended but Non-fair-use Model

It is clear from the preceding discussion that, unless the challenges to the constitutional grounds can be overcome, the SPC judicial interpretations and other similar initiatives as solutions to the problems of AI analysis and data mining are not ideal for China. Furthermore, according to civil law tradition, any judgments that aim to create new laws will come to nothing until the rules created are absorbed by the law.

Fortunately, a third revision of the CLC has just been passed on 11 November 2020, and the NCAC has proposed several drafts since 2012.[72] However, the following discussions are based on the proposed copyright exceptions model of the third draft for review of the CLC published by the NCAC on 2014[73] rather than the 2020 CLC, as the former is more ambitious than the latter, in that you can see a proposal of an open-ended copyright exception model which is discussed below. Surprisingly, the 2020 CLC has taken a big step back by only replacing the sentence 'the other rights enjoyed by the copyright owner in accordance with this Law are not prejudiced' of the first paragraph of Article 24 with the following: 'the normal use of the work is not prejudiced and the lawful rights and interests of the copyright owner are not unreasonably prejudiced', which is basically a verbatim copy of Article 21 of the RICL and added '[o]ther circumstances provided for by laws and administrative regulations' as the thirteenth exception. In effect, nothing much will be changed about the copyright exception model of the 2020 CLC as the added part of the first paragraph will serve the original function of Article 21 of the RICL, and the newly added thirteenth exception is not an instant functioning one as it merely opens the possibility of new exceptions set by future laws and administrative regulations.[74] In contrast, the third draft of the CLC has proposed a bold amendment to its copyright exception part, termed Article 43 (the equivalent of Article 24 in the current CLC).[75] Table 9.2 provides a comparison between the settings.

The third draft has added an open-ended provision: it inserted 'other circumstances' in Article 43 as a 'catch-all' exception as Article 43.1(13). In addition, the third draft included a sub-section as Article 43.2: 'the use of a published work pursuant to the above provisions may not prejudice the normal use of the work and may not unreasonably prejudice the lawful rights and interests of the copyright owner'.[76]

[72] The first draft was made officially available for public consultation by the NCAC on 31 March 2012. The NCAC subsequently published the second draft on 2 July 2012 and the third draft on 6 June 2014. The fourth and final draft was published for public consultation on 30 April 2020. See 'Revision proposal for the Copyright Law of China full text' (*IPRDaily*, 2020) <http://www.iprdaily.cn/article_24614.html>.

[73] Legislative Affairs Office of the State Council P.R. China, 'Notice About Circular of the Legislative Affairs Office of the State Council on Promulgating the Copyright Law of the People's Republic of China (Draft Revision for Review) for Public Consultation' (2014) <http://www.gov.cn/xinwen/2014-06/10/content_2697701.htm> (hereafter CLC (Draft Revision for Review)).

[74] CLC (2020) (PRC) Art 24.

[75] CLC (Draft Revision for Review) (n 73) Art 43.

[76] Ibid.

Table 9.2: Comparison Between the Article 24 and the Proposed Article 43

2020 CLC Article 24	2014 Revision Draft of CLC Article 43
In the following cases, a work may be exploited without permission from, and without payment of remuneration to, the copyright owner, provided that the name or appellation of the author and the title of the work are mentioned, and the normal use of the work is not prejudiced and the lawful rights and interests of the copyright owner are not unreasonably prejudiced:	In the following cases, a work may be exploited without permission from, and without payment of remuneration to, the copyright owner, provided that the name or appellation of the author, and the source and title of the work shall be mentioned and the other rights enjoyed by the copyright owner by virtue of this Law shall not be prejudiced:
(1) use of another person's published work for purposes of the user's own personal study, research or appreciation;	(1) copy snippets from another person's published work for purposes of the user's own personal study, research.
(2) appropriate quotation from another person's published work in one's own work for the purpose of introducing or commenting on a certain work, or explaining a certain point;	(2) appropriate quotation from another person's published work in one's own work for the purpose of introducing or commenting a certain work, or explaining a certain point, but the quoted part should not constitute a major or substantial part of the original work.
(3) unavoidable inclusion or quotation of a published work in the media, such as in a newspaper, periodical and radio and television program, for the purpose of reporting current events;	(3) unavoidable inclusion or quotation of a published work in the media, such as in a newspaper, periodical, radio, television program, and Internet for the purpose of reporting news;
(4) publishing or rebroadcasting by the media, such as a newspaper, periodical, radio station and television station, of an article published by another newspaper or periodical, or broadcast by another radio station or television station, etc on current political, economic or religious topics, except where the declares that such publishing or rebroadcasting is not permitted;	(4) publishing or rebroadcasting by the media, such as a newspaper, periodical, radio station, television station, and Internet of an article published by another newspaper or periodical or online, or broadcast by another radio station or television station, etc on current political, economic or religious topics, except where the author declares that such use is not permitted;
(5) publishing or broadcasting by the media, such as a newspaper, periodical, radio station and television station of a speech delivered at a public gathering, except where the author declares that such publishing or broadcasting is not permitted;	(5) publishing or broadcasting by the media, such as a newspaper, periodical, radio station, television station, and Internet of a speech delivered at a public gathering, except where the author declares that such use is not permitted;
(6) translation, adaptation, compilation, playing, or reproduction in a small quantity of copies of a published work by teachers or scientific researchers for use in classroom teaching or scientific research, provided that the translation or the reproductions are not published for distribution;	(6) translation, or reproduction in a small quantity of copies of a published work by teachers or scientific researchers for use in classroom teaching or scientific research, provided that the translation or the reproductions are not published;
	(7) use of a published work by a State organ to a justifiable extent for the purpose of fulfilling its official duties;

Table 9.2: Continued

2020 CLC Article 24	2014 Revision Draft of CLC Article 43
(7) use of a published work by a State organ to a justifiable extent for the purpose of fulfilling its official duties; (8) reproduction of a work in its collections by a library, archive, memorial hall, museum, art gallery, cultural halls, etc for the purpose of display, or preservation of a copy, of the work; (9) gratuitous live performance of a published work, for which no fees are charged to the public, nor payments are made to the performers and there is no aim to profit; (10) copying, drawing, photographing or video-recording of a work of art put up or displayed in an outdoor public place; (11) translation of a published work of a Chinese citizen, legal entity, or other organization from the standard written Chinese language into minority nationality languages for publication and distribution in the country; and (12) providing published works in an accessible fashion that can be perceived by people with print disabilities. (13) Other circumstances provided for by laws and administrative regulations. The provisions of the preceding paragraph apply to restrictions on copyright-related rights.[77]	(8) reproduction of a work in its collections by a library, archive, memorial hall, museum, art gallery, etc for the purpose of display, or preservation of a copy, of the work; (9) gratuitous live performance of a published work, for which no fees are charged to the public, nor payments are made to the performers, and no economic benefits are gained in any other ways; (10) reproducing, drawing, photographing or video-recording, copying, distributing and making available to the public of a work of art put up or displayed in an outdoor public place, provided that it is not reproduced, displayed, or publicly distributed in the same manner as the work of art; (11) translation of a published work of a Chinese natural person, legal entity or other organization from Han language into minority nationality languages for publication in the country; and (12) transliteration of a published work into braille for publication; (13) Other circumstances. The use of a published work pursuant to the above provisions may not prejudice the normal use of the work and may not unreasonably prejudice the lawful rights and interests of the copyright owner.[78]

This sub-section replicates the wording of Article 21 of the 2013 RICL. The addition of these parts is essential, as it will turn the closed-list model into an open one.[79] Ideally, one can arguably combine Article 43.1(13) and sub-section 2 and claim that paragraph (13) was inserted to cover not just AI analysis and data mining but also other new utilizations in the future.

The actual effect of this setting is similar to the current setting of the Copyright Act of Taiwan, in which the 'two-step' test in sub-section 2 will serve as the 'ceiling' for all the limitations and exceptions. Theoretically, if AI analysis and data mining

77 CLC (2020) (PRC), Art 24.

78 CLC (Draft Revision for Review) (n 73) Art 43.

79 Peter K Yu, 'Customizing Fair Use Transplants' (2018) 7 Laws 1, 10 (hereafter Yu, 'Customizing Fair Use Transplants').

are not covered by any listed exceptions, then paragraph (13) of 'other circumstances' will act as a catch-all clause to assess these new utilizations with the help of the 'two-step' test in sub-section 2. However, even if AI analysis and data mining can be covered by the newly added 'other circumstances' exception, this kind of setting is still too broad to be deemed a 'certain special case', which is required by the first step of the Berne three-step test. This raises a concern about the Berne compliance of the proposed Article 43, causing some to suggest that the newly added 'other circumstances' should be rephrased as 'other specific occasions'.[80]

4.3 The Possible Model for China

In order to make the CLC become a facilitator rather than a hindrance to the development of AI technology, China is facing two options: first, to pick a side between the closed-list model and the open-ended model; second, to introduce a hybrid model that combines features from both models.

4.3.1 A US-style fair use model for China?

It is obviously a choice between certainty on one hand, and flexibility on the other. However, as the proposed drafts of the CLC demonstrates that, China has no intention to introduce the US fair use test verbatim. As demonstrated above, Taiwan, South Korea, and Japan all managed to retain their original setting to a degree when broadening their closed-list settings. According to research conducted by Peter Yu, only a few of the jurisdictions investigated have introduced the US fair use model verbatim or substantially verbatim.[81] Moreover, of all the jurisdictions that have changed their closed-list model to an open one, most chose to avoid a marked change to the current setting by retaining 'a considerable part of the status quo, including pre-existing fair dealing provisions'.[82] According to Peter Yu, the causes underlying this 'conscious choice to retain a considerable part of the status quo'[83] range 'from economic to social and from legal to technological'.[84]

Are there any economic, social, legal, or even technological causes that prevent China from adopting the US fair use model? Obviously, the continental-European civil law tradition of the CLC is not a key factor preventing China from introducing the US four-factor fair use test directly, as South Korea and Taiwan have managed to introduce fair use in a sense. However, if viewed from an international relationship perspective, legislators of China, which faces repeated pressure from the US in

80 Zhang, 'Introducing the Open Clause to Improve Copyright Flexibility in Cyberspace?' (n 41) 86.
81 Yu, 'Customizing Fair Use Transplants' (n 79) 11.
82 Ibid.
83 Peter K Yu, 'Fair Use and Its Global Paradigm Evolution' (2019) University of Illinois Law Review 111, 141.
84 Ibid, 155.

relation to IP issues and has no historical connection with the fair use paradigm, will be more inclined to build from their current setting and establish a regime based on local conditions. Moreover, when considering legal transplants, Chinese legislators tend to check the message underlying the foreign regime to see if it accords with China's policies. It is believed that the US fair use test 'reaffirms that copyright law poses a First Amendment paradox that cannot be ignored',[85] and the US Supreme Court has held that 'fair use defense affords considerable latitude for scholarship and comment ... even for parody'.[86] However, these internal links do not exist in the Chinese legal system.[87] Accordingly, if the underlying messages include Western interpretations of values such as freedom of speech, which can be used to utter dissent that is not welcomed by government officials, then this might be a big hurdle for China to transplant the US fair use model directly, as direct transplant will inevitably lead to indirect adoption of the US jurisprudence into Chinese law.[88]

Moreover, with respect to AI analysis and data mining, a flexible general clause not specifically provided for the needs of these new exploitations may not be able to provide the degree of certainty that they are asking for. Specifically, without the *stare decisis* principle, any judgments given by the Chinese courts that provide that AI analysis and data mining can be covered by the open-ended clause would have almost no precedential effect. In other words, a clearly provided exception for AI analysis and data mining is much more preferable under the context of CLC.

4.3.2 Recommendation: A semi-open copyright exceptions model

In order to accommodate use of copyright materials by AI analysis and data mining, the CLC needs a copyright exceptions design that is not only flexible enough to keep pace with any technological changes in the future, but also relatively certain to help Chinese judges to better adjudicate. From a theoretical point of view, China should adhere to and refine the proposed flexible model, thereby developing its own precedents and copyright jurisprudence.

Experiences from other civil law jurisdictions in East Asia such as Taiwan, Korea, and Japan can be used as a reference point while deciding the future path towards refinement. Technically speaking, the approaches taken by Taiwan and Korea can both serve as the right model for China to introduce, as both can resolve the issue raised by AI analysis and data mining. However, as discussed above, unlike Taiwan, Korea, and Japan, which have maintained good relationships with the US, currently China is having a trade dispute with the US, and it is believed that it

[85] Neil Weinstock Netanel, 'First Amendment Constraints on Copyright after Golan v. Holder' (2013) 60 UCLA Law Review 1128.

[86] *Eldred v Ashcroft*, 537 US 186, 219–20 (2003).

[87] Tianxiang He, 'Control or Promote? China's Cultural Censorship System and Its Influence on Copyright Protection' (2017) 7 Queen Mary Journal of Intellectual Property 95–7.

[88] Helman, 'Session IV: Fair Use and Other Exceptions' (n 50) 397. (Helman pointed out that when Israeli introduced the US fair use test, '[M]ost likely, by incorporating the U.S. four factor test, Israel also indirectly adopted the U.S. jurisprudence into Israeli law'.)

'represents a struggle for global technological leadership as well as a new type of institutional competition in the post-Cold War era.'[89] In other words, a friendly environment that would help to introduce a purely US doctrine into the CLC does not exist in China. Taking into consideration the underlying message and the need for the AI analysis and data mining exception to be more specified, as discussed above, the Japanese model is preferable. Therefore, to refine the current copyright exceptions setting to further promote the development of AI technology, Chinese legislators could learn from the Japanese model by nominating a new exception and then consolidating cognate ones under a broader theme, providing them with the 'general clause—list—catch-all' setting such as the following:

> Article 24: In the following cases, a work may be exploited without permission from, and without payment of remuneration to, the copyright owner, provided that the name or appellation of the author, and the source and title of the work shall be mentioned and the other rights enjoyed by the copyright owner by virtue of this Law shall not be prejudiced:
>
> ...
>
> (X) Within a reasonable scope, exploitation of copies of a lawfully accessed published work for use in scientific research purposes, such as:
>
> (X.1) Translation, or reproduction in a small quantity of copies, of a published work for use by teachers or scientific researchers, in classroom teaching or scientific research, provided that the translation or reproduction shall not be published or distributed;
> (X.2) Reproduction, and adaptation of published works in the course of data analysis and mining, in order to uncover new knowledge or insights;
> (X.3) ...
> (X.4) In addition to the cases set forth in the preceding items, exploitation for using the work in the course of computer data processing or any other scientific research.
>
> ...
>
> (13) other reasonable circumstances.
>
> The use of a published work pursuant to the above provisions may not prejudice the normal use of the work and may not unreasonably prejudice the lawful rights and interests of the copyright owner.

[89] Jyh-An Lee, 'Shifting IP Battlegrounds in the U.S.–China Trade War' (2020) 43 Columbia Journal of Law & the Arts 194.

The new design has kept the setting proposed by Article 43 of the Draft Revision for Review, and embraces the Japanese approach to further develop the existing exceptions.[90] Specifically, the suggested new drafting contains the following changes:

For the proposed scientific research exception, a general rule that encompasses a purpose element (exploitation of copies of a lawfully accessed published work for use in scientific research purposes) and a degree element (within a reasonable scope) are provided. The proposed two-step test in Article 43.2 of the Draft Revision for Review (the use of a published work pursuant to the above provisions may not prejudice the normal use of the work and may not unreasonably prejudice the lawful rights and interests of the copyright owner) as Article 24.2 is kept along with the Article 24.1(13) 'other circumstances' so that an open-ended general clause can be established. This kind of setting is definitely required, as it can provide the degree of flexibility that is needed to accommodate unexpected future challenges. It is believed that Chinese judges have to play an active role 'in concretizing legal rules of general nature and in substantiating such rules with more detailed and precise specifications in the process of adjudicating individual cases and making legal rules compatible with social development'.[91] In an era of rapid social and economic changes, an open-ended general clause will provide Chinese courts with the flexibility they desire.

The original Article 24(6) of the CLC that concerns 'translation, or reproduction in a small quantity of copies, of a published work for use by teachers or scientific researchers, in classroom teaching or scientific research' and the newly added exception that concerns 'exploitation for using the work in the course of data analysis and mining' are provided in (X.1) and (X.2) as examples of 'scientific research purposes'. For (X.1), the jurisprudence related to the original article developed throughout history could therefore be retained. Furthermore, the wording of (X.2) provides clearly that only the acts of reproduction and adaptation of copyrighted works during the data analysis and mining process could be exempted. In other words, the exception must come with certain restrictions so that a delicate balance between the interests of the copyright owners and the public can be maintained.[92] Furthermore, a flexible circumstance was inserted as the last sub-paragraph to cover any future 'computer data processing' uses and any other future scientific uses that are deemed reasonable. Lastly, the two-step test in the second paragraph of the proposed Article 24 will make sure that the exploitation of published works in (X.2) can only serve their original purpose, that is to facilitate data analysis and

[90] For a broader application of the Japanese model concerning copyright exceptions for text and data mining, see Kung-Chung Liu and Shufeng Zheng, Chapter 16 in this volume.

[91] Chenguang Wang, 'Law-making Functions of the Chinese Courts: Judicial Activism in a Country of Rapid Social Changes' (2006) 1 Frontiers of Law in China 524, 548.

[92] Jie Hua, 'The Dilemma and Solution concerning Application of Copyright Exceptions to Artificial Intelligence's Creation' (2019) Electronics Intellectual Property (4)29, 36 (华劼, '合理使用制度运用于人工智能创作的两难及出路', 《电子知识产权》, 2019年第4期, 第36页).

mining that aim to uncover new knowledge or insights. Moreover, it does not limit 'scientific research' to those of non-commercial nature; commercial research can and should also be included, as long as the use satisfies the two-step test.[93] If the user subsequently commercializes the reproduced copies, it will definitely be a copyright infringement due to the fact that it fails the enshrined two-step test, as it amounts to a market substitution.

With this setting, the CLC could achieve flexibility with a semi-open clause that covers not only AI analysis and data mining but also any similar future technological advancements, as the legislature could add more 'examples' under the exception when necessary. These listed examples can then provide a higher degree of certainty.

5. Conclusion

This chapter demonstrates that copyright laws could act as an impediment to the development of AI technology. Because the data set for AI training or mining typically concerns a huge amount of copyrighted works, the machine processing involving reproduction and adaptation of them is likely to be deemed copyright infringement. If this tension cannot be alleviated, it is possible that the development of AI technology will be greatly hampered, and that the result will be biased due to incomplete data collection. Even though the Chinese government has promoted the development of big data and AI with its national policies for many years and a new revision of the CLC has just been published, its copyright law is still lagging behind in terms of providing exceptions to such uses. Considering the fact that many East Asian jurisdictions have either taken the move to introduce specified exceptions for AI analysis and data mining, or have a flexible fair use test that allows the local courts to cover such cases, China should learn from these experiences and revise the copyright exceptions part of the CLC accordingly. In view of the social, cultural, and political environments in China, the design of the AI analysis and data mining copyright exception should follow a semi-open style in order to strike the right balance between flexibility and certainty.

[93] Jinping Zhang, 'On the Dilemma and Solution of the Fair Use of Copyrighted Works by AI' (2019) 41 Global Law Review 120, 131 (张金平, '人工智能作品合理使用困境及其解决', 《环球法律评论》, 2019年第3期, 第131页).

10

A Taxonomy of Training Data

Disentangling the Mismatched Rights, Remedies, and Rationales for Restricting Machine Learning

*Benjamin Sobel**

1. Introduction

We are worried about 'AI problems'. We worry about economic harms: what will long-haul truckers, radiologists, and journalists do for a living if their vocations become automated? We also worry about dignitary harms: how will new means of synthesizing realistic videos, or 'deepfakes', harm vulnerable populations or deceive the body politic?[1] We worry about invasions of privacy: how will we live rich, contextualized lives if pervasive facial recognition obviates obscurity in public?[2] Law and policy responses to our varied concerns about AI are broad-ranging. Some restrict specific technologies.[3] Some emphasize *ex post* redress: eg, draft and enacted legislation in the US imposes new criminal and/or civil penalties on malicious deepfakes.[4] Others propose counterbalancing automation with more systemic changes, like a universal basic income.[5]

* The author is grateful for the support of the Harvard Law School Summer Academic Fellowship. He thanks his editors and co-contributors, as well as Julia Reda, Joel Sobel, and Kathryn Woolard, for their helpful comments. All online materials were accessed before 25 December 2019.

[1] Robert Chesney and Danielle Citron, 'Deepfakes and the New Disinformation War: The Coming Age of Post-Truth Geopolitics' (2019) 98 Foreign Affairs 147.

[2] Ben Sobel, 'Facial recognition technology is everywhere. It may not be legal' (*Washington Post*, 11 June 2015) <https://www.washingtonpost.com/news/the-switch/wp/2015/06/11/facial-recognition-technology-is-everywhere-it-may-not-be-legal/>.

[3] 'POR 2019 #255 That the amendment to Chapter 2.128 Surveillance Ordinance Technology be forwarded to the Public Safety Committee for a hearing' (*Cambridge City, MA*) <http://cambridgema.iqm2.com/Citizens/Detail_LegiFile.aspx?Frame=&MeetingID=2399&MediaPosition=&ID=9847&CssClass=>; Sarah Wu, 'Somerville City Council passes facial recognition ban—the Boston Globe' (*Boston Globe*, 27 June 2019) <https://www.bostonglobe.com/metro/2019/06/27/somerville-city-council-passes-facial-recognition-ban/SfaqQ7mG3DGulXonBHSCYK/story.html>.

[4] H.R. 3230, 116th Cong. (2019); S. 3805, 115th Cong. (2018); Caitlin Morris, 'Virginia general assembly expands revenge porn law to include fake nudes' (*WTKR.com*, 28 February 2019) <https://wtkr.com/2019/02/28/virginia-general-assembly-expands-revenge-porn-law-to-include-fake-nudes/>.

[5] 'What is Universal Basic Income?' (*Andrew Yang for President*) <https://www.yang2020.com/what-is-freedom-dividend-faq/> ('Andrew Yang wants to implement [a universal basic income] because we are experiencing the greatest technological shift the world has ever seen. By 2015, automation had already destroyed four million manufacturing jobs, and the smartest people in the world now predict that a third of all working Americans will lose their jobs to automation in the next 12 years').

Benjamin Sobel, *A Taxonomy of Training Data* In: *Artificial Intelligence and Intellectual Property*. Edited by: Jyh-An Lee, Reto M Hilty, and Kung-Chung Liu, Oxford University Press (2021). © The several contributors.
DOI: 10.1093/oso/9780198870944.003.0011

The variety of these proposals is appropriate: different applications of AI pose distinct harms that demand distinct legal responses. But despite wreaking dramatically different harms through dramatically different mechanisms, worrisome applications of AI frequently share a common feature: they rely on unauthorized uses of copyrighted 'training data'.[6] In major jurisdictions like the US, very few of these applications of AI to copyrighted data are on firm legal ground.[7] This uncertainty jeopardizes the development of artificial intelligence technology. It jeopardizes the rights of deserving potential plaintiffs and over-deters law-abiding potential defendants. And if left unclarified, this uncertainty also threatens to undermine the purpose and administrability of copyright law.

To the extent lawmakers and commentators conceive of AI as a challenge for intellectual property (IP) law, the focus is often on issues distinct from protected training data, such as copyright in computer-generated works and potential IP protections for algorithms, software, or trained models.[8] Those that do examine training data, in turn, typically characterize today's legal uncertainties as a deficiency in copyright's exceptions and limitations.[9] If we could only strike the right balance in our systems of exceptions and limitations, the thinking goes, we could resolve our current predicament.

This chapter argues that, in fact, the current predicament is a product of systemic features of the copyright regime that, when coupled with a technological environment that turns routine activities into acts of authorship, have caused an explosion of media subject to broad, long, and federated ownership claims. Thus, equilibrating the economy for human expression in the AI age requires a solution that focuses not only on exceptions to *existing* copyrights, but also on the doctrinal features that determine the ownership and scope of copyright entitlements *at their inception*.

Because the most pressing issues in AI frequently implicate unauthorized uses of copyrighted training data, this chapter taxonomizes different applications of machine learning according to their relationships to their training data. Four categories emerge: (1) public-domain training data, (2) licensed training data, (3) market-encroaching uses of copyrighted training data, and (4) non-market-encroaching uses of copyrighted training data.

Analysing AI in this way illuminates a conundrum. Copyright is paradigmatically an economic entitlement. Thus, copyright primarily regulates

[6] Anthony Man-Cho So, Chapter 1 in this volume.

[7] Benjamin LW Sobel, 'Artificial Intelligence's Fair Use Crisis' (2017) 41 Columbia Journal of Law & the Arts 45, 66–7 (hereafter Sobel, 'Artificial Intelligence's Fair Use Crisis').

[8] Jyh-An Lee, Chapter 8 in this volume.

[9] 2019 OJ (L 130/92) 94 ('In certain instances, text and data mining can involve acts protected by copyright, by the sui generis database right or by both, in particular, the reproduction of works or other subject matter, the extraction of contents from a database or both which occur for example when the data is normalised in the process of text and data mining. *Where no exception or limitation applies*, an authorisation to undertake such acts is required from rights holders') (emphasis added).

market-encroaching uses of data—that is, uses of copyrighted expression that endanger the market for that very expression, rather than for some non-expressive aspect of a source work.[10] However, market-encroaching uses represent just a narrow subset of AI applications. Moreover, copyright's economic focus makes it a poor fit for redressing some of the most socially harmful uses of copyrighted materials in AI, like malicious deepfakes. Even more paradoxically, copyright's property-style remedies are ill-suited to addressing market-encroaching uses, and are in fact much more appropriate remedies for the categories of AI that inflict dignitary harms that fall outside copyright's normative mandate. In other words, copyright's property-style remedies are inappropriate for the AI applications that copyright can appropriately regulate. Meanwhile, those remedies *are* appropriate for the AI applications that it would be substantively *inappropriate* for copyright to regulate. Identifying this mismatch helps explain why some commentators have been eager to apply copyright where it does not belong, and eager to dismiss copyright where it rightly governs.

Finally, this chapter discusses a variety of remedies to the 'AI problems' it identifies, with an emphasis on facilitating market-encroaching uses while affording human creators due compensation. It concludes that the exception for TDM in the EU's Directive on Copyright in the Digital Single Market represents a positive development precisely because it addresses the structural issues of the training data problem that this chapter identifies. The TDM provision styles itself as an exception, but it may in fact be better understood as a formality: it requires rights holders to take positive action to obtain a right to exclude their materials from being used as training data. Because of this, the TDM exception addresses a root cause of the AI dilemma rather than trying to patch up the copyright regime post hoc. The chapter concludes that the next step for an equitable AI framework is to transition towards rules that encourage *compensated* market-encroaching uses of copyright-protected training data. Such rules could offer industry a less risky strategy for expansion, facilitate remunerated uses that transaction costs might otherwise impede, and compensate rights holders more proportionally than the outsized, property-style remedies that copyright affords in other contexts.

2. Diagnosing AI's Copyright Problem and Copyright's AI Problem

Insofar as lawyers and scholars treat AI as a problem for copyright law to respond to, they often focus on the inadequacy of copyright's existing exceptions and limitations. However, tensions between copyright entitlements and AI methodologies

[10] See Section 3.3.

are better understood as the results of *systemic* features of global copyright regimes. Machine learning's methods and values clash with broad copyright entitlements that automatically protect even the most banal exertions of human creative effort. Thus, it is inappropriate to blame the friction at the AI-copyright interface on an inadequate exception or limitation to copyright, without interrogating the larger reasons for that safety valve's inadequacy. Accordingly, solutions that present themselves as post hoc safety valves may not fully rectify the problems they purport to address.

Tension between copyright law and AI is in fact a consequence of several interlocking phenomena that should be analysed distinctly from copyright's exceptions and limitations. The root of many copyright-and-AI concerns is the proliferation of bloated copyright entitlements. This phenomenon, in turn, stems from low legal thresholds for protectable originality coupled with information technology that turns routine communications into acts of authorship. In other words, AI has a copyright problem: machine learning may often entail nominal violations of thousands of different copyrights. At the same time, *copyright* has an *AI* problem: now that nearly every scrap of digital expression is copyright-protected *ab initio*, machine learning technology exposes the practical and theoretical shortcomings of a copyright regime that combines strong rights, low originality standards, and no formalities. This section tracks how copyright law has developed to protect vast amounts of online media and encumber AI development. It also explains why, despite a proliferation of copyright entitlements, copyright does not protect some of the highest-stakes training data.

2.1 Everyone Owns Something and Someone Owns Everything

Most of the data that train AI are banal. Indeed, some of these data are just 'data exhaust', the information logged as by-products of technology usage.[11] This kind of data is not copyrightable. No matter how valuable they are to tech companies, the movements of a cursor on a webpage, or geolocation data, or the patterns in one's Netflix browsing, are not works of authorship. But just as banality does not preclude commercial value, neither does banality preclude copyrightability. Minimally creative emails or chat messages are copyrightable literary works, and it is these messages that train state-of-the-art text-generation AI.[12] The digital photographs that train image recognition networks are almost always protectable, even if they're throwaways. As a result, a great deal of the information that powers state-of-the-art

[11] Shoshana Zuboff, *The Age of Surveillance Capitalism* (PublicAffairs 2019) 68.

[12] Anjuli Kannan and others, 'Smart Reply: Automated Response Suggestion for Email' in *Proceedings of the 22nd ACM SIGKDD International Conference on Knowledge Discovery and Data Mining* (KDD '16, New York, NY, USA, ACM 2016).

AI is *owned* by ordinary Internet users. Widespread ownership of training data reflects an unexpected convergence of trends that unfolded over the twentieth century: the abolition of formalities for copyright ownership, the lowering of originality requirements for copyright protection, and the proliferation of technologies that fix expressive activity that until then had been unfixed.

2.1.1 Formalities

Copyright protects so much training data today because copyright now vests automatically in a creator. A century or so ago, complying with numerous formal requirements was essential to copyrighting a work in the US. These hurdles arguably helped allocate copyright entitlements to valuable works, while avoiding the social costs of protecting works whose creation was not incentivized by economic rights.[13] An American novelist in the year 1910 would have forfeited her copyright if, eg, she published her work without a copyright notice.[14] In contrast, the Berne Convention provides that the enjoyment of copyrights 'shall not be subject to any formality'.[15] Beginning with the Copyright Act of 1976, the US shifted away from formalities, a trend that continued through its accession to the Berne Convention in 1989.[16] US copyright law no longer requires notice or registration as prerequisites to a valid copyright, and foreign authors need not even register their works before bringing suit for infringement.[17] Such 'unconditional' copyright means that, by default, anyone who authors a minimally creative email, text message, or photograph becomes its legal owner for decades to come.[18]

2.1.2 Low originality standards

The second trend is international gravitation towards a relatively low standard for 'originality' in copyright law.[19] Leading up to the twentieth century, American copyright cases recited fairly demanding originality requirements: a work needed to manifest an author's 'original intellectual conceptions' to enjoy protection.[20]

[13] To some degree, of course, this system operated at the expense of creators who lacked the sophistication to comply with formalities. Christopher Sprigman, 'Reform(Aliz)Ing Copyright' (2004–05) 57 Stanford Law Review 485, 514 (hereafter Sprigman, 'Reform(Aliz)Ing Copyright').

[14] An Act to Amend and Consolidate the Acts Respecting Copyright (1909) § 9 <https://www.copyright.gov/history/1909act.pdf>.

[15] Berne Convention for the Protection of Literary and Artistic Works, Art 5(2).

[16] Berne Convention Implementation Act of 1988, Pub.L. 100–568.

[17] 17 US Code § 411; *Fourth Estate Pub. Benefit Corp. v Wall-Street.com, LLC*, 139 S. Ct. 881, 891 (2019) ('Noteworthy, too, in years following the 1976 revisions, Congress resisted efforts to eliminate § 411(a) and the registration requirement embedded in it. In 1988, Congress removed foreign works from § 411(a)'s dominion in order to comply with the Berne Convention for the Protection of Literary and Artistic Works' bar on copyright formalities for such works. See § 9(b)(1), 102 Stat. 2859. Despite proposals to repeal § 411(a)'s registration requirement entirely, however, see S. Rep. No 100-352, p. 36 (1988), Congress maintained the requirement for domestic works, see § 411(a)').

[18] Sprigman, 'Reform(Aliz)Ing Copyright' (n 13) 539.

[19] William W Fisher, 'Recalibrating Originality' (2016–17) 54 Hous L Rev 437, 438 (hereafter Fisher, 'Recalibrating Originality').

[20] *Burrow-Giles Lithographic Co. v Sarony*, 111 US 53, 58 (1884).

These standards diminished considerably in the mid-1900s. Today, the prevailing test in the US requires only a 'minimal degree of creativity'.[21] As Peter Jaszi cannily observes, an expansive conception of copyright 'offers no sound basis for distinguishing between oil paintings, art reproductions, motion pictures, lamp bases, poems, and inflatable plastic Santa Clauses'.[22]

In comparison to the US, continental Europe's originality requirements are more exacting. However, Europe has relaxed its standards in recent years. Before the harmonization of European copyright law, some jurisdictions imposed stringent originality standards. Austria, eg, required that a copyrightable photograph differ substantially from pre-existing photographs.[23] The standard promulgated by the European Court of Justice 'is widely seen as an effort to forge a compromise between the more stringent rules previously in force in many continental countries and the more relaxed approach previously in force in Ireland and the United Kingdom'.[24] Thus, while copyright today may not protect rote drudgery, it will attach to most other fixations of mundane expression.

2.1.3 New fixation technologies

The third trend is the proliferation of technologies that fix in tangible form expression that would have gone unrecorded in previous eras. Typically, copyright regimes require protected works to be 'fixed'.[25] Today, it is easier than ever to record, store, and transmit large amounts of text, images, video, and audio. These technologies mediate and memorialize interpersonal interactions. Instructions to employees might be fixed in emails instead of announced verbally, flirtatious conversation might take place on a dating app instead of in a bar, and friends might share jokes and skits as videos sent to a group messaging thread. Expressive interactions that were heretofore unfixed are now fixed. Under most copyright regimes, media like this will be both sufficiently original and sufficiently fixed to receive full copyright protections. As Joseph Miller wrote in 2009, 'technological change is as much a part of copyright's conquest of daily life as any legal rule. Low-cost computers (with word processing, e-mail, photo, music, drawing, and browsing applications) linked to a global, high-speed communications network routinely transform us into gushing copyright and infringement fountains'.[26] If the lowering

21 *Feist Publications, Inc. v Rural Tel. Serv. Co.*, 499 US 340, 345 (1991).

22 Peter Jaszi, 'Toward a Theory of Copyright: The Metamorphoses of "Authorship"' (1991) 1991 Duke Law Journal 455, 485.

23 Roman Heidinger, 'The Threshold of Originality under EU Copyright Law' (Co-Reach Intellectual Property Rights in the New Media, Hong Kong, 20 October 2011); cited in Fisher, 'Recalibrating Originality (n 19) 439.

24 Fisher, 'Recalibrating Originality' (n 19) 443.

25 17 USC § 102(a); Copyright, Designs and Patents Act 1988, s 3(2); Berne Convention for the Protection of Literary and Artistic Works, Art 2(2).

26 Joseph Scott Miller, 'Hoisting Originality' (2009) 31 Cardozo Law Review 451, 459.

of originality standards democratized authorship, then new fixation technologies and the abolition of formalities democratized *ownership*.

2.2 Copyright as Accidental Obstacle: Some AI Needs neither 'Works' nor 'Authorship'

The confluence of unconditional copyright, low originality standards, and networked technology has precipitated an explosion of owned data. But that ownership is, in many cases, merely a nominal obstacle to using those data in AI. This is because, despite being nominally copyrightable, many of the data that train AI fit uneasily within copyright's cosmology and do not lend themselves to uses that copyright can control.

Copyright protects 'works' by 'authors'.[27] A work connotes a freestanding, ascertainable product of deliberate intellectual labour.[28] Michelangelo's *David* is a work. *Pride and Prejudice* and *Die Zauberflöte* are works—even though, unlike the *David*, they lack a single, authoritative embodiment. A stroke of paint on a canvas can be a work. So can an email to a friend or a text-message to a lover. 'Authorship', in turn, suggests some measure of deliberate creative investment, originating from the author. As the US Supreme Court noted in *Feist Publications v Rural Telephone Service*, citing the copyright scholar Melville Nimmer, 'since an author is the "creator, originator[,]" it follows that a work is not the product of an author unless the work is original'.[29] The *Feist* decision remains the authoritative statement that US copyright law requires protectable works to evidence a modest amount of creativity.

Copyright law already has difficulty assimilating information that resembles a work or appears to be authored, but for some reason does not amount to a 'work of authorship'. Transient performances, eg, often evidence authorial creativity, but that authorship may not easily reduce to a unified work. Unsurprisingly, then, copyright law struggles to protect performance, and often ends up premising protection on the details that make a performance a 'work'—choices made by a sound engineer recording an improvised solo or a cameraman recording a dance routine—rather than the substantive creativity in the performance itself.[30]

Many AI training data are an even poorer fit for copyright law because their utility depends *neither* on any authorial qualities *nor* on any resemblance to a

[27] US Constitution, Art I, s 8 (referring in pertinent part to protecting the 'Writings' of 'Authors'); Beijing Treaty on Audiovisual Performances, Art 2(a) ('"performers" ... perform literary or artistic *works* or expressions of folklore'); 17 USC § 101.

[28] The *Oxford English Dictionary*'s pertinent definitions are: 'A literary or musical composition, esp. as considered in relation to its author or composer', and 'A product of any of the fine arts, as a painting, statue, etc.' 'Work, N.', *OED Online* (Oxford University Press, no date).

[29] *Feist Publications, Inc. v Rural Tel. Serv. Co.*, 499 US 340, 351–2 (1991).

[30] Rebecca Tushnet, 'Performance Anxiety: Copyright Embodied and Disembodied' (2013) 60 Journal of the Copyright Society of the USA 209, 210.

work. Indeed, some of the richest data for AI are information that copyright law traditionally disfavours, and the copyright-protected status of which is largely accidental. A highly expressive, stylized photograph could well be *less* valuable as training data for a facial recognition algorithm than a full-frontal mugshot. For training voice-synthesis AI, a recording of someone reciting every word in the dictionary, or enunciating every combination of phonemes, would probably be no less useful than a dramatic soliloquy. Are one's involuntary facial movements a work? Are they authored? Is one's gait a work of authorship? What about facial features, speaking cadence, or vocal timbre? It is true, of course, that these attributes *sometimes* evince authorship, but they certainly are not *always* authored. A recording of someone reading a banal sentence, or just enunciating a series of random syllables, is a performance without meaningful indicia of copyrightable authorship. If that recording were made by someone other than the speaker, there would be few, if any, hooks in contemporary doctrine that could give the speaker a copyright interest in the recording itself. In short, it is a legal and technological accident that such large amounts of training data are copyright-protected today.

Moreover, technological progress may obviate the need to fix training data at all, or at least in any form that resembles a work. Already, digital personal assistants learn to recognize our voices and faces without requiring us to supply photographs or sound recordings that we have created ourselves.[31] Google's 'federated learning' technology trains AI models without reproducing training data on cloud servers.[32] Thus, it is neither the qualities of 'authorship' nor of 'works' that make training data valuable for a number of current AI applications. And it is quite easy to imagine that the powerful, valuable training data of the future will be neither authored nor works, and therefore that copyright's somewhat accidental relevance could wane.

3. A Taxonomy of Training Data

Because one of the most distinctive aspects of contemporary AI is its reliance on large quantities of training data, it is illuminating to characterize 'AI problems' in terms of the legal status of their training data.[33] These training data are often copyrighted, and the individuals who develop or deploy an AI system may not be the rights holders, or even the licensees, of the data. As a result, copyright law sometimes seems like a viable counterweight to a number of AI problems. On other occasions, copyright seems like it might stifle salutary applications of AI. Often, copyright's involvement in this process is accidental—a model might learn from

[31] 'About face ID advanced technology' (*Apple Support*) <https://support.apple.com/en-us/HT208108>.

[32] 'Federated learning: collaborative machine learning without centralized training data' (*Google AI Blog*, 6 April 2017) <https://ai.googleblog.com/2017/04/federated-learning-collaborative.html>.

[33] Sobel, 'Artificial Intelligence's Fair Use Crisis' (n 7) 58.

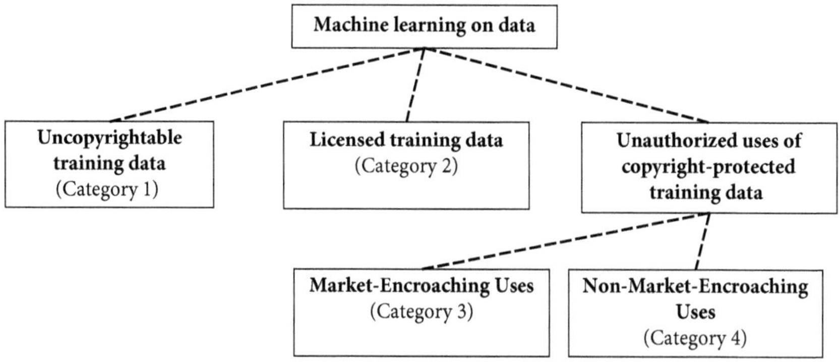

Figure 10.1 Categories of training data used in machine learning

copyrighted data but have little to do with the information that copyright protects, or with copyright's animating principles.

This section identifies four different categories of machine learning on data, set forth in Figure 10.1: (1) uses involving uncopyrightable training data, including expression that has fallen into the public domain, (2) uses involving copyrightable subject matter that has been released under a permissive licence or licensed directly from rights holders, (3) market-encroaching uses, and (4) non-market-encroaching uses. The first of these categories is straightforward: it encompasses uses of AI that do not implicate copyrighted training data at all. These uses may be worrisome for any number of reasons, but they do not invite control through copyright law. The second category is similar: it comprises AI that trains on data that are authorized for such a use, and therefore raises no copyright issues at the initial stages of AI development.

The third category is 'market-encroaching' uses: uses of copyrighted training data undertaken for a purpose that threatens the market for those data. The fourth category is 'non-market-encroaching' uses, which do rely on copyrighted training data, but for purposes unrelated to copyright's monopoly entitlement. Of these four categories, only market-encroaching uses are properly controlled by copyright law—and yet, paradoxically, copyright law seems worst-equipped to regulate them.

3.1 Uncopyrightable Training Data

Many consequential uses of artificial intelligence have neither a formal nor a substantive relation to copyright law.[34] In other words, existing copyright law provides

[34] Of course, underlying software or algorithms may themselves be the subject of a copyright interest, as might their outputs, but those relationships are the focus of other chapters of this book.

no 'hook' for regulating the technology, and the technology's application does not relate to the normative purposes of copyright law. This is most likely to be the case for applications that rely on uncopyrightable training data.

AI that trains on uncopyrightable, non-expressive information is probably more significant than AI that trains on expression that is in the public domain. Fraud-detection or creditworthiness models analyse factual or uncreative data to make inferences that impact individuals' livelihoods. Predictive policing techniques, eg, deploy AI to analyse factual information, like location data, call logs, or criminal records.[35] These technologies can threaten civil liberties, and there is every reason to regulate them in some fashion. But there is essentially no reason for *copyright* to be the regulatory mechanism: factual training data do not implicate copyright, and the applications of the trained models, while consequential, usually do not relate to copyright's purposes.

Public-domain expression might include government work products and out-of-term literary or musical works. Such data have plenty of uses: proceedings of the European Parliament, eg, make for a rich machine-translation training corpus because they offer a voluminous dataset in many parallel translations.[36] Out-of-copyright music can train AI to generate novel songs,[37] and the long-deceased painter Rembrandt van Rijn's oeuvre can teach an AI to generate a novel Rembrandt.[38]

AI trained on material in the public domain may implicate branches of IP other than copyright. The *sui generis* database right, in the jurisdictions that recognize it, might protect certain training corpora.[39] Trade secret law, too, could protect valuable troves of data. As mentioned in the introduction above, some IP regimes might protect an algorithm, a software implementation, a weighted model, or the outputs thereof, rather than training data. And a model trained on unprotected materials may nevertheless create outputs that are similar to copyrighted works. But uses of uncopyrightable data and public-domain expression to train artificial intelligence are properly beyond the reach of copyright law.

[35] Walter L Perry and others, 'Predictive policing: forecasting crime for law enforcement' (*Rand Corporation*, 2013) 2 <https://www.rand.org/pubs/research_briefs/RB9735.html>.

[36] 'Europarl parallel corpus' <https://www.statmt.org/europarl/>.

[37] Jukedeck R&D Team, 'Releasing a cleaned version of the Nottingham dataset' (*Jukedeck Research*, 7 March 2017) <https://research.jukedeck.com/releasing-a-cleaned-version-of-the-nottingham-dataset-928cdd18ec68>.

[38] Tim Nudd, 'Inside "The Next Rembrandt": how JWT got a computer to paint like the old master' (*Adweek*, 27 June 2016) <http://www.adweek.com/brand-marketing/inside-next-rembrandt-how-jwt-got-computer-paint-old-master-172257/>.

[39] Directive 96/9/EC of the European Parliament and of the Council of 11 March 1996 on the legal protection of databases [1996] OJ L 77/20.

3.2 Licensed Training Data

Permissively-licensed, in-copyright works—such as those published under Creative Commons licences—offer substantially the same opportunities for training AI as public-domain expressive material. As uses of permissively-licensed works become more prominent, however, litigation may test how the terms of common licences govern certain uses in machine learning. Licensors may also begin to adopt licences that purport to restrict controversial uses, such as the training of facial recognition algorithms.[40] And, of course, perhaps the most valuable applications of AI are those that train on licensed, non-public corpora of copyrighted data, like Facebook's trove of Instagram photos or Google's store of emails, all of which are licensed from end users.[41]

Even authorized uses of training data may raise issues for copyright law. A model trained on authorized copies of training data may create output that appears to be substantially similar to prior copyrighted media.[42] Present-day doctrines concerning 'improper appropriation' might underemphasize AI's ability to appropriate difficult-to-articulate expressive style.[43] Existing law might not establish who, if anyone, owns these outputs. And a different paradigm for producing expressive works may require updating the received wisdom about the ways in which copyright incentivizes creative production.[44] But because these uses raise no copyright issues at the training stage, they are not the focus of this chapter.[45]

3.3 Market-Encroaching Uses of Copyrighted Works

Some uses of machine learning are 'market-encroaching': these uses of AI plausibly threaten the market for the copyrighted works that comprise their training data. In market-encroaching uses, economic harms to rights holders predominate over dignitary harms. But not all uses that might diminish the value of their copyrighted training data constitute market-encroaching uses. For example, AI

[40] 'Facial recognition's "dirty little secret": social media photos used without consent' (*NBC News*, 17 March 2019) <https://www.nbcnews.com/tech/internet/facial-recognition-s-dirty-little-secret-millions-online-photos-scraped-n981921>.

[41] For examples of the licences platforms like Google and Facebook secure from their users, see 'Google terms of service—privacy & terms—Google' (*Google*) <https://policies.google.com/terms?fg=1>; 'Terms of use | Instagram help center' (*Instagram*) <https://help.instagram.com/581066165581870>.

[42] Sobel, 'Artificial Intelligence's Fair Use Crisis' (n 7) 66.

[43] Benjamin LW Sobel, 'Elements of Style: Emerging Technologies and Copyright's Fickle Similarity Standards' (unpublished manuscript, 2019).

[44] Pamela Samuelson, 'The Future of Software Protection: Allocating Ownership Rights in Computer-Generated Works' (1986) 47 University of Pittsburgh Law Review 1185, 1224.

[45] Of course, a given licence may not speak unequivocally about whether it would permit certain uses as training data. This uncertainty, however, would be a matter of contractual interpretation rather than of copyright law.

text-mining techniques might help identify a novelist as a plagiarist. Analysing the novels might require reproducing them without permission, and a revelation of plagiarism could damage the market for the author's works. This is not, however, a market-encroaching use.[46] Rather, a market-encroaching use is one that encroaches upon markets *over which copyright grants a monopoly*: they use protected expression for purposes that usurp the market for that very expression.[47]

Royalty-free or 'stock' music is a vivid example of market-encroaching AI. State-of-the-art technology can generate novel musical works and sound recordings. Startups like Aiva and Jukedeck[48] advertise AI-generated soundtracks for media producers, with different pricing tiers for non-commercial and commercial uses and different copyright ownership schemes.[49] Another startup, Melodrive, offers machine learning technology that can dynamically generate soundtracks for video games.[50] Commercial use of this AI-generated music is more than just academic conjecture. In mid-2019, Jukedeck was reportedly acquired by the Chinese firm Bytedance, a major player in entertainment AI that produces the TikTok app.[51]

AI-generated music does not rival the artistry of human composers and performers, but it doesn't need to.[52] Stock music tracks guard against uncomfortable silences at hotel bars or provide aural backdrops to commercials—they do not deliver artistic revelations on their own. Today's AI-generated music is a perfectly appropriate space-filler for, say, a virtual tour of a real estate listing. In the past, humans would have had to compose, perform, and record this background music, or at least create a composition and input it into sequencing software. It may not require visionary genius to write and record a track called 'Dark Background Piano Tones', but it does demand the sort of expressive act that copyright law protects.

It is likely that some AI music startups train their models on copyright-protected music, possibly without rights holders' authorization.[53] Even if no

[46] *A.V. ex rel. Vanderhye v iParadigms, LLC*, 562 F.3d 630 (4th Cir. 2009). The author used a variation of this example in comments submitted to the US Patent and Trademark Office on 15 December 2019, and to the World Intellectual Property Organization on 14 February 2020.

[47] Judge Pierre Leval of the US Court of Appeals for the Second Circuit, a leading jurist on fair use, has in his analysis limited fair use's market-substitution factor to the 'protected aspects' of the works used. *Authors Guild v Google, Inc.*, 804 F.3d 202, 229 (2d Cir. 2015); Sobel, 'Artificial Intelligence's Fair Use Crisis' (n 7) 55, 56.

[48] Jukedeck went offline sometime between 15 June and 24 June 2019. Compare 'Jukedeck—create unique, royalty-free AI music for your videos' (*Internet Archive*) <https://web.archive.org/web/20190615121143/https:/www.jukedeck.com/> with 'Jukedeck is offline' (*Internet Archive*) <https://web.archive.org/web/20190624100130/https://www.jukedeck.com/>.

[49] 'AIVA—the AI composing emotional soundtrack music' (*AIVA*) <https://aiva.ai/>; 'Jukedeck—create unique, royalty-free soundtracks for your videos' (*Jukedeck*) <http://www.jukedeck.com/make>.

[50] 'Melodrive | adaptive AI solutions' (*Melodrive*) <http://melodrive.com/>.

[51] 'AI-music firm Jukedeck's CEO now runs AI lab of TikTok owner Bytedance' (*Music Ally*) <https://musically.com/2019/07/23/ai-music-startup-jukedecks-ceo-now-runs-the-ai-lab-of-tiktok-owner-bytedance/>.

[52] Here, this chapter refers only to music produced on-demand by an AI engine designed to eschew human input, rather than musicians who use artificial intelligence technologies to achieve particular artistic effects.

[53] Sobel, 'Artificial Intelligence's Fair Use Crisis' (n 7) 77–9.

companies in this space currently make unauthorized uses of copyrighted music, they certainly *could* do so without difficulty. To the extent this training requires reproducing source music in order to assemble datasets, it is *prima facie* infringement. Moreover, as this author has argued elsewhere, because such a use of data harnesses expressive works *for expressive purposes*, it is possible that even the US's relatively permissive fair use doctrine would not excuse it.[54] Jurisdictions that lack an exception or limitation as flexible as fair use would be even less likely to excuse such a market-encroaching use of copyrighted materials.[55]

Thus, copyright may indeed be a barrier to commercial music synthesis, as it would be for other market-encroaching uses of AI. But this is sensible. Whether copyright *ever* ought to impede expressive activity is worth interrogating.[56] To the extent that copyright should obstruct downstream creativity, however, it is under circumstances more or less like these. AI-generated stock music could very well displace much of the market for human-created stock music. If it does, it will almost certainly be because the technology has appropriated some expressive value from its training data.

3.4 Non-Market-Encroaching Uses of Copyrighted Works

True market-encroaching uses represent a small fraction of AI endeavours. Far more concerning applications of AI rely on data, sometimes copyrighted data, in order to accomplish purposes that have no bearing on rights holders' legitimate markets. Arguably more prominent than market-encroaching machine learning is AI that learns from potentially copyrighted training data for purposes unrelated to the expressive aspects of those data. Facial recognition technology, eg, trains on digital photographs of human faces, which are likely to be copyright-protected.[57] But the data that facial recognition algorithms analyse are unrelated to the expression in a photograph that copyright protects. Facial geometry, like other biometric data, raises such urgent privacy concerns precisely because it is innate and immutable, *not* authored.[58] The best facial recognition training data are close-cropped pictures of faces, edited to leave essentially no room for copyrightable expression.[59] To the extent expressive details like lighting and angle appear in training data, it is

[54] Ibid, 78, 79.

[55] Arts 3 and 4 of the recent EU Directive on Copyright in the Digital Single Market may change this calculus. See Section 4.1.2.

[56] David L Lange and H Jefferson Powell, *No Law: Intellectual Property in the Image of an Absolute First Amendment* (Stanford University Press 2008).

[57] Sobel, 'Artificial Intelligence's Fair Use Crisis' (n 7) 67. The author used a variation of this example in comments submitted to the US Patent and Trademark Office on 15 December 2019.

[58] Benjamin LW Sobel, 'Countenancing Property' (unpublished manuscript, 2019) (hereafter Sobel, 'Countenancing Property').

[59] Sobel, 'Artificial Intelligence's Fair Use Crisis' (n 7) 67, 68.

so that algorithms' performance becomes invariant to differences in the presentation of an underlying human subject. Thus, facial recognition does not encroach upon a copyright-protected interest in source photographs.

Substantially the same analysis applies to 'deepfakes', AI-synthesized video and audio that reproduce the human likeness.[60] Deepfake technology allows relatively unsophisticated actors to synthesize verisimilar media using only photographs or videos of a target subject's face, which can then be superimposed over unrelated video footage. Unlike facial recognition, it is likely that *someone* could have a copyright claim arising out of an unauthorized deepfake. But this rights holder, who might own the video into which someone is falsely inserted, is unlikely to be the person most harmed by the synthesized media. The principal victim—the person inserted into falsified media—will have little recourse in copyright. For one, that person may not own the rights to the photos and videos that trained the AI. More fundamentally, deepfakes reproduce immutable, non-authored information about the human likeness. Much like facial recognition, then, deepfakes do not by necessity appropriate expressive information, and may therefore lie outside copyright's scope.[61]

It is obvious that facial recognition and deepfakes encroach on legitimate personal interests. Facial recognition facilitates state surveillance and invasive corporate marketing, and deepfakes can fuel abuse, extortion, and fraud. Even in the business-friendly—or, euphemistically, innovation-friendly—US, some academics are calling for a moratorium on facial recognition.[62] At least two US cities have banned facial recognition use by local government.[63] Federal and state legislators in the US have proposed deepfake-specific legislation.[64] In other words, the public is clamouring for a way to bridle these technologies. Described generally, copyright is a legal entitlement to control the data that train recognition and synthesis models; in these terms, copyright seems like the perfect countermeasure to overreaching facial recognition and deepfake technology.

But a recent controversy over facial recognition data illustrates that copyright is the wrong vehicle for constraining facial recognition. Some background: insofar as facial recognition software's training data mis- or under-represent particular groups of people, the resulting algorithms are liable to perform less accurately on

[60] Danielle Keats Citron, 'Sexual Privacy' (2019) 128 Yale Law Journal 1870, 1922.

[61] In a recent analysis of a deceptive use of likeness, albeit a less technologically sophisticated one, the US Court of Appeals for the Ninth Circuit reasserted copyright's role as an economic entitlement, rather than a privacy protection. *Garcia v Google, Inc.*, 786 F.3d 733, 745 (9th Cir. 2015).

[62] Woodrow Hartzog, 'Facial recognition is the perfect tool for oppression' (*Medium*, 2 August 2018) <https://medium.com/s/story/facial-recognition-is-the-perfect-tool-for-oppression-bc2a08f0fe66>.

[63] Tim Cushing, 'Somerville, Massachusetts becomes the second US city to ban facial recognition tech' (*Techdirt*, 1 July 2019) <https://www.techdirt.com/articles/20190627/21011442491/somerville-massachusetts-becomes-second-us-city-to-ban-facial-recognition-tech.shtml>.

[64] H.R. 3230, 116th Cong. (2019); S. 3805, 115th Cong. (2018).

those groups.[65] Indeed, flagship facial recognition algorithms may be notably worse at recognizing people who are not white men than they are at recognizing white men.[66] In early 2019, IBM published a dataset designed to mitigate these biases and increase diversity in facial recognition training data.[67] IBM's dataset comprised images uploaded to the Flickr photo-sharing service under permissive Creative Commons (CC) licences. Some Flickr users were surprised and dismayed to learn that their photographs ended up in the IBM dataset; one news article quoted several photographers who expressed frustration that IBM had not given them notice before using their CC-licensed photographs in a facial recognition tool.[68]

If using a photograph to train facial recognition aligned well with the interests that copyright protects—and the photographers on Flickr understood the terms of their CC licences—we would not expect photographers to bristle at IBM's use of their photographs. But the interests at stake here do not align with copyright at all, and have much more to do with the privacy of the photographs' subjects than with the economic interests of the photographers. Addressing the kerfuffle, Creative Commons' then-CEO Ryan Merkeley wrote, 'copyright is not a good tool to protect individual privacy, to address research ethics in AI development, or to regulate the use of surveillance tools employed online'.[69] Merkley is correct both normatively and descriptively. Copyright law as it exists today is the wrong tool to further the urgent and legitimate goal of regulating facial recognition. To begin with, blackletter copyright law would not entitle most authors to reserve rights to control how photographs are used for facial recognition, because facial recognition is not a market-encroaching use. [70] The technology most likely does not implicate protected expression in the source photographs that train algorithms, which means that it may not even amount to a *prima facie* infringement. And even if using photographs to train facial recognition does nominally encroach upon an exclusive right, that use would likely be excused as fair use in the US.

In sum, the most worrisome non-market-encroaching AI uses training data that copyright law disfavours, for purposes outside copyright's ambit. Images and videos that train facial recognition or deepfake models need not be expressive. In fact, the more these media evidence 'facts' of a person's physical appearance, rather than a photographer's expressive contributions, the better. Synthesizing someone's

[65] Steve Lohr, 'Facial recognition is accurate, if you're a white guy' (*The New York Times*, 11 February 2018) <https://www.nytimes.com/2018/02/09/technology/facial-recognition-race-artificial-intelligence.html>.

[66] Claire Garvie and others, 'The Perpetual Line-Up' (18 October 2016).

[67] Michele Merler and others, 'Diversity in Faces' (2019) arXiv:1901.10436 [cs.CV].

[68] 'Facial recognition's "dirty little secret": social media photos used without consent' (*NBC News*, 17 March 2019) <https://www.nbcnews.com/tech/internet/facial-recognition-s-dirty-little-secret-millions-online-photos-scraped-n981921>.

[69] Ryan Merkley, 'Use and fair use: statement on shared images in facial recognition AI' (*Creative Commons*, 13 March 2019) <https://creativecommons.org/2019/03/13/statement-on-shared-images-in-facial-recognition-ai/>.

[70] Sobel, 'Artificial Intelligence's Fair Use Crisis' (n 7) 67, 68.

voice does not require a recording of that person 'performing' a 'work'. A recording of a banal, extemporaneous conversation could work just as well as a recording of a dramatic reading. Moreover, none of these data need to be fixed under the authority of the people whose privacy and dignitary interests they implicate—and, at least in the case of photographs and videos, they often are not. These applications of AI engender wrongs that compel some sort of legal intervention. But the substantive law of copyright would be difficult to deploy to redress these harms, and copyright's normative underpinnings suggest that this difficulty is no accident.

4. Solving AI's Copyright Problem and Copyright's AI Problem

Copyright may not be the appropriate means of redressing the bulk of our concerns about AI—even AI that trains on copyrighted data. Copyright can, however, mitigate the injuries presented by market-encroaching uses of copyrighted works. This section describes several ways of addressing the tensions between present-day copyright doctrine and commercial realities. It concludes that, of the regimes practically available, the EU's new TDM exceptions do a surprisingly good job of balancing the various interests that market-encroaching uses implicate. Nevertheless, this section also describes farther-reaching reforms that could address the gaps in the EU exception. Finally, even though copyright seems like an obvious means of controlling harmful, non-market-encroaching machine learning, this section reminds readers why deploying copyright to address these problems would be both doctrinally awkward and normatively unwarranted.

4.1 Market-Encroaching Uses

Copyright should support robust technological progress without steamrolling legitimate, present-day legal entitlements. Copyright should *not*, however, serve to wring a few more years of unnecessary profit from otherwise obsolete endeavours. In other words, it is not copyright's place to stop AI from eating the stock music business; rather, copyright's place is to ensure that AI's human trainers get their due as AI begins to displace them.

An ideal system, then, would give the appropriate creators some appropriate compensation for their service to market-encroaching AI, and it would do so with minimal transaction costs. Such a system is easy to write about and difficult to implement. As this chapter argued above, duly compensating expressive activity without throttling innovation would require reexamining fundamental features of copyright protection in addition to redrawing existing exceptions and limitations. Without progress in both arenas, it is unlikely that these problems will be resolved.

Indeed, the differences between US and EU law illustrate different ways of failing to address the AI problem. To the extent that EU member states impose slightly higher bars to initial copyright interests in the form of higher originality requirements, those jurisdictions thereby mitigate aspects of the copyright regime that may inhibit the progress of AI. At the same time, the EU offers only a few rigid carveouts for unauthorized uses of copyrighted media, which means that it is likely to over-deter machine learning that does not threaten rights holders' legitimate economic interests. The US, on the other hand, encumbers training data with its rock-bottom criteria for copyright protection. Yet it shows a greater solicitude for uses that do not prejudice rights holders' economic interests because of its flexible fair use doctrine.

4.1.1 Fair use is ill-equipped to address market-encroaching uses

The US's fair use doctrine,[71] and regimes like it, set forth a flexible, case-by-case standard that allows courts to immunize certain unauthorized uses of copyrighted works. Fair use's open-endedness permits the doctrine to adapt to technological change more nimbly than a closed-list approach might.[72] Indeed, other contributions to this volume advocate more open-ended exceptions frameworks for precisely this reason.[73]

It is difficult to deny that more rigid exceptions regimes restrict the salutary, non-market-encroaching uses of artificial intelligence already flourishing under the US's fair use regime.[74] With respect to *market-encroaching* uses of AI, however, fair use is not ideal. Fair use is all-or-nothing: either the defence succeeds and the use in question is unreservedly legal, or the defence fails and leaves the defendant liable for infringement. Neither situation makes sense for market-encroaching uses of AI because of the way AI alters traditional balances of equities.[75] Treating market-encroaching AI just like other forms of copyright infringement would obstruct technological progress by offering rights holders property remedies like statutory damages and injunctions, which would far overcompensate for the harms authors are likely to suffer from having their work included in training datasets. At the same time, categorizing market-encroaching AI as fair use would fail to compensate rights holders for valuable commercial uses of their *expression*. A more equitable approach would encourage—and perhaps even reward—authorized uses of copyrighted works in market-encroaching AI. The EU's new TDM exception, while far from perfect, represents a tentative step towards such a system.

[71] 17 USC § 107.

[72] See, eg, Ian Hargreaves, 'Digital Opportunity: A Review of Intellectual Property and Growth' (May 2011) 43–4 (comparing and contrasting the fair use doctrine with the European enumerated-exceptions approach in the TDM context) (hereafter Hargreaves, 'Digital Opportunity').

[73] Tianxiang He, Chapter 9 in this volume.

[74] Hargreaves, 'Digital Opportunity' (n 72) 43, 44.

[75] Sobel, 'Artificial Intelligence's Fair Use Crisis' (n 7) 79–82.

4.1.2 The EU TDM exception: better for market-encroaching uses, worse for non-encroaching uses

The most significant recent development in the AI-and-copyright field is the EU's Digital Single Market (DSM) Directive of 2019. The DSM Directive mandates two pertinent exceptions to member state copyright laws. The first, in Article 3 of the Directive, requires member states to permit certain reproductions of copyrighted materials by research and cultural heritage organizations, undertaken for the purposes of text and data mining (TDM) research.[76] The second, in Article 4, extends that same exception to *any entity* seeking to perform TDM.[77] However, the Article 4 exception does not apply when rights holders expressly reserve their TDM rights.[78]

Despite calling itself an 'exception', Article 4 appears to operate more like a formality.[79] The language of exceptions makes sense, because framing Article 4 as a formality would invite scrutiny as a possible violation of the Berne Convention. Nonetheless, because Article 4 prescribes steps an author must take in order to possess a particular exclusive right, it redraws the default bundle of copyright entitlements in a way that an exception does not. Like a formality, and unlike an exception, Article 4 focuses on an author's behaviour, rather than on an evaluation of a particular use. Article 4 thus subverts unconditional copyright by making a TDM right conditional on an owner's express reservation. In other words, Article 4 requires an author affirmatively to reserve a right to exclude uses of her works to train AI, if she wishes to exercise that right.

In spite of, or maybe because of, its possible incongruence with the Berne Convention's prohibition on formalities, Article 4 represents a positive development for copyright law and for AI. Indeed, Article 4's formality-like qualities allow it to operate more effectively than a pure exception. Article 4 solves part of the AI-and-copyright problem by facilitating the confident development of artificial intelligence using data that are not subject to reserved rights.

Article 4 falls short, however, in establishing an effective scheme for authors who do not object to their works training AI, but who want to be compensated. Presumably, a sizeable portion of rights holders would be willing to license their works for use as training data, but unwilling to extend the gratis licence that Article 4 creates by default. In theory, a centralized registration regime, coupled with collective licensing arrangements, could lubricate this market. However, AI training combines massive corpora of works with low per-use payoffs, which together mean

[76] 2019 OJ (L 130/92) 113.

[77] Ibid, 113, 114.

[78] Ibid.

[79] A blog post by Neil Turkewitz brought Art. 4's formality-like qualities to the author's attention. Neil Turkewitz, 'Sustainable text and data mining: a look at the recent EU Copyright Directive' (*Medium*, 16 May 2019) <https://medium.com/@nturkewitz_56674/sustainable-text-and-data-mining-an-look-at-the-recent-eu-copyright-directive-9ea13ba05f60>.

that incentives to register works will probably be too low to sustain a conventional government-run registration system. The private sector may be able to fill this lacuna: private entities like the PLUS registry organize media and licences to lower search and transaction costs.[80] What may distinguish AI training data from these other licensing systems, however, is the premium on secrecy that data command. A company's AI can only be as good as the data on which it trains. Thus, there will be few parties that have unilateral control over large datasets *and* an incentive to license those datasets widely. This suggests that compensated uses of authored training data—other than by platforms that receive licences from their end users—will be unlikely to flourish without some form of government intervention to lubricate the market. Finally, there is a risk that Article 4 unduly burdens *non*-market-encroaching uses to the extent that its opt-out regime empowers rights holders to exclude others from making non-market-encroaching TDM uses of copyrighted materials.

4.2 Beyond Exceptions and Limitations

Resolving the disharmony between artificial intelligence and intellectual property regimes requires more than an exception or limitation to copyright. This subsection briefly introduces three doctrinal areas that more ambitious reforms might target: originality, formalities, and remedies.

4.2.1 Tweaking originality

Redrawing copyright's originality requirements could mitigate the potential copyright liabilities associated with some machine learning. Delineating copyright in a manner that unambiguously excluded emails, throwaway photographs, or short comments left on an Internet forum might alleviate some worries about impeding the progress of TDM. Moreover, originality-based reforms would not jeopardize the economic protections that more creative endeavours would receive. As a practical matter, originality-oriented reforms are particularly appealing because they are comparatively unlikely to conflict with international treaties. The US, eg, is not party to a treaty that places a 'ceiling' on the stringency of copyright's originality requirements.[81] However, heightened originality requirements would also eliminate a rare source of leverage for the humans whose run-of-the-mill expression currently trains the AI that may replace them in the workplace.[82] Copyright may not be the best tool to ensure distributive equity in the age of artificial intelligence,

[80] 'PLUS Registry: about the Registry' (*Plus Registry*) <https://www.plusregistry.org/cgi-bin/WebObjects/PlusDB.woa/2/wo/Z2vbrwAumsxHHQToC5sz1w/0.111.27>.
[81] Fisher, 'Recalibrating Originality' (n 19) 457, 461.
[82] Sobel, 'Artificial Intelligence's Fair Use Crisis' (n 7) 97.

and low originality requirements may never have been wise policy. But raising originality standards now, without social support for the workers who may soon be displaced by AI, could exacerbate the difficulties some human labourers face in an automated economy.

4.2.2 Formalities

Prior sections of this chapter have suggested that formalities regimes could mitigate risks associated with commercial AI without abridging the rights of sophisticated authors. Indeed, despite its framing as an exception, Article 4 of the EU DSM Directive may also be understood as a formalities regime. While Article 4 does not condition copyright protection on a formality, it does establish a formal prerequisite to asserting a right to exclude uses in text and data mining. As a practical matter, traditional formalities regimes would be difficult to implement in a manner consistent with major international treaties. However, it is worth noting that the technological architecture of the internet already has a well-established permissions standard that augurs well for a TDM-focused formality. The robots.txt standard for webpages sets forth the instructions that automated software should observe when indexing or archiving a given page.[83] Because this convention is fundamental to the Internet, a robots.txt-like standard dictating permissible uses for AI might be more straightforward to implement than other copyright formalities regimes, and less likely to penalize the legally unsavvy.

4.2.3 Rethinking remedies

Copyright punishes infringers with stiff penalties that can include statutory damages and injunctive relief. These remedies may be appropriate to deter some unauthorized uses of copyrighted materials, but they are utterly inapt for addressing unauthorized uses of copyrighted materials in training data. Machine learning technology learns from hundreds of thousands of data points at a time, each of which makes some small contribution to a trained model. Injunctive relief and high damages awards will over-deter technological development and overcompensate plaintiffs. Indeed, these remedies would be much more appropriate for the types of non-market-encroaching uses that lie beyond copyright's scope, such as the creation of simulated nonconsensual pornography using deepfakes technology.[84]

In contrast to conventional property-style entitlements, liability-style rules in copyright can promote commerce that would otherwise be too costly, and promote access to expressive works that a market system might not otherwise provide.[85]

[83] 'Robots Exclusion Standard', *Wikipedia* (2019).

[84] Representative Clarke's DEEPFAKES bill, H.R. 3230, 116th Cong. (2019), proposes a slate of remedies strikingly similar to those codified in the United States Copyright Act of 1976, 17 USC § 504. For further discussion of the resemblances between some deepfakes-related privacy proposals and moral rights, see Sobel, 'Countenancing Property' (n 58).

[85] Jacob Victor, 'Reconceptualizing Compulsory Copyright Licenses' (2020) 72 Stanford Law Review 915, 920.

Indeed, a liability-style rule may be the only way of fulfilling the function that Article 4 fails to fulfil: facilitating compensated, market-encroaching uses of copyrighted training data. Authors who would otherwise opt out of the Article 4 exception might instead opt into a licensing regime that offers their works for market-encroaching AI uses at a set licensing rate.

4.3 What Copyright Cannot Do

This chapter has shown that many worrisome uses of AI depend on copyright-protected training data. However, it has also shown that only a significant revision of contemporary copyright law would allow it to regulate the applications of AI that implicate non-economic interests. Attempts to deploy copyright in service of non-economic interests like privacy, dignity, and reputation are nothing new. In the nineteenth century, an English publisher surreptitiously obtained etchings created by Queen Victoria and Prince Albert. When the publisher released a pamphlet describing the etchings, Prince Albert invoked a 'common law right to the copy' to enjoin the pamphlet's publication.[86] In fact, it was partially from this jurisprudence of common-law copyright that Samuel Warren and Louis Brandeis famously distilled a 'right to privacy' in Anglo-American law.[87] This privacy-protective, dignity-protective conception of copyright transposes to contemporary concerns. For instance, Kim Kardashian reportedly used a copyright takedown to remove a deepfake video depicting her.[88]

But the preceding sections of this chapter have described numerous reasons why copyright probably cannot redress the harms that non-market-encroaching uses of AI entail. First, many of these uses require neither works nor authorship. Instead, these uses implicate data that are not protected by copyright in the first place, or whose protection is merely incidental to a fixation step that future technologies can probably eschew. Second, even if these uses do rely on copyrighted training data, they use those data in a manner unrelated to any expressive information in the data. Indeed, it is *precisely* because these uses implicate facts of personal identity—rather than expression—that they can be so harmful.

Mechanisms like the TDM opt-out found in Article 4 may allow rights holders to control even non-expressive uses of information in copyrighted works. To the extent that a copyright regime restricts non-expressive uses, however, it at best

[86] *Prince Albert v Strange* (1849) 2 De G. & Sm. 652, 64 ER 293.

[87] Samuel D Warren and Louis D Brandeis, 'The Right to Privacy' (1890–91) 4 Harvard Law Review 193.

[88] 'Kim Kardashian deepfake taken off of YouTube over copyright claim' (*Digital Trends*, 17 June 2019) <https://www.digitaltrends.com/social-media/kim-kardashian-deepfake-removed-from-youtube/>; Tiffany C Li, 'This backdoor approach to combating deepfakes won't work' (*Slate Magazine*, 18 June 2019) <https://slate.com/technology/2019/06/deepfake-kim-kardashian-copyright-law-fair-use.html>.

stifles the flow of non-proprietary information, and at worst, it encroaches upon the functions served by different causes of action designed to protect privacy and dignitary interests. Claims designed to prevent harmful uses of non-expressive information should be founded in tort or privacy law, not in the economic rights that copyright grants authors.

5. Conclusion

AI has a copyright problem: valuable business practices implicate the unauthorized reproduction of countless copyrighted works. AI's copyright problem, in turn, exposes copyright's AI problem: vast amounts of digital media are copyright-protected essentially due to historical accident. Despite adding uncertainty to AI development, the copyright protections attached to many training data cannot, and should not, regulate many applications of AI. Only those applications of AI that encroach upon the market for their copyrighted training data—such as royalty-free music generation—are properly within copyright's ambit.

This is difficult news for two reasons. First, copyright seems at first glance like it could help prevent harmful uses of AI that involve copyrighted training data, but that do not threaten the market for those data. But copyright's economic focus makes it a poor vehicle for redressing harms to privacy or dignity. Second, copyright's remedies are a bad fit for the AI-related economic injuries that copyright *can* appropriately regulate.

Thus, copyright's role in addressing AI is limited but nevertheless significant. Successful interventions will focus not simply on exceptions to copyright entitlements, but also on the nature and scope of copyrights in the first instance. The EU's recent Directive on the Digital Single Market begins to effectuate some of these reforms, although it is drafted in a way that obscures its own significance. But the problem of *compensating* authors for market-encroaching uses will persist after the Directive's implementation. The international copyright system will have to reshape itself if it is to address this problem. Whether it can do so remains to be seen.

PART IV
ARTIFICIAL INTELLIGENCE AND IP ADMINISTRATION

11

Patent Examination of Artificial Intelligence-related Inventions

An Overview of China

*Jianchen Liu and Ming Liu**

1. Introduction

Artificial intelligence (AI), as opposed to natural intelligence displayed by humans, is the simulation of human intelligence processes by machines, especially computer systems.[1] With the ability to conduct learning, reasoning, and self-correction, AI machines have caused, among other things, fundamental changes in inventing processes.[2] Inventions generated solely by or relating to AI (collectively referred to as 'AI-related inventions') represent an important part of future technologies, and yet very few countries' patent regimes address the issue of whether and under what circumstances AI-related inventions are patentable. As a world leader in the AI industry, China has the second largest number of patent filings concerning AI-related inventions in the world, with strong potential to be the first.[3] Therefore, the National Intellectual Property Administration of China (CNIPA) has accumulated rich experience in the examination of AI-related inventions, and at the same time, still needs to learn from the rest of the world.

This chapter provides an overview of China's experience and latest regulatory movements on the examination of AI-related inventions, with a main focus on the

* All online materials were accessed before 1 May 2020.

1 These processes include learning (the acquisition of information and rules for using the information), reasoning (using rules to reach approximate or definite conclusions), and self-correction. Particular applications of AI include expert systems, speech recognition, and machine vision. Ed Burns and Nicole Laskowski, 'Special report on artificial intelligence apps come of age' (*SearchEnterpriseAI*, April 2019) <https://searchenterpriseai.techtarget.com/definition/AI-Artificial-Intelligence>.

2 It is argued that AI may overtake human inventors as the primary source of new discoveries, leading to debate over whether AI could meet the requirements of inventorship under the current patent regime. See, eg, Ryan Abbott, 'I Think, Therefore I Invent: Creative Computers and The Future of Patent Law' (2016) 57 Boston College Law Review 1079. This chapter does not intend to cover this issue, and instead discusses the patentability of AI-related inventions with a particular focus on China's attitude.

3 See World Intellectual Property Organization, Technology Trends 2019—Artificial Intelligence (WIPO 2019, https://www.wipo.int/edocs/pubdocs/en/wipo_pub_1055.pdf) 85–7.

Jianchen Liu and and Ming Liu, *Patent Examination of Artificial Intelligence-related Inventions* In: *Artificial Intelligence and Intellectual Property.* Edited by: Jyh-An Lee, Reto M Hilty, and Kung-Chung Liu, Oxford University Press (2021).
 DOI: 10.1093/oso/9780198870944.003.0012

patentability issue. To adjust its patent regime to AI-related inventions, China has revised its Guidelines twice. Section 2 takes a retrospective view on the barriers to the patentability of AI-related inventions and illustrates how the first revision to the Guidelines mitigates those barriers. Section 3 discusses some experience that the CNIPA has gained in the practice of patent examination on AI-related inventions. In Section 4, some key revisions to the Guidelines are addressed to show China's recent position in the examination of AI-related inventions.

2. Amendment to the Guidelines for Patent Examination

The current Chinese patent regime can be roughly divided into three tiers. At the top level lie the Patent Law and its interpretation made by the Supreme People's Court; at the middle level are regulations promulgated by the State Council, such as Rules for the Implementation of the Patent Law ('Implementation Rules'); at the bottom are some operational documents enacted by the CNIPA. The most representative among those legal sources made by the CNIPA are the Guidelines for Patent Examination (the 'Guidelines'), which are made in accordance with, but provide a more detailed interpretation of, the provisions of the Patent Law and the Implementation Rules. More specifically, the Guidelines define some vague terms contained in the two laws, and use plenty of examples to guide examiners on how to examine certain kinds of patent applications. Patent examiners are bound by the Guidelines, which play a critical role in the practice of patent examination, determining whether an application can be granted a patent right.

The patentability of AI-related inventions is, of course, subject to the provisions stipulated in the Guidelines. It used to be difficult for such inventions to meet the requirements of patent eligibility until the revised Guidelines took effect on 1 April 2017. A brief look back at the revision history of the Guidelines may illustrate the decisive effect of the Guidelines on the patentability of AI-related inventions. Prior to that, however, a quick glance at those barriers set by China's patent regime to restrict the patentability of computer software inventions will better position readers to understand the revisions. Therefore, Section 2 will first identify the barriers and then discuss how the revised Guidelines mitigate them to facilitate the approval of patent filings of AI-related inventions.

2.1 Barriers to Inventions Relating to Computer Programs Under China's Patent Regime

Chinese Patent Law tries to make clear the patentability issue through a combination of positive definition and negative enumeration. Article 2.2 of the Patent Law, by defining invention patent in a positive way, sets out a key requirement for an invention to be patentable. As required by this article, an invention patent shall contain technical solutions which, by following natural rules, exploit technical means to solve technical problems. A technical solution is an aggregation of technical means applying the laws of nature to solve a technical problem. Usually, technical means are embodied as technical features.[4] In contrast, Article 25 of the Patent Law takes a different approach from Article 2.2 by negating the patentability of six kinds of subject matters, one of which is rules and methods for mental activities.[5] Following this article, the Guidelines further clarify that a claim concerning only rules and methods for mental activities is not patentable.[6] In the context of patent law, computer software and business methods inventions can be easily associated with rules and methods, which had long been the stumbling block to the patentability of computer software inventions and business-model ones[7] before the Guidelines were revised in April 2017. Due to this negation, a patent application of computer software cannot be granted if what has been claimed in the application merely contains algorithms, mathematical rules, a computer program itself, or game rules. In this case, the claims do not contain any technical solution, because neither technical fields nor technical features are embodied therein. Without satisfying the key requirement for an invention patent, such application is of course not patent-eligible. In practice, Articles 2.2 and 25 are closely related, and patent examiners frequently refer to both of them when examining applications relating to computer programs.[8]

The standard that a claim concerning only rules and methods for mental activities is not patentable is mainly for computer program inventions and business model ones, and AI-related inventions are no exception. For example, supervised learning and semi-supervised learning are typical learning methods for machine learning, a sub-field of AI that is concerned with the automated detection of meaningful patterns in data and using the detected patterns for certain tasks.[9] But an

[4] Guidelines for Patent Examination 2014, Art 2, Chapter 1, Part 2 (hereafter Guidelines 2014).

[5] This article provides that for any of the following, no patent right shall be granted: (1) scientific discoveries; (2) rules and methods for mental activities; (3) methods for the diagnosis or for the treatment of diseases; (4) animal and plant varieties; (5) substances obtained by means of nuclear transformation; and (6) design, which is used primarily for the identification of pattern, colour, or the combination of the two on printed flat works. For processes used in producing products referred to in item (4) of the preceding paragraph, a patent may be granted in accordance with the provisions of this Law. Patent Law of China 2008, Art 25 (hereafter PL 2008).

[6] Guidelines 2014 (n 4) Art 4.2, Chapter 1, Part 2.

[7] According to the Guidelines for Patent Examination, business model is a broader term than business methods, because a business model invention may contain business methods and business rules. Ibid.

[8] See Li Ke and Liu Di, 'How to Determine the Patentability of Inventions relating to Computer Programs' (2016) 8 China Invention & Patent 102, 113.

[9] Supervised machine learning algorithms are trained on datasets that include labels that guide algorithms to understand which features are important to the problem at hand, while unsupervised machine learning algorithms, on the other hand, are trained on unlabelled data and must determine feature importance on their own based on inherent patterns in the data. Semi-supervised learning algorithms are trained on a combination of labelled and unlabelled data. For detailed discussion of different types of machine learning, see Anthony Man-Cho So, Chapter 1 in this volume.

application claiming these learning methods is non-patentable if such methods merely relate to numerical calculation and do not improve the performance of hardware. An example in this regard is a patent application named 'A Training Method for the Classifier of Support Vector Machine based on Semi-Supervised Learning'. It first uses some marked sample sets to train a support vector machine (SVM) classifier which, after identifying the characteristics thereof, will then single out and mark high-confidence sample sets from among unmarked ones. In return, the classifier will be further trained by the updated marked sample sets.[10] This application was, however, rejected by the CNIPA based on lack of patentability as rules and methods for mental activities.[11] The Patent Reexamination Board (PRB) affirmed CNIPA's decision by holding that what is being claimed in the application is, in essence, a function to classify set elements via mathematical algorithm on a sample set and thus falls into the scope of rules and methods for mental activities under Article 25 of the Patent Law.[12]

Rejecting the patentability of rules and methods for mental activities is actually an internationally common practice, mainly because they are the basic tools of scientific and technological innovation, and monopolizing these tools by granting patent rights may impede innovation rather than promoting it.[13] The United States Patent and Trademark Office (USPTO) rules out the patentability of a claimed invention which is directed to abstract ideas, laws of nature, and natural phenomena.[14] Likewise, the European Union (EU) deems mathematical methods, schemes, rules and methods for performing mental acts, and programs for computers non-eligible for patent protection.[15] This is also the same in Japan. The Examination Guidelines of Japan Patent Office (JPO) enumerate the subject matters in which the laws of nature are not utilized, and mathematical formula is one of those not eligible for patent.[16] Therefore, an invention relating to computer programs, to qualify as an invention patent, needs to contain technical features in addition to rules and methods for mental activities. More specifically, patent-eligible inventions relating to computer programs generally solve certain problems via, either in whole or in part, running computer programs, to control or process the external or internal objects of a computer.[17] Technical effects achieved

[10] See Patent Application No 201310231254.4.

[11] Art 41 of the Patent Law provides that if any patent applicant is dissatisfied with the decision of the CNIPA on rejecting the application, he may, within three months of receipt of the notification, appeal to the Patent Re-examination Board for review. PL2008 (n 4), Art 41.

[12] See No 120841 Decision of PRB (29 March 2017).

[13] See *Alice Corp v CLS Bank Int'l*, 134 S. Ct. at 2354, 110 USPQ2d at 1980; *Mayo Collaborative Servs. v Prometheus Labs., Inc*, 566 US 66, 71, 101 USPQ2d 1961, 1965 (2012).

[14] See the Manual of Patent Examining Procedure 2018, Art 2106.04(a)(2) (hereafter MPEP 2018).

[15] See the European Patent Convention 2016, Art 52(2), Chapter I.

[16] See the Examination Guidelines for Patent and Utility Model in Japan 2015, Section 2.1.4, Chapter 1, Part III.

[17] Control or processing of external objects means controlling an external operating process or external operating device, or processing or exchanging external data, while control or processing of internal objects refers to improvement of internal performance of computer systems, management of

in this way shall be in conformity with natural rules as well as those rules governing computers.

2.2 Revisions to the Guidelines to Pave the Way for AI-related Inventions

China's AI industry has boomed since 2012, and the total number of AI companies reached its peak in 2015.[18] Accordingly, AI-related inventions have been on the rise, and therefore more and more patent applications in this regard have begun swarming into the CNIPA. However, the deep-rooted effect of Article 25 of the Patent Law on the patentability of AI-related inventions, as well as the long-established examination practice, have impeded those applications from being granted patent rights. As more and more jurisdictions have gradually realized, granting legal certainty and stronger patent protection to AI-related inventions will undoubtedly lead to more investments and research and development in this ground-breaking field. In view of this, China has been determined to strengthen IP protection for creations in emerging areas, such as the Internet, e-commerce, and big data, so as to develop those industries.[19] Faced with these situations, the CNIPA felt obliged to amend the Guidelines in response to those applications arising from emerging areas, and the first step to move forward was, without any doubt, to reconsider the Guidelines, especially those provisions that easily lead examiners to reject the patentability of AI-related inventions.

Two major changes have been made in this regard. The first one relates to a business model which can easily be regarded as rules and methods for mental activities and thus falls within the scope of Article 25 of the Patent Law. However, business methods improved by AI can increase the efficiency of business activities. To deal with this problem, a new clause has been added to the Guidelines. The clause provides that if a claim related to a business model contains both business methods and technical features, its patentability shall not be excluded under Article 25 of the Patent Law.[20] Even though this clause is not specifically made for AI-related inventions, it can also be applied to a business model invention employing AI. That being said, an application of big data and AI-related invention

internal resources of computer systems, and improvement of data transmission. See Guidelines 2014 (n 4) Art 1, Chapter 9, Part 2.

[18] See Research Center for Chinese Science and Technology Policy at Tsinghua University, 'The status quo and future of China's artificial intelligence' (*Sohu*, 11 October 2018) <http://www.sohu.com/a/258848488_468723>.

[19] See State Council's opinions on Accelerating the Construction of Great Power via Intellectual Property under the New Circumstances (2015) Section 11, Part 3.

[20] Guidelines for Patent Examination 2017, Art 4.2(2), Chapter 1, Part 2 (hereafter Guidelines 2017).

can be patent-eligible if its claims harness natural rules or computer rules to achieve technical effects.

For instance, a patent application named 'A Method for Targeted Advertising Based on the Big Data regarding User Habit in a Region' claimed an intelligent system consisting of several data processing modules. The system, via invoking those modules, can remind merchants to stock up on products that customers will buy in a short period and also notify customers of buying those products before they run out. Efficiency of transactions would be raised significantly by this business method because the system functions are based on big data collected, which include target customer data (location information and transaction records), merchant data (location and product information), and other customer data (the frequency and quantity of buying the products).[21] The CNIPA found this patent application patentable on the basis that even if the claims thereof contain rules and methods, they have achieved technical effects. As the rules embodied and exploited by AI-related inventions are extended from natural rules to other objective laws, such as consumer behaviour, more and more business model patents are likely to be submitted and approved.[22]

Another change is that the Guidelines distinguish computer-program-implemented inventions from computer programs themselves, allowing the claims of the former to be written in a way that combines the medium or hardware with the flow path of computer programs. According to the previous version of the Guidelines, computer programs themselves fall into the scope of rules and methods for mental activities, and thus are unpatentable. Even if they defined 'computer program itself', they did not differentiate computer-program-implemented inventions and 'computer program itself' in the section titled 'Examination Benchmark for the Application of Invention Patent related to Computer Programs'.[23] This made it fairly easy for examiners to misunderstand that inventions relating to computer programs are unpatentable. To deal with this, the Guidelines have made clear that a computer program itself is unpatentable but inventions relating to computer programs might be patentable.[24] Because AI-related inventions are all implemented by computer programs, they are not necessarily deemed by examiners to be 'rules and methods for mental activities' simply because they include computer programs, and thus their potential for being approved has risen significantly.

[21] See Patent Application No 201811482899.X.

[22] See Qiang Liu, 'A Study on the Patentability of AI-related Inventions' (2019) 17 Presentday Law Science 4, 21 (hereafter Liu, 'Patentability of AI-related Inventions').

[23] See Guidelines 2014 (n 4) Sections 1 and 2, Chapter 9, Part 2.

[24] Guidelines 2017 (n 20) Art 2.1 (1), Chapter 9, Part 2.

2.3 Representative Approved AI-related Inventions After the Revised Guidelines

Technically, the key innovation for AI-related inventions lies in the improvement of algorithms. However, algorithms are a double-edged sword for the purpose of patent law. On the one hand, with the help of algorithms, the functional effects of technical solutions which could be better applied in industry can be improved. On the other hand, algorithms, as mentioned above, can be easily associated with rules and methods for mental activities, which will eliminate their patentability. This concern has been greatly lessened since the revised Guidelines came into force on 1 April 2017. Below are two typical AI-related invention applications whose approval by CNIPA could be a harbinger of the increasing approval rate of such applications thereafter.

One of the most typical applications of AI is imitating the ways humans perceive information—through vision. The first representative case revolves around image recognition and processing. A chief segment of the vision field involves understanding images by categorizing, filtering, editing, and parsing image data.[25] Narrowing down to the area of smart healthcare, AI algorithms can be used to enhance the display effect of medical images, which is helpful for auxiliary diagnosis. Generally, such algorithms are used to detect patterns in training data in order to automate complex tasks or make predictions, and are designed to improve in performance over time on a particular task as they receive more data.[26] In this case, a patent application involved a method to enhance the display effect of medical images by using correctional and multiscale retinex algorithms. The claims consist of four steps: The first one is to obtain, by making use of various image-capture armamentaria, image sequences in a nidus or of a target part; the second step deals with those image sequences with the help of image enhancement methods; the third step is to mix together all the enhanced image sequences; and the last step focuses on the treatment of all the mixed image sequences, producing the finished image sequences.[27] Image-enhanced algorithms are mainly used in the second step. Such algorithms convert the grey value of the image sequences acquired in the first step to floating-point type, use functions and formulas to enhance the grey level image of all image sequences, and obtain images with enhanced edges. The CNIPA's opinion was that those technical solutions claimed in the application enhanced the display effect of the image edge and thus increased the visibility of a nidus or target part. Since it is helpful for doctors to distinguish organs with identical or similar shape and to improve the accuracy rate of treatment, the claims have technical

[25] See Paramvir Singh, 'AI capabilities in image recognition' (*Towards Data Science*, 12 November 2018) <https://towardsdatascience.com/ai-capabilities-in-image-recognition-7d79aec5222f>.

[26] See Harry Surden, 'Machine Learning and Law' (2014) 89 Washington Law Review 87, 89–91.

[27] See Patent Application No 201710007475.7. This application was submitted to CNIPA on 5 January 2017 and approved on 15 March 2019.

effects and are able to satisfy the requirements set in Article 2.2 of the Patent Law. Therefore, the application was approved by CNIPA.

The second one is concerned with convolutional neural networks (CNNs). As deep-learning algorithms, CNNs can take in an input image and assign importance (learnable weights and biases) to various aspects or objects in the image, and are able to differentiate one from the other.[28] Obviously, both CNNs and deep learning fall under the umbrella of AI. CNNs are most commonly applied to analysing visual imagery.[29] This application mainly claimed a network training method of hand gesture detection. More specifically, it first trains the first CNNs with sample images including marked human hands and gets predictive information in the candidate region, then modifies such information, and trains the second CNNs with the modified information and sample images. In this process, the first and second CNNs share the same layer of characteristic extraction, and the parameters of this layer remain the same in the process of training the second CNNs.[30] The CNIPA believed that this application could increase the accuracy rate of detecting hand gestures by the second CNNs and could also reduce the computational burden in the process of training. Therefore, this patent application was approved.

What has been claimed in both of the above patent applications is a method that employs AI algorithms to recognize and process images. It is worth reiterating that the key element for their patentability is whether their claims could achieve technical effects. Our observation from the above two cases is that AI algorithms for image recognition, compared with those for other purposes like training algorithms (eg, the SVM case mentioned in Section 2.1), may have an advantage in terms of patentability. The output of AI algorithms for image recognition usually involves processed images with better display effects or trained algorithms with higher detection accuracy. Such output could be further used in other areas like medical treatment, and thus adds some value to the technical effects of those AI algorithms. However, even if living examples can provide us with some clues on the technical effects of AI-related inventions, it is still difficult to draw a line between those with technical effects and those without. Patent applicants still need to focus on the examination practice of IP offices and size up their trend and policy on the patentability of AI-related inventions.

[28] See Sumit Saha, 'A comprehensive guide to convolutional neural networks—the ELI5 way' (*Towards Data Science*, 16 December 2018) <https://towardsdatascience.com/a-comprehensive-guide-to-convolutional-neural-networks-the-eli5-way-3bd2b1164a53>.

[29] See Wiki, Convolutional Neural Network (*Wiki*, 17 February 2018) <https://en.wikipedia.org/wiki/Convolutional_neural_network>.

[30] See Patent Application No 201610707579.4. This application was submitted to CNIPA on 19 August 2016 and approved on 22 February 2019.

3. China's Experience on the Examination of AI-related Inventions

With an increasing number of patent applications of AI-related inventions,[31] Chinese patent examiners have accumulated plenty practical experience in this process and also reached some consensus on applying the Patent Law, the Implementation Rules, and the Guidelines to examining the applications. Among such areas of consensus are three significant ones, namely, the required embodiment of the application field in both description and claims, the broad interpretation of technical effects for AI-related inventions, and how to define the scope of protection of AI-generated inventions. These will be discussed one by one in detail.

3.1 Application Fields Shall be Clearly Specified in Both Claims and Description

To qualify as patentable inventions, AI-related applications must be of actual applicability to certain fields of technology, otherwise, they will fall into the scope of rules and methods for mental activities if they are merely potentially applicable.[32] However, a wide range of application fields can be a Gordian knot to AI-related inventions, because, on the one hand, AI-related inventions may be applicable to a wide range of fields of technology, which will have negative effect on their patentability. If such applications get approved, their protection scope would be so broad that it would be very difficult for subsequent applications with similar functions to be approved, leaving limited room for competitors to innovate around, and as a consequence, innovation would be stifled.[33] On the other hand, due to fear of unpatentability, applicants sometimes have to leave out some application fields of the AI-related inventions, meaning that they lose the opportunity to obtain the appropriate protection scope that they deserve. In this sense, it is a great challenge for examiners to determine an appropriate range of application fields commensurate with the degree of innovation of AI-related inventions.

As for China's position in this regard, our observation, as evidenced by the following examples, is that the CNIPA favours those applications whose application

[31] According to a report issued by IThinkTank on 27 December 2019, the number of patent filings of AI-related inventions has been 918.38 million up to November 2019 with an annual rate of growth of around 35.9%. See IThinkTank, 'A report on the value and competitiveness of Chinese AI-related inventions' (*CNR*, 27 December 2019) <http://www.cnr.cn/rdzx/cxxhl/zxxx/20191227/t20191227_524916028.shtml>.

[32] Liu, 'Patentability of AI-related Inventions' (n 22) 24.

[33] Taking this factor into consideration, Julie Cohen and Mark Lemley argue that in light of the special nature of innovation within the software industry, courts should narrow the protection scope of software patent by applying the doctrine of equivalents narrowly in infringement cases. See Julie E Cohen and Mark A Lemley, 'Patent Scope and Innovation in the Software Industry' (2001) 89 California Law Review 1, 37–40.

fields can be supported by what has been specified in the claims and description thereof. That being said, it will be easier for applications of AI-related inventions to be approved if their application fields coincide with what can be summarized from their claims and description. According to our observations, examiners are inclined to approve those AI-related invention applications whose specific application fields are unequivocally embodied in both their claims and description. This can be explained well by some cases. One application claimed a device that could charge smart phones quickly by connecting with smart phones via a USB interface. The device contains a CPU chip that can identify each phone model and then work out the maximum current suitable for it.[34] In this way the efficacy of charging improves. Obviously, such a USB interface cannot connect with and charge laptops. Therefore, its application field shall, in its claims and description, be limited to a specific one, namely, charging smart phones, thus making its protection scope match those problems which could be solved by the claims.

Some AI-related patent applications may specify application fields which are narrower than what they are really capable of. Under certain circumstances, applicants should broaden the application fields in the procedure of office action. A case in point is an intelligent-agriculture device based on the internet of things (IoT). The technical solutions claimed achieve an integration of automated control over areas of modern agriculture such as greenhouse planting, fishery, and farmland. The working process begins with collecting data from sensor units installed in greenhouses, and at fishponds and on farmland. The next procedure is to transmit those data to the device's central processing unit, which will process them and then transmit the processed data to a monitor terminal. After receiving the processed data, workers at the monitor terminal can then take necessary measures such as operating controllers of shade rolling shutters, automatic spraying, and water changing devices.[35] For this application, it is inappropriate to limit the application field to automatic spraying and describe it as 'An Automatic Spraying Device based on IoT technology', because such a description cannot cover those problems that could be solved by the claimed technical solution. Instead, its application field should be 'An Intelligent-Agriculture Device based on IoT technology'.

3.2 Broad Interpretation of Technical Effects for AI-related Inventions

As mentioned above, Article 2.2 of the Patent Law requires that an invention patent use technical solutions to solve technical problems by following natural rules. In other words, the solved problems are a technical effect. For instance, some

[34] See Patent Application No CN201620623756.6.
[35] See Patent Application No CN201620523181.0.

AI-related invention applications aim mainly to improve the user experience, rather than solve a 'technical' problem. If, however, technical effect is strictly interpreted in the context of technology, then a significant number of applications of AI-related inventions are not patentable. In practice, examiners have taken this problem into consideration, and some approved applications of this kind, like the target advertising method, have made clear that improvement or optimization of user experience can be deemed a technical effect. It is worth mentioning that, as widely held by examiners, such experience should be an objective effect arising from a combined action of natural rules and humans' biological attributes, and shall not be judged solely based on users' subjective feeling.

Two issues related to such broad interpretation have to be addressed. First, for a patentable AI-related invention, this broad interpretation does not, in any event, lessen the importance of technical means. That being said, the claims shall specify the technical means used to improve the user experience. From the perspective of how this kind of invention comes about, it begins with an idea of solving a problem confronting users. In the next step, inventors need to figure out which kind of technology could be used to achieve the intended effect. Obviously, the second step matters in the context of patent law. Without this step, the idea would definitely fall into the scope of rules and methods for mental activities and thus be not patent-eligible. For example, the bicycle-sharing industry is booming in China. The general business model for this industry is that there are many bicycles widely spread throughout a city, and users may locate and rent them with the help of their mobile phones. Payment to bicycle owners is also made via their mobile phones after each ride. Clearly, this is only an idea, because it does not disclose what technical means have been used to make it a reality. To qualify as invention patent, a patent application in this regard shall, in its claims and description, specify the technical means of computer programs, such as how to locate a bicycle, how to unlock it, and how to pay and ensure payment safety.[36]

The second issue is that the Guidelines have, to some extent, facilitated the approval of AI-related invention applications. AI-related inventions are, of course, computer-implemented inventions (CII) which, according to the Guidelines, may function in three ways. They could control external industry processes, improve computers' internal performance, or process external technical data.[37] The last one is bound up with AI-related inventions in the sense that AI relies heavily on training data to modify and perfect its algorithms to process more data. As mentioned in Section 2.3, typical instances are AI-related inventions for image recognition, an important applied field of AI. First, huge amounts of image data are collected and analysed, enabling identification and classification of objects in a specific image; the system can then identify and classify objects in a specific image.

[36] See, eg, Patent Application No CN201710743121.9.
[37] See Guidelines 2017 (n 20) Art 1, Chapter 9, Part 2.

Improving user experience is also related to the collection, analysis, and processing of data, be they user data or product data. Therefore, the recognition of CII's function as a technical means, independently or together with the extensive interpretation mentioned above, has increased the likelihood of approval for applications of AI-related inventions.

3.3 Defining the Protection Scope of AI-generated Inventions

As provided by the Patent Law, the protection scope of an invention patent shall be determined in accordance with its claims, and its description can be used to interpret the claims.[38] Therefore, the key step for defining the protection scope of a traditional patent lies in claim construction. This is the same case for AI-related inventions. However, when interpreting their claims, examiners have to take into consideration, among other things, one aspect—the application field. That's because for CII inventions (including AI-related ones), different application fields generally lead to different technical means exploited in computer program structure (like algorithms) and hardware.[39] For example, the application field for the charger mentioned in Section 3.1 is mobile phones, and the charger is connected with a mobile phone via a USB interface. Changing the application field from mobile phones to laptops would require a replacement of interface technologies, namely, from USB to Type-C or AC that is suitable for laptops. As a consequence, the application field is an important consideration factor when drafting and constructing claims.

In order to clearly express its protection scope, a patent application for an AI-related invention, as mentioned above, shall unequivocally specify the application fields of the claimed technical solution, and describe, within the specified application fields, the technical means used to make the technical solution function. The application fields can and shall be utilized to limit the scope of protection of the AI-related invention, and thus to ensure that its protection scope is proportionate to the degree of innovation made by the claimed technical solution. In fact, the introduction of the application field makes it possible for persons skilled in the art to implement the technical solution as claimed. Associating this with those rules providing how to interpret claims, the PRB has put forward a proposal particularly for interpreting CII claims. That is 'If an accused infringing technical solution cannot apply to the application field specified in the claims, a people's court shall not hold that the technical solution falls under the umbrella of the patent in question. To determine whether it could apply or not, the differences between application fields

38 See PL 2008 (n 5) Art 59.1.

39 See Patent Re-examination Board of the CNIPA, 'Research Report on the Protection of Innovations in the New Form Industry' (2019) 18 (unpublicized).

shall be taken into account, and when such application requires major changes to the computer programs or hardware, a people's court shall hold that the accused infringing plan does not fall into the protection scope of the patent.'[40]

Additionally, the technical means used to make a technical solution functional may include both technical plans and non-technical plans whose function is mainly to describe the application field. Therefore, the claim construction of CIIs (including AI-related inventions) shall involve a combined specification of both technical plans and non-technical plans. Under certain circumstances, non-technical plans may well affect the inventive step of an AI-related invention. For example, if an application of such invention contains both technical plans and non-technical ones in its claims and it only differs from prior art in those non-technical plans, examiners will then pay close attention to them. In the case where they have no technical relationship with those technical plans, meaning such difference from prior art does not, on the whole, facilitate the technical solution to solve technical problems and makes no contribution to prior art, the application in question lacks an inventive step. If, however, those non-technical plans have a technical relationship with the technical ones, that is to say, they have a technical effect on the latter, then examiners shall not ignore them and deny the inventive step of the application.

4. Brief Introduction to the New Examination Rules for AI-related Inventions by the CNIPA

On the basis of the above-mentioned experience and in order to unify examination standards for AI-related inventions, the CNIPA amended the Guidelines again in 2019. It released a draft amendment to solicit public opinion on 12 November 2019 and passed the draft on 31 December 2019, with the amendment taking effect as of 1 February 2020.[41] Under the new Guidelines, a new section has been added to Chapter 9, Part 2 of the Guidelines, and those examination rules newly added are particularly for inventions patents containing algorithms or business rules and methods. As specified by the amendment, such patents may involve AI (AI-related inventions), 'Internet Plus', big data, blockchain, etc.[42] The basic rule provided by the new Guidelines for examining AI-related inventions is that all the contents recited in a claim, including technical plans and non-technical ones (algorithmic characteristics or business rules and methods), shall be deemed a whole, and then the technical means exploited, technical problems to be solved, and technical

[40] Ibid.

[41] See CNIPA, 'Explanation on the Draft Amendment to Chapter 9, Part 2 of the Guidelines for Patent Examination' (2019) 1–2.

[42] For the purpose of this chapter, the focus is solely on AI-related inventions which are used to illustrate some key provisions of the amendment.

effects thereby acquired in the claim shall be analysed.[43] Some key provisions of the new Guidelines are briefly introduced below.

4.1 Provisions Regarding Patentability

Patent application of AI-related inventions may apply to a specific field, such as image analysis, search engine, smart translation, or face recognition, and may be wholly based on the process flow of computer programs. AI-related inventions may adjust, control, or process the external or internal objects of computers by running computer programs, and they may also make changes to computer hardware, like robots, self-driving cars, and unmanned aerial vehicles. As pointed out by the CNIPA, the major difference of application of AI-related inventions from that of other inventions lies in the uniqueness of the claim which contains both technical plans and non-technical ones like algorithms and business methods. Since algorithms and business methods are easily associated with rules and methods for mental activities, the patentability of AI-related invention is a key issue in the new Guidelines.

4.1.1 The two-step test under the new Guidelines

The new Guidelines provide a two-step test to determine whether an application of AI-related invention is patentable or not. The two-step test is very similar to the test used for determining the patentability of computer program inventions and business model inventions. The first step starts with examining whether it falls into the scope of Article 25.1 of the Patent Law, namely, rules and methods for mental activities. In the event that the claims of AI-related inventions only contain algorithmic characteristics or business rules and methods, such claims will fall under the umbrella of rules and methods for mental activities and thus are not patentable. A case in point is where an application of AI-related invention involves rules for choosing stocks, and when executing the rules, users cannot determine, without any doubt, whether or not these rules are implemented by computers. In essence, it only applies artificial rules of choosing stocks and does not contain any technical plan, meaning that it cannot fulfil the patentability requirement. If, however, the claims of an AI-related invention application contain both technical plans and algorithmic characteristics or business rules and methods, they are not, on the whole, a kind of rules and methods for mental activities, and their patentability is not ruled out.[44]

[43] See the Guidelines for Patent Examination 2020, Art 6.1, Chapter 9, Part 2 (hereafter Guidelines 2020).

[44] Ibid, Art 6.1.1.

If the answer to the first step is negative, then in the second step, the claim will be further examined on whether it could satisfy the requirements set out in Article 2 of the Patent Law. As required by this article, a patentable invention shall contain at least one technical solution which must solve a technical problem by using technical means and achieve technical effects. Solving problems relating to the improvement of user experience can also be deemed technical effects. If an AI-related invention application exploits algorithms to solve a technical problem and can achieve technical effects, then it could fulfil those requirements for patentability under Article 2 of the Patent Law.[45] For instance, if algorithms contained in a claim have a close relationship with the technical problems to be solved, such as the data processed by those algorithms having practical function in technical fields, the execution of such algorithms could directly embody the process of utilizing natural laws to solve technical problems and thus acquire technical effects. In this case, the claim could, of course, meet the requirements under Article 2 of the Patent Law.

4.1.2 EPO and USPTO's practice on how to determine the patentability of AI-related inventions

The European Patent Office (EPO) updated its Guidelines for Examination, which came into force on 1 November 2018, adding a new sub-section under mathematical methods (Section 3.3 of the Guidelines) in the part of patentability (Part G). The newly added sub-section is particularly made for evaluating the patentability of AI and machine learning (ML) technologies, taking the initiative to define its position on the patentability of AI-related inventions among its peers. It has made clear that AI and ML are based on computational models and algorithms which are per se of an abstract mathematical nature, regardless of whether they can be trained on training data. Hence, the EPO instructs its examiners to look carefully at certain expressions within a claim, such as 'support vector machine', 'reasoning engine', or 'neural network', because they 'usually refer to abstract models devoid of technical character'.[46] According to the EPO, the patentability requirements for mathematical-method applications can be applied to examining the patentability of AI—and ML-related applications. As with the patentability requirements under Article 2 of the Patent Law of China, those requirements under the EPO's guidelines pay close attention to whether a claimed invention has technical character.[47]

Since the newly added sub-section appears within the section of mathematical methods, test standards for determining the patentability of mathematical methods could also be generally applied to that of computational models and algorithms, which are key components of AI-related inventions. Put simply, a claim

[45] Ibid, Art. 6.1.2.

[46] See EPO Guidelines for Examination 2018, Art 3.3.1, Chapter II, Part G (hereafter EPO Guidelines 2018).

[47] Ibid, Art 3.3.

would be excluded from patentability if it is directed to a purely abstract mathematical method and it does not require any technical means. In contrast, if the claim is directed either to a method involving the use of technical means (eg, a computer) or to a device, its subject matter has a technical character as a whole and is thus not excluded from patentability. As indicated by the EPO's guidelines, the technical character of an invention means it contributes to producing a technical effect that serves a technical purpose by its application to a field of technology and/or by being adapted to a specific technical implementation. On the one hand, the key feature of technical application is that it serves a technical purpose, which must be a specific one, meaning that a generic purpose such as 'controlling a technical system' is not sufficient to confer a technical character to the mathematical method. On the other hand, where a claim is directed to a specific technical implementation of a mathematical method which is particularly adapted for such implementation, the mathematical method may still contribute to the technical character of the invention even if it is independent of any technical application.[48]

The USPTO revised its Patent Subject Matter Eligibility Guidance in January 2019 to make clear how to determine whether a subject matter is patent-eligible or not. Even though the revision is not made especially for AI-related inventions, the revised manual provides examiners with guidance on how to determine the patent eligibility of AI-related inventions. The revised guidance revises Step 2A of the *Alice–Mayo* framework into a two-prong approach. It starts with examining whether a claim falls into one of the three categories of abstract idea, namely, mathematical concepts, certain methods of organizing human activity, and mental processes (Step 2A, prong one). If yes, then examiners will jump to step two; if not, the claim should typically not be treated as an abstract idea and is instead patent-eligible. In the second prong, examiners determine whether the abstract idea embodied in a claim is integrated into a practical application (Step 2A, prong two). More specifically, examiners consider whether the claim overall integrates the abstract idea into a practical application that imposes meaningful limits on the abstract idea, thus trying not to monopolize the abstract idea. Limitations that are indicative of integration into a practical application include, among other things, improvements to the functioning of a computer or to another technology or technical field, use or application of a particular machine, effecting a transformation or reduction of a particular article to a different state or thing, and applying or using the abstract idea in some other meaningful way beyond generally linking it to a technological environment. If examiners conclude that there is no 'practical application', then Step 2A fails, and the analysis moves to Step 2B, in which if the abstract idea is not integrated into a practical application, examiners further look into whether the claim provides an inventive concept that is significantly more

48 See EPO T 1358/09 (Classification/BDGB Enterprise Software) of 21 November 2014.

than an abstract idea itself.[49] In general, the revised manual mainly contributes to patent examination in two aspects: One is clarifying the definition of abstract idea; the other is that the direction to practical application does not lead to judicial exception.[50]

4.1.3 The key requirement of patentability of AI-related inventions

The above discussion indicates that the key requirement for an AI-related invention, either under the CNIPA's new Guidelines or the EPO's guidelines or the USPTO's manual, rests on whether its claim has technical effects. The second step of the two-step test under the new Guidelines emphasizes technical solution as a requirement for patentability and echoes Article 2 of the Patent Law of China. The EPO's guidelines follow a typical European technicality-oriented tradition that an application of AI-related invention, to satisfy the requirement for patentability, shall illustrate how the AI technology solves a technical problem by employing technical means, and achieves technical effects. This reflects a long-standing practice among member states of the European Patent Convention, which requires that a patentable invention have technical effects.[51] In addition, the requirement of practical application under the USPTO's manual also pays close attention to technical effects.

How to define technical effects then becomes an important issue. It is easy to make a judgement on whether technical effects achieved by following natural laws exist or not, but this is not the case for AI-related inventions, because their technical effects, if any, are generally implemented by computers. In fact, it is a tall order to draw a line between technical effects and non-technical ones within AI-related inventions. That's why the new Guidelines, the EPO's guidelines, and the USPTO's guidance all enumerate some examples to clarify patentable AI-related inventions or CII. The new Guidelines listed six examples to help examiners determine under what circumstances AI-related inventions are patentable or non-patentable.[52] The EPO enumerated some examples for reference to indicate which fields of technology could be claimed by AI.[53] The USPTO's guidance also provides

[49] The USPTO guidance revised in January 2019 also defines mathematical concepts as 'mathematical relationships, mathematical formulas or equations, and mathematical calculations'. 2019 Revised Patent Subject Matter Eligibility Guidance (2019 PEG).

[50] The US courts' precedents provide three specific exceptions to Section 101 of the US Patent Law's broad patent-eligibility principles: laws of nature, physical phenomena, and abstract ideas. See MPEP 2018 (n 14) Art 2106.04.

[51] See Xu Huina, 'How to Determine the Examination Standards for the Subject Matter of AI-related Inventions?' *China Intellectual Property Newspaper* (Beijing, 8 December 2019).

[52] The new Guidelines list an example of patentable AI-related inventions concerning a training method for a Convolutional Neural Network (CNN) model. Aiming to solve the technical problem of how to make a CNN model capable of identifying images in different sizes, instead of a fixed size, the invention claims a method to process images in different convolutional layers and train the model with adjusted image parameters. As a result, the invention achieves a technical effect by acquiring a well-trained model that can identify images in any size. See Guidelines 2020 (n 43) Art. 6.2, Chapter 9, Part 2.

[53] Eg, the EPO points out that the use of a neural network in a heart-monitoring apparatus for the purpose of identifying irregular heartbeats makes a technical contribution. The classification of digital

a hypothetical example to address the patent eligibility of AI-related inventions, which is directed to a computer-implemented method of training a neural network for facial detection.[54] These examples are no doubt non-exhaustive and far from enough, but in this way, the CNIPA's new Guidelines, the EPO's guidelines, and the USPTO's guidance remain flexible and leave enough room to deal with future problems caused by the development of AI technologies.

4.2 Provisions Regarding Novelty, Inventive Step, and Practicability

For the purpose of patent law, novelty requires that a patent application be different from prior art, meaning that all plans recited in the claims, either technical plans or non-technical ones, will be compared with prior art. If they are substantially similar to prior art, then the novelty requirement cannot be satisfied and thus the application is not patentable. For applications containing both technical plans and non-technical ones like algorithms or business rules and methods, all of those plans shall also be taken into consideration by examiners when judging the novelty. In accordance with a prior undisclosed version of the draft guidelines, if the application differs from the prior art only in the non-technical plans, then examiners will scrutinize whether those non-technical plans have a relationship and work together with the technical plans, for instance, whether they limit the protection scope of the claimed technical solution. If the answer is positive, then it may well satisfy the novelty requirement.[55]

images, videos, audio, or speech signals based on low-level features (eg, edges or pixel attributes for images) are further typical technical applications of classification algorithms. Classifying text documents solely in respect of their textual content is, however, not regarded *per se* as a technical purpose but as a linguistic one (T 1358/09). Classifying abstract data records or even 'telecommunication network data records' without any indication of a technical use being made of the resulting classification is also not per se a technical purpose, even if the classification algorithm may be considered to have valuable mathematical properties such as robustness (T 1784/06). See EPO Guidelines 2018 (n 46) Art 3.3.1, Chapter II, Part G.

[54] The hypothetical Example 39 accompanies the issuance of the USPTO's revised guidance in January 2019. The claimed method uses two training sets to train a neural network for facial detection. The first training set includes digital facial images, and transformed versions of those images and digital non-facial images, and the second one includes the first training set and digital non-facial images that are incorrectly detected as facial images after the first stage of training. In applying the abovementioned analysis, the USPTO concludes that this claim is eligible for patent protection under Step 2A, prong one, because it is not directed to an 'abstract idea'. The USPTO further explains that the claim does not recite mathematical relationships, formulas, or calculations (although some of the limitations may be based on mathematical concepts), the claim does not recite a mental process because 'the steps are not practically performed in the human mind', and the claim also does not recite organizing human activity such as a fundamental economic concept or managing interactions between people. See Subject Matter Eligibility Examples: Abstract Ideas, 2019 Revised Patent Subject Matter Eligibility Guidance (2019 PEG).

[55] See Examination Rules for CII Patent Application 2019, Art 4 (unpublicized draft) (hereafter CII Rules 2019).

As for the examination of inventive step for an AI-related invention, the invention cannot pass the inventive step test if it contains mere application of AI or replaces the estimation method from a conventional one to a trained neural network model, while adding training data to the invention may change this conclusion.[56] Here we focus on a specific scenario. If the claim of an AI-related invention contains both technical plans and non-technical ones like algorithms or business rules and methods which are mutually supportive of and interact in function with technical plans, all those plans shall be deemed to constitute a whole. By 'mutually supportive of and interact in function with technical plans', the new Guidelines means that those algorithms or business rules and methods are closely related to technical plans and they jointly constitute a technical means to solve a technical problem and achieve technical effects. For example, if the algorithms recited in the claim can be applied to a specific field and solve a specific technical problem, or the implementation of the business rules and methods requires the adjustment or improvement of technical plans, then those algorithms or business rules and methods are mutually supportive and interactional in function with technical plans and shall be taken into consideration by examiners when determining whether the application satisfies the requirement of inventive step.[57]

Compared with the new Guidelines, the prior undisclosed version of the draft guidelines made a more detailed provision on how to examine the inventive step of AI-related inventions. According to it, non-technical plans having a relationship and working together with technical plans shall be taken into account as a whole by examiners when judging the inventive step of an AI-related invention application. More specifically, two scenarios are worth addressing. First, if the application differs from the closest prior art to the subject matter of its claim only in non-technical plans, then examiners, in the same way as they do in evaluating the novelty requirement,[58] will examine whether those non-technical plans have a relationship and work together with technical plans and could solve the technical problems as claimed. In the other case, if an AI-related invention application differs from prior art in both technical plans and non-technical ones (like algorithms), and if both plans have a relationship and work together with each other, then the inventive step requirement shall be examined by taking into consideration both of them as a whole. Under both circumstances, if the distinctive features are used to solve the problems as claimed in an AI patent application and the problems are application field ones that are dependent on solving a technical problem, achieving the effects of application fields also rests with those of the technical

[56] For more details of the requirement of inventive step for AI-related inventions, see Ichiro Nakayama, Chapter 5 in this volume.

[57] See Guidelines 2020 (n 43) Art 6.1.3, Chapter 9, Part 2.

[58] The difference here is that novelty examination only requires comparison between the patent application and one closest patent as prior art, while the examination of inventive step could involve the combination of two or more patents as prior art.

effect. In this case, examiners shall further decide whether prior art could provide a person skilled in the art with a ready clue on applying the distinctive feature to the closest prior art. In the event the answer is positive, then the application fails to satisfy the requirement of inventive step.[59]

The new Guidelines do not mention how to examine the requirement of practicability for AI-related inventions, while the prior undisclosed version of the draft guidelines did. In respect of practicability, they require that an AI-related invention application be used in a relevant industry and create a positive effect. The industries mentioned here include but are not limited to: agriculture, forestry, aquaculture, animal husbandry, transportation, commerce, service, finance, recreation and sports, articles of daily use, and medical apparatuses and instruments. When it comes to the practicability requirement for AI-related inventions, a technical solution satisfying this requirement shall not violate natural rules and shall have certainty and reproducibility. For example, a solution claimed will be deemed to be lacking in practicability if the technical effect claimed relating to user experience varies from person to person. An application also cannot meet the requirement if the technical effect can be achieved in theory but with uncertain results. A case in point is to determine samples or models via black-box AI algorithms and get uncertain results, or using AI or virtual reality technology to conduct mental intervention.[60]

5. Conclusion

AI technology is challenging the current patent regime and represents the future of innovation. Most countries have yet to address the issue of how and whether to issue AI-related patents.[61] As this chapter indicates, the field of patent examination has to respond to those issues raised by AI. Some major jurisdictions are moving in this direction. The CNIPA has accumulated plenty experience in examining patent application of AI-related inventions, and has modified its Guidelines with a focus on the examination rules on AI-related inventions, in order to unify the practice of examining such applications. Patentability of AI-related inventions, under the current Patent Law, is subject to rules and methods for mental activities as well as the requirements for technical solution, and a patent application thereof without using technical means to solve technical problems so as to achieve technical effects cannot meet the patentability requirement. Application field(s) shall be unequivocally specified in both the claims and description of an AI-related

[59] See CII Rules 2019 (n 55) Art 5.
[60] Ibid, Art 6.
[61] See W Michael Schuster, 'Artificial Intelligence and Patent Ownership' (2018) 75 Wash & Lee L Rev 1945, 2004.

invention application, and may be used to limit the protection scope of the application. If the claims of such an application contain technical plans and non-technical ones like algorithms or business rules and methods, they should, according to the new Guidelines, be taken into consideration by examiners when evaluating the application's inventive step, provided that those non-technical plans are in function mutually supportive to and interactional with technical plans. Even though China's experience can be a benchmark for other jurisdictions, a long road still lies ahead for the patent office of each individual country. AI itself is also evolving, making the situation uncertain even in the near future.

12
Artificial Intelligence and Trademark Assessment

*Anke Moerland and Conrado Freitas**

1. Introduction

Artificial intelligence (AI) and its impact on society is being intensively studied, including by legal scholars, who assess the need for regulation on the use of AI in various fields, eg, e-commerce, press, art, democratic processes, judicial activities, etc, and what types of rules should be installed. Other researchers focus on the possibilities AI offers for legal professionals in carrying out some of their tasks. For instance, researchers from the University of Liege, Sheffield, and Pennsylvania have developed software based on AI that can predict decisions of the European Court of Human Rights with up to 79% accuracy.[1]

This chapter analyses the potential of AI in facilitating IP administration processes, in particular in the context of examining trademark applications (eg, descriptiveness or immorality of terms) and assessing prior marks in opposition and infringement proceedings (eg, assessing the likelihood of confusion with another sign). We compare the functionality of AI-based algorithms used by trademark offices in a series of tests and evaluate their ability to carry out, without human input, (parts of) the legal tests required to register a trademark. We use doctrinal research methods and interviews with fourteen main stakeholders in the field, including software developers, trademark examiners, judges, and in-house trademark counsels and attorneys from different jurisdictions, to highlight the functionality and limits of AI tools for trademark assessment.

Our results suggest that only a few trademark offices are currently applying AI tools to assess trademark applications on their compatibility with absolute grounds for refusal or in relation to prior marks; no trademark judge reported that they are using AI tools. As discussed in Section 2, the AI tools currently used do not have

* All online materials were accessed before 27 October 2019.

[1] The algorithm mainly relied on the language used by the Court in previous judgments, as well as the topic and circumstances mentioned in the text of the case. This was made possible because of the nature of European Court of Human Rights judgments that rely predominantly on facts rather than legal arguments. UCL, 'AI predicts outcomes of human rights trials' (*UCL*, 24 October 2016) <https://www.ucl.ac.uk/news/2016/oct/ai-predicts-outcomes-human-rights-trials>.

Anke Moerland and Conrado Freitas, *Artificial Intelligence and Trademark Assessment* In: *Artificial Intelligence and Intellectual Property*. Edited by: Jyh-An Lee, Reto M Hilty, and Kung-Chung Liu, Oxford University Press (2021).
 DOI: 10.1093/oso/9780198870944.003.0013

decision-making capabilities and are predominantly focused on very specific and often simple tasks, such as assessing similarity of signs with prior registered marks, and classifying goods and services. The quality of the assessments made by the AI tools differs, with some performing strongly on image recognition and others doing well on descriptiveness checks.

We argue in Section 3 that it is very difficult for the subjective and more complex tests enshrined in trademark law to be carried out autonomously by an AI tool, and this is unlikely to change in the near future. Assessing the likelihood of confusion and whether a third party has taken unfair advantage of a mark without due cause are obvious examples of subjective and complex tests that rely on various factors to be examined. We find that so far, AI tools are unable to reflect the nuances of these legal tests in trademark law. Even in the near future, we argue that AI tools are likely to carry out merely parts of the legal tests and present information that humans will have to assess.

Even though the current state of AI technology seems to allow only for specific applications in trademark assessment, the rapid development of technology may swiftly change this scenario, and within a few years' time, more complex tasks could be carried out by AI. Section 4 discusses how professionals working in trademark administration, examination, and the judiciary see the future and which developments are taking place to make AI tools better appreciate the circumstances of the case as well as market information.

1.1 Artificial Intelligence: Terminology and Development

AI is not a new concept, and its applications date back to the 1950s. With the proliferation of the term in the 1980s, pioneers such as Marvin Minsky and John McCarthy described an AI as 'any task performed by a program or a machine that, if a human carried out the same activity, we would say the human had to apply intelligence to accomplish the task'.[2] Since then, different AI applications have flourished, and various techniques such as machine learning (ML), deep learning (DL), and natural language processing have been developed.

A definition for AI is not settled yet, as it is evolving over time.[3] It varies from an entire field of science involving the creation of complex

[2] Heikki Vesalainen and others, 'Artificial intelligence in trademark software A PRIMER' (*Trademark Now*) <https://www.trademarknow.com/artificial-intelligence-in-trademark-software>.

[3] Josef Drexl, Retho Hilty, Francisco Beneke, Luc Desaunettes, Michèle Finck, Jure Globocnik, Begoña Gonzalez Otero, Jörg Hoffmann, Leonard Hollander, Daria Kim, Heiko Richter, Stefan Scheuerer, Peter R. Slowinski, and Jannick Thonemann, 'Technical Aspects of Artificial Intelligence: An Understanding from an Intellectual Property Law Perspective' (8 October 2019) Max Planck Institution for Innovation & Competition Research Paper N.19-13, 2 <https://ssrn.com/abstract=3465577> (hereafter Drexl, Hilty, Beneke, Desaunettes, Finck, Globocnik, Gonzalez Otero, Hoffmann, Hollander, Kim, Richter, Scheuerer, Slowinski, and Thonemann, 'Technical Aspects of Artificial Intelligence').

algorithms[4] to any task performed by a computer that mimics human intelligence. For this chapter, we follow the latter definition of AI technologies as enabling machines to mimic human behaviour.[5]

Currently the most common form of AI is ML, which comprises techniques that allow machines to make decisions and to learn without being specifically programmed to do so. To be precise, several steps are required for developing a machine learning model. First, a programmer provides a model architecture, which is used to feed training data sets through a training algorithm. The purpose is to find the best combination of the model parameters in order to reduce the error rate. When sufficient training data have been run through the system, a model will be determined. The developed model will now be able to predict a certain output when being presented with new data. A subset of ML is deep DL, which allows machines to solve more complex problems by using multilayer neural networks designed to work like human brains.[6]

Andrew Burgess has categorized AI according to the different objectives it pursues.[7] The first objective would be to capture information correctly, by classifying documents and extracting relevant information, speech, or images. Technologies used for this are image analytics, speech recognition, search functionality, text generation, and content extraction software. Through ML, these technologies automatically search emails, generate automated responses, or classify texts according to self-learned categories. The second objective is to make sense of the information identified and to predict the next step, based on previous actions. Such prediction requires DL, as it is more complex and involves a semantic element. The third objective is to understand why something is happening. This requires general cognitive AI, which does not exist yet.

It is important to distinguish ML from rule-based systems, in which reactions are pre-programmed and therefore not adaptive.[8] Many of the trademark assessment tools currently used by trademark offices are rule-based rather than learned by machines. In other words, a business rule is a predefined rule that is not trained on past data. According to IP Australia, business rules are used where one can define the problem and relate a consequence to it, in a rather linear form of 'If … then … '. The advantage of business rules is that one can explain exactly what the logic is and what parameters determine the outcome. On the other hand,

[4] Tania Sourdin, 'Judge v Robot? Artificial Intelligence And Judicial Decision-Making' (2018) 41(4) University of New South Wales Law Journal l 38 <http://www.austlii.edu.au/au/journals/UNSWLJ/2018/38.html#fnB1>.

[5] Drexl, Hilty, Beneke, Desaunettes, Finck, Globocnik, Gonzalez Otero, Hoffmann, Hollander, Kim, Richter, Scheuerer, Slowinski, and Thonemann, 'Technical Aspects of Artificial Intelligence' (n 3) 3.

[6] For a more elaborate explanation of the different steps involved in ML models, ibid, 5 ff.

[7] Andrew Burgess, *The Executive Guide to Artificial Intelligence: How to Identify and Implement Applications for AI in Your Organization* (Palgrave Macmillan 2018) 3–4.

[8] Drexl, Hilty, Beneke, Desaunettes, Finck, Globocnik, Gonzalez Otero, Hoffmann, Hollander, Kim, Richter, Scheuerer, Slowinski, and Thonemann, 'Technical Aspects of Artificial Intelligence' (n 3) 3.

an ML model is trained on past data and learns the rules from those data itself. Explaining ML decisions can be a challenge, depending on the complexity of the model. This has driven the emergence of explainable artificial intelligence (XAI). According to IP Australia, the decision as to whether a business rule is used or an AI tool will be developed depends on a number of factors, including the nature and complexity of the problem and the availability of structured training data.[9]

This chapter does not aim to analyse and identify the exact type of AI technology that is used for a specific trademark assessment. Rather, we rely on the information gathered from the tools' developers. We are more interested in the results the technology produces and in describing their functionality as correctly as possible.

To the best of our knowledge, no previous studies assessing the application of AI to trademark law have been published, nor the use of AI tools to assist the administration of trademarks by IP offices and/or courts. Only one author appreciates that AI tools for IP administration will ultimately generate better filings, with less potential grounds for refusal; this is expected to render trademark offices' work more efficient and productive and thereby reduce backlogs.[10] This chapter will analyse the functionality of the identified AI tools in a comparative manner and discuss their limitations for trademark assessment.

1.2 Methodology

In order to describe the functionality of the tools used for trademark search and assessment by trademark offices in Section 2, we have identified the online search tools available on trademark offices' websites. We have also identified private companies that have developed the technology used by some trademark offices. While some explicitly claim to use AI, other trademark offices do not identify the type of software used. We decided to describe the functionality of all, in order to compare the results currently achieved by commonly available AI tools.

The main stakeholders identified were (1) TrademarkNow, (2) CompuMark and Trademark Vision from Clarivate, (3) the Norwegian IP Office (NIPO), (4) the Word Intellectual Property Organisation (WIPO), (5) the European Union Intellectual Property Office (EUIPO), (6) IP Australia (IPA), and (7) the Singapore IP Office (IPOS). We have also contacted the Chinese Trademark Office, the Benelux Office of IP, and the Korean IP Office, but we did not receive responses. The US Patent and Trademark Office (USPTO) informed us that it currently does

[9] Interview with Thomas Murphy, Member of the Cognitive Futures team IP Australia, Skype, 20 September 2019 (hereafter Interview with Thomas Murphy).

[10] Alexander Supertramp, 'How IP offices use artificial intelligence' (*World Intellectual Property Review*, 22 May 2019) <https://www.worldipreview.com/contributed-article/how-ip-offices-use-artificial-intelligence>.

not use any AI to carry out trademark examination but is testing several tools for possible implementation if found to be reliable.[11]

The District Courts of Amsterdam (Rechtbank Amsterdam) and The Hague (Rechtbank Den Haag), the German Federal Patent Court, the District Court of Hamburg and Munich, and the EUIPO Boards of Appeal have been contacted because of the number of trademark cases they hear.[12] However, they informed us that they do not operate AI-based systems for trademark assessment. It is important to highlight that the list of assessed tools is therefore not exhaustive. The results presented here are based on the responses we received and the tools available online.

We successfully completed fourteen interviews with AI developers, users of AI tools, and persons responsible for the AI development at TrademarkNow, Darts-ip, private law firms and companies, for instance Noerr and Unilever, the EUIPO (Digital Transformation Department and Boards of Appeal), IPA (Policy and Governance Group, Innovation & Technology Group, Cognitive Futures Team), USPTO (Office of Policy and International Affairs and Department of Commerce) and NIPO (Communication and Knowledge). The majority of interviews were conducted on the phone (two interviews took place in person) between April and October 2019.

The interviews were conducted based on three slightly different semi-structured questionnaires, addressing the target group of users (trademark attorneys and trademark counsels of companies), AI developers and trademark offices or judges. The questions addressed the following five issues: (1) the tools' functionalities and the specific use by interviewees; (2) the tools' ability to perform different legal tests (eg, similarity of signs, likelihood of confusion); (3) experience with the reliability of such tools; (4) the tools' limitations; and (5) expected future performance.

Upon conclusion of the interviews, seven search tests were performed on the databases of (1) WIPO, (2) EUIPO, (3) IPA, and (4) IPOS. These offices were chosen based on the results of the scoping exercise among stakeholders as well as the responses from the interviewees. The EUIPO and WIPO tools are considered important search tools. The IPA and IPOS are considered to be most advanced in their use of AI technology for trademark search and examination. The NIPO tool is currently transitioning to an AI tool and could not yet provide reliable results for our tests. Whether all online search tools are based on AI technology could not be fully verified. This is due to the difficulty of defining when a technology involves a form of AI instead of a business rule.

[11] Interview with Senior Trademark Advisor Kathleen Cooney-Porter at Department of Commerce, 26 September 2019, Alicante and email exchange with Senior Counsel Amy Cotton at Office of Policy and International Affairs USPTO, 8 October 2019 (hereafter email exchange with Amy Cotton).

[12] Darts-ip has been used to determine the frequency of cases per court and country.

Table 12.1: Test for AI Tools for Trademark Assessment

Test	Inputs / Variations	Purpose
1) Image recognition	 The above image was inserted, without specification of goods and services. **Variation:** With the same image, we used the keywords 'brick' and/or 'block', in the relevant classes for games.	Test the software's ability to identify with precision similar figurative marks, regardless of the goods and services. **Variation:** Test the systems' capability in disclosing very precise hits.
2) Conceptual similarity of images	The Apple image mark was uploaded, searching for figurative marks in all classes. **Variation:** Using the same image, now searching only trademarks in the relevant classes for software and hardware.	Examine the software's power to pinpoint signs that are not owned by Apple Inc., but visually and conceptually similar.
3) Conceptual similarity between different types of marks	We searched for figurative trademarks using only the word 'APPLE', in all classes.	Assess the programmes' capability of identifying a similar figurative mark merely with a word-based search
4) Conceptual similarity – foreign scripts	蘋果 We uploaded the above image, which is the Chinese translation for apple (according to Google Translate), searching for figurative marks, first in the relevant classes for computers, software and hardware, then in the relevant classes for fruit products. **Variation:** We repeated the test above, but this time including the English translation 'apple' as a keyword.	Test the tools' ability to understand foreign scripts.
5) Descriptiveness	Searched for the word 'apple' in the relevant class for fruit products.	Test the tools' ability to flag descriptiveness.
6) Morality	We uploaded the term FXXX, in all classes of goods and services.	Test the tools' ability to flag scandalous/immoral terms.
7) Classification	Searched for the word 'apple', for fruit products and for software/hardware.	Test the tools' ability to suggest the appropriate Nice classes for identical/similar goods/services.

The tests carried out are relevant in the context of identifying absolute and relative grounds for refusal for trademark applications.[13] We aimed at comparing the ability of the different search tools to generate relevant results regarding (a) identical or similar images, (b) descriptiveness of signs; (c) conceptually similar signs; (d) morality concerns, and (e) classification of goods or services. These tests allowed us to categorize each examined tool as yielding relevant or irrelevant results. Apart from minor variations when conducting the tests in each tool, the seven tests conducted are reflected in Table 12.1.

For Sections 3 and 4, we have used interview data as well as doctrinal legal methods to analyse how the overarching principles and rules of trademark law in European Union (EU) law could conceivably be performed by AI tools and what its limitations are. While limited to EU law, we believe the analysis is also relevant for other jurisdictions due to substantial similarities in substantive trademark rules.

2. Current Performance of AI-Tools for Trademark Search and Assessment

The AI tools currently employed by trademark offices allow users and trademark examiners to assess similarity of image and word marks with previous signs, classifying goods and services in the relevant classes and checking descriptiveness and morality concerns of signs. The purpose of this section is to assess the functionality of these AI tools based on the tests described in Section 1.2.

The search tool operated by WIPO is entitled Global Brand Database.[14] This incorporates the databases of several national trademark offices as well as international registrations. The EUIPO tool is called eSearch Plus and allows searching for EU trademarks.[15] The IPA adopts two different tools: Australian Trademark Search[16] and Trademark Assist (TM Assist).[17] The main AI-based functionalities are present in TM Assist, for instance to search images, determine if an image contains copyright material or a registered symbol like flags for example, and to help the user find relevant goods and services in the Nice classification. Finally, the IPOS search tool is available both through a website[18] and a smartphone application called IPOS Go. The smartphone app is the one claimed to run on AI, and it is where the general public can use the image recognition feature.

[13] However, these tests are also relevant in the process of clearing a name for use in the market, without registration intentions. One could even rely on the above elements when undertaking market surveillance of competitors and policing one's trademarks.

[14] <https://www3.wipo.int/branddb/en/>.

[15] <https://euipo.europa.eu/eSearch/>.

[16] <https://search.ipaustralia.gov.au/trademarks/search/advanced>.

[17] <https://assist.ipaustralia.gov.au/trademarks/welcome>.

[18] <https://www.ip2.sg/RPS/WP/CM/SearchSimpleP.aspx?SearchCategory=TM>.

Table 12.2 presents remarkable results: the IPA search tool has presented the strongest performance overall, as it scores high on image recognition for similar marks and carries out, as the only tool tested, a morality and descriptiveness test. However, for conceptual similarity between words and images, it scored lower than other tools. A strong image search tool enabling conceptual similarity between words and images is present in the WIPO and the IPOS tools: both provided relevant figurative marks containing an apple as results when the word 'apple' was searched for. This was even the case for figurative marks that did not contain any apple-bearing word element.

2.1 Test 1: Image Recognition

All tools examined revealed mostly irrelevant results when running the shape similarity test with a nonverbal image of the Lego brick. The results were not related to the subject matter and displayed practically all forms and shapes. This was unexpected for the WIPO tool, as it allows users to choose the strategy to be applied during the search, such as assessing similarity on the basis of conceptual, shape, or colour similarity, or a combination of those. Users can also select the specific type of image inserted (verbal, nonverbal, combined, and unknown).

From the two million hits generated by the WIPO search tool, the majority were not related to the subject matter, and practically all forms and shapes were listed. When the search was limited to the relevant classes of toys and games, the list was reduced to approximately 30,000 results, with various still unrelated hits. At least for shape marks, these results suggest that the tool is unable to precisely pinpoint the most similar trademarks.

We observed another interesting outcome for the IPA tool. For the first stage of the test, without goods and services classification, 2,000 hits comprised any type of shape. When we restricted the search to the relevant classes for games and toys, 224 trademarks were disclosed, but still comprising several unrelated shapes. However, when the keyword 'brick' was inserted, only two hits were found, one of them owned by LEGO. These results suggest that the underlying image recognition technology is moderate, as the tool only produced the Lego brick shape mark when the keyword 'brick' was inserted.

The results for the IPOS tool suggest an even less developed image recognition technology. The search for similar signs without a description of goods and services yielded more than 2,000 hits, comprising any trademark in a rectangular, or even other shape. Including the relevant classes for toys and games did not make much of a difference for the outcome. When the keyword 'brick' was used, only thirteen trademarks were disclosed, none of them owned by LEGO. Overall, the tool available by IPOS did not produce the registered LEGO shape mark, even after limiting the class of goods, and thereby failed the test.

Table 12.2: Comparison of AI Tools for Trademark Assessment

	WIPO	EUIPO	IPA	IPOS
1) Image recognition	Irrelevant results. Various different shapes in all phases of the test.	Irrelevant results. Various different shapes in all phases of the test.	Relevant results only when including the keyword 'brick'.	Irrelevant results. Various different shapes in all phases of the test and did not disclose the actual Lego trademark.
2) Conceptual similarity of images	Relevant results. Many conceptually similar signs containing apples and other fruits.	Relevant results. Many conceptually similar signs containing apples and other fruits.	Relevant results only for computer-related classes. Irrelevant results for fruit-related classes, even with 'apple' keyword.	Relevant results. Many conceptually similar signs containing apples and other fruits.
3) Conceptual similarity between different types of marks	Relevant results. Figurative marks contain an apple without any apple-bearing word element.	Irrelevant results. Figurative marks always contain the word element 'apple', and several other hits unrelated to apples.	Irrelevant results. Figurative marks always contain the word element 'apple', and several other hits unrelated to apples, but containing apple in the description (eg, pineapple).	Relevant results. Figurative marks contain an apple without any apple-bearing word element.
4) Conceptual similarity—foreign scripts	Relevant results, representing apple logos and fruits (eg, images containing an apple or resembling an apple), only when keyword 'apple' included.	Relevant results only when keyword 'apple' included.	Relevant results only when keyword 'apple' included.	Relevant results only when keyword 'apple' included.
5) Descriptiveness	No descriptive-ness check.	No descriptive-ness check.	Relevant results.	No descriptive-ness check.

Table 12.2: Continued

	WIPO	EUIPO	IPA	IPOS
6) Morality	No morality check.	No morality check.	Relevant results.	No morality check.
7) Classification	Relevant results.	No classification suggestion.	Relevant results.	No classification suggestion.

It is important to highlight that none of the tools allows users to search for non-traditional marks. The only exception is WIPO's database, which allows for a search strategy based on colour similarity. We conducted a parallel test using an image file containing only the orange colour of the logo (without the word element 'orange'), in class 38 in all databases. Only the WIPO and IPOS tools were able to identify the actual registrations owned by Orange Brand Services Limited. The results contained all types of marks and many unrelated ones. However, both tools' ability to identify Orange's actual registration is relevant.

The rather weak performance of the image recognition technology used by all offices has been attributed by one interviewee[19] to the difficulties of recognizing specific elements within a larger sign (word or figurative), different colours, and images with low contrast, and to the fact that only a part of an image or text was searched for.[20]

In conclusion, IPA's tool performed best regarding image recognition for the purpose of similarity assessment.

2.2 Test 2: Conceptual Similarity

This test used the Apple, Inc. logo to identify similar signs in classes for fruit products and computers. In fact, all tools performed well in Test 2. Almost all results were relevant, depicting conceptually similar images of fruit when uploading the Apple logo. Among the tools with the most striking performance were the IPOS and IPA tools. The results of both tools included the Apple Inc. logo, and similar signs of apples and other fruits, even without any keyword. The surprising element in the IPOS tool was that it not only identified the closest prior trademarks, but also displayed other signs from the same right holder, even signs that did not contain the Apple logo, like the logos for Safari and FaceTime.

[19] Email correspondence with Miguel Ortega, Advisor at the Digital Transformation Department, EUIPO, 1 August 2019 (hereafter email correspondence with Miguel Ortega).

[20] Ibid.

2.3 Test 3: Conceptual Similarity between Different Types of Marks

During this test, we inserted the term 'apple' to search for conceptually similar figurative marks. Only the WIPO and IPOS tools performed well on this test. The results of both tools revealed several registrations for trademarks that consist of an apple, even without any reference to the word element 'apple' in the logo. The results revealed also the figurative mark owned by Apple Inc., confirming the tool's ability to compare words with figurative similar signs. EUIPO's and IPA's tools did not produce relevant results, depicting merely figurative marks that contain the word element 'apple' and several unrelated hits.

2.4 Test 4: Conceptual Similarity—Foreign Scripts

We used the Chinese translation of apple and searched for figurative marks in the classes for food products and computers. Subsequently, we supplemented the search with the English translation 'apple' as a keyword. The results were predominantly irrelevant in all tools. They only revealed relevant results after including the English term 'apple' as a keyword. Even at this stage, most results contained the term 'apple' in the description of the trademark. This suggests that the tools executed the searches based on the English keyword 'apple', and not on the basis of the Chinese script.

2.5 Test 5: Descriptiveness

We searched for the word 'apple' in the relevant class for fruit products. Only the IPA tool flagged descriptiveness concerns. Through its link with dictionaries, the goods or services for which the sign is applied can be compared to the meaning of the sign. If it is identical or similar, a flag appears. The IPA tool will, however, also flag descriptiveness even if the term has acquired distinctiveness. IPA's current tool scans synonyms to assess a sign's descriptiveness in relation to the goods or services applied for.

2.6 Test 6: Morality

During this test, we uploaded the term FXXX, in all classes of goods and services. The only tool that checks a sign for morality concerns is the one developed by IPA. It indicates a possible problem with the absolute ground of morality. According to IP Australia, a list of terms has been defined previously that is checked when a term is inserted.[21] This feature, however, is based on a business rule rather than an AI tool. IP Australia will not use an AI if a simple business rule can easily identify words as those commonly deemed immoral, according to accepted dictionaries. Such results of the TM Assist tool are perceived as relevant from a user perspective, but cannot be attributed to AI technology.

2.7 Classification

The IPA and WIPO tools were able to suggest the relevant Nice classes as soon as the goods and services were entered by the user; EUIPO and IPOS have not yet integrated such a feature in their tools.[22] As part of IPA's business transformation and technology agenda,[23] one of the tools developed was the Goods & Services Assistant tool. It does not simply indicate the class for the exact good or service claimed; it also reveals similar classes, by comparing semantically similar goods or services. For instance, when the user inserts 'gelato', the tool will suggest sorbets, ice cream desserts, and ice desserts (class 30), as well as cream desserts (class 29), and sorbet beverages (class 32). AI technology incorporated in this tool thus can identify semantically similar goods and services. Similarly, when searching for software, TM Assist suggests classes 9 (software), 42 (design of software), 16 (manuals for software), and 45 (licensing of software).

The performance of WIPO's tool was very relevant. It also suggests the relevant classes for identical and similar goods and services. It is worth noting that the tool was able to recommend service classes when the user inserts a similar good. For instance, when searching for software or hardware, the tool recommended not only class 9, but also 42 and 45.

2.8 Trademark Administration

The interviews carried out during the present study also revealed that AI features are used to facilitate the administration of trademarks. For example, EUIPO uses a tool which applies algebraic algorithms to group similar trademarks to be evaluated by the same examiner.[24] The purpose is to allow examiners to work on similar cases, leading to more agile, coherent, and harmonized decisions.

[21] Interview with Thomas Murphy (n 9).

[22] The EUIPO is currently also developing a proof of concept that aims at creating a classification model for goods and services in trademark applications <http://euipo.europa.eu/ec2>.

[23] 'IP Australia system upgrade for trade marks' (*IP Australia*, 2 April 2019) <https://www.ipaustralia.gov.au/about-us/about-this-site/system-availability/rio-release>.

[24] Email correspondence with Miguel Ortega (n 19).

EUIPO also applies AI technology to read letters from applicants or opposing parties in different languages and to extract relevant information. The information currently extracted relates to formality and classification deficiency and opposition decisions. It is then made available to EUIPO's examiners in the form of dashboards, which facilitates examiners' work. Very basic letters regarding deadlines, acknowledgment of receipt of documents, etc are sent automatically.[25] The possibilities to use AI for other administrative purposes are discussed in Section 4.2.

2.9 Features Not Yet Present in AI Tools

To date, the reviewed AI tools do not yet assess issues that involve more complex assessment of signs. From our tests, it is clear that the distinctiveness of signs or the presence of a reputation are features not yet available in the assessed search tools. The similarity of goods is not carried out either, which is necessary to eventually determine the likelihood of confusion. From the interview data collected, it has also become clear that opposition or cancellation divisions of trademark offices do not yet make use of AI tools that could help in assessing likelihood of confusion, unfair advantage, detriment to distinctive character or repute, or whether the EU law requirement of 'without due cause' is fulfilled.

2.10 Interim Conclusions

From the tests carried out for the assessed tools and the interviews, we conclude that the current state of AI technologies used by trademark offices only performs simple tasks, such as image recognition and comparison, conceptual similarity, classification of goods and services, and descriptiveness and morality checks.

Some of the tools performed better than others. None of them so far has been set up to undertake complex legal tests in trademark law, in particular for the distinctiveness of signs, reputation, similarity of goods and services, likelihood of confusion, unfair advantage, detriment to distinctive character or repute, or whether the requirement of 'without due cause' is fulfilled. The next section will discuss the current impediments for AI tools to improve their performance.

[25] Phone interview with Sven Stürmann, Chairperson of the Second EUIPO Board of Appeal and programme manager for the development of the new IT back office for the Boards of Appeal, 4 October 2019 (hereafter Interview with Sven Stürmann).

3. Current Limitations of AI Tools to Accurately Predict Outcome

Even though the current use of AI technologies is still limited to mostly (1) image recognition, (2) classifying goods and services according to the Nice classes, and (3) identifying descriptive terms, we can foresee that within five to ten years, trademark examiners will rely on AI technology to assist them in many more steps of trademark assessment. AI technologies will become more accurate, as computer vision for indexing pictures, attributing meaning to texts, and identifying text within a figurative mark, among others, develops into sophisticated tools. For example, for 3D shape marks, a precise comparison of a registered mark and a trademark application, or potentially a shape on the market, can be carried out if several images exist from the various angles that produce the complete 3D picture. Technology is not far from producing accurate results in this respect.

Already now, AI tools are being experienced by many as having positive aspects, even though their current use is still limited. According to Miguel Ortega, when AI technology is used as a tool by examiners, the quality and consistency in examiners' assessment will increase, as well as their efficiency.[26] Already with the classification model for goods and services under development at EUIPO, or the pairing of similar goods and services based on previous case law at IPA, examiners can use the suggestions made to them and thereby avoid duplicating work.

The ability of AI technology to yield positive results for the work of examiners and judges, however, highly depends on its reliability. In this context, one of the most important challenges is to acquire huge volumes of data that is structured for the purpose of training the AI. Next to this challenge, we argue that there are more impediments for AI technology to play a major role in trademark assessment. We highlight the subjectivity of trademark law as an important challenge for AI technology: predicting distinctiveness, likelihood of confusion, unfair advantage, detriment, or 'without due cause' is complex, context-dependent and requires the potential to suggest new solutions.

3.1 Unregistered Prior Rights Currently not Covered in Similarity of Signs

While the search for similar signs is probably the number one area where AI technology already produces very good results, there are still a number of aspects in the AI technology that can be improved. The most obvious limitation is that the AI technologies used by different offices currently only search prior registered

[26] Email correspondence with Miguel Ortega (n 19).

signs; there is no tool yet that 'surfs the Internet' or has access to relevant databases in order to identify which signs are in use but not registered. Another limitation relates to non-traditional marks, which cannot be searched for at this point. Extending the search function to such marks will be highly relevant in the future.

Including unregistered rights would require an AI algorithm to have access to certain predefined datasets, such as those of online retailers, supermarkets, or important search engines. At least at this point in time, it seems very unlikely that such data will be (freely) available for public registries' AI tools. Data about the use of brands and signs, and even more so about competitors and consumers' behaviour, is one of the most valuable assets, and their owners are likely to keep them exclusive.

3.2 Accurate Data

The accuracy of the results produced by AI technology in trademark assessment has been mentioned by several stakeholders as one of the most important areas of improvement. This is not an obstacle that cannot be overcome with time and investment. However, even where AI technologies become more sophisticated, Anna Ronkainen, a former co-founder and developer of the TrademarkNow tool, warns that perfect information provided by an algorithm is unrealistic.[27] But the threshold for using AI technologies may not necessarily have to be full reliability of the outcome; a high percentage of accuracy can be very valuable information, certainly if it is provided in a fraction of the time humans need for it.[28] It may also mean that one needs to be aware and prepared to take a risk that decisions are not made on the basis of full information but on the basis of very high probabilities. Without being explicit about this, trademark examiners also cannot claim that they are making decisions on full information—humans may even miss more information than AI.

Nevertheless, while some acceptance of such a risk may be needed, one should strive towards improving the technologies to the extent that the remaining risks are as small as possible. The determining factor for improving AI technologies is the availability of structured and reliable training data, in particular in relation to multi-jurisdictional contexts, in order to allow for the exchange of such data among offices. We distinguish between legal and market-based data.

[27] Interview with Anna Ronkainen, former Co-founder of TrademarkNow, Skype, 24 May 2019 (hereafter Interview with Anna Ronkainen).

[28] Also acknowledged at IP Horizon 5.0 conference in Alicante, organized by EUIPO and McCarthy Institute, 26–27 September 2019 (hereafter IP Horizon 5.0 conference).

3.2.1 Legal data

In order for AI tools to facilitate substantive trademark assessment by legal attorneys, examiners, and judges, the technology needs to be trained with data that reflects the legal concepts, tests, and case law of the relevant legal system. For such data to be available and fed into an AI tool, trademark offices will have to digitize all examination decisions, opposition and invalidity proceedings, decisions by the Boards of Appeal, case law from relevant courts, etc. Those documents will have to be structured according to points of fact and law that play a role in determining trademark registrability as well as infringement at a later stage.

A database to which interviewees have often referred as a model for that is Darts-ip, a commercial database that covers IP case law on a global level. The database is limited to case law only. But its approach has merit for trademark registration questions as well. According to Evrard van Zuylen from Darts-ip, its database contains case law of a specific court in a specific country that is analysed according to predetermined points of fact and law.[29] In other words, the outcome of cases is classified per court in a country, thereby reflecting differences at the court level. The AI technology they use focuses on language processing in order to extract legal context and legal issues automatically. It is only applied to courts where there is enough training data available from previous decisions. For some courts, there may never be enough decisions to train the AI properly, due to a low volume of case law in trademarks.[30]

Since October 2019, Darts-ip has started cooperating with the Benelux Office of IP on integrating case law data in the registration phase. The purpose is to improve the assessment of similarity of trademarks, by using millions of cases that have determined similarity of signs, relying on shape, colour, and use of letters as relevant factors, among others. On the basis of that training data, the AI tool can identify rules that it needs to follow when presented with new signs.[31] The training is continuous and subject to high standards of reliability. Error measures are used as well as pilot studies on unseen data in order to determine how the AI tool performs its tasks.[32]

A similar experience has been reported by IP Australia, which explained that the AI technology IP Australia has developed is based on ten years of training data consisting of trademark examiners' responses in Australia. Only a sufficient amount of high-quality data as well as continuous training lead to a reliable outcome that can augment examiners' experience.[33]

[29] Interview with Evrard van Zuylen, Managing Director of Darts IP, Skype, 23 September 2019 (hereafter Interview with Evrard van Zuylen).

[30] Darts-ip has introduced an AI similarity check in the summer of 2019. It is based on mathematical processing of trademarks, without any semantic checks through a link to dictionaries. Darts-ip is currently working on incorporating a semantic element in order to enable conceptual similarity or a descriptiveness check.

[31] 'Darts-ip image search technology licensed to Benelux Office for Intellectual Property' (*Darts-IP*, 2 October 2019) <https://www.darts-ip.com/blog-darts-ip-boip-image-search/>.

[32] Interview with Evrard van Zuylen (n 29).

[33] Email exchange with Michael Burn, Senior Director of the Innovation & Technology Group from IP Australia, 4 October 2019 (hereafter email exchange with Michael Burn).

Working towards a multi-jurisdictional search or assessment by an AI tool is a next step that requires the subtle differences between legal systems to be reflected in the training data of the AI tool. Different users of the commercial AI tool TrademarkNow have pointed out that so far, this detailed information about the relevant tests and case law per jurisdiction is not yet well-reflected in the tool, which aims to have a multi-jurisdictional application. For example, the various trademark offices of important jurisdictions deal differently with the registrability of a descriptive term in combination with a figurative element (involving the question of determining the dominant element). Another example is whether a term in English can be descriptive of the product in eg, the German or French market.[34] For users of such AI tools, it currently means that they have to carefully review the results for these regional differences.

According to IP Australia, it is an immensely challenging task to collect the right data in the right way from different jurisdictions, as the data need to be structured in a similar way to use it for training purposes.[35] Slightly different legal requirements may already inhibit an accurate assessment by the AI tool if it is to assess similarity of signs in different jurisdictions.

Another related problem is the bias in data, and the reinforcing nature of AI technology. In the case of supervised learning, humans have classified the data. This increases the risk of bias when classifying the data, even when consciously trying to avoid that. For instance, when teaching an AI to establish a pattern of similarity of signs, one could easily ascertain a similarity between two given signs, while someone else would not. Even if case law regarding similarity of signs is used as training data, courts sometimes come to differing outcomes for the same cases. Bias in data will be replicated when used by the AI technology, as it lacks the ability to filter out slightly incorrect interpretations. However, with large amounts of data, incidental bias may not influence the rule that the AI learns from the data. This is at least the case where the vast majority of decisions follow a similar pattern.

3.2.2 Market-based data

Market-based data provides information about the preferences and purchasing behaviour of customers. In particular, it includes information about what type of consumers purchase which type of products, how consumers are attracted by certain marks when looking at shelves containing products with trademarks from competing undertakings, etc. This type of information is required in order for an AI tool to make any type of assessment related to the market. Examples are the use of a mark in the market, the relevant public, distinctiveness, reputation, detriment to distinctive character or repute, etc.

[34] Interview with Michael Rorai, Lead of IP department, Unilever, telephone, 12 June 2019.
[35] Interview with Thomas Murphy (n 9).

Privacy considerations, data protection laws, and the sensitivity of market-based data, however, seem to be key impediments for having access to such data. It seems unlikely that customers will consent to the use of their personal data for such purposes or that owners of such data will share the data with trademark offices or competitors.[36]

Also, whether an AI tool could be trained to find such information itself is doubtful. Of course, one could imagine that the training data could contain a description of the context of a case that led to a judicial decision, but such input would have to be provided by a human who studied the case facts. If a human, however, is necessary for such information to be available to an AI tool, it may reduce the usefulness of AI to perform this task in the first place. Thus, it is questionable whether it is efficient to build an AI tool to carry out such context-dependent tests, or whether those should better be left to economic data analysts and then be interpreted by humans.

3.2.3 Cooperation

The level of cooperation between IP offices at the current stage still presents an impediment for AI technology to develop at the level that it can perform complex tests. So far, IP offices are not yet or are merely at the beginning of investigating the potential of AI for trademark examination.[37] This also means that expertise on generating training data that can be shared with others is still in its infancy. However, in order to speed up the development of reliable AI technology to assist trademark examiners and judges, cooperation among offices regarding commonly structuring and eventually sharing training data seems to be needed.[38] Such cooperation requires commonly structured legal data, which is, as discussed in Section 3.2.1, not easy to generate in a multi-jurisdictional context with subtle legal differences.

Australia is by far the most advanced trademark office in terms of cooperating with other offices. IP Australia works with WIPO and its member states in Task Forces under the Committee on WIPO Standards, eg, the XML4IP Task Force, in order to standardize formats for data dissemination in a structured manner under ST.96.[39] Such standards are used at all stages of the industrial property prosecution process, in order to provide IP information in a harmonized way.[40]

In addition, IP Australia recently launched a prototype platform named IPGAIN (Intellectual Property Global Artificial Intelligence Network). IPGAIN is a simple, secure, and cloud-hosted service (Amazon Web Services) to expose, host, and

[36] Interview with Benjamin Mitra Kahn, General Manager of Policy & Chief Economist, IP Australia, skype, 10 July 2019 (hereafter Interview with Benjamin Mitra Kahn).

[37] Email correspondence with Miguel Ortega (n 19); email exchange with Amy Cotton (n 11).

[38] Acknowledged by panel 'Bringing the IP world closer together' at IP Horizon 5.0 conference in Alicante, organized by EUIPO and McCarthy Institute, 26–27 September 2019; IP Horizon 5.0 conference (n 28).

[39] Email exchange with Michael Burn (n 33).

[40] Committee on WIPO Standards (CWS), 'Proposal for JSON specification' [2019] CWS/7/5.

provide access to AI and ML tools from IP Australia and third parties, including other intellectual property offices.[41] As IPGAIN is still in its infancy, it remains to be determined how much cooperation between offices regarding the sharing and exchange of training data will be established.

3.3 Complexity and Subjectivity of Tests in Trademark Law

From the results presented in Section 2, it is obvious that the technology currently used by the assessed trademark offices is limited to image recognition, classification of goods and services, and descriptiveness analysis. They assist trademark users and examiners in carrying out very specific and rather simple tasks, such as searching for prior registered signs based on mostly visual similarity.

An important impediment for AI technology to provide reliable outcomes is the complexity and often subjectivity inherent in some trademark tests. The following legal tests have been identified as involving significant complexity and/or subjectivity: the level of distinctiveness of a mark, immoral terms, similarity of goods and services, likelihood of confusion, unfair advantage, and detriment to distinctive character and repute, including an assessment of 'without due cause'.

Before assessing those individual concepts, some general remarks can be made about complex and subjective elements in trademark law. Trademark law is about consumers, and its purpose is to avoid consumers being confused about the origin of products in the marketplace. The sign used in relation to a product, ie, the trademark, therefore should not be confusing. What is considered to be confusing, however, is determined by the overall impression the relevant public gets when seeing the mark on a product in a specific context. Many of these elements require a holistic and human-centric approach: how does a human perceive a mark?[42] This leads us to the finding that the assessment is one of degree and requires reasoning from the perspective of the relevant public.[43] It is questionable as to how far AI technology can reflect this human-centric approach.

Another general challenge lies in the relevance of the context and circumstances of the case for the assessment of various concepts. In order to assess whether eg, a consumer is confused, good knowledge is required of the market of specific products, who the relevant consumer of such products is, the right holders' competitors, the circumstances of purchase, the end use of a product, etc. These are often factual circumstances that an AI tool is unlikely to acquire from databases by itself. That information would have to be provided to the AI tool. It would equally require

[41] Email exchange with Michael Burn (n 33).

[42] Dr Ilanah Fhima, Associate Professor, University College London at conference 'AI: Decoding IP'; IP Horizon 5.0 conference (n 28).

[43] Confirmed by the panel 'Regulation & Incentives Breakout Session 1: Registered rights' at the conference 'AI: Decoding IP'; IP Horizon 5.0 conference (n 28).

sufficient information from previous case law for the AI tool to accurately compare situations and determine a likely outcome. So far, this type of classification of facts for previous judicial or administrative decision and for the situation to be assessed by the AI tool is not yet under development. It is a challenging task to (1) acquire this information (see Section 3.2.2) and (2) to structure it in such a manner that it can be automatically processed by the AI software.

3.3.1 Distinctiveness test

Determining the distinctiveness of a mark is relevant for various assessments. It is required for the registration of a mark, and for determining its reputation and the likelihood of confusion, among others. A mark can have different levels of distinctiveness, from generic or descriptive to suggestive, arbitrary, or fanciful.

An AI technology would need to be able to identify from the vast amount of data the parameters that play a role in assessing the distinctiveness of a sign. A first approach to assessing distinctiveness would be to check whether a term has a meaning in the languages understood by the consumers in the country of registration. If it does and the meaning corresponds with the type of goods registration is sought for, the sign is descriptive and therefore not distinctive. If it has no meaning that corresponds with the products, it can be considered distinctive.[44]

However, this becomes more complex when composite marks are at issue. A relevant parameter will be whether the dominant element of the mark is distinctive, while other parts of the sign could be descriptive or generic. In order to identify the dominant element in a mark, the AI tool would have to be able, from the decisions and case law it was trained on, to identify the rules for how the dominant element in a mark is identified. However, these rules are not always straightforward and depend on the relevant public that purchases this category of products, their language proficiency, etc. Such assessment requires a good knowledge of the market of such products and who the relevant consumers are. The challenges related to market-based information have been pointed out above; determining the relevant public is another complex endeavour discussed below.

3.3.2 The relevant public

The concept of the relevant public is highly relevant for the determination of distinctiveness, likelihood of confusion, and detriment to the distinctive character and repute. The case law on what constitutes the relevant public of a good or service in the EU alone is vast and relatively diverse. According to the Court of Justice of the European Union (CJEU), the relevant public can be the general public, usually an average consumer, or a specialized public, namely a professional in a certain area, such as a yoga practitioner.[45] An average consumer is reasonably well-informed,

[44] Interview with Sven Stürmann (n 25).
[45] *Prana Haus GmbH v EUIPO* [2009] CJEU C-494/08 ECR I-00210.

circumspect, and observant, but has an imperfect recollection of marks, of which (s)he only assesses the overall impression, not details. However, her/his level of attentiveness depends on the category of products. For example, the average EU consumer does not pay as much attention to food products as they do to cars.

It is difficult to imagine that an AI can be taught to assess in a case at hand who the relevant public is and what its level of attentiveness for a specific category of goods in a relevant market is, taking its imperfect recollection of signs into account. If market-based information about the consumers who purchase the product and, eg, their (foreign) language proficiency to understand the meaning of a word would be available, one can envisage that an AI tool could be of use. However, judges in the EU currently do not readily apply surveys or other statistical data when determining, eg, the level of language proficiency.[46] Such data, however, would be necessary for the AI tool to determine the relevant public. If an AI tool, hence, were to assist judges in such a determination, they may need to adapt their practice as to what type of evidence would be acceptable.

3.3.3 Similarity of goods and services

The similarity of goods or services of a trademark application with those of a prior mark is often relevant in an opposition procedure or an infringement action.

While it seems that so far, no trademark office or judges use AI tools to assist them in carrying out this assessment, IPA's tool does flag similarity of the type of goods entered by an applicant if they constitute an abbreviation of goods or services listed in the picklist (eg, the Nice classification of goods and services), or come from a similar word family.[47] This assessment is, however, used at the application phase and merely to classify goods according to the Nice classes.

Assessing what type of goods/services a sign is used for on the market (relevant in an opposition or infringement procedure) is more difficult, as it is a factual question. It is currently not feasible that an AI tool would be able to determine, on the basis of a picture of a product offered in online marketplaces, what category of good that is. From the state of technology of the trademark office tools tested, image recognition is far from recognizing a brick as such, without any additional information. The description of the product, which is also available in the online marketplace, may possibly make this assessment easier, which is nevertheless a complex exercise.

Even when knowing what the type of good at issue is, this does not yet reflect the full scope of the similarity of goods and services assessment required by EU law in opposition or infringement cases. The CJEU has clarified that several determine

[46] Interview with Gordon Humphreys, Chairperson of the Fifth Board of Appeal, and Member of the Third Board of Appeal—EUIPO, 6 June 2019, Maastricht (hereafter Interview with Gordon Humphreys).

[47] Interview with Benjamin Mitra Kahn (n 36).

the similarity of goods and services. Information about the market of the goods, their physical nature, their end use, method of use and competitive nature, the points of sale, the relevant public, and the usual origin of the goods is required and needs to be weighed and balanced.[48] Such factual information does not seem to be readily available and may be left to data analysts in the first place.[49]

3.3.4 Likelihood of confusion

While some AI tools simplify the concept of likelihood of confusion to merely relate to a high percentage of similarity of signs,[50] the legal assessment required goes beyond pure similarity of signs. A likelihood of confusion results from a situation where the signs are similar, the goods and services are similar, and the consumer is likely to believe that the products come from an undertaking other than the true undertaking. Such confusion can arise pre- or post-sale and depends on how the signs are used in the market. Mere association is not enough; the assessment of a likelihood of confusion is based on the overall impression, and in particular the most dominant features of the sign.

Whether the consumers merely associate a product with another based on similar signs and goods or whether they are confused requires a weighing of all factors involved in the case. Such weighing and balancing does not follow strict rules but is a case-by-case assessment. Because of its complex and contextual nature, weighing of all factors seems to be out of reach of AI technology for the near future.[51]

3.3.5 Unfair advantage, detriment to distinctive character and repute

So far, the developers of AI software interviewed do not yet focus on the assessments of taking unfair advantage of or causing detriment to the distinctive character or repute of a mark. Such assessment seems to be out of the scope of current and future technology. The assessments are complex, rather vague, and involve a high degree of subjectivity. It requires market-based information about a sign's use in the market and competing products. More importantly, the interpretation of those concepts has evolved with time and continues to do so. This raises the question as to whether AI will ever be able to produce 'new' and evolving applications of the law.

For unfair advantage, one needs to determine whether a third party uses a brand's selling power to launch a product and entice more consumers to purchase the product, by benefitting from a 'transfer of image' of the renowned brand to the

[48] *Canon Kabushiki Kaisha v Metro-Goldwyn-Mayer Inc.* [1998] CJEU C-39/97 ECR I-5507; *EUIPO*, Trademark Guidelines, Part C, Section 3 (2017) <https://euipo01app.sdlproducts.com/1004922/903949/trade-mark-guidelines/part-c-opposition>.

[49] See challenges listed in Section 3.2.2.

[50] Eg, Trademark Now.

[51] Interview with Evrard van Zuylen (n 29).

later mark and product.[52] The actionable behaviour lies in the fact that a third party tries to free ride on a mark's distinctive character and reputation without sharing in the efforts undertaken by the mark owner to gain such reputation. Such notions of benefitting from a transfer of image or riding on the coat tails of another mark's reputation are not particularly concrete and consistent in the CJEU's case law. It would be difficult for an AI tool to learn the assessment required.

The same is true for determining whether actual detriment has been caused. The current test by the CJEU requires a change in the economic behaviour of the relevant public, which very much entails a market analysis. Such data can of course be generated, but if a data analyst gathers this data, an AI tool may no longer be needed to interpret it.

Another highly flexible concept is that of 'without due cause'. Only when an unfair advantage is taken or a detriment is caused without due cause, is a trademark infringed. This flexibility incorporated in EU law is meant to balance the need to protect reputed marks with other fundamental rights, such as the freedom of competition and freedom of artistic and commercial expression.[53] This balancing act requires knowledge not only about previous case law where 'without due cause' has been interpreted, but also about the broader field of fundamental rights and their interpretation in the EU context. In addition, maybe the most prominent impediment is the fact that this concept has evolved over time. Depending on the facts of the case, judges tend to look for solutions in the law in order to reach the outcome they find to be just. It is through this activity that law has developed, which seems unfeasible for an AI technology to imitate.

3.4 Interim Conclusions

We have found that one of the biggest impediments for the use of AI technology in the field of trademark assessment lies in the limited availability of accurate and structured data and its exchange among trademark offices. Only with an abundant amount of relevant data will AI technology be able to produce reliable results. Legal data from various jurisdictions faces the difficulty of correctly representing subtle legal differences. Market-based data most likely needs to be collected by data analysts, which may make the need for AI technology to be used in context-dependent tests rather low.

The other difficulty of using AI technology in trademark law is in respect to the tests that are rather complex and subjective. Whether the training data will always allow for the technology to identify a clear rule or weighing of parameters is

[52] Guy Tritton, *Intellectual Property in Europe* (5th edn, Sweet & Maxwell 2018) para 3-367.

[53] *Interflora Inc. and Interflora British Unit v Marks & Spencer plc and Flowers Direct Online Ltd* [2011] CJEU C-323/09 ECR I-08625, para 91.

questionable. More importantly, concepts have evolved over time, depending on the circumstances of the case and advances in technology. It is hard to imagine that an AI could perform such evolving interpretation of the law.

4. Future Outlook

AI as a final decision-maker is not a realistic option. As IP Australia suggests, it is unlikely that there will be AI systems in the near future that outperform human teams.[54] Currently, most developers of AI tools for trademark examination agree that the gold standard is the combination of AI tools with human judgement—the synergy between machines and humans is what one should focus on.[55] Gordon Humphreys from the Fifth EUIPO Board of Appeal also emphasizes that AI is a great help to decision-makers but will not replace them.[56] The more complex decisions should be left to humans. As Bernt Boldvik from the Norwegian Trade Mark Office highlighted, from the list of similar trademarks provided by AI, it will still be humans who will select the confusingly similar trademarks.[57]

4.1 Future Tools for Substantive Assessment

Several interviewees suggested that the way forward is to identify the areas of trademark assessment most feasible to be accomplished by AI technology now and in the near future.[58] With a view to the upward trend in trademark registrations every year, examiners (and trademark attorneys) will have no other choice than to rely on technological tools that assist them in handling the amount of data that is relevant and needs to be checked. Therefore, the tasks for which AI technology is useful are those that involve the assessment of large amounts of data in a very short time frame.

Sven Stürmann from EUIPO suggests focusing the next steps on developing and training AI technology applied to databases that already exist.[59] Useful databases would be the approximately 35,000 decisions in the EUIPO of the last twenty years and some 1,000 cases from the General Court. According to him, there is much potential to make search results more effective.[60]

WIPO's database for marks resembling emblems and badges recognized by Article 6*ter* of the Paris Convention, the EU databases for geographical indications, and registered plant varieties are instances of relevant sources. Connecting

54 Interview with Benjamin Mitra Kahn (n 36).
55 Interview with Anna Ronkainen (n 27).
56 Interview with Gordon Humphreys (n 46).
57 Email exchange with Bernt Boldvik, Director Communication and Knowledge, 3 September 2019.
58 Interview with Sven Stürmann (n 25).
59 Ibid.
60 Ibid.

to those databases during the examination of absolute grounds for refusal of trademark registration seems feasible with current technologies, as applied for classifying goods or services according to the Nice classification system.[61]

Another area for AI technology is the pre-application stage. TM Assist from IPA is an educational tool that informs applicants about the chances of registering a trademark. In this way, AI technology has the potential to provide greater certainty for developers of new marks.[62] Also after having registered one's mark, right holders will find it easier to monitor potentially misleading or conflicting new registrations. Another important effect of pre-application tools is to decrease the workload of examiners by identifying flaws in the application that are easy to detect and thereby limits the incoming trademarks to those that stand a chance of being registered.

What is, however, important to point out to the users of these publicly accessible pre-application tools is that the outcome of the system is an indication and that in case of doubt, an application should be filed nevertheless. Otherwise, such a system may discourage applications of trademarks that are not easy to examine but nevertheless stand a chance of being protected if examined by an experienced examiner. The cost of foregoing possible trademark registrations that would otherwise have benefitted society by avoiding confusion among consumers should be reduced as much as possible.

Regarding the more complex tasks, the first step is to collect more data on the context of a mark's use. Partly, this could be provided by the user. But it would also require the availability of analyses of the relevant market. In addition, one would need to structure the context in relation to all previous decisions and case law in order for an AI technology to compare and predict.[63] Agreeing on a common structure for the context would be the first step in this endeavour.

Other tests may never be supported by AI. The morality test per se is very subjective and depends greatly on the culture and societal views at the time of assessment. What could be deemed immoral for one person in one culture at a certain time could easily be perceived differently by another person in the same culture and time. This assessment by a human can of course be supported by a tool that flags signs previously classified as immoral.[64] However, it does not provide a tool for terms that have not yet been assessed.

[61] Ibid.
[62] Email correspondence with Miguel Ortega (n 19).
[63] Interview with Evrard van Zuylen (n 29).
[64] IP Australia has already incorporated such a tool in TM Assist.

4.2 Future Tools for Administration

So far, the tools used in the administration of trademark applications and cases at the EUIPO Boards of Appeal mainly rely on the current state of technology. AI is well-suited to further facilitate case administration according to the legal issues raised. While very basic letters are already drafted automatically with classic software programmes, AI could be trained to draft letters to parties also in relation to costs, restrictions, or informing them about the withdrawal of a party, which would lead to the closure of the proceedings.[65]

In particular, AI would be useful to respond to requests by parties to make limitations. According to Sven Stürmann, there is a vast amount of data about limitations that have been accepted or rejected and for which reasons.[66] This previous data would lend itself to training an AI tool in assessing those parameters that are relevant to determine whether the requested limitations can be accepted or not.

5. Concluding Remarks

Ultimately, the impact of AI tools on trademark assessment will clearly be significant, even if they are unlikely to replace human assessment. This chapter has highlighted the challenges that the assessment of trademarks by AI tools presents. In particular, the determination of complex and subjective tests in trademark law is likely to be reserved for humans. But the more administrative tasks involved in trademark registration, examination, opposition, and judicial procedures are already being performed by AI tools, and are likely to become so even more. The implications for today's workforce and students being trained in this field are significant. It is one of the fundamental challenges for our society, and in particular education institutions, to address these changes and train people on how to judge and use the output created by AI technologies, and to focus on skills that are not performed well by AI tools.

[65] Interview with Gordon Humphreys (n 46).
[66] Interview with Sven Stürmann (n 25).

13

Detecting and Prosecuting IP Infringement with AI

Can the AI Genie Repulse the Forty Counterfeit Thieves of Alibaba?

*Daniel Seng**

1. Introduction

It was August 2016 and it seemed like any other ordinary day for electronic commerce. But something was amiss. Amazon was receiving thousands of negative reviews from angry customers who received defective goods, or never received what they paid for.[1] Under Amazon's customer-friendly A to Z Guarantee policy, they would be refunded,[2] but complaints about shoddy or poor quality products that shattered on first use, melted, or did not work, would translate into negative reviews and impact seller ratings.[3] Customers would blame the manufacturer or authorized distributor for this snafu instead of the resellers, causing significant loss of sales for the real thing.[4] And as manufacturers and authorized distributors combat the 'cheap fakes' to protect their brand reputations against the tide of poor reviews, their cost of doing business increases significantly. This even led established brands to pull out of the Amazon marketplace and not authorize third party merchants to sell on the website.[5] As the Birkenstock CEO David Kahan explained in a confidential memo sent to its retailer partners:

* I wish to thank my research assistant, Shaun Lim, for his invaluable assistance in reviewing and proofreading this chapter. All errors however remain mine. All online information was accessed before 10 January 2020.

[1] Wade Shepard, 'Amazon scams on the rise as fraudulent sellers run amok and profit big' (*Forbes*, 2 January 2017) <https://www.forbes.com/sites/wadeshepard/2017/01/02/amazon-scams-on-the-rise-in-2017-as-fraudulent-sellers-run-amok-and-profit-big/>.

[2] Amazon, 'Help: About A-to-Z Guarantee' <https://www.amazon.com/gp/help/customer/display.html?nodeId=200783670>.

[3] Jeff Bercovici, 'Small businesses say Amazon has a huge counterfeiting problem. This "shark tank" company is fighting back' (2019) March/April Issue, Inc., Magazine https://www.inc.com/magazine/201904/jeff-bercovici/amazon-fake-copycat-knockoff-products-small-business.html.

[4] Ibid.

[5] Ari Levy, 'Birkenstock quits Amazon in US after counterfeit surge' (*CNBC*, 20 July 2016) <https://www.cnbc.com/2016/07/20/birkenstock-quits-amazon-in-us-after-counterfeit-surge.html>.

Daniel Seng, *Detecting and Prosecuting IP Infringement with AI* In: *Artificial Intelligence and Intellectual Property*.
Edited by: Jyh-An Lee, Reto M Hilty, and Kung-Chung Liu, Oxford University Press (2021).
DOI: 10.1093/oso/9780198870944.003.0014

> The Amazon marketplace, which operates as an 'open market,' creates an environment where we experience unacceptable business practices which we believe jeopardize our brand. Policing this activity internally and in partnership with Amazon.com has proven impossible.[6]

This is not a problem unique to the Amazon platform. The Organisation for Economic Co-operation and Development (OECD) estimated that trade in counterfeit and pirated goods amounted to as much of 3.3% of world trade,[7] and noted that China, Hong Kong (China), India, the United Arab Emirates, and Singapore together exported almost 73% of fake goods traded worldwide in 2016.[8] While the OECD report acknowledged that online retail was fuelling the rapid rise in sales of fake goods, in its statistics, it did not distinguish between goods sold via traditional platforms and goods sold via digital platforms. On the other hand, the Global Brand Counterfeiting Report 2018 estimated that losses suffered due to online counterfeiting globally amounted to USD 323 billion in 2017.[9] In the US, the Customs and Border Patrol seized 31,560 shipments of IPR-infringing goods worth an estimated USD 1.38 billion, with approximately 90% of such seizures coming from interdictions of imports via express carriers and international mail.[10] As the US Government Accountability Office report pithily explained, this rise in counterfeit goods and products is made possible by the growth of e-commerce platforms and, through them, the ability of counterfeiters to gain direct access to consumers by delivery of shipments via mail packages or express carrier services.[11]

Nor is the problem limited to counterfeit goods. As consumers take to the online environment and increasingly acquire and experience copyrighted content such as music, films, series, books, and games via the Internet, this has led to decreases in the sale of copyright-protected content on physical media such as CDs, DVDs, and print books.[12] In a survey of 35,000 respondents conducted in 2017, the per capita consumption of illegal content ranges from a low of 23% in Japan and 29% in Germany to 64% in Spain, 73% in Thailand and 84% in India.[13] The annual global losses from the displacement of legal sales through these illicit channels have been

[6] David Kahan, 'Birkenstock products on the Amazon.com marketplace' (*Scribd*, 5 July 2016) <https://www.scribd.com/document/318842235/Birkenstock-Letter#from_embed>.

[7] 'Trends in trade in counterfeit and pirated goods' (*OECD*, 18 March 2019) http://www.oecd.org/gov/risk/trends-in-trade-in-counterfeit-and-pirated-goods-g2g9f533-en.htm.

[8] Ibid, Table 4.3.

[9] R Strategic Global, 'Global Brand Counterfeiting Report 2018' (*Research and Markets*, December 2017) <https://www.researchandmarkets.com/research/hzjb9c/global_brand?w=4>.

[10] US Government Accountability Office, 'Agencies Can Improve Efforts to Address Risks Posed by Changing Counterfeit Market' (GAO-18-216, January 2018) 12–14 https://www.gao.gov/assets/690/689713.pdf.

[11] Ibid.

[12] 'Global Online Piracy Study', 11 (Figure 2) (*IViR*, May 2018) <https://www.ivir.nl/publicaties/download/Global-Online-Piracy-Study.pdf> (hereafter 'Global Online Piracy Study').

[13] Ibid, 13 (Figure 5).

estimated to be around USD 37.4 billion for TV and movies,[14] around USD 12.5 billion for music piracy,[15] and around USD 300 million for ebook piracy[16] for the US economy. However, unlike counterfeit goods, much of this online piracy is driven by the activities of end users or peers, who, through the use of online intermediaries such as peer-to-peer exchanges,[17] cyberlockers,[18] and streamripping platforms,[19] illegally supply and make available copyrighted content for consumption by other end users.[20]

How does the law address the issues with the sale of counterfeit goods and the availability of pirated content in the online environment?

2. The Role of Reporting Systems

A review of the law of trademark and copyright liability, both in direct[21] as well as indirect liability,[22] shows that the primary onus is on the right holder to detect and report infringing materials online,[23] regardless of whether the infringing activity is conducted by the sellers or end users, or facilitated by intermediaries such as advertisers,[24] electronic commerce,[25] search engines,[26] or content hosting

[14] 'Online TV and movie revenue lost through piracy worldwide 2010–2022' (*Statista*, 22 January 2019) <https://www.statista.com/statistics/778338/global-online-tv-movie-revenue-loss-piracy/>.

[15] 'The true cost of sound recording piracy to the U.S. economy' (*RIAA*, 2019) <https://www.riaa.com/reports/the-true-cost-of-sound-recording-piracy-to-the-u-s-economy/> (citing a report from Stephen E Siwek, 'The True Cost of Sound Recording Piracy to the U.S. Economy' (Institute for Policy Innovation, August 2007).

[16] Adam Rowe, 'U.S. publishers are still losing $300 million annually to ebook piracy' (*Forbes*, 28 July 2019) <https://www.forbes.com/sites/adamrowe1/2019/07/28/us-publishers-are-still-losing-300-million-annually-to-ebook-piracy/>.

[17] Eg, Morpheus, Gnutella, LimeWire, eMule, and BitTorrent.

[18] Eg, Megaupload, Mega, and Rapidshare.

[19] Eg, Popcorn Time.

[20] 'Global Online Piracy Study' (n 12) 19.

[21] See Singapore Trade Marks Act, s 27(1); Singapore Copyright Act, s 26(1).

[22] See, eg, *Inwood Laboratories, Inc. v Ives Laboratories, Inc.* 456 US 844, 854, 102 S Ct 2182, 2188 (1982); *Sony Corp. of America v Universal City Studios, Inc.* 464 US 417, 439 n 19, 104 S Ct 774, 78 L Ed 2d 574 (1984) (contributory trademark infringement requires that the defendant 'intentionally induc[ed] its customers to make infringing uses' of the marks or 'suppl[ied] its products to identified individuals known by it to be engaging in continuing infringement'); Case-494/15 *Tommy Hilfiger Licensing v Delta Center a.s.* (7 July 2016) para 37 (an injunction may be addressed against a market hall for alleged intellectual property infringement when its market-traders sold counterfeits).

[23] *Hard Rock Cafe Licensing Corp. v Concession Servs., Inc.* 955 F.2d 1143, 1149 (7th Cir. 1992); 17 USC § 512(m)(1); EU Copyright Directive, Art 8; EU E-Commerce Directive, Art 15.1; Singapore Copyright Act, s 193A(3)(a).

[24] See Case C-324/09 *L'Oreal SA v eBay International AG*, para 92 and *Rosetta Stone Ltd v Google, Inc.* 676 F.3d 144 (4th Cir. 2012), both holding that the use of a third party's marks by the customer of a service provider establishes a link between the mark and the service offered by the service provider.

[25] *Tiffany (NJ) Inc. v eBay Inc.* 576 F Supp 2d 463 (hereafter *Tiffany I*), aff'd on appeal, *Tiffany (NJ) Inc. v eBay Inc.* 600 F.3d 93 (2nd Cir. 2010) (hereafter *Tiffany II*).

[26] See *Google France SARL and Google v Louis Vuitton Malletier SA.*, joined Cases C-236/08 to C-238/08, paras 51 and 52 ('With regard, firstly, to the advertiser purchasing the referencing service and choosing as a keyword a sign identical with another's trade mark, it must be held that that advertiser is using that sign within the meaning of that case-law') (hereafter *Google France*).

platforms.[27] For copyright infringement, the US Digital Millennium Copyright Act (DMCA) safe harbours enshrine the takedown obligation in legislation and also prescribe the contents of a takedown notice and steps for managing the takedown notice. Although it had a quiet start,[28] research has shown that since 2011, content providers have relied greatly on it to manage the growing issue of online piracy, and manage it effectively.[29] Starting with hundreds of takedown notices each year, today, millions of takedown notices are sent each *day* to all types of network services providers, especially content hosting companies and information aggregators, by individual right holders, industry groups, and trade organizations and their agents—known as reporters.[30] In particular, the music industry, represented by the British Phonographic Industry (BPI), the International Federation of the Phonographic Industry (IFPI), and the Recording Industry Association of America (RIAA) has been the largest and most prolific user of takedown notices, ahead of the adult entertainment industry, movie studios, software and games developers, and book publishers.[31]

While the reporting system in copyright law is prescribed by legislation, the reporting system in trademark law started as an organic and endogenous effort between the right holders and the intermediaries. In the absence of legislative sanction, this has led right holders to complain that they are required to police the '[online platform or intermediary's] website—and many others like it—"24 hours a day, and 365 days a year," … a burden that most mark holders cannot afford to bear'.[32] However, the 2nd Circuit in *Tiffany II* disagreed, noting that placing the burden on the intermediary is inappropriate. Citing extensively from the District Court, the 2nd Circuit said:[33]

> Because eBay 'never saw or inspected the merchandise in the listings,' its ability to determine whether a particular listing was for counterfeit goods was limited … Even had it been able to inspect the goods, moreover, in many instances it likely would not have had the expertise to determine whether they were counterfeit … '[I]n many instances, determining whether an item is counterfeit

[27] See, eg, *RecordTV Pte Ltd v MediaCorp TV Singapore Pte Ltd* [2010] SGCA 43, [2011] 1 SLR 830.

[28] See, eg, Jennifer Urban and Laura Quilter, 'Efficient Process or "Chilling Effects"? Takedown Notices under Section 512 of the Digital Millennium Copyright Act' (2006) 22 Santa Clara Computer and High Technology Law Journal 621.

[29] See Daniel Seng, 'The State of the Discordant Union, An Empirical Analysis of DMCA Takedown Notices' (2014) 18 Virginia Journal of Law and Technology 369 http://ssrn.com/abstract=2411915 (hereafter Seng, 'The State of the Discordant Union').

[30] Ibid, 380–1. See also generally Daniel Seng, 'Trust but verify—an empirical analysis of errors in takedown notices' (2015) https://papers.ssrn.com/sol3/papers.cfm?abstract_id=2563202 (hereafter Seng, 'Trust but verify').

[31] Ibid, 385.

[32] *Tiffany II* (n 25) 109.

[33] Ibid, 98.

will require a physical inspection of the item, and some degree of expertise on the part of the examiner'.

But this responsibility to remove infringing listings or content is neither passive nor is it to be executed in isolation. Reminiscent of the four modalities argument made by Lessig in his seminal thesis,[34] the 2nd Circuit in *Tiffany II* also opined that private market forces will give bona fide intermediaries operating as businesses a strong incentive to minimize counterfeit goods sold on their websites, as they do not wish to alienate their end users.[35] A similar argument has been made in relation to intermediaries hosting or enabling access to copyrighted content.[36] As such, at common law, the burden remains largely on the right holders to detect and report the infringements, which serves as the trigger for accreting to the intermediaries the requisite knowledge that may expose them to indirect trademark or copyright liability if they fail to act on the complaints. This approach has since seen legislative support in the EU E-Commerce Directive, by way of the requirement that the 'information society service' provider has to act expeditiously to remove or disable access to the allegedly infringing listing to preserve his immunity.[37] It has also received sanction in the PRC E-Commerce Law, which gives the intellectual property right holder who 'believes that its intellectual property right has been infringed' the *right* to send a takedown notice to the e-commerce platform to 'delete or block the relevant information, disable relevant links and terminate transactions and services'.[38] It further subjects the intermediary who fails to take the aforesaid measures 'in time' to joint liability with the allegedly infringing sellers for 'the increased part of the damage'.[39]

The corollary therefore is for intermediaries to develop adequate reporting systems to enable right holders to report their trademark or copyright complaints to the intermediaries that will enable the intermediaries to accurately and reliably receive, track, and act on the complaints expeditiously.

Most established online marketplaces have some form of complaint system that enables legitimate sellers or customers to raise issues or concerns about counterfeit goods or illicit copyrighted content with the marketplace operator. Alibaba and Taobao have their Intellectual Property Protection system (IPP),

[34] Lawrence Lessig, *Code version 2.0* (Basic Books 2006) 80, available in pdf at <http://codev2.cc/download+remix/Lessig-Codev2.pdf>.

[35] *Tiffany II* (n 25) 109.

[36] See *Columbia Pictures Industries, Inc. v Fung* 2009 WL 6355911 (C D Cal 2009); *RecordTV Pte Ltd v MediaCorp TV Singapore Pte Ltd* [2009] SGHC 287 at [91]. But see *Columbia Pictures Industries, Inc. v Fung* 710 F.3d 1020, 1039, 1043 (9th Cir. 2013) (inducing infringement also constitutes 'red flag' knowledge of infringement).

[37] EU E-Commerce Directive, Art 14.

[38] PRC E-Commerce Law, Art 42(1).

[39] Ibid, Art 42(2).

which was previously known as AliProtect.[40] eBay has an anti-counterfeit program known as VeRO (Verified Rights Owner), which was launched in 1998.[41] Even Amazon, which is well-regarded for its customer-centric support services, has its Amazon Report Infringement system.[42] What all these systems have in common is a mechanism to allow owners of intellectual property rights and their authorized representatives to report alleged infringements of their intellectual property on various listings and products on the marketplaces.[43] These are typically instances of trademark infringements because the listed products are illicit counterfeits, or because the listings involved brand name or trademark misuse, or contain misrepresentations regarding an item's warranty.[44] They could also be instances of the sale of unauthorized copies of media, software, movies, or paintings, or involve the illicit use of copyrighted images or text in the listings.[45] And there could be instances of design rights infringement or patent rights infringement.[46] Upon validating the reports,[47] the marketplace operators would typically remove the listings as soon as possible, typically within twenty-four hours (for eBay,[48] Amazon,[49] and Alibaba[50]), and the seller would be sent information about why the listing was taken down and be provided with contact information of the rights owner or right holder.[51]

Another solution adopted by many large manufacturers is called 'brand gating'. For products which are known to have a high risk of counterfeiting, large manufacturers may force e-commerce sites such as Amazon to grant them the power to approve third-party sellers of their products.[52] Unfortunately, such an option

[40] Alibaba Group, 'IP Protection ("IPP") Platform Enhancement—Important Guidelines' (7 December 2018) <https://ipp.alibabagroup.com/infoContent.htm?skyWindowUrl=ippSystemUpdate-en>.

[41] eBay, 'Verified Rights Owner Program' <https://pages.ebay.com/seller-center/listing-and-marketing/verified-rights-owner-program.html>. As of 2009, about 31,000 right holders are participants. See Cyndy Aleo-Carreira, '2 million counterfeit items removed from eBay' (*PCWorld*, 24 March 2009) <https://www.pcworld.com/article/161848/ebay_counterfeit.html>. See also *Tiffany I* (n 25) 478 (describing the VeRO program).

[42] Amazon, 'Report infringement' <https://www.amazon.com/report/infringement>.

[43] See, eg, *Tiffany I* (n 25) 478.

[44] See n 41.

[45] Ibid.

[46] Ibid.

[47] *Tiffany I* (n 25), noting that eBay would first verify that the report contained all of the required information and had indicia of accuracy.

[48] Ibid, noting the practice to remove reported listings within twenty-four hours, and that ¾ of listings were removed within four hours of the making of reports.

[49] *Tre Milano, LLC v Amazon.com, Inc.* 2012 WL 3594380, 13* (2nd Dist. CA), at *2 (hereafter *Tre Milano*).

[50] Alibaba Group, '2018 IPR Protection Annual Report 4' (11 June 2019) <https://ipp.alibabagroup.com/infoContent.htm?skyWindowUrl=news-20190625-en> (hereafter Alibaba Group, '2018 IPR Protection Annual Report 4').

[51] See n 41.

[52] Jeff Bercovici, 'Small businesses say Amazon has a huge counterfeiting problem. This "shark tank" company is fighting back' (*Inc.*, April 2019) <https://www.inc.com/magazine/201904/

is not typically available to all legitimate sellers, only those with sufficient market power such as Nike.[53] And Amazon has also not publicly detailed the criteria it uses for gating brands, which puts small time sellers at a disadvantage.[54]

These solutions have had an impact. Although eBay has not published detailed reports on its actions, an eBay spokesperson disclosed that eBay removed 2.1 million listings based on VeRO reports, and suspended 30,000 sellers in 2008.[55] Considering that eBay saw about 2.7 billion live listings globally during that time,[56] this is not an insignificant number.

Similarly, between 2010 and 2012, Amazon has blocked about 5,900 sellers a year whom it suspected of infringing conduct, and in 2011, cancelled over 4 million seller listings.[57] About 75% of such sellers were identified by Amazon itself, with the remainder identified after Amazon received a 'notice of claimed infringement', a DMCA notice or a customer complaint.

However, these were obviously not enough in Amazon's case. Amazon's counterfeit reporting system relied on legitimate sellers themselves making test purchases of the counterfeiter's products to confirm their inauthenticity, and then forwarding both items as physical evidence to Amazon.[58] But legitimate sellers still do not have information about the identity of the counterfeiters to pursue an enforcement action, as Amazon would not share this information with sellers.[59] This could also be an ultimately futile process, as illegitimate sellers who found their listings being purged could quickly set up new accounts and relist the same items,[60] as Nike recently discovered.[61]

The problem of counterfeits was growing, and the reliance on reporting systems did not scale well or work quickly enough. A new solution was required—an automated solution.

jeff-bercovici/amazon-fake-copycat-knockoff-products-small-business.html> (hereafter Bercovici, 'Small businesses say Amazon has a huge counterfeiting problem').

[53] Jeff Bercovici, 'Amazon's counterfeit crackdown: what it really means' (*Inc.*, 28 February 2019) https://www.inc.com/jeff-bercovici/amazon-project-zero.html (hereafter Bercovici, 'Amazon's counterfeit crackdown').

[54] Ibid. See also Bercovici, 'Small businesses say Amazon has a huge counterfeiting problem' (n 52).

[55] Cyndy Aleo-Carreira, '2 million counterfeit items removed from eBay' (*PCWorld*, 24 March 2009) https://www.pcworld.com/article/161848/ebay_counterfeit.html (Aleo-Carreira, '2 million counterfeit items removed from eBay').

[56] Ibid.

[57] *Tre Milano* (n 49) *2.

[58] Ibid, 23.

[59] Bercovici, 'Small businesses say Amazon has a huge counterfeiting problem' (n 52).

[60] Sarah Young, 'Nike to stop selling shoes and clothing on Amazon' (*The Independent*, 14 November 2019) https://www.independent.co.uk/life-style/nike-amazon-stop-selling-clothes-trainers-a9202561.html.

[61] Ibid.

3. The Rise of the Machines

3.1 Automated Detection Systems for Counterfeits

The solution which Amazon came up with is called Project Zero, and it has three key components: a product serialization requirement,[62] a self-service counterfeit removal service, and an automated protection system.

The product serialization component requires enrolled brands to apply a unique code to every unit for an enrolled product. This allows Amazon to scan and confirm the authenticity of each product sold.[63] Product serialization is not free: the codes have a per-unit cost based on volume.[64] Nor is it a new concept: it has been mandatory for drugs and many types of foods, to provide supply and distribution chain control and verification, and enable authentication and monitoring for quality control and traceability purposes. What is novel is that the same techniques for ensuring food and drug safety are now being deployed to combat counterfeits.

The self-service counterfeit removal service is an extension of the existing reporting system. Instead of having right holders submit a complaint, which is then investigated before being acted on, enrolled brands are themselves allowed to remove counterfeit listings from Amazon stores, rather than waiting for Amazon to do so.[65] However, not all right holders are entitled to this pilot service, as Project Zero is currently only available by way of invitation from Amazon, with brand owners having to apply to be added to the waitlist. As such, it will be unable to protect many legitimate sellers.

Arguably the most novel component of Project Zero is its automated protection system. This uses machine learning systems to continuously scan Amazon stores and proactively remove suspected counterfeits.[66] To do this, enrolled brands will provide key data points about themselves—such as their trademarks and logos, product descriptions, and other materials—to establish an authoritative record

[62] Andre Pino, 'Product serialization: the key to protecting your supply chain—and your brand' (*Serrala*, 2 January 2009) <https://sapinsider.wispubs.com/Assets/Articles/2009/January/Product-Serialization-The-Key-To-Protecting-Your-Supply-Chain-And-Your-Brand>. The product serialization requirement is a separate programme from Amazon's existing Transparency Programme. See Amazon, 'Transparency: helping prevent counterfeit & verify authenticity' <https://brandservices.amazon.com/transparency>; Chaim Gartenberg, 'Amazon's Project Zero will let brands remove counterfeit listings of their products' (*The Verge*, 28 February 2019) <https://www.theverge.com/2019/2/28/18244603/amazon-project-zero-counterfeit-listing-remove-products> (hereafter Gartenberg, 'Amazon's Project Zero').

[63] Amazon, 'Project Zero: empowering brands against counterfeits' <https://brandservices.amazon.com/projectzero> (hereafter Amazon, 'Project Zero').

[64] See Bercovici, 'Amazon's counterfeit crackdown' (n 53); Alibaba Group, '2018 IPR Protection Annual Report 4' (n 50) 15–16 (describing Alibaba's management of malicious notice and takedown submissions by IP trolls).

[65] Bercovici, 'Amazon's counterfeit crackdown' (n 53).

[66] Ibid.

against which infringements can be tracked.[67] Automated systems will scan over 5 billion daily listings to look for suspected counterfeits.[68] In addition, based on how enrolled brands themselves remove suspected counterfeits, the machine learning algorithm will identify the characteristics of counterfeit listings and 'use this data to strengthen our automated protections to better catch potential counterfeit listings proactively in the future'.[69] Some of these characteristics, which have been identified by the Amazon sellers' community, include changes in crucial seller information such as contact details, physical addresses, bank accounts, and IP addresses.[70]

Alibaba appears to have implemented an impressive, state-of-the-art automated protection system as well. Calling it 'effective proactive monitoring efforts', Alibaba describes it as built upon technology to proactively identify and remove potentially problematic listings. It uses 'product intelligence, image and semantic recognition algorithms, real-time monitoring and interception, bio-identification, and algorithms to detect abnormal merchant behaviour'.[71] In 2018, it added three new features to determine leads for further investigation: analysis of negative emotions and semantics of user comments and feedback, searches for anomalous traffic data and unusual transactions, and recognition algorithms to control and monitor the sellers' live broadcasting of product demonstrations and information for counterfeiting activity.[72] Based on these technologies, Alibaba touted that '96% of Alibaba's proactive removals in 2018 occurred before a single sale took place, protecting consumers and brand owners alike'.[73]

To be clear, the use of algorithms to scan listings for issues is not per se novel. eBay has had its own 'Fraud Engine' since 2002, which uses rules and complex models that automatically search for activity that violates eBay policies, including illegal and counterfeit listings, blatant disclaimers of genuineness, or statements that the seller could not guarantee the authenticity of the items.[74] It has been documented that the Fraud Engine uses more than 13,000 different search rules, 'and was designed in part to capture listings that contain indicia of counterfeiting apparent on the face of the listings without requiring expertise in rights owners' brands or products'.[75] Listings that offered 'knock-off', 'counterfeit', 'replica', or 'pirated' items were flagged as instances of potentially infringing or otherwise problematic activity.[76] Although the engine could not determine whether a listed item

[67] Bercovici, 'Small businesses say Amazon has a huge counterfeiting problem' (n 52). This is also referred to as a Brand Registry.

[68] Amazon, 'Project Zero' (n 63).

[69] Ibid.

[70] Talya Friedman, '3 tips for complying with Amazon's antifraud measures' (*Payoneer Blog*, 17 July 2017) <https://blog.payoneer.com/e-sellers/marketplaces/amazon-anti-fraud-measures/>.

[71] Alibaba Group, '2018 IPR Protection Annual Report 4' (n 50) 9.

[72] Ibid, 9–10.

[73] Ibid, 5.

[74] *Tiffany I* (n 25) 477.

[75] Ibid.

[76] Ibid.

was actually counterfeit, it would combine that listing with other information, such as the seller's Internet protocol address, issues and history associated with the seller's eBay account, feedback and ratings received from other eBay users and past buyers, the language and sophistication of the listing, the seller's business model and its eBay registration information,[77] and send it to eBay's approximately 2,000 customer service representatives for review and possible further action. These customer service representatives who could remove the listing, send a warning to the seller, place restrictions on the seller's account, or refer the matter to law enforcement, based on eBay's standards and guidelines. eBay removes 'thousands of listings per month' via this process,[78] which is a sizeable number compared to the 2.1 million listings that it removed based on VeRO reports in 2008.[79]

The use of automated or semi-automated detection systems for illicit items on electronic marketplaces is genuinely impressive, and should be encouraged as complements to efforts by right holders. However, it is important to note that eBay itself concedes that its ultimate ability to make infringement determinations is limited because eBay never saw or inspected the merchandise in the listings.[80] The possible consequences from this limitation will be explored in the next section.

3.2 Automated Takedown Systems for Content Providers

In many respects, the takedown mechanism for online merchants to manage counterfeit products bears similarities to, and appears to be inspired by, the DMCA notice and takedown mechanism.[81] Nonetheless, there are substantial differences between the counterfeit detection systems and detection systems for online copyright piracy.

First, as noted above, the DMCA mechanism mandates that a reporting system be set up by the intermediary to allow right holders to report for copyright infringement. In addition to spelling out the procedural requirements and processes for managing takedown notices,[82] the DMCA also requires the intermediary to designate a registered agent to receive infringement notices as a prerequisite to the DMCA safe harbours.[83] The identity of the registered agent together with its contact details must be made publicly available by the Intermediary, and provided to the copyright office.[84] Having a reporting mechanism therefore justifies the intermediary's reliance on the safe harbour defences.

[77] Ibid.
[78] Ibid.
[79] Aleo-Carreira, '2 Million Counterfeit Items Removed From EBay' (n 55).
[80] *Tiffany I* (n 25) 478.
[81] See, eg, *Tiffany II* (n 25) 99 (describing eBay's VeRO Program as a 'notice-and-takedown' system).
[82] Seng, 'The State of the Discordant Union' (n 29) 379.
[83] 17 USC § 512(c)(2); Copyright (Network Service Provider) Regulations, Reg. 5.
[84] Ibid.

Secondly, just as there is a designated agent for the intermediary, the DMCA explicitly enables a designated agent of the right holder to report the infringing work or activity to the intermediary.[85] This designated agent may be the right holder's own representative such as its attorney, its copyright licensee or its industry representative. These may even be specialist third-party vendors who were contracted to help the right holders in their anti-piracy efforts. Described as an 'undeniable trend', since 2011, these 'reporting agents' have dominated the DMCA takedown scene. In 2008, reporting agents accounted for only 36.8% of all takedown notices served. By 2012, this number rose to 59.6%.[86] Of the top thirty reporting agents by volume of notices identified in the 2014 study, twenty-one are reporting agents that are not industry or trade representatives.[87]

Thirdly, because reporting agents are allowed to *file* takedown notices on behalf of right holders, it is only a small step to also enable reporting agents to *detect* instances of online infringement on behalf of the same right holders. Since the advent of the Internet, right holders have always used a variety of semi-automated, automated, and intelligent systems to detect instances of infringement to police the online environment. These typically involve one or more of the following methods:

- Sampling: The agent randomly samples the files of their users on the targeted online resource and conducts a detailed examination of the random sample to identify which of the files were copyrighted works, and ascertain how many of them were reproduced or distributed without authorization.[88] Typically, the agent downloads the file to verify that the file was not authorized. Based on the sampling, general conclusions such as the percentage of unauthorized files are made about the targeted resource.[89]
- Searches: The agent accesses the targeted website and searches it for infringing content, which is then flagged for removal.[90] It may also search for linking sites (sites that link to content on the targeted site),[91] especially where the targeted site itself has no search feature that allows users to locate files.[92] These searches are typically effected via keyword searches based on the names of the

[85] 17 USC § 512(c)(3)(A)(i) ('a person authorized to act on behalf of the owner of an exclusive right that is allegedly infringed'); Singapore Copyright Act, ss 193C(2)(b)(i), 193D(2)(b)(iii)(A), (4)(b)(iii)(A).

[86] Seng, 'The State of the Discordant Union (n 29) 388.

[87] Ibid, 387.

[88] See, eg, *A&M Records v Napster*, 114 F Supp 2d 896, 902 (N D Ca 2000).

[89] See, eg, Tobias Lauinger and others, 'Clickonomics: Determining the Effect of Anti-Piracy Measures for One-Click Hosting' (2013) Proceedings of NDSS Symposium 2013 (conducting a random sample on 'release blogs' that provided links to files shared on cyberlockers sites; though also noting that many files were incorrectly categorized or password-protected, which the researchers could not open and verify).

[90] See, eg, *Disney Enterprises, Inc. v Hotfile Corp* [2013] WL 6336286 (SD Fla, 2013) *14–*15 (hereafter *Disney v Hotfile*).

[91] Ibid, *15.

[92] Ibid, *28.

files, titles of the works, and their authors/artists, variations thereof,[93] as well as categories or classifications of the files in question.[94] This appears to be the predominant method used by reporting agents to identify infringing content.

- Digital fingerprinting: Fingerprinting technology enables a file to be identified by analysing its file contents rather than by meta data about the file such as its filename, title, or artist/author.[95] This non-text based technology is not vulnerable to textual variations in the filenames (as well as other meta data).[96] An example of such a technology that is being deployed on a large scale by an Internet intermediary to police its platform is ContentID, developed and used by YouTube for audio and video content.[97] For such a system to work, the right holder has to first register its content for fingerprinting. This information is stored in a database. When any video is uploaded, it is checked against this database, and flagged as a copyright violation if a match is found.[98]
- Real-time detection: Using the ability of the platform, typically a file sharing system built on peer-to-peer technologies, to share files with others, the agents develop tools that track and record the instances of specific copyrighted files[99] that are being uploaded and the IP addresses of those who download the files in real-time.[100] (In BitTorrent parlance, the original file sharer and those who have the complete file and are sharing it are the 'seeds' and those who are downloading the files are the 'peers'.)[101] The IP addresses are then translated into actual identities of subscribers and their contact information, pursuant to a court order for pre-action discovery[102] or statutory request[103] directed at the relevant Internet Service Provider.[104]

Combining automated detection mechanisms with automated reporting and enforcement mechanisms means that copyright enforcement actions can be pursued on a large scale against various infringers. For instance, after

[93] *A&M Records, Inc. v Napster, Inc.* [2001] WL 227083 (N D Ca 2001).
[94] See, eg, 'Technical report—an estimate of infringing use of the Internet 3' (*Envisional*, January 2011) <http://documents.envisional.com/docs/Envisional-Internet_Usage-Jan2011.pdf> (evaluating 10,000 most popular content managed by torrents, and concluding that 63.7% of non-pornographic BitTorrent content was copyrighted and shared illegitimately).
[95] See, eg, *A&M Records, Inc. v Napster, Inc.*, 284 F 3d 1091, 1097–8 (9th Cir. 2002).
[96] Ibid.
[97] 'Content ID (system)' (*Wikipedia*) https://en.wikipedia.org/wiki/Content_ID_(system) .
[98] Ibid.
[99] The specific copyrighted files can be identified by their filenames, torrent files, or hash values. See *Roadshow Films Pty Ltd v iiNet Ltd* [2012] HCA 16, [29].
[100] See, eg, *Odex Pte Ltd v Pacific Internet Ltd* [2008] SGHC 35, [4];*Roadshow Films Pty Ltd v iiNet Ltd* [2012] HCA 16, [28]–[29]; and *Dallas Buyers Club LLC v iiNet Limited* [2015] FCA 317, [8], [25]–[27].
[101] *Wikipedia*, 'Glossary of BitTorrent terms' <https://en.wikipedia.org/wiki/Glossary_of_BitTorrent_terms>.
[102] See, eg, *Odex Pte Ltd v Pacific Internet Ltd* [2008] SGHC 35.
[103] See, eg, 17 USC § 512(h).
[104] See, eg, *Recording Industry Ass'n of America, Inc. v Verizon Internet Services, Inc.* 351 F.3d 1229 (DCCA 2003).

Napster, the recording and motion pictures industries commenced large scale actions against end users, in an effort to stem the flood of illicit file sharing on peer-to-peer platforms.[105] It has been estimated that as of July 2006, the RIAA has sued over 20,000 people for file sharing,[106] but this has been largely abandoned since 2008.[107]

Instead, attention is now focused on the intermediaries—content hosts, cyberlockers, streaming sites, and information location aggregators—for possible indirect copyright liability for facilitating infringements. Combining the detection of online infringement with automated mechanisms for reporting infringements have led to an explosion of activity. These so-called 'robo-takedowns'[108] have been responsible for an exponential increase in the number of takedown notices issued across the years, from 125,000 in 2011 to 1.31 million in 2015, which represents a year-on-year increase of 79.8% in notices *each year*.[109] Using the number of takedown requests within each takedown notice as a proxy for enforcement action, the data show that the number of online resources targeted for takedown has more than *doubled* each year.[110] If there are around 50 billion individually indexed web pages in the world in 2015, this works out to the fact that in 2015, 565 million or at least 1.13% of web pages worldwide are alleged to contain unlicensed online resources,[111] an extraordinary statistic that represents the sheer scale and intensity of the largely automated enforcement action on the Internet.

4. Issues with Enforcement in the Online Environment

When presented with these statistics, it would appear that machine-driven enforcement is the solution to the management and control of large scale online trademark and copyright piracy. However, lest it be thought that automation is the cure to all online issues, it is suggested that a more circumspect view of both the promises and limitations of automated enforcement should be adopted.

[105] 'RIAA v. The People: four years later' (*EFF*, August 2007) <https://www.eff.org/files/filenode/riaa_at_four.pdf>.

[106] 'How to not get sued for file sharing' (*EFF*, 1 July 2006) <https://www.eff.org/wp/how-not-get-sued-file-sharing>.

[107] Sarah McBride and Ethan Smith, 'Music industry to abandon mass suits' (*Wall Street Journal*, 19 December 2008) <https://www.wsj.com/articles/SB122966038836021137>.

[108] See US Copyright Office, 'Section 512 Study: Notice and Request for Public Comment' 80 FR 251 at 81862 (31 December 2015) <https://www.copyright.gov/fedreg/2015/80fr81862.pdf> (hereinafter 'Section 512 Study'); *Disney Enterprises, Inc. v Hotfile Corp.* 2013 WL 6336286 (SD Fla, 2013).

[109] See Seng, 'Trust But Verify' (n 30).

[110] Ibid.

[111] Ibid.

4.1 Collaboration, Coordination, and Oversight

Distilled into its essence, the reason why the problem of online counterfeits has been so intractable is because counterfeiters thrive by exploiting trust. The reputation of the online platform and its ratings system have largely replaced the traditional forms of trust from dealings with physical platforms and known traders. This makes the standing of the intermediary[112] and the indication of origin and quality of the product as guaranteed by its brand[113] even more important. Public education by way of media outreach efforts to remind consumers about the dangers of purchasing counterfeit products[114] is helpful but is limited in its utility. Simply put, there will always be a psychological gap between the customer's moral values and desire to save money,[115] as well as the limitations of how he can verify that the product is what he wants, especially in a fast-changing market.[116] Therein lies the utility of the trademark as a guarantee of quality, the reputation of the intermediary as a guarantee of trustworthiness, and the importance of strong anti-counterfeiting laws and public education in their totality.

It is thus surprising that although it is in the common interests of both right holders and bona fide intermediaries to cooperate to better understand and manage this issue, until recently, this level of cooperation has been minimal. The problem of counterfeits and fake goods can only be solved with greater transparency and cooperation between right holders, intermediaries, and public institutions, and not less. In this regard, Alibaba's recently constituted Anti-Counterfeiting Alliance (AACA), a collaboration between Alibaba and right holders on new online enforcement practices, offline investigations such as conducting investigation purchases from suspect sellers, litigation strategies and tactics, and IPR-protection efforts, is to be lauded.[117] Among the information exchanged is knowledge about counterfeit-detection techniques, which Alibaba has incorporated into its

[112] See Amazon.com, Inc., 'Form 10-K: Annual Report Pursuant to Section 13 or 15(d) of the Securities Exchange Act of 1934' (For the fiscal year ended December 31, 2018) at 14, <https://www.sec.gov/Archives/edgar/data/1018724/000101872419000004/amzn-20181231x10k.htm>; Bercovici, 'Amazon's Counterfeit Crackdown' (n 53).

[113] See Case C-487/07 *L'Oreal and Others v Bellure NV* [2009] ECR I.0000, para 58 (trademarks not only guarantee to consumers the origin of the goods or services, but also *inter alia* the quality of the goods or services in question and those of communication, investment, or advertising). See, eg, Ari Levy, 'Amazon's Chinese counterfeit problem is getting worse' (*CNBC*, 8 July 2016) <https://www.cnbc.com/2016/07/08/amazons-chinese-counterfeit-problem-is-getting-worse.html> ('"As long as the logo looks legit, people assume you have that item," said a Canada Goose seller').

[114] Alibaba Group, '2018 IPR Protection Annual Report 4' (n 50) 19; *The Counterfeit Report*, 'Counterfeit products alert' <http://www.thecounterfeitreport.com/>.

[115] See, eg, Gene Grossman and Carl Shapiro, 'Counterfeit-product Trade' (1988) 78 American Economic Review 59; Ryan Williams, '5 personality traits that make people buy counterfeits' (*Red Points*, 23 October 2018) <https://blog.redpoints.com/en/5-personality-traits-that-make-people-buy-counterfeits>.

[116] Williams, '5 personality traits that make people buy counterfeits' (n 115) (distinguishing between 'non-deceptive' counterfeits and 'deceptive' counterfeits).

[117] Alibaba Group, '2018 IPR Protection Annual Report 4' (n 50) 17–19.

automated detection systems.[118] In turn, Alibaba has 'provided timely feedback to brand members about the effectiveness of Alibaba's proactive-monitoring controls'.[119] It is this feedback that is essential to enable both right holders and intermediaries to stay ahead of counterfeiters. Of course, this arrangement itself entails building a high level of trust between the right holders and intermediaries to coordinate their efforts. In this regard, it could be argued that the relatively open-textured nature of indirect trademark liability as observed above has actually contributed (indirectly) to fostering this coordination and cooperation between the right holders and intermediaries.

While the relationship between copyright content providers and Internet intermediaries has been largely antagonistic, a similar level of coordination and cooperation has arisen in the context of policing online piracy on YouTube. By empowering right holders who have registered their content via the Content ID digital fingerprinting system to block the whole uploaded video from being viewed, track its viewership statistics or monetize the video by running advertisements against it, and even opting to share revenue with the uploader,[120] Content ID affords right holders the intermediate option of opting-in or tolerating the use of its copyrighted content,[121] an option not otherwise available in law. In consequence, this has been described as a 'DMCA Plus' system because it extends the statutory ambit of the DMCA.[122]

While the aforesaid voluntary arrangements help to narrow the gap between the problem of infringement and the interests of the parties, these arrangements deserve a higher level of legal scrutiny. There could be concerns about whether these arrangements exclude the participation of other stakeholders such as consumers, end users, and other website operators.[123] There could also be concerns about the discriminatory nature of these arrangements, especially where only certain right holders will qualify for these reporting arrangements,[124] or where right holders and intermediaries enter into side agreements to exclude items such as second-hand goods or certain types of copyright content from their trademark or copyright review.

These arrangements could also have potential anti-competitive effects,[125] where intermediaries or IP owners use their market power to cooperate to the detriment of smaller competing intermediaries or IP owners, in the form of

[118] Ibid, 19.

[119] Ibid.

[120] Google, 'How Content ID works' <https://support.google.com/youtube/answer/2797370?hl=en>.

[121] Tim Wu, 'Tolerated Use' (2008) 31 Columbia Journal of Law & the Arts 617 available at <https://ssrn.com/abstract=1132247> or <http://dx.doi.org/10.2139/ssrn.1132247>.

[122] Annemarie Bridy, 'Copyrights Digital Deputies—DMCA-Plus Enforcement by Internet Intermediaries' in John A Rothchild (ed), *Research Handbook on Electronic Commerce Law* (2016) at https://osf.io/grzeu/download/?format=pdf.

[123] Ibid.

[124] *Google*, 'Qualifying for Content ID' <https://support.google.com/youtube/answer/1311402>.

[125] John Schoppert, 'The need to regulate DMCA-Plus agreements: an expansion of Sag's Internet safe harbors and the transformation of copyright law' <https://siliconflatirons.org/wp-content/uploads/2018/10/The-Need-to-Regulate-DMCA-Plus-Agreements-An-Expansion-of-Sags-Intern....pdf>.

agreements, decisions, or practices that have as their object or effect the appreciable prevention, restriction, or distortion of competition.[126] For instance, arrangements by intermediaries that grant only certain owners access to the reporting system but not others would arguably be applying dissimilar conditions to equivalent transactions with other owners, thereby placing them at a competitive disadvantage.[127] The active intercession of the competition regulator may be critical to ensure that there remains a level playing field between all stakeholders in the electronic commerce and digital content distribution industries. This could, eg, be achieved by declaring the detection technologies and arrangements developed jointly by the right holders and the intermediaries as 'essential facilities'.[128] Under the 'essential facilities' doctrine, if it becomes, among others, 'uneconomical for anyone to develop another facility to provide the [detection] service',[129] third parties will be able to have access to, and benefit from, the same detection technologies as the original right holders and lead intermediaries, while ensuring that there is an equitable compensation provided to the developers of these technologies.

4.2 Transparency and Explainability

One of the most frequent complaints of trademark takedowns is that sellers have no clear rights to appeal their listings removal or their suspension from sales. Additionally, there is no clear mechanism for these aggrieved sellers to seek redress against the right holders or, as is more frequently the case, the platform intermediaries. Even when contacted, intermediaries may defer to the complaining right

[126] Singapore Competition Act (Cap. 50B, 2006 Rev. Ed.) s 34(1). These reporting arrangements are not arrangements which relate to the conditions under which the seller and the intermediary may 'purchase, sell or resell certain products' because the intermediary's role is not to be directly involved in the purchase or sale of the products, and thus would not fall within the exclusion under para 8 of the Third Schedule, Competition Act, as an excluded vertical agreement. See Competition and Consumer Commission of Singapore (hereinafter 'CCCS') Guidelines on the Treatment of Intellectual Property Rights in Competition Cases 2016, paras 3.10–3.12.

[127] Singapore Competition Act (Cap. 50B, 2006 Rev. Ed.) s 34(2)(d).

[128] While there has yet to be a decision on the essential facilities doctrine in Singapore, reference was made to it in the CCCS Guidelines on the Section 47 Prohibitions 2016, para 10.14, <https://www.cccs.gov.sg/-/media/custom/ccs/files/legislation/legislation-at-a-glance/cccs-guidelines/cccs-guidelines-on-the-section-47-prohibitions-2016.pdf> ('There will be circumstances in which difficulties accessing inputs or resources constitute an entry barrier without those assets or resources meeting the strict criteria required to be defined as "essential facilities"'). For a general discussion of the tensions inherent in promoting innovation and the essential facilities doctrine in other jurisdictions, namely the EU, US, and Japan, see Toshiaki Takigawa, 'Super Platforms, Big Data, and the Competition Law: The Japanese Approach in Contrast with the US and the EU' presented at the 13th Annual Conference of the Academic Society for Competition Law <https://www.law.nyu.edu/sites/default/files/upload_documents/Takigawa.pdf>.

[129] See, eg, *The Pilbara Infrastructure Pty Ltd v Australian Competition Tribunal* [2012] HCA 36.

holders, and aggrieved sellers may neither be provided with any reasons for the takedown, nor a mechanism to appeal directly to the right holders.[130]

Over here, the electronic commerce industry can take a page from the DMCA. The DMCA provides that when a takedown notice is received, the copyright intermediary enjoys immunity from taking down[131] (and putting back[132]) the material only if the following conditions are met. The copyright intermediary must take reasonable steps to promptly notify the content uploader (referred to as the subscriber). If the copyright intermediary receives a counter-notification, it must give the reporter ten business days' notice (as well as a copy of the counter-notice), and then restore the material within a further four business days after that (unless it has received a court order taken out by the reporter to bar or restrict access to the material, in which case it need not restore the material).[133] 'The put-back procedures were added to balance the incentives created in new Section 512 for service providers to take down material against third parties' interests in ensuring that material not be taken down.'[134] In short, while the DMCA observes and preservers the subscriber's due process rights, the counterfeit policies of electronic commerce platforms do not necessarily similarly protect sellers.

Due process also requires information about the reasons for the removal of the material. In the case of copyright infringement, the 'reasonable steps' to notify the subscriber[135] are to include information necessary to enable the subscriber to file a counterclaim such as the identity of the copyright owner, the description of the work whose copyright is allegedly infringed and the location of the infringing work. In relation to a trademark notice, what information will suffice for the aggrieved seller? If a right holder is the party issuing a trademark notice, it is right that the alleged seller should receive the notice and be given the opportunity to challenge the allegation. This is explicitly provided for in the PRC E-Commerce Law.[136]

[130] See, eg, *The eBay community*, 'Item INACCURATELY Removed as "Counterfeit" and selling privileges suspended. Ebay no help in resolvi [sic]' (29 April 2016) <https://community.ebay.com/t5/Archive-Selling/Item-INACCURATELY-Removed-as-quot-Counterfeit-quot-and-selling/td-p/25514073>. But see *eBay*, 'Verified Rights Owner Program: what happened to my listing?' <https://pages.ebay.com/seller-center/listing-and-marketing/verified-rights-owner-program.html#m17-1-tb1> (indicating that, contrary to the complaint on the community, eBay will notify the seller of the details about why the listing was reported and the right holder's contact information, but requiring the seller to further contact eBay if the right holder does not reply after five business days).

[131] 17 USC § 512(g)(1); Singapore Copyright Act, s 193DA(1).

[132] 17 USC § 512(g)(4); Singapore Copyright Act, s 193DA(4).

[133] 17 USC § 512(g)(2); Singapore Copyright Act, s 193DA(2).

[134] House of Representatives Report 105–551 Part 2, 59.

[135] 17 USC § 512(g)(2)(A).

[136] PRC E-Commerce Law, Art 42(2) (providing that the operator of the e-commerce platform shall forward the takedown notice it has received from an intellectual property rights owner to the operators on its platform). Note, however, it does *not* provide for the situation where the takedown is effected by the e-commerce platform rather than by the right holder.

If manual processes for deciding that a listing will be disabled are used, there should be no difficulty for the reasons to be supplied to the user. Most of the time, these manual processes are supplemented with systems that automatically identify suspect listings, or systems that implement human-designed rules that can be explicated and elucidated. An example of such a 'human-in-the-loop' implementation is eBay's Fraud Engine, which sets out a series of search rules 'designed to capture listings that contain indicia of counterfeiting apparent on the face of the listings without requiring expertise in rights owners' brands or products'.[137]

That said, even eBay acknowledged that the Fraud Engine rules had to be modified and updated (weekly), presumably to keep up with the counterfeiters and also with changing patterns of counterfeit activities. It is only a small step to move from that to a system such as Project Zero and Alibaba's where algorithms have replaced the rules. Perhaps the initial setup of the rules will be by way of supervised machine learning, based on the previous (manual) removals of problematic listings and the suspension of recalcitrant sellers. However, as described, the subsequent, iterative revisions to the rules will be based on *current* removals, suspensions, and reports from right holders. Because the rules are constantly changing with real-time feedback, do we as humans know the precise 'reasons' for the algorithms to have singled out the listing or seller in question? And, more importantly, if humans are still in the loop in relation to making the final decision for suspending the listing or seller, do we have enough information, or even gumption to decline to follow the recommendation of the algorithms, let alone justify this decision to the aggrieved seller to protect his due process rights?[138] After all, the intermediary owes contractual obligations to the seller for using its platform as a subscriber.

With the advent of machine learning and its implementation in 'AI' systems, concerns have been rightly raised as to whether autonomous or intelligent detection systems are 'traceable, explicable and interpretable'[139]—often referred to in short as 'explainability'. The requirement of explainable autonomous or intelligent systems, reflected as the Principle of Transparency in IEEE's rulebook on Ethically Aligned Design, ensures that the operation of such systems is transparent to a wide range of stakeholders.[140] But transparency may operate at different levels to different stakeholders. Thus, automated detection systems have to be transparent to the right holders whose IP interests these systems are primarily designed to protect, to the intermediaries who often take the lead role in designing and implementing such systems and therefore need such systems to absolve them of liability and

[137] *Tiffany I* (n 25) 477.

[138] See, eg, *IEEE*, 'Ethically Aligned Design' at 97, 102, 108, 123 (March 2018) (discussing the need for information symmetry through proper interface design in order for there to be proper situational awareness, understandability, and knowability of system goals, reasons, and constraints) https://standards.ieee.org/content/dam/ieee-standards/standards/web/documents/other/ead_v2.pdf.

[139] Ibid, Principle 4—Transparency, 29.

[140] Ibid.

responsibility, to the sellers or distributors, who are the clients or subscribers of the intermediaries and who need their transactions consummated, and to the end users, purchasers, and consumers, who need a simple assurance that the system is operating to protect them from harm.

In addition, depending on the type of machine learning algorithms used and actually implemented, the degree and extent of explainability of the results from such algorithms may vary greatly. Statistical multivariate regression or random forest models built on existing takedown data may be more traceable, explicable, and interpretable, by virtue of their algorithmic design,[141] but may lack the requisite accuracy and prediction power.[142] On the other hand, deep learning neural network models with their higher dimensionality architectures may produce models that have the necessary prediction power,[143] but may suffer from issues of explicability due to their relative opacity (think hidden layers, neural network architectures, and hyperparameters) and an inability to generalize or deal with corner cases.[144] For instance, many of these algorithms track changes to crucial information about the seller and correlate changes to such information with a prelude to counterfeit activity. There could however be legitimate reasons for crucial information to be revised, for instance, where the seller moved, used a different warehouse, or changed banks. Any such changes could be totally innocuous, or be triggered by human or systemic error, or could be an actual prelude to counterfeit activity. A properly trained algorithm has to be sensitive to the nuances of interpreting such data, and to the possibility of alternative explanations indicative of non-illicit activities.

Coupled with the fact that different stakeholders place different demands on autonomous or intelligent detection systems, perhaps it is more realistic to start with the conclusion that automation cannot really make a determination as to whether or not a product is infringing: algorithms can only *approximate* the probability that a seller or a listing is counterfeit. Short of actually having right holders and their experts examine the item in question, which is an impossibility for an online platform, all else being equal, there is no way to tell definitively if an item is a counterfeit.[145] Machines and algorithms operating in their endogenous environment

[141] See, eg, Rich Caruana and Alexandru Niculescu-Mizil, 'An Empirical Comparison of Supervised Learning Algorithms', ICML 2006, Proceedings of 23rd International Conference on Machine Learning, 161–8 <https://www.cs.cornell.edu/~caruana/ctp/ct.papers/caruana.icml06.pdf>; Khadse, Mahalle, and Biraris, 'An Empirical Comparison of Supervised Machine Learning Algorithms for Internet of Things Data', 2018 Fourth International Conference on Computing Communication Control and Automation (ICCUBEA) <https://ieeexplore-ieee-org/stamp/stamp.jsp?tp=&arnumber=8697476>.

[142] See, eg, Connor Shorten, 'Machine Learning vs. Deep Learning' (*Medium*, 7 September 2018) <https://towardsdatascience.com/machine-learning-vs-deep-learning-62137a1c9842>.

[143] See, eg, Holger Lange, 'Pathology AI: deep learning vs decision trees' (*Flagship Biosciences*, 19 February 2019) <http://www.flagshipbio.com/blog/pathology-ai-deep-learning-vs-decision-trees/>.

[144] But see Geoffrey Hinton, Oriol Vinyals, and Jeff Dean, 'Distilling the knowledge in a neural network' in *NIPS Deep Learning Workshop* (2015); M Kahng, P Y Andrews, A Kalro, and D H Chau 'Activis: Visual exploration of industry-scale deep neural network models' (2017) <http://arxiv.org/abs/1704.01942>.

[145] *Tiffany I* (n 25) 472 ('To determine if an item is authentic Tiffany silver jewelry, Tiffany quality inspectors must be able to physically inspect each item ... n 7: Of course, in many instances, determining

cannot be a substitute for good, old-fashioned human investigation that involves the exogenous collection of evidence. The fact that a suspicious item for sale has been detected is not evidence of trademark infringement. As the courts remind us repeatedly, detection is not infringement.[146]

4.3 The Limits of Technology

As noted above, an absence of transparency on well-used intermediary platforms makes it difficult to ensure the accountability of such automated and intelligent systems to all the aforesaid stakeholders. In turn, the opacity and approximate nature of such systems may hinder attempts to achieve a requisite level of transparency after the fact. The use (and abuse) of such systems on well-patronized intermediary platforms effecting billions of dollars in transactions and sales each day also has the potential of increasing the risk and magnitude of harm to all parties concerned. The use of machine learning therefore must be tempered with a huge dose of realism, especially since these are deployed in operational, open-ended environments that have real impacts on individuals and society.

4.3.1 The sociological dimension

One such example can be found in the promises (and over-promises) of digital fingerprinting. With digital fingerprinting, it has been possible to identify a work which has infringed copyright with a high level of accuracy.[147] However, it is precisely because of this high level of accuracy that concerns have been expressed about the over-inclusiveness of the use of such technologies. Operating such automated takedown systems in the form of Content ID on YouTube has led to a multiplicity of anecdotal instances of rampant overmatching. Public domain material such as NASA's Mars videos used in science discussion videos have been claimed to be copyrighted by news channels.[148] School performances of compositions by classical composers such as Bach, Beethoven, Bartok, Schubert, Puccini, and Wagner were all claimed to be protected by copyright, because filters could not distinguish between the commercially performed recordings by music labels and

whether an item is counterfeit will require a physical inspection of the item, and some degree of expertise on the part of the examiner').

[146] Ibid, 477 ('For obvious reasons, the fraud engine could not determine whether a listed item was actually counterfeit'), 477–8 ('Nevertheless, eBay's ultimate ability to make determinations as to infringement was limited by virtue of the fact that eBay never saw or inspected the merchandise in the listings'), and 492 ('[Tiffany's expert] conceded that his methodology would not be able to actually identify counterfeit Tiffany items on eBay').

[147] See *EFF*, 'Testing YouTube's Audio Content ID System' (23 April 2009) at <https://www.eff.org/deeplinks/2009/04/testing-youtubes-aud>.

[148] Timothy B Lee, 'How YouTube lets content companies "claim" NASA Mars videos' (*ArsTechnica*, 9 August 2012) <https://arstechnica.com/tech-policy/2012/08/how-youtube-lets-content-companies-claim-nasa-mars-videos/>.

the copyright-free musical composition underlying the recording.[149] More disturbingly, sounds of nature like dogs barking, birds chirping, motorcycle engines revving,[150] white noise, and even silence[151] have been claimed to be copyrighted by the Content ID system.

It would seem that 'copyright filters' designed with state-of-the-art fingerprinting technologies are simply not up to the task of discriminating between what is copyrighted and what is not, and what is licensed and what is fair use. As one author has noted, 'there is no bot that can judge whether something that does use copyrighted material is fair dealing. Fair dealing is protected under the law, but not under Content ID.'[152] In fact, as YouTube itself admitted, 'Automated systems like Content ID can't decide fair use because it's a subjective, case-by-case decision that only courts can make'.[153] Indeed, it is already a very difficult machine learning task to equip the system to exclude sounds of nature and public domain works from its ambit, let alone equip it to recognize the ever-changing sociological context in which an allegedly infringing work is used and assess it for fair use. Given the current state of technology, we have to acknowledge that machines cannot be easily trained to recognize between outright instances of blatant infringement, and reviews, comments, criticisms, parodies, news reporting, and personal events. To claim otherwise is disingenuous.

Similar arguments could likewise be made about the difficulty or infeasibility of algorithms to detect grey-market products or parallel imports that are sold on electronic commerce platforms.

4.3.2 Gaming the system

Another limitation of the use of automated systems, particularly algorithms that rely strongly on feedback, is the possibility that such systems can be gamed. Witness

[149] Ulrich Kaiser, 'Can Beethoven send takedown requests? A first-hand account of one German professor's experience with overly broad upload filters' (*Wikimedia Foundation*, 27 August 2018) <https://wikimediafoundation.org/2018/08/27/can-beethoven-send-takedown-requests-a-first-hand-account-of-one-german-professors-experience-with-overly-broad-upload-filters/>.

[150] Nancy Messiem, 'A copyright claim on chirping birds highlights the flaws of YouTube's automated system' (27 February 2012) <https://thenextweb.com/google/2012/02/27/a-copyright-claim-on-chirping-birds-highlights-the-flaws-of-youtubes-automated-system/>.

[151] Daniel Nass, 'Can silence be copyrighted?' (*classicalMPR*, 2 December 2015) <https://www.classicalmpr.org/blog/classical-notes/2015/12/02/can-silence-be-copyrighted> (alleging that SoundCloud removed a DJ's song because it infringed on John Cage's composition, 4'33", which is a score instructing the performers not to play their instruments, and the 'music' comes from the environment in which the performance occurs, such as a creaking door, a cough from the audience, a chirping bird, and so on).

[152] Cory Doctorow, 'How the EU's copyright filters will make it trivial for anyone to censor the Internet' (*EFF*, 11 September 2018) <https://www.eff.org/deeplinks/2018/09/how-eus-copyright-filters-will-make-it-trivial-anyone-censor-internet>.

[153] YouTube, 'Frequently asked questions about fair use' <https://support.google.com/youtube/answer/6396261?hl=en>.

the numerous reports of runaway feedback loops such as flash crashes[154] and astronomical online prices of products set by bots.[155] In addition, where Alibaba noted that its algorithms removed 96% of problematic listings before a single sale took place,[156] did the removed listings appear in another form? The machine-driven solution could have simply converted the problem of easily detected problematic listings into more surreptitious problematic listings.[157] If so, the problem did not go away—it just took another form because enterprising sellers had 'gamed' the system.

In the competitive environment of online sales, there are many less-than-ethical sellers who are already taking steps to 'game' the system. Some counterfeiters pay for positive reviews to 'jump' or 'inflate' their listings or credibility ratings over legitimate sellers.[158] Self-service takedowns assume the good faith of the claimants, but scammers can take advantage of this by reporting rival sellers' real products as counterfeit.[159] It is not inconceivable for brand owners to use this service to excise secondary market goods[160] or grey-market goods[161] from existing listings, perhaps to enable its own discount sales.[162] Likewise, it is also possible for legitimate merchants to file malicious or false takedown claims against their competitors to harm them.[163] Under the rubric of 'IP trolls', Alibaba has documented these instances in its Annual Report, and in response, has indicated that it would conduct the requisite due diligence when vetting takedown requests.[164] Yet this seems at odds with its policy of 'reduced evidentiary requirements for their takedown requests' for right holders with good takedown records.[165]

Likewise, we are already witnessing the same phenomenon in the copyright space. Under the guise of copyright infringement, takedown notices have been

[154] US Commodity Futures Trading Commission and US Securities & Exchange Commission 'Findings regarding the market events of May 6, 2010' (30 September 2010) <https://www.sec.gov/news/studies/2010/marketevents-report.pdf>.

[155] See, eg, Olivia Solon, 'How a book about flies came to be priced $24 million on Amazon' (*Wired*, 27 April 2011) <https://www.wired.com/2011/04/amazon-flies-24-million/>.

[156] Alibaba Group, '2018 IPR Protection Annual Report 4' (n 50).

[157] See, eg, *Tiffany I* (n 25) 492 ('[Tiffany's expert] further admitted that his methodology might easily be circumvented over time because counterfeiters typically adapt to evade such anti-counterfeiting measures').

[158] See, eg, Ari Levy, 'Birkenstock quits Amazon' (n 5); *Big Commerce*, 'The Definitive Guide to Selling on Amazon 2019' at 97 <https://www.bigcommerce.com/blog/wp-content/uploads/2018/12/The-Definitive-Guide-to-Selling-on-Amazon-2019.pdf>; Ari Levy, 'Amazon's Chinese counterfeit problem is getting worse' (*CNBC*, 8 July 2016) <https://www.cnbc.com/2016/07/08/amazons-chinese-counterfeit-problem-is-getting-worse.html>.

[159] Bercovici, 'Small businesses say Amazon has a huge counterfeiting problem' (n 52).

[160] See *Polymer Tech. Corp. v Mimran*, 975 F.2d 58, 61–62 (2d Cir.1992) ('As a general rule, trademark law does not reach the sale of genuine goods bearing a true mark even though the sale is not authorized by the mark owner').

[161] These are legal but inexpensive variants of the original products, often legitimately produced for sale in other countries or for a mass discounter.

[162] Bercovici, 'Small businesses say Amazon has a huge counterfeiting problem' (n 52).

[163] Alibaba Group, '2018 IPR Protection Annual Report 4' (n 50) 15.

[164] Ibid.

[165] Ibid, 8.

used as tools to smother competition[166] and stifle discussion about public issues.[167] Right holders may behave in an 'overzealous and overreaching' manner, by attempting to take down non-copyrighted content, or copyrighted content which it did not own, in an attempt to stymie the network service provider.[168] The rise of opportunistic 'copyright trolls', where right holders (and their complicit lawyers) engage in 'speculative invoicing' in an attempt to strike sufficient fear, uncertainty, and doubts about possible criminal prosecution and large amounts of damages in the minds of targeted consumers to get them to settle for disproportionately large sums of money,[169] is really enabled by a combination of automated detection and large scale enforcement against consumer piracy.

4.3.3 Misrepresentations and the inevitability of errors in notices

It is a serious matter to issue a copyright takedown notice. Under the DMCA, right holders and reporters issuing takedown notices are required, by law, to attest to the accuracy of the information supplied in the notice,[170] namely, the identification of the infringed work, the location of the infringing material and their contact information. A takedown notice is not to be a blinkered view by the right holder of the infringing activity. They are to assess if the activity in question is not 'authorized by the law',[171] and only then can they be said to hold a *subjective* good faith belief[172] that the allegedly offending activity is infringing. In *Lenz v Universal Music Corp.*, the 9th Circuit ruled that:

> Copyright holders cannot shirk their duty to consider—in good faith and prior to sending a takedown notification—whether allegedly infringing material constitutes fair use, a use which the DMCA plainly contemplates as authorized by the law ... [T]his step imposes responsibility on copyright holders [and was] intended by Congress in striking an appropriate balance between the interests of [the right holders] and the need for fairness and accuracy with respect to information disclosed ...[173]

Under the DMCA, the seriousness of issuing a false takedown notice is further reinforced by holding a reporter who wilfully makes a misrepresentation as to his authority to perjury,[174] and subjecting a reporter who 'knowingly materially

[166] See generally n 28.
[167] See, eg, *Online Policy Group v Diebold, Inc.* 337 F Supp 2d 1195, 1204 (N D Cal 2004).
[168] *Disney v Hotfile* (n 90) 16.
[169] See, eg, *Dallas Buyers Club LLC v iiNet Limited* [2015] FCA 317, [82]–[83].
[170] 17 USC § 512(c)(3)(A)(v), (vi).
[171] 17 USC § 512(c)(3)(A)(v).
[172] *Rossi v Motion Picture Ass'n of Am. Inc.* 391 F.3d 1000, 1104 (9th Cir. 2004).
[173] *Lenz v Universal Music Corp.*, 815 F.3d 1145, 1157 (9th Cir. 2015) (hereafter *Lenz v Universal Music*).
[174] 17 USC § 512(c)(3)(A)(vi); Singapore Copyright Act, s 193DD(1)(a).

misrepresents' that the material or activity is infringing to damages incurred by the alleged infringer[175] or by the service provider.[176] The PRC E-Commerce Law echoes the same sentiments by additionally providing that if the takedown notice is 'erroneous' and thus causes damage to the alleged sellers, the sellers are entitled to remedies in civil law[177] (presumably from either the right holder or the e-commerce platform), a requirement not found in the EU E-Commerce Directive. This in turn ensures that network service providers or intermediaries have to evaluate the received notices for legal compliance eg with the DMCA formalities (though it is unclear what evaluations an e-commerce platform provider could make). Under the DMCA, service providers are not required to act on notices that fail to comply substantially with *all* the formalities[178] as they are not legally effective.[179]

Even so, empirical analysis has shown that at least 5.5% of all takedown notices between 2011 and 2015 (the bulk of which were directed at search engines) are missing descriptions of the infringed copyright work. In addition, at least 9.8% of the notices fail to identify the locations of the infringing works.[180] (Another study concluded that 4.2% of takedown requests from a random sample of 2013 notices were flawed for mismatches in copyrighted and infringing content, and 28% raised issues about statutory non-compliance and fair use.)[181] This is both a surprising and worrisome result. It is surprising because search engines have consistently reported very high takedown rates—above 98% for Google in 2015,[182] and more than 99.75% for Bing for the second half of 2018.[183] It is worrisome because it suggests that search engine intermediaries were *ignoring* the formalities errors in the notices they received and were processing legally ineffective takedown notices that were in breach of the DMCA, and were, as a consequence, *themselves in breach* of the DMCA.[184]

[175] 17 USC § 512(f)(1); Copyright Act, s 193DD(1)(b). See also *Lenz v Universal Music Corp.* 2013 WL 271673 at 9 (N D Cal, 24 January 2013) ('any damage' in § 512(f) encompasses damages even if they do not amount to substantial economic damages); *Automattic Inc. v Steiner* 2015 WL 1022655 (N D Cal, 2 March 2015) (the online service provider is entitled to recover damages for time and resources incurred in dealing with the defective takedown notices, in the form of employees' lost time and attorneys' fees).

[176] *Rosen v Hosting Services, Inc.* 771 F Supp 2d 1219 (C D Cal 2010).

[177] PRC E-Commerce Law, Art 42(3).

[178] *Perfect 10, Inc. v CCBill LLC*, 488 F.3d 1102, 1112 (9th Cir. 2007) ('substantial compliance means substantial compliance with *all* of § 512(c)(3)'s clauses, not just some of them').

[179] 17 USC § 512(c)(3)(A); Singapore Copyright Act, s 193D(3), (5).

[180] Seng, 'Trust But Verify' (n 30).

[181] Jennifer Urban, Joe Karaganis, and Brianna L Schofield, 'Notice and Takedown in Everyday Practice' (30 March 2016) <https://papers.ssrn.com/sol3/papers.cfm?abstract_id=2755628>.

[182] Google, 'Report: How Google Fights Piracy' at 38 (2016) <https://drive.google.com/file/d/0BwxyRPFduTN2TmpGajJ6TnRLaDA/view>.

[183] Microsoft, 'Content Removal Requests Report' <https://www.microsoft.com/en-us/corporate-responsibility/content-removal-requests-report>.

[184] See, eg, 17 USC § 512(g)(1) (a service provider has immunity from taking down the material *only if* it acts in good faith to disable access to or remove the material or activity claimed to be infringing, or based on facts or circumstances from which infringing activity is apparent).

The same types of errors appear to befall trademark complaints as well. For instance, it was observed that Tiffany had occasionally reported allegedly infringing listings by submitting a Notice of Claimed Infringement (NOCI) to eBay.[185] In the NOCI, a right holder had to attest that it 'possessed a "good faith belief that the item infringed on a copyright or a trademark"'[186] (since changed to 'good faith belief, and so solemnly and sincerely declare, that use of the material complained of is not authorised by the IP owner, its agent or the law' with a declaration of accuracy and, under penalty of perjury, authorization to act).[187] Even then, the judge in *Tiffany* noted that approximately *one quarter* (or 25%) of the items flagged by Tiffany as counterfeit Tiffany jewellery turned out to be authentic or could not be determined to be counterfeit,[188] and had to have eBay reinstate the listings[189] This certainly gives pause for thought on Alibaba's much touted claim that its algorithms removed 96% of problematic listings before a single sale took place,[190] which has to have *zero* false positives in order not to subject Alibaba to any claims from aggrieved sellers under the PRC E-Commerce law.

If Tiffany's 'error rate' of takedowns at the time of the litigation in 2008 is representative of that of trademark right holders in general, an unanswered question is whether these error rates have changed with the advent of automatic takedowns driven by algorithms. Given that estimates of the error rates of copyright notices range from 4.2% to 28%, and that these were essentially robo-takedown notices, the experience of reporting agents using takedown algorithms in the copyright content space does not augur well for right holders operating in the trademark space. It is not often discussed, but erroneous takedowns can have deleterious effects on legitimate sellers[191] and small time content providers,[192] who will lose essential business and advertising revenue respectively during their downtime. Because of this, an argument that the disabled listing or taken down content can be restored just simply does not cut it.

[185] *Tiffany I* (n 25) 478.

[186] eBay, 'Notice of claimed infringement' <https://ir.ebaystatic.com/pictures/aw/pics/pdf/us/help/community/EN-NOCI.pdf>.

[187] *Tiffany I* (n 25) 478.

[188] Ibid, 487 (noting that this jewellery was actually purchased and verified by Tiffany experts pursuant to a special buying program that was designed to seek out counterfeit jewellery).

[189] Ibid. There have also been anecdotal complaints from sellers about eBay's removal of listings and their refusal to reinstate them. See, eg, The eBay Community, 'Item INACCURATELY removed as "counterfeit" and selling privileges suspended. Ebay no help in resolvi [sic]' (29 April 2016) <https://community.ebay.com/t5/Archive-Selling/Item-INACCURATELY-Removed-as-quot-Counterfeit-quot-and-selling/td-p/25514073>.

[190] Alibaba Group, '2018 IPR Protection Annual Report 4' (n 50).

[191] See, eg, *Tiffany I* (n 25) 489 (noting that suspension of legitimate eBay seller accounts was very serious, 'particularly to those sellers who relied on eBay for their livelihoods', and also to innocent infringers).

[192] See, eg, Hacker News, 'Lon Seidman gets YouTube takedown notice for public domain video from NASA' <https://news.ycombinator.com/item?id=4354720>.

Even with the DMCA provision that specifically enables aggrieved alleged copyright infringers to sue for damages,[193] it has been neither easy nor straightforward to seek redress from the recalcitrant right holder.[194] On the one hand, it may seem like there are limits to having right holders consider whether or not the allegedly infringing activity is 'authorized by law'. For a trademark right holder, this could require the right holder to rule out considerations such as whether the allegedly infringing seller was selling imported or second-hand goods, or was using the trademark in a descriptive or comparative manner—what US jurisprudence would describe as 'normative fair use'. On the other hand, the requirement of subjective good faith is a really low standard to satisfy: it does not matter if the right holder is ultimately proven wrong.[195] All that is required is for the right holder to apply his mind to the possibility that the allegedly infringing activity in question is authorized, so that it can form a good faith belief that the alleged activity in question is infringing.[196] But this also means that once a right holder has ostensibly applied its mind to this possibility and dismissed it, the innocent copyright infringer (or aggrieved seller, if the DMCA formulation is applied to the electronic commerce environment) would be left with no remedies.

Removing the good faith defence *or* the knowledge requirement, which is the approach taken in the PRC E-Commerce Law,[197] would however appear to tilt the balance too far in favour of the aggrieved seller. While it is in principle correct to afford the aggrieved seller redress in civil liability law for losses it suffered for a wrong takedown, and these losses in the form of expectation damages from lost sales could be not insubstantial, this could have the opposite effect of chilling any attempted takedowns by right holders of counterfeit goods. This problem is exacerbated by the fact that, as noted above, many of these takedowns will be affected by algorithms, which will take down suspected counterfeit listings *by design*. Furthermore, there is no easy way for the right holders (through automated takedowns) to avoid the problem of false positives, short of actually purchasing the suspect products and submitting them for expert analysis.

[193] See n 175.

[194] For instance, see *Lenz v Universal Music* (n 173) (allowing plaintiff to recover nominal damages from right holders, with a jury yet to determine if the plaintiff would prevail at trial); *Disney v Hotfile* (n 90) *48 (observing that economic damages to plaintiff intermediary from misrepresented notice was necessarily difficult to measure with precision).

[195] *Lenz v Universal Music* (n 173) 1154.

[196] See, eg, *Johnson v New Destiny Christian Centre Church* 2019 WL 1014245 (D C Fl).

[197] PRC E-Commerce law, Art 42(3) cl. 1 ('Where the notice issued is erroneous and thus causes damage to the operators on the platform, civil liability shall be borne according to the law. Where an erroneous notice is issued maliciously, which causes losses to the operators on the platform, the compensation liability shall be doubled').

5. Proposals for Reform

The problem of false positives is a difficult problem in the copyright context. For the electronic commerce context, it is made harder by the need to balance the economic interests of two aggrieved parties—the right holders and legitimate sellers—against the need to expeditiously protect the consuming public by curtailing counterfeit products sold on platforms. Failure to act on counterfeit goods only further jeopardizes right holders, legitimate sellers, and consumers.

However, changes to the law can help stakeholders make correct decisions about the design and use of automated and intelligent enforcement systems.

5.1 Recognizing Indirect Liability

For starters, recognizing indirect liability rather than absolving intermediaries of all responsibilities ensures that the economic returns from intermediation come with responsibilities to right holders and to consumers and end users. Intermediaries must be encouraged to invest in improving their platforms. A more nuanced line must be drawn: instead of *not* requiring intermediaries to monitor their systems,[198] legal incentives should be given to intermediaries to shield them from liability to right holders where they deploy 'explainable' automated and intelligent systems to keep their systems free of counterfeit products or illicit content. The net result arrived at in *Tiffany*, where eBay developed an endogenous system for detecting and removing counterfeit listings *sans* a DMCA-like safe harbour which absolves them of indirect trademark liability, is an attractive one and should be replicated in the legislation. Indeed, this rebalancing of the obligations of the intermediary is correctly captured in Article 17 of the Directive on Copyright in the Digital Single Market,[199] though its exact mechanism, which requires online intermediaries to implement filtering technologies, is highly suspect because of the problems of the sociological dimensions outlined above.[200]

[198] See, eg, *Fair Housing Council of San Fernando Valley v Roommates.com, LLC*, 521 F.3d 1157 (9th Cir. 2008), and see also Ryan Gerdes, 'Scaling Back ss230 Immunity: Why the Communications Decency Act Should Take a Page from the Digital Millennium Copyright Act's Service Provider Immunity Playbook' (2012) 60(2) Drake Law Review 653, 667.

[199] Directive (EU) 2019/790 of the European Parliament and of the Council of 17 April 2019 on copyright and related rights in the Digital Single Market and amending Directives 96/9/EC and 2001/29/EC, Recital 66.

[200] See, eg, Michael Sawyer, 'Filters, Fair Use and Feedback: User-Generated Content Principles and the DMCA' (2009) 24(1) Berkeley Technology Law Journal 363; Lauren D Shinn, 'Youtube's Content ID as a Case Study of Private Copyright Enforcement Systems' (2015) 43(2/3) AIPLA Quarterly Journal 359, 362. Even the European Parliament, in its official press release on the Digital Copyright Directive, admits that '[t]he criticism that [filters] sometimes filter out legitimate content may at times be valid', but goes on to assert that the platforms designing and implementing these filters should be made to pay for material it uses to make a profit: 'Questions and answers on issues about the digital copyright directive' (27 March 2019) <https://www.europarl.europa.eu/news/en/press-room/20190111IPR23225/questions-and-answers-on-issues-about-the-digital-copyright-directive>.

An 'explainable' system is one that is designed to provide traceable, explicable, and interpretable enforcement results. As this is a condition for the revamped safe harbour protection, intermediary platforms will be encouraged to introduce legally robust takedown systems, after they have understood the capabilities and limitations of their own AI systems. To further promote the 'explainability' of such systems, platforms could take a page from the copyright online service providers and periodically issue 'takedown reports' that detail the quantities and types of products or content that have been taken down.[201] The contents of the original takedown requests or reports could be made available to accredited researchers or independent third parties for review and research, to further promote transparency in and credibility of such systems,[202] especially if the full details of such systems cannot be revealed for commercial or strategic reasons.

At the same time, there must be new legal rules for trademark takedowns and clear processes for put-back notifications for innocent subscribers and sellers to apply for a review and restoration. This is to ensure that right holders do not abuse these automated processes, especially since the manual takedowns can themselves be used as feedback and reference points for future machine-driven takedowns. Only responsible right holders should qualify for accessing such processes. For Amazon's takedown system, currently being beta-tested, 'brands must maintain a high bar for accuracy in order to maintain their Project Zero privileges'.[203] This author has examined the issue of erroneous takedowns in the context of DMCA notices, and proposed a tiered reporting system for copyright takedowns.[204]

Likewise, the intermediaries will be denied their shield from indirect liability if they fail to exercise their oversight over the takedowns, for not reviewing them for legal compliance with processes, just as they will lose their safe harbour protections if they fail to take the requisite action when they have actual or 'red-flag' knowledge of instances of infringement.[205]

5.2 Insurance and the Essential Facilities Doctrine

Because the statutory declarations of good faith belief in the infringement and accuracy of the DMCA takedown requests were not being observed,[206] coupled with the requirement to prove subjective bad faith on the part of the right holder, it was difficult to pursue effective redress against right holders for egregiously bad

201 See, eg, Google, 'Requests to delist content due to copyright' <https://transparencyreport.google.com/copyright/overview?hl=en>.

202 See, eg, James Grimmelman, 'Regulation by Software' (2004) 114 Yale Law Journal 1719.

203 Gartenberg, 'Amazon's Project Zero' (n 62).

204 Seng, 'Trust But Verify' (n 30).

205 See *Viacom Int'l, Inc. v YouTube, Inc.*, 676 F.3d 19 (2d Cir. 2012).

206 Ibid.

takedowns. However, holding right holders (and arguably intermediaries) liable in damages for all erroneous takedown notices, even if done in good faith, may discourage right holders and intermediaries from taking pre-emptive measures to stop the sale and distribution of counterfeit products, pending further investigations. It may be that a preferred solution is to set up some kind of insurance scheme[207] funded jointly by right holders, sellers, and consumers to compensate legitimate sellers (and blameless content uploaders) for innocent takedowns in what is really a 'no-fault' situation by all parties concerned. Dealing with counterfeits and piracy will ultimately be a cost borne by everyone, until the problem is minimized extrinsically to the digital platform.

If this cost is best shared through the use of a common autonomous or intelligent infringement detection facility that the right holders and intermediaries jointly develop, there is no reason why the operators of such a facility should discriminate between certain chosen brands or right holders. To ensure that there are no accessibility inequalities, the essential facilities doctrine could be deployed to ensure that there is equitable and fairly compensated access to this detection facility by all relevant stakeholders.

6. Conclusions

There is no denying that automated enforcement is here to stay, but it is also wrong to make overly broad promises about the use of machine learning. Claiming that a machine learning system can detect counterfeits is simply marketing hype. All that an algorithm can do is to identify suspicious sellers and listings *deemed* to be suspicious. It would have been better to acknowledge the current limitations of technology in this regard and find ways to ameliorate that lacuna. These may include clearer rules for rapid appeals and restoration of erroneous takedowns, coupled with compensation for the aggrieved parties. While the use of automated systems to address the inefficiencies of a manually driven process to detect counterfeit products in a rapidly changing electronic commerce market is laudable, errors or unexpected situations can lead to a cascade of other, more serious problems that will engender overall mistrust of the marketplace. The use of automated and intelligent systems must therefore be encompassed within an entire enterprise framework of rules and processes to keep that overall trust intact.

[207] Counterfeit insurance is already available for online platforms. See Zurich, 'Keeping it real: Insurers have a role in helping manage the risks of counterfeiting' <https://www.zurich.com/en/media/magazine/2019/keeping-it-real>; Aon, 'Comprehensive crime insurance' <https://www.aon.com/singapore/risk-services/products-services/crime-insurance.jsp>.

PART V

LEGAL ASPECTS OF SOFTWARE

14

Copyright Protection for Software 2.0?

Rethinking the Justification of Software Protection under Copyright Law

*Hao-Yun Chen**

1. Introduction

'Software 2.0', a catchy and memorable phrase coined by the director of artificial intelligence (AI) at Tesla, Andrej Karpathy, denotes how artificial neural networks are playing a vital role in writing software these days.[1] In contrast to handicraft codes of the so-called 'software 1.0' written by programmers, the code of software 2.0 is in part generated intelligently, without programmers' intervention, by neural networks with inputs of data sets. In theory, the technical benefits of software 2.0 include, according to Karpathy, computational homogeneity, simplicity of implementation ('simple to bake into silicon'), constant running time, constant memory use, high portability, agility, interactive modules ('Modules can meld into an optimal whole'), and better code quality when compared to Software 1.0. Traditionally, software programmers create explicit instructions for a computer to execute by writing thousands and thousands of lines of source code. However, instead of giving step-by-step instructions in the code, programmers can now, with the help of a neural network, write a rough skeleton to build an artificial neural network structure, and then 'train' it with data sets collected for specific purposes, in order to have the computational resources generate the necessary code that could result in a specified outcome.[2] Despite some technical limitations,[3] software 2.0

* This research is funded by the Ministry of Science and Technology (Taiwan) Research Project 'Intellectual property law issues arising in the collection, processing and value addition of big data' (Project Number 'MOST 108-2410-H-305-041-MY2'). All online materials were accessed before 20 March 2020.

[1] Andrej Karpathy, 'Software 2.0' (*Medium*, 12 Nov 2017) <https://medium.com/@karpathy/software-2-0-a64152b37c35> (hereafter Karpathy, 'Software 2.0').

[2] For a concise explanation of how machine learning works, see Josef Drexl and others, 'Technical Aspects of Artificial Intelligence: An Understanding from an Intellectual Property Law Perspective' (2019) Max Planck Institute for Innovation & Competition Research Paper No 19-13 <https://ssrn.com/abstract=3465577> (hereafter Drexl and others, 'Technical Aspects of Artificial Intelligence').

[3] Current limitations, eg, difficulties in analysing biased, trained AI and eliminating gender, sexual, or racial prejudice in algorithms, can be attributed mostly to inherent technical constraints. To completely decipher the function of each neuron in neural networks is at present close to mission impossible in most cases, and some scholars are thus focusing on improving interpretability by humans. See Samek

Hao-Yun Chen, *Copyright Protection for Software 2.0?* In: *Artificial Intelligence and Intellectual Property*.
Edited by: Jyh-An Lee, Reto M Hilty, and Kung-Chung Liu, Oxford University Press (2021). © The several contributors.
DOI: 10.1093/oso/9780198870944.003.0015

seems to provide a promising alternative or complement for Software 1.0, and is being experimented with and deployed in various ICT fields, including visual and speech recognition, machine translation, and spam detection. It is expected to be further applied not only in industry but also in agriculture and service sectors.[4]

In view of the rosy prospects of machine learning based on neural networks and its attendant applications,[5] IT giants have been investing heavily in constructing neural networks and collecting data sets suitable for training purposes. Both a rough but well-designed neural network model and large volume and variety of data are indispensable for building a machine learning system, but the associated building and training costs are extremely high, especially those associated with collecting and organizing huge volumes of data. Besides, even a pre-trained neural network model needs frequent and constant updates of new training data to ensure the accuracy of analysis,[6] particularly when the analytical targets embrace wide diversity or are situated in a rapidly changing environment. This undoubtedly raises the cost of building software via a neural network. Given these enormous and recurring costs, it is understandable that the securing of IT companies' R&D investment in building and training neural networks and the protection of outputs (not only software 2.0 as an immediate output of the training process, but also the results produced by software 2.0, etc) thus emerge as crucial issues which attract attention from the perspective of intellectual property (IP) law, especially patent and copyright law. With respect to patent protection, given that the execution of a machine learning system requires some form of computer implementation, many of the patentability issues relating to computer-implemented inventions are germane to discussions on protecting machine learning-related inventions under patent law, as noted in the USPTO's Request for Comments on Patenting Artificial Intelligence Inventions.[7] On the other hand, with respect to copyright

Wojciech and others, 'Explainable Artificial Intelligence: Understanding, Visualizing and Interpreting Deep Learning Models' (2017) ITU Journal: ICT Discoveries, Special Issue No 1. Nevertheless, there are also empirical studies pointing out that the increased transparency of a machine-learning model may hamper people's ability to detect and correct a sizeable mistake made by the model due to information overload. Forough Poursabzi-Sangdeh and others, 'Manipulating and Measuring Model Interpretability' (2019) arXiv:1802.07810v3 [cs.AI].

[4] For an overview of AI application fields, see WIPO, 'WIPO Technology Trends 2019: Artificial Intelligence' (2019) Figure 1.3 <www.wipo.int/edocs/pubdocs/en/wipo_pub_1055.pdf>.

[5] A McKinsey study found that three deep learning techniques, namely, feed forward neural networks, recurrent neural networks, and convolutional neural networks, together could enable the creation of between USD 3.5 trillion and USD 5.8 trillion in value each year in nine business functions in nineteen countries. See Michael Chui and others, 'Notes from the AI Frontier: Insights from Hundreds of Use Cases' Discussion Paper (McKinsey Global Institute 2018) 17 http://www.mckinsey.com/~/media/mckinsey/featured%20insights/artificial%20intelligence/notes%20from%20the%20ai%20frontier%20applications%20and%20value%20of%20deep%20learning/notes-from-the-ai-frontier-insights-from-hundreds-of-use-cases-discussion-paper.ashx.

[6] Ibid, 16.

[7] USPTO, Request for Comments on Patenting Artificial Intelligence Inventions (Doc No PTO-C-2019-0029, 2019) <www.federalregister.gov/documents/2019/08/27/2019-18443/request-for-comments-on-patenting-artificial-intelligence-inventions>.

protection, there are heated debates on whether and how to protect works created semi-autonomously or autonomously by such systems, as human involvement will likely be unnecessary during the process of creating works with software 2.0 in the foreseeable future.[8] This chapter, however, tackles this copyright issue from a different angle, focusing on the necessity of protection of software 2.0 that contains neural networks and other essential elements.[9] Should software 2.0 and the like be protected under copyright law? What are the obstacles and challenges in applying copyright law to software 2.0? More importantly, do these obstacles and challenges offer persuasive reasons for introducing new rules and regulations in addition to existing regimes? Are there any alternatives available under the existing legal regimes that may satisfy the needs of protection of software 2.0?

In the following, this chapter will first review the current scope of computer program protection under copyright laws and international treaties, and point out the potential inherent issues arising from the application of copyright law to software 2.0. After identifying related copyright law issues, the chapter will then examine the possible justification for protecting computer programs in the context of software 2.0, aiming to explore whether new exclusivity should be granted or not under copyright law, and if not, what alternatives are available to provide protection for the investment in the creation and maintenance of software 2.0.

2. Computer Program Protection Under Copyright Law

It is undisputed that software creators and investors deserve appropriate legal protection for their effort and should be allowed to recoup investment in creating software. The form of legal protection for computer programs is, however, a long-debated issue. The rapid development of software has sparked academic discussions since the mid-1970s on whether the patent system, the copyright system, or a sui generis system should provide protection for computer program.[10] There

[8] See, eg, Tim W Dornis, 'Artificial Creativity: Emergent Works and the Void in Current Copyright Doctrine' (2020) 22 Yale Journal of Law & Technology 1 (hereafter Dornis, 'Artificial Creativity'); Shlomit Yanisky-Ravid, 'Generating Rembrandt: Artificial Intelligence, Copyright, and Accountability in the 3A Era—The Human-Like Authors Are Already Here—A New Model' (2017) 2017 Michigan State Law Review 659 (hereafter Yanisky-Ravid, 'Generating Rembrandt').

[9] It is theoretically possible to develop a sui generis regime for protecting computer programs that contain neural networks for the purpose of encouraging and protecting investment in software development. Similar arguments occurred in debates several decades ago on the sui generis right for databases and discussions on whether to protect software with a sui generis bundle of rights. However, given the fact that computer programs may be protected under current IP laws and that computer programs do not change their instructive nature when neural networks are used for training such programs, analysing the application of IP laws to software 2.0 seems to be a prerequisite for revisiting such arguments.

[10] Google's Ngram Viewer shows a soaring increase in the 1970s and a peak in the 1990s with the keyword phrase 'computer program protection'. Google Books Ngram Viewer <https://books.google.com/ngrams/graph?content=computer+program+protection&year_start=1960&year_end=2013&corpus=15&smoothing=3&share=&direct_url=t1%3B%2Ccomputer%20program%20protection%3B%2Cc0#t1%3B%2Ccomputer%20program%20protection%3B%2Cc0>.

has been widespread debate on whether or not computer programs should be protected under copyright law, because computer programs are mainly characterized as functional works rather than artistic ones. Generally, consumers purchase software for its utilitarian value in accomplishing certain functions, not for its aesthetic appeal or originality.[11] In addition, the nature of computer programs makes them susceptible to copying,[12] and the application of copyright law to a computer program has a minimal, if any, effect on preventing competitors from adopting the same idea in their software products. All these facts make computer programs less compatible with protection under copyright law when compared with other kinds of works, eg, literary or artistic ones.

There are, however, plausible reasons for protecting computer programs under copyright law. Computer programs are basically textual expressions, irrespective of their unique dual nature as both expression and applied innovation, the latter of which is in general protected by patent rather than copyright. Their expressive nature enables them to be protected as literary works provided that they are original intellectual creations made by programmers. Their innovative nature should not, at least on a superficial level, have a negative effect on their qualifying as literary work.[13] In addition, computer programs in object code are unintelligible due to their binary format, but they share the copyright status of other literary works stored in computer systems in machine-readable form, because they can be decompiled into the form of source code, where they are intelligible to programmers.[14]

As one of the earliest countries to extend its copyright protection to computer programs, the US had a decisive influence on other countries' choices of the form of computer program protection. In 1974, the US Congress created the National Commission on New Technological Uses of Copyrighted Works (CONTU) to address computer-related copyright law issues. In the legislative history of the Copyright Act of 1976 (1976 Act),[15] serious concerns were raised over the extension of copyright protection to computer programs, given their technical and

[11] John C Phillips, 'Sui Generis Intellectual Property Protection for Computer Software' (1992) 60 George Washington Law Review 997, 1009.

[12] Ibid, 1010.

[13] However, the innovative nature does have a certain effect on the protection of computer programs under copyright law in practice. An example of this is the application of the merger doctrine, which states that an expression merges with an idea and is thus unprotected under copyright law if the idea can be expressed only in one way or in a limited manner. In the context of computer programs, some functions may be coded in limited ways with specific programming languages for reason of functional efficiency. In such cases, the corresponding expressions may not protected in those jurisdictions where the merger doctrine is introduced. See Pamela Samuelson, 'Reconceptualizing Copyright's Merger Doctrine' (2016) 63 Journal of the Copyright Society of the U.S.A. 417; Pamela Samuelson, 'Staking the Boundaries of Software Copyrights in the Shadow of Patents' (2019) 71 Florida Law Review 243, 276–8 (hereafter Samuelson, 'Staking the Boundaries of Software Copyrights'); Christopher Buccafusco and Mark A Lemley, 'Functionality Screens' (2017) 103 Virginia Law Review 1293, 1325 (hereafter Buccafusco and Lemley, 'Functionality Screens').

[14] WIPO, *Intellectual Property Handbook: Policy, Law and Use* (2nd edn, WIPO 2008) paras 7.12–7.13.

[15] Pub L No 94-553, 90 Stat. 2541 (codified as amended at 17 USC §§101–1401 (2012)).

functional nature.[16] However, although there were still doubts about whether object codes (machine-executable forms of programs) were copyright-protectable after the passage of the 1976 Act, the CONTU issued its final report (hereafter 'CONTU Report') in 1978, stating that '[f]lowcharts, source codes, and object codes are works of authorship in which copyright subsists'.[17] The CONTU Report reached a conclusion that 'the continued availability of copyright protection for computer programs is desirable'.[18] Based on the CONTU Report's recommendations, the US Congress amended the 1976 Act in 1980[19] to define the meaning of 'computer program',[20] and created a limitation enabling owners of a copy of such a program to adapt the program for utilization or archival purposes.[21] Many countries, including European and Asian ones, subsequently adopted an approach similar to that of the US,[22] conferring copyright protection on computer programs. Eventually, as a sign of global consensus on this issue, international treaties have been signed to ensure copyright protection of computer programs.

With respect to international treaties on this issue, two international treaties, Article 10(1) of the TRIPs Agreement and Article 4 of the WIPO Copyright Treaty, are applicable in this regard. Both provisions provide that computer programs should be protected as literary works under the Berne Convention.[23] Prior to the advent of the TRIPs Agreement, Article 2(1) of the Berne Convention specified that literary and artistic works are protected 'whatever may be the mode or form of its expression'. There were, however, diverging views and arguments on the issue of whether it is appropriate to consider computer programs in the form of object code to be works of authorship, because object codes are machine-readable and in most cases incomprehensible to human beings.[24] Article 10(1) of the TRIPs Agreement settled this argument by clarifying that computer programs, 'whether in source or object code', are similar to literary works and protected under the

[16] Samuelson, 'Staking the Boundaries of Software Copyrights' (n 13) 253–4.

[17] National Commission on New Technological Uses of Copyrighted Works, *Final Report* (1978) 21.

[18] Ibid, 11.

[19] Computer Software Copyright Act of 1980, Pub L No 96-517, 94 Stat. 3015.

[20] 'A set of statements or instructions to be used directly or indirectly in a computer in order to bring about a certain result.' Ibid, 3028 (codified at 17 USC § 101).

[21] Ibid, 3028 (codified at 17 USC § 117).

[22] Eg, the UK enacted the Copyright, Designs and Patents Act 1988 to deal with computer program-related issues under copyright law. The European Commission later introduced the EC Software Directive (Counsel Directive of 14 May 1991 on the Legal Protection of Computer Programs, 91/250/EEC, O.J. L 122/42 (1991)), which has led to the harmonization of copyright laws of all EC member states. In Asia, Japan amended its Copyright Act in 1985 to explicitly include computer programs as a form of copyrightable subject matter. See Art 10(1)(ix) of the Japan Copyright Act (Act No 48 of 6 May 1970). The definition of computer program is provided in Art 2(1)(x)-2 of the Copyright Act as 'something expressed as a set of instructions written for a computer, which makes the computer function so that a specific result can be obtained'.

[23] Berne Convention for the Protection of Literary and Artistic Works, of 9 September 1886, last revised at Paris on 24 July 1971, and amended on 28 September 1979 (hereafter Berne Convention).

[24] Sam Ricketson and Jane C Ginsburg, *International Copyright and Neighbouring Rights: The Berne Convention and Beyond* (2nd edn, Oxford University Press 2005) vol. 1, 516–17 (hereafter Ricketson and Ginsburg, *International Copyright and Neighbouring Rights*).

Berne Convention, together with the requirement of effective enforcement mechanisms.[25] The wording of 'whether in source or object code' made it clear that all member states of the treaties should protect computer programs irrespective of whether the form is directly comprehensible to humans or not.

It is worth noting that Article 9(2) of the TRIPs Agreement prohibits member states from extending copyright protection to 'ideas, procedures, methods of operation or mathematical concepts as such'.[26] This principle is known as the idea–expression dichotomy. To put it differently in the context of computer programs, copyright protection extends only to literal expressions of computer programs, in the form of either source or object code. The protection, however, does not extend to ideas, methods, and procedures, processes of operation, or even algorithmic concepts embedded in the computer programs. The combined interpretation of Articles 9(2) and 10(1) of the TRIPs Agreement directs member states to maintain the principle that computer programs are copyright protectable, and meanwhile emphasizes that member states need to ensure that 'protection of program does not result in monopolization of the functions the program executes'.[27]

After briefly reviewing the rationale for copyright protection and the history of the introduction of computer program protection, it seems that the copyright issues surrounding computer programs have, to some extent, been resolved. However, the rise of software 2.0 may bring these issues back to the table. In the next section, this chapter turns the spotlight on the potential issues arising from the application of copyright law to software 2.0.

3. Copyright Challenges Presented in the Context of Software 2.0

3.1 What is Software 2.0?

To offer a background for the following analysis in this chapter, it is essential to understand the basic concepts of software 2.0 and recognize the key differences between software 1.0 and 2.0. As briefly explained above, software 1.0 denotes computer programs in a conventional sense, which are a set of statements or instructions to be used directly or indirectly in a computer in order to bring about a certain result.[28] These explicit instructions are manually developed and written by programmers, which is one of the reasons computer programs are copyrightable subject matter—programmers do understand and appreciate the source code.

[25] TRIPs Agreement, Arts 41–61.

[26] WIPO Copyright Treaty, Art 2 reiterates the identical doctrine.

[27] Ricketson and Ginsburg, *International Copyright and Neighbouring Rights* (n 24) 517.

[28] 17 USC § 101.

Therefore, the expression, ie, the code of software 1.0, reflects the programmers' intellectual creation. By contrast, software 2.0, which still has the nature of computer programs as the instructions to computers, has as a special feature its development process. It can be automatically formulated in much more abstract, human-unfriendly language, such as the weights of a neural network.[29] The term 'software 2.0' used in this chapter then refers to computer programs containing models trained with machine learning (ML). Such an ML-trained model is the immediate output of the ML process, and can be grasped as an algorithm based upon a mathematical function that generates a desired outcome based on the patterns learned from the training data.[30] However, in contrast to algorithms articulated by programmers in the case of Software 1.0, the ML-trained model embedded in software 2.0 is in most cases difficult to interpret due to the complexity of the calculations. Even programmers cannot explain how an ML-trained model combines the different features of the input data to produce a prediction rule. This is why an ML-trained model is often dubbed a 'black box' and is the reason there has been growing interest in interpretable ML.[31]

When programmers build software 2.0, the degree of the human effort involved in the ML training mainly depends upon the type of ML tasks they choose to perform. While the degree varies from one to another, human-dependent factors are at present still necessary for all the ML training process.[32] For instance, in the scenario of supervised learning, a basic neural network architecture, including neurons, the links between the neurons, and the functions implemented on the neurons, needs to be built by programmers prior to the ML training process. It is expected, though, that human involvement will be gradually reduced, eventually becoming unnecessary during the ML training process in the foreseeable future.

3.2 Challenges for Software 2.0 Protection Under Copyright Law

As mentioned in Section 1, with the recent dramatic progress in ML technology, IT companies are eager to develop software 2.0 in order to provide services that have been so far operated by humans in various sectors. Given the competitive advantages software 2.0 may offer to a company, it is likely that competitors will endeavour to gain access to the software and its core part—the ML-trained model. Nevertheless, if software 2.0 developers want to protect the economic value derived from software 2.0, they may face legal challenges under copyright law. In this

29 Karpathy, 'Software 2.0' (n 1).

30 Drexl and others, 'Technical Aspects of Artificial Intelligence' (n 2) 5. It should be noted that the focus of this chapter is on the protection of computer programs containing ML-trained models rather than the subsequent output of the application of software 2.0.

31 Anthony Man-Cho So, Chapter 1 in this volume.

32 The principle and process of ML is plainly explained in this volume, ibid.

section, these challenges will be emphasized and examined from a copyright law perspective.

3.2.1 Challenges in terms of copyrightable works

The first challenge that software 2.0 developers may encounter is copyrightability. Computer programs may be subject to copyright protection, as briefly explained in Section 2. Since software 2.0 is a kind of computer program, it seems copyrightable. To be more concrete, the development process of the manually-written architecture part of software 2.0 bears a resemblance to that of Software 1.0 on the whole. Programmers devote efforts to choosing or developing a training algorithm, setting the hyperparameters, data labelling, and developing the model architecture. The code of the architecture part, if it meets the minimal threshold of originality, constitutes protectable expression (a literary work) under copyright law, and should be accordingly protected in the same manner as Software 1.0.[33] On the other hand, it seems questionable whether an ML-trained model is copyrightable.

The idea–expression dichotomy, as previously mentioned in Section 2, specifies that copyright protection is given only to the expression of an idea, not the idea itself. However, when it comes to computer programs, how to apply this long-established doctrine to computer programs is far from an easy task in practice. The utilitarian nature of computer programs makes the delineation between idea and expression a difficult one.[34] As commentators have pointed out, the value in a computer program lies in its technical functionality, rather than its creative expression.[35]

To illustrate the difficulty in distinguishing idea from expression in computer programs, a quick review of the landmark cases in the US and the European Union (EU) may be of help. In the US, the current Copyright Act explicitly stipulates that 'In no case does copyright protection for an original work of authorship extend to any idea, procedure, process, system, method of operation, concept, principle, or discovery, regardless of the form in which it is described, explained, illustrated, or embodied in such work'.[36] But how to distinguish idea from expression in cases involving nonliteral software copyright infringement remains highly controversial. Case law once expanded the eligibility for software copyright protection by stating that 'the purpose or function of a utilitarian work would be the work's idea, and everything that is not necessary to that purpose or function would be part of the

[33] In practice, many ML architectures have been released under open source licences, which are based on copyright law. See, eg, TensorFlow <https://github.com/tensorflow>; or DeepMind <https://github.com/deepmind/lab>.

[34] Frederick M Abbott, Thomas Cottier, and Francis Gurry, *International Intellectual Property in an Integrated World Economy* (4th edn, Wolters Kluwer 2019) 750.

[35] Lothar Determann and David Nimmer, 'Software Copyright's Oracle from the Cloud' (2015) 30 Berkeley Technology Law Journal 161, 165; Buccafusco and Lemley, 'Functionality Screens' (n 13) 1320; Samuelson, 'Staking the Boundaries of Software Copyrights' (n 13) 291–2.

[36] 17 USC § 102(b) (2012).

expression of the idea'.[37] However, many commentators and software developers have expressed concern that overbroad protection of software by copyright law might harm competition and ongoing innovation in the software industry.[38] In the landmark decision *Computer Associates International, Inc. v. Altai, Inc.* (hereafter '*Altai*'), the Second Circuit narrowed copyright scope by adopting a 'abstraction, filtration, and comparison' (AFC) test to avoid protecting functional elements of programs.[39] The test required filtering out the unprotectable elements of programs, which include aspects of programs that are dictated by efficiency, elements dictated by external factors, and elements of programs that are taken from the public domain, such as commonplace programming techniques, ideas, and know-how.[40] After *Altai*, courts invoked several approaches to avoid extending copyright protection to code's functional components.[41] However, recently the Court of Appeals for the Federal Circuit (CAFC)'s decision in *Oracle America, Inc. v Google Inc.*[42] raised furious disputes concerning the copyrightability of the Java application program interface.[43] The law is not entirely clear on how to filter the software's functional components from copyright protection.

Likewise, in the EU, Article 1(2) of Directive 91/250 (hereafter 'the Computer Programs Directive')[44] provides that 'Protection in accordance with this Directive

[37] *Whelan Associates, Inc. v Jaslow Dental Laboratory, Inc.*, 609 F. Supp. 1307 (E.D. Pa. 1985), aff'd, 797 F.2d 1222 (3d Cir. 1986) 1236.

[38] For a detailed introduction to the concerns and opinions expressed against overbroad copyrights and software patents, see Samuelson, 'Staking the Boundaries of Software Copyrights' (n 13) 260–4.

[39] 982 F.2d 693 (2d Cir. 1992). For a discussion of how to apply the AFC test to distinguish function from expression, see Pamela Samuelson, 'Functionality and Expression in Computer Programs: Refining the Tests for Software Copyright Infringement' (2017) 31 Berkeley Technology Law Journal 1215, 1223–31 (hereafter Samuelson, 'Functionality and Expression in Computer Programs').

[40] *Computer Associates International, Inc. v Altai, Inc.*, 982 F.2d 693 (2d Cir. 1992) 707–10; Samuelson, 'Functionality and Expression in Computer Programs' (n 39) 1231.

[41] Eg, Pamela Samuelson identified five doctrinal strategies that courts have adopted to avoid software copyright and patent overlaps: the layering approach, the § 102(b) exclusion approach, the thin protection approach, the merger approach, and the explanation/use distinction approach. Samuelson, 'Staking the Boundaries of Software Copyrights' (n 13) 268–81 (noting that 'in numerous cases, the courts invoked more than one of these strategies'). On the other hand, Buccafusco and Lemley identified three separate functionality screens (exclusion, filtering, and thresholds) used in IP law, and suggest that, while literary works are subject to filtering under copyright law, in the case of highly functional literary works such as software, the filtering regime will tend toward over-protection, and thus strengthening the application of the functionality threshold to deny copyright protection when it invokes the merger doctrine may be a better way to balance the costs and benefits (See Buccafusco and Lemley, 'Functionality Screens' (n 13) 1366–8).

[42] 750 F.3d 1339 (Fed. Cir. 2014), cert. denied, 135 S. Ct. 2887 (2015).

[43] This decision is criticized by many commentators (see, eg, Samuelson, 'Staking the Boundaries of Software Copyrights' (n 13) 246; Buccafusco and Lemley, 'Functionality Screens' (n 13) 1323; Peter Menell, 'Rise of the API Copyright Dead? An Updated Epitaph for Copyright Protection of Network and Functional Features of Computer Software' (2018) 31 Harvard Journal of Law & Technology 307, 421); but see Ralph Oman, 'Computer Software as Copyrightable Subject Matter: Oracle v. Google, Legislative Intent, and the Scope of Rights in Digital Works' (2018) 31 Harvard Journal of Law & Technology 639, 646 (arguing that 'the Federal Circuit in the *Oracle v. Google* case reached the right decision'). Currently, the US Supreme Court has agreed to review CAFC's decisions as to both copyrightability and fair use. 'Google LLC v. Oracle America Inc.' (*SCOTUS blog*) <http://www.scotusblog.com/case-files/cases/google-llc-v-oracle-america-inc/>.

[44] Council Directive 91/250/EEC of 14 May 1991 on the legal protection of computer programs.

shall apply to the expression in any form of a computer program. Ideas and principles which underlie any element of a computer program, including those which underlie its interfaces, are not protected by copyright under this Directive.' In addition, recital 14 of the Computer Programs Directive indicates that 'logic, algorithms and programming languages' may be categorized as potential (unprotectable) ideas and principles. In one landmark case, *SAS Institute Inc v World Programming Ltd*, the Court of Justice of the European Union (CJEU) made it quite clear that, 'neither the functionality of a computer program nor the programming language and the format of data files used in a computer program in order to exploit certain of its functions constitute a form of expression of that program for the purposes of Article 1(2) of Directive 91/250'.[45] The court noted that 'to accept that the functionality of a computer program can be protected by copyright would amount to making it possible to monopolise ideas, to the detriment of technological progress and industrial development'.[46] On the other hand, the court held that 'the SAS language and the format of SAS Institute's data files might be protected, as works, by copyright under Directive 2001/29 if they are their author's own intellectual creation (see *Bezpečnostní softwarová asociace*, paragraphs 44 to 46)'.[47] However, it also should be noted that in *Bezpečnostní softwarová asociace*, the CJEU held that, 'where the expression of those components is dictated by their technical function, the criterion of originality is not met, since the different methods of implementing an idea are so limited that the idea and the expression become indissociable'.[48] In other words, even if the code (the expression of those components) is considered a form of expression, in cases where the idea and expression have been merged, it is not protected by copyright.

With reference to software 2.0, the main difference of software 2.0 before and after the ML training process lies in the so-called parameters (the weights and the interrelations between the neurons), as demonstrated in Chapter 1 of this book. A question then naturally arises as to whether the parameters constitute copyrightable work.

In the development process of software 2.0, the key element of it for the programmer is the trainable parameters (ie, the weights connecting neurons in a given

[45] Case C406/10 *SAS Institute Inc v World Programming Ltd* [2012] para 39. For a comment on this case, see Daniel Gervais and Estelle Derclaye, 'The Scope of Computer Program Protection after SAS: Are We Closer to Answers?' (2012) 34 European Intellectual Property Review 565 (hereafter Gervais and Derclaye, 'The Scope of Computer Program Protection after SAS').

[46] Case C406/10 *SAS Institute Inc v World Programming Ltd* [2012] para 40.

[47] Ibid, para 45. Commentators pointed out that the CJEU's statements at paras 39 and 45 are 'facially hard to reconcile' (suggesting that one of the two possible ways to reconcile the two paragraphs is to say that the court meant that 'the actual *code* underlying the language and data formats can be protected' but also pointing out that in this situation, 'the code must be analysed to see if it embodies original expression and if then to ensure there is no merger between idea and expression.') See Gervais and Derclaye, 'The Scope of Computer Program Protection after SAS' (n 45) 568–9.

[48] Case C-393/09 *Bezpečnostní softwarová asociace—Svaz softwarové ochrany v Ministerstvo kultury* [2010] para 49.

architecture), which are optimized with the help of computational resources and data during the ML training process. Although the initial value of the parameters and algorithms adopted to proceed with the optimization (training) are chosen by the programmer, the process of optimizing the weights is a purely mathematical operation aiming to minimize the loss function by finding the best combination of trainable parameters.[49] Such trainable parameters embedded in software 2.0 are the components dictated solely by their technical functions, and thus could be categorized as the nonliteral elements of computer programs, which tend in court practice to be excluded from copyright protection according to the case law precedents in the US and the EU. Consequently, although software 2.0 as a whole may be protected as literary work(s) under copyright law, it is highly possible that the trainable parameters might be excluded from copyright protection owing to their purely functional nature.

3.2.2 Challenges in terms of authorship

Software 2.0 developers need to tackle the issue of authorship as a second challenge. As Karpathy pointed out, the code of software 2.0 is automatically 'written in much more abstract, human unfriendly language, such as the weights of a neural network' and '[n]o human is involved in writing this code because there are a lot of weights (typical networks might have millions), and coding directly in weights is kind of hard'.[50] If the code was not written directly by the programmers, do they still qualify as the authors of software 2.0?

According to a WIPO Committee of Experts, the only mandatory requirement for a literary or artistic work to be protected by the Berne Convention is that it must be original.[51] As for the question of what constitutes originality, in most jurisdictions, it requires that the work be created by a human being. For example, the US Copyright Office has made it quite clear that to qualify as a work of authorship 'a work must be created by a human being'.[52] In the EU, the originality criterion also requires the work to be the author's own intellectual creation, which suggests that the originality requirement involves some degree of human authorship.[53] However, it should be noted that there are a few exceptions where computer-generated works are protected by the copyright law, such as in the UK.[54]

[49] Anthony Man-Cho So, Chapter 1 in this volume (n 31); see also Drexl and others, 'Technical Aspects of Artificial Intelligence' (n 2) 7.

[50] Karpathy, 'Software 2.0' (n 1).

[51] Daniel J Gervais, 'Exploring the Interfaces Between Big Data and Intellectual Property Law' (2019) 10 Journal of Intellectual Property, Information Technology and Electronic Commerce Law 22, 26 (hereafter Gervais, 'Exploring the Interfaces Between Big Data and Intellectual Property Law').

[52] US Copyright Office, Compendium of U.S. Copyright Office Practices § 313.2 (3rd edn 2017).

[53] Andres Guadamuz, 'Do Androids Dream of Electric Copyright? Comparative Analysis of Originality in Artificial Intelligence Generated Works' (2017) 2 Intellectual Property Quarterly 169; Enrico Bonadio, Luke McDonagh, and Christopher Arvidsson, 'Intellectual Property Aspects of Robotics' (2018) 9 European Journal of Risk Regulation 655, 666–7.

[54] For a thorough analysis of the copyright protection of computer-generated work under the Copyright, Designs and Patents Act (CDPA) 1988 in the UK, see Jyh-An Lee, Chapter 8 in this volume.

In the case of software 2.0, the issue lies in whether the programmers merely used the machine as a tool to support the writing of the code. For example, if a person draw a picture using painting software, there is no doubt that she created the work (the picture), because in this case the software's involvement is evaluated as merely a supporting tool or instrument.[55] In contrast, with the help of a machine, if the outcome of the 'creation' is contingent upon uncontrollable processes (which cannot be controlled or completely foreseen by the 'creator'), and this kind of 'accidental' outcome is intended by the 'creator', can we say that the person delegating the execution to the machine still qualifies as the author of the work?[56] This issue is not a completely new one. A similar discussion appeared in disputes concerning human creation with the involvement of animals.[57] For example, if someone put colored ink on a cat's feet, then put the cat on a canvas on the ground so that the cat stepped on the canvas and produced a painting, it seems difficult to conclude that the person who put the cat with inked feet on the canvas qualifies as the author of the painting, because the person who put the cat onto the canvas cannot anticipate how the cat will step on the canvas at all. In other words, the person's control over the 'creative process' is too limited, and thus it is more appropriate to evaluate that the person merely made a creative plan, but was not involved in the execution of the creation process.[58]

In the context of software 2.0 and the ML process, as mentioned in Section 3.1, the programmer formed the basic architecture of the neural network, chose the appropriate algorithm and the initialization strategies, and prepared the training data sets, and the codes of software 2.0 are compiled via the ML process based on above-mentioned factors. Although the codes (the expression of the literary work) are not directly written by the programmers, how software 2.0 will be coded depends on the above factors determined by programmers. Consequently, it seems fair to say that at least under current practice, the programmer is still involved in the execution of creation (ie, writing the code) with the support of a computer, and the programmer can anticipate the outcome of the work (ie, the code of software 2.0) during the ML process. The fact that the programmer of software 2.0 cannot explain the correlation between the above factors does not prevent her from becoming the author of the software, because copyright does not necessarily require the author to understand exactly the mechanism of how the work is created.[59]

[55] In this way, creating computer-aided works is no different from the use of cameras for photography. Dornis, 'Artificial Creativity' (n 8) 7.

[56] For a thorough analysis of this issue, see Jane C Ginsburg and Luke Ali Budiardjo, 'Authors and Machines' (2019) 34 Berkeley Technology Law Journal 343, 363 ff (hereafter Ginsburg and Budiardjo, 'Authors and Machines').

[57] A recent example concerns the famous monkey selfie case. See *Naruto v Slater*, 888 F.3d 418 (9th Cir. 2018).

[58] Ginsburg and Budiardjo, 'Authors and Machines' (n 56) 364–7 (discussing the issue from the context of the US Copyright Act, meeting the criterion of authorship requires conception and execution).

[59] Ibid, 407 (arguing that even in the context of deep learning, 'the machine still proceeds through a process fundamentally controlled by its programmers', therefore the so-called 'black-box problem' is irrelevant to the authorship question).

4. Justification for New Protection for Software 2.0?

As examined in Section 3, while software 2.0 as a whole may be protected as literary works under copyright law, it is highly possible that the functional components of software 2.0, which are exactly the most valuable parts, may be ineligible for protection under copyright law. The next question is whether the copyright protection should be expanded to cover these functional components or not. In this section, this chapter reviews the justification for granting IP protection, as a prerequisite, before diving into discussing whether some kind of new exclusivity should be granted or not.

The theoretical grounds for justifying IP protection can be roughly divided into two categories: (1) natural rights theories and (2) utilitarian theories.

4.1 Natural Rights Theories

The English philosopher John Locke provided one of the cornerstones of property rights theories. According to Locke's labour theory, people who mixed their labour with an object from the commons should have property in it, 'at least where there is enough, and as good left in common for others'.[60] Locke's philosophy was used to justify the granting of property rights in the physical world.[61] From an historical view, scholars have suggested that Locke's philosophy has been used to justify the protection of an author's or inventor's right, and eventually influenced the development of modern copyright law in the eighteenth and nineteenth centuries.[62] Several important studies argue that Locke's theory can be used as a basis to justify IP.[63] On the other hand, there are scholars who disagree about applying Locke's

[60] John Locke, *Second Treaties on Government* (1690) ch 5, para 26. The quoted phrase has been referred to as the 'Lockean proviso' and was used as a basis for limiting the scope of intellectual property. See Wendy J Gordon, 'A Property Right in Self-Expression: Equality and Individualism in the Natural Law of Intellectual Property' (1993) 102 The Yale Law Journal 1533, 1562–70 (hereafter Gordon, 'A Property Right in Self-Expression'); Wendy J Gordon, 'Intellectual Property' in Peter Cane and Mark Tushnet (eds), *The Oxford Handbook of Legal Studies* (Oxford University Press 2003) 624 (hereafter Gordon, 'Intellectual Property').

[61] See, eg, Carol M Rose, 'Possession as the Origin of Property' (1985) 52 The University of Chicago Law Review 73 (pointing out that Lockean theory is one of the most familiar theories to explain property law in the US).

[62] Benjamin G Damsted, 'Limiting Locke: A Natural Law Justification for the Fair Use Doctrine' (2003) 112 The Yale Law Journal 1179, 1179. For a discussion of how the notion of authorship arose and how it has influenced the law, see, eg, Peter Jaszi, 'Toward a Theory of Copyright: The Metamorphoses of "Authorship"' (1991) 41 Duke Law Journal 455. For a detailed discussion of how Lockean theory influenced the development of modern patent doctrines from a historical view see, eg, Adam Mossoff, 'Rethinking the Development of Patents: An Intellectual History, 1550–1800' (2001) 52 Hastings Law Journal 1255.

[63] See Justin Hughes, 'The Philosophy of Intellectual Property' (1988) 77 Georgetown Law Journal 287 (hereafter Hughes, 'The Philosophy of Intellectual Property'); Edwin C Hettinger, 'Justifying Intellectual Property' (1989) 18 Philosophy & Public Affairs 31; Gordon, 'A Property Right in Self-Expression' (n 60); Peter Drahos, *The Philosophy of Intellectual Property* (Dartmouth 1996) 41–72; Robert P Merges, *Justifying Intellectual Property* (Harvard University Press 2011) 31–67.

theory to intangible IP.[64] Intangible goods such as information are non-exclusive and their consumption is nonrivalrous; these characteristics differ significantly from tangible goods. Therefore, even if we are convinced by Locke's theory that whoever invests her labour in picking an apple from a tree can make the apple her property, this does not mean that it can justify the protection of ideas exactly like apples.[65]

Another crucial justification for this is personality theory, which describes property as an expression of the self, and copyright protection is a right that accrues to the author in possession of, and reflection and development of his personality in the intellectual work.[66]

With respect to software 2.0, as mentioned in Section 3.1, while the degree of the human effort involved in ML training varies depending on upon the type of ML tasks creators choose to perform, human-dependent factors are at present still necessary for all the ML training process. For example, the scenario of supervised learning requires programmers to invest labour in order to build the basic neural network architecture and preparing training data sets prior to the ML training process. Therefore, at first glance, labour theory seems to provide some justification for protection. Nevertheless, Locke's labour theory is flawed when applied to intangible goods as discussed above, thus this theory alone cannot justify protection.

In addition, it is arguable whether software code can be characterized as an expression of a programmer's personality, given software's utilitarian nature, in the first place. When it comes to software 2.0, the ML-trained model is modified as a result of a mathematical operations aiming to minimize the loss function by finding the best combination of trainable parameters. Programmers' personality rarely matters here. Consequently, personality theory cannot provide justification for protection, either.

This chapter argues that natural right theories do not provide grounds justifying protection of the functional aspects of software 2.0 (including ML-trained models). Although programmers do devote efforts to choosing or developing a training algorithm, setting the hyperparameters, data labelling, and developing the model architecture, the functional aspects of software 2.0 can hardly be characterized as

[64] Jacqueline Lipton, 'Information Property: Rights and Responsibilities' (2004) 56 Florida Law Review 135, 179 (explaining that 'the Lockean notion of property is grounded in the realities of the physical world, where a key concern is optimizing society's use of tangible resources'. On the other hand, intangible goods like information can exist in more than one place, as opposed to tangible, rivalrous goods); Mark A Lemley, 'Property, Intellectual Property, and Free Riding' (2005) 83 Texas Law Review 1031, 1050–1 (explaining that 'information is what economists call a pure "public good," which means both that its consumption is nonrivalrous' and that 'information does not present any risk of the tragedy of the commons').

[65] Mark A Lemley, 'Faith-Based Intellectual Property' (2015) 62 UCLA Law Review 1328, 1339 (hereafter Lemley, 'Faith-Based Intellectual Property').

[66] Hughes, 'The Philosophy of Intellectual Property' (n 63) 288; Justin Hughes, 'The Personality Interest of Artists and Inventors in Intellectual Property' (1998) 16 Cardozo Arts & Entertainment Law Journal 81, 116; Yanisky-Ravid, 'Generating Rembrandt' (n 8) 706.

an expression of a programmer's personality, because those aspects are determined by utility functionality. It seems that we cannot rely on natural rights theories to justify why additional protection should be granted.

4.2 Utilitarian Theories

The utilitarian theories hold that the law should promote the greatest good (utility) for the greatest number.[67] Copyright can be viewed as performing both incentive and prospect-like functions.[68] The incentive theories suggest that, owing to two distinctive features of intangible goods (non-rivalrous and non-excludable), others may free ride upon the efforts of the creators, and thereby the number of works created would be less than optimal because creators would be unable to recoup their investment in creation.[69] IP rights are a form of government intervention in the free market to achieve the purpose of encouraging innovation and creation.[70] Nevertheless, the exclusive protection of copyright is not costless.[71] By granting exclusive copyright to right owners, it also creates deadweight loss such as transaction cost, and may even deter further creations which are built upon earlier works.[72] Therefore, in addition to providing incentives to authors, it is equally important to make sure that the public (including consumers and potential new authors who need to copy in order to implement their own creativity and skill) still have proper access to earlier works.[73] In sum, under the utilitarian theories, the protection of IP can be justified only when the extent of protection is limited to an extent that is consistent with the overarching purpose of benefiting the public.[74]

However, does IP protection really promote greater efficiency and benefit for society? This is extremely difficult to verify. While many sophisticated empirical

[67] Thomas F Cotter, *Patent Wars: How Patents Impact our Daily Lives* (Oxford University Press 2018) 39. For a thorough introduction to and analysis of the utilitarian economic justification of IP rights, see Reto M Hilty, Jörg Hoffmann, and Stefan Scheuerer, Chapter 3 in this volume.

[68] Roger D Blair and Thomas F Cotter, *Intellectual Property: Economic and Legal Dimensions of Rights and Remedies* (Cambridge University Press 2005) 30 (hereafter Blair and Cotter, *Intellectual Property*).

[69] Ibid, 30; Craig Allen Nard, *The Law of Patents* (4th edn, Wolters Kluwer 2017) 31. There are various incentive-based theories focusing on different aspects, eg, incentive to invent theory (focusing on efficiency gains and the internalizaion of externalities), incentive to disclose theory (focusing on the perspective of inducing the inventors to seek patent protection instead of trade secret protection), and incentive to innovate and commercialize theory. For a brief introduction to these theories and the weakness of these rationales, see ibid, 34–40.

[70] Lemley, 'Faith-Based Intellectual Property' (n 65) 1331.

[71] William M Landes and Richard A Posner, *The Economic Structure of Intellectual Property Law* (The Belknap Press of Harvard University Press 2003) 16–21.

[72] Blair and Cotter, *Intellectual Property* (n 68) 31.

[73] Gordon, 'Intellectual Property' (n 60) 619.

[74] For a general analysis of how policymakers can improve the innovation/deadweight loss tradeoff by carefully tailoring the intellectual property monopoly for each individual industry, see Stephen Maurer, 'Intellectual Property Incentives: Economics and Policy Implications' in Rochelle Cooper and Justine Pila (eds), *The Oxford Handbook of Intellectual Property Law* (Oxford University Press 2018) 144–68.

studies have been published in the past two decades, the empirical evidence demonstrates that the relationship between IP and both innovation and creation is extremely complicated, and it is difficult to conclude that IP is doing the world more good than harm.[75] The fact that there are alternatives to granting property rights (eg, the first-mover advantage, and trade secret protection) makes the assessment even more difficult.

In the context of software 2.0, as discussed in Section 3.1, in order to develop a sophisticated ML-trained model, programmers devote efforts to choosing or developing a training algorithm, setting the hyperparameters, data labelling, and developing the model architecture. One might argue that these investments and efforts should be protected, otherwise the incentive to develop or improve ML-trained models will be undermined. Nevertheless, while granting exclusive protection may enhance the incentives to create to a certain degree, it also creates some social cost at the same time. If there are alternatives available for the creator to recoup their investment in creation, there is no need for granting copyright protection. Therefore, unless there is market failure due to free riding and thus additional incentive is indispensable, there is no necessity for the government to intervene in the market by granting copyright protection in the first place. In addition, even if market failure does exist, before jumping to expanding protection, we should take into account social welfare losses that creating a new exclusivity might cause, such as increased transaction and licensing costs.[76]

Under this view, do programmers of software 2.0 really need additional incentives to do what they do? It seems that investment in AI projects is already plentiful.[77] Many neural network architectures are provided as open source software (OSS), which lowers the threshold for the public to participate in developing their own ML systems and trained models.

Furthermore, ML-trained models can be applied to new data to generate a certain output. Depending on the business model and strategy of the developer, it may be possible to use contract in combination with technological protection to prevent others from extracting or copying an ML-trained model from the software. For example, if an ML-trained model is provided as cloud-based SaaS (software as a service), the service provider does not need to provide the software to its users, thus making it easier to protect the ML-trained model by a combination of trade secrets protection, contracts and technological protection.[78] In a case where an

[75] In Lemley, 'Faith-Based Intellectual Property' (n 65) 1334–5. For a summary for the empirical studies of the benefits and costs of the patent system, see Lisa Larrimore Ouellette, 'Patent Experimentalism' (2015) 101 Virginia Law Review 65, 75–84.

[76] Gervais, 'Exploring the Interfaces Between Big Data and Intellectual Property Law' (n 51) 24.

[77] Daryl Lim, 'AI & IP: Innovation & Creativity in an Age of Accelerated Change' (2018) 52 Akron Law Review 813, 829–30. Reto M Hilty, Jörg Hoffmann, and Stefan Scheuerer, Chapter 3 in this volume (n 67) ('[O]n a general level one can presently observe that AI innovation appears to be thriving', suggesting that market failure in AI-related industries is not apparent).

[78] Dornis, 'Artificial Creativity' (n 8) 25 (suggesting that the misappropriation doctrine is not unfit for providing basic protection for AI-generated works).

ML-trained model is provided as a core part of software (sometimes incorporated in products), it is also possible for the programmer to collect new data from its users, which in turn may help the programmer to improve the model or use these data for other potential business opportunities, allowing the programmer to recoup investment of developing software 2.0 and the ML-trained model.

In addition, the 'first-mover advantage' may allow the first-mover on the market with a new service or product incorporating software 2.0 to recoup its investments.[79] Theoretically, others may imitate the first mover and develop the same model by putting the same neural network architecture through the same training process (using the same input data sets). However, in the context of software 2.0, if the developer keeps its training method and training data sets in secret,[80] and if the cost of repeating the same training process is high, the 'first-mover advantage' is likely to help the programmer to recoup her investments in software 2.0. The availability of alternatives to copyright protection should not be ignored when evaluating the costs and benefits of expanding protection.

Based on the above-mentioned reasons, currently, it seems that the incentives for developing software 2.0 and the ML-trained models are not insufficient. If there is inadequate evidence demonstrating the need to create a new type of legal exclusivity, we should not expand current IP protection.[81] By expanding copyright protection for the functional components of software 2.0, the benefit of public access to such technology may be jeopardized. And once an amendment has been made to expand the protection, it will be extremely difficult to terminate or abolish such regulation even if significant flaws are found afterwards.

5. Conclusion

With the dramatic progress in machine learning technology, the rise of software 2.0 has brought new challenges to copyright law from the perspectives of copyrightability and authorship. Specifically, the functional components of software 2.0 including ML-trained models may be ineligible for protection under current copyright law. While ML-trained models are expected to generate huge economic value, neither natural rights theories nor utilitarian theories can provide sufficient grounds to justify granting additional protection to them.

As discussed in this chapter, currently, there are no obvious signs of underinvestment in AI-related industries, and the availability of alternatives to copyright protection such as trade secrets with combinations of contracts and technological

[79] Blair and Cotter, *Intellectual Property* (n 68) 15.

[80] Drexl and others, 'Technical Aspects of Artificial Intelligence' (n 2) 10 (suggesting that complete reverse-engineering of all the parts of the machine learning system does not seem realistic currently).

[81] Peter K Yu, 'Data Producer's Right and the Protection of Machine-Generated Data' (2019) 93 Tulane Law Review 859, 895–6.

measures also implies that the necessity of granting a new protection to ML-trained models is relatively low.

Taking the costs and benefits of expanding copyright protection into consideration, this chapter argues that currently the empirical evidence and theoretical grounds are insufficient to justify additional, exclusive legal protection; therefore, we should not expand the protection. Otherwise the public access to the works will be limited, which in turn would deter further creation and cause larger negative social costs to society than the benefits it could add.

15

Rethinking Software Protection

*Peter R Slowinski**

1. Narrowing It Down: What is AI?

The term artificial intelligence (AI) is somewhat ambiguous and often appears to be much more than it actually is. On a very high level of abstraction, it is technology that attempts to mimic at least parts of what we regard to be human intelligence[1]—although it must be said that even the definition of human intelligence is not agreed upon by neurologists and other disciplines.[2] On the level of particular applications, most, although not all, AI applications come down to predictions made based on available information and software that has, in one way or another, been trained to make these predictions.[3] Other forms of AI are basically search machines that try to find a certain optimal result within a large number of possibilities.[4] Both can also be combined. Just imagine an AI playing a game of chess or go. It will learn from data that are presented to it, but it may also try to 'find' new moves that are possible but that no one has taught it. The training is usually only possible due to the availability of large amounts of data, which is one of the reasons why this field of computer science has made an enormous leap forward in the past few years: data are now available in quantities and levels of quality not previously known.[5]

This chapter focuses on this type of AI and particularly on machine learning (ML) and evolutionary or genetic algorithms, since these seem to be applicable in a wide range of areas and real-life uses. In contrast, it does not take a particular

* All online sources were accessed before 10 May 2020.

[1] See Stuart J Russel and Peter Norvig, *Artificial Intelligence, A Modern Approach* (3rd edn, Prentice Hall 2011) 1 ff, breaking it down to different perspectives on what machines can do or are perceived to be doing (hereafter Russel and Norvig, *Artificial Intelligence*).

[2] It is quite remarkable that various scientific disciplines arrive at different conclusions regarding what intelligence is. For examples from philosophy, economics, neuroscience, and psychology, and the application to computer science, see ibid 5 ff.

[3] Panos Louridas and Christof Ebert, 'Machine Learning' (2016) 33 IEEE Software 110; Matt Taddy, 'The Technological Elements of Artificial Intelligence' in Ajay Agrawal, Joshua Gans, and Avi Goldfarb (eds), *The Economics of Artificial Intelligence: An Agenda* (University of Chicago Press 2019) 61.

[4] Russel and Norvig, *Artificial Intelligence* (n 1) 64 ff.

[5] Other reasons include the constantly rising computing power and the desire to automatically connect machines and appliances in the internet of things (IoT) or the internet of everything (IoE), which requires smart applications.

Peter R Slowinski, *Rethinking Software Protection* In: *Artificial Intelligence and Intellectual Property.* Edited by: Jyh-An Lee, Reto M Hilty, and Kung-Chung Liu, Oxford University Press (2021).
DOI: 10.1093/oso/9780198870944.003.0016

look at final products such as robotics or autonomous driving that implement AI technology, with the exception of the last part of the chapter, which looks at some selected use cases. While other chapters of this book are focused on the technical aspects of AI,[6] this chapter limits itself to explaining those parts that are important for software protection and to providing examples that allow the transfer of known legal concepts to AI and thus enable us to *rethink* software protection.[7]

1.1 Machine Learning

When journalists, politicians, and intellectual property (IP) lawyers discuss AI, they usually mean machine learning (ML). The reason is not that ML is the best AI solution or some kind of one-size-fits-all AI solution, but because it is the type of AI application that is currently most commonly used for a wider range of tasks in practice.[8] In rather simplistic terms, ML is a way to apply statistical models and pattern recognition to large amounts of data. This allows the system to make predictions regarding similar but new situations. There are various examples of ML in practice. One rather famous example is the use of ML in the context of autonomous driving, and particularly image or object recognition. Other examples include speech recognition or automated translations.[9]

Let us take a closer look at autonomous driving. Letting a car drive on its own is not much of a challenge. The difficulties start as soon as the car meets objects that it needs to avoid, such as other cars, trees, cats, or other human beings. A (real) human of the age that is required to drive a car usually has no difficulties in distinguishing these different kinds of objects. In fact, a child learns the process of distinguishing them at a very early age. However, how can one teach this to a car? In essence, the process is the same: the child and the car need examples of objects to learn to distinguish them.[10] We may think that in the case of the child it is the

[6] See Anthony Man-Cho So, Chapter 1 in this volume; Ivan Khoo Yi and Andrew Fang Hao Sen, Chapter 2 in this volume.

[7] A similar approach has been taken by Plotkin but with a much stronger focus on patent protection based on software as something that is engineered. See Robert Plotkin, 'Computer Programming and the Automation of Invention: A Case for Software Patent Reform' (2003) 7 UCLA Journal of Law and Technology (hereafter Plotkin, 'Computer Programming and the Automation of Invention').

[8] Studies have shown that publications in the area of ML have been rising in the last decade compared to other sub-fields of AI. See Iain M Cockburn, Rebecca Henderson, and Scott Stern, 'The impact of artificial intelligence on innovation' (*The National Bureau of Economic Research*, 2018) <http://nber.org/papers/w24449> (hereafter Cockburn, Henderson, and Stern, 'The impact of artificial intelligence on innovation').

[9] Michael I Jordan and Tom M Mitchell, 'Machine Learning: Trends, Perspectives and Prospects' (2015) 349 Science 201, 255.

[10] Ahmad El Sallab and others, 'Deep Reinforcement Learning Framework for Autonomous Driving, Electronic Imaging, Autonomous Vehicles and Machines' (2017)

child that is distinguishing, while in the case of a car it is software, but this is not entirely correct. Processes in the child's brain are responsible for learning and distinguishing, while software in the car is responsible for the learning and distinguishing in the machine. There is, however, one important difference between the child or any human being and AI. The child may understand what a car is after seeing just a few types of cars or maybe even just one car. The AI application needs hundreds or thousands of examples, but it can process the large amount of examples much faster than any human ever could.

An ML application consists of various components that, by interacting with each other, form the AI.[11] At the core of the ML application are one or more training algorithms and training data. However, before the training algorithm can be implemented, a model architecture needs to be created by the developer. This model architecture provides the general parameters—the structures for the ML application. In a second step, the developer uses training data to teach the application via the training algorithm. The result of the teaching process is a trained model that can be used in an application to fulfil a specific task. In this respect it is worth mentioning that describing ML as general purpose technologies that basically can be used for any task is currently only true on an abstract level. It is correct that the concept of ML can be used for tasks ranging from image recognition through creation of new music, to automated translation of high accuracy.[12] However, as far as this author is aware and as discussions with experts have confirmed, changing the area of expertise requires changing the model and architecture and of course retraining the application so that it can be used for automated translation instead of image recognition. But even using a model and architecture designed for one image-recognition-related task to solve a different problem will often create results that are far from the desired one. So an application which has been set up to recognize stop signs for the purpose of being used in autonomous driving cannot just be used with new data sets for the recognition of skin cancer based on pictures and vice versa. The differences are too large for this to be feasible. This seems to be another difference between human and artificial intelligence: a human brain can be trained for different tasks, and therefore a surgeon is able to recognize both stop signs and skin cancer with high accuracy.

Electronic Imaging 2017(19):70–76 DOI: 10.2352/ISSN.2470-1173.2017.19.AVM-023 compare the development of skills in a human being from childhood through adolescence to the features required in autonomous driving.

[11] For a concise explanation, see Josef Drexl and others, 'Technical Aspects of Artificial Intelligence: An Understanding from an Intellectual Property Law Perspective' (2019) Max Planck Institute for Innovation & Competition Research Paper No 19-13 <https://ssrn.com/abstract=3465577>.

[12] For a discussion of ML/DL as general purpose technology and/or the invention of a method of invention, see Cockburn, Henderson, and Stern, 'The impact of artificial intelligence on innovation' (n 8).

1.2 Evolutionary Algorithms

The results and solutions that ML-based applications can come up with are mostly limited to scenarios in which the process can rely on data (ie, experience) and the result that is expected is in one way or another a variation of this experience or based on it. If the result goes beyond this experience, the application may face its limits. For example, a self-driving car that has learned to recognize brick walls may stop in front of a concrete wall but crash into a glass wall, lacking data on transparent but still solid objects. While deep neural networks (DNN) have shown promising results in detecting skin cancer, they reach their limitation when they are trained on high-definition pictures taken under perfect environmental conditions and then used in ordinary surroundings of a hospital or on pictures taken at home.[13] Similarly, ML-based applications may be not suited to 'think' outside the box and come up with solutions that differ substantially from previously presented examples. This latter scenario is one where evolutionary algorithms can be used and in the past have been used with a certain degree of success.

According to AI literature, evolutionary algorithms, sometimes also called genetic algorithms, are programmed after the way evolution comes up with new solutions to existing problems.[14] First, a population of potential solutions is created. These solutions are then tested for their fitness to accomplish a task (ie, survive). The best-suited candidates are then mutated (ie, changed in some more or less random way) or mated (ie, their characteristics mixed to result in a new individual). This new generation is again tested for fitness. This cycle is repeated for a predefined number of times or until a predetermined degree of fitness is reached. As in nature, the probability of finding a 100%-perfect solution is relatively low. However, the goal is to come as close as possible to such a solution.

While on the level of designing and programming it makes sense to compare this kind of AI to evolution and genetic change, from a (human) cognitive perspective these cycles of change and testing very much resemble the way a human would brainstorm for new solutions to a predefined problem. It is the way engineers and other innovators have come up with ideas and solutions for ages: by designing concepts, changing them, and testing them. In computer sciences, evolutionary algorithms are classified as search approaches, as compared to learning approaches as represented by ML or deep learning (DL).[15]

[13] Manu Goyal and others, 'Artificial Intelligence-Based Image Classification for Diagnosis of Skin Cancer: Challenges and Opportunities' (2019) arXiv:1911.11872 [eess.IV].

[14] See for an explanation Russel and Norvig, *Artificial Intelligence* (n 1) 127 ff.

[15] Ibid, 127.

1.3 Artificial Neural Networks

Many publications discuss artificial (or deep) neural networks (ANN or DNN) in the context of ML or DL. In fact, a DNN transforms ML into DL. However, ANN are not limited to these sub-fields of AI theory and technology. Instead, they can also be combined with evolutionary algorithms.[16] In fact, when it comes to the training of ANN, traditional ML methods and particularly methods of reinforced learning find themselves in direct competition with evolutionary algorithms.[17]

ANN try to mimic the way our brain functions. While the human brain has billions of neurons that help us to store knowledge and to process incoming information, ANN use artificial neurons in the form of coded mathematical formulas. Each neuron has a certain value, and when the input information passes through a neuron, its value will decide which path it will take after it leaves the neuron and which new value it will have. A DNN, as the word 'deep' suggests, consists of multiple layers of neurons and thus provides more possibilities to fine-tune the way the input travels through the network to become the output and thus (hopefully) provides better results and therefore better applications. However, having more layers does not automatically mean better results. The setup of a DNN, including the number of layers, is as much an art as a science, and also requires a lot of steps back and forth to find an optimally balanced system. Recent developments show that AI applications may actually be better at achieving the task of designing a DNN than human software engineers are.[18]

2. The Software in AI

At first, it may seem puzzling why the question of software in AI has to be discussed at all, since it seems that AI *is* software. While it is true that AI includes software code in one way or another, it is the question of the nature of the software and the investment required to implement it that is actually important for the assessment of AI's intellectual property protection.

[16] Felipe Petroski Such and others, 'Deep Neuroevolution: Genetic Algorithms are a Competitive Alternative for Training Deep Neural Networks for Reinforcement Learning' (2018) arXiv:1712.06567 [cs.NE] (hereafter Salimans and others, 'Deep Neuroevolution'); Tim Salimans and others, 'Evolutions Strategies as a Scalable Alternative to Reinforcement Learning' (2017) arXiv:1703.03864 [stat.ML].

[17] Salimans and others, 'Deep Neuroevolution' (n 16).

[18] Hanzhang Hu and others, 'Efficient Forward Architecture Search' (2019) arXiv:1905.13360 [cs.LG].

2.1 Algorithms

First, an AI, just as any computer program, consists of algorithms. While this term seems to be mystified to some degree outside of the technical community, it is a rather simple concept: an algorithm is a set of instructions to achieve a certain result. The Merriam-Webster dictionary puts it like this: 'a step-by-step procedure for solving a problem or accomplishing some end'.[19] In principle, this can be written down on a piece of paper, explained orally or written in a code that a computer can understand and implement. It is worth understanding that a programmer can write the same algorithm in different programming languages and still achieve the same result. Therefore, the algorithm is at first a concept not tied to a computer program and only becomes part of the computer program once it has been coded. In addition, only deterministic algorithms present the same results when run multiple times, while so-called non-deterministic algorithms will present different results on each run. This means that simply looking at an outcome does not allow an expert to determine the algorithm that came up with the result. With respect to AI, algorithms are present in all the AI categories described above and coded in the form of software.

2.2 Mathematical Models

Second, the structures of AI, including the algorithm, are based on mathematical models. Actually, it can be argued that AI is much more mathematics than traditional programming ever was. From the point of view of experts, 'getting the math right' is about one third of the overall work required to build an AI application. However, since this estimate relates to applications that have been coded more or less from scratch, the importance of the mathematical part can be substantially higher in cases where the AI developer is using a preprogrammed tool.[20] The models as such are the theoretical background of an AI application. For example, such a model can include a mathematical function for evaluating the quality of the results, it can decide the number of required layers in a DNN, or it can set the number of input neurons based on the task that needs to be achieved. A simple example from image recognition is the number of pixels in a digitally stored picture. If it is 100, then a DNN can have 100 input neurons—one for each pixel. This will, with some likelihood, increase the probability of correct results, since the picture will be analysed pixel by pixel. However, if the computing power is limited, the developer can decide to group the pixels and, for example, compare clusters of ten

[19] See <https://www.merriam-webster.com/dictionary/algorithm>.

[20] For an overview of such tools see 'Top 18 artificial intelligence platforms' (*Ppat Research*) https://www.predictiveanalyticstoday.com/artificial-intelligence-platforms/.

pixels, resulting in ten input neurons. The overall mathematical model ends up in the code of the AI application, but as values instead of programming expressions (ie, words).

2.3 Framework

The framework is basically the environment in which the AI application is created, trained, and evaluated. In some cases, it may be proprietary and used within a company on their own computers or in the lab of a research institution. However, there are numerous examples of frameworks that are being used on the web as services stored on servers of a provider. One of the most prominent frameworks is TensorFlow, operated by Alphabet, the parent company of Google. Others include Microsoft Azure, Rainbird, and Premonition.[21]

2.4 Weights and Biases

Weights and biases play an integral role in DNN. They have enormous influence on the way in which information moves from the input layer to the output layer and thus on the quality of the final output. Similar to mathematical models, they are included in the code but as numbers and not as literary expressions.

2.5 Fitness Functions and Other Evaluation Mechanisms

Just like a child or a learning adult, an AI application, irrespective of whether it is based on ML or evolutionary algorithms, can continue with its task without any regard to the quality of the outcome. An application for image recognition may continue to see cats in dog pictures, and an application to design a new toothbrush or space antenna may come up with results that cannot be used in real life. You can imagine a toothbrush with a head 5 cm long and a handle just 1 cm. What AI needs to distinguish good from bad outputs, without or at least with limited human intervention, are mechanisms for evaluation. One example of such a mechanism is a fitness function, which, in mathematical terms, sets parameters for evaluation of output. Therefore, such a function may pre-specify that the head of a toothbrush may not be longer than 1.5 cm and the handle should be sufficiently long for the average human hand to use it. A space antenna may have predefined characteristics regarding energy input and output and the material that can be used. Here again,

[21] For further frameworks see ibid.

the parameters are predefined by the developers and translated into mathematical terms (ie, numbers and functions). Once they can be expressed in mathematical terms, they are included in the code. It is worth mentioning that modern programmers do not code every mathematical function from scratch. Instead they rely on pre-programmed routines and thus are able to work at a higher level of abstraction to achieve certain tasks through programming.[22]

2.6 Summary

At this point, we can summarize that the parts of an AI application that include most of the coding work are the framework and the transformation of the algorithm into executable code. Both parts are also similar to work that has been done in 'classical software development' although with some differences. The other parts, while of enormous importance, are mostly mathematical concepts that require a lot of thinking and preparation, but which can in many cases be implemented in the code by including numbers and functions at the appropriate places. This distinction is important to keep in mind when we now turn to the legal framework for software as it existed in the past and still exists, with its strengths, limitations, and flaws.

3. Traditional Software Protection and Its Flaws

While the practical application of AI may be a relatively new development, software as such has existed for decades, and has been the subject of IP protection and sometimes fierce litigation. Over the decades, flaws in the protection of traditional software that do not foster innovation but instead have the potential to create dysfunctional, innovation-hampering effects have become visible. Just for the sake of clarity, it should be mentioned that IP rights do not protect software in general, but only executable computer programs instead of code or coded information. While this distinction may not have been of great importance in the past, it may become much more so with respect to AI application.

3.1 Copyright Protection

Software or computer programs have always been part of a technical field. Software runs on machines, and those who design, code, and implement software are called

[22] See Plotkin, 'Computer Programming and the Automation of Invention' (n 7).

software engineers.[23] To compare a software engineer and his or her creation, the software code, to a painter or writer and a painting or novel seems pretty far-fetched at first sight. Nevertheless, software has been explicitly protected by copyright at the international level as well as in various national laws from the 1970s[24] onwards.[25] Understanding how this came about is important to understand the problems and insufficiencies of this protection and the subsequent shift to the patent regime. It is also an important basis for analysing the applicability of copyright protection to the software parts of AI.

To understand the historical development and current situation of legal software protection, it is important to understand the technical history of software and software development.[26] Generally speaking, according to computer sciences, software is everything that is not hardware, meaning that software are those parts of a computer system that can be moved from one system to another. Another distinction is that software is the part of a computer system that turns the general purpose machine (the hardware) into a special purpose machine with the purpose being defined by the software.[27] However, in the very beginning, software was still tangible and 'hard' and either firmly wired into the hardware or moveable in the form of punch cards. These punch cards replaced rigid wiring of computer systems and thus allowed for much more flexibility, since the rigid wiring had to be rearranged to make the computer perform a different operation. What the wiring and the punch cards could do was activate (or not activate) switches resulting in the flow of current. Two different situations were possible: current is flowing (1) or current is not flowing (0). These two binary possibilities are still the basic 'language' that a computer understands, and that is called machine code. Writing software in machine code is at least difficult and perhaps even impossible for a human programmer. Therefore, programming languages have been developed that allow the programmer to use a language very similar to natural language to write instructions for a computer, called the source code.

[23] Of course there are also other job descriptions such as programmer or developer, but those neither confirm nor counter the technical nature of software, and merely describe on a more or less abstract level what the person is doing. Plotkin, eg, provides a comparison between the classical (electrical) engineering process and the process of engineering a computer program. See ibid.

[24] In 1979 the Commission on New Technological Uses of Copyrighted Works (CONTU), which was established by the US Congress five years earlier, came to the conclusion that the US Copyright Act of 1976 already protected computer programs, but recommended changes including the insertion of a definition of 'computer program' in the Copyright Act, s 10, which was implemented in 1980. See Mark A Lemley and others, *Software and Internet Law* (4th edn, Wolters Kluwer 2011) 32.

[25] On the international and EU level see WIPO Copyright Treaty of December 20, 1996, Art 4; TRIPs, Art 10(1); Art 1 of the Directive 91/250 dated 14 May 1991 on the legal protection of computer programs at 42 expressly states: 'In accordance with the provisions of this Directive, Member States shall protect computer programs, by copyright, as literary works within the meaning of the Berne Convention for the Protection of Literary and Artistic Works'.

[26] For an historical overview see Robert Plotkin, *The Genie in the Machine: How Computer-Automated Inventing is Revolutionizing Law and Business* (Stanford Law Books 2009) 18 ff (hereafter Plotkin, *The Genie in the Machine*).

[27] Ibid, 30.

In the early days of programming languages, this source code was actually written in a text editor and then transferred first to an assembler that would make a first translation into an assembler language, which would then be translated by a compiler into the machine code understandable by a computer. So looking just at the first stage of programming at that time, the source code was just a long text. It was not readable by an average person, but it was close to this and used words from the English language.[28] Back in the 1960s and 1970s the source code for a computer program could consist of several hundred pages of text. One example of such a program is that for the Apollo 11 space mission. The code for the control of the capsule consisted of hundreds of pages of code and was vital in the success of the mission.[29] Today this source code is publically available to everyone.[30] The appearance of source code as text may have been a first reason why, in the 1970s, copyright was considered and introduced as the (primary) way to protect software through IP rights.

A second reason can be related to the way software was transferred at that time. If stored on a portable medium, which was often a floppy disk at that time, instead of the hard drive or memory of the computer, the software was copied from one floppy disk to another using two floppy drives. This method very much resembled the copying of text from one piece of paper to another piece of paper by the first Xerox photocopying machines or music from one magnetic tape to another using a tape recorder for two tapes. So the product resembled a work category known in copyright (literary works), and the method of copying was one relevant to copyright infringement as well.

While copyright protection was initially sought by software programmers and after intensive lobbying was introduced first in the US and then on a global scale, it left one vital part of software unprotected: the idea. According to the idea-expression dichotomy, copyright law protects only the expression laid down in a work but not the general idea behind the work.[31] While it is true that particularly in the early ages a substantial part of the investment in software development went into programming (ie, labour), the real value for the buyer of the software came from the idea and the functionality. Neither was directly protected by copyright, leaving a gap that could be exploited by competitors when the market became more diverse.[32]

[28] There are also programming languages using terms based on other languages such as French, German, or Mandarin Chinese to mention just a few, but most of the commonly used languages rely on English.

[29] Maia Weinstock, 'Scene at MIT: Margaret Hamilton's Apollo code' (*MIT News*, 17 August 2016) <https://news.mit.edu/2016/scene-at-mit-margaret-hamilton-apollo-code-0817>.

[30] Github <https://github.com/chrislgarry/Apollo-11>.

[31] *Brown Bag Software v Symantec Corp.* 960 F.2d 1465; David I Bainbridge, *Information Technology and Intellectual Property* (7th edn, Bloomsbury Professional 2019) 88 (hereafter Bainbridge, *Information Technology and Intellectual Property*).

[32] *Apple Computer, Inc. v Microsoft Corp.* 35 F.3d 1435.

3.2 Patent Protection

It was the gap in the protection through copyright that led to a shift by software developers to obtain patents on their products. However, patent laws contain either literally or through case law an exclusion of, inter alia, computer programs. The reason for this exclusion can be traced to different arguments.[33] A first one is the belief that software is a building block of modern industries and science, and should therefore not be monopolized in the strong form of idea protection but only with respect to the form in which it was laid down. A second argument stems from the belief that software resembles thought processes or mental acts, and that mental acts as abstract ideas should not be patentable. While there is the general belief that the legal situation is quite different between the US and Europe, the practical consequences in litigation are more or less the same.

3.2.1 The situation in the EPO

For a long time, it was an often-repeated myth that computer programs or software were not patentable under the European Patent Convention (EPC). The reason for this misbelief lies in Article 52(2) and (3) EPC. It is worth taking a closer look at both paragraphs of this article:[34]

> (2) The following in particular shall not be regarded as inventions within the meaning of paragraph 1:
> (a) discoveries, *scientific theories* and *mathematical methods*;
> (b) aesthetic creations;
> (c) schemes, *rules and methods for performing mental acts*, playing games or doing business, and *programs for computers*;
> (d) presentations of information.
>
> (3) Paragraph 2 shall exclude the patentability of the subject-matter or activities referred to therein only to the extent to which a European patent application or European patent relates to such subject-matter or activities *as such*.

With respect to computers, the case law of the European Patent Office (EPO) and the examination guidelines that derive from this case law make it clear that the exclusion does not apply when the computer program has a technical character.[35] This limitation of the exclusion—which cannot be found in the wording of the EPC—is the very needle eye through which software developers try to squeeze

[33] Rudolf Krasser and Christoph Ann, *Patentrecht* (7th edn, CH Beck 2016) 184 ff.
[34] Emphasis added.
[35] Guidelines for Examination Part G II 3.6; EPO T 1173/97 and EPO G 3/08.

their products to obtain a patent. The EPO assesses the technical effect without taking into consideration the prior art. Therefore, simply replacing a process or the acts of a human being, which are not considered to be technical, does not suffice to give the invention a technical character.[36] As the guidelines and the case law further set out: 'Further technical considerations beyond merely finding a computer algorithm to perform a task are needed'.[37]

However, controlling the functioning of a computer by means of a computer program may have the required technical character. The EPO guidelines list computer programs implementing security measures for protecting boot integrity or countermeasures against power analysis attacks as examples of technical character. Also the programs specifying a method of controlling anti-lock braking in a car, determining the emissions by an X-ray device, compressing videos, restoring a distorted digital image, or encrypting electronic communications have been considered to have a technical effect by the case law of the EPO.[38]

So overall, while each case has been decided on its own merits, there is a rather clear line to decide whether an invention has the required technical character: computer programs, or more precisely, their underlying algorithms, are methods to accomplish tasks or solve problems. As long as the method remains abstract, it cannot be patented under the rules of the EPC even if it runs on a computer. As soon as the method is put to a specific, technical use, it will be treated just like any other solution for a problem and subjected to the further patent requirements of novelty and inventive step. In principle, these rules apply also to AI applications.

3.2.2 The situation in the US

For a long time, the common opinion was that it is a lot easier to obtain patents on computer programs, software, or computer-implemented business models in the US than in Europe and particularly at the EPO. To some extent this is true. On the one hand, neither the black letter law nor the case law in the US excluded computer programs per se or as such from patentability. Instead, US courts only exclude 'mathematical formulas' and 'abstract ideas' from patentability.[39] So, as a starting point, the general approach towards protecting computer programs by means of patents was not as negative as it seemed to be in Europe. The leniency of the US courts reached its highest point with the decision in *State Street Bank & Trust Co. v Signature Financial Group, Inc.* by the US Court of Appeals for the Federal Circuits (CAFC) in 1998, which was regarded as carte blanche for business

[36] EPO T 1227/05; EPO T 1784/06; EPO T 1370/11; EPO T 1358/09.

[37] Guidelines for Examination Part G II 3.6; G 3/08.

[38] Guidelines for Examination Part G II 3.6.1.

[39] Bainbridge, *Information Technology and Intellectual Property* (n 31) 490 f.

idea patents and software patents.[40] This development lasted throughout the first decade of the twenty-first century, when the US Supreme Court stepped in. In the cases of *Bilski*,[41] *Alice*,[42] and *Mayo*[43] the court had the opportunity to provide guidance on the question of patentable subject matter. Subsequent case law by the CAFC provides additional guidance as to when a patent may be granted for an invention using a computer program, but overall—as in the EPO—this is an area of law very much defined on a case-by-case basis.[44]

3.2.3 Trans-jurisdictional issues

Irrespective of the specific legal situation in the US and at the EPO, there are several issues regarding the protection of computer programs through patents which are problematic and may cause dysfunctional effects in the market.

The first issue that has been brought up in the legal literature is the question of sufficient disclosure. Particularly, it has been argued that patents for computer programs cannot be granted if the patent applicant does not include the software code with the patent application.[45] The argument is that the patent must enable the person skilled in the art to create the invention based on the patent claims, the description, and drawings. While the lack of the source code may be a serious issue in some cases, it will not be so in others. Depending on the description and the flow charts that are usually included in the drawings, a person skilled in the art may indeed be able to write the required code themselves. This may happen in a different programming language than the inventor used, but it may be sufficient to create the same functionality. This issue therefore needs to be decided on a case-by-case basis.

A second important issue is the general breadth of patents involving computer programs. Patents including computer programs are, at least in cases where the computer program is at the heart of the invention, per se process patents since the computer program and the algorithm behind the computer program are processes.[46] If the process is described in the patent claims in very abstract terms, this

[40] Mark A Lemley and Samantha Zyontz, 'Does Alice target patent trolls?' (2020) <https://ssrn.com/abstract=3561252>.

[41] *Bilski v Kappos*, 130 S.Ct. 3218.

[42] *Alice Corp. Pty. Ltd. v CLS Bank Intern.*, 134 S.Ct. 2347.

[43] *Mayo Collaborative Services v Prometheus Laboratories, Inc.*, 132 S.Ct. 1289.

[44] For an overview see Bainbridge, *Information Technology and Intellectual Property* (n 31) 490 ff.

[45] Reto M Hilty, 'Softwareurheberrecht statt Softwarepatente? Forderungen der Deutschen Politik unter der Lupe' in Christian Alexander and others (eds), *Festschrift für Helmut Köhler zum 70. Geburtstag* (CH Beck 2014) 288, 291; Reto M Hilty and Christophe Geiger, 'Patenting Software? A Judicial and Socio-economic Analysis' (2005) IIC 615, 646; Joachim Weyand and Heiko Hasse, 'Patenting Computer Programs: New. Challenges' (2005) IIC 647, 660; Thomas P Burke 'Software Patent Protection: Debugging the Current System' (1994) Notre Dame Law Review 1115, 1158.

[46] Reto M Hilty and Christophe Geiger, 'Towards a New Instrument of Protection for Software in the EU? Learning the Lessons from the Harmonization Failure of Software Patentability' in Gustavo Ghidini and Emanuela Arezzo (eds), *Biotechnology and Software Patent Law: A Comparative Review on New Developments* (Edward Elgar 2011) 153; Plotkin, 'Computer Programming and the Automation of Invention' (n 7).

will result in an overly broad protection, possibly covering uses and therefore outputs that the programmer may not even have dreamt of. And since examples included in the description are sufficient for enablement while not limiting the scope of the claims, any other use of the process even for a different purpose would be blocked by the patent. Particularly in relatively young and developing markets, such patents can stifle innovation. And as mentioned earlier, it was the fear of such a development that was the reason behind the intended limitation of patents on computer programs.

4. AI and Software Protection

Based on the previous parts of this chapter, the question now is: how should software protection be designed with respect to AI applications and their software parts? We have seen that copyright protects only the code, and patents protect the idea as far as it goes beyond the mere software code. In fact, we have seen that the code is not even included in either the claims or the description or drawings of the patent application and granted patent. To understand where potential dangers of the application of the current software protection to AI lie and to what extent the current protection regimes probably will not create any (additional) dysfunctional effects, it is helpful to take a closer look at specific examples of AI applications (Section 4.2).

But before that, the chapter provides a more abstract look at the various parts of AI applications as laid out in Section 2 of this chapter and attempt to establish whether they are protected by either copyright or patents (Section 4.1).

4.1 AI in Copyright and Patent Law

4.1.1 Framework

The framework is coded in a specific programming language. This as such, however, does not make it a computer program in the sense of the law. However, the framework consists of executable commands that can run on a computer system. Even if it is provided over the Internet and accessible through the use of a website, this does not change. The code runs on a server—which is a computer—and the result of the computation is then displayed through the Internet on a client. With respect to the current law, this does not make a difference. Therefore the framework can be protected by copyright.[47]

[47] Patrick Ehinger and Oliver Stiermerling, 'Die urheberrechtliche Schutzfähigkeit von Künstlicher Intelligenz am Beispiel von Neuronalen Netzen' (2018) Computer Recht 761, 769.

4.1.2 Algorithm

As explained above, the algorithm is a set of instructions. As such it can be protected by copyright as far as it is coded in a programming language and meets the requirements of originality and individuality.[48] With respect to patent law, neither the abstract algorithm nor the code can be protected as such.[49] However, according to the EPO and the case law in the US an algorithm implemented in a computer program in a way that meets the additional requirements of technicality in the EPO or goes beyond a mere abstract idea in the US can be protected by a patent.[50] In the abstract, this is true for ML algorithms as well as for evolutionary algorithms. However, as with most computer programs the decision has to be made on a case-by-case basis, and it can only be concluded that algorithms are not excluded from protection per se.

4.1.3 Model and mathematical functions

As explained above, an AI's model, weights, and biases as well as fitness functions and other evaluation mechanisms are based on numbers and mathematical functions and included in the AI application as such. Therefore, a priori, they are excluded from both copyright and patent protection. However, with respect to patent law this conclusion is not entirely without limitations. While it is true that the specific function or the numbers used for biases and weights are excluded from patentability in the US and at the EPO, this does not prevent the application for and granting of a patent that includes the function and numbers while fulfilling all the other requirements of patent protection. In fact, here the situation may not be so different from other areas of technology. Just as the use of a mathematical function may be patented with respect to software determining the state of an airplane[51] or the correct dosage of a drug,[52] they may be part of a patent for an AI application and therefore their use in the same context may be protected.

4.1.4 Data

Although there has been some discussion in recent years regarding IP rights to data, this development has fortunately slowed down.[53] While data are of tremendous importance not only for machine learning but also for many other aspects of

[48] Ibid; Thomas Söbbing, 'Algorithmen und urheberrechtlicher Schutz' (2020) Computer Recht 223, 228.

[49] Ronny Hauck and Baltasar Cevc, 'Patentschutz für Systeme Künstlicher Intelligenz?' (2019) Intellectual Property Journal 135, 147 f.

[50] Ibid, 148 f.

[51] German Federal Court of Appeal, decision of 30 June 2015 case no X ZB 1/15—*Flugzeugzustand*.

[52] EPO Decision of the Enlarged Board of Appeal G 2/08 dated 19 February 2010—*Dosierungsanleitung/ABBOTT RESPIRATORY* ECLI:EP:BA:2010:G000208.20100219.

[53] For a general discussion of rights in data see Drexl and others, 'Data Ownership and Access to Data—Position Statement of the Max Planck Institute for Innovation and Competition of 16 August 2016 on the Current European Debate' (2016) Max Planck Institute for Innovation & Competition Research Paper No 16-10.

the industry of things, there are risks in assigning exclusive right to a commodity that is of crucial importance for entire industries and where general access may be much of greater benefit to everyone than exclusion. This is particularly true since we do not see any shortage in data creation without exclusive rights, and various approaches to how data can be shared on a large scale are being discussed.[54] This leaves the situation with respect to AI application such that the data used for the training of the AI are not protected under the current regimes unless it can be established that it is a database and therefore protected either by copyright or in the EU through the sui generis database protection regime. However, quite often this may not be the case for various reasons.[55] In practice, it is in fact difficult to imagine how this may play a role. Quite often, what the customer or the competitor gets to see is the trained algorithm that is used in the AI application. It is very difficult to reverse engineer the data from any output, particularly in cases where DNN are used. So this suggests that legal protection beyond technical measures combined with trade secret or unfair competition law protection may not be required.

4.1.5 Overall AI application

The overall AI application consisting of the parts described above will either be presented as coded software in a product or as a service via the Internet. With respect to copyright law, only those parts that actually meet the requirements of copyright protection will be protected[56] Therefore, infringement will be found in cases where the overall code of the application has been copied. With respect to patent law, the rules on patentability of computer programs as described above apply. This means that as long as the product meets the requirement of technical effect (at the EPO) or goes beyond a mere mental act (in the US), it may be protected by patent law.

4.1.6 Summary

Based on the above legal analysis, not all, but substantial parts of AI applications can be protected under the current IP regimes through either copyright or patent law. Some parts, such as the data and the mathematical and logical models behind the applications, as well as the labour associated with the testing and implementing of the models, cannot be protected by traditional IP rights, but may obtain protection as trade secrets or through de facto protection in cases where reverse engineering is not feasible. In the abstract, the available protection seems therefore to be sufficient, and the question arises as to whether or not the granted protection may indeed have negative effects such as those that we have seen with respect to classical computer programs but also other types of subject matter protected

[54] There may, however, be a need to distinguish between raw big data and labelled data prepared for the use in AI application, see Kung-Chung Liu and Shufeng Zheng, Chapter 16 in this volume.

[55] For a detailed analysis see Matthias Leister, Chapter 17 in this volume.

[56] Ehinger and Stiermerling (n 47) 769.

by IP rights. In the abstract, IP rights may seem justified and helpful. The real dysfunctionalities and market failures become apparent when we take a look at real usage cases and examples, and their interplay with the protection regimes.

4.2 Specific Examples

The above analysis shows that AI applications and at least some of their parts are not excluded from IP protection per se. However, beyond the question of actual patentability or protection by copyright, a far more important question is whether or not protection is actually required, since we know from experience that IP rights not only provide benefits and reduce market failure, but also can create dysfunctionalities themselves and thus be detrimental to innovation. This question can be approached from the perspective of IP theories and justifications.[57] But when a technology is relatively new and developing rapidly, broad experience and empirical studies are scarce. Additional value can therefore come from the analysis of specific examples. Therefore, in this section a few examples will be used to highlight some important aspects regarding the protection of AI applications through IP rights.

4.2.1 Patents on the application of AI

As explained in Section 3.2, the reason behind the excluded subject matter in patent law is mostly the fear that basic concepts of science may be monopolized and therefore protection granted can stifle the overall development in an area of technology for up to twenty years. Therefore, patenting broad concepts, possibly even without a sufficiently enabling disclosure, must be prevented. Without attempting to provide a detailed patentability analysis including enablement and prior art, this section points to two examples that demonstrate where the dangers lie with respect to AI patents.

The first example is US 5,659,666 (the '666 patent'). The patent claims a 'Device for the Autonomous Generation of Useful Information'. At first, this reads very much like the patent on a search or brainstorming device in general. The 666 patent contains a total of four independent claims and thirteen dependent claims. It is of course possible to discuss in general whether or not claims directed to such computer program-based inventions should be patentable. However, this would not enrich the debate beyond what has already been discussed at length in jurisdictions around the globe prior to the rise of AI applications. Instead, it promises much more value to analyse the possible effect of the patent and its claims on AI applications and their future development.

[57] See Reto M Hilty, Jörg Hoffmann, and Stefan Scheuerer, Chapter 3 in this volume.

In essence, what a device based on the first independent claim of the 666 patent does is produce suggestions, eg, for new designs by using a trained ANN and sending those for evaluation regarding fitness to a second ANN. The second ANN can send back the results by way of feedback to the first ANN. What is crucial from the point of view of the patent and the 'creative' or 'innovative' aspect of the claimed invention is the perturbation involved, which gradually removes 'thinking' boundaries from the pre-trained knowledge of the first ANN. This leads, in the words of the patent, to 'hybridized or juxtaposed features'.[58] Or to use an example from the patent description, pictures of cows and birds may gradually result in cows with wings. So far, this sounds very much just like the process of human creativity or innovation. The ANN learns to think outside the box and ignore previously acquired knowledge as long as the second ANN agrees with the fitness of the new creations for the intended purpose. This is very similar to the process of trial and error that every child and most engineers and designers go through when they try to come up with something new.

So far, the innovation engine seems to be a desirable and useful tool to support engineers and designers in their work. In fact, the patent presents a coffee mug, a musical composition, and designs for the automobile industry as examples of things that have been created by a device based on the patent. The problem, however, lies in the breadth of such a patent. As described earlier in this chapter and in previous chapters of this book, AI applications based on artificial neural networks consist of several key elements that are required for every such application.

In essence, the 666 patent claims a method of thinking and/or inventing implemented in an ANN setup. By this, it claims a basic building block of research and thus may be a crucial obstacle to any future research based on ANN for the purpose of innovation.[59] In addition, the 666 patent does not disclose any details regarding the setup of the two ANN or how exactly the perturbation is accomplished. It just discloses the basic idea and setup of the device. Neither the weights and biases nor the number of layers in the ANN are described. Therefore, it seems difficult to set up such a network based on the patent. It remains an abstract idea implemented in the form of a software setup.

But there are also examples of patents that may meet the criteria for patentability by providing sufficient disclosure and also avoid the risks to general innovation by being directed to specific uses of AI technologies. One such example is patent US 7,117,186 B2 (the '186 patent'). The patent claims a method and apparatus for automatic synthesis of controllers. The invention uses genetic algorithms to come up with new designs for controllers. So, first of all, it is limited to a relatively specific purpose and meets the requirements of technicality. Furthermore, the description

58 Patent US 5,659,666 Col. 4, Lines 45–46.

59 Further examples of patents on basic buildings blocks of AI technology and possible approaches to reduce the number of such patents, see Raphael Zingg, Chapter 4 in this volume.

and drawings provide detailed information regarding the setup of the invention including a mathematical function and even source code.[60] This demonstrates that it is possible to obtain protection while not expanding the boundaries of protection in ways that monopolize very general concepts. This limits itself to the specific application of such concepts.

4.2.2 Patents on the output of AI

While it is not exactly a question of software protection, it makes sense to take a look at the protection of 'outputs' generated by AI applications. The innovation machine described above has apparently come up with various different 'inventions', some of which have been patented. One of the first appears to be a toothbrush that has later been marketed as the 'Oral-B Crossaction'.[61] The concept for the toothbrush was designed by the AI based on some data regarding the design and effectiveness of previous toothbrush designs and by the system described in the 666 patent trying out different new designs, evaluating them for fitness and presenting a final output. It is not absolutely clear from the patents and the literature what kind of algorithm has been used in the DNN, but it can be assumed that it was a form of reinforced learning. It is also clear that the 'Oral-B Crossaction' toothbrush has been patented.[62] So in principle, AI as a general purpose thinking machine does not require patent protection from a commercial point of view since the output can be protected and used for remuneration. As long as all other requirements for patent protection are met, there is no reason to exclude the toothbrush as an output from patentability just because a human used a machine to support the process of invention. At this point we need to keep in mind once again that there is no such thing as an autonomous inventor. The idea of the toothbrush comes from a human being, as do the model, architecture, and data including previous toothbrushes and parameters for fitness, and it is a human being that decides whether the output is indeed satisfactory, since the machine will not brush anyone's teeth to see whether the toothbrush is good or not. What the AI application essentially does is speed up the design process by creating more designs in a short period of time than a human being ever could and to some extent by eliminating the bias in the human designer's thinking process which comes from the designer's past experience.

This is particularly apparent in another example, the new NASA antenna. Here, it is well-established that the technology used to design the antenna was based on evolutionary algorithms.[63] And it has also been established that the final design,

[60] See Figure 10 of the patent US 7,117,186 B2.

[61] For a history of this invention see Plotkin, *The Genie in the Machine* (n 26) 51 ff.

[62] See US 6,564,416, although it is not clear whether or not the first design suggested by the AI has been patented.

[63] Gregory S Hornby and others, 'Automated antenna design with evolutionary algorithms' (2006) Collection of Technical Papers—Space 2006 Conference <https://ti.arc.nasa.gov/m/pub-archive/1244h/1244%20(Hornby).pdf>.

while meeting all the requirements of NASA, would have never been presented by either a single designer or a team of designers. It is simply so far outside of any previous design that only chance could have led to it. Admittedly, the amount of labour that went into the preparation of the AI application that finally came up with the new antenna was enormous. But does this require patent protection for the AI application itself? This is doubtful. First of all, most of the thinking and trying out came once again from the mathematical parts of the AI, and it is not clear whether or not the AI as such—compared to other AIs—has been innovative. Second, as with the toothbrush, it seems that sufficient economic incentives result from the possibility of using and maybe licensing or selling the antenna that additional incentives with respect to the AI application are not necessary. And if the real work and ingenuity went into the mathematical part of the application and not the art expressing the code, there is also no basis—and no requirement—for copyright protection.

4.2.3 AI without patent protection

Interestingly, many AI applications currently discussed seem to originate from the US and the major players in the markets for IT and data. This includes DABUS and the space antenna, but also self-driving cars by Wanyo, another Alphabet subsidiary, and the AI applications included in Siri, Cortana, Alexa, and any platform that uses AI to provide better tailored services to customers such as music play lists or video streaming recommendations. Nevertheless, one interesting company that in its business area is a not-so-hidden champion comes from Europe. Experts are of the opinion that the AI-based translation services provided by DeepL are far better than those by well-known competitors. The interesting thing is that DeepL is not providing any details regarding its technology and apparently also has not patented its technology.

This suggests several things that are important regarding the discussion on software protection with respect to AI. For one, it seems that it is not easy to reverse engineer the setup of the AI behind DeepL, or else competitors would already have done so. Furthermore, the lack of patents or patent applications indicates that the company does not seem to regard such protection as vital for their technology-based business model. It may even be that patent application that indeed fulfils all the requirements of sufficient disclosure may be detrimental to the company by reducing the current lead time advantage that DeepL has.

4.2.4 Analysis

The examples show several things. First, patents on the basic concepts of the use of AI may not meet the requirements for patenting, either because they do not enable a person skilled in the art to actually build an AI based on the patent, or by being mere concepts or business methods and thus excluded from patentability. At least the chosen examples, however, do not suggest that AI applications do not deserve patent protection because they are implemented as software. There is some probability that there are also patents for which this exclusion will apply, but this requires additional extended research in the patent databases. Second, in those cases where the output of an AI application can be commercialized as a product or service, it is doubtful that patent protection is indeed required to prevent market failure. Instead, it is very plausible that the market will provide sufficient incentives to invest in AI and to use it if the quality of the products or services increases in a way that provides advantages in the market. Third, at least some usage cases do not rely on patent protection at all while keeping a technological and competitive advantage.

One conclusion that can be drawn from this is that there is some anecdotal evidence suggesting that patent protection may not be required, while at the same time it may be detrimental if it covers basic concepts of AI. Furthermore, it is evident that discussion of the pros and cons of protection on a theoretical level does not bear any merit. Instead, extensive empirical research starting from qualitative descriptive and exploratory work and moving to quantitative, large-scale studies is required.

5. Conclusions

At first sight, AI applications seem to be just like any other computer program, and the same rules seem to apply with respect to both patent and copyright protection. However, the main difference between 'ordinary' programs and AI applications is the higher complexity and the fact that the value behind the AI application is not just in the code or the general idea, and those are the subjects of copyright and patent protection. Because AI applications rely to a large extent on mathematical concepts and are currently at least difficult or even impossible to reengineer, the core value can be better protected through trade secrets. Nevertheless, if the requirements for a protectable computer program are met, copyright and patents may also play a role. In this respect there are two important points to highlight. The first one is that copyright protection seems in fact to be desirable not so much for the protection but for the exceptions and limitations included in copyright law. Those apply only if protection is recognized in the first place. With respect to patent law the core issue seems to be that a more purpose-bound form of protection is required. As demonstrated above, some of the current patents are so abstract that they may be obstacles to follow-on innovation, without actually demonstrating specific applications. Furthermore, in those examples, the 'inventor' may not even require patent protection, since the real value is in the output of the AI application, and this can be provided as a service instead of being sold. Rethinking software protection thus means limiting the protection in patent law to specific applications and appreciating the limitations of copyright protection. Since most AI platforms are currently offered based on open-source licences, this seems to be even more important.

PART VI
PROTECTION OF AND ACCESS TO DATA

16

Protection of and Access to Relevant Data—General Issues

*Kung-Chung Liu and Shufeng Zheng**

1. Introduction

The development of AI has evolved from technology driven to data driven.[1] The advancement of the Internet of things (IoT), supercomputers, and cloud technologies enable us to collect and process huge amounts of data, as well as to perform complicated calculations at the speed of light. The enormous amount of data further enhances machine learning and data-based innovations. Machine learning technology together with big data has been applied widely in all areas of our daily lives.[2] Data have become the raw materials of production, a new source of economic and social value.[3] The issue of the protection of and access to relevant data will have a tremendous impact on the future of AI. However, this chapter is not directed at any specific jurisdiction and could be used as the groundwork for the next chapter which discusses possible suggestions how to revise the database sui generis right.

The chapter is divided into five sections. After the introduction, Section 2 discusses typology of data and classifies data according to several criteria or dimensions. Section 3 deals with the issue of whether it is justified and necessary to provide protection for relevant data. Section 4 weighs the issues surrounding access to relevant data. Section 5 wraps up with some preliminary conclusions.

* All online materials were accessed before 10 April 2020.

[1] See Kai-Fu Lee, *AI Superpowers: China, Silicon Valley, and the New World Order* (1st edn, Houghton Mifflin Harcourt 2018) 14.

[2] Omer Tene and Jules Polonetsky, 'Big Data for All: Privacy and User Control in the Age of Analytics' (2013) 11 Northwestern Journal of Technology and Intellectual Property 240; Deloitte, 'Global Artificial Intelligence Industry Whitepaper' <https://www2.deloitte.com/cn/en/pages/technology-media-and-telecommunications/articles/global-ai-development-white-paper.html>.

[3] Tene and Polonetsky, 'Big Data for All' (n 2) 240, 238.

Kung-Chung Liu and Shufeng Zheng, *Protection of and Access to Relevant Data—General Issues* In: *Artificial Intelligence and Intellectual Property*. Edited by: Jyh-An Lee, Reto M Hilty, and Kung-Chung Liu, Oxford University Press (2021).
 DOI: 10.1093/oso/9780198870944.003.0017

2. Typology of Data: What Type of Data are We Talking About?

Currently, there is no generally accepted definition of data in the legal world due to their complex and diverse nature. The *Cambridge Dictionary* provides a basic understanding of data: 'information, especially facts or numbers, collected to be examined and considered and used to help decision-making or information in an electronic form that can be stored and used by a computer'.[4] As data have become the primary building blocks for the information society, they have gained more new applications and contain more complex connotations.

The European Commission (EC) does not use a clear definition of the term 'data'. Instead, the European Union (EU) focuses on certain types of data with critical economic value or potential legal issues, and provides targeted regulations.[5] The most influential one is the General Data Protection Regulation (GDPR), which provides privacy protection, guarantees a high level of personal data protection, and helps to establish digital trust and preconditions for sustainable business models that rely on the collection and processing of personal data. Other regulations include legislation on the free flow of non-personal data (focusing on non-personal data),[6] a directive on the re-use of public sector information (focusing on public data),[7] a recommendation on access to and preservation of scientific information (focusing on data specified for scientific research),[8] and guidance on sharing private-sector data (focusing on data controlled by private sectors).[9]

The widely read and referenced Position Statement of the Max Planck Institute for Innovation and Competition on Data Ownership and Access to Data (hereafter 'Position Statement') does not provide a definition of data either, which it considers a 'complex question'.[10]

[4] See *Cambridge Dictionary* <https://dictionary.cambridge.org/dictionary/english/data>.

[5] See Communication from the Commission to the European Parliament, the Council, the European Economic and Social Committee and the Committee of the Regions, 'Towards a common European data space' COM (2018) 232 final; European Commission, 'Building a European data economy' (22 May 2019) <https://ec.europa.eu/digital-single-market/en/policies/building-european-data-economy>.

[6] Regulation (EU) 2018/1807 of the European Parliament and of the Council of 14 November 2018 on a framework for the free flow of non-personal data in the European Union (2018) OJ L 303/59; Communication from the Commission to the European Parliament and the Council Guidance on the Regulation on a framework for the free flow of non-personal data in the European Union, COM (2019) 250 final.

[7] Council Directive 2019/1024/EC of 20 June 2019 on Open Data and the Re-Use of Public Sector Information [2019] OJ L 172/26.

[8] Commission Staff Working Document Accompanying the document Commission Recommendation on access to and preservation of scientific information C(2018)2375 final.

[9] Commission Staff Working Document Guidance on Sharing Private Sector Data in the European Data Economy Accompanying the Document Communication from the Commission to the European Parliament, the Council, the European Economic and Social Committee and the Committee of the Regions 'Towards a common European data space', SWD/2018/125 final.

[10] Paragraphs 2 and 8 of the Position Statement.

How about classifying data based on a single variable? Data classification is often used by companies as a method for data management,[11] and refers to labelling or grouping existing data according to data set requirements for various objectives to make data easily searchable and trackable.[12] However, our discussion angle is legal rather than data management.

Drawing from the above, a one-size-fits-all approach to data is simply not the right way to go. Our approach to data is one of typology, which is more flexible and allows for classifying data according to several criteria or dimensions.[13] Typology may not appear at first to be particularly as 'systematic' or 'scientific' as a means of providing a definition, but is nonetheless of considerable heuristic importance.[14] Various types of data have different methods of generation, functions, and legal issues. Differentiated legal judgement should be worked out for different types of data.

In the context of discussing ownership of data, Professor Reto Hilty identified three types of data, mainly according to the connection with and closeness to natural persons. The three types are 'data of purely technical or factual nature' (eg, machine data); 'person-related data' (data that involve a 'reference' or 'connection' to individual people such as personal data and consumer behaviour data); and data not directly 'attributed' to an individual person, but which can easily produce the relation to a person ('personenbeziehbar' data).[15] He rightly points out that 'Depending on the category we are talking about, data can be subject to fundamentally different conditions, whether in terms of collection, processing, function, or downstream uses of data'.[16]

We do not disagree with the three types Professor Hilty identified. However, for the purpose of viewing data as an instrument to facilitate AI development, we identify three types of data, which have different issues in protection and access. The first type is data specifically generated for AI, namely data tailor-made as the training materials for machine learning, which are critical to AI technology development.

The second type is big data. Big data are generated and collected by netizens, platforms, and smart devices (such as smart phones, metres, grids, etc) interconnected

[11] Wikipedia Introduction, <https://en.wikipedia.org/wiki/Data_classification_>(data management), data classification is used as a tool in data management for categorization of data to enable/help organizations to effectively know more background information of data>.

[12] See Techopedia <https://www.techopedia.com/definition/13779/data-classification>; Juliana De Groot, 'What is data classification? A data classification definition' (*DataInsider*, 15 July 2019) <https://digitalguardian.com/blog/what-data-classification-data-classification-definition>.

[13] Alberto Marradi, 'Classification, Typology, Taxonomy' (1990) 24 Quality & Quantity 129 (hereafter Marradi, 'Classification, Typology, Taxonomy').

[14] Kurt Hoehne, 'Classification vs Typology, A Difference of Practical Importance' (1980) 244(10) Journal of the American Medical Association 1099.

[15] Reto Hilty, 'Big Data: Ownership and Use in the Digital Age' in Xavier Seuba, Christophe Geiger, and Julien Pénin (eds), *Intellectual Property and Digital Trade in the Age of Artificial Intelligence and Big Data*, Trade in the Age of Artificial Intelligence and Big Data, Global Perspectives for the Intellectual Property System (CEIPI-ICTSD, 2018) 90, 91 (hereafter Hilty, 'Big Data').

[16] Ibid.

via the Internet and IoT. Big data have 'volume, veracity, velocity, and variety' as their technical features: data with huge size (volume), rapid change or updating for data collection and analysis (veracity and velocity), and various data sources, which include Internet browsers, social media sites and apps, cameras, cars, and a host of other data-collection tools (variety).[17] In addition, big data also has its huge socio-economic value dimension (value).[18]

The third type of data is copyright-protected data. Text and data mining (hereafter TDM) is the basic tool for data analysis and machine learning in various areas and would require copying, and therefore is faced with risks of infringing copyright-protected data.

It is admitted that the three types of data are not mutually exclusive of each other, as they involve different criteria. Copyright-protected data refers to legal status, and big data is according to the method of generation. Therefore, some copyright-protected data and big data can also be data specifically generated for AI as long as they are organized for AI purposes.[19] Cutting across these three types of data are both personal and non-personal data; this chapter focuses, however, more on the latter.

3. The Protection of Relevant Data

Copyright-protected data by the very name already enjoy the legal protection of copyright, and do not warrant further investigation at this juncture. In the following, our discussion will focus more on data specifically generated for AI and big data.

3.1 Data Specifically Generated for AI

Supervised machine-learning is dependent on labelled data (or a training data set (training data)).[20] However, in many cases, and especially when developing AI

[17] Daniel Rubinfeld and Michal S Gal, 'Access Barriers to Big Data' (2017) 59 Arizona Law Review 345–7 (hereafter Rubinfeld and Gal, 'Access Barriers to Big Data').

[18] OECD, *Supporting Investment in Knowledge Capital, Growth and Innovation* (2013) 325 <https://www.oecd-ilibrary.org/industry-and-services/supporting-investment-in-knowledge-capital-growth-and-innovation_9789264193307-en> (hereafter OECD, *Supporting Investment*); Daniel Gervais, 'Exploring the Interfaces Between Big Data and Intellectual Property Law' (2019) 22 Journal of Intellectual Property Information Technology and Electronic Commerce Law (JIPITEC) para 2 (hereafter Gervais, 'Exploring the Interfaces').

[19] However, some scholars point out that classes of a typology need to be mutually exclusive and jointly exhaustive. See Marradi, 'Classification, Typology, Taxonomy' (n 13) 129; Kenneth D Bailey, *Typologies and Taxonomies: An Introduction to Classification Techniques* (1st edn, SAGE Publications, Inc 1994) v.

[20] For more see Anthony Man-Cho So, Chapter 1 in this volume.

systems for specific applications, labelled data are scarce and costly to obtain.[21] Data augmentation is a common strategy for handling scarce data situations. It works by synthesizing new data from existing training data, with the objective of improving the performance of the downstream model. This strategy has been a key factor in the performance improvement of various neural network models, mainly in the domains of computer vision and speech recognition. Specifically, for these domains there exist well-established methods for synthesizing labelled data to improve classification tasks.[22]

Data labelling is a contribution of data generators as they collect data from various sources, select data and improve relevance, organize them in certain groups, and adjust data into a machine-readable format. The accumulation and consolidation (agglomeration, organization, selection, and processing) of data require intellectual and professional creations. Without sufficient protection the business of data labelling will be crippled. Therefore, labelled data should qualify as works worthy of copyright protection as compilation.[23]

The Q&A on Technical Aspects of Artificial Intelligence: An Understanding from an Intellectual Property Law Perspective (hereafter 'Q&A on Technical Aspects of AI') prepared by the Max Planck Institute for Innovation and Competition reminds us that 'A distinction should be made between the *direct output of a model* and the *potential practical applications of this output*.... from an intellectual property law perspective, distinct legal issues can arise with regard to direct outputs and their applications' (emphasis added) of a machine learning model, without however pointing out what distinct IP issues can arise with regard to direct outputs and their application respectively. Nevertheless, the output of a machine learning model is in principle deterministic and traceable, and often not human-explainable due to the complexity of the calculations, especially in the case of artificial neural networks (the 'black box' issue).[24] Technology startups like AiFi, May Mobility, Mapillary, etc, produce and use synthetic data for their machine learning to compensate for the lack of real data.[25] In the area of self-driving, where the data for real life experiments is hard to get, industry leaders like Google have been relying on simulations to create millions of hours of synthetic driving data to

[21] Ateret Anaby-Tavor, Boaz Carmeli, Esther Goldbraich, Amir Kantor, George Kour, Segev Shlomov, Naama Tepper, and Naama Zwerdling, 'Not Enough Data? Deep Learning to the Rescue!' (2019) 1911.03118 ArXiv 1.

[22] Ibid, 2; Rubinfeld and Gal, 'Access Barriers to Big Data' (n 17) 370.

[23] TRIPs, Art 10(2): '2. Compilations of data or other material, whether in machine readable or other form, which by reason of the selection or arrangement of their contents constitute intellectual creations shall be protected as such. Such protection, which shall not extend to the data or material itself, shall be without prejudice to any copyright subsisting in the data or material itself.'

[24] Drexl, Hilty, and others, 'Technical Aspects of Artificial Intelligence: An Understanding from an Intellectual Property Law Perspective' (October 2019) Max Planck Institute for Innovation & Competition Research Paper No 19-13 <https://papers.ssrn.com/sol3/papers.cfm?abstract_id=3465577>.

[25] Evan Nisselson, 'Synthetic data will democratize the tech industry' (*TechCrunch*, 12 May 2018) <https://techcrunch.com/2018/05/11/deep-learning-with-synthetic-data-will-democratize-the-tech-industry/>.

train their algorithms.[26] A thus synthesized data corpus is in essence the result of the operation of a certain algorithm or data augmentation method, similar to data generated from software and therefore does not deserve the same copyright protection as the software involved.[27]

However, such a synthesized data corpus, when satisfying all the necessary requirements (secrecy, commercial value, and reasonable steps taken to protect the secrecy), can be subject to trade secret protection.

3.2 Big Data

Although the Position Statement did not mention specifically that it was dealing with the legal treatment of big data (in fact it mentioned big data twice in addition to 'individual data', 'customer data', 'personal data', 'raw data', 'data set', and 'big data' when discussing specific issues),[28] it was clearly targeting big data. Basically, the Position Statement did not see any need or justification for creating exclusive rights in big data,[29] or for applying the sui generis right of database in the EU to big data.[30] It did however recognize that data are protectable against tortious conduct via 'regulation against unfair competition'.[31] The Position Statement further opined that 'one can conclude that even if individual data might not constitute a trade secret, the combination of data or information (that as such is not publicly available) might well do so'.[32]

Professor Hilty, a co-drafter of the Position Statement, has recently reminded people to be cautious with regard to the creation of 'data ownership', as legal ownership protection of databases in the EU has more negative effects, such as interference with the freedom to conduct a business and competition and impeding the development of downstream data markets, than positive effects, and Europeans at least should not repeat the legislation mistake when dealing with big data.[33] Indeed, statistics show that data markets keep growing rapidly without the blessing of an exclusivity right.[34]

[26] 'Synthetic data: an introduction & 10 tools [2020 update]' (*AI Multiple*, 1 January 2020) <https://blog.aimultiple.com/synthetic-data/#benefits>; Jordan Golson, 'Google's self-driving cars rack up 3 million simulated miles every day' (*The Verge*, 1 February 2016) <https://www.theverge.com/2016/2/1/10892020/google-self-driving-simulator-3-million-miles>.

[27] Daniel Gervais seems to have a similar reservation: '[T]he question whether machine-created productions can qualify as copyright works is either still open, or resolved in favour of a need for human authorship.' See Gervais, 'Exploring the Interfaces' (n 18) para 28.

[28] Position Statement, paras 9–11 (individual data), 25 (customer data), 3, 5, 39 (personal data), 13, 34, 39 (raw data), and 12 and 37 (big data) of the Position Statement.

[29] Ibid, paras 4–8.

[30] Ibid, paras 9–11.

[31] Ibid, paras 18–20.

[32] Ibid, para 26.

[33] Hilty, 'Big Data' (n 15) 90.

[34] According to the research from International Data Corporation, worldwide revenues for big data and business analytics (BDA) solutions are forecasted to reach USD 189.1 billion in 2019, an increase

We believe that the issue of 'protection of big data' should not be addressed in the sense or direction of giving proprietary entitlement over big data to any entity, which has some control over part of it, given the diverse nature, sources, and parties involved in the creation of big data. If data have become the raw materials of production, a new source of economic and social value, even more so are big data. Big data, as the single most valuable capital of our society for economic and technological innovation, are of crucial importance to human beings. Therefore, we must ensure that big data are not prevented from forming, accumulating, and flowing freely (accessing big data is another issue that we will come back to in the next section), including big data from both the private and public sectors.

3.2.1 Looking at the private-sector components of big data

There are at least two issues that hinder the formation, accumulation, and free flow of big data, namely, divergent national laws on personal data protection and on cross-border data transfer. There are two other issues that help big data to form, accumulate, and flow freely, namely, data standardization and trading.

3.2.1.1 Divergent national laws on personal data protection

Private-sector components of big data are under all sorts of state regulations, which might obstruct or slow down the formation, accumulation, and free flow of big data. For one thing, according to the United Nations Conference on Trade and Development (UNCTAD), as of April 2016 there were 108 countries which had implemented personal data protection laws governing collection and cross-border transfer of personal data.[35] It remains to be seen whether and to what extent personal data would be needed and could be used for the development of AI (eg, is profiling of specific individuals allowable?) and whether international efforts should be made to make national regulations on personal data harmonized in an AI-friendly way.

3.2.1.2 Divergent national regulations on cross-border transfer of non-personal data

For another thing, there are divergent national regulations on cross-border transfer of non-personal data. According to a study by Information Technology

of 12% over 2018. It also predicts BDA revenues will maintain this growth throughout the 2018–22 forecast, with a five-year compound annual growth rate (CAGR) of 13.2%. See IDC, 'IDC forecasts revenues for big data and business analytics solutions will reach $189.1 billion this year with double-digit annual growth through 2022' (*IDC*, 4 Aril 2019) <https://www.idc.com/getdoc.jsp?containerId=prUS44998419>.

[35] UNCTAD, 'Data Protection Regulations and International Data Flows: Implications for Trade and Development' (2016) 42.

and Innovation Foundation (ITIF), 'Cross-Border Data Flows: Where Are the Barriers, and What Do They Cost?', 'a growing number of countries are enacting barriers that make it more expensive and time-consuming, if not illegal, to transfer data overseas. Some nations base their decisions to erect such barriers on the mistaken rationale that it will mitigate cybersecurity concerns; others do so for purely mercantilist reasons'.[36] The study shows that *data localization*, which requires certain types of data to be stored within the country, has been adopted by thirty-four countries or regions, namely Argentina, Australia, Belgium, Brazil, Bulgaria, Canada, China, Colombia, Cyprus, Denmark, the EU, Finland, France, Germany, Greece, India, Indonesia, Iran, Kazakhstan, Kenya, Luxembourg, Malaysia, the Netherlands, Nigeria, New Zealand, Poland, Romania, Russia, South Korea, Sweden, Taiwan, Turkey, the UK, and the US. In addition, China requires security assessments for cross-border data transfer.[37]

The US actively promotes free cross-border data transfer through bilateral and multilateral free trade agreements (FTA). For example, Article 15.8 of the US-Korea FTA mandates that parties shall refrain from imposing or maintaining unnecessary barriers to electronic information flows across borders. Article 14.11.2 of the Trans-Pacific Partnership (TPP) and the Comprehensive and Progressive Agreement for Trans-Pacific Partnership (CPTPP) prescribes that members shall allow cross-border data flow and prohibits data localization. The World Trade Organization (WTO) has launched, at the eleventh WTO Ministerial Conference in Buenos Aires, an e-commerce initiative which can address the issue of cross-border data transfer, in December 2017. In January 2019 a Joint Statement on Electronic Commerce was launched by fifty WTO members (including the EU, the US, and China), representing over 90% of global trade. It is noteworthy that China has changed its conservative stance on this issue and has signed the Joint Statement.

We are of the opinion that strict cross-border data transfer rules (data localization) threaten big data, as they increase costs and add complexity to the collection and maintenance of data, and reduce the size of potential data sets supply, eroding the informational value that can be gained by cross-jurisdictional studies.[38]

36 ITIF, 'Cross Border Data Flows: Where Are the Barriers, and What Do They Cost?' (2017).

37 According to Arts 8 and 37 of China's Cyber Security Act, operators of critical information infrastructure need to conduct security assessment when transferring data out of China.

38 Anupam Chander and Uyin Lj, 'Data Nationalism' (2015) 64 Emory Law Journal 677, 730. For a more comprehensive analysis of these concerns, see Jyh-An Lee, 'Hacking into China's Cybersecurity Law' (2018) 53 Wake Forest Law Review 57, 78–87.

3.2.1.3 Data standardization

There is huge demand for data trading (discussed in the following sub-section), which will immensely facilitate machine learning, algorithm training, etc. A unified standard for the data format,[39] granularity, structure, internal organization, quality,[40] data portability,[41] and interoperability.[42] etc is the precondition for data trading. Standardization of data could also help limit duplication of data collection, storage, and analysis.[43]

However, the promotion of data standardization would incur huge costs and face practical difficulties in convincing market players to apply that standard. Once adopted, monopoly risks may arise when the standard is controlled by limited parties via intellectual property rights (IPR) or trade secret. Besides, the market may be locked in by the outdated standard and face high switching cost if a new one were to be adopted. Therefore, these concerns make the open data format highly desirable.[44]

[39] With a unified standard of data format, market players can use data from other sources without data transformation. See Unification Foundation, 'Why unified data is inevitable—the relevance to enterprise [part 3]' (*Unification*, 28 July 2018) <https://medium.com/unificationfoundation/why-unified-data-is-inevitable-the-relevance-to-enterprise-part-3-68202c79cd7>; Oracle White Paper 2017, 'A unified approach to data processing and analytics' <https://www.oracle.com/technetwork/database/options/advanced-analytics/oracleapproachtodataandanalytics-3761912.pdf> 2.

[40] The quality of data refers to the integrity and veracity of data as well as metadata disclosure. Minimum standards for data quality can help to solve the issue of metadata uncertainty and missing data. See Michal S Gal and Daniel L Rubinfeld, 'Data Standardization' (2019) 94(4) NYU Law Review 737, 747 (hereafter Gal and Rubinfeld, 'Data Standardization'). Metadata in data sets contain critical information about the properties of the data (attributes, history, unit, etc). They enable processors to track, group, and analyse data with detailed information. When metadata in a big data set are partial or unknown, erroneous processes may arise. Data receivers cannot fully understand the meaning or attributes of the data for processing without complete metadata. See David Marco, 'Implementing data quality through metadata, part 1' (*TDAN*,1 April 2006) <https://tdan.com/implementing-data-quality-through-metadata-part-1/5024>; 'Behind the data: investigating metadata' (*Exposing the Invisible*) <https://exposingtheinvisible.org/guides/behind-the-data-metadata-investigations/>; Scott Gidley, 'What is metadata and why is it critical in today's data environment?' (*DZone*, 20 February 2017) <https://dzone.com/articles/what-is-metadata-and-why-is-it-critical-in-todays>.

[41] Data portability refers to the ability to transfer data without affecting their content. In 2018, Apple, Facebook, Google, Microsoft, and Twitter founded the Data Transfer Project (DTP) to facilitate data standardization. The DTP uses services' existing Application Programming Interfaces (APIs) and authorization mechanisms to access data. It then uses service-specific adapters to transfer those data into a common format, and back into the new service's API. For more information see the Data Transfer Project website <https://datatransferproject.dev>.

[42] Interoperability refers to the ability to join up data from different sources in a standardized and contextualized way. See the Joined-Up Data Standards (JUDS) project, The Frontiers of Data Interoperability for Sustainable Development (November 2017) <https://www.publishwhatyoufund.org/wp-content/uploads/2017/11/JUDS_Report_Web_061117.pdf>.

[43] Gal and Rubinfeld, 'Data Standardization' (n 40) 737, 747.

[44] Jyh-An Lee 'Licensing Open Government Data' (2017) 13 Hastings Bus LJ 207, 213–14.

3.2.1.4 Data trading

There are three main data trading models: industrial data platforms,[45]marketplace for data transactions,[46] and companies' open data policy.[47] Data brokers are emerging and developing rapidly in the US, and make up the majority of data trading players.[48] Ideally, data transaction platforms could form a data transaction ecosystem with comprehensive services covering data transaction negotiation, transaction processing, data assets packaging, etc with unified standards on a large scale. According to one study by McKinsey, cross-border data flows grew by forty-five times between 2004 and 2014 and generated USD 2.8 trillion in global economic revenue in 2014.[49] To further enhance data trading, we need to ascertain whether there are other obstacles apart from standard-related (technical) obstacles that are impeding data trading, and find solutions to overcome those obstacles.

3.2.2 Looking at the public-sector components of big data

A large part of big data comes from the public sector, including public-funded education and R&D institutions, public utilities, government agencies, etc. As a result, the importance of having open access to those components of big data cannot be emphasized enough, which is also true for the development of AI. Huge amounts of open data could be used to facilitate machine learning applications

[45] Typical examples include Skywise and RIO. Skywise is an aviation data platform developed by AIRBUS which provides centralized and secure aviation data sharing to facilitate equipment design and service improvement in the aerospace area. RIO is the platform launched by MAN Truck & Bus as the platform to provide connectivity services on all commercial vehicles of MAN Truck & Bus's brands. By providing an exchange place for operation data, contract-, product-, and service-related data, etc, it serves multiple users, ranging from startups, manufacturers, telematics providers, original equipment manufacturers, and digital service providers.

[46] Such platforms act as independent third parties to provide a marketplace for data transactions by providing comprehensive services. Services ranging from transaction matching and data pricing, to data anonymization, and can cover the whole process of data transactions. DAWEX, a famous data-trading platform, connects companies with the end goal of selling and buying data, and providing user-friendly technical solutions to ease the process to monetize and acquire data. It also provides data pricing and API services. Talking Data is another data-trading platform developed by a pure data-processing technology company. Apart from providing technology service for data analysis and management, it now provides a smart data market to facilitate data exchange through tag data, user group data, risk detection, and secure data-sharing services. For more information see its website (<https://www.talkingdata.com/>). In China, to facilitate data trading, the government has established several data platforms, such as GBDEX (贵阳大数据交易所), the Changjiang Data exchange platform (长江大数据交易所), etc.

[47] Some companies apply B2B open data policy or form data-sharing alliances. But many of the companies are legally bound to make data available to third parties. Eg, Elering shares its data under legal obligation for free. Considering the competitive advantage for data resources and security requirements, companies which choose an open data policy are quite limited.

[48] Famous data brokers include Acxiom, Corelogic, Datalogix, eBureau, Recorded Future, etc. Different from data platforms, data brokers collect data by themselves and directly sell them to buyers online.

[49] McKinsey Global Institute (MGI), Digital globalization: The new era of global flows, 2016 <https://www.mckinsey.com/business-functions/mckinsey-digital/our-insights/digital-globalization-the-new-era-of-global-flows> 8–9.

and AI.[50] Currently, there are also many public databases specifically collected for AI research.[51] The various open government (public) data initiatives are of high importance to AI development.[52] The OECD Council 2008 Recommendation on Enhanced Access and More Effective Use of Public Sector Information (PSI) suggests openness, access, and transparent conditions for re-use, quality control (to ensure methodical data collection and curation practices to enhance quality), and safeguarding the integrity of PSI. It also prescribes other means to achieving effective use of PSI: exercising copyright in ways that facilitate re-use (eg, waiving copyright and creating mechanisms that facilitate waiving of copyright and use of orphan works); pricing PSI transparently and consistently within and across different public sector organizations if PSI is not provided free of charge; setting up redress mechanisms; facilitating public-private partnerships; and furthering international access and use.[53]

Following the call of the OECD, the EU has recently promulgated Directive (EU) 2019/1024 on open data and the re-use of public sector information (20 June 2019). This requires its members to ensure that documents to which this Directive applies and those documents on which libraries, including university libraries, museums, and archives hold IPRs and documents held by public undertakings, are re-usable for commercial or non-commercial purposes (Article 3). It set up principles governing pricing (Article 6), standardized licences (Article 8), and restriction on exclusive licences (Article 12), among other things. This is a welcome move in the right direction and of high reference value for the international community.

4. The Access to Relevant Data

Data access is the precondition for data collection and data processing. There are however legal mechanisms and obstacles that control or prevent data collection and mining, or raise the costs thereof.

[50] 'AI and open data: a crucial combination' (*European Data Portal*, 7 April 2018) <https://www.europeandataportal.eu/en/highlights/ai-and-open-data-crucial-combination>. There is one well-known project that uses public crime data to develop an algorithm identifying 'hotspot' areas where certain crimes are likely to occur in future. The algorithm successfully reduced burglaries by 33% and violent crimes by 21% in the city where it was applied. See the project information, 'Crime prevention through artificial intelligence' (*Data analytics*) <https://www.policyconnect.org.uk/appgda/research/crime-prevention-through-artificial-intelligence>.

[51] Kamalika Some, 'Working on AI? get these free public data sources for 2019' (*Analytics Insight*, 7 February 2019) <https://www.analyticsinsight.net/working-on-ai-get-these-free-public-data-sources-for-2019/>; Meiryum Ali, 'The 50 best free datasets for machine learning' (*Lionbridge*, 8 July 2019) <https://lionbridge.ai/datasets/the-50-best-free-datasets-for-machine-learning/>.

[52] See OECD, *Supporting Investment* (n 18) 339.

[53] OECD Legal Instruments, Recommendation of the Council for OECD Legal Instruments Enhanced Access and More Effective Use of Public Sector Information, OECD/LEGAL/0362.

4.1 Access to Data Specifically Generated for AI

We hold that with current legal tools, including flexible contractual arrangements and trade secret protection law, together with technical measures, data holders could keep control of access to their data specifically generated for AI by granting a licence. Unauthorized disclosure made by a contracting party could be sanctioned as contract violation. For unauthorized use by third parties, data holders could seek protection from trade secret law and/or unfair competition remedy.[54] However, whether and to what extent we need to enhance access to data specifically generated for AI is a completely different issue. If data specifically generated for AI are PSI, then we should take measures that may facilitate the widest re-uses of public data, such as compulsory obligations on public institutions to adopt open data policy,[55] disclose their data, and make rules that require public institutions to unify their data format to improve data interoperability.

However, if data specifically generated for AI are from the private sector, we then need to explore whether these data are of critical importance and whether there are scenarios in which the use of competition law and/or ex ante regulation will be needed to ensure access to data specifically generated for AI.

4.2 Access to Copyright-Protected Data

The development of technologies like TDM and natural language processing allows machines to extract information, tendencies, and knowledge from complicated data including articles, pictures, videos, and audios. Prior to that, data processors first need to digitalize data into a machine-readable format. Then, machines will read the texts or videos to locate and extract features, and finally, recombine these features to identify patterns and trends. As these data are under copyright protection, necessary copying, digitization, and processing in the mining process could incur infringement risks.

4.2.1 Major jurisdictions are applying fair use or fair dealing rule to AI

Getting copyright owners' permission for data mining and analysis would, in some cases, be 'an insurmountable obstacle, preventing a potentially significant quality of research from taking place at all'.[56] Actually, necessary copying, digitization, and

[54] Japan revised its Unfair Competition Prevention Act in 2018 and offers protection to data. According to Art 2.1(11)–(16), wrongful acquisition, use, or disclosure of data protected by electromagnetic measures is considered an act of unfair competition. See Japan Ministry of Economy, Trade and Industry, 'Revision of Unfair Competition Prevention Act' <https://www.meti.go.jp/english/policy/economy/chizai/chiteki/>. For more, see Matthias Leistner, Chapter 17 in this volume.

[55] Jyh-An Lee, 'Licensing Open Government Data' (2017) 13 Hastings Business Law Journal 207.

[56] UK Government, 'Modernising Copyright: A Modern, Robust and Flexible Framework. Government Response to Consultation on Copyright Exceptions and Clarifying Copyright Law' (2012) 37.

processing during data mining should not constitute copyright infringement, as it does not 'use' the works in the traditional sense, namely for personal enjoyment, appreciation, comprehension, or inspiration (non-expressive use), and would therefore not affect the economic results of those works (non-consumptive use or non-market-encroaching use).[57] Furthermore, TDM has the potential benefits of creating tools for education and research, fostering innovation and collaboration, boosting the impact of open science, improving population health and wealth, addressing grand challenges such as climate changes and global epidemics, and accelerating economic and social development in all parts of the globe,[58] and should enjoy exemptions from copyright liability.

In the US, the use of copyrighted text for TDM purposes is permitted under fair use because it is transformative and does not serve as a substitute to the original work, but enhances information-gathering techniques and serves a new purpose.[59] For the purpose of the use, although TDM can be used for commercial purposes, necessary copying for commercial purposes could still be regarded as fair use.

With the development of AI, providing legal certainty to researchers and market players of TDM is becoming increasingly critical to the development of machine learning. Major jurisdictions have recently introduced specific clauses to exempt data mining from copying infringement. For example, the UK adopted a clause which provides that copying for 'computational analysis' is not copyright infringement, and in a contract which purports to prevent or restrict the making of such copies, that term is unenforceable.[60] However, the exemption is limited for non-commercial use, and thus far, the clause remains unapplied by case law.[61] In 2019, the EU adopted the Directive on Copyright and related rights in the Digital Single Market and introduced specific clauses which allow reproduction and extraction for TDM. However, the Directive foresees substantial limitations: (1) If TDM is done by research organizations and cultural heritage institutions and of works or other subject matter to which they have lawful access (Article 3(1)), it must be for

[57] Matthew Sag, 'Orphan Works As Grist for the Data Mill' (2012) 27(3) Berkeley Technology Law Journal 1502, 1523, 1544; Deloitte Access Economics, 'Copyright in the digital age (2018)' 26 <https://www2.deloitte.com/content/dam/Deloitte/nz/Documents/Economics/dae-nz-copyright-fair-use-final.pdf>. See also Benjamin Sobel, Chapter 10 in this volume.

[58] See 'The Hague Declaration on Knowledge Discovery in the Digital Age' (2015) <https://www.ifla.org/publications/node/91863> (hereafter The Hague Declaration); United Nations Industrial Development Organization, 'World Statistics on Mining and Utilities' (*UNIDO*, 2018), available at <https://www.unido.org/resources/publications/cross-cutting-services/world-statistics-mining-and-utilities>.

[59] *Kelly v Arriba-Soft*, 336 F.3d 811 (9th Cir. 2003); *Authors Guild v Google*, 770 F.Supp.2d 666 (SDNY 2011); *Authors Guild v HathiTrust*, 755 F.3d 87 (2nd Cir. 2014).

[60] Copyright Designs and Patents Act 1988, s 29A(1), (5) which prohibits copyright holders from making reservations: copyright owners cannot prevent or restrict copying for text and data analysis for non-commercial research through contracts.

[61] See Eleonora Rosati, 'Copyright as an Obstacle or an Enabler? A European Perspective on Text and Data Mining and its Role in the Development of AI Creativity' (2019) Asia Pacific Law Review 17.

the purposes of scientific research, which excludes commercial uses;[62] (2) If TDM is done generally by all those who enjoy lawful access to underlying mined materials, reproductions and extractions can only be made when the use of works and other subject matter has not been expressly reserved by their right holders (opt-out option) in an appropriate manner, such as machine-readable means in the case of content made publicly available online (Article 4(1) and (3)).

Japan first provided the exception of recording works in information analysis by computer for both commercial and non-commercial purposes in 2009,[63] which is criticized for its vague and outdated rules.[64] In 2018, Japan amended the Copyright Act (effective since 2019) and introduced detailed clauses exempting related activities in data mining and analysis. The amendment allows electronic incidental copies of works (Article 47-4) and the use of copyrighted works for data verification (Article 47-5). Most noteworthy is Article 30-4, which allows all users to 'exploit work in any way' for 'experiments of realization of technologies' and 'data analysis', as long as it 'does not involve perceiving the expression in such work through human sense'. By using words broadly termed like 'exploit' and 'in any way', this article allows a wide range of uses in data mining activities. Some have also expressed the opinion that this article permits the business model of 'creating a learning data set consisting of third parties' works, and then transferring and disclosing it to an unspecified third party who intends to develop AI'.[65] Clearly, Japan's broad wording provides more freedom for TDM compared to the EU.[66]

[62] Christopher Geiger and others have stated 'Within these limitations, the TDM exception's scope is very inclusive as it applies both to commercial and non-commercial uses' (Policy Department for Citizens' Rights and Constitutional Affairs, Directorate General for Internal Policies of the Union, *The Exception for Text and Data Mining (TDM) in the Proposed Directive on Copyright in the Digital Single Market—Legal Aspects*, 2018, PE 604.941, 19). However, as Recital (12) of the Directive clearly indicates otherwise: 'Despite different legal forms and structures, research organisations in the Member States generally have in common that they act either on a not-for-profit basis or in the context of a public-interest mission recognised by the State. Such a public-interest mission could, for example, be reflected through public funding or through provisions in national laws or public contracts.'

[63] Japan's Copyright Act, Art 47*septies*.

[64] 'Japan amends its copyright legislation to meet future demands in AI and big data' (*European Alliance for Research Excellence*, 3 September 2018) <http://eare.eu/japan-amends-tdm-exception-copyright/>.

[65] Nakamura & Partners, 'The Copyright Act revised in 2018 will further improve the machine learning environment in Japan' (*Nakamura & Partners*, 23 March 2019) <http://www.nakapat.gr.jp/en/legal_updates_eng/the-copyright-act-revised-in-2018-will-further-improve-the-machine-learning-environment-in-japan/>.

[66] Some commentators predict that Japan will surpass EU in attracting more AI developments as a result of this reform. See Christian Troncoso, 'Copyright proposal threatens to undermine Europe's AI ambitions' (*BSA TechPost*, 5 September 2018) <https://techpost.bsa.org/2018/09/05/copyright-proposal-threatens-to-undermine-europes-ai-ambitions/>. Some scholars criticize the current exemption scope for TDM as too narrow in the EU; see Christophe Geiger, Giancarlo Frosio, and Oleksandr

4.2.2 To construct a specific fair dealing clause that is more conducive to AI

To promote the development of the data mining industry, a specific exemption clause in copyright law is preferred, as it would provide more certainty. The design of this specific clause must be directed towards facilitating the development of AI. However, an explicitly fixed clause runs the risk of lagging behind technology development. We agree with the call for an open clause to promote flexibility and future incorporation possibility.[67] In identifying allowable uses, legislators in Japan use 'exploitation' to incorporate future uses under mining technology with broad room for interpretation. In contrast, the EU uses 'reproductions and extractions' to provide more certainty for practitioners with less flexibility. We are of the opinion that the Japanese approach should be preferred.[68]

In addition, regarding the relationship between exemption and copyright holders' interests, a question arises as to whether the copyright holders can make reservations (opt-out) to prevent data mining as Article 4(2) of the EU Digital Single Market Directive allows.[69] Allowing copyright holders to make reservations might seem to be a balance between copyright protection and new technology development, but would cripple the effect of the exemption. Data processors would have to find out whether the copyright holders have made reservations and then locate them. This could be time-consuming and difficult, considering the various sources of data and a lack of registration for copyright. To allow reservation would open the door for right holders to refuse to provide access to data mining. A similar attitude is reflected in The Hague Declaration on Knowledge Discovery in the Digital Age launched by Ligue des Bibliothèques Européennes de Recherche (LIBER) in 2015[70] and the UK exemption clause.

Bulayenko, 'Crafting a Text and Data Mining Exception for Machine Learning and Big Data in the Digital Single Market' in Xavier Seuba, Christophe Geiger, and Julien Pénin (eds), *Intellectual Property and Digital Trade in the Age of Artificial Intelligence and Big Data* (CEIPI-ICTSD 2018) 95, 110 (hereafter Geiger, Frosio, and Bulayenko, 'Crafting a Text and Data Mining Exception').

[67] Geiger, Frosio, and Bulayenko, 'Crafting a Text and Data Mining Exception' (n 66) 95, 110.

[68] Daniel Gervais is of the opinion that any TDM exception should be set against the three-step test principle, the third step of which 'may be met by compensating right holders. This would allow the imposition of a compulsory license for specific TDM uses that overstep the boundary of free use, for example to make available significant portions of, or even entire, protected works that are no longer commercially exploited.' See Gervais, 'Exploring the Interfaces' (n 18) para 61. See also Tiangxian He, Chapter 9 in this volume.

[69] Directive 2019/790 of 17 April 2019 on copyright and related rights in the Digital Single Market and amending Directives 96/9/EC and 2001/29/EC. However, such reservation must be 'expressly reserved by their rightholders in an appropriate manner'.

[70] The Hague Declaration (n 58).

4.3 Access to Big Data

Daniel Rubinfeld and Michal Gal analyse the issue of accessing barriers to big data in accordance with the big data value chain, namely barriers to the collection, storage, synthesis and analysis, and usage of big data.[71] However, the last three barriers are more an issue of 'protection' of big data that has been dealt with in Section 3 and will therefore not be discussed here. In the following, the focus will be on behavioural barriers to the collection of big data,[72] as firms may use a variety of strategies in order to erect entry barriers, such as exclusive dealing, pricing and conditioning access, disabling competitor's data-gathering mechanisms, etc.[73]

The UK Competition and Markets Authority (CMA) pointed out in 2015 that 'Two-sided markets, as with other markets with network effects, often have high levels of concentration, as customers gravitate toward companies that already have large numbers of customers. Two-sided data markets may therefore feature large firms holding a position of market power.'[74] The CMA further alludes to 'Markets in which data is a significant input into products and services' as indicator that suggests 'a greater likelihood of competition concerns'.[75]

The Japanese Fair Trade Commission states in its Report of the Study Group on Data and Competition Policy (2017) that unjust data hoarding, ie, refusal to admit access to data which are essential to competitors' business and for which it is technically or economically difficult for competitors and/or customers to obtain substitutable data, without justifiable grounds, by monopolistic or oligopolistic enterprises may be an issue under the Antimonopoly Act.[76]

Indeed, scale economy and network effect are present in the data market and favour market concentration and dominance. This is more obvious in two-sided markets where most consumers with data are concentrated in limited big

[71] Rubinfeld and Gal, 'Access Barriers to Big Data' (n 17) 349.

[72] Daniel Rubinfeld and Michal Gal identify three types of barriers to collection of big data, technological, legal, and behavioural, which can exist in parallel and can reinforce one another. However, the first two have been considered in Section 3.2.1 and will not be discussed again here.

[73] Rubinfeld and Gal, 'Access Barriers to Big Data' (n 17) 362–3.

[74] UK Competition and Markets Authority, 'The Commercial Use of Consumer Data' (2015) 3.24 (80) <https://www.gov.uk/government/uploads/system/uploads/attachment_data/file/435817/The_commercial_use_of_consumer_data.pdf>. While there are one-sided consumer data markets where a firm collects consumer data purely for its own use, and does not share this further, there are also two-sided consumer data markets where a firm collects data from consumers and shares these data with third parties, such as advertisers, and interacts with these two groups of customers.

[75] Ibid, 3.78.

[76] Japan Fair Trade Commission Competition Policy Research Center, *Report of Study Group on Data and Competition Policy* <https://www.jftc.go.jp/en/pressreleases/yearly-2017/June/170606.html>. In 2015, the Paris Court of Appeals upheld the French Competition Authority's decision to sanction the refusal of a vertically integrated editor of software to grant access to its database to its downstream competitor (Cegedim). See Concurrences Antitrust Publications & Events, 'Related EU and national case law on essential facility' (*Concurrences*) <https://www.concurrences.com/en/glossary/Essential-facility>.

platforms.[77] Competition scrutiny is necessary to avoid data monopoly and to lower the entry barriers for small companies. Access to data under competition law can be obtained as a remedy in cases of abuse of market dominance. In that context, the modalities of access, in particular the formats in which the data at issue should be made accessible and the issue of interoperability of data formats and standardization, will have to be addressed (see Section 3.2.1).

However, as the Position Statement rightly concludes, antitrust law is in most cases not suitable to address the issue of access to big data for the following reasons: Competition law solves the problem by ex post measures, which is time-consuming, case specific, and therefore less effective than ex ante regulation, and cannot keep abreast with the fast-developing data market. Rather, as the Position Statement opines, only sector-specific regulations may be required, if at all.[78] One possible regulation is a rule requiring data holders to make data widely available at a reasonable and non-discriminatory cost when barriers are structurally inherent and hard to solve and the sharing of data is socially beneficial. A potentially instructive model might be FRAND (fair, reasonable, and non-discriminatory) licensing-rate requirements that are central to the operation of standard-setting organizations.[79]

5. Findings and Conclusions

This chapter identifies three major types of data that are of relevance to the development of AI. It then explores and discusses issues on the protection of and access to those three types of data respectively. First and foremost, when we talk about data for AI, we have to be very clear about what type of data we are discussing: are they data specifically generated for AI, big data with huge size (volume), rapid changes or updates (veracity and velocity), and various data sources (variety), or copyright-protected data?

Data specifically generated for AI should qualify as works worthy of copyright protection as compilations. With regards to whether and to what extent we need to enhance access to data specifically generated for AI, it is suggested that if data specifically generated for AI are PSI, measures that may facilitate the widest re-uses of public data, such as open data, data disclosure, and data interoperability, should be taken. If data specifically generated for AI are from the private sector, we then need to explore whether these data are of critical importance and whether there are scenarios in which the use of competition law and/or ex ante regulation will be needed to ensure access to data specifically generated for AI.

[77] Rubinfeld and Gal, 'Access Barriers to Big Data' (n 17) 377.
[78] Position Statement, paras 32–8. Also Hilty, 'Big Data' (n 15) 92.
[79] Rubinfeld and Gal, 'Access Barriers to Big Data' (n 17) 373.

Regarding the issue of 'protection of big data', it should not be addressed in the sense or direction of giving proprietary entitlement over big data to any entity, which is simply as infeasible as it is unjustified. Big data, as the single most valuable capital of our society for economic and technological innovation, should be permitted to form, accumulate, and flow freely. When looking at the private-sector components of big data, we have found legal, technical, and market factors that work against the formation, accumulation, and free flow of big data: divergent national laws on personal data protection and cross-border transfer of non-personal data, the lack of standardization and interoperability of data, and the data-trading market place. When looking at the public-sector components of big data, both the importance of open data and the re-use of public sector information come to the fore. Concerning the issue of accessing big data, there are barriers to its collection, storage, synthesis, analysis, and usage. However, behavioural barriers to the collection of big data, such as exclusive dealing, pricing and conditioning access, disabling competitors' data-gathering mechanisms, etc, warrant special scrutiny. In that regard, competition law as an ex post remedy can be relied upon to confront abuse of a dominant position, but is of limited use; therefore sector-specific regulation might be needed, such as a FRAND licensing arrangement.

As for copyright-protected data, the real issue is more about access than protection. TDM is the most important tool for accessing copyright-protected data and is neither expressive use nor consumptive use. Therefore, we need to work on a specific fair use clause for TDM that is more conducive to AI development. In that regard, the Japanese model is preferable.

17
Protection of and Access to Data under European Law

*Matthias Leistner**

1. Introduction

When the European Union (EU) Commission launched its 2017 consultation 'Building the European Data Economy'[1] many commentators were rightly concerned that this might lead to the creation of a new data producer's right in the EU although doctrinal or empirical evidence on the need for any such right was completely lacking. In particular, the subsequent discussion has shown clearly that a data producer's right would not contribute to the solution of the very specific problems which have to be solved in order to foster the development of functioning data markets in the EU.[2] Since then, the discussion has increasingly focused on access rights. Consequently, and rightly, the EU after the initial fact finding followed a very limited, targeted approach in the data economy sector by first enacting the Regulation on free flow of non-personal data in the EU,[3] applicable as of 28 May 2019, whose main objective is to remove any remaining national law obstacles to the free movement of non-personal data within the EU, ie, an almost complete abolition of national data localization requirements in the EU market.

* The author thanks his research assistant *Lucie Antoine* and his student research assistant *Sandra Stadler* for valuable help with research for this chapter. All Internet sources were accessed before 27 April 2020.

[1] See EU Commission, 'Public consultation on Building the European Data Economy' (2017) <https://ec.europa.eu/digital-single-market/en/news/public-consultation-building-european-data-economy>.

[2] Josef Drexl and others, 'Position Statement of the Max Planck Institute for Innovation and Competition of 26 April 2017 on the European Commission's "Public consultation on Building the European Data Economy"' (2017) Max Planck Institute for Innovation & Competition Research Paper No 17-08 1 et seq. <https://www.ip.mpg.de/fileadmin/ipmpg/content/stellungnahmen/MPI_Statement_Public_consultation_on_Building_the_EU_Data_Eco_28042017.pdf> (hereafter Drexl and others, 'Position Statement of the Max Planck Institute'); Wolfgang Kerber, 'A New (Intellectual) Property Right for Non-Personal Data? An Economic Analysis' (2016) GRUR International Journal of European and International IP Law 989; Wolfgang Kerber, 'Governance of Data: Exclusive Property vs. Access' [2016] International Review of Intellectual Property and Competition Law 759.

[3] Regulation (EU) 2018/1807 on a framework for the free flow of non-personal data in the European Union [2018] OJ L303/59 (hereafter Regulation on free flow of non-personal data).

Matthias Leistner, *Protection of and Access to Data under European Law* In: *Artificial Intelligence and Intellectual Property*. Edited by: Jyh-An Lee, Reto M Hilty, and Kung-Chung Liu, Oxford University Press (2021). © The several contributors.
DOI: 10.1093/oso/9780198870944.003.0018

Apart from this targeted and useful legislative project, intense academic discussion on access rights has continued since 2017 and developed more specific depth.[4] In that regard, EU policy increasingly focuses on the role of the Database Directive[5] in different typical big data and AI use scenarios. The Evaluation of the Database Directive by the Commission,[6] as well as the underlying academic Evaluation Report[7] in particular, have shown that the Database Directive is a case for imminent reform.

This chapter will focus on three aspects of the recent access discussion. First, the *infrastructural framework* will be discussed: Namely, general copyright law should guarantee that certain infrastructures, such as data file formats, application programming interfaces (APIs), as well as interfaces in general remain freely accessible (see Section 2.1). Secondly, as regards protection of databases, *copyright protection* should certainly not be over-extended but should instead be reserved for databases which genuinely reflect their authors' original, personal creativity; this largely reduces the role of copyright protection in the realm of big data but might lead to limited protection for outstanding achievements in the selection and/or combination of different training data, algorithms, and weighing factors (see Section 2.2). Thirdly, the existing sui generis protection regime for databases under the Database Directive seems problematic and in need of imminent reform. This topic has been discussed more generally by this author several times.[8] This chapter does not repeat these and other more general contributions to the ongoing discussions, but instead follows a more targeted approach: At Section 3.2.2, the chapter will exclusively focus on different areas and case groups, where *access rights* are discussed and will try to categorize these access rights from an intellectual property (IP) perspective as a sound basis for making specific proposals on the *contextual accommodation of such (new) access*

[4] See, eg, Jacques Crémer, Yves-Alexandre de Montjoye, and Heike Schweitzer, 'Competition Policy for the digital era. Final report' (2019) <https://ec.europa.eu/competition/publications/reports/kd0419345enn.pdf> (hereafter Crémer, de Montjoye, and Schweitzer, 'Competition Policy for the digital era'); Josef Drexl, 'Data Access and Control in the Era of Connected Devices. Study on behalf of the European consumer organisation BEUC' (2018) <https://www.ip.mpg.de/fileadmin/ipmpg/content/aktuelles/aus_der_forschung/beuc-x-2018-121_data_access_and_control_in_the_area_of_connected_devices.pdf> (hereafter Drexl, 'Data Access and Control in the Era of Connected Devices').

[5] Directive (EC) 1996/9 on the legal protection of databases [1996] OJ L77/20 (hereafter Database Directive).

[6] EU Commission Staff Working Document, 'Executive Summary of the Evaluation of Directive 96/9/EC on the legal protection of databases', SWD (2018) 146 final (hereafter EU Commission, 'Evaluation of Directive 96/9/EC').

[7] Lionel Bently, Estelle Derclaye, and others, 'Study in support of the evaluation of Directive 96/9/EC on the legal protection of databases. Final Report' (2018) (hereafter Database Directive Final Evaluation Report).

[8] Cf Matthias Leistner, 'Big Data and the EU Database Directive 96/9/EC: Current Law and Potential for Reform' in Sebastian Lohsse, Reiner Schulze, and Dirk Staudenmayer (eds), *Trading Data in the Digital Economy: Legal Concepts and Tools* (Baden-Baden: Nomos 2018) 27 et seq. (hereafter Leistner, 'Big Data and the EU Database Directive').

rights with sui generis protection for databases and for respective *targeted reform* of the Database Directive.

2. General Copyright Law: Computer Programs and Database Works (Compilations)

2.1 Freedom of Interfaces and Data Exchange Infrastructures under European Law

Access to data and the development of data markets in general require that there be free and accessible infrastructures for the exchange of data between different market players.[9] Copyright protection for computer programs can be a problem in that regard if protection is extended to interface structures or data file formats as such (eg, in the highly controversial Federal Circuit's *Google/Oracle* case which will now be ultimately resolved by the US Supreme Court).[10]

In Europe, the situation seems comparatively stable and less problematic. The relevant EU Computer Program Directive of 2009 (originally enacted in 1993)[11] acknowledges the need for interoperability inter alia in its Recitals 19, 11, and 15. Accordingly, the Court of Justice of the EU (CJEU) has decided in its *SAS Institute* judgment[12] that programming languages and data file formats as such are not copyright protected under EU protection for computer programs. Although this is still under discussion in Europe, many authors have derived inter alia from that judgment that API infrastructures or other infrastructures as such should not be copyrightable under EU copyright law.[13]

[9] See, eg, Crémer, de Montjoye, and Schweitzer, 'Competition Policy for the digital era' (n 4) 83 et seq. On interoperability generally Jason Furman, 'Unlocking digital competition—Report of the Digital Competition Expert Panel' (2019) <https://www.gov.uk/government/publications/unlocking-digital-competition-report-of-the-digital-competition-expert-panel> 64 et seq.

[10] See *Oracle Am., Inc. v Google LLC*, 886 F.3d 1179 (Fed. Cir. 2018); pending proceedings *Google LLC v Oracle Am., Inc.* before the US Supreme Court under Docket No 18-956.

[11] Directive (EC) 2009/24 on the legal protection of computer programs [2009] OJ L111/16 (hereafter Computer Program Directive).

[12] *SAS Institute v World Programming* [2012] ECLI:EU:C:2012:259, paras 29 et seq.

[13] Jochen Marly, 'Der Schutzgegenstand des urheberrechtlichen Softwareschutzes' (2012) Gewerblicher Rechtsschutz und Urheberrecht 773, 779; more open in the prognosis Simonetta Vezzoso, 'Copyright, Interfaces, and a Possible Atlantic Divide' (2012) 3 Journal of Intellectual Property, Information Technology and Electronic Commerce Law 153, para 40, who however herself requests freedom of interface structures; with a useful distinction between the interface structures and their specific implementation and programming in code Pamela Samuelson, Thomas Vinje, and William Cornish, 'Does Copyright Protection Under the EU Software Directive Extend to Computer Program Behaviour, Languages and Interfaces?' (2012) 34 European Intellectual Property Review 158 et seq, 163 et seq; similarly Christian Heinze, 'Software als Schutzgegenstand des Europäischen Urheberrechts' (2011) 2 Journal of Intellectual Property, Information Technology and Electronic Commerce Law 97, para 8.

2.2 Big Data and AI as Compilations

By contrast, the typical creativity involved in the development of AI models and applications based on big data, ie, the structuring and weighing of the cost functions, selection and combination of training data, etc[14] seems on principle eligible for protection as a database work under EU copyright law, ie, potentially copyrightable compilation of independent elements. Given that in particular in the EU the exceptions to copyright are too narrow and rigid to accommodate the dynamic and multipolar use of training data and weighing factors in different contexts and problem-specific combinations (data biotopes), copyright law could be a significant source of additional transaction costs and contribute to lock-in and even holdup potential under certain circumstances. However, the CJEU has specified the condition of copyright protection in Europe in a rather strict and targeted way in its more recent case law. Hence, according to the CJEU's judgment in *Football Dataco/Yahoo* mere intellectual effort, skill, judgement, and labour in the selection and structuring of the elements of a database work will not suffice for copyright protection; in particular technical considerations will not qualify if they do not leave room for the expression of personal creativity in an original manner by making free and creative choices and thus stamping the database with a 'personal touch'.[15] Similarly, in the very recent *Funke Medien/ Germany* judgment, the Court has applied strict criteria to potential copyright protection for mere factual reports and their structure when it is guided by the underlying practical purpose.[16]

For all these reasons, it seems that database copyright protection in the EU, while in principle, capable of protecting certain outstanding achievements in the area of AI and big data, will not protect the typical selection and combination of data in order to compile and combine optimized training data sets and the respective weighing of factors to optimize the used cost functions in everyday cases. Copyright in computer programs and compilations in Europe therefore is not a significant cost factor for the future development of AI and big data in Europe as such will presumably not pose a substantial obstacle for future technological development.

By contrast, with regard to underlying *materials* which are *used* for the compilation of training data and which might be protected by copyright law, the question has to be asked whether the existing exceptions to copyright law in Europe are sufficient. Since the topic of this chapter is access to and protection of data, suffice it to say in this regard that even the new text and data mining exceptions in Articles 3 and 4 of the DSM Directive[17] do not seem sufficient. Further reform

[14] See further Drexl and others, 'Position Statement of the Max Planck Institute' (n 2).

[15] *Football Dataco v Yahoo* [2012] ECLI:EU:C:2012:115, paras 31 et seq, in particular paras 38 et seq.

[16] *Funke Medien NRW GmbH v Federal Republic of Germany* [2019] ECLI:EU:C:2019:623.

[17] Directive (EU) 2019/790 on copyright and related rights in the Digital Single Market and amending Directives 96/9/EC and 2001/29/EC [2019] OJ L130/92 (hereafter DSM Directive).

seems imminent and it is submitted that the Japanese copyright law exception for text and data mining (as a case example in the larger realm of irrelevant uses which do not allow the enjoyment of the work as such) could be a model in that regard.[18]

3. Sui Generis Right for Databases under European Law

3.1 Introduction: The Scope and Impact of the EU Sui Generis Right in Big Data Scenarios

The recent discussion of the function and relevance of the Database Directive's[19] sui generis right for database makers for the European data economy has been partly characterized by the assumption that in most big data situations the crucial condition of a 'substantial investment' will not be fulfilled.[20] This author has shown elsewhere that this assumption might be mistaken under current European case law.[21] Instead, one should be aware that database sui generis protection might potentially come into play in numerous different typical big data and AI use scenarios and with regard to a large variety of big data relevant raw material. Compilations of independent elements such as geographical data, certain kinds of sensor-measured data (although a number of differentiations has to be made in this case group), sales data, etc can potentially qualify for protection depending on the circumstances of the case. This is not to say that investments in the compilation of such data *should* be protected in all these different case groups. Instead, this analysis should serve as a *warning* that the database sui generis right might be more relevant than generally thought for both the protection and the access aspects of big data use case scenarios.[22]

While investments into the compilation of data via sensor or other measurement might qualify, depending on the circumstances of the case,[23] as investments into the refining, combining, and weighing of these data and into the specific combination with certain algorithms, further analysis will typically not be relevant

[18] Japanese Copyright Act, Art 30-4; see further Tatsuhiro Ueno: 'A General Clause on Copyright Limitations in Civil Law Countries: Recent Discussion toward the Japanese-style "Fair Use" Clause' in Shyam Balganesh and others (eds), *Comparative Aspects of Limitations and Exceptions in Copyright Law* (Cambridge University Press 2020) forthcoming.

[19] Database Directive (n 5).

[20] EU Commission, 'Evaluation of Directive 96/9/EC' (n 6) 2.

[21] Leistner, 'Big Data and the EU Database Directive' (n 8) 27 et seq. With the same conclusion and a rigorous analysis see also Drexl, 'Data Access and Control in the Era of Connected Devices' (n 4) 67 et seq; more differentiated also Database Directive Final Evaluation Report (n 7) 29 et seq.

[22] Cf also Database Directive Final Evaluation Report (n 7) 29 referring to Leistner.

[23] See further Leistner, 'Big Data and the EU Database Directive' (n 8) 27 et seq; Drexl, 'Data Access and Control in the Era of Connected Devices' (n 4) 73 with a differentiation between sensor-produced data on the working of machinery and devices as such and sensor-measured data of certain outside factors.

because these cases concern typical cases of mere (irrelevant) generation of data;[24] only indirect protection is conceivable in such cases if investments into the underlying measured data can be shown and are still reflected in the resulting data set. This rough overview picture shows already at the outset that the database *sui generis right has significant potential* to hamper the development of future big data and AI applications in certain cases.[25]

This is aggravated by the fact that the *exclusive rights* under Article 7(2) of the Database Directive, ie, extraction and re-utilization, have been construed *broadly* in the CJEU's case law. In fact, practices such as indirect extraction and even extraction for the compilation of substantially changed, value-added databases of a more or less different nature will be covered by these exclusive rights.[26] Moreover, the activities of typical meta-databases or meta-search websites, ie, the automated gathering and compiling of data from a multitude of different sources are potentially infringing the sui generis right.[27]

Compared to this rather broad construction of the exclusive rights, the *limitation* of the protected subject matter, ie, the limitation to the use of *substantial parts* of a database or systematic and repeated extraction of insubstantial parts which add up to be a substantial part of the database,[28] is not an efficient means to protect freedom of competition and to prevent leveraging potentials in respect of typical big data uses. This is because most of these uses which compile and process large, and ideally *complete* data sets from different sources will accordingly need *complete data* and not only *insubstantial parts* of databases in order to produce sensible results from the previously unprocessed underlying data sets. Consequently, the limitation of the protected subject matter to substantial parts of databases does not solve potential problems with access to data, which might arise in these contexts.[29]

In short, as regards access to data in big data and AI use cases in the EU, the database sui generis right can raise serious *information and transaction cost problems* in its current state. Moreover, it can worsen *lock-in problems* and even lead to *holdup potential* in certain situations.[30] In sum, depending on the development of future case law in the area, this could substantially aggravate the existing and acknowledged access problems which already follow from factual control over different

[24] Cf *Fixtures Marketing v Organismos prognostikon* [2004] ECLI:EU:C:2004:697, ECR I-10549, paras 40–53; *Fixtures Marketing v Oy Veikkaus AB* [2004] ECLI:EU:C:2004:694, ECR I-10365, paras 34–49; *Fixtures Marketing v Svenska Spel AB* [2004] ECLI:EU:C:2004:696, ECR I-10497, paras 24-37; and Leistner, 'Big Data and the EU Database Directive' (n 8) 28.

[25] See comprehensively Leistner, 'Big Data and the EU Database Directive' (n 8) 27 et seq.

[26] *Directmedia Publishing v Albert-Ludwigs-Universität Freiburg* [2008] ECLI:EU:C:2008:552, paras 29 et seq.

[27] *Innoweb v Wegener* [2013] ECLI:EU:C:2013:850, paras 37 et seq.

[28] *The British Horseracing Board v William Hill Organization* [2004] ECLI:EU:C:2004:695, paras 87 et seq.

[29] Cf also Leistner in Database Directive Final Evaluation Report (n 7) 57.

[30] See further Section 3.2.2.1.

data sources.[31] The existing database sui generis regime is thus in need of reform or should be abolished altogether. At the same time the existing 'tradition' of database sui generis protection in Europe might in the future also offer the *opportunity* to address certain very well defined and targeted protection needs, in particular for high quality training data, if these needs can in fact be validated and if the right was rigorously reformed. However, this latter aspect shall not be discussed in what follows. Instead, the following sections focus on the more imminent *access issues* and *reform* of the existing sui generis regime in this particular regard.[32]

3.2 Access to Data and the Sui Generis Right—the Case for Immediate Reform

3.2.1 Exceptions to the sui generis right

Considering access to IP-protected subject matter, the exceptions to the concerned IP right come into focus. In the overarching general framework of EU fundamental rights, such exceptions express genuine *user rights* to freedom of expression and information which have to be fairly balanced with the right to protection of IP.[33] On a more detailed, technical level, the existing exceptions to the sui generis right (Article 9 of the Database Directive) are undoubtedly too narrowly designed, in particular in comparison to the broader general copyright exceptions.[34] In fact, this critique becomes even more pertinent with respect to the challenges of the data economy.

First, it seems to have been ignored in the legislative process that the sui generis right, by virtue of its autonomous nature, would not be subject to certain traditional limitations set out in national laws with regard to works protected under copyright. This leads inter alia to a significant problem in respect of databases established by *public authorities*, which are covered by exclusive sui generis protection even in countries where *official works by public bodies* are generally exempted from copyright under certain conditions. This issue should be solved by an analogy to the copyright exception for official databases by public bodies.[35] However, the

[31] Cf Drexl and others, 'Position Statement of the Max Planck Institute', 1 et seq (n 2); EU Commission, 'Communication Building the European data economy', COM(2017) 9 final, 9 et seq.

[32] Cf similarly Drexl, 'Data Access and Control in the Era of Connected Devices' (n 4) 69.

[33] *Funke Medien NRW GmbH v Federal Republic of Germany* [2019] ECLI:EU:C:2019:623, paras 57 et seq.

[34] Annette Kur and others, 'First Evaluation of Directive 96/9/EC on the Legal Protection of Databases—Comment by the Max Planck Institute for Intellectual Property, Competition and Tax Law, Munich' (2006) International Review of Intellectual Property and Competition Law 551, 556 et seq (hereafter Kur and others, 'First Evaluation'). See also Leistner in Database Directive Final Evaluation Report (n 7) 59.

[35] Cf Matthias Leistner, 'Anmerkung zu BGH, Beschluß vom 28.9.2006, I ZR 261/03—Sächsischer Ausschreibungsdienst' (2007) European Union Private Law Review 190, 193 et seq; with an overview of the current status of the debate whether the exception of German copyright law for 'official' copyrighted

CJEU never explicitly decided on that question, hence this issue remains legally uncertain on the level of EU law. This also results in considerable tensions between the framework for access and use under the PSI Directive and possible sui generis protection for databases created by public bodies.[36]

This specifically odd example points, secondly, to a more general problem. In fact, the narrow exceptions to the sui generis right should at the very least be *aligned and dynamically linked with the exceptions to copyright law* under the Information Society Directive.[37] It is therefore of considerable practical interest to enable and oblige member states to extend, *mutatis mutandis*, the exemptions and limitations applying to works protected under copyright to sui generis protection of non-original databases.[38] The obligation should be phrased so as to establish a dynamic link between both fields, to the effect that limitations set out in new copyright legislation would automatically also become applicable, under suitable terms and circumstances, to the sui generis right. The new copyright provisions for text and data mining and certain other exempted uses in Articles 3–6 and 8 of the DSM Directive are examples in point: Rightly, they explicitly extend the scope of the newly proposed exceptions to the database maker's sui generis right. However, the problem is of a more general nature and should be solved in a general way when revising the Database Directive by simply mandatorily aligning the exceptions to the sui generis right with the general exceptions to EU copyright law.

In this context, it should also be clarified that permitted use under the exceptions also covers use acts in respect of *complete* databases. This is because the current wording of Article 9 of the Database Directive seems to suggest that even exempted acts shall be limited to the use of substantial parts. However, a limitation of the exempted uses to the use of only substantial parts of a database could hardly be accommodated with the access needs in the context of big data activities. Moreover, the limitation of the personal scope of application of the exceptions to 'lawful users of a database' should be abolished. This qualification is inconsistent with the system of general copyright law exceptions which do not contain an additional legitimacy test since the considerations whether the use is legitimate are already embedded in the very definition of the scope of the exceptions as such. Therefore, an additional condition of lawful user is systematically inconsistent and unnecessarily endangers the practical utility of the rules on exceptions.

Finally, the strict limitation of the exceptions to *non-commercial uses* certainly has to be placed under scrutiny. This is a more general problem of certain

works can be extended by way of analogy: Martin Vogel in Ulrich Loewenheim, Matthias Leistner, and Ansgar Ohly (eds), *Urheberrecht: Kommentar* (6th edn, CH Beck 2020) § 87b UrhG paras 67 et seq.

[36] Directive 2003/98/EC on the re-use of public sector information [2003] OJ L 345/90 (hereafter PSI Directive). See further Section 3.2.2.3.

[37] Kur and others, 'First Evaluation' (n 34), 556 et seq.

[38] Leistner, in Database Directive Final Evaluation Report (n 7) 16; Drexl, 'Data Access and Control in the Era of Connected Devices' (n 4) 81.

exceptions in EU copyright law, which will have to be discussed generally in the future as it is also inherent to the exception for text and data mining under Articles 3 and 4 of the DSM Directive.[39] As a more general and by no means new proposition, another future consideration should be whether to make some of the optional exceptions and limitations in the Information Society Directive *mandatory* in nature.[40] Article 17(7) of the DSM Directive, with its somewhat arbitrary and therefore insufficient selection of certain now mandatory exceptions, and its limited sector-specific scope, can only be a beginning in that regard.[41]

3.2.2 Access rights, exceptions, and/or compulsory licences in the reform of the Database Directive

3.2.2.1 Basic considerations: access rights and justification of use

As has been described above, the limitation of the exclusive rights to uses in respect of substantial parts of a database cannot effectively accommodate the possible need for access to comprehensive machine—or sensor-generated use or other data which in certain situations might be necessary for third parties in order to develop, produce, market, or distribute value-added products or services based on big data analysis. Arguably, the entire concept of a limited closed-shop catalogue of exceptions for certain well-defined cases which is typical for EU copyright law does not fit with the more utilitarian industrial property character of the sui generis right.

In an early analysis of the regulatory need in this context, the Max Planck Institute for Innovation and Competition had emphasized that a possible future solution to the problem of *de facto* control of data might be the provision of area-specific, non-waivable access rights for parties with a legitimate interest in the use of the data.[42] This approach has been further developed and generalized for connected devices in a recent study by Drexl.[43] In that regard, two concepts have to be distinguished. Drexl's recent proposal focuses on *access* and a right to disclose and *use* data. Such access rights which encompass the right to require *disclosure* of confidential data have to be conceptually distinguished from exceptions or compulsory licences in the realm of IP rights, such as the sui generis right, which generally only give a right to *use* data without giving a right to access including disclosure.[44]

Generally, Drexl argues against the background of balanced economic incentives which should not go beyond that which is necessary to sufficiently incentivize

[39] Cf Section 2.2.

[40] Leistner, 'Big Data and the EU Database Directive' (n 8) 47 et seq; Drexl, 'Data Access and Control in the Era of Connected Devices' (n 4) 81.

[41] Matthias Leistner, 'European Copyright Licensing and Infringement Liability Under Art. 17 DSM-Directive Compared to Secondary Liability of Content Platforms in the U.S.—Can We Make the New European System a Global Opportunity Instead of a Local Challenge?' (2020) 12 Intellectual Property Journal (forthcoming).

[42] Drexl and others, 'Position Statement of the Max Planck Institute' (n 2) 11 et seq.

[43] Drexl, 'Data Access and Control in the Era of Connected Devices' (n 4).

[44] See rightly Database Directive Final Evaluation Report (n 7) 41 et seq.

the creation of databases in certain situations. Consequently, eg, in regard to sensor-produced data and in particular in regard to smart devices, he fundamentally questions the premise whether remuneration will be needed in all situations where data access is necessary and justified.[45] Problems which might require data access can occur inter alia in situations of lock-in or where data access is needed by a competitor or another business to offer another product or service. For this and other cases Drexl's concept is expressly based on future sector-specific *access* rights. That means on the basis of the distinction established in the preceding paragraph, it focuses on both access to/disclosure of data *and* use of data. In this context, it seems consistent that Drexl regards such access rights as independent from the legal status of the concerned data, in particular possible IP protection for the concrete form in which these data are collected and stored, and instead proposes sector-specific access regimes which 'should prevail over any sui generis database right'.[46] The details concerning such data access and use shall then be regulated in the context of these sector-specific access regimes including the question whether and in which cases such use should be remunerated and in which form. Consequently, the Database Directive would only need to be complemented with what may be called a passive 'interface provision', ie, a general exception which clarifies that the sui generis database right 'does not apply where, and to the extent to which' sector-specific regulations require access to data.[47]

In a similar vein, already existing regulation on the re-use of public sector information, namely the PSI Directive, requires alignment of such IP-external obligations concerning public sector information with possible sui generis right protection for databases of public bodies.[48] In fact, in this field holdup problems and certain dysfunctional effects even of the PSI regime can already be seen in the markets in some member states so that respective reform to align the sui generis right with the regulatory purpose behind the PSI framework is not just a task for future research on certain sector-specific needs but instead an imminent need for immediate revision of the Database Directive.[49]

3.2.2.2 Details of the interface with IP protection, in particular sui generis protection

While leaving further regulation of such access rights to the existing or possible future sector-specific access regimes (such as in the context of the planned EU Data Act) is a generally sound and consistent approach, the devil of course is in the details. Thus, while the concept seems systematically consistent and deserves

[45] Drexl, 'Data Access and Control in the Era of Connected Devices' (n 4) 82.
[46] Ibid.
[47] Ibid, 83.
[48] Which generally qualify for sui generis database protection, cf German Federal Supreme Court (Bundesgerichtshof) *Autobahnmaut* [2010] Gewerblicher Rechtsschutz und Urheberrecht 1004 (hereafter *Autobahnmaut*) paras 13 et seq, 22 et seq (on public-private partnerships).
[49] Database Directive Final Evaluation Report (n 7) 115 et seq. Cf critically on *Autobahnmaut* (n 48), also Drexl, 'Data Access and Control in the Era of Connected Devices' (n 4) 72 et seq.

approval as far as *access* as such is concerned, in regard to subsequent (commercial) *use* of the accessed data, in this author's view, the interface with existing IP protection still deserves further attention and refinement.

From a contextual point of view, in case groups where incentives are typically not necessary in order to foster dynamic competition in production and dissemination of data, respective investments should not be covered by the sui generis right in the first place. Access regimes do not seem the appropriate solution here. Instead, investments in such cases should be excluded from the protectable subject matter and consequently should not qualify as relevant for sui generis protection. The *BHB v Hill* case, which concerned a spin-off situation where the relevant databases resulted from another (main) commercial activity and an additional protection of the investment to create the database was therefore obviously not necessary, is a case in point.[50] In such cases, sui generis protection should be denied from the start. By contrast, in the remaining cases where relevant investments are protected by a sui generis regime because incentives seem necessary and reasonable to foster creation and structured dissemination of databases, this expresses the will of the legislator that use of the resulting data shall generally not be for free. It is possible to overrule this basic balancing of rights and interests in certain case groups but this requires thorough analysis and the burden to establish free use of such data would generally be on the parties requiring such entirely free use.

3.2.2.3 Different case groups

In fact, it seems possible to further distinguish certain categories of access and use interests[51] and provide for some initial guideposts where use should be remunerated and where use should be free. First, *customers* whose devices collect certain use data (machine- or sensor-produced data on the very functioning and maintenance of the device) generally seem to have a justified interest in access to such customer data as well as in use of such data, in particular to prevent lock-in situations, even if these data have been gathered independently and are therefore potentially sui generis-protected, eg, for the provider of the device in question. In these cases, individual access and use for such *lawful customers (users)* should be free, as the business offering the smart device is perfectly at liberty to factor these use possibilities into the sales or service contract underlying the use of the devices.[52] Also, individual customers should be at liberty to transfer such data to competitors of the database maker or other businesses in order to switch their existing service contract or for any other legitimate purpose.

[50] *The British Horseracing Board v William Hill Organization* [2004] ECLI:EU:C:2004:695.

[51] Similarly Database Directive Final Evaluation Report (n 7) 39 et seq; see also Drexl, 'Data Access and Control in the Era of Connected Devices' (n 4) 81 et seq.

[52] Drexl, 'Data Access and Control in the Era of Connected Devices' (n 4) 83.

Secondly, *competitors* of the database maker or other businesses might need access to and use of large databases beyond individual customer data in order to offer certain new products or services. This is the case group which is generally well-known from EU competition law.[53] In regard to the sui generis right, access and use should be granted if a competitor with comparable economic resources as the original database maker would not be able to collect the same data independently without being faced with prohibitive costs. However, if this condition was met (*sole source data*), further conditions, such as the emergence of a new product or service in a new market, should not apply. Instead, the additional offer of cheaper or more efficient products or services in the same market thereby significantly enhancing competition should generally suffice for an access and use right.

Thirdly, in the case of databases created by public bodies, a specific regulatory framework already exists in EU law, namely the PSI Directive, which at present does not sit well with existing sui generis protection for databases made by public bodies. In addition, it has raised some problems of its own, in particular concerning certain licensing practices of public bodies in some Member States. In these cases, the interplay with existing sui generis protection aggravates certain problems which are already based in specific flaws of the PSI regime.[54]

The question now is: how should these three very basic cases (*individual access to customer data* inter alia to prevent lock-in; *general access to complete databases by competitors or businesses* to enhance competition; *databases created by public bodies*) be treated from the viewpoint of IP and in particular from the viewpoint of the sui generis right?

3.2.2.4 Certain identifiable 'anchors' in EU IP law, particularly in the Database Directive

The crucial question is how to accommodate these case groups with existing IP protection in general and with existing database sui generis protection in particular. In fact, any plan to introduce a regime of non-waivable access rights has to specifically deal with the interface to IP protection and will have to answer 'the question of whether the person seeking access to data has to pay a price to the data holder'[55] or not, whether in the context of the respective different sector-specific access regimes or in the context of the affected IP rights.

3.2.2.4.1 Access rights for individual 'lawful customers' in regard to sensor-produced data of smart devices As these are not entirely new questions, it is not surprising that existing 'anchors' in EU IT-related copyright law can be identified

[53] Cf *RTE v Commission (Magill)* [1995] ECLI:EU:C:1995:98; *IMS Health v NDC Health* [2004] ECLI:EU:C:2004:257.

[54] Cf Database Directive Final Evaluation Report (n 7) 115 et seq.

[55] Drexl, 'Data Access and Control in the Era of Connected Devices' (n 4) 82.

for all three case groups distinguished in the preceding paragraph. The case group concerning individual customer access and use (by transferring the received data to third parties) in the realm of smart devices, sensor-produced data, etc is systematically related to the legal figure of the so-called *lawful user* in both the Computer Program[56] and the Database Directive. Accordingly, the Database Directive contains a provision on mandatory minimum rights of *lawful users* of databases, which cannot be overridden by contract (Articles 8(1) and 15 of the Database Directive). From a broader perspective, another example in the wider context of such mandatory minimum rights of customers outside IP law is Article 16(4) of the Digital Content Directive[57] which in turn was modelled on the General Data Protection Regulation (GDPR).[58]

In fact, the regulatory technique already used in European IP law, ie, the provision of certain *mandatory minimum rights of legitimate users*, has the potential to substantially streamline the function of IP rights in online networks. This is because legally these minimum rights '*travel*' with the legitimate user who may perform certain minimum acts which are deemed necessary to effectively use the respective databases.[59] It is this very mechanism which could easily be extended to cover access to data and use rights concerning the transfer to other providers for lawful users of smart devices and machinery which produce sensor-generated sui generis protectable data. Naturally, for such use no additional remuneration should be foreseen since the database producer has the opportunity to factor the associated costs into the conditions of the underlying sales or service contract. The provisions on the minimum rights of *lawful users* therefore provide for the ideal, functional context to implement possible *sector-specific individual customer access and porting rights in the area of smart devices*, etc where these are deemed necessary and possibly provided in sector-specific regulation. Of course, the main challenge for such sector-specific regulation is to make access and use rights of individual customers functional in practice. In that regard, the model of Article 20 GDPR should be closely followed and IP law should contribute to functional, accessible infrastructures by safeguarding free access to API's data formats and other comparable infrastructural technical elements.[60]

[56] See Computer Program Directive, Art 5 (n 11).

[57] Directive (EU) 2019/770 on certain aspects concerning contracts for the supply of digital content and digital services [2019] OJ L136/1 (hereafter Digital Content Directive).

[58] Regulation (EU) 2016/679 on the protection of natural persons with regard to the processing of personal data and on the free movement of such data, and repealing Directive 95/46/EC [2016] OJ L 119/1 (hereinafter GDPR).

[59] See fundamentally *UsedSoft v Oracle International Corp.* [2012] ECLI:EU:C:2012:407; although the CJEU in *Nederlands Uitgeversverbond v Tom Kabinet* [2019] ECLI:EU:C:2019:1111, refused to generalize the UsedSoft doctrine for all categories of copyright-protected works under the InfoSoc Directive, it might still be extended to the area of databases where minimum rights of lawful users are expressly foreseen in the Database Directive for both copyright and the sui generis right.

[60] See also Section 2.1.

Future reform of the Database Directive should keep this overall context in mind. Admittedly, implementing possible access rights in this context and consequently granting access, portability, and subsequent use for free, result in a certain cross-subsidization of users which rely on these rights and actually actively use them for switching their providers at the expense of less active users which do not utilize these possibilities. However, in sectors where such regulation seems necessary and proportionate to prevent existing or likely lock-in problems, this very effect would actually be desirable. After all, it would enable and enhance competition in the interest of *all* customers by nuancedly subsidizing the more active customers in their switching endeavours. Further details, such as a possible definition of the minimum non-waivable use rights and their 'portability', should be regulated in possible future sector-specific access regulation where and to the extent that this is reasonable and necessary.

3.2.2.4.2 Compulsory licences Access rights to entire databases or substantial parts of a database for *competitors* or other *businesses* in order to enhance competition in the area of *sole source data* follow different principles. Typically, such use should be remunerated as it seems that the incentives ratio behind the sui generis right will generally be intact in such cases, whereas it is only a specific market situation which requires that the property rule be turned into a liability rule.[61]

In fact, compulsory licences have been considered since the very beginning of policy discussions about a possible need for database protection in the 1990s.[62] In that regard, it is of particular interest that an earlier Proposal for the Database Directive indeed explicitly included provisions on *compulsory licences* (see Article 8 of the original Commission's Proposal for the Database Directive[63]).[64] Article 8 of the Proposal provided for a compulsory licence on 'fair and non-discriminatory' terms for publicly available *sole source databases* as well as for publicly available databases compiled by *public bodies*. In fact, it seems that such compulsory licences would at least be useful in cases where the mere generation/collection distinction fails to proactively prevent sole source situations, eg, because 'collected' databases develop into an industry standard, independent obtainment becomes impossible because of ex post network effects or subsequent public regulation, etc.[65] Whether additional cases are conceivable in the wake of big data and the multi-polar data economy remains to be seen and should be left to sector-specific analysis and

[61] Cf also Leistner, 'Big Data and the EU Database Directive' (n 8) 42 et seq.

[62] Jane C Ginsburg, 'Creation and Commercial Value: Copyright Protection of Works of Information' (1990) 90 Columbia Law Review 1865 (hereafter Ginsburg, 'Copyright Protection of Works of Information').

[63] Proposal for a Council Directive on the legal protection of databases, COM(1992) 24 final (hereafter Proposal for the Database Directive).

[64] See further Database Directive Final Evaluation Report (n 7) 36 et seq with further references.

[65] Cf on possible reasons and case groups for compulsory licences Database Directive Final Evaluation Report (n 7) 39 et seq.

regulation. As regards the *sole source* criterion, the definition of indispensability should follow the CJEU's definition in *Bronner* (concerning a physical newspaper distribution scheme). Hence, a successful claim to a compulsory licence should require that the creation of a comparable database not be viable under reasonable economic conditions for a competitor of comparable size and resources as the original database maker.[66] Moreover, access to the data would under these circumstances have to be indispensable for access to a secondary market (in relation to the (hypothetical) licensing market for the data).[67] By contrast, the additional criteria from general competition law for compulsory licences (in particular, prevention of the offer of a new product or service) should not apply. Remuneration should be set on fair and non-discriminatory terms.[68] Depending on the circumstances of the case, this might also result in free access to data where reasonable parties would have negotiated a zero licence fee. In the broader context of the discussion to turn the sui generis right into a registered industrial property right[69] one might consider whether it would be recommendable that the EUIPO be responsible for the granting of such compulsory licences for use in the EU market.[70] In that context an arbitration mechanism and, ultimately, an appeal to the General Court should be foreseen in order to set the conditions of such compulsory licences. With regard to the sui generis right which is a genuinely unitary EU protection right and did as such not previously exist in the member states, such provisions and corresponding procedures would be possible and should at least be considered.

Compulsory licences under this mechanism should also extend to *non-published databases*, ie, should take the form of genuine *rights to access* where needed to enable competition.[71] Naturally, this raises intricate issues of third party rights and interests, in particular concerning privacy protection, protection of personal data, and confidentiality in regard to natural persons, but also in regard to businesses, whose data are stored in such databases.[72] Remarkably, even the original Proposal of the Commission which still foresaw compulsory licences only for published databases, already dealt with the relationship to other legislation concerning privacy, protection of personal data, and confidentiality. As for *protection*

[66] Cf *Bronner v Mediaprint* [1998] ECLI:EU:C:1998:569, paras 46 et seq.

[67] Consequently, the so-called secondary market could also be the market where the database maker already offers its own services to customers, since the (hypothetical) primary market would be the licensing market in such cases. See similarly already *IMS Health v NDC Health* [2004] ECLI:EU:C:2004:257.

[68] Cf also Drexl, 'Data Access and Control in the Era of Connected Devices' (n 4) 82.

[69] Cf Leistner, 'Big Data and the EU Database Directive' (n 8) 49 et seq, 56; Leistner, in Database Directive Final Evaluation Report (n 7) 65, 84.

[70] Cf Database Directive Final Evaluation Report (n 7) 42 et seq.

[71] Still differently and limiting compulsory licences to published databases, Ginsburg, 'Copyright Protection of Works of Information' (n 62) 1929; Art 8 of the original Commission's Proposal for the Database Directive (n 63).

[72] Cf, eg, Drexl and others, 'Position Statement of the Max Planck Institute' (n 2) 18 et seq; Database Directive Final Evaluation Report (n 7) 42; Drexl, 'Data Access and Control in the Era of Connected Devices' (n 4) 82.

of personal data, today it follows mandatorily from the GDPR that respective information duties in relation to, and a veto right of, affected individual persons must be foreseen in cases of upstream compulsory licensing when a business which has stored data relating to these natural persons is concerned. At first sight, this might seem like a considerable practical trammel on compulsory licensing. On the other hand, customers would probably rather seldom veto such upstream compulsory licences if they allowed for the offer of new or more efficient products or services. Also, if only individual customers vetoed such licensing this would not entirely devalue the utility of the remaining parts of the database, subject to compulsory licensing.

As for *trade secrets* it seems that as far as these were concerned, compulsory licences should only be granted under the additional circumstances of the CJEU's *IMS Health* decision[73] and the Court's *Microsoft* ruling,[74] ie, in this cases compulsory licences would require that access to the data in question be indispensable to offer a *new product or service* in a secondary market in relation to the (hypothetical) licensing market and that the denial of access would effectively foreclose workable competition on that market.

Whether further conditions or qualifications would be needed should be a matter for future research.[75] This might concern issues such as additional guide posts for the specification of fair, reasonable, and non-discriminatory (FRAND)-terms in certain cases, procedural backing for the process of specifying FRAND-terms, such as possible specific rights of information and other procedural rules and the possible need for a mandatory provision on cross-licences to be granted by the licensee. Given that one of the main problems in the current data marketplace is also the lack of information on provenance and quality of data, one might consider whether possible compulsory licences would have to be complemented by provisions on the obligation to provide certain additional *information on provenance, quality and methodology of given data sets*. At the same time, any such regulation would have to keep in mind that necessary incentives for providing such meta-data to the market participants generally should not be undermined by any sector-specific compulsory licensing regimes.[76]

3.2.2.4.3 Databases created by public bodies Finally, in the case group of databases created by public bodies, where certain imminent contextual tensions within the overall framework of EU copyright law[77] as well as with the existing EU PSI

[73] *IMS Health v NDC Health* [2004] ECLI:EU:C:2004:257.

[74] *Microsoft Corp. v Commission* [2004] ECLI:EU:T:2004:372.

[75] See, from the more recent literature comprehensively on compulsory licensing, Reto M Hilty and Kung-Chung Liu (eds), *Compulsory Licensing* (Springer 2015).

[76] On the general problem see Michael Mattioli, 'The Data-Pooling Problem' (2017) 32 Berkeley Technology Law Journal 179.

[77] See Section 3.2.1.

regime[78] have been identified in this chapter, it seems that the appropriate solution straightforwardly follows from a contextual comparison to general copyright law.

In general copyright law, such creations authored by public bodies are exempted from copyright law if the very policy or legal purpose of the creation is to be disseminated to the public to the maximum extent. As has been already pointed out from a contextual viewpoint in this chapter, it seems that under that same condition (ie, *legal or policy interest in maximum dissemination of certain data*), databases created by public bodies should also be *excepted from possible sui generis protection under the Database Directive*. Only in the remaining cases where a direct legal or policy interest in maximum dissemination does not exist, but instead access only seems reasonable in order to increase dynamic efficiency, alternative access regimes, such as FRAND licences could be considered as far as they are compliant with the regime under the PSI Directive.

4. Conclusion

After an initial phase of insecurity, the current legal and policy discussion of protection of and access to data in the EU data economy has become more and more focused. The academic discussion meanwhile mainly centres on sector-specific access rights, contract law, and portability, and the provision of generally and easily accessible data exchange infrastructures. The discussion of general copyright law (concerning computer programs and compilations) in this chapter has shown that copyright protection for computer programs and compilations (database works) in Europe in general provides for a balanced and reasonable legal framework for the data economy. Reform is mainly needed in regard to certain exceptions to copyright protection, where in particular the very new exceptions for text and data mining in the DSM Directive already seem outdated and insufficient to deal comprehensively with the challenges and opportunities of the data economy.

On the policy side, after the enactment of the Regulation on free flow of non-personal data in the EU meanwhile, the main focus seems to be on the planned EU Data Act 2021 and a possible reform of the EU Database Directive. In that regard, the present chapter has chosen a targeted and specific perspective. Academic proposals for sector-specific access rights have been analysed in the legal context of the existing copyright and sui generis protection regime in order to further specify and deepen the academic discussion. As a result, the different justifications and mechanisms for access and use rights have been categorized in order to develop specific proposals for the accommodation of such rights with the IP law framework in general and with the database sui generis right in particular.

[78] See Section 3.2.2.1.

Three different case groups have emerged for which the respective results of this chapter shall be briefly summarized here. First, certain minimum rights of the lawful users of connected devices should comprise access and portability rights with regard to possibly sui generis-protected databases resulting from the data collecting activity of such devices and their sensors. Such sector-specific access and porting rights of lawful users should be granted for free. The 'anchor' for such access rights within the EU copyright system are the existing mandatory minimum rights of lawful users provided for in Article 5 of the Computer Program Directive as well as in Articles 8(1) and 15 of the Database Directive.

Secondly, in certain remaining cases of sole source databases, competitors as well as other businesses should have a right of access to and use of complete databases where the database is an indispensable element for the development of products and services. This case group would essentially further develop and extend existing compulsory licences under Article 102 of the Treaty on the Functioning of the European Union (TFEU) by providing for a sector-specific compulsory licensing mechanism for the Database Directive's sui generis right. Generally speaking, in these cases, access and use should only be granted on FRAND terms, ie, generally the users should pay for such use licences. However, even in this case group there might be cases where reasonable parties would have negotiated a zero licence fee—in such cases, access under FRAND-terms should consequently be granted for free. As for the details and necessary institutional arrangements, specific proposals have been developed in this chapter.

Thirdly, under certain conditions, databases created by public bodies should be exempted from possible sui generis protection under the Database Directive. The need for revision of the Directive in this area is particularly pressing, as the current regime already produces certain dysfunctional results in some member states as regards the overlap with existing PSI regulation in European law.

Certainly, in order to optimize the legal institutional conditions for the future development of the data economy in Europe, the complete abolition of the sui generis protection right seems a serious alternative worth considering. However, if for certain constitutional law as well as policy reasons, this option were not followed by the EU Commission, as regards access to and use of data in the EU, the proposals made in this chapter should be seriously considered in any future reform of the Database Directive.

PART VII
THE BIGGER PICTURE

18

Competition and IP Policy for AI—Socio-economic Aspects of Innovation

*Anselm Kamperman Sanders**

1. Introduction

The Fourth Industrial Revolution (4IR), coined by Klaus Schwab of the World Economic Forum,[1] may lead to disruptive innovation that is rooted in the convergence of physical, virtual, and biological spheres that affect the entire industrial value chain. The 4IR is articulated in technologies such as smart devices, artificial intelligence (AI), additive manufacturing, 3D printing robotics, and sensory devices, where data analytics and cloud computing will dramatically alter the way in which information is collected, processed, analysed, shared, and used. In assessing whether 4IR can spur innovation in sensitive sectors such as energy production and storage, carbon emission reduction, sustainable food production, and environmental preservation, equality in access to technological progress will be key in providing a competitive and sustainable development path for future generations.

AI is a key component of the 4IR. It is capable of detecting patterns in data that humans cannot and rather than simply generating a synthesis of findings, it also attributes meaning to the information assessed. Many specialists currently temper the high expectations of AI in light of the adage 'garbage in results in garbage out'. It is, however, clear that AI, in addition to pure data trawling resulting in data sets that may be subject to database rights or proprietary information, is likely to find solutions to technical problems that may be patentable, create works that may be considered equal or even superior to works of human authorship. AI itself, being a neural network learning algorithm, may also be subject to intellectual property rights (IPRs) in terms of the code, as well as in terms of the weights, being the 'parameter within a neural network that transforms input data within the network's hidden layers'.[2]

* All online materials were accessed before 1 April 2020.

[1] Klaus Schwab, 'The Fourth Industrial Revolution' (2016 World Economic Forum).

[2] A neural network is a series of nodes, or neurons. Within each node is a set of inputs, weight, and a bias value. See 'Weight (Artificial Neural Network)' (*DeepAI*) <https://deepai.org/machine-learning-glossary-and-terms/weight-artificial-neural-network>.

Anselm Kamperman Sanders, *Competition and IP Policy for AI—Socio-economic Aspects of Innovation*
In: *Artificial Intelligence and Intellectual Property.* Edited by: Jyh-An Lee, Reto M Hilty, and Kung-Chung Liu,
Oxford University Press (2021). © The several contributors. DOI: 10.1093/oso/9780198870944.003.0019

AI is also likely to change the way in which consumers receive information on their needs and wants and how they make purchasing decisions. Apart from scientific breakthroughs, AI is also likely to impact all aspects of R&D and thus industrial and economic life. Furthermore, AI impacts all aspects of economic and social life,[3] most notably labour markets,[4] which may lead to social unrest. Due to the convergence of various scientific disciplines, 4IR will also raise the share of intellectual property in products and services offered across technological fields and in global value chains.[5] The 2017 overview of the 'inventions behind the digital transformation' by the European Patent Office (EPO) in cooperation with the Handelsblatt Research Institute[6] displays a growth of 54% in terms of patent applications over three years in 4IR technologies. However, since patent applications do not yet lead to a massive uptake of technology in the market, the effects of patenting activity on actual innovation will only become visible in the years to come. Concentration in AI-dominated platform technology undertakings is becoming increasingly visible, with Google, Amazon, Facebook, and Apple (GAFA) representing the western world, and Baidu, Alibaba, Tencent, and Huawei (BATH) representing the parallel Chinese economic powerhouse. Platform dominance is the result of vertical integration of Internet of Things (IoT) devices, data capture and analytics of user contents and consumer behaviour, big data analysis, and self-learning neural networks (AI).

Societal acceptance of new technology is very much dependent on the level of education and development of an economy, as well as the trust that its population has in the regulatory system that underpins innovation and the deployment thereof in society.[7] Ownership of data, regulatory and ethical issues of data-mining,[8] effects of AI-generated works and inventions on labour, how to ensure that black-box algorithms are free from bias and do not distort the patent bargain, and the

[3] OECD, 'Key issues for digital transformation in the G20', Report prepared for a joint G20 German Presidency/OECD conference (2017) <http://www.oecd.org/g20/key-issues-for-digital-transformation-in-the-g20.pdf>; see also European Commission, Definition of a research and innovation policy leveraging cloud computing and IoT combination (EU 2014) <https://ec.europa.eu/digital-single-market/en/news/definition-research-and-innovation-policy-leveraging-cloud-computing-and-iot-combination>.

[4] Erik Brynjolfsson and Andrew McAfee, *The Second Machine Age—Work, Progress, and Prosperity in a Time of Brilliant Technologies* (W. W. Norton & Company 2014).

[5] WIPO, 'World Intellectual Property Report 2017—Intangible Capital in Global Value Chains' (2017).

[6] EPO, 'Patents and the Fourth Industrial Revolution—the inventions behind the digital transformation' (2017) <http://www.epo.org/4IR>.

[7] A key factor recognized in the Communication for the Commission to the European Parliament, The Council, The European Economic and Social Committee and the Committee of the Regions, Shaping Europe's digital future, Brussels, 19 February 2020 COM(2020) 67 final (hereafter European Commission, Shaping Europe's digital future 2020).

[8] See Communication for the Commission to the European Parliament, The Council, The European Economic and Social Committee and the Committee of the Regions, A European strategy for data, Brussels 19 February 2020, COM(2020) 66 final (hereafter European Commission, A European strategy for data 2020).

mitigation of the effects of dominant monopolies, are all issues that AI is likely to affect in positive and negative ways alike.[9]

Intellectual property has long been recognized as a key driver for innovation, but its ability to act as a regulatory instrument for trustworthy industrial policy is increasingly challenged. One of the reasons for this development is that the socio-economic impact of frontier technologies is no longer measured against the yardstick of economic and financial gains only, but also against sustainable development goals and societal acceptance of innovation. Societal acceptance is often measured by consumer interests and the regulatory framework that market and competition authorities can bring in terms of technical, environmental, safety, and antitrust standards.

This chapter therefore deals with the intellectual property system and how it may have to be adapted for its continued acceptance as instrument to engender trust in the sustainable development of 4IR platform technologies, and AI in particular. It is argued that competition policy that recognizes and safeguards consumer interests in AI-dominated markets is key to the smooth functioning of such a platform economy.

2. AI and Trust

Arthur Samuel first coined the term 'machine learning' in 1959 when he was working at IBM[10] at computer checkers, defining it as 'the field of study that gives computers the ability to learn without being explicitly programmed'.[11] Whereas AI has progressed from game-based rules that were at the basis of machine learning, one aspect is still true about AI, and that is that 'the most powerful algorithms being used today haven't been optimized for any definition of fairness; they have been optimized to perform a task'.[12] In other words, the problem with machine learning is that rather than bringing order to the world, machines absorb all of humanities' shortcomings, leading to AI bias in outputs.[13] Where such bias results in unfair decisions that affect humans,[14] it will undermine the acceptance of the use of

[9] See European Commission, White Paper On Artificial Intelligence—A European Approach to Excellence and Trust, Brussels, 19 February 2020 COM(2020) 65 final (hereafter European Commission, White Paper on Artificial Intelligence).

[10] After retirement in 1966 he became a professor at Stanford University.

[11] Arthur. Samuel, 'Some Studies in Machine Learning Using the Game of Checkers' (1959) 3(3) IBM Journal of Research and Development 210–29 <https://ieeexplore.ieee.org/document/5392560>.

[12] UC Berkeley School of Information Associate Professor D. Mulligan, as quoted by Jonathan Vanian, 'Unmasking A.I.'s bias problem' (*Fortune*, 25 June 2018) <https://fortune.com/longform/ai-bias-problem/>.

[13] For examples see Cassie Kozyrkov, 'What is AI bias?' (*Towards Data Science*, 24 January 2019) <https://towardsdatascience.com/what-is-ai-bias-6606a3bcb814>.

[14] For an analysis see UN Department of Economic and Social Affairs, 'World Economic and Social Survey 2018, Frontier Technologies for Sustainable Development' (2018) 59–64 <https://www.un.org/development/desa/dpad/document_gem/wess-report/>.

AI.[15] In the context of intellectual property, or even de facto control over personal data, private individuals expect that their privacy is secure and that AI decisions are transparent. This implies that there is a form of oversight over AI algorithms and how they are trained and execute automated decisions, so that these are not 'black box'. [16] For the purpose of this chapter, however, privacy and data-subject control over the accuracy, privacy, and impact of AI decisions are not further elaborated.[17] Rather, the intellectual property-antitrust interface, or competition policy aspects will be considered. In a data-driven society, the data sets, algorithms, and weights that drive AI are often proprietary and subject to trade secrecy. This means that in the interest of societal acceptance of AI technologies, transparency and competition policy in relation to intellectual property is equally important.[18]

2.1 Competition Policy—Trust in AI and IP, Digital Twins?

Since AI is primarily dependent on the data sets to train these neural networks, the presence of any patents and copyright may not be immediately problematic, but the combination with the access to data and the related gathering and processing means it is very likely to be.[19] Data as such are, however, neither patentable, nor an original work of copyright. In most instances trade secrecy may be the best method of protecting databases and weights that make Big Data analysis possible.[20] Some

[15] Aaron Rieke, Miranda Bogen, and David Robinson, *Public Scrutiny of Automated Decisions: Early Lessons and Emerging Methods* (Omidyar Network and Upturn 2018) <https://omidyar.com/wp-content/uploads/2020/09/Public-Scrutiny-of-Automated-Decisions.pdf>.

[16] For these aspects please see Michael Mattioli, '(Dis)Trust and the Data Society—AI and other Biases' in Christopher Heath, Anselm Kamperman Sanders, and Anke Moerland (eds), *Intellectual Property Law and the 4th Industrial Revolution* (Kluwer Law International 2020).

[17] See European Commission, A European strategy for data 2020 (n 8) 10, where the empowerment of individuals to decide what is done with their data by means of nascent (technical) tools that allow for consent and personal information management is positively received and in need of further support.

[18] European Commission, Shaping Europe's digital future 2020 (n 7) articulates the need for 'creating ecosystems of excellence and trust in the field of AI, based on European values'.

[19] European Union Agency for Fundamental Rights, 'Data Quality and Artificial Intelligence—Mitigating Bias and Error to Protect Fundamental Rights' (2019, FRA) <https://fra.europa.eu/en/publication/2019/artificial-intelligence-data-quality> with the abstract at p. 1: 'Algorithms used in machine learning systems and artificial intelligence (AI) can only be as good as the data used for their development. High quality data are essential for high quality algorithms. Yet, the call for high quality data in discussions around AI often remains without any further specifications and guidance as to what this actually means. Since there are several sources of error in all data collections, users of AI-related technology need to know where the data come from and the potential shortcomings of the data. AI systems based on incomplete or biased data can lead to inaccurate outcomes that infringe on people's fundamental rights, including discrimination. Being transparent about which data are used in AI systems helps to prevent possible rights violations. This is especially important in times of big data, where the volume of data is sometimes valued over quality.'

[20] For an analysis of the data and competition aspects of the 4IR see Anselm Kamperman Sanders, 'Data and Technology Transfer Competition Law in the Fourth Industrial Revolution' in Christopher Heath, Anselm Kamperman Sanders, and Anke. Moerland (eds), *Intellectual Property Law and the 4th Industrial Revolution* (Kluwer Law International 2020) (hereafter Sanders, 'Data and Technology Transfer Competition Law').

jurisdictions, most notably the European Union (EU), have sui generis legislation for the protection of databases.[21] This legislation protects the investment in the obtaining, verification, and presentation of data, and provides the right holder with the possibility to object to unauthorized extraction and re-utilization of data. This also means that the linking-up of data sets also falls within the ambit of this sui generis database right. Nothing, however, prevents third parties from gathering, verifying, and presenting their own data.[22] In view of the fact that many databases will in future be filled through IoT devices, however, the practical ability to gather information will be firmly in the hands of platform providers (Google, Facebook, Apple, etc), as well as IoT device manufacturers and service providers.[23]

In the world of Big Data, information is the currency that is required to have access to services. This is made possible by means of 'digital twinning',[24] where IoT devices can be expressed as a virtual representation of a physical object in a computer system. Take, eg, vehicles that are equipped with sensory devices that monitor not only the vehicle and its engines in operation, but also monitor road and traffic situations and log the driver's behaviour. When this information is relayed for analysis to the manufacturer, it is possible to have each individual vehicle expressed in the form of a digital twin. An AI system capable of comparing a fleet of vehicles is able to learn from the driving experiences of each and every digital twin and update the software that can then be sent remotely to the real-life vehicles.[25] Digital twinning in IoT and AI creates a platform environment on the basis of which connected products can be continuously monitored and updated. It also allows for continuous analysis of customer information, so that additional services can be offered based on real-time consumer behaviour and preferences. Digital twinning is also the type of computer-implemented invention that is capable of meeting the patentability threshold where 'software as such' does not.[26] This is due to the fact that further technical effects going beyond the mere running of

[21] Directive 96/9/EC Of the European Parliament and of the Council of 11 March 1996 on the legal protection of databases, OJ L77, 27 March 1996 (hereafter legal protection of databases).

[22] See DG for Communications Networks, Content and Technology, Study in support of the evaluation of Directive 96/9/EC on the legal protection of databases (2018) <https://op.europa.eu/en/publication-detail/-/publication/f10f8ee0-597e-11e8-ab41-01aa75ed71a1> citing positive effects of harmonization of the legal framework, but finding no positive or negative effects of the Directive on the competitiveness of the EU database industry.

[23] See European Commission, A European strategy for data 2020 (n 8) 12, calling for the operationalization of the principles of Findability, Accessibility, Interoperability and Reusability (FAIR) of data.

[24] See Bernard Marr, '7 amazing examples of digital twin technology in practice' (*Forbes*, 23 April 2019) <https://www.forbes.com/sites/bernardmarr/2019/04/23/7-amazing-examples-of-digital-twin-technology-in-practice/#5215765c6443>.

[25] Tesla can serve as a perfect example here. See Bernard Marr, 'The amazing ways Tesla is using artificial intelligence and big data' (*Forbes*, 8 January 2018) <https://www.forbes.com/sites/bernardmarr/2018/01/08/the-amazing-ways-tesla-is-using-artificial-intelligence-and-big-data/#649338774270>.

[26] Kemal Bengi and Christopher Heath, 'Patents and Artificial Intelligence Inventions' in Christopher Heath, Anselm Kamperman Sanders, and Anke Moerland (eds), *Intellectual Property Law and the 4th Industrial Revolution* (Kluwer Law International 2020).

the software can be achieved through the digital reach into the physical domain.[27] Patents in AI technologies are therefore growing fast and have a reach into biological, knowledge, material, and mathematical sciences.[28]

2.2 AI Governance—A Horizontal and Technologically Neutral Approach

Due to the enormous amount of human work and effort AI can replace, and the need for governance structures on AI in relation to liability and risk, the Committee on Legal Affairs of the European Parliament adopted a Motion for a European Parliament Resolution.[29] It encompasses a number of recommendations to the Commission on Civil Law Rules on Robotics and AI to support a 'horizontal and technologically neutral approach' to intellectual property applicable to the various sectors in which robotics could be employed, as well as a 'balanced approach to IPRs when applied to hardware and software standards and codes that protect innovation and at the same time foster innovation'. Of course, IPRs are merely a small issue in the wider context of the regulation of AIs.[30] As a matter of fact, in terms of patenting AI and neural networks, AI is facing the same issues that computer programs do.[31]

In their more basic form IPRs fulfil three basic functions: the 'creation of competitive markets' for human, industrial, and intellectual creativity that is novel or original, where consumers can make rational choices about which goods or services to buy; 'insurance' for innovators, safeguarding the fruits of their labour from abuse by free riders; and a 'commercial gateway' through which innovators can exploit and benefit from their creations. This implies that market participants and society at large can somehow learn from the industrious activities of their competitors. The patent system recognizes the need for enabling disclosure as part of the social contract under which the patentee requests a temporary monopoly in exchange for openness.

[27] See Benjamin Sanderse and Edgar Weippl (eds), Special theme issue of the European Research Consortium for Informatics and Mathematics, 'Digital Twins' 115 (*ERCIM News*, October 2018) <https://ercim-news.ercim.eu/images/stories/EN115/EN115-web.pdf>.

[28] Hidemichi Fujii and Shunsuke Managi, 'Trends and priority shifts in artificial intelligence technology invention: a global patent analysis' (*VOX CEPR's Policy Portal*, 16 June 2017) <http://voxeu.org/article/trends-artificial-intelligence-technology-invention>.

[29] Report with recommendations to the Commission on Civil Law Rules on Robotics (2015/2103(INL)) A8–0005/2017 (of 27 January 2017) <http://www.europarl.europa.eu/sides/getDoc.do?pubRef=-//EP//NONSGML+REPORT+A8-2017-0005+0+DOC+PDF+V0//EN>.

[30] Wider issues include liability, corporate and civic responsibility, etc. See Peter Stone and others, 'Artificial intelligence and life in 2030' (Stanford University, 2016) <http://ai100.stanford.edu/2016-report>.

[31] Randall Davis, 'Intellectual Property and Software: The Assumptions are Broken', AI Memo No 1328 (Massachusetts Institute of Technology Artificial Intelligence Laboratory, 1991).

The inherently closed and proprietary nature of trade secrecy and in many respects self-learning algorithms and the data sets that they learn from do present real challenges of access for the purpose of access, learning, and regulatory oversight. Naturally, IPRs also have limitations and boundaries, not least due to the problems that may arise from the considerable market power that IPRs provide to their owners. Since patent applications do not yet lead to a massive uptake of technology in the market, the effects of patenting activity on actual innovation and market power will only become visible in the years to come. In this context it is important to note that at present only twenty-five companies are responsible for 50% of the 4IR applications at the EPO between 2011 and 2016, with the US, Europe, and Japan leading, and the Republic of Korea and China rapidly catching up. Among the biggest patent filing firms, traditional ICT corporations like Samsung, Apple, Sony, and Philips are still present, but Google and Huawei are among of the biggest climbers. In 2017 the Economist published an article[32] under the title 'The world's most valuable resource is no longer oil, but data', arguing that competition authorities ought to be much more critical of relation to data platform operators, such as GAFA as they had been with Microsoft in the past. Microsoft's dominance in the market for operating systems enabled them to control the market for mainframe systems, and to bundle browser and media player software to the detriment of alternatives provided by competitors. This behaviour was held to be abusive by competition authorities.[33]

3. Competition Law and Abuses of Market Dominance

In the EU, the Commission as competition authority can initiate antitrust actions based on Articles 101 and 102 of the Treaty on the Functioning of the European Union (TFEU).[34] Article 101 TFEU prohibits anticompetitive agreements and decisions of associations of undertakings that prevent, restrict, or distort competition within the EU's Single Market. Article 102 TFEU prohibits the abuse of a dominant position.[35]

Under this regime it is possible to hold that denial of access to infrastructures is anticompetitive. The test employed is one where a company with a dominant

[32] 'The world's most valuable resource is no longer oil, but data. The data economy demands a new approach to antitrust rules' (*The Economist*, 6 May 2017) <https://www.economist.com/leaders/2017/05/06/the-worlds-most-valuable-resource-is-no-longer-oil-but-data>.

[33] See inter alia *United States v Microsoft Corporation*, 253 F.3d 34 (D.C. Cir. 2001); and EGC Case T-201/04 *Microsoft Corp. v Commission*, ECLI:EU:T:2007:289.

[34] Note that part of this section is based on the case analysis in Sanders, 'Data and Technology Transfer Competition Law' (n 20).

[35] Articles 101 and 102 TFEU were previously known as Arts 81 and 82, see Council Regulation (EC) No 1/2003 of 16 December 2002 on the implementation of the rules on competition laid down in Arts 81 and 82 of the Treaty.

position in supplying facilities, products, or services that are indispensable for the functioning of a downstream market abuses its position if it refuses, without justification, to grant access to these facilities, products, or services, resulting in the elimination of competition in the downstream market.[36] A refusal to grant a licence to intellectual property also falls within the definition of this test, albeit that the party seeking the licence must offer a new product.[37]

ICT platform operators have increasingly come under scrutiny from the Commission. Google has already been fined repeatedly for abusing its dominance, in 2017 and 2018 for its search engine, in relation to its own comparison-shopping service, and in relation to its Android mobile devices. Fines of EUR 2.42 billion and EUR 4.34 billion have been levied for each of these abuses. In 2019 Google was fined yet again for abusive practices in relation to its online advertising for EUR 1.49 billion.[38] Platform dominance is likely to occupy competition authorities in the future as well. In July 2019, the Commission announced that it had opened an investigation[39] into the conduct of Amazon in relation to accumulated marketplace seller data that it analyses to position its own products in relation to those of third-party retailers using its platform. The central question being whether this data set and algorithm is open to inspection and use by those third-party retailers. After all, the pricing algorithm will eventually allow for contracts to be concluded in an automated fashion and verified by use of blockchain technology.[40] In fact, we already see the emergence of pricing algorithms that seemingly facilitate smart contracts.[41]

Such pricing algorithms may result in benefits to consumers. In the *Webtaxi* case, the Luxemburg competition authority decided[42] that a pricing algorithm that automatically determines the price of a taxi fare in a fixed and non-negotiable manner

[36] CJEU Case C-7/97, *Bronner*, EU:C:1998:569; CJEU Case T-167/08, *Microsoft v Commission*, EU:T:2012:323.

[37] CJEU Case C-418/01, *IMS Health*, ECLI:EU:C:2004:257 and Joined Cases C-241/91 P and C-242/91 P, *RTE and ITP v Commission*, EU:C:1995:98. Conversely, however, see CJEU Case T-167/08, *Microsoft v Commission*, EU:T:2012:323.

[38] For an overview of cases on Google Android see <https://ec.europa.eu/competition/elojade/isef/case_details.cfm?proc_code=1_40099>; for Google Search (shopping) <https://ec.europa.eu/competition/elojade/isef/case_details.cfm?proc_code=1_39740>; for Google advertising <https://ec.europa.eu/commission/presscorner/detail/en/IP_19_1770>.

[39] Case number AT.40462.

[40] With its reliance on 'proof of work' that requires crypto computing with every entry in the distributed ledger, blockchain technology is, however, rather energy consuming. Many AI applications are, see Will Knight, 'AI can do great things—if it doesn't burn the planet' (*Wired*, 21 January 2020) <https://www.wired.com/story/ai-great-things-burn-planet/>.

[41] For a rather critical analysis of self-executing software contracts that typically comprise coded parameters written into a blockchain, see Andres Guadamuz, 'Smart Contracts, Blockchain and Intellectual Property: Challenges and Reality' in Christopher Heath, Anselm Kamperman Sanders, and Anke Moerland (eds), *Intellectual Property Law and the 4th Industrial Revolution* (Kluwer Law International 2020).

[42] Webtaxi S.à.r.l, 'Décision no 2018-FO-01' (7 June 2018) <https://concurrence.public.lu/dam-assets/fr/decisions/ententes/2018/decision-n-2018-fo-01-du-7-juin-2018-version-non-confidentielle.pdf>.

based on geo-location of clients and the number of close-by taxis participating in the app resulted in higher efficiencies for participating taxi drivers and customers alike. Efficiencies were found to exist in terms of reduced fares, reduced number of empty taxis, reduced pollution, and reduced waiting times. A critical point, however, is that there does not appear to be competition in terms of presenting alternatives to the ones presented in the Webtaxi app and the automated process prevents price differentiation. The system rather results in parallel pricing due to a *de facto* agreement on collective pricing within a bandwidth determined by the algorithm for all competitors that use the system. Pricing algorithms may then also result in algorithmic price fixing, a form of collusion between undertakings operating in the same market.[43] Illustrative in this regard is Accenture's Partneo algorithm that identifies the maximum price consumers would be willing to pay for car parts such as fenders, mirrors, and bumpers.[44] This software is used by a number of car manufacturers, most notably Renault, Nissan, Chrysler, Jaguar Land Rover, and Peugeot, resulting in a price increase of 15% on average of their inventory between 2008 and 2013. The manufacturers all claim not to collude, because they are not in direct contact with each other.[45] After all, in the absence of any communication between competitors, no agreement or concerted practice may be identified, and so no violation of Article 101 TFEU can be established either. The European Court of Justice (ECJ) has clarified that in the context of Article 101 TFEU market participants need to operate with independence, so that for concerted practices to occur: 'any direct or indirect contact between such operators, the object or effect whereof is either to influence the conduct on the market . . . or to disclose to such a competitor the course of conduct . . . on the market'[46] is precluded.

The car manufacturers' decision to use the software arguably results in price fixing in the market for car parts, but there is no 'contact' between the market participants in the traditional sense. It is the AI that facilitates an analysis and pricing that is not yet defined as 'communication' within the scope of Article 101 TFEU.[47] The common use results in parallel price increases,[48] and unless Accenture actually held out its software as a means of exchange of sensitive pricing information

[43] See Antonio Capobianco, Pedro Gonzaga, and Anita Nyesö, *Algorithms and Collusion—Competition Policy in the Digital Age* (OECD 2017) <http://www.oecd.org/competition/algorithms-collusion-competition-policy-in-the-digital-age.htm>.

[44] See Tom Bergin and Laurence Frost, 'Software and stealth: how carmakers hike spare parts prices' (*Reuters Business News*, 3 June 2018) <https://www.reuters.com/article/us-autos-software-pricing-insight/software-and-stealth-how-carmakers-hike-spare-parts-prices-idUSKCN1IZ07L>.

[45] CJEU Case C-74/14 21 January 2016, *Eturas UAB* et al. *v Lietuvos Respublikos konkurencijos taryba*, ECLI:EU:C:2016:42, paras 44–5.

[46] CJEU 16 December 1975, Joined Cases 40–48, 50, 54–56, 111, 113, and 114/73, *Suiker Unie and Others v Commission*, 1668–2044.

[47] CJEU Case C-8/08 4 June 2009 *T-Mobile Netherlands BV*, et al. *v Raad van bestuur van de Nederlandse Mededingingsautoriteit*, ECLI:EU:C:2009:343, para 51.

[48] CJEU Case 48/69 14 July 1972, *Imperial Chemical Industries Ltd. v Commission*, ECLI:EU:C:1972:70, paras 64–6.

through the common use of Partneo, it will be hard to establish liability.[49] If no undertaking is to blame since no anticompetitive intent can be shown, the question is whether the use of self-learning algorithms that may lead to an exchange of (price-)sensitive information between undertakings ought to be caught by Article 101 TFEU so that the users may be liable for market collusion that such algorithms create.[50] This is a form of attribution that is after all not uncommon in relation to employees and agents.

4. The *Facebook* Case and Germany's Competition Law

In the case of *Facebook*, the Commission investigated Facebook's attempts to squeeze rivals out of the market. An example involves the 'copying' of features of Snapchat, which in 2003 had turned down a take-over offer by Facebook of reportedly more than USD 3 billion. Facebook's plan to launch a cryptocurrency called Libra is also underway, raising questions on access and use of information and customer data and the integration of the Libra wallet in Facebook's WhatsApp and Messenger services to the detriment of competitors in these downstream markets. The German competition regulator, the Bundeskartellamt, has meanwhile imposed restrictions on Facebook prohibiting it from collecting information outside the Facebook website and assigning it to a single user's Facebook account. This is achieved by combining user data gathered from the (third party) websites and smart devices apps, including Facebook-owned services such as WhatsApp and Instagram. What is interesting about this decision is that the Bundeskartellamt has taken into consideration that the EU's General Data Protection Regulation (GDPR)[51] plays a central role in the exploitative abuse that is to the detriment of consumers and moreover also impedes competitors from collecting and utilizing a similar amount of data to advertise and thus create a competitive market. Upon appeal, however, the Oberlandesgericht (OLG) Düsseldorf has ruled that Facebook's behaviour does not violate section 19 of the German Competition Act (GWB), as

[49] See case brought by Laurent Boutboul, the creator of the Partneo pricing software, against Accenture pending before the Paris Commercial Court for misuse of the software after Boutboul sold it to Accenture in 2010.

[50] For such an argument see Jan Blockx, 'Antitrust in Digital Markets in the EU: Policing Price Bots' (Radboud Economic Law Conference, 9 June 2017) <https://ssrn.com/abstract=2987705>; Ariel Ezrachi and Maurice Stucke, 'Artificial Intelligence & Collusion: When Computers Inhibit Competition' Working Paper CCLP (L) 40 <https://www.law.ox.ac.uk/sites/files/oxlaw/cclpl40.pdf> at 37: 'In a digitalised universe in which the law's moral fabric is inapplicable, any game theories are constantly modelled until a rational and predicable outcome has been identified. Given the transparent nature of these markets, algorithms may change the market dynamics and facilitate tacit collusion, higher prices, and greater wealth inequality. In such a reality, firms may have a distinct incentive to shift pricing decisions from humans to algorithms. Humans will more likely wash themselves of any moral concerns, in denying any relationship and responsibilities between them and the computer.'

[51] Regulation (EU) 2016/679 (General Data Protection Regulation), OJ L119, 4 May 2016; cor. OJ L127, 23 May 2018 (hereafter EU General Data Protection Regulation).

it cannot be established whether Facebook's terms of use refer to the additional data that would restrict actual or potential competitors in the market for social networks that the Bundeskartellamt identified. In this context it is relevant, according to the OLG, that it cannot be excluded that the processing of additional data by Facebook does not result in the ability to foreclose the market to competition. This is due to the fact that the network is financed by advertising revenues and that the quality of the user data is relevant for the generation of additional revenue. Whether this does in fact lead to unjustified restrictions on competition requires closer examination. According to the OLG the market position of Facebook is reinforced through network effects resulting from the large number of 32 million new private users per month:

> The benefit of Facebook's network for its users increases with the total number of connected people to the network, because increasing user numbers also lead to increased communication possibilities for each individual user. As a result, the market position of Facebook as a provider of a social network can only be successfully challenged if the competitor succeeds, within a reasonable amount of time, to attract a sufficient number of users to its network for it to be attractive, which in turn depends on whether he is capable to offer an attractive social network compared to Facebook.com. This is the crucial barrier to entry … In the contested decision, the Bundeskartellamt has not yet substantiated and comprehensibly demonstrated which concrete—going beyond the Facebook data—extra data is at issue and what influence the processing and linking of this additional data for the purposes of the social network would have on the (in) ability for competing network providers to enter the market. Likewise, there is a lack of reliable explanations as to how far and to what extent the use of the disputed additional data would enable Facebook to noticeably increase advertising revenue to finance its social network and to what extent this will shield Facebook's market position against future market entries.

The decision is currently under appeal before the German Supreme Court, and the tenth revision of the German Competition Act (GWB-Digitalisierungsgesetz), which deals with digitization, provides the clues on the arguments that will be presented by the Bundeskartellamt. The draft explicitly includes the access to data relevant to competition as a factor for the assessment of a position of dominance and possibilities for abuse. Section 18(3)(2) dealing with market dominance adds 'access to data relevant to competition' to financial strength, and also sections 18(3a) and 18(3b) GWB-Digitalisierungsgesetz consider multi-sided markets and networks and undertakings acting as intermediaries in multi-sided markets in the assessment. Furthermore, the supply of products or services may be abusive in the context of section 19(4) GWB-Digitalisierungsgesetz, including 'access to data, networks or other infrastructure, the supply of which is objectively necessary in order to operate on an upstream or downstream market and the refusal to supply threatens to eliminate effective competition on that market'. Finally, a new provision in the form of section 19a is foreseen to deal with 'Abusive conduct of undertakings with paramount significance for competition across markets'.

While the Bundeskartellamt and European Commission have clearly taken the lead in regulating platform ICT industries, the US appears to follow suit, with Attorneys General in a number of states opening antitrust investigations into Facebook and Google. The US Department of Justice and the Federal Trade Commission do not, however, seem to see eye to eye on competence and approach.[52]

5. The EU's Latest Communications and White Paper

5.1 'Shaping Europe's Digital Future' Communication

On 19 February 2020, the European Commission issued two communications and a White Paper, outlining its vision on Europe's digital future. Its general publication entitled 'Shaping Europe's digital future'[53] highlights the need for 'European technological sovereignty'.[54] This is terminology that has an interesting connotation in a time where the role of Huawei in the construction of 5G networks is an issue of intense debate and Atlantic divide between the US[55] and European countries.[56] The EU already claims sovereignty over privacy-related issues, as is clearly visible in the GDPR, but there is an openness towards non-EU operators in that: 'The EU will remain open to anyone willing to play by European Rules and meet European standards, regardless where they are based'.[57] The sentiment that European citizens value their privacy and need to be able to have a sense of control over what happens with their personal data, is reflected in the fact that the Commission places trust at the heart of its digital future agenda (see Figure 18.1).

A fair and competitive digital economy with a level playing field is also one of the three key objectives for the digital transformation. Platform dominance is one of the issues that is to be addressed in this context, and apart from an 'enhanced

[52] Justin Sherman, 'Oh sure, big tech wants regulation—on its own terms' (*Wired*, 28 January 2020) <https://www.wired.com/story/opinion-oh-sure-big-tech-wants-regulationon-its-own-terms/>.

[53] See European Commission, Shaping Europe's digital future 2020 (n 7).

[54] Ibid, 2.

[55] See Nick Statt, 'US pushing tech and telecom industries to build 5G alternative to Huawei' (*The Verge*, 5 February 2020) <https://www.theverge.com/2020/2/5/21124888/us-5g-huawei-white-house-trump-china-alternative-telecom-standard>.

[56] Alicia Hope, 'France authorizes the use of Huawei equipment in its 5G network while plans for a new factory are underway' (*CPO Magazine*, 20 March 2020) <https://www.cpomagazine.com/cyber-security/france-authorizes-the-use-of-huawei-equipment-in-its-5g-network-while-plans-for-a-new-factory-are-underway/>.

[57] EU General Data Protection Regulation (n 51).

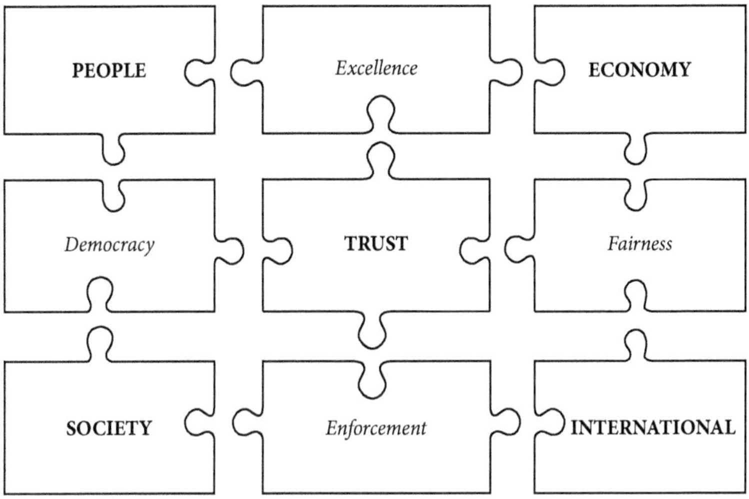

Figure 18.1 Source: Shaping Europe's digital future[58]

framework for platform workers',[59] the reform of EU competition law is on the cards[60] to address B2C and B2B concerns over trust and abuse of dominance, especially in relation to platforms.[61] A sector enquiry is already ongoing and an exploration of stronger ex ante rules, in the context of the so-called Digital Services Act package, has been announced 'to ensure that markets characterised by large platforms with significant network effects acting as gate-keepers, remain fair and contestable for innovators, businesses, and new market entrants'.[62] These policy statements are presently further articulated in two documents: 1) A European strategy for data;[63] and 2) White Paper on Artificial Intelligence—A European approach to excellence and trust.[64]

5.2 'A European Strategy for Data' Communication

The Commission's data strategy emphasizes the need for access to (private sector) data of general interest, but also specific secondary uses of health and social data

[58] European Commission, Shaping Europe's digital future 2020 (n 7) 3.
[59] Ibid, 6.
[60] See in this respect the earlier Commission's report, Competition policy for the digital era (doi: 10.2763/407537, 2019) https://op.europa.eu/en/publication-detail/-/publication/21dc175c-7b76-11e9-9f05-01aa75ed71a1/language-en (hereafter Commission's report, Competition policy for the digital era).
[61] Ibid, 53–77.
[62] European Commission, Shaping Europe's digital future 2020 (n 7) 10.
[63] European Commission, A European strategy for data 2020 (n 8).
[64] European Commission, White Paper on Artificial Intelligence (n 9).

that is currently regulated at member state level.[65] Business interest in access to data is also recognized and is, according to the Commission, subject to imbalances in market power due to platform dominance and data co-generated through use of IoT from industrial and consumer devices. The Commission's data strategy incorporates the recommendation of the report, 'Competition policy for the digital era'[66] that calls for regulatory experimentation (sandboxes) that is sector-specific and in line with the principles of Findability, Accessibility, Interoperability, and Reusability (FAIR).[67] In this context a possible revision of the EU's Database[68] and Trade Secrets Protection[69] Directives is tabled, and indeed necessary. The Commission states that data sharing should in principle be subject to contract, but that in case of identified or foreseeable market failure in a given sector, access to data should be made compulsory. The examples provided are information resulting from the testing of chemicals,[70] and motor vehicle repair and maintenance information.[71] These instruments are interesting, as they introduce a standard of fair, transparent, reasonable, proportionate, and/or non-discriminatory conditions under which providing data access is mandatory.[72]

The application of these principles may require sector-specific technological standard-setting in terms of software and data protocols, leading to the pooling or even setting aside of IPRs and compelling transfer of trade secrets and confidential information. It is expected that the newly established Observatory of the Online

[65] See European Commission, A European strategy for data 2020 (n 8) at fnn 14 and 15, where French and Finnish examples are mentioned.

[66] Commission's report, Competition policy for the digital era (n 60).

[67] European Commission, A European strategy for data 2020 (n 8) 12.

[68] Legal protection of databases (n 21).

[69] Directive (EU) 2016/943 of the European Parliament and of the Council of 8 June 2016 on the protection of undisclosed know-how and business information (trade secrets) against their unlawful acquisition, use and disclosure, OJ L 157, 15.6.2016, 1–18.

[70] Regulation 1907/2006 of the European Parliament and of the Council of 18 December 2006 concerning the Registration, Evaluation, Authorisation and Restriction of Chemicals (REACH), OJ L 396, 29.5.2007, 3–280.

[71] See in this respect the new Regulation (EU) 2018/858 of the European Parliament and of the Council of 30 May 2018 on the approval and market surveillance of motor vehicles and their trailers, and of systems, components and separate technical units intended for such vehicles, amending Regulations (EC) No 715/2007 and (EC) No 595/2009 and repealing Directive 2007/46/EC, which entered into force on 1 September 2020.

[72] Eg, Art 6 of Regulation (EU) 2018/858 provides the following:

> Manufacturers' obligations to provide vehicle OBD information and vehicle repair and maintenance information
>
> 1. Manufacturers shall provide to independent operators unrestricted, standardised and non-discriminatory access to vehicle OBD information, diagnostic and other equipment, tools including the complete references, and available downloads, of the applicable software and vehicle repair and maintenance information. Information shall be presented in an easily accessible manner in the form of machine-readable and electronically processable datasets. Independent operators shall have access to the remote diagnosis services used by manufacturers and authorised dealers and repairers. Manufacturers shall provide a standardised, secure and remote facility to enable independent repairers to complete operations that involve access to the vehicle security system.

Platforms Economy[73] will provide further analysis and recommendations for a Digital Services Act and further regulatory efforts to create common European data spaces for: manufacturing, green deal,[74] mobility, health, financial, energy, agriculture, public administration, and skills.[75] These data spaces are likely to be subject to differentiating rules operating under the common FAIR principle. This principle is a very open-ended norm that will require interpretation and case law to develop.

Where AI is concerned, measures to establish data pools for data analysis and machine learning will require competition guidelines, as these measures amount to horizontal cooperation, thus potentially resulting in collusion.[76]

5.3 White Paper on Artificial Intelligence

The European Commission White Paper on Artificial Intelligence sets out the policy options on how to promote the uptake of AI and of addressing the risks associated with certain uses of this technology.[77] In line with the Commission's data and digital future strategies, 'trust' is the central tenet for the White Paper, especially where human-centric AI is concerned. This is relevant not only to address socio-economic aspects,[78] but also from the perspective that computing facilities, that are currently predominantly cloud-based, are set to shift close to the user (Edge Computing) in the form of AI of Things (AIoT).[79] This means that users will increasingly be co-creators of intellectual property contents, as the AIoT devices that users use and wear process their inputs and information locally and individually. As a result, the individual user of an AIoT device will also demand a stake in the access and positive outputs of such devices, even though AIoT devices are part of a larger connected web of centralized AI and digitally twinned networks. The adoption of 'responsible data management practices and compliance with FAIR principles will contribute to build trust and ensure re-usability of data',[80] and in

[73] See <https://platformobservatory.eu>.

[74] On the EU Green Deal and the ambition to be carbon-neutral by 2050, The European Green Deal, Communication from the Commission, 11 December 2019, COM(2019) 640 final <https://ec.europa.eu/info/strategy/priorities-2019-2024/european-green-deal_en>.

[75] See the appendix to European Commission, A European strategy for data 2020 (n 8) 26–34.

[76] For this purpose, the Commission announces an update of the Horizontal Co-operation Guidelines, Guidelines on the applicability of Article 101 of the Treaty on the Functioning of the European Union to horizontal co-operation agreements, OJ C 11, 14.1.2011, 1–72.

[77] European Commission, White Paper on Artificial Intelligence (n 9).

[78] See the report from the High-Level Expert Group, 'Ethics guidelines for trustworthy AI' (*European Commission*, 8 April 2019) <https://ec.europa.eu/futurium/en/ai-alliance-consultation/guidelines#Top> (hereafter European Commission, 'Ethics guidelines for trustworthy AI').

[79] See for an explanation Keith Shaw, 'What is edge computing and why it matters' (*Networkworld*, 13 November 2019) <https://www.networkworld.com/article/3224893/what-is-edge-computing-and-how-it-s-changing-the-network.html>.

[80] European Commission, White Paper on Artificial Intelligence (n 9) 8.

doing so address the asymmetries of power or information, such as between employers and workers, or between businesses and consumers.[81]

Inherent to AI is that the product it is embedded in or interacts with will change its functionality and behaviour throughout its lifecycle. This means that the more the AIoT user has interacted with it, the more the device becomes personalized. The user's traits, labour, and skill, and ultimately the personality of the user will be indelibly stamped onto the AIoT device. It is foreseeable that, like with telephone number portability before, the demand for personal data sets that contain a semblance of works of authorship to become personal property will increase. These data sets can after all be ported to the next AI to speed up learning. Accuracy and openness to independent audit is furthermore necessary to verify compliance with applicable rules but may also be used for appropriate attribution of data sets to corporations, users, and individuals that all interact in a co-creation setting through an AI. It would not engender trust if all intellectual property would accrue only with the corporate entities that market AI products, especially with those that also command the platforms for IoT and AIoT business, commerce, and social interaction.

6. Conclusion

With a rapidly developing AI landscape, it is important for the uptake and acceptance in society of new applications in this domain that there is clear regulatory oversight in respect of data sets used to train neural networks (AI), as well as the algorithms themselves as and when they self-adapt (learn). This means that there is a need for continuous supervisory access to data sets and algorithms, so that the general public maintains trust in automated information and decision systems. In this respect bias leading to unjustifiable decisions and outcomes must be prevented. Black-box algorithms must be open to an independent audit for this purpose.

Due to the economic dominance of platform providers, competition authorities will have to provide the necessary regulatory oversight, ex ante and ex post, so as to ensure equal access to data sets and the means of gathering, and in some cases even the processing, of information. This requires a very different view on intellectual property and related trade secrets than before, namely one where the exercise of IPRs is viewed in a connected environment of sensory devices, data sets, trade secrets, and platform dominance. Co-creation in such an environment will result in a complex web of claims of use and re-use, but also of co-created intellectual property contents. In order to maintain trust in AI technologies, an intellectual property paradigm that serves the public interest in transparency and openness will be more relevant than ever before.

[81] See European Commission, 'Ethics guidelines for trustworthy AI' (n 78) 13 for a test of proportionality 'between user and deployer [of AI], considering the rights of companies (including intellectual property and confidentiality) on the one hand, and the rights of the user on the other'.

19

AI as a Legal Person?

*Eliza Mik**

1. Introduction

This chapter critically examines the recurring claim that sophisticated algorithms—or artificial intelligence (AI) in general—require recognition as discrete legal entities. Historically, technological advancements have posed challenges to intellectual property (IP) law by providing superior abilities to copy and disseminate protected works. In the case of AI, the challenge lies in technology being *creative* or *inventive*—having the ability to generate its 'own' output. In effect, due to, the sophistication of the AI (including its purported ability to operate without human intervention), the output produced thereby can no longer be attributed to the person who created the AI. It has been claimed, eg, that 'autonomous, creative, unpredictable, rational, and evolving' AIs can create innovative, new, and non-obvious products and services that, 'had they been generated by humans, might be patentable inventions'.[1] Purportedly, such AIs are capable of operating independently, rather than following digital orders.[2] It is thus claimed that, as there is no human being behind the invention (ie, the AI 'created' it by itself), no human is entitled to such invention and/or it falls outside of the scope of traditional patent law.[3] Some call for considering the AI to be an inventor and granting them patent rights; others state that patent law is simply inapplicable to technologies invented by the AI.[4] Similar claims are made in the context of copyright, where 'innovative and autonomous' AIs create art, write stories, and compose symphonies.[5] Seemingly then, the Turing test, according to which computers exhibit intelligent behaviour if they are capable of generating human-like responses during natural language conversations, is superseded by the Lovelace test—computers can be believed to have

* All online materials were accessed before 1 May 2020.

[1] Shlomit Yanisky-Ravid and Xiaoqiong Liu, 'When Artificial Intelligence Systems Produce Inventions: The 3a Era and an Alternative Model for Patent Law' (2017) 39 Cardozo Law Review 2215, 2222 (hereafter Yanisky-Ravid and Liu, 'When Artificial Intelligence Systems Produce Inventions').

[2] Ryan Abbott, 'I Think, Therefore I Invent: Creative Computers and the Future of Patent Law' (2016) 57 Boston College Law Review 1079, 1080.

[3] Yanisky-Ravid and Liu, 'When Artificial Intelligence Systems Produce Inventions' (n 1) 2221.

[4] Ibid.

[5] Burkhard Schafer, 'A Fourth Law of Robotics? Copyright and the Law Ethics of Machine Co-Production' (2017) 23 Artificial Intelligence and Law 207, 219–20; Carys J Craig and Ian R Kerr, 'The death of the AI author' (25 March 2019) <https://ssrn.com/abstract=3374951>.

Eliza Mik, *AI as a Legal Person?* In: *Artificial Intelligence and Intellectual Property.* Edited by: Jyh-An Lee, Reto M Hilty, and Kung-Chung Liu, Oxford University Press (2021). DOI: 10.1093/oso/9780198870944.003.0020

minds once they are capable of *originating* things.[6] Given that such claims are only made if the AI in question is 'autonomous', it is necessary to explain and demystify this fundamental concept. It is also necessary to place autonomy in its original, technical context and examine the actual capabilities of systems that are considered autonomous. After all, autonomy is used as a simplistic proxy for creativity, which implicitly underlies the 'inventive ingenuity' behind patents and the originality, however minimal, implicit in copyright. This chapter aims to provide a background for other discussions of AI in the area of intellectual property law. More specifically, it attempts to provide an improved 'intellectual toolbox' to counter the popular argument that where an algorithm produces creative or inventive output without human involvement, it becomes necessary to grant some form of legal personality to the algorithm.[7] The very formulation of this statement can, however, be criticized as departing from the unproven assumption that the algorithm is (or *can be*?) creative or inventive in the first place and that it can operate without any human involvement. Moreover, as stated in the context of computer-generated works under the UK Copyright Designs and Patent Act 1988, the assumption often seems to be that if there is no human author,[8] the author must be the computer. To put an end to such arguments, it is necessary to explore the purpose of creating autonomous systems as well as the purpose(s) of granting legal personhood to non-human entities.

1.1 Terminology

Some terminological conventions must be introduced. While legal arguments tend to acquire a sheen of novelty whenever they reference AI, it must not be forgotten that ultimately the term refers to and encompasses computer programs that form part of larger, interconnected systems. AI, in its embodied or disembodied form, never exists in isolation. Similarly, the term 'create' is easily replaced with the more prosaic 'produce', piercing the bubble of technological excitement. As this chapter aims to eliminate sensationalistic elements from scholarly discussions, the term AI

[6] Alan M Turing, 'Computing Machinery and Intelligence' (1950) 59 Mind 433; the Lovelace test insists on a restrictive epistemic relation between an artificial agent A, its output O, and the human architect H of A. Roughly speaking, the test is passed when H cannot account for how A produced O. See S Bringsjord, P Bello, and D Ferrucci, 'Creativity, the Turing Test, and the (Better) Lovelace Test' (2011) 11 Minds and Machines 3.

[7] The idea of granting legal personality to robots gained currency in 2015, when the Committee on Legal Affairs of the European Parliament in January 2015 established a Working Group for legal questions related to the development of Robotics and Artificial Intelligence. On 16 February 2017, the Committee's Motion in respect of robotics and artificial intelligence was adopted as the Civil Law Rules on Robotics; see also Samir Chopra and Laurence F White, *A Legal Theory for Autonomous Artificial Agents* (The University of Michigan Press 2011).

[8] William Cornish, David Llewelyn, and Tanya Aplin, *Intellectual Property: Patents, Copyright, Trade Marks and Allied Rights* (Sweet & Maxwell 2013) 853; see also Jyh-An Lee, Chapter 8 in this volume.

is used interchangeably with algorithm, program, or machine. Depending on the context and for the sake of technical accuracy, more detailed distinctions are made in individual arguments. In the majority of instances, even the most sophisticated algorithms or AIs are designed not to emulate human intelligence but to optimize a certain process or to replace humans in hostile environments.[9]

1.2 Caveats

Some caveats are required to clarify the scope of the discussion. First, attempts to recognize autonomous systems as distinct from their creators or operators have been largely driven by the purported need to protect such creators or operators from liability in the event the system malfunctioned, produced unforeseen output, caused losses, and/or harmed third parties. The attribution of the operations of a computer *to* the computer was hence driven by the need to shift or apportion liability for such operations away from whoever created or operated the machine.[10] In the present context, the recognition of the system as a legal person is driven by the need to acknowledge its 'creativity'. The system becomes a subject, not only an object of IP rights. Second, the discussion does not concern ownership *of the AI* but ownership of the output created *by the AI*.

2. Demystifying Autonomy and Computer 'Creativity'

It is necessary to commence the discussion with the concept of autonomy, the term describing the level of human involvement in the operation of a computer system. Autonomy can also be regarded as the best technical and hence objective proxy for other important concepts such as creativity. If 'something' is autonomous, then it is independent from humans, it operates without human control, and it makes 'its own' decisions and produces 'its own' output. A popular view is that once computers become autonomous, they must be separated from their human operators and recognized as legal persons of their own.[11] The granting of legal personhood

[9] Rajarshi Das and others, 'Agent-Human Interactions in the Continuous Double Auction,' in conference: Proceedings of the International Joint Conferences on Artificial Intelligence (IJCAI), Seattle, USA (August 2001); Brookshear and Brylow observe that most AI research is commercially driven, the objective being to create products meeting certain performance goals, see J Glenn Brookshear and Dennis Brylow, *Computer Science* (13th edn, Pearson 2020) 597.

[10] See Iria Giuffrida, 'Liability for AI Decision-Making: Some Legal and Ethical Considerations' (2019) 88 Fordham Law Review 439, 440, 443–5; Bert-Jaap Koops and Mireille Hildebrandt, 'Bridging the Accountability Gap: Rights for New Entities in the Information Society?'(2010) 11 Minnesota Journal of Law, Science & Technology 2.

[11] Laurence B Solum, 'Legal Personhood for Artificial Intelligences' (1992) 70 North Carolina Law Review 1231; Ignacio N Cofone, 'Servers and Waiters: What Matters in the Law of AI' (2018) 21 Stanford Technology Law Review 167.

is usually justified by the technological sophistication of the algorithm, indiscriminately labelled as the 'autonomy'. Autonomy is, however, an elusive and ill-defined concept. Using Minsky's terminology, it is a 'suitcase word' that can be shaped to support various arguments. The danger in this approach lies in the fact that legal theories built on ambiguous (and largely misunderstood) concepts are doctrinally fragile and unlikely to survive in the long run. The author does not necessarily support the view that autonomy constitutes the best criterion for distinguishing between those entities that require legal personhood and those that do not. The point is that the dominant theories advocating such personhood for AIs regard this concept as central. Given the fundamental importance of autonomy, it is surprising that legal scholarship has been using the term in a haphazard manner. The following paragraphs describe the discrepancy between the legal and the technical understanding of autonomy—and its resulting decontextualization.

The Normative Context of Autonomy

In its broadest sense, one that is familiar to any lawyer, autonomy denotes self-governance or self-rule, the ability to act independently of external directions or influences. The concept is associated with personhood, both in the legal and philosophical sense. It is commonly assumed that a founding feature of any person is the ability to make his or her own decisions based on his or her own authentic motivations, as well as the ability to reason and make judgements. Autonomy is also a core concept of liberal democratic traditions, which regard persons as autonomous agents capable of bearing legal liability.[12] Without autonomy, it may in fact be impossible to speak of legal rights and obligations.[13] Even in this broad normative context, however, autonomy is ridden with controversies, as it is difficult to specify its conditions and/or prerequisites. While it is implicitly assumed that every human person is autonomous (at least in theory), it is increasingly recognized that humans are not necessarily rational beings—our independence from external factors and our ability to withstand hidden influences has been overestimated.[14] Despite these limitations, however, autonomy can be regarded as instrumental in determining (or *justifying*?) moral and causal responsibility. Somewhat illogically,

[12] Roger Brownsword, 'Agents in Autonomic Computing Environments' in Mireille Hildebrandt and Antoinette Rouvroy (eds), *Law, Human Agency and Autonomic Computing—The Philosophy of Law Meets the Philosophy of Technology* (Routledge 2011) 68.

[13] Merel Noorman, *Mind the Gap* (Universitaire Pers Maastricht 2008) 1–24 (hereafter Noorman, *Mind the Gap*).

[14] Kelly Burns and Antoine Bechara, 'Decision-making and Free Will: A Neuroscience Perspective' (2007) 25 Behavioral Sciences & the Law 2, 26; Benjamin Libet, 'Unconscious Cerebral Initiative and the Role of Conscious Will in Voluntary Action' (1985) 8 Behavioral & Brain Sciences 4, 529; cf Nita A Farahany, 'A Neurological Foundation For Freedom' (2011) 11 Stanford Technology Law Review 1, 29–30.

when 'autonomy' is used to describe a computer system, the trend is to assume that the system is *like* a human or *independent* from humans.

The Technical Context of Autonomy

The normative understanding of autonomy must be distinguished from its technical meaning—and it is the technical meaning of the term that is of paramount importance in the present discussion. AI derives from and has always been part of computer science: an engineering discipline aimed at creating software products to meet human needs.[15] In its original, technical context, autonomy is devoid of any normative or philosophical connotations and constitutes a quantifiable attribute used to describe the relationships of control between biological or mechanical systems and their environments.[16] The technical meaning of autonomy is inextricably linked to—and often synonymous with—automation, ie, the mechanization of tasks and the translation of routine actions into formalized structures.[17] Autonomy is generally regarded as an advanced form of automation. Automation concerns the relationship between humans and technologies, in which control over tasks is distributed or delegated according to the capacities of both.[18] Automation comes in various degrees, with autonomy connoting the broader sense of self-determination than simple feedback loops.[19] Automation differs in type and complexity, from organizing information sources, to suggesting decision options that best match the incoming information or even carrying out the necessary action.[20] Interestingly, even in the technical context, automation and autonomy are not uniformly defined terms but come in various levels. Sheridan has famously introduced a gradual scale of automation to illustrate the incremental levels of control that can be *shared* between human operators and computers.[21] A minimal level of automation leaves it to the human to make all the decisions and perform all actions. The higher the level

[15] Keith Frankish and William M Ramsey (eds), *The Cambridge Handbook of Artificial Intelligence* (Cambridge University Press 2014).

[16] Stuart J Russell and Peter Norvig, *Artificial Intelligence: A Modern Approach* (3rd edn, Pearson 2016) 38 (hereafter Russel and Norvig, *Artificial Intelligence*).

[17] For a detailed explanation of the distinction between autonomy and automation see Cristiano Castelfranchi and Rino Falcone, 'Founding Autonomy: The Dialectics Between (Social) Environment and Agent's Architecture and Powers' (2004) 2969 Lecture Notes in Computer Science 40 (hereafter Castelfranchi and Falcone, 'Founding Autonomy').

[18] See definition in *Oxford English Dictionary*.

[19] David Mindell, *Our Robots, Ourselves* (Random House 2015) 195 (hereafter Mindell, *Our Robots, Ourselves*).

[20] See generally Parasuraman Raja, Thomas B Sheridan, and Christopher D Wickens, 'A Model for Types and Levels of Human Interaction with Automation' (2001) 30(3) IEEE Transactions on Systems, Man, and Cybernetics—Part A: Systems and Humans 286 (hereafter Raja, Sheridan, and Wickens, 'A Model for Types and Levels of Human Interaction with Automation').

[21] Thomas B Sheridan and William Verplank, *Human and Computer Control of Undersea Teleoperators* (1978) Cambridge, MA: Man-Machine Systems Laboratory, Department of Mechanical Engineering, Massachusets Institute of Technology.

of automation, the more the decision-making opportunities for humans are constrained by the actions of the computer. Consequently, the more a system is capable of collecting, analysing, interpreting, and acting on information—be it sensory information or symbolic representations of knowledge—the more autonomous it is considered to be. Complete autonomy, assuming such exists, is on the far end of a continuous scale of increasing automation, where tasks are delegated to machines to be completed without direct and continuous human control (the key words being 'direct' and 'continuous').[22]

Demystifying Autonomy

It must be remembered, however, that even autonomous systems that rely on non-deterministic (ie, unpredictable) software, display emergent properties, or engage in learning behaviours, are always designed, programmed—and controlled in some form or manner—by people. In fact, '[a]utonomy is *human action removed in time*. This, in a sense, is the essence of the term "programming"—telling the computer what to do at some point in the future, when the program is run'(emphasis added).[23] All machine learning techniques, both supervised and unsupervised, rely on human programmers for their structure and input. Even the most autonomous system has not created or programmed itself. Moreover, even in the technical area, the meaning of autonomy—and hence its practical implications—is always context-dependent. Technical scholarship speaks of 'autonomy' (or automation) as a relationship between elements in a larger system—with humans *always* being regarded as parts of such a system. To complicate matters, autonomy is regarded as an important attribute of so-called artificial agents, which are capable of finding their 'own solutions'.[24] Taking these expressions too literally, legal scholarship has ignored the fact that the concept of 'autonomous agents' concerns a particular way of thinking about how one component of a software program relates to other components[25] and fixated on the agents' ability to pursue *their own* goals or make *their*

[22] The ten levels of automation range from complete human control to complete computer control. Interestingly, technical writings consider systems at or above level 6 as autonomous, see: Raja, Sheridan, and Wickens, 'A Model for Types and Levels of Human Interaction with Automation' (n 20) 292; Thomas B Sheridan, *Telerobotics, Automation and Human Supervisory Control* (MIT Press 1992).

[23] Mindell, *Our Robots, Ourselves* (n 19) 220.

[24] Castelfranchi and Falcone, 'Founding Autonomy' (n 17) 13; the term 'agent' refers to a wide array of technologies, ranging from word processors, browsers, chat bots, and mail servers to trading algorithms and software operating satellites, see J Glenn Brookshear and Dennis Brylow, *Computer Science* (13th edn, Pearson 2020) 576; Russel and Norvig, *Artificial Intelligence* (n 16) 34; for an alternative definition see David L Poole and Alan K Mackworth, *Artificial Intelligence, Foundations of Computational Agents* (Cambridge University Press 2017).

[25] Nick R Jennings and Michael J Wooldridge, *Agent Technology: Foundations, Applications and Markets* (Springer 1998).

own decisions.[26] Oblivious to the original, *technical* context of such statements and to the fact that control over a system need not be direct or continuous, legal scholarship started advocating personhood for autonomous agents.

2.1 The Purpose of Autonomy

The present discussion requires an understanding of the purpose(s) of creating autonomous systems. Contrary to popular beliefs, autonomous systems are generally created not to replicate human intelligence but to solve specific problems or, to be more precise, to enable or optimize the performance of pre-defined tasks if such tasks are too complex, dangerous, or time-critical for direct human control.[27] Often, the task itself may be simple (eg, collection of soil samples) but the environment in which it must be performed is dangerous, beyond human reach, and/or prone to communication challenges.[28] The design of autonomous systems is task-oriented. As autonomy is closely related to control, two clarifications are required.

First, as the concept of control recurs in nearly all discussion of autonomy, one would assume that its clear definition could assist in simplifying debates surrounding the required level of control over an AI for a human still to be considered an 'author' or 'inventor' of whatever output is produced by such 'autonomous' AI. After all, autonomous AIs are supposed to operate without human intervention and must hence be regarded as being beyond human control. Unfortunately, despite its technical and seemingly objective character, the term 'control' is used inconsistently and remains difficult to define.[29] Conventional control theory speaks of a goal-oriented action by a subject upon an object.[30] In practice, however, the definition of control depends on a precise description of the system being controlled. A 'system' is commonly defined as a 'group, set or aggregates of things, natural or artificial, forming a collected or complex whole'.[31] As indicated, an AI never exists in isolation but forms part of a larger whole that, by definition, involves hardware and humans. Consequently, the term 'control' requires a case-specific re-evaluation every time it is used. A determination of whether 'something is under control of something or someone' becomes difficult when the system is complex and interconnected with other systems. In sum, control is difficult to define and

[26] This misunderstanding becomes apparent when one analyses the technical literature on human-machine interaction, where it is acknowledged that engineers must re-think interaction design if the system does not require supervision. In such instances, 'autonomy' is a design concept; see generally Erwart J de Visser, Richard Pak, and Tyler H Shaw, 'From "Automation" to "Autonomy": the Importance of Trust Repair in Human-machine Interaction' (2018) 61(10) Ergonomics 1409.

[27] Noorman, *Mind the Gap* (n 13) 105.

[28] Mindell, *Our Robots, Ourselves* (n 19).

[29] See Bryant Walker Smith, 'Lawyers and Engineers Should Speak the Same Robot Language' in Ryan Calo, A. Michael Froomkin, and Ian Kerr (eds), *Robot Law* (Edward Elgar 2016) 78.

[30] James Ron Leigh, *Control Theory, A Guided Tour* (3rd edn, IET 2012).

[31] System definition 4 OECD.com.

context specific—it depends on the system being controlled and the relationship between the human and the individual components of the system. The statement that an 'AI was operating without human control' must never be taken at face value, but requires an analysis of the environment in which the AI is operating.

Second, control over a system presupposes the ability to continuously communicate with the system in order to give instructions and to receive feedback regarding their execution. If the ability to communicate is constrained, it becomes technically difficult to convey instructions. In this instance, the system must be capable of operating 'by itself', ie, without ongoing instructions. The preceding sentence must not be interpreted simplistically as implying that the system is 'beyond control' or 'truly autonomous'. Control need not be direct or exercised in real-time. Control can also be indirect, exercised remotely, and with degrees of delay. Everything depends on the system, the communication environment, and the task at hand. Human decisions may be made in real-time or they may precede the action performed by the AI by seconds, minutes, months, or even years. Each action is, however, dependent on and preceded by human input. Control can be exercised at an earlier stage, before the system is left to operate. It can also be exercised remotely and can be based on prior human actions or instructions. This point is made by Mindell, who emphasizes that autonomy comes on a scale: during communication delays, an unmanned underwater vehicle is 'more autonomous' than when it communicates with the control centre.[32] Depending on the context, autonomy can be periodic or mediated by regular human control. Three illustrations best convey the practical applications of autonomous systems.

2.2 Autonomous Systems in Practice

Noorman discusses autonomy in the context of space exploration. Her example concerns software on board the Earth Observing 1 satellite ('EO1'), called an 'autonomous science agent'.[33] Built by NASA, the software uses machine learning and pattern recognition to scan images of the Earth for anomalies. As human operators in the control centre on Earth have limited opportunities to instruct EO1 to perform tasks given the physical constraints, the satellite is designed to operate for extended periods of time without human intervention and 'make decisions' about the ongoing sub-tasks that it must perform during the communication delays or interruptions. Controlling such systems is difficult given the distance and the small data set about their surrounding environment. Human operators must allow for latency in communicating with the satellite and for the limited amount of information about EO1's operating environment. The same picture emerges from

[32] Mindell, *Our Robots, Ourselves* (n 19) 196.

[33] Noorman, *Mind the Gap* (n 13) 29.

Asimov's famous book, *I, Robot*.[34] With few exceptions,[35] Asimov's robots operate in extreme and dangerous conditions, such as the sunny side of Mercury, solar stations, or asteroid mines. Each robot is capable of unsupervised, autonomous operations while, at the same time, returning for instructions (and maintenance!) to its human master. Stories of extreme environments are interlaced with sketches of communication problems—and an overreaching desire to delegate *all* work to the sturdy robots so that the vulnerable humans can return to the comforts of Earth. In less far-fetched scenarios, Mindell describes autonomous underwater vehicles and unmanned aerial vehicles—systems operating independently in hostile conditions, such as the ocean floor or war theatres. Although automated and autonomous systems are 'self-acting', the success of the operations depends on people and machines working together. Even in autonomous systems, people are always present—'they just exist in a different place and time'.[36] In sum, equating autonomy with an absence of human control or intervention is technically incorrect. As indicated, control need not be direct or continuous.

2.3 A Word on Computer 'Creativity'

Initially, it was inconceivable for a computer program to get any further than its initial programming—that is, to generate or produce anything more or different than it was programmed to do. Short of unforeseen (and unwanted!) malfunctions, output could not 'transcend' prior input. Gradually, however, programmers have attempted to mimic or replicate human creativity in computers, mainly by introducing randomness into the process of generating whatever 'artistic' output the program was set up to generate. Randomness has been associated with the loss of human control and with unpredictability.[37] It has been theorized that 'anything that doesn't have randomness programmed into it, that is deterministic, must still really be the creation of the programmer, regardless of the surprise the programmer might get at the outcome'.[38] The use of chance has been the main strategy in many early attempts to build creative algorithms that could pass the Lovelace test. For example, in AARON, a computer program designed to generate original images, the algorithm was making decisions based on a complex sequence of prior if-then statements but was also equipped with a random number generator.[39]

34 Isaac Asimov, *I, Robot* (Gnome Press 1950).

35 Where robots operated as nannies ('Robbie'), mind-readers ('Herbie'), or calculators of industrial output ('The Machines').

36 Mindell, *Our Robots, Ourselves* (n 19) 204.

37 Marcus du Sautoy, *The Creativity Code* (4th Estate 2019) 102 (hereafter du Sautoy, *The Creativity Code*).

38 Ibid, 112.

39 AARON was created in the mid-seventies to answer the question: 'what is the minimum condition under which a set of marks functions as an image?' See Harold Cohen, 'Parallel to Perception: Some Notes on the Problem of Machine-generated Art' (1973) 4 Computer Studies 3, 4.

Randomness was used to create a sense of autonomy or agency in the machine.[40] Some observations come to mind. First, it is unclear why randomness is associated with (or treated as equivalent to) creativity. It could be argued that creativity involves choices, be they conscious or subconscious, intuitive or calculated. Human choices are not, however, random in the same technical sense as a random number generator.[41] Moreover, as creativity is an amorphous concept, its 'replication' by means of randomness is premised on a prior definition or 'scientific description' of the term. Taking an undefined attribute (ie, 'creativity') and claiming that it can be reproduced by means of another attribute (ie, 'randomness') is unconvincing. Second, it has been suggested that if the programmer does not understand how the program works, it is unclear who is making decisions, ie, the AI operates as a 'black box'. This unpredictability has, again, been linked to creativity and independence. Arguably, an artist's inability to explain or articulate where his or her ideas come from does not mean that he or she does not follow any rules. After all, human creativity remains ill-defined and can be regarded as a 'black box'—even if the human artist follows rules (intuitively or subconsciously). If, then, it is impossible to define or explain human creativity it should be irrelevant that we cannot explain how a given AI produces a certain output. It is also impossible to associate this 'inexplicable' creativity with the aforementioned randomness. This line of argumentation inevitably leads into a blind alley, as it always depends on the definition of creativity and on some objective, computable metric. It can also be regarded as redundant altogether. The broader question is whether creativity is a strictly human attribute or whether it could be displayed by computers, at least theoretically. An answer would, however, require a treatise exceeding the length of this book. It must be acknowledged that technical literature lacks clarity on the issue of whether they are trying to replicate human creativity in computers or making computers creative in their own way.

To briefly digress on the 'black box' argument: it may often be impossible to establish how a particular artwork or invention originated, whether it was 'created' by a human or by a machine. The origins of the computer-generated output, the method of operation, the algorithm used, etc may not be apparent from the output itself. A human may not be able to tell by looking at a painting or listening to an opera that such art has been 'created' by an AI. A painting may be the output of an autonomous AI that has been fed with the entire collection of modern art or 'of' a heartbroken Eliza having a sleepless night painting away her emotions. At the expense of some oversimplification, it can be stated that although IP law rewards creativity, it disregards the creative process itself and, consequently, the fact that a particular output was generated by a 'creative' algorithm. The AI's programming

[40] du Sautoy, *The Creativity Code* (n 37) 117.

[41] Of course, we could go into different theories of the mind, but this might be an academic waste of time in the present context, which is ultimately pragmatic.

and the complexity of its underlying algorithm are as unimportant as the level of emotional turmoil experienced by the painter at the time his or her work is created. At the present state of technological advancement, an 'artwork' generated by an autonomous supercomputer may be indistinguishable from an artwork created by a human artist. This fact is, however, legally irrelevant. It is equally irrelevant that a particular AI operates in a manner that cannot be explained in retrospect or even understood from a technical perspective.[42] The same can be said of the creative process deployed by artists or inventors. What must be remembered, however, is that the operations of the AI have been programmed by humans.[43]

2.4 'Creative' Systems in Practice

Most importantly, it must be acknowledged that any 'creativity' displayed by an AI derives from a staggering amount of human labour, including the creation of a knowledge base and the fine-tuning of the underlying algorithm(s). One must recall the large team of programmers, data analysts, art historians, AI professors, and 3D specialists that was involved in creating *The Next Rembrandt*, a collaboration of multiple companies and universities tasked by its corporate sponsor, ING, to produce a new painting 'by' the long-deceased artist.[44] The famous 'The Painting Fool', a program 'aspiring' to be painter, was designed to 'exhibit behaviors that might be deemed as a skillful, appreciative and imaginative'.[45] Yet, its creator emphasized that only about 10% of 'creativity' came from the algorithm itself.[46] The remaining 90% was human in terms of input and control. An even better illustration of the role humans play in computer 'creativity' can be gleaned from a description of so-called algorithmic art (ie, art that cannot be created without the use of programming). In traditional algorithmic art, the artist-programmer must write the code specifying detailed rules for the aesthetics of the desired output. In the new wave of algorithms, the artists '*set up*' the system to 'learn' the aesthetics by looking at many images using machine learning technology. 'The algorithm only then generates new images that follow the aesthetics it has learned.'[47] For example, in generative adversarial networks, or GANs, the artist chooses the images to feed the

[42] J Burrell, 'How the Machine "Thinks": Understanding Opacity in Machine Learning Algorithms' (2016) 3 Big Data & Society 1.

[43] D Lehr and P Ohm, 'Playing with the Data: What Legal Scholars Should Learn about Machine Learning' (2017) 51 UCLA Davis Law Review 653; Amitai Etzioni and Oren Etzioni, 'Keeping AI Legal' (2016) 19 Vanderbilt Journal of Entertainment & Technology Law 133, 137–8; Tal Zarsky, 'The Trouble with Algorithmic Decisions: An Analytic Road Map to Examine Efficiency and Fairness in Automated and Opaque Decision Making' (2016) 41 Science, Technology and Human Values 118, 121.

[44] <https://www.nextrembrandt.com>.

[45] <http://www.thepaintingfool.com>.

[46] du Sautoy, *The Creativity Code* (n 37) 121.

[47] Ahmed El Gamal and Marian Mazzone, 'Art, Creativity, and the Potential of Artificial Intelligence' (2019) 8 Arts 26.

generative AI algorithm.[48] The artist then examines the output to curate a final collection. In GANs, the creative process is primarily done by the artist in the pre- and post-curatorial phases, as well as in tweaking the algorithm.[49] In the case of the more advanced creative adversarial networks, or CANs, the person(s) setting up the process 'designs a conceptual and algorithmic framework, but the algorithm is fully at the creative helm when it comes to the elements and the principles of the art it creates'.[50] The CAN chooses the style, the subject, and the principles of the art it creates. It is designed to deviate from copying or repeating what has been seen (the GAN function) and to produce new combinations and new choices based on a knowledge of art styles (the CAN function). It is emphasized, however, that the system is not directed at replicating creativity but intended to 'learn whether it can produce work that is able to qualify as art and if it exhibits qualities that make it desirable to look at'.[51] The same authors acknowledged that 'AI is really very limited and specific in what it can do in terms of art creation'.[52] After all, irrespective of the CANs' impressive output, they are *designed* to produce unforeseen combinations, and their goals are set by the artist-programmer. To a CAN, each painting is only a collection of data points from which the algorithm must deviate.

3. Legal Personhood

Legal personhood is an artificial construct. To state that an entity has legal personhood is to state that a legal system addresses its rules to such an entity, giving it rights and also subjecting it to certain obligations. Legal personhood derives from a decision in the legal system to endow an entity with it.[53] The central question for any legal system is whether such endowment advances or hinders its objectives. Being an aggregate of legal rights and obligations, legal personhood is divisible. Different entities enjoy different rights and obligations. Consequently, if a legal system chose to confer legal personality on an AI, it would have to state which specific legal rights and obligations accompany such conferral. Moreover, it is possible to enjoy certain rights without being recognized as a legal person. There is historical precedent for granting certain narrowly defined rights to non-persons, such as temples and relics. Similarly, the law often recognizes rights and protections of non-human animals, such as livestock or wildlife.[54]

[48] Goodfellow and others, 'Generative Adversarial Nets,' in Advances in Neural Information Processing Systems, (2014) Conference Proceedings 2672.
[49] Ibid, 2.
[50] Ibid, 5.
[51] Ibid, 5.
[52] Ibid, 6.
[53] Joanna J Bryson, Mihailis E Diamantis, and Thomas D Grant, 'Of, For, and By the People: The Legal Lacuna of Synthetic Persons' (2017) 25 Artificial Intelligence and Law 273.
[54] David Favre, 'Equitable Self-ownership of Animals' (2000) 50 Duke Law Journal 473.

3.1 Conditions of Legal Personhood

Legal personhood is generally attached to human beings and corporations. There is no 'in-between' position, as entities are categorized as persons in a binary, 'all-or-nothing' fashion. All animals and robots, regardless of their level of autonomy, intelligence, or consciousness, are property.[55] For the purposes of liability, robots and similar entities are generally regarded as 'products'.[56] While legal personhood is not confined to human beings,[57] its main purpose is to regulate *human* conduct.[58] Questions of legal personhood are, of course, outside of the scope of IP law. While the ability to hold copyright or own a patent is premised on legal personhood, none of the areas of IP law decide which entities 'deserve' such personhood or state that 'anything' or 'anyone' else but a human person or a corporation can be the subject of IP rights. For present purposes it is necessary to differentiate between the questions of when do AIs *deserve* legal personhood and when is it *required* to grant legal personhood to AIs. It is also necessary to abandon debates inspired by movies like *Blade Runner* or *Ghost in the Shell* (where the human-like nature of androids forces us to re-think what it means to be human) and focus on concrete, commercial goals. Legal personhood is a means to an end: to enable natural persons to achieve their goals more efficiently.[59] What goal—and *whose* goal—would be achieved if AIs were recognized as legal entities or granted certain rights? The philosophical possibility of recognizing AIs as *human* persons has been discussed elsewhere.[60] Suffice it to say, philosophical approaches to personhood diverge from legal ones.[61] This chapter addresses the practical necessity and consequences of recognizing an AI as a legal person. Two opposing approaches exist.

3.1.1 The restrictive, 'human-attributes' approach

The first approach is restrictive and anchored in metaphysical arguments. No matter how 'intelligent' or 'conscious' the AI, it can never become a legal person. Certain innate properties of human beings, eg, intentionality, free will, or consciousness, are regarded as the prerequisites of legal (and moral) responsibility but are absent in any machine. It is possible, of course, to doubt the metaphysical

[55] F Patrick Hubbard, '"Sophisticated Robots": Balancing Liability, Regulation, and Innovation' (2014) 55 Florida Law Review 1803.

[56] Y H Weng, C H Chen, and C T Sun, 'Toward the Human–Robot Co-existence Society: On Safety Intelligence for Next-Generation Robots' (2009) 1 International Journal of Social Robotics 267.

[57] *Byrn v New York City Health & Hosp Corp* [1972] 286 N E 2d 887.

[58] Smith B 'Legal Personality' (1928) 37 Yale Law Journal 283.

[59] Brian L Frye, 'The Lion, the Bat & the Thermostat: Metaphors on Consciousness' (2018) 5 Savannah Law Review 13.

[60] Lawrence B Solum, 'Legal Personhood for Artificial Intelligences' (1992) 70 North Carolina Law Review 1231; F Patrick Hubbard, 'Do Androids Dream? Personhood and Intelligent Artifacts' (2011) 83 Temple Law Review 405.

[61] Gerhard Wagner, 'Robot, Inc.: Personhood for Autonomous Systems?' (2019) 88 Fordham Law Review 591, 595–6 (hereafter Wagner, 'Robot, Inc.').

foundations of this approach. Although legal responsibility is usually premised on intentionality and free will,[62] 'intention' and 'free will' tend to be reified as if they physically existed in the real world. In reality, purely human characteristics—including intention and free will—are only 'things' that we attribute to one another to maintain structure in our social interactions. They are conceptual constructs, not 'real' phenomena the existence of which can be established and measured. As such, they cannot constitute preconditions of legal (or moral) responsibility. From a legal perspective, the existence of certain human attributes, including consciousness and self-awareness, has been held as irrelevant[63] so that the restrictive approach is easily discarded. Some human beings have historically been denied legal personhood, while other entities, such as corporations or states, have been endowed with such personhood despite the absence of *any* human characteristics.[64] Consequently, it is not a question of establishing what computers must be able to do (in terms of replicating human characteristics or abilities) or what attributes they must possess to be treated as persons or recognized as authors or inventors.[65] The granting of legal personhood is not the result of meeting any criteria, but a normative choice dictated by commercial expediency, which brings us to the next approach.

3.1.2 The permissive and pragmatic approach

The second approach is permissive and pragmatic. The law can endow anyone or anything with rights. Historically, certain legal systems have precluded some human beings from being recognized as legal persons or denied them basic rights while, at the same time, recognizing other entities as persons or granting them rights—despite the fact that the latter lacked any human attributes (eg, Whanganui river in New Zealand).[66] Since legal personhood is a fiction, 'the inherent characteristics of a thing are not determinative of whether the [legal] system treats it as a legal person.'[67] Consequently, legal personhood could be granted to any object—including algorithms and computer systems—irrespective of whether it is creative, intelligent, or conscious. It must be re-emphasized that this granting is not derived from or premised on any innate attributes of the machine or algorithm: 'the legislator is free to introduce any legal construction that may serve their goals.'[68]

[62] J Hage, 'Theoretical Foundations for the Responsibility of Autonomous Agents' (2017) 25 Artificial Intelligence and Law 255.

[63] *Matter of Nonhuman Rights Project, Inc v Stanley* [2015] NY Slip Op 31419(U).

[64] Bartosz Brozek and Marek Jakubiec, 'On the Legal Responsibility of Autonomous Machines' (2017) 25 Artificial Intelligence and Law 293 (hereafter Brozek and Jakubiec, 'On the Legal Responsibility of Autonomous Machines'); Joanna Bryson, Thomas D Grant, and Mihailis Diamantis, 'Of, For and By the People: The Legal Lacuna of Synthetic Persons' (2017) 25 Artificial Intelligence and Law 273 (hereafter Bryson, Grant, and Diamantis, 'Of, For and By the People').

[65] M Bain, 'E-commerce Oriented Software Agents: Legalising Autonomous Shopping Agent Processes' (2003) 19 Computer Law Security Review 5.

[66] Abigail Hutchison, 'The Whanganui River as a Legal Person' (2014) 39 Alternative Law Journal 179.

[67] Bryson, Grant, and Diamantis, 'Of, For and By the People' (n 64).

[68] Brozek and Jakubiec, 'On the Legal Responsibility of Autonomous Machines' (n 64) 296.

Notwithstanding the foregoing, there must be concrete justifications or 'good reasons'[69] to grant legal personhood to anything that is not human.

The following questions arise: What would be the purpose of granting personhood to an algorithm? What would be the benefits and risks? Given that there are no natural or legal prerequisites of personhood,[70] it would be necessary to decide on the criteria for distinguishing between those algorithms that require personhood and those that do not. As the ill-defined concept of autonomy seems unsuitable—if only due to the fact that it comes in gradations and requires the selection of the level of autonomy that justifies personhood—a different attribute would have to be adopted. Would it be a question of the quality of output produced by an AI, as evaluated in terms of originality, inventiveness, or … emotional impact? From a technical perspective, which part of the system would be regarded as a person? It must not be forgotten that an AI never exists in isolation, and instead forms part of a larger system. To what extent, if any, would the creator of the algorithm remain liable for its operation? It must also be assumed that algorithms do not self-create, and autonomous systems are not the product of the technological equivalent of an immaculate conception. In sum, the granting of legal personhood to AIs creates a myriad of practical and technical questions. Lastly, the need to maintain internal consistency in the law must not be forgotten. Is it admissible to recognize algorithms as legal persons in a single legal area, while other legal areas fail do so?

3.2 Comparing AIs with Corporations

The personhood of corporations is often regarded as a template for the personhood of robots or other artificial entities.[71] It is necessary to briefly explore this proposition, if only to demonstrate its futility and doctrinal weakness. A corporation is a legal person composed of humans with the objective of advancing certain interests.[72] While it is unnecessary to delve into the different theories underpinning corporate legal personhood,[73] it is important to recall its purposes. Legal personhood enables the artificial entity to enter into almost all legal relations with other persons.[74] It also combines and demarcates its assets in order to shield them from

69 Wagner, 'Robot, Inc.' (n 61) 599.

70 Leaving aside registration requirements that incorporate the company.

71 G Hallevy, 'Virtual Criminal Responsibility' (2010) 6 Original Law Review 6; A Bertolini, 'Robots as Products: The Case for a Realistic Analysis of Robotic Applications and Liability Rules' (2013) 5 Law Innovation and Technology 214; Simon Chesterman, 'Artificial Intelligence and the Limits of Legal Personality' (2020) 69 International and Comparative Law Quarterly 819, 823.

72 J C Gray, *The Nature and Sources of the Law* (Columbia University Press 1909).

73 S K Ripken, 'Corporations Are People Too: A Multi-Dimensional Approach to the Corporate Personhood Puzzle' (2010) 15 Fordham Journal of Corporate Finance Law 97.

74 R Kraakman and others, *The Anatomy of Corporate Law—A Comparative and Functional Approach* (Oxford University Press 2009); the separate personhood of corporations is recognized in all legal systems, based on *Salomon v Salomon & Co Ltd* [1897] AC 22.

its owners or their personal creditors.[75] Apart from pooling resources and protecting assets, legal personhood also facilitates the procedural and financial aspects of liability.[76] Corporations can be sued as a single entity and, in principle, have 'deeper pockets' than their individual shareholders. At the same time, it must also be acknowledged that corporations are formed *by* and *for the benefit* of humans. Consequently, the rights and duties of the latter effectively relate to those of the former. When it comes to any wrongdoings, both physical and mental elements of humans directing or acting on behalf of the company are attributed to the company.[77] In this sense, the separate legal personhood of corporations is not absolute, as it may be ignored by lifting the corporate veil. A corporation can be penalized as a way of directly or indirectly punishing the people who manage, direct, and/or own it.[78] Both corporations and individuals wearing the veil of incorporation can be held liable under administrative, civil, and even criminal liability regimes.[79]

3.2.1 Accountability

It is often forgotten is that legal personhood results in the conferral of legal rights *and* in the imposition of legal duties. If an entity is not capable of fulfilling the obligations imposed upon it by law or private agreement, it cannot be a person in the legal sense.[80] Obligations are meaningless if the AI cannot be held accountable. After all, corporations consist of legal persons who can be held personally liable in certain circumstances. The AI, as an artificial person, could be required to hold a minimum of assets or compulsory liability insurance. At the same time, other legal tools that are usually available to hold persons to account (anything from an apology to jail time) would be unavailable or ineffective. Moreover, from a broader regulatory perspective, AI-legal persons would remain unreceptive to financial or moral incentives to avoid harm in the way humans are.[81] Consequently, it would also be necessary to establish the entities that could be held legally liable when 'piercing the veil of AI-personhood'. Would it be the coder(s), the operator, or the legal entity (human or otherwise) that derives financial benefits from the operations of the AI? Given the complexity of AI systems, this question would require a thorough investigation of such systems to establish the adequate apportionment of liability. Alternatively, legislators would have to decide on a default allocation to a specific person that could subsequently be refined by means of private agreement. All of those questions must be answered in addition to and irrespective

[75] H Hansmann, R Kraakman, and S Richard, 'Law and the Rise of the Firm' (2006) 119 Harvard Law Review 1335.

[76] Ibid.

[77] Celia Wells, *Corporations and Criminal Responsibility* (Oxford University Press 2001).

[78] A W Machen Jr, 'Corporate Personality' (1911) 24 Harvard Law Review 253.

[79] *Tesco Supermarkets Ltd v Nattrass* [1972] AC 153.

[80] *People ex rel Nonhuman Rights Project, Inc v Lavery* [2014] 124 A D 3d 148.

[81] Wagner, 'Robot, Inc.' (n 61) 610–11.

of the practical, commercial, and policy issues pertaining to the specific areas of copyright and patent law.

3.2.2 Protecting operators

At this stage, it necessary to recall why legal scholarship has repeatedly advocated the legal separation of AI (or advanced algorithms in general) from their operators or creators. In a nutshell, suggestions to grant legal personhood to AIs largely derive from the purported need to protect operators from the incorrect or unplanned operation of autonomous systems, ie, to shield them from liability for such operations.[82] Legal scholarship rightly observes that computer-generated output may not reflect the operator's intention or that it may function in an unexpected manner causing physical or financial harm to third parties.[83] Such 'unintended' output/operation may derive from design and/or programming errors,[84] unexpected input, unexpected interactions with other systems, external interference (eg, hacking), or from a correct albeit unexpected operation of the program, especially in the case of non-deterministic, self-learning systems.[85] In the last instance, it is possible to speak of emergent behaviour, the system demonstrating novel capabilities that prima facie exceed those comprised in the original programming.[86] Attributing the output of an incorrect operation of the computer to the computer would automatically absolve the operator from liability. Logically, such attribution would require that the computer be a legal entity. It has been suggested that the conferral of personhood on 'fully autonomous machines' would resolve problems of liability, as the machines could 'insure themselves' to meet any legal obligations arising from the damage caused by their conduct. At the same time, it has been claimed that owners or operators of such machines would participate in funding such insurance.[87] If 'fully autonomous machines' are legal persons, why should *other* persons be liable for their operations? Ultimately, as computers do not 'have' assets, their separation would be pointless because legal liability is premised on the ability to pay compensation or obeying the court's orders for specific remedies.[88] Moreover, while other

[82] T Allen and R Widdison, 'Can Computers Make Contracts?' (1996) 9 Harvard Journal of Law & Technology 25, 36 (hereafter Allen and Widdison, 'Can Computers Make Contracts?').

[83] See Tianxiang He, Chapter 9 in this volume; Benjamin Sobel, Chapter 10 in this volume.

[84] The distinction between coding errors and faulty design of the system was expressly made in a recent decision on software errors; see *B2C2 Ltd v Quoine Pte Ltd* [2019] SGHC(I) 3.

[85] Iria Giuffrida, Fredric Lederer, and Nicolas Vermeys, 'A Legal Perspective on the Trials and Tribulations of AI: How the Internet of Things, Smart Contracts, and Other Technologies Will Affect the Law' (2018) 68(3) Case Western Law Review 747, 751–2; for a technical description see Raja, Sheridan, and Wickens, 'A Model for Types and Levels of Human Interaction with Automation' (n 20) 293.

[86] Ryan Calo, 'Robotics and the Lessons of Cyberlaw' (2015) 103 California Law Review 513, 532.

[87] D C Vladeck, 'Machines without Principals: Liability Rules and Artificial Intelligence' (2014) 89 Washington Law Review 117.

[88] Jean-Francois Lerouge, 'Symposium: UCITA: The Use of Electronic Agents Questioned Under Contractual Law: Suggested Solutions on a European and American Level' (1999) 18 John Marshall Journal Computer and Information Law 403, 410; but note proposals for a 'digital peculium' for artificial agents, modelled after the Roman institution, see Ugo Pagallo, *The Laws of Robots* (Springer 2013) 79, 82; European Parliament, Committee on Legal Affairs, 31.05.2016 Draft Report with recommendations

legal areas, such as tort or contract law, focus their concerns on malfunctions and errors in the operation of the AI, in the context of IP, such concerns do not arise. In the latter context, the 'problems' created by the AI cannot be described in terms of loss or harm. What would be the harm of a GAN creating an 'unexpected painting' or composing a symphony that is unpleasant from an auditory perspective? A disappointed audience? It can be broadly assumed that in the context of IP, problems of harm or loss are secondary. In practice, they may concern situations where the autonomous, 'creative' AI (ie, the output produced thereby) infringed the IP rights of someone else.[89] Such would be the case, eg, if a CAN 'created' a painting that constitutes an unauthorized adaptation of another.

4. A Better Tool?

The best solution (assuming such is necessary) to the problems created by autonomous AIs (assuming such problems are in fact *created* by those sophisticated technologies) is to treat AIs as tools—irrespective of their technological complexity. This approach preserves technological neutrality and the legal status quo. The ability to maintain the status quo seems generally underappreciated. Sensationalistic headlines and a superficial understanding (if any) of the technologies involved have led many to believe that the laws in a particular area are insufficient or outdated. The computer's autonomy—including its propensity to display emergent behaviour or 'creativity'—does not, however, change the fact that it has been programmed, initiated, and/or controlled by *some* human being.[90] This reasoning is reflected in the statutory provisions that treat the technological tools deployed by authors and inventors as legally transparent.[91] In the area of contract law,[92] most decisions derive from the US and involve ATMs, coin-operated lockers, and ticketing machines.[93] The cases converge on the same conclusion: computers are tools deployed for the purpose of entering into transactions of varying degrees

to the Commission on Civil Law Rules on Robotics (2015/2103 (INL), which contemplated the possibility of robots earning wages and having 'their own' assets.

[89] Tianxiang He, Chapter 9 in this volume; Benjamin Sobel, Chapter 10 in this volume (n 83).

[90] Allen and Widdison, 'Can Computers Make Contracts?' (n 82) 46.

[91] See, eg, UK Patent Act 1977, which does not contemplate the possibility of non-human inventions and is indifferent to the manner in which the invention is created; similarly, the UK computer-generated works regime makes no attempt at attributing the works to the computer, irrespective of its sophistication.

[92] *Cushing v Rodman* 82 F 2d 864 n29 (DC Cir 1936); *Child's Dinning Hall Co v Swingler* 197 A 105 (Md 1938); *Seattle v Dencker* 108 P 1086 (Wash 1910).

[93] See *Bernstein v Northwestern National Bank in Philadelphia* 41 A2d at 442; *American Meter Co v McCaughn* 1 F Supp 753 (E D Pa 1932); *Marsh v American Locker Co* 72 A 2d 343 (NJ Super Ct 1950); *Ellish v Airport Parking Co of America* 345 NYS 2d 650 (NYAD 1973); *Lachs v Fidelity & Casualty Co of NY* 118 NE 2d 555 (NY 1954); *State Farm Mutual Automobile Insurance Co v Bockhorst* 453 F 2d 533 (USCA 10th Cir. 1972); *Thornton v Shoe Lane Parking Ltd* [1971] 2 QB 163; *R (Software Solutions Partners Ltd) v HM Customs & Excise* [2007] EWHC 971, para 67.

of complexity.[94] More recently, in *B2C2 Ltd v Quoine Pte Ltd*, two highly sophisticated trading algorithms operated without any human supervision. Nonetheless, the court did not attempt to ascribe the output of their faulty operations to anyone else but their operators.[95] In contract and tort, treating the computer as a tool 'puts the risk of unpredicted obligations on the person best able to control them—those who program and control the computer'.[96] This approach encourages diligent programming and supervision.

Arguably, ignoring the technological sophistication of an AI and treating it as a 'mere' tool equates paintbrushes with creative adversarial networks.[97] On a doctrinal level, this appears to be a minor sacrifice for doctrinal integrity and the avoidance of creating technology-specific regimes. Such regimes would be based on gradations of autonomy[98] and necessitate the formulation of technical criteria for a clear, technology-specific line beyond which the AI must be separated from its creator or operator and regarded as a legal entity. Regrettably, those who claim that autonomous computers cease to be 'mere tools' do not propose any such criteria.

The progressive refinement of our tools or the fact that such tools enhance not only our physical but also our artistic capabilities must lead to legal differentiations. Mechanized looms increase the economic efficiency of textile production and AI-CANs enable the generation of new forms of art—and an exploration of the very concept of creativity. Neither the loom nor the algorithm requires legal personhood, though. Humans have been 'supplementing' their muscles and brains with various forms of external assistance, with the tasks and the tools used to achieve them becoming increasingly complex and sophisticated.[99] Even the most complex algorithms, however, have no goals of their own. Humans 'put the purpose into the machine', as AI pioneer Norman Wiener would say.[100] Humans may specify a goal, without providing detailed instructions on how to achieve it—for the very reason that they may not be able to predict the exact conditions in which the computer will operate.[101] The computer may develop sub-goals. Such goals are not, however,

[94] Michael Chissick and Allistair Kellman, *Electronic Commerce: Law and Practice* (Thompson Professional 2000) 77.

[95] *B2C2 Ltd v Quoine Pte Ltd* [2019] SGHC(I) 3.

[96] Allen and Widdison, 'Can Computers Make Contracts?' (n 82) 46.

[97] A tensor processing unit is an application-specific integrated circuit purposefully created for neural network machine learning.

[98] Eg, the EU Civil Law Rules state: '[T]he more autonomous robots are, the less they can be considered simple tools in the hands of other actors (such as the manufacturer, the owner, the user, etc); ... this, in turn, questions whether the ordinary rules on liability are insufficient or whether it calls for new principles and rules to provide clarity on the legal liability of various actors concerning responsibility for the acts and omissions of robots ...'.

[99] Antone Martinho-Truswell, 'To Automate is Human' *AEON Magazine*, 13 February 2018.

[100] Norman Wiener, 'Some Moral and Technical Consequences of Automation' (1960) 131 Science 1355.

[101] Russel and Norvig, *Artificial Intelligence* (n 16) emphasize that it is more advisable to design agents according to what one wants in the environment, rather than in terms of how the agent should behave, 37.

the computer's—they only serve as a means to achieve the operator's original goal. Operators can either explicitly formulate a task and the instructions to be followed to achieve the task, or program the system to achieve the same task by creating its own instructions.[102] In the words of Bostrom, 'software simply does what it is programmed to do. Its behavior is mathematically specified by the code.'[103]

5. Conclusion

As described above, autonomous systems have been designed for the safety and/or convenience of humans. Moreover, irrespective of their technical sophistication, they always remain dependent on their human makers (or operators) for information, energy, maintenance, and further instructions. Arguably, fully autonomous machines that require no human input whatsoever will remain beyond reach for the foreseeable future. The idea of an AI being *fully* independent from humans must be abandoned. An autonomous system will always act within the constraints originally imposed by its designers. At the present stage of technological development, most of the automation comes *after* humans have designed and built the system.[104] The need to create autonomous systems derives from the need to automate a task that is difficult or dangerous for a human to do. The task is pragmatic and utilitarian, devoid of emotional or creative undertones. In contrast, in the context of applications that would fall under the scope of IP law, the goals and the tasks are different. The aim is not to facilitate human labour but to 'originate' art, to create, or to innovate. While artists-programmers might be exploring the very concept of creativity, the technology itself and technological premises of the AI remain the same, irrespective of the task at hand. Crucially, the latter is always set by a human 'artist-programmer.'

Many legal narratives have taken an abstraction used to describe system behaviour and equipped it with normative connotations. The resulting decontextualization of autonomy has contributed to the popular narrative that 'autonomous computers' should be endowed with legal personhood and recognized as separate rights-and-duties-bearing units. It is overlooked that such systems set out to accomplish 'their own goals and realize their own plans' only in the figurative sense.

It must always be remembered that the granting of legal personhood has never been premised on the existence of autonomy, creativity, consciousness, or intelligence. Consequently, even an exponential increase in any of those attributes that would 'spawn' a superior computer intelligence capable of creating breathtaking art

[102] Nick Bostrom, *Superintelligence* (Oxford University Press 2014) 169.

[103] Ibid, 184; see also Neil M Richards and William D Smart, 'How Should the Law Think about Robots?' in Ryan Calo, A Michael Froomkin, and Ian Kerr (eds), *Robot Law* (Edward Elgar 2016) 3.

[104] Monika Zalnieriute, Lyria Bennett Moses, and George Williams, 'The Rule of Law and Automation of Government Decision-Making' (2019) 82(3) Modern Law Review 9.

or groundbreaking inventions would remain legally irrelevant. AIs are tools which are no different from hammers.[105] It is always a human being that can be attributed with or is responsible for the AI's operations.[106] Humans decide which processes to automate, what level of automation to deploy, what technologies to use, and in what type of environment to deploy the system.[107] Humans decide whether to use a particular technology in space exploration, submarine drilling, or in the 'creation' of art. Ultimately, absent some compelling moral or commercial necessity in any of the areas falling under IP law, the idea of granting legal personhood to or endowing an AI with any rights and/or obligations should be abandoned. After all, what would be the purpose or the benefit of granting personhood to an AI in the context of IP law? The question is not what rights AI should possess, but what for?

[105] L Floridi, 'Artificial Companions and Their Philosophical Challenges' (2009) 19 *Dialogue and Universalism* 31–6.

[106] R Leenes and F Lucivero, 'Laws on Robots, Laws by Robots, Laws in Robots: Regulating Robot Behaviour by Design' (2014) 6 Law Innovation and Technology 193.

[107] This is emphasized by Raja, Sheridan, and Wickens, 'A Model for Types and Levels of Human Interaction with Automation' (n 20) 287.

Index